Applied Issues in Investigative Interviewing, Eyewitness Memory, and Credibility Assessment

Barry S. Cooper · Dorothee Griesel
Marguerite Ternes
Editors

Applied Issues in Investigative Interviewing, Eyewitness Memory, and Credibility Assessment

Editors
Barry S. Cooper
The Forensic Alliance
Vancouver, BC, Canada

Dorothee Griesel
Gesellschaft für Wissenschaftliche
Gerichts- und Rechtspsychologie
München, Germany

Marguerite Ternes
Department of Psychology
University of British Columbia
Vancouver, BC, Canada

ISBN 978-1-4614-5546-2   ISBN 978-1-4614-5547-9 (eBook)
DOI 10.1007/978-1-4614-5547-9
Springer New York Heidelberg Dordrecht London

Library of Congress Control Number: 2012950359

© Springer Science+Business Media New York 2013
This work is subject to copyright. All rights are reserved by the Publisher, whether the whole or part of the material is concerned, specifically the rights of translation, reprinting, reuse of illustrations, recitation, broadcasting, reproduction on microfilms or in any other physical way, and transmission or information storage and retrieval, electronic adaptation, computer software, or by similar or dissimilar methodology now known or hereafter developed. Exempted from this legal reservation are brief excerpts in connection with reviews or scholarly analysis or material supplied specifically for the purpose of being entered and executed on a computer system, for exclusive use by the purchaser of the work. Duplication of this publication or parts thereof is permitted only under the provisions of the Copyright Law of the Publisher's location, in its current version, and permission for use must always be obtained from Springer. Permissions for use may be obtained through RightsLink at the Copyright Clearance Center. Violations are liable to prosecution under the respective Copyright Law.
The use of general descriptive names, registered names, trademarks, service marks, etc. in this publication does not imply, even in the absence of a specific statement, that such names are exempt from the relevant protective laws and regulations and therefore free for general use.
While the advice and information in this book are believed to be true and accurate at the date of publication, neither the authors nor the editors nor the publisher can accept any legal responsibility for any errors or omissions that may be made. The publisher makes no warranty, express or implied, with respect to the material contained herein.

Printed on acid-free paper

Springer is part of Springer Science+Business Media (www.springer.com)

Preface

In July 2007, we co-chaired a Festschrift—German for celebration of career—conference as a tribute to John Yuille when he became a Professor Emeritus at the University of British Columbia (UBC) in Vancouver, British Columbia, Canada. Co-chaired with Donald Dutton and Judith Daylen, the conference at UBC celebrated the illustrious and pioneering forensic psychology career of John Yuille. Together with Donald Dutton and Robert Hare, John Yuille formed the first forensic psychology program in Canada in the mid-1980s at UBC. Also pioneering is the reality that John Yuille spent his academic and applied career as a forensic psychologist breaking new ground in the areas of investigative interviewing, eyewitness memory, and credibility assessment—domains that, not surprisingly, formed the themes for the present volume. Indeed, John Yuille developed and subsequently revised the Step-Wise Interview Guidelines, an investigative tool used around the world by interviewers tasked with eliciting accounts of alleged crimes from a variety of types of forensic interviewees. Together with Judith Daylen (formerly Cutshall), he conducted the first field study of eyewitness memory with actual eyewitnesses in the late 1980s. John Yuille has subsequently challenged the status quo in the eyewitness memory arena, and has made calls for more ecologically valid research in order for psychology to be in a better position to assist the triers of fact in their decisions. As well, he was instrumental in bringing a European developed method for assessing credibility of statements to North America (e.g., he organized a NATO funded conference in Italy in 1988, which was attended by both European and North American participants); he has since refined the approach and has conducted extensive research on the topic.

In many ways, the areas of investigative interviewing, eyewitness memory, and credibility assessment are inherently interrelated. For example, an effective investigative interviewer uses knowledge of memory processes and patterns to ask memory and interviewee compatible questions while using knowledge of empirically based tools and skills to assess the credibility of the interviewee's statement. John Yuille has researched these areas extensively in addition to providing related training and consulting to every type of professional involved in the criminal justice system—from law enforcement to the Judiciary. Although his academic career has come to an end, he remains active in his role as Chief Executive Officer for The Forensic Alliance, a company that provides research, training, and consulting services to various facets of the criminal justice system, typically concerning the intertwined areas of investigative interviewing, eyewitness memory, and credibility assessment.

The Festschrift conference and the present volume were both meant to honor John Yuille. In addition to a talk by John Yuille, a number of professionals from a variety of disciplines that were, in some way, influenced by his work or, conversely, have influenced his work, provided talks at the Festschrift conference. These included Donald Dutton, Robert Hare, Judith Daylen, John Pearse, Ian Prescott, John Yarbrough, Wendy van Tongeren Harvey, Chief Judge Gerald Seniuk, Paul Ekman, Hugues Hervé, and the editors of this volume. Some of the speakers in addition to a number of other recognized professionals, including John Yuille, provided chapters for the present volume.

This volume is organized into four parts: *(1) Historical Views and Broad Perspectives; (2) Investigative Interviewing; (3) Eyewitness Memory; and (4) Credibility Assessment.* In the opening chapter, John Yuille provides a historical yet critical analysis of the science of psychology, in particular the field of eyewitness memory, and makes a renewed call for more field research on the topic. The second chapter, by Chief Judge Seniuk, discusses certain challenges associated with credibility assessment from the perspective of the Judiciary and provides suggestions for redress by applying insight from the phenomenon of fuzzy logic. In the third chapter, Dave Walsh and Ray Bull review the area of investigative interviewing of benefit fraud suspects in the United Kingdom and promote effective interviewing through a discussion of the PEACE model. The fourth chapter, authored by John Yarbrough, Hugues Hervé, and Robert Harms, discusses the sins of investigative interviewing and offers suggestions for effective interviewing from the perspectives of science and the experience of seasoned law enforcement professionals.

In the fifth chapter, Hugues Hervé, Barry Cooper, and John Yuille attempt to explain the memory variability observed in eyewitness research and practice from the perspective of a biopsychosocial model of eyewitness memory. Following is a review of the scientific case study research on children's memory for sexual abuse by Pedro Paz-Alonso, Christin Ogle, and Gail Goodman, during which they promote a multi-method approach to examining eyewitness memory issues. In the seventh chapter, Ronald Fisher, Aldert Vrij, and Drew Leins provide a review of research and theoretical perspectives on inconsistent witness accounts to answer the empirical question of whether inconsistency is suggestive of deception and/or inaccurate memory. Deborah Connolly and Heather Price then further review the research on the effects of repeated interviews on memory consistency and discuss the results of a related novel field study.

In the first chapter in the fourth part of the present volume, Leanne ten Brinke and Stephen Porter discuss their Dangerous Decisions Theory of examining credibility and promote empirically valid training in the area via the amalgamation of field and laboratory research on the topic. In the next chapter, the late and beloved Maureen O'Sullivan reviews her research on Truth Wizards and offers insight into how such experts of evaluating truthfulness make their decisions. As she died since the submission of her chapter, her contribution is presented in a relatively unedited form, in part, as a tribute to her. May Maureen O'Sullivan rest in peace and her legacy of high quality research be continued by the next generation of deception researchers. In that vein, her contribution is followed by chapter eleven, authored by Kevin Colwell, Cheryl Hiscock-Anisman, and Jacquelyn Fede, who introduce a novel approach to assessing credibility through their research paradigm of Differential Recall Enhancement.

In the twelfth chapter, Dorothee Griesel, Marguerite Ternes, Domenica Schraml, Barry Cooper, and John Yuille dispel some misperceptions about Criteria-Based Content Analysis and provide examples of how to apply this complex procedure via examples from field research and actual credibility assessments. Finally, the book fittingly ends with the thirteenth chapter by Jeffrey Hancock and Michael Woodworth who review the relatively new and very promising area of detecting online deception.

As can be seen, the present volume is an amalgamation of theoretical, research, and practical perspectives from individuals from different countries and from a variety of different disciplines in the criminal justice system, all of whom are concerned with the interplay between investigative interviewing, eyewitness memory, and credibility assessment.

This volume would not have been completed without the dedication, encouragement, and hard work of a number of different individuals. Thanks to Simone Viljoen and Erin Hutton for assisting in the organizing of the Festschrift conference, which resulted in the present volume. Melody Nelson deserves special credit as she was of tremendous assistance during the early stages of the editing process. Similarly, we appreciate the contributors for the present volume who served as peer reviewers. As well, thanks to Sharon Panulla, Sylvana Ruggierllo, and Ethiraju Saraswathi from Springer Science+Business Media for their patience, assistance, and unwavering confidence. Finally, thanks to Mario, owner of a Vancouver coffee shop, where much of this volume was edited, with free espresso to boot. Grazie, Mario!

Vancouver, BC, Canada	Barry S. Cooper
München, Germany	Dorothee Griesel
Vancouver, BC, Canada	Marguerite Ternes

Contents

Part I Historical Views and Broad Perspectives

1 The Challenge for Forensic Memory Research: Methodolotry 3
   John C. Yuille

2 Credibility Assessment, Common Law Trials and Fuzzy Logic 19
   Gerald T.G. Seniuk

Part II Investigative Interviewing

3 The Investigation and Investigative Interviewing of Benefit Fraud
   Suspects in the UK: Historical and Contemporary Perspectives 33
   Dave Walsh and Ray Bull

4 The Sins of Interviewing: Errors Made by Investigative
   Interviewers and Suggestions for Redress 59
   John Yarbrough, Hugues F. Hervé, and Robert Harms

Part III Eyewitness Memory

5 Biopsychosocial Perspectives on Memory Variability
   in Eyewitnesses 99
   Hugues F. Hervé, Barry S. Cooper, and John C. Yuille

6 Children's Memory in "Scientific Case Studies"
   of Child Sexual Abuse: A Review 143
   Pedro M. Paz-Alonso, Christin M. Ogle, and Gail S. Goodman

7 Does Testimonial Inconsistency Indicate Memory Inaccuracy
   and Deception? Beliefs, Empirical Research, and Theory 173
   Ronald P. Fisher, Aldert Vrij, and Drew A. Leins

8 Repeated Interviews About Repeated Trauma from the
   Distant Past: A Study of Report Consistency 191
   Deborah A. Connolly and Heather L. Price

Part IV   Credibility Assessment

9 Discovering Deceit: Applying Laboratory and Field Research
   in the Search for Truthful and Deceptive Behavior 221
   Leanne ten Brinke and Stephen Porter

10 Is *Le Mot Juste*? The Contexualization of Words by Expert
   Lie Detectors 239
   Maureen O'Sullivan

11 Assessment Criteria Indicative of Deception: An Example
   of the New Paradigm of Differential Recall Enhancement 259
   Kevin Colwell, Cheryl Hiscock-Anisman, and Jacquelyn Fede

12 The ABC's of CBCA: Verbal Credibility Assessment in Practice 293
   Dorothee Griesel, Marguerite Ternes, Domenica Schraml,
   Barry S. Cooper, and John C. Yuille

13 An "Eye" for an "I": The Challenges and Opportunities
   for Spotting Credibility in a Digital World 325
   Jeff Hancock and Michael Woodworth

Index 341

About the Editors

Dr. Barry S. Cooper is a Registered Psychologist in Vancouver, BC, Canada, practicing in the forensic arena. He received an M.A. and Ph.D. in Forensic Psychology at the University of British Columbia (UBC) where he met and was mentored by Dr. John Yuille. A former Senior Psychologist for the Correctional Service of Canada, Dr. Cooper is a Psychologist for the Forensic Psychiatric Services Commission at the BC Forensic Psychiatric Hospital. He is a Clinical Instructor in the Department of Psychiatry at UBC and an Adjunct Professor in the Departments of Psychology at UBC-Okanagan and Simon Fraser University. In addition, Dr. Cooper is in private practice which involves assessment and consultation services to law enforcement, lawyers, corrections, and the Judiciary. He is also a founding Partner and Director of Research and Development for the Forensic Alliance, a research, training, and consulting company headed by Dr. Yuille. Dr. Cooper's research and clinical-forensic interests include investigative interviewing, eyewitness memory, credibility/malingering assessment, risk assessment, and psychopathy. He has provided training to various groups including law enforcement, child protection, mental health professionals, lawyers, corrections, and the judiciary. Dr. Cooper has also provided evidence at BC Review Board hearing and has served as an expert witness in court for both the prosecution and defence.

Dr. Dorothee Griesel belongs to the Gesellschaft für Wissenschaftliche Gerichts- und Rechtspsychologie (GWG) in Munich, Germany—a network of forensic psychologists and psychiatrists. As an expert witness, she provides credibility assessments in the context of criminal law, family law, and compensation claims. In this line of work, she benefits tremendously from her training with Dr. John Yuille. She was first introduced to his research on autobiographical memory for violent events during a practicum in the Forensic Psychology Lab at the University of British Columbia (UBC) in 2001. In 2002, she completed her Diploma in Psychology at Mannheim University in Germany and entered the Ph.D. program in Forensic Psychology at UBC under John's supervision. She also received training in Counseling Psychology and completed a predoctoral internship at the Health and Counseling Centre at Simon Fraser University. Dr. Griesel's dissertation was a field investigation of sex trade workers' narratives of sexual violence. She completed her Ph.D. in 2008. In 2007, when John became a Professor Emeritus, she participated in organizing his Festschrift conference at UBC, which set the stage for the present book.

Dr. Marguerite Ternes has worked for the Correctional Service of Canada's Addictions Research Centre since 2009. Since 2011, she has also been a lecturer of Forensic Psychology at the University of Prince Edward Island. After completing her undergraduate degree at St. Francis Xavier University, she began graduate studies in Forensic Psychology at the University of British Columbia. She completed her Masters in 2003 and her Ph.D. in 2009, both under the supervision of Dr. John Yuille. Mentored by Dr. Yuille, her research interests include autobiographical memory, suggestibility, investigative interviewing, and credibility assessment. Her Masters research investigated eyewitness identification performance in a group of adults with intellectual disabilities, while her dissertation explored verbal credibility in the memory accounts of violent offenders. Dr. Yuille instilled in Dr. Ternes an appreciation for the importance of ecological validity in forensic psychological research, values which Dr. Ternes practices and advocates in her current positions. When Dr. Yuille retired in 2007, she was part of the team that organized a Festschrift conference in his honor, which led to the present volume.

List of Contributors

Ray Bull is Professor of Forensic Psychology at the University of Leicester. His major research topic is investigative interviewing. In 2010, Ray was "Elected by acclaim" an Honorary Fellow of the British Psychological Society "for the contribution made to the discipline of psychology." In 2010, he received from the Scientific Committee of the Fourth International Conference on Investigative Interviewing a "Special Prize" for his "extensive contributions to investigative interviewing." In 2009, Ray received from the "International Investigative Interviewing Research Group" the "Senior Academic Award" for his "significant lifetime contribution to the field of investigative interviewing." In 2008, Ray received from the European Association of Psychology and Law an "Award for Life-time Contribution to Psychology and Law." In 2005, he received a Commendation from the London Metropolitan Police for "Innovation and professionalism whilst assisting a complex rape investigation." He has advised a large number of police forces in several countries on the interviewing of witnesses and of suspects, and he has testified as an expert witness in a considerable number of trials. He has authored and coauthored a large number of papers in quality research journals and has coauthored and coedited many books including Investigative Interviewing: Psychology and Practice (1999—a second edition is now being written) and Witness Identification in Criminal Cases (2008). He has been an invited speaker at a variety of meetings around the world. In recognition of the quality and extent of his research publications, he was in 1995 awarded a higher doctorate (Doctor of Science).

Dr. Kevin Colwell is an Associate Professor in the Department of Psychology at Southern Connecticut State University in New Haven, CT. He began studying investigative interviewing and credibility assessment in 1994 as a member of Dr. Hiscock-Anisman's CBCA grant. This was the beginning of their long and productive collaboration. This early work was made possible by information and materials provided by Dr. John Yuille. The first series of studies focused upon college students and inmates who witnessed staged thefts. The results of the study were not powerful, but the things they learned were. What they learned was that interviewing was the most important aspect of detecting deception. Because of this, Kevin's Master's Thesis (1997) and his Doctoral Dissertation (2002) both focused on matching interviewing to facilitate the detection of deception with content criteria derived from motivation and memory. Dr. Hiscock-Anisman was the Chair of both efforts. They created the Reality Interview and compared it to the Cognitive and Step-Wise interviews to study how mnemonics and forced-choice questions interact with the relative cognitive and interpersonal demands of honest vs. deceptive responding. This research led directly to the ACID system, which is literally a synthesis of the interviews and content criteria studied during the thesis and dissertation. They have been continually involved in studying investigative interviewing to detect deception, and training others how to do so. Kevin, along with Dr. Hiscock-Anisman, has also conducted a number of studies examining the subjective experience of participants during investigative interviews to learn how people attempt impression management and deception, across cultures. He hopes that it can inform a general theory of interpersonal deception during interpersonal interactions at some point in the future.

Dr. Deborah A. Connolly earned her Ph.D. and her LL.B. from the University of Victoria. She is currently an Associate Professor of Psychology at Simon Fraser University. Dr. Connolly's research focuses on memory for repeated events: how are repeated events organized in memory? What does the criminal justice system expect of memory reports from witnesses who report having been repeatedly victimized? Are the expectations reasonable, and how can we help victims to report details of the offence in a way that is consistent with the needs of the criminal justice system? We are indebted to Professor John Yuille for challenging us to test our beliefs about memory for crime with participants who have a memory for crime. Applied work is essential if we are to have an impact on the criminal justice system.

Dr. Barry S. Cooper (see About the Editors)

Jacquelyn Fede received her B.A. in Psychology from Southern Connecticut State University where she is a graduate student. For the past 2 years, she has worked with Dr. Kevin Colwell as a research assistant studying the use of forced-choice questions for witness selection as well as distinguishing between honest and deceptive children's statements. She has also assisted in studies of ACID and deception via the Internet. Jacquelyn is currently working towards her Master's degree and intends to continue education thereafter.

Dr. Ronald P. Fisher is currently a Professor of Psychology and is a member of the Legal Psychology Ph.D. program at Florida International University. He received his Ph.D. from Ohio State University and has held academic positions at the University of Toronto and UCLA. Ron has published extensively in both theoretical and applied aspects of memory, and currently serves as the editor-in-chief of the Journal of Applied Research in Memory and Cognition. Ron is best known for developing the Cognitive Interview technique to enhance witness recollection (Fisher & Geiselman, 1992: Memory-Enhancing Techniques for Investigative Interviewing). He has conducted many training workshops on the Cognitive Interview with investigative agencies such as the FBI and the National Transportation Safety Board. He has also worked with several federal agencies both in the U.S. and abroad, including NASA, the U.S. Army and Navy, the British and Australian Police, and the Israeli Air Force. Ron served on the Planning and Technical Working Groups of the U.S. Department of Justice to develop national guidelines on collecting eyewitness evidence (Eyewitness Evidence: A Guide for Law Enforcement). His current research also examines the areas of detecting deception and understanding the causes and implications of witnesses recalling events inconsistently.

Dr. Gail S. Goodman is Distinguished Professor of Psychology and Director of the Center for Public Policy Research at the University of California, Davis. Her research concerns memory development, child maltreatment, trauma and memory, and children in the legal system. She has received many awards for her research and writings, including the James McKeen Cattell Award for Lifetime Contributions to Applied Psychological Research from the Association for Psychological Science; Urie Bronfenbrenner Award for Lifetime Contribution to Developmental Psychology in the Service of Science and Society; and two Distinguished Contributions awards from the American Psychological Association (the Distinguished Contributions to Research in Public Policy Award and the Distinguished Professional Contributions to Applied Research Award). Dr. Goodman is the upcoming president of Division 7 (Developmental Psychology) of the American Psychological Association and has served as president of several other divisions/sections, including the American Psychology-Law Society. She has published widely and received many federal, state, and foundation grants, and her research has been cited in U.S. Supreme Court decisions. Dr. Goodman's Center for Public Policy Research brings science to policy on behalf of children and families in California. She obtained her Ph.D. in Developmental Psychology from UCLA and conducted postdoctoral studies at the University of Denver and the Université René Descartes in Paris, France. Dr. Goodman has served on the faculty of the University of Denver, the State University of New York, and the University of Oslo, Norway. She has consulted with numerous governments and agencies throughout the world on policies and research concerning child victims in the legal system. She first heard of Dr. Yuille's research on eyewitness memory as a postdoctoral fellow, was honored to meet with him to discuss child witness research, and has followed his writings and studies ever since.

Dr. Dorothee Griesel (see About the Editors)

Dr. Jeff Hancock is an Associate Professor in the Departments of Communication and Information Science. He is currently the Chair of the Information Science Department and the Co-Director of Cognitive Science at Cornell University. He is also Associate Editor of Discourse Processes. His work is concerned with how social media affect psychological and interpersonal processes, with a particular emphasis on understanding how language can reveal psychological and social dynamics, such as deception and credibility, emotional contagion, intimacy and relationships, and social support. Funding from the National Science Foundation and the Department of Defense supports his research, which has been frequently featured in the popular media, including the New York Times, CNN, NPR, and the BBC. Dr. Hancock earned his Ph.D. in psychology at Dalhousie University, Canada, and joined Cornell in 2002.

Robert Harms was a 31-year veteran of the Los Angeles County Sheriff's Department and held the rank of Detective Sergeant. During his career, he had worked a wide range of assignments, including the Crime Lab, Custody, Patrol, Vice, Intelligence, Organized Crime, Narcotics, and as a Coroner's Investigator. He has instructed at the Los Angeles County Sheriff's Training Academy, the Federal Law Enforcement Training Center, and before other Federal, State, and Local Law Enforcement personnel, civilian groups and organizations on various subjects. He is a national instructor in Analytic Interviewing, Hate and Bias Crimes, Undercover Investigative Techniques, and Case Management. He has trained personnel from U.S. State Department—Foreign Service Institute, National Counter Intelligence Executive, The U.S. Army, Federal Bureau of Investigations, The Department of Defense, Central Intelligence Agency, U.S. Secret Service, and the Bureau of Alcohol, Tobacco, Firearms and Explosives, to name a few. He was profiled three times on the show "L.A. Detectives" (A & E Television). The "Human Interaction Laboratory" at the University of California, San Francisco, has identified him as a "Truth Wizard." The "Wizard Project" (conducted by the late Dr. Maureen O'Sullivan) is researching people who are excellent at detecting deception and reading emotion. He is in the top 2% of people who are accurate in telling whether others are truthful. He has been profiled in the New Yorker Magazine (August, 2002), the Smithsonian Magazine (January, 2004) and other publications. Sergeant Harms retired from the Los Angeles Sheriff's Department on January 30, 2012.

Dr. Hugues F. Hervé is a Registered Psychologist in British Columbia, Canada, who specializes in forensic and medical-legal assessments. A former psychologist for the Correctional Service of Canada and the Forensic Psychiatric Services Commission, he is currently a Partner and Director of Consulting Services for The Forensic Alliance. Committed to the investigation, application, and dissemination of sound clinical-forensic practice, he is actively involved in providing consulting, training, and research services to various professionals groups and organizations on such topics as effective interviewing, evaluating truthfulness, malingering assessments, risk assessments, eyewitness memory, and psychopathology.

Dr. Cheryl Hiscock-Anisman is a Professor in the Department of Psychology at National University in La Jolla, CA. She began work in the area of Forensic Psychology with the study of malingering. This research helped in bringing the two-alternative, forced-choice paradigm into the mainstream of psychological assessment. As a result, she became interested in the detection of deception in general. In 1993, Cheryl participated in a training workshop provided by Dr. John Yuille in investigative interviewing and SVA/CBCA. She then established an interviewing and statement analysis lab, largely with materials provided by Dr. Yuille. He provided laboratory manuals, training materials, and a wealth of theoretical and practical information. Without enthusiastic support, the research that followed could not have happened. She first met her coauthor, Dr. Kevin Colwell, as an Undergraduate Research Assistant working on this CBCA study. Unfortunately, CBCA did not work very well with adult inmates who witnessed a staged theft. However, this experience led to the study of interviewing techniques that enhance honest recall while making deception more difficult. Dr. Hiscock-Anisman was Chair of Kevin's Master's Thesis (1997) and Doctoral Dissertation (2002). Both of these projects compared the relative effects of mnemonics and two-alternative, forced-choice questions detecting deception. She has worked to synthesize the ACID system, along with Kevin. This has naturally led into the training of professionals in the process of investigative interviewing and detecting deception, and also the study of these trainings. These studies have also provided a chance to gain insight into the subjective strategies of impression management and deception that are used during an investigative interview. She hopes to continue studying ACID and deception across cultures, and to study manipulation of information in the media.

Dr. Drew A. Leins is currently a Research Psychologist for Applied Research Associates, Inc. He holds graduate degrees from Northeastern University and Florida International University. He has worked in multiple domains of psychology, including vocational rehabilitation, forensic counseling, geriatric cognition, and psychology-law. Drew's general research interests are in social cognition and include exploring the roles of social dynamics and memory in investigative interviewing. One of his specific interests is in developing methods for protecting innocent suspects from incriminating themselves during interrogations—by enhancing their ability to recall and report accurate alibis—while also improving interviewers' ability to detect deception. In part to that end, he is currently engaged in field testing methods of human intelligence gathering and detecting deception in military contexts. Drew would like to thank Dr. John Yuille for conducting seminal work in so many interesting and important areas of applied psychology.

Dr. Christin M. Ogle is a postdoctoral associate at the Center for the Study of Aging and Human Development at Duke University, where she is currently funded by a National Institutes of Health research training grant. Christin earned her B.A. in Psychology from Reed College in Portland, Oregon. While working under the mentorship of Daniel Reisberg at Reed, Christin first developed an interest in the fallibility of eyewitness memory and later completed an undergraduate thesis concerning eyewitness identification procedures. She went on to receive her doctorate from the University of California, Davis, where she conducted several lines of research on topics related to psychology and the law under the direction of Dr. Gail S. Goodman. Christin's current program of research investigates the impact of trauma exposure on autobiographical memory and psychological health from a lifespan development perspective.

The late Dr. Maureen O'Sullivan was Professor Emeritus at the University of San Francisco. Dr. O'Sullivan completed her undergraduate degree at Fordham University in 1960, and her Masters and Ph.D. at the University of Southern California in 1963 and 1965, respectively. Dr. O'Sullivan spent much of her career researching social-emotional intelligence—the ability to manage, recognize, communicate, detect, and decipher emotions in others. In particular, Dr. O'Sullivan worked for many years on aspects of facial expressions of emotion in honest and deceptive situations, completing a multiyear project on individual differences among highly accurate human lie detectors. In addition to her research on social-emotional intelligence, lie detection, and facial expression recognition, Dr. O'Sullivan studied cross-cultural differences in romantic love. Much of her research over the last few years before her death focused on the Truth Wizard Project, as discussed in her contribution to the present volume. During her illustrious career, in addition to being an active researcher, Dr. O'Sullivan also served as a consultant to many national and international law enforcement groups, including the FBI, CIA, TSA, and Scotland Yard.

Dr. Pedro M. Paz-Alonso (BA '98; MA '01; PhD '04; U Basque Country, Spain) examined misinformation effects and memory accuracy for emotional events in children and adult eyewitnesses in his doctoral dissertation. During his postdoctoral positions, at Dr. Gail S. Goodman's Developmental Research Center at the University of California (UC) Davis and at Silvia A. Bunge's Development and Cognitive Control lab at the Helen Wills Neuroscience Institute at UC Berkeley, he investigated neurodevelopmental changes over childhood in true and false memories and intentional retrieval inhibition processes using MRI. Currently, he is a Research Scientist at the Basque Center on Cognition, Brain and Language (BCBL) where he conducts developmental cognitive neuroscience studies on higher cognitive functions and language. Professor Yuille's research greatly inspired Dr. Paz-Alonso's doctoral dissertation. Dr. John Yuille's landmark case study of adult eyewitness memory from a tragic shooting showed that, in contrast to the results from many lab studies, witnesses' memories were highly accurate and resistant to false information, highlighting the importance of using field research to evaluate the external validity of laboratory experiments. In dedication to Professor Yuille's work, Paz-Alonso, Ogle, and Goodman's chapter in this volume reviews "scientific case studies" of the accuracy of children's reports of sexual abuse. The research described in this review was inspired to a great extent by Professor Yuille's groundbreaking and innovative research.

Dr. Stephen Porter received his Ph.D. in forensic psychology under Dr. John Yuille's supervision at UBC. John and Steve ultimately became close friends and colleagues, and complemented their scholarly work together with equally important pursuits, such as fly-fishing. He currently is an academic and consultant in the area of psychology and law. After working as a prison psychologist, Steve spent a decade as a professor at Dalhousie University. In 2009, he transferred to UBC-Okanagan where he assumed a position as a professor of psychology and the Co-Director of the Centre for the Advancement of Psychological Science & Law (CAPSL). Steve has published numerous scholarly articles on psychopathy and violent behavior, deception detection, and forensic aspects of memory with funding from the Social Sciences and Humanities Research Council of Canada (SSHRC) and the Natural Sciences and Engineering Research Council of Canada (NSERC). As a registered forensic psychologist in British Columbia, Steve has been consulted by Canadian courts and has been qualified as an expert witness in various areas, including "dangerousness and risk for violence" and "memory and the factors involved in credibility assessments." He has been consulted by police in serious crime investigations and provides training to law enforcement, mental health professional groups, government agencies, journalists, trial judges, and other adjudicators. He hails from Deer Lake, Newfoundland.

Dr. Heather L. Price is an Associate Professor at the University of Regina. After completing her undergraduate degree at the University of Victoria, she entered Simon Fraser University's Psychology and Law program where she finished her Master's and Ph.D. She then undertook concurrent postdoctoral fellowships at the University of North Carolina at Chapel Hill and Wilfrid Laurier University before accepting her current position at the University of Regina in 2007. Heather's primary research interests relate to child victims and witnesses, but she studies the many ways in which memory is related to the justice system. One of her first practical experiences as a graduate student was taking a Step-Wise Interviewing course through Dr. Yuille at UBC. The course provided the introduction to several years of work investigating how investigators question young witnesses.

Domenica Schraml (formerly Schwind) received her Diploma in Psychology from Konstanz University, Germany. Her studies and practicums were focused on the topic of credibility assessments. Since 2007, she has been part of the Gesellschaft für Wissenschaftliche Gerichts- und Rechtspsychologie (GWG) in Munich, Germany, and has provided credibility assessments for prosecutions, criminal courts, as well as in the context of family law and compensation claims. She is currently receiving additional training in various fields of forensic psychology in the Berufsverband Deutscher Psychologinnen und Psychologen (BDP).

Gerald T.G. Seniuk is a retired Canadian judge who collaborated with Dr. Yuille on a judicial research project. Judge Seniuk was a judge of the Provincial Court of Saskatchewan for 30 years, the last seven as Chief Judge of the court, before retiring in 2007. In 1982, he initiated a judicial research project into the fact-finding aspect of judicial reasoning and legal methodologies. In about 1989, Dr. Yuille was requested to advise the project on aspects of forensic and cognitive psychology that were relevant to judicial fact determination. Dr. Yuille became a close collaborator with Judge Seniuk. Together they wrote and published articles on the topic of decision-making. Dr. Yuille took part in many of the project's Credit Model of Analysis

Workshops presented to judges in and outside of Canada. In retirement, Judge Seniuk has continued developing aspects of the research project, most currently in collaboration with experts in fuzzy logic and fuzzy neural networks.

Dr. Leanne ten Brinke received her Ph.D. from the University of British Columbia (UBC) in 2012 under the supervision of Dr. Stephen Porter, examining the behavioral consequences of emotional, high-stakes deception. Prior to studying at UBC, she completed her Bachelor of Science with Honours in Psychology, and a Certificate in Forensic Psychology, at Dalhousie University in 2007. She was awarded the University Medal upon graduation from this program, and has been funded by the Social Sciences and Humanities Research Council of Canada (SSHRC) throughout her graduate career. As a Ph.D. student, she has conducted research at the London Business School, and quickly is establishing herself as an international and cross-disciplinary psychological scientist. She recently received a SSHRC Postdoctoral Fellowship to pursue further research at the Haas School of Business at UC Berkeley. Leanne has over twenty published articles in leading academic journals in the areas of deception, interpersonal intuition, human decision-making, and criminal psychopathy, several of which have attracted national and international media attention. She was born and raised in Antigonish, Nova Scotia.

Dr. Marguerite Ternes (see About the Editors)

Dr. Aldert Vrij is a Professor of Applied Social Psychology. His main research interests lie in deception, and he examines (1) nonverbal and verbal correlates of deception and (2) people's ability to detect deceit. He received grants from the British Academy, Economic and Social Research Council, Engineering and Physical Sciences Research Council, Federal Bureau of Investigation, Innovation Group, Leverhulme Trust, Nuffield Foundation, and Dutch, British and American Governments, totaling >£2,200,000. His research has a strongly applied quality, and he has been working closely with practitioners (police, security services, and insurers) for the last 20 years, both in terms of conducting collaborative research and in disseminating the research findings via seminars and workshops. He has published almost 400 articles and seven books on the above topics, including his 2008 book, *Detecting lies and deceit: Pitfalls and opportunities* (published by Wiley), a comprehensive overview of research into nonverbal, verbal and physiological deception and lie detection.

Dr. Dave Walsh obtained his Ph.D. from the University of Leicester in 2011. His thesis concerned an examination of the practices of investigators from nonpolice agencies in the UK when interviewing their suspects. Dave is a senior lecturer in the School of Law and Criminology at the University of Derby in the UK. Prior to his current role, he was involved for over 20 years as an investigations professional in several government departments in the UK, either as an investigator or later in his career as a senior investigations manager. He has published several articles in peer-reviewed journals and presented at many international conferences on the subject of interviewing suspects. He is editor of the journal, Investigative Interviewing;

Research and Practice, being a founder member of the International Investigative Interviewing Research Group. Dr. John Yuille's work has inspired and influenced his work, both as an investigations professional, looking towards researchers to provide solutions to problems that confront investigations practitioners in the field, and also as a researcher. In particular, John Yuille's research, which has created frameworks for the interviewing of children in order to gain reliable and fulsome information, has been influential. It is a privilege to him, therefore to have been asked to contribute to this book in John Yuille's much deserved honor.

Dr. Michael Woodworth is an Associate Professor at UBC-Okanagan. His primary areas of research include psychopathy, criminal behavior, and deception detection. Along with his colleagues, Dr. Stephen Porter, and Dr. Zach Walsh, Dr. Woodworth was awarded Canadian Foundation for Innovation (CFI) funding to create the "Centre for the Advancement of Psychological Science and Law (CAPSL)." This facility is a state-of-the-art research center in which faculty and students conduct cutting-edge studies with relevance to the legal system. The center was officially opened in a ceremony on February, 2012. Dr. Woodworth will also be the first Director of the created Clinical Psychology Graduate Program from January 2013 to January 2015. He was recently awarded a 3-year SSHRC Insight Grant (2012–2015) to study language and psychopathy. He regularly presents at national and international psychology conferences, consults with law enforcement agencies such as the RCMP and the FBI, and serves as an expert witness for the courts. Dr. Woodworth has over 25 publications in top tier journals such as Law and Human Behavior, Criminal Justice and Behavior, and Journal of Abnormal Psychology. Dr. Woodworth was the recipient of the UBC Teaching Excellence and Innovation Award (presented at convocation in June, 2010). In the last 7 years, Dr. Woodworth has supervised over 25 undergraduate and graduate student thesis projects and directed studies. Finally, Dr. Woodworth is a Registered Psychologist who currently provides clinical services to citizens primarily residing in the Okanagan.

Retired Sergeant John Yarbrough was a sworn peace officer for nearly 30 years, specializing in homicide investigations for 16 years. He served as his department's criminal profiler for 8 years, and was certified in criminal investigative profiling and crime scene analysis by the Federal Bureau of Investigation (FBI) and the International Criminal Investigative Analysis Fellowship (ICIAF) in 1995. Sergeant Yarbrough conducted research on homicides of the elderly and was an advisor for a Los Angeles County Sheriff's Department training film entitled *Predators of the Elderly*. He also conducted research on "police-assisted suicide" and was a coauthor of a published article entitled "Suicide By Cop" (*Annals of Emergency Medicine*, December 1998). Also in 1998, Sergeant Yarbrough served on a technical working group that developed and published *Crime Scene Investigation: A Guide for Law Enforcement* for the National Institute of Justice (NIJ) in Washington, D.C. He coauthored "Crime Specific Consultation: A Law Enforcement and Psychology Partnership", an article published by the California Psychological Association (June, 2000) on personality, evaluating truthfulness, and interviewing. Sergeant

Yarbrough remains active in the research community by engaging in collaborative investigations on applied topics within the areas of credibility, eyewitness memory, and criminal conduct, with special emphasis being placed on the mediating/moderating roles of mental illness and personality (including psychopathy).

Dr. John C. Yuille, Professor Emeritus, University of British Columbia, is a Registered Psychologist with a private forensic practice. Dr. Yuille has conducted research with children and adults for over 40 years. His research has included the areas of human memory, interviewing, credibility assessment, and psychopathy. He regularly provides training to law enforcement, lawyers, child protection workers, and judges on interviewing and credibility assessment. He has served as an expert witness in criminal, family, and civil court for over 30 years. He is the Chief Executive Officer for The Forensic Alliance.

Part I
Historical Views and Broad Perspectives

Chapter 1
The Challenge for Forensic Memory Research: Methodolotry

John C. Yuille

The aim of this chapter is to describe a major challenge facing contemporary forensic psychology: the reliance on laboratory-based research at the expense of field research. I argue that the reliance on laboratory research has had a profound negative effect on the discipline, retarding our understanding of many psychological phenomena in the forensic field. My focus is on the area of eyewitness memory, although I believe that the arguments presented here are valid for a number of forensic areas of enquiry. This chapter begins with a review of some of the historical roots for the reliance on the laboratory. This is followed by an examination of the consequences of the reliance on the laboratory as the appropriate venue for the study of eyewitness memory. I conclude with some thoughts on how we can meet this challenge; how we can overcome our belief in the ultimate value of the laboratory and develop more appropriate methodologies for the study of eyewitness memory, as well as other aspects of forensic psychology.

In the title to this chapter I used the term "methodolotry." I use this term to characterize the reliance among psychologists on the use of a standard experimental design in laboratory-based research (see Plante, Kiernan, & Betts, 1994 for a similar concern in educational research). This method—conducting research in a relatively sterile context and manipulating some factors while other factors are controlled—is the dominant method of conducting psychological research. When the focus of research is on some aspect of psychology that is context free—that is, that functions the same in all contexts—the controlled laboratory is the perfect venue for research. However, much of human behavior is context dependent—the way we think, feel, and act is deeply affected by the context we are in and our interpretation of that context. For context dependant aspects of psychology, the laboratory may be an inappropriate context to conduct research. However, researchers have such a deep

---

J.C. Yuille (✉)
The Forensic Alliance, PO Box 600,
Saltspring Island, BC, Canada V8K 1J2
email: jyuille@theforensicalliance.com

seated belief in the appropriateness of the standard laboratory method that it can be caricatured as a worship of method: methodolotry. I argue in this chapter that this methodolotry has placed eyewitness research in the wrong context (i.e., the laboratory). It has blinded many psychologists to the need for unique methodologies to study eyewitness memory in situ rather than the artificial context of the lab. Making the method paramount has forced researchers to take the interesting questions about memory in the forensic context and distort them to fit the methodology.

A Brief History of Methodolotry

The origin of psychology as a science is usually dated to 1879. This is the year that Wilhelm Wundt (1832–1920) opened the first psychology laboratory at the University of Leipzig. Wundt was convinced that the success of the scientific method in such fields as physics, chemistry, and medicine also could be achieved in psychology (e.g., Wundt, 1904). That said, he felt that the unique aspect of psychology (i.e., the mind studying itself) required a mix of methods. He proposed that those aspects of the mind that were observable to a person (i.e., the contents of consciousness) could be studied using a modification of standard laboratory techniques. However, he was of the belief that more complex mental processes—those outside immediate observation—required a unique methodology (Wundt, 1912).

In effect, Wundt proposed that psychology needed two distinct methodologies: an experimental methodology for what he called the outer aspects of mind and a nonexperimental approach for the study of what he called the inner aspects of mind. The outer aspects of mind could be researched by training observers to report on the contents of their consciousness in the same way that trained physicists report on their observations of the physical world. However, Wundt argued that those aspects of mind not available to consciousness required a different method of study, one that he called Folk Psychology. Folk Psychology would study language, creativity, social behavior, etc., and would employ methods related to history, and what would later become sociology. Unfortunately, subsequent generations of psychologists were only interested in the laboratory-based part of Wundt's psychology. The Folk Psychology seemed too arcane and unnecessary. If more effort had been devoted to developing a tailored methodology for psychological research, the discipline might have developed in a more productive direction. However, most of Wundt's students emphasized his experimental work and little attention was given to his argument for a Folk Psychology. The strong influence of Positivism in the late nineteenth century was too great: for most researchers in the new discipline, it was clear that laboratory research provided the path to knowledge.

Before leaving this brief examination of history, I turn to a discussion of two of Wundt's students. One of Wundt's students was an Englishman named Titchener (1867–1927). He was quite taken with the experimental aspect of Wundt's work but either did not understand or dismissed Wundt's more extensive work on the inner aspects of the mind. After completing his studies with Wundt, Titchener was unable to find a sympathetic reception for the notion of an experimental psychology in his native Britain. Titchener took advantage of a job offer from Cornell University and moved to the USA. He became the main source in the USA for the dissemination of his version of Wundtian psychology (e.g., Titchener, 1898). Titchener advocated for the use of a particular type of trained introspection for the systematic study of the contents of the conscious mind. While many in the newly developing field of psychology were attracted to the concept of an experimental psychology, they rejected both the trained introspection method of Titchener and his focus on the contents of consciousness as the proper concern of psychology. Instead, many academic American psychologists became enamored with the laboratory and the promise they saw in a purely objective behavioral science. During the first three decades of the twentieth century, they began to shape psychology so that psychological questions could be studied by experimental methods. This was the beginning of the phenomenon I have labeled methodolotry: the dedication to a particular method and the consequent distortion of psychology to fit the method. By the 1930s, academic psychology had become predominantly behavioristic and wedded to an experimental methodology. This approach to psychological research succeeded for a number of reasons, including the following:

1. The earlier success of experimental methodologies in chemistry, physics, and medicine provided an attractive model for the new science of psychology.
2. The strong influence of Logical Positivism (e.g., Ayer, 1936) as a philosophy of science was leading some to advocate that all science should be objective (i.e., based as much as possible solely on observation).
3. The Progressive Movement (e.g., Gould, 2000) in American politics at the time promised a bright future based on the results of empirical science and technology.
4. American researchers viewed the new science of psychology as representative of the innovation of the New World and a rejection of the failures of the philosophical speculations of the Old World.

Whatever the reasons for its appeal, advocates for an external psychology became increasingly vocal in the early twentieth century in the USA. Chief among them was John B. Watson (1878–1958). Watson advocated for a strictly experimental psychology with the goal of predicting and controlling human behavior. Watson began to advocate his position in print in 1913 (Watson, 1913) and, as noted above, by the 1930s, Behaviorism had become the dominant approach to academic psychology in the USA. It was the ascendancy of Behaviorism that assured the adoption of methodolotry in psychology. As MacKenzie (1972) observed:

> "The revolution that produced Behaviorism was, in short, a methodological revolution. Behaviorism was not born from a solution, even a tentative solution, to a major problem. It was born from of an uncompromising faith in a particular objective methodology, a faith that (as is well known) required a rejection and denial of those phenomena and foci of research which could not be made compatible with the methodology" (p. 228).

The discipline of psychology had become attached to laboratory research as the method to deal with all psychological questions. All research would have to conform to the method and the widely held belief was that the method could and would answer all questions. The field of eyewitness memory research was equally swept up in the enthusiasm for the experimental methodology. It was another student of Wundt, in fact, who played a critical role in applying experimental procedures to the study of eyewitnesses. Hugo Munsterberg (1863–1916) became Wundt's research assistant and completed a Ph.D. with Wundt at the University of Leipzig in 1885. He then completed a medical degree and opened a psychology lab at the University of Freiburg (for a history of Munsterberg, see Spillmann & Spillmann, 1993). While there, he met William James at a conference and ultimately accepted an invitation from James to join the faculty at Harvard University. He was eager to apply the new experimental methodology to the study of eyewitness memory. He staged events in front of students or provided them with written descriptions of crimes and then tested their memory. He was convinced that this served as an appropriate analogue for the study of victims and witnesses to crimes. Munsterberg did not pioneer this area of research but he became its principal advocate in the USA. He believed there was no difference between a student observing an event in the comfort and security of the classroom and a victim of a violent act. By 1908, he believed that he and others had acquired a sufficiently large database to permit the direct application of the laboratory results to real crime situations. He advocated for expert testimony by psychologists in criminal cases in order to inform the triers of fact of the insights gained in the laboratory. To this end, he published a book: *On the witness stand* (1908). Munsterberg asserted that the laboratory study of witnesses had produced a body of knowledge that was of value to the criminal justice system.

The legal community did not respond positively to Munsterberg's assertion that the experimental studies of eyewitnesses were of value in court. The primary critic of Munsterberg's work was John Wigmore (1863–1943). Wigmore was the leading authority on rules of evidence and became dean of the law school at Northwestern University. His 1904 landmark text on the Anglo-American system of evidence (Wigmore, 1904) is still used in many law schools to this day. Wigmore (1909) wrote a devastating review of Munsterberg's book, *On the witness stand*. He argued that the psychological research was in its infancy and that it was premature to even consider its application in court. He also pointed out that the artificiality of the experimental procedures employed to study witnesses made it questionable that the results of such work would ever prove of value to the criminal justice system. More than a century ago, a legal scholar had more insight than many psychologists into the context dependent nature of human psychology.

This brief look at the early history of experimental psychology serves two points:

1. The new discipline rapidly adopted a dedication to laboratory-based research that would characterize the field to this day.
2. The new discipline assumed that psychological processes are context free: for example, eyewitnesses perform and react the same whether they are students in a lab or victims of a violent crime. This unwarranted and untested assumption would also continue to the present.

Before leaving this excursion into history, I want to note how short the life of experimental psychology has been. The brevity of psychology's existence as an experimental science is demonstrated by the short link between Wundt and many of the chapter

Table 1.1 A professor/student brief history of psychology

Wilhelm Wundt (1832–1920)—University of Leipzig
Alfred Lehmann (1858–1921)—Denmark
Helge Lundholm (Ph.D., 1919)—Stockholm
Harold McCurdy (1909–1999)—Duke University
Wallace Lambert (1922–2009)—McGill University
Allan Paivio (1925–)—University of Western Ontario
John Yuille (1941–)—University of British Columbia

authors in this book. Table 1.1 (see below) lists the thesis advisors from Wundt to me. One of the students who studied with Wundt was Lehmann who spent his career in Denmark. One of Lehmann's students was Lundholm who spent his career in Stockholm. The next branch of this academic tree is found with McCurdy who studied with Lundholm and then spent his career at Duke University in North Carolina. One of McCurdy's students was Wallace Lambert; he was a professor at McGill University and supervised my supervisor, Alan Paivio. Paivio spent most of his career at the University of Western in Ontario where I had the privilege of doing my graduate work. I should note that I also did a postdoctoral fellowship with Lambert at McGill University. So, in my case, I can trace the history of contemporary psychology in just seven generations from the founder, Wilhelm Wundt.

Eyewitness Research Hiatus

The emerging methodolotry of North American psychology had been readily echoed in the new field of eyewitness testimony. However, the viability of the experimental study of eyewitnesses was short-lived. Few studies were conducted between the end of World War I and the 1960s. Two factors combined to end the interest in the laboratory study of eyewitnesses:

1. Behaviorism, which became the dominant view in academic psychology by the 1950s, generally eschewed the study of more complex phenomena in favor of simple stimulus-response contexts. Lab rats and pigeons were a regular focus of attention together with mazes and reward delivery apparatuses. The study of eyewitness memory was simply not attractive to those working on the development of basic behavioral laws.
2. The rejection of Munsterberg's (1908) work by Wigmore (1909) and others curbed the enthusiasm for such work. Also, Munsterberg's early death at age 53 left no strong advocate for this area of research in North America.

In summary, when psychology first emerged as a science, there was a debate concerning the proper methodology for this new discipline. Many argued that the unique nature of psychological phenomena required a unique methodology. However, these arguments were ultimately futile and the desire to develop a "purely experimental branch of natural science" triumphed. The consequence was that the experimental method, as psychologists came to define it, became the ultimate concern. Any psychological issue worthy of study had to be framed in a manner that fit the method with the focus on control and systematic manipulation. The fact that the laboratory might not be the appropriate context for many psychological issues never arose. I believe that this was a profound error for psychology in general and for forensic psychology in particular. This error had at least three major consequences:

1. During the past century, there has been limited progress in our understanding of many psychological phenomena. Many psychological processes are simply not amenable to study in the experimental context. So much of human thinking, emotions, and behavior is context dependent and the context of the lab is too artificial (i.e., an inappropriate or ineffective analogue) to permit the study of many complex phenomena. I expand on this point in more detail below with respect to forensic psychology in particular.
2. A consequence of relying on experimental design and the associated statistical procedures employed to analyze the results has been a focus on mean differences. Results of research are typically summarized by comparisons of group means. Yet, it is often the variability within the groups that reflects the more interesting aspects of psychology. Individual differences and the factors causing those differences are often ignored or trivialized. This point is also elaborated below.
3. Another consequence of being wedded to an inappropriate methodology has been a division between researchers and practitioners. The past century has been witness to a growing gap between the minority of psychologists who research psychological issues and the substantial majority of psychologists who provide psychological services. This also has had implications for forensic psychology which are elaborated in the following pages.

Contemporary Eyewitness Research

As reviewed above, the early twentieth century interest in the laboratory study of eyewitness memory was followed by a long period of disinterest. When interest in the topic was rekindled in the 1960s, the methodolotry of the general field of psychology persisted. Consequently, the modern era of research on eyewitness memory has the same basic flaws as the work in the early twentieth century. Although the label for the research was "eyewitness memory" and the application of the work has been consistently focused on the criminal justice context, none of this research involved actual witnesses to actual crimes. Instead, the research involved questionable/inappropriate analogues to real eyewitness circumstances. Thus, in the typical study, a group of students is presented with an event, either via a recording (e.g., audio, video, film) or a staged live event. The memory of the student observers is questioned typically immediately after seeing the event. For obvious ethical reasons, the events can have no physical or emotional impact on the observers. Thus, these studies are an analogue, at best, for an unaffected bystander watching an innocuous event. However, there has been no hesitation to apply this to any witness, including victims, and to any context, regardless of the nature of the impact. The questionable face validity of the research had not limited the willingness of the researchers to apply the results to the criminal justice context (e.g., Loftus, 1979). The justification for the reliance on the laboratory has primarily been based on the need for control. Researchers have argued that the real world context is simply too complex and that the development of scientific knowledge requires more precision and control (e.g., "the implication that tests in the real world permit greater generalizability is false once the immense variability from one real world situation to another is recognized"; Banaji & Crowder, 1989, p. 1189). While there is no question that the laboratory provides much greater control and precision than conducting research in real world contexts, it does so, I believe, at the expense of utility. That is, the context of the laboratory is so different from the context of many crimes, particularly violent crimes, that using the lab to study memory in the forensic context is pointless. The gain in control and precision is vacuous.

While the laboratory researchers acknowledge that there is a lack of sufficient field research, they argued that the generalization of their laboratory results to the forensic context is justified: "we do not have the luxury of waiting until researchers get around to completing all the studies that would be desirable" (Loftus, 1986, p. 249). Expert testimony should be based upon relevant and appropriate evidence, not simply a belief that the findings are relevant. It is not a luxury to have field research but rather it is a necessity. The time and effort spent in studying an inappropriate analogue is wasted time and effort. However, the new generation of laboratory researchers of eyewitness memory are as eager as Munsterberg was to bring their analogue findings to the criminal justice system. Like Wigmore, I believe that much of the current laboratory-based research is of limited value in understanding the psychological processes that occur in the forensic context. However, in the final analysis, it is an empirical question: we must study the behavior of real witnesses to actual crimes. Then and only then will we have a foundation for a psychology of eyewitnesses.

In the following paragraphs, I explore several examples of phenomena studied in the lab that I believe are not and cannot be analogues of phenomena in the real world.

Effect of Stress

Real-life events in the forensic context often have a strong emotional component. Victims, witnesses, and, at times, offenders may feel fear or be traumatized by an event. Because of the central importance of emotion in the criminal context, laboratory researchers have tried to create an analogue for use in the laboratory. The results have been poor. For example, one analogue has involved the use of white noise as a stressor (e.g., Deffenbacher, 1983). That is, white noise is played to the laboratory witnesses while they observe an event. It should be obvious that this is not, in any sense, an analogue of the stress experienced by a witness to or a victim of violence. First of all, white noise is annoying but it is not a threat to life or limb (e.g., the emotional responses are entirely different). Secondly, white noise is a distractor that may draw attention away from the event. In the real world, violence has a variety of effects but distraction is not one of them (see Hervé, Cooper & Yuille, 2007). Other researchers have attempted to manipulate stress through varying the violent content of a film (e.g., Clifford & Hollin, 1981). It is stunningly naïve to think that violence in a film can serve as an analogue for directly experiencing violence (Yuille & Cooper, 2012; Yuille, Daylen, Porter, & Marxsen, 1995). Violent content on television and in films has inured most people to media violence. There simply is no possibility of creating a laboratory-based analogue for the kind of emotional response that a victim of violence (e.g., sexual assault) can experience. The laboratory studies of "stress" have not contributed at all to our understanding of how emotion impacts memory of witnesses to crime; the important questions related to the impact of violence have largely gone unanswered.

More recently, some researchers have attempted to exploit circumstances with strong emotional content to help in our understanding of the impact of emotions on memory. For example, Morgan et al. (2004) studied the memory of active duty military personnel enrolled in mock prisoner of war (POW) training. The focus of this study was on the ability of the trainees to recognize someone who had interrogated them during training. If one examines the average differences, low stress participants were better able to make identifications than those in the high stress condition. However, the more interesting result from this study was the variability in the manner in which trainees responded to interrogation stress: only 45 % of the witnesses made more accurate identifications under lower stress; for 42 % of the participants, variation in stress appeared to have no effect, while for 13 % of the witnesses, higher stress improved their identification performance. That is, for some, their memory was negatively affected by stress while, for others, the stress appears to have no effect or even improved their memory. This kind of variability is what one observes when working with victims, witnesses, and offenders in the criminal justice system. There is no typical or average way of responding to violence, threats of violence, sexual assault, hostage taking, etc. Instead, there is a range of the impact of stress all the way from a completely debilitating effect on memory to improving memory. It is this variability that should be the focus of forensic research (see Hervé, Cooper, & Yuille, 2007, present volume) and not average differences that ignore this variability. As noted earlier, this is one of the negative consequences of the methodolotry that characterizes contemporary eyewitness research. Mean differences provide little information to inform a psychologist, or triers of fact, about the impact of stress on eyewitness memory. The triers of fact need to understand the factors that cause the variable responses to stress. It is the individual differences that are informative, not the means.

Weapon Focus Effect

The weapon focus effect provides another excellent example of the problem of trying to develop an analogue in the lab for real world situations. This term—weapon focus—was developed to refer to a series of findings that showed a negative impact from the presence of a weapon in studies of experimental witnesses (e.g., Loftus, Loftus, & Messo, 1987). It was reported that laboratory witnesses who saw a film of a perpetrator carrying a weapon were less able to identify him compared to witnesses who saw the perpetrator without a weapon. The argument was that the weapon took a witness' attention away from facial features and on to the weapon. Once again, researchers saw no problem applying these results to the forensic context: they claimed that the presence of a weapon has a detrimental effect on eyewitness identification. It is a stunning leap of faith to make such an assertion without actually studying the impact of weapons in actual crime contexts.

Fortunately, more recently, several studies have examined the weapon focus phenomenon in the forensic context (e.g., Behrman & Davey, 2001; Cooper, Kennedy, Hervé, & Yuille, 2002; Griesel & Yuille, 2012; Tollestrup, Turtle, & Yuille, 1994). These studies have reported the results from examining police files of identifications or by interviewing actual victims and witnesses to determine the effect of the presence of a weapon on eyewitness memory. These real world studies have found no support for a consistent weapon focus effect. Thus, a weapon may attract attention away from the person holding it in a film but it doesn't appear to have the same effect in the real world; better put, the presence of a weapon appears to have variable effects in the real world. I'm not suggesting that the presence of a weapon does not have an impact—clearly it does. The presence of a weapon may make the situation more emotional and result in a variety of psychological changes in a victim or witness. However, those changes don't include a simplistic change in perceptual focus.

In an attempt to bolster the generalizability of laboratory findings to the criminal justice system Kassin, Ellsworth, and Smith, (1989) and Kassin, Tubb, Hosch, and Memon, (2001) have reported the results of surveys of experimental psychologists concerning the reliability of the laboratory findings. They concluded that researchers agree about the negative impact of a weapon on eyewitness memory. Researchers may agree on the reliability of the laboratory findings but the field research with actual witnesses to criminal events suggests that the weapon focus effect is not a reliable phenomenon in the real world. What is the value of agreement on the reliability of an analogue finding when the analogue does not compare to the real world situation?

Eyewitness Identification

A major focus of research in the modern era has been on eyewitness identification. Once again, rather than studying how witnesses to actual crimes perform when presented with photo spreads or lineups, researchers have primarily used videos and mock crimes with laboratory witnesses. The researchers have been so enthusiastic about the value of their laboratory research to the forensic context that they have advocated for widespread acceptance of changes in police practices based on the research outcomes (e.g., Wells, 1988; Wells et al., 1998). Once again, this advocacy was based entirely on laboratory studies and not on the variety of forensic contexts in which identifications are made. Subsequently, a single field study of actual eyewitness identifications was conducted (Wells, Steblay, & Dysart, 2011). Wells et al. found some results that appeared consistent with the laboratory findings and other results that were inconsistent. This should have led researchers to temper their enthusiasm about the generalizability of the laboratory findings (see Clark, 2012a). However, the laboratory researchers are so blinded by their methodolotry that they were forced to find faults with any applied studies when the findings of the field research did not match laboratory-based expectations (Wells, Steblay, & Dysart, 2012). These researchers are so convinced of the efficacy of their laboratory research that any inconsistent findings from field research must be wrong. This demonstrates how methodolotry has turned empiricism on its head. Our understanding of eyewitness psychology must stem, primarily, from studies of actual witnesses and not presumed analogues. Also, public policy requires a solid and appropriate research foundation (see Clark, 2012b); that is, field research. We cannot rely on the belief of laboratory researchers in the correctness of their methodology.

Similar examples could be provided for other eyewitness phenomena studied in the laboratory: the relationship between witness confidence and accuracy; the effects of delay on memory; cross racial identification issues; interview procedures; etc. In each case, the point would be the same (and redundant with the above examples): the context of the laboratory cannot serve as an analogue for forensic events. This is not an argument against laboratory-based research; such research can play a useful role. For example, studying the impact of alcohol (e.g., Read, Yuille, & Tollestrup, 1992) and other drugs (e.g., Yuille, Tollestrup, Porter, Marxsen, & Hervé, 1998) on memory may benefit from a combination of lab and field studies. However, when the purpose of conducting eyewitness research is to understand how victims, witnesses, and offenders respond to criminal events, then such events must be the focus of that research, not laboratory analogues. Occasionally, an experimental study could supplement the field-based literature when appropriate (e.g., to provide some precision about the amount of alcohol in the blood stream and the impact on memory). However, such efforts should be the exception rather than the rule.

The issue concerning the appropriate type of research is both empirical and ethical in nature. The only way that we can understand eyewitnesses to real events is to study them (Yuille, 1993). Asserting a belief in the generalizability of laboratory findings is simply that: a belief. It is not a proper foundation for scientific knowledge. Also, we are obliged, when providing testimony in court, to clearly indicate any limitations in the application of our knowledge to the case at trial. Claiming that our laboratory knowledge applies to the criminal justice context because we would like it to is not only empirically unjustified but also unethical.

Research with Witnesses to Actual Crimes

Although the vast majority of studies of eyewitness memory have employed the experimental methodology that characterizes the methodolotry of the field during the past 25 years, there have been increasing efforts to develop non-laboratory approaches for the study of memory in the forensic context. I was involved in the first such study (Yuille & Cutshall, 1986): my research team and I interviewed witnesses to a shootout between a gun store owner and a thief that occurred on a major public thoroughfare. We were able to compare the recall the witnesses provided to us several months after the event with the information they had reported to the police immediately after the event. Also, there was sufficient physical evidence at the scene of the crime to permit an assessment of the accuracy of witnesses' recall. This study became a template for a number of such studies which gave us the privilege of talking to victims and witnesses to a variety of criminal events. What has emerged from this body of work is a picture of eyewitness performance that is more complex than what had emerged from the thousands of laboratory studies. As noted earlier in this chapter, the major finding with respect to real world witnesses is the variability in their performance. That is, one witness to a violent event may provide very poor recall (e.g., either little detail or highly inaccurate detail) while another witness to the same event may display a detailed and accurate memory for the event. In addition, some findings from the lab (e.g., weapon focus) simply are not found in the field. The findings from the limited amount of field research provide a different picture of eyewitness performance and confirm that the lab simply cannot serve as an analogue for many aspects of eyewitness performance. Although the amount of field work is limited, it has led my colleagues and I to develop a model to explain the variety of factors that contribute to the variable pattern of real eyewitness memory (Hervé et al. 2007, present volume). The laboratory research on its own has never provided a foundation for the development of this type of model.

The fact that the Yuille and Cutshall (1986) study was the first of its kind (i.e., studying actual witnesses of criminal events), provides further evidence of the negative impact that methodolotry has had on this field. The appearance of this study followed decades of research and thousands of articles allegedly concerned with eyewitness memory and not one of them focused on actual eyewitness. It speaks volumes about the dependency on a particular methodology that no one even attempted to study what was reportedly the purpose of the research: eyewitnesses of crime.

The Reasons for Methodolotry

If the interest of researchers is the understanding of eyewitness behavior, why are they so reliant on studying analogue witnesses instead of the real thing? There are many reasons for this including the following:

1. It is a lot more convenient to bring students into the lab than it is to find real victims and witnesses for research. As someone who has conducted studies with real witnesses, I can attest to how difficult it is to do this type of research. It is difficult to obtain the cooperation of law enforcement and other agencies in order to conduct the research. One then has to obtain the cooperation of victims, witnesses, or offenders to participate in the research. For example, my colleagues and I have been studying the memory for sexual assault experiences in street sex trade workers (Cooper et al., 2002; Cooper, Yuille, & Kennedy, 2002; Griesel & Yuille 2012; Griesel, Ternes, Schraml, Cooper, & Yuille, present volume). Obtaining the cooperation of these participants—mostly women—was a difficult task requiring considerable sensitivity and community work. I should add, however, that it was a privilege that these individuals were willing to share their narratives of very difficult experiences with us.
2. Not only is the cooperation of students more easily obtained, a laboratory project can be conducted in a relatively short period of time. Research with real witnesses, whether it involves interviews or the use of file information, is very time-consuming. For example, my colleagues and I have been studying the memory of offenders for their crimes (Cooper, Cuttler, Dell, & Yuille, 2006; Cooper, Hervé, & Yuille, 2007; Cooper & Yuille 2007). In one study, we interviewed violent offenders in prison about their memories for a number of incidents, both violent and nonviolent. These interviews required many hours for each inmate—some interviews lasted as long as 2 days. Not only did the data collection require a great deal of time but the transcription and coding of the audiotaped interviews demanded even more time. The academic pressure to publish encourages the continued commitment to laboratory studies. Real world research would not allow the generation of enough publications to support tenure, promotion, and provision of grant funds. Only a tenured full professor can conduct this kind of field research and even then he or she might have difficulty getting or maintaining grant funds.
3. Most research is conducted by research assistants and volunteers. Conducting research with undergraduate students is relatively straightforward for the assistants. In contrast, research with victims of crime or with offenders can be difficult and emotionally taxing. My colleagues and I have found it necessary to spend time and effort preparing research assistants and volunteers before they are permitted to work with these populations. Furthermore, it is important to provide debriefing support for the assistants and volunteers as they conduct the research.
4. While the above factors play a role in continuing the preference for laboratory as opposed to field research, the primary reason for the preference for the lab is control. The training and the thinking of research psychologists convinces them that the control and precision provided by the laboratory are essential to the scientific enterprise. As noted earlier, the variability in real world contexts is perceived as too great to permit proper science. The irony is that the central feature of eyewitness behavior in the real world—variability—is used as an excuse to remove the variability and use the laboratory. This is the main consequence of the methodolotry: the questions that really matter about eyewitness behavior are ignored or distorted so that the questions can be examined in the lab.

The sad truth is that questions such as: What is the impact of trauma on memory? How accurate are real eyewitnesses? What are the factors that result in the substantial variability in eyewitness memory? etc., are ignored. These questions have not been answered because they can't be examined in the lab. As noted above, there have been a few studies in the past 25 years of real witnesses to actual crimes. Instead of these studies being the exception and a small minority in the field, they must become the standard if we are to learn about actual eyewitness behavior.

The Broader Impact of Methodolotry on Psychology

A recent report by Mitchell (2012) has suggested that the problem of generalizing laboratory findings to the real world extends to many areas of psychology outside that of eyewitness memory. Mitchell compared laboratory and field study findings across a number of subfields of psychology. He reported that the generalizability of findings from the laboratory to the field varied considerably from one area of psychology to another. One of the areas with relatively poor correspondence between laboratory and field findings is social psychology—the area probably most closely related to eyewitness memory research. Not only were many lab findings dissimilar from those in field research, but 26 % of the findings were in the opposite direction in the field compared to the laboratory. The laboratory is often a poor choice as an analogue for the study of a broad range of psychological phenomena. Mitchell concluded that:

> "Applied lessons are often drawn from laboratory research before any cross validation work has occurred, yet many small effects from the laboratory will turn out to be unreliable, and a surprising number of laboratory findings may turn out to be affirmatively misleading about the nature of relations among variables outside the laboratory" (p. 115).

Mitchell's conclusion about how misleading laboratory findings are is certainly substantiated in the area of eyewitness memory.

The Methodolotry Cure

The forensic context provides an opportunity to study aspects of human memory, emotion, behavior, etc., that is difficult or impossible to study in other contexts. Emotional criminal events have a profound effect on memory. Furthermore, variability in the memory of actual witnesses provides an opportunity to study the many factors that positively and negatively affect memory.

The cure for methodolotry is that we have to abandon our faith in the laboratory/experimental method as the appropriate methodology for studying forensic questions. We have to stop forcing the questions to conform to the methodology and instead adapt the methodologies to the needs of the particular question. The majority of studies should be field studies—based on archival analysis police files or field studies of actual victims, witnesses, and offenders. We can occasionally return to the laboratory to answer specific questions if and only if we can convincingly demonstrate that the laboratory is providing an appropriate analogue for the question under consideration. By focusing on research on field studies, we should be able to focus more time on developing new methodologies to facilitate the analysis of field findings. The evaluation of academic productivity of researchers doing this type of work will have to be adjusted to accommodate the additional time and resources, as well as the fewer publications that such research entails.

In addition to abandoning the laboratory as the primary venue for forensic research, we should develop an interest in individual differences that affect the variability in performance rather than a focus on average or mean performance. Means or averages can be of some use to the criminal justice system, but it is much more important to understand the range of responses and the causes for this variability.

I appreciate that moving from the lab to the field will not be easy for most of my colleagues. To do so requires an acknowledgement of the limited success of our current approach to research and a rejection of a deeply held belief in the efficacy of the experimental methodology as the appropriate path to knowledge about forensic eyewitnesses. However, we have to face the fact that we simply cannot develop a knowledge base of these witnesses through the use of analogues: it has not worked and it cannot work.

Finally, expert witnesses should follow standard ethical guidelines and provide the triers of fact with relevant research findings and not with analogue results. Expert witnesses should clearly delineate the limitations of their knowledge base.

The following chapters in this book are an encouraging sign of the changing focus of forensic research. Many of the studies/reviews reported in these chapters are the result of a move away from the laboratory toward the proper exploration of psychological phenomena in the forensic context. Although it is unfortunate that we devoted more than a century trying to force forensic questions into the laboratory—a context where they do not fit—it is encouraging to see an increasing realization that there is no analogue for the forensic context: in order to understand the victims, witnesses, and perpetrators of crime, we must study the victims, witnesses, and perpetrators of crime in situ.

References

Ayer, A. J. (1936). *Language, truth and logic*. New York: Dover.
Banaji, M. R., & Crowder, R. R. (1989). The bankruptcy of everyday memory. *American Psychologist, 44*(9), 1185–1193.
Behrman, B. W., & Davey, S. L. (2001). Eyewitness identification in actual criminal cases: An archival analysis. *Law and Human Behavior, 25*(5), 475–491.
Clark, S. E. (2012a). Costs and benefits of eyewitness identification reform: Psychological science and public policy. *Perspectives on Psychological Science, 7*, 238–259.
Clark, S. E. (2012b). Eyewitness identification reform: Data, theory, and due process. *Perspectives on Psychological Science, 7*, 279–283.
Clifford, B. R., & Hollin, C. R. (1981). Effects of the type of incident and the number of perpetrators on eyewitness memory. *Journal of Applied Psychology, 66*, 364–370.

Cooper, B. S., Cuttler, C., Dell, P., & Yuille, J. C. (2006). Dissociation and amnesia: A study with male offenders. *International Journal of Forensic Psychology, 1*(3), 69–83.
Cooper, B. S., Hervé, H. F., & Yuille, J. C. (2007). Psychopathy and memory for violence. *International Journal of Forensic Mental Health, 6*(2), 123–135.
Cooper, B. S., Kennedy, M. A., Hervé, H., & Yuille, J. C. (2002). Weapon focus in sexual assault memories of prostitutes. *International Journal of Law and Psychiatry, 25*(2), 181–191.
Cooper, B. S., & Yuille, J. C. (2007). Offenders' memories for instrumental and reactive violence. In S.-A. Christianson (Ed.), *Offenders' memories of violent crimes* (pp. 75–97). Chichester: Wiley.
Cooper, B. S., Yuille, J. C., & Kennedy, M. A. (2002). Divergent perspectives in prostitutes' autobiographical memories: Trauma and dissociation. *Journal of Trauma and Dissociation, 3*(3), 75–96.
Deffenbacher, K. A. (1983). The influence of arousal on reliability of testimony. In S. M. A. Lloyd-Bostock & B. R. Cliffors (Eds.), *Evaluating witness evidence* (pp. 235–251). New York: Wiley.
Gould, L. L. (2000). *America in the progressive era, 1890–1914*. New York: Milton.
Griesel, D., & Yuille, J. C. (2012). Sex trade workers narratives of sexual violence: A field investigation. *Memory.* doi:10.1080/09658211.2012.654797.
Hervé, H. F., Cooper, B. S., & Yuille, J. C. (2007). Memory formation in offenders: Perspectives from a biopsychosocial theory of eyewitness memory. In S.-A. Christianson (Ed.), *Offenders' memories of violent crimes* (pp. 37–74). Chichester: Wiley.
Kassin, S. M., Ellsworth, P. C., & Smith, V. L. (1989). The 'general acceptance' of psychological research on eyewitness testimony: A survey of the experts. *American Psychologist, 44*, 1089–1098.
Kassin, S. M., Tubb, V. A., Hosch, H. M., & Memon, A. (2001). On the 'general acceptance' of eyewitness testimony research: A new survey of the experts. *American Psychologist, 56*, 405–416.
Loftus, E. F. (1979). *Eyewitness testimony*. Cambridge, MA: Harvard University Press.
Loftus, E. F. (1986). Ten years in the life of an expert witness. *Law and Human Behavior, 10*, 241–264.
Loftus, E. F., Loftus, G. R., & Messo, J. (1987). Some facts about 'weapon focus'. *Law and Human Behavior, 11*(1), 55–62.
MacKenzie, B. (1972). Behaviorism and positivism. *Journal of the History of the Behavioral Sciences, 8*, 222–231.
Mitchell, G. (2012). Revisiting truth or triviality: The external validity of research in the psychological laboratory. *Perspectives on Psychological Science, 7*, 109–117.
Morgan, C. A., Hazlett, G., Doran, A., Garrett, S., Hoyt, G., Thomas, P., et al. (2004). Accuracy of eyewitness memory for persons encountered during exposure to highly intense stress. *International Journal of Law and Psychiatry, 27*, 265–279.
Munsterberg, H. (1908). *On the witness stand: Essays on psychology and crime*. New York: Doubleday.
Plante, E., Kiernan, B., & Betts, D. G. (1994). Method or methodolotry: The qualitative/quantitative debate. *Language, Speech, and Hearing Services in Schools, 25*(1), 52–54.
Read, J. D., Yuille, J. C., & Tollestrup, P. (1992). Recollections of a robbery: Effects of arousal and alcohol upon recall and person identification. *Law and Human Behavior, 16*(4), 425–446.
Spillmann, J., & Spillmann, L. (1993). The rise and fall of Hugo Munsterberg. *Journal of the History of the Behavioral Sciences, 29*, 322–338.
Titchener, E. B. (1898). The postulates of a structural psychology. *Philosophical Review, 7*, 449–465.
Tollestrup, P. A., Turtle, J. W., & Yuille, J. C. (1994). Actual victims and witnesses to robbery and fraud: An archival analysis. In D. Ross, D. Read, & S. Ceci (Eds.), *Adult eyewitness testimony: Current trends and developments* (pp. 144–160). New York: Press syndicate of the University of Cambridge.
Watson, J. B. (1913). Psychology as the behaviorist views it. *Psychological Review, 20*, 158–177.

Wells, G. L. (1988). *Eyewitness identification: A system handbook.* Toronto: Carswell Legal Publications.
Wells, G. L., Small, M., Penrod, S., Malpass, R. S., Fulero, S. M., & Brimacombe, C. A. E. (1998). Eyewitness identification procedures: Recommendations for lineups and photospreads. *Law and Human Behavior, 22,* 603–647.
Wells, G. L., Steblay, N. M., & Dysart, J. E. (2011). *A test of the simultaneous vs. sequential lineup methods: An initial report of the AJS national eyewitness identification field studies.* Des Moines, IA: American Judicature Society.
Wells, G. L., Steblay, N. M., & Dysart, J. E. (2012). Eyewitness identification reforms: Are suggestiveness-induced hits and guesses true hits? *Perspectives on Psychological Science, 7,* 264–271.
Wigmore, J. (1904). *Treatise on the Anglo-American system of evidence in trials at common law.* Boston: Little, Brown and company.
Wigmore, J. (1909). Professor Munsterberg and the psychology of testimony. *Illinois Law Review, 3,* 399–445.
Wundt, W. (1904). *Principles of physiological psychology (E. Titchener trans.).* London: Swan Sonnenschein.
Wundt, W. (1912). *An introduction to psychology (Trans. Pub. 1973).* New York: Arno Press.
Yuille, J. C. (1993). We must study forensic eyewitnesses to know about them. *American Psychologist, 48*(3), 572–573.
Yuille, J. C., & Cooper, B. S. (2012). Challenging the eyewitness expert. In D. Faust & J. Ziskin (Eds.), *Coping with psychiatric and psychological testimony* (6th ed., pp. 685–695). New York: Oxford University Press.
Yuille, J. C., & Cutshall, J. L. (1986). A case study of eyewitness memory of a crime. *Journal of Applied Psychology, 71*(2), 291–301.
Yuille, J. C., Daylen, J. L., Porter, S., & Marxsen, D. (1995). Challenging the eyewitness expert. In J. Ziskin & D. Faust (Eds.), *Coping with psychiatric and psychological testimony* (5th ed., pp. 1266–1298). Los Angeles, CA: Law and Psychology Press.
Yuille, J. C., Tollestrup, P., Porter, S., Marxsen, D., & Hervé, H. (1998). An exploration on the effects of marijuana on eyewitness memory. *International Journal of Law and Psychiatry, 21*(9), 117–128.

Chapter 2
Credibility Assessment, Common Law Trials and Fuzzy Logic

Gerald T.G. Seniuk

Judges or juries make decisions about the credibility of witnesses, decisions that might send one person to prison for years, strip another of her fortune or deny a parent full access to his children. An on-going judicial research project has been studying how such questions of contested fact are determined in a trial (Seniuk, 1994). The project reached out to experts from outside the legal profession to assess what knowledge or insight these other disciplines might shed on this question. For example, knowledge of forensic psychology and what the discipline has learned of credibility assessment and lie detection has greatly assisted this project (see Seniuk & Yuille, 1996; ten Brinke & Porter, present volume).

The purpose of this chapter is to reflect on that knowledge exchange and, as such, the focus here is on that type of trial where key witnesses disagree under oath about the essential facts of the case. These are not cases deductively reasoned toward legal principles or public policy positions. What are examined here are those kinds of cases where the trier must determine if the factual elements of a case have been proven. Furthermore, these are cases where there is no independent evidence that determines that question of fact. Although other pieces of evidence are considered in making the ultimate decision, in such cases, the fact finder, either judge or jury, ultimately makes the decision by relying on one witness over the other.

Although the forensic psychologists and the judges in the on-going judicial research project (Seniuk, 1994) considered various aspects of this question, one example is sufficient to illustrate my conclusion, which is that, while much can be learned by such exchanges, the essential issues are not resolved. Instead, new insights raise new issues for the trial process. The example I would choose for this purpose is the use of demeanour evidence. There has been awareness within the legal profession of the frailties of relying on demeanour evidence but, in my

G.T.G. Seniuk (✉)
Provincial Court of Saskatchewan,
Visiting Scholar, College of Law, University of Saskatchewan.
Saskatoon, SK, Canada
e-mail: seniuk@sasktel.net

experience, that was a dim awareness that resulted primarily in an anxious, impotent wringing of hands. For example, it was argued many years ago that such fact finding amounted to nothing better than guesses (Frank, 1949), but the practice of fact finding continued as before. Generations ago, a leading Canadian jurist, Chief Justice O'Halloran, repeatedly warned about the dangers of making decisions on the basis of which witness was believed. Phrases from his decisions such as, "The judge is not given a divine insight into the hearts and minds of witnesses appearing before him. Justice does not descend automatically upon the best actor in the witness box." (R. v. *Presley*, 1948), are quoted in decisions to this day, but the call he made for general reform more than 50 years ago did not lead to that.

Up until recent years, judges generally continued to explain their reliance on a witness because of "the demeanour of the witnesses" or because "the testimony had the ring of truth to it." However, it now appears that is changing, and such explanations for findings of fact are becoming rarer. Although there were changes in the law that also led to this growing concern with demeanour evidence, I think the change is at least in part due to the work of the judicial research project and the kind of credible scientific information forensic psychologists have brought into that discussion (see Seniuk and Yuille, 1996). One example that leads me to this observation is the use within judicial circles of a quotation that I first encountered only through the input of psychologists. Although the following idea by Ekman (1992) may have been well known in psychology circles, it was new to many of us in the 1980s:

> "It is amazing to many people when they learn that all of the other professional groups concerned with lying—judges, trial attorneys, police, polygraphers who work for the CIA, FBI or NSA (National Security Agency), the military services, and psychiatrists who do forensic work—did no better than chance. Equally astonishing, most of them didn't know they could not detect deceit from demeanour" (p. 285).

Presenting that quote and idea in judicial project workshops in those years did, in fact, bring amazement to many. It may have been saying essentially the same thing that Jerome Frank and Chief Justice O'Halloran had been cautioning everyone about decades before, but this warning had the rigor of science to back it up, and it commanded attention. Over the years, the quote began to surface in other workshops or presentations, and eventually has been joined to a list of other similar scientific reports, adding more emphasis to the message and gaining wider circulation within the legal community. The muted response to the jurisprudential cautions has now become conventional wisdom within the profession, thanks in part, to the work of the project.

Recent developments in the legal universe, such as changes to rules on corroboration (see Seniuk, 1992, for a summary of the history of these changes) and new theories in evidence scholarship (Allen, 1994a, 1994b) were also amplifying the previously muted concerns raised by legal writers such as Frank and O'Halloran. However, the ability to now point to scientific research, to be guided by quantified conclusions rather than to rhetorical warnings, strengthened the arguments of those, who for decades, previously might have been whistling in the jurisprudential wind.

Of course, psychologists did more than demonstrate the dangers of relying on demeanour evidence. They have also made advances in credibility assessment techniques (see Colwell, Hiscock-Anisman, & Fede, present volume; Griesel, Ternes, Schraml, Cooper, & Yuille, present volume; Hancock & Woodworth, present volume;

O'Sullivan, present volume; ten Brinke & Porter, present volume) which the North American courts have not been able to incorporate into their decision making on credulity matters. One problem is that these new techniques require specialized training (see Yarbrough, Hervé, & Harms, present volume). But even if a fact finder were trained in these new techniques, the new techniques are not recognized in law as something appropriate for application by a judge or a jury. The law looks to common human abilities as the primary intellectual tool fact finders should use to assess credibility. The law is wary of specialized knowledge (*R. v. Belland and Phillips*, 1987), especially newer scientific knowledge that has not been universally adopted by the particular discipline and proven over time. Thus, if a fact finder in a trial presumed to apply these techniques, lawyers on the losing side may very well use that as a ground of appeal. The law jealously guards this human function of the fact finder and is wary of allowing expert evidence that may supplant the fact finders role in determining the truthfulness of a witness.

In addition, the new techniques are geared more for investigative or interview processes (see Yarbrough et al., present volume) rather than the formalized and restricted courtroom environment. To the extent that they may have an application in the courtroom, it is the cross-examining lawyer who could use these skills in assessing which line of questioning to pursue with a witness. Judges and jurors are assigned a more passive, listening role. Finally, there is the question of the degree of reliability achievable by any of the current techniques. It may be that new technologies on credibility assessment might reflect the kind of certainty and reliability that we have experienced with DNA evidence, which is relied upon in the courts. But so far, advances in credibility assessment techniques do not make claims to that type of measurement of reliability. Although credibility assessment techniques do report improved accuracy above the 50% level (e.g., Ekman, 1992; Colwell et al., present volume; ten Brinke & Porter, present volume), the level achievable by chance or via the use of demeanour evidence, they do not claim to attempt to achieve levels of 90%, the threshold level many would assign to proof beyond reasonable doubt. However, even if such techniques were successful over 90% of the time, that kind of statistical, frequency measurement of accuracy is not useable by courts in assessing the credibility of a particular witness. Frequencies and statistical or subjective estimates of probabilities are not used in trials to establish the reliability of any particular witness.

The example of demeanour evidence is intended to demonstrate that, while the evolving knowledge in psychology can help myth-busting in the trial, those advances do not resolve the main issue in question. Although no longer using the lens of demeanour evidence alone, judges and jurors are still making decisions about whether a witness is truthful. We have made important gains in removing that error but that gain alone has not resolved the fundamental problem. If anything, it has raised more uncertainty. Removing that faulty lens helped us realize we were seeing things that were not there, namely reliable indicia of credibility, but our vision without the lens is not made more crisp or focused. If anything, everything is fuzzier now. As a result, we have brought a new issue into greater focus—the issue of indeterminism in the process generally. This can be seen as Appellate Courts review Trial Court decisions on credibility. In Canada, there has been a history of some Provincial Appellate Courts seeking more deterministic explanations by trial judges of their findings on credibility assessment. Generally these attempts by Provincial Appellate Courts have been reversed by the Supreme Court of Canada (see Allen & Seniuk, 1997, for a review of some of these cases in the latter half of the last; see *R. v. J.H.S.*, 2008, for a current example).

As we continue to grapple with this issue of indeterminacy, there are likely other new developments that could assist in our understanding of the interplay of credibility assessment with other aspects of the trial process—for example, the relatively new lens of *fuzzy logic*. Dr. Lotfi Zadeh, from the University of California, is the originator and leader of fuzzy logic and, his colleague, Dr. Madan Gupta, from the University of Saskatchewan, is an international leader in the field of neural networks and fuzzy systems. In their explanations of fuzzy logic, two important points are made right off the start. Fuzzy logic is not fuzzy but rather is a precise way to deal with imprecision (e.g., Ding & Gupta, 2000; Kaufmann & Gupta, 1985; Zadeh, 2004). Fuzzy logic has been and still is to a lesser degree an object of controversy, but one that is gaining more attention.[1]

Although it is precise, fuzzy logic is very different from traditional logic, and traditional logic is the basis of judicial reasoning. Traditional logic is bivalent, implying that every proposition is true or false with no degrees of truth allowed. This logic would seem to fit well in criminal law where you are either *guilty* or *not guilty*, and you are always *not guilty* unless the prosecution has proven beyond a reasonable doubt that you are guilty. In fuzzy logic everything is, or is allowed to be, partial (a matter of degree), imprecise (approximate), granular (linguistic) and perception based. Kaufmann and Gupta (1985) describe the distinction by using the example of illumination from a light bulb and a light switch. Bivalent logic is like having a light switch that you turn on or off. There is either zero illumination from the light, or full illumination. In law, you are either guilty or not guilty. Fuzzy logic is akin to using a dimmer switch to turn the illumination up or down, and there are degrees of illumination from zero to one. In between, there can be 0.2, or 0.4 or 0.7 or any degree of illumination between. In addition, we can use natural language to describe the degrees without requiring mathematical precision. The lighting may be very dim, somewhat dim, just right or too bright. In law, with the exception of the unique Scottish additional verdict of *not proven*, the switch is either on or off, *guilty* or *not guilty*, and there are no such degrees. Could there be? Should there be? By using this new lens of fuzzy logic as a framework for analysis, we can explore that question. Legal evidence scholarship has already begun looking at related questions.

In evidence scholarship, there has been recognition of insights similar to those of fuzzy logic, although legal scholarship has certainly not embraced fuzzy logic. However, there is recognition in evidence scholarship that fact finding and the logic of proof is not as crisp and precise as formalized legal reasoning makes it appear (Allen & Seniuk, 1997). From that perspective, the conventional view of legal proof

---

[1] Count of papers containing "fuzzy" in the title as compiled by Engineering Library, UC Berkley to October 2005 from INSPEC databases: 1970–1979=569; 1980–1989=2,404; 1990–1999=23,211; October 2000. 2005=17,785.

that focuses on the elemental structure of liability is replaced by a holistic view, from deciding the truth or falsity of particular elements to deciding the relative plausibility of opposing stories. This is analogous to the earlier shift in scientific thinking from the view that science is embarked on a march toward truth (i.e., just as trials are seen as a search for truth; *R. v. B. [K.G.]*, 1993), to the view that "progress" is measured by the articulation of better theories, where "better theories" means "better than the available alternatives" (Allen & Seniuk, 1997). The relative plausibility theory of evidence recognizes that evidence in a trial is not invested with only two probabilities—1.0 and 0.0—but rather views those as the end points of an infinite range of possibilities. One can hear evidence, not believe it to 1.0 probability, and still be influenced by it (Allen & Seniuk, 1997; see also *R. v. Mackenzie*, 1993, for a distinction between "facts" and "evidence of facts"). Thus, despite the conventional theories of legal adjudication which has a crisp framework, there is recognition that both the reality of the world and the trial process are fuzzy. While there is a growing recognition of this fuzziness, we lack an accepted method to reason in this uncertain mode, and that is where fuzzy logic might help.

Fuzzy logic is aimed at a formalization of modes of reasoning which are approximate rather than exact. As Zadeh (2004) explains, in the exact mode, we reason that "all men are mortal, Socrates is a man, and therefore Socrates is mortal." In approximate mode, we reason that "most Swedes are tall, Magnus is a Swede, and therefore it is likely that Magnus is tall." Criminal law forbids that kind of reasoning in the fact finding process, and instead insists that the question is whether Magnus is tall regardless of the incidence of tallness among other Swedes. The fundamental legal question that needs to be addressed is what use, if any, can be made of the generalization about most Swedes?

Related questions in law were the subject of debate 20–30 years ago (e.g., Anderson & Twinning, 1991). For example, say your degree of proof was 97% (note, however, that proof beyond reasonable doubt is not a matter of probabilities) and you knew that 98 of a group of 100 people each stole an apple; could you just convict any one of those 100 people of theft since the probability of you being right is 98%? I have not seen a similar degree of interest about such questions in legal literature in recent years. The initial flurry of discussion generated insight into the complexity of the fact-finding process, but it never provided any practical applications. Judges were still reliant on the basic tests established by legal precedent over the decades; and there is little or no guidance in legal precedent, other than the standard of reasonable doubt, as to appropriate modes of reasoning where the law allows fact finders the discretion to convict under uncertain and ambiguous conditions. Because of the developments outlined above concerning demeanour evidence, there is now great pressure on trial judges to demonstrate the path of their reasoning to a conclusion about facts that are in dispute, facts that are often resolved by reliance on a witness telling the truth. However, while there is this growing expectation to demonstrate highly accurate findings of fact, there is precious little in the way of criteria or framework to guide a fact finder in the work of concretely demonstrating the correctness of such findings when they are based on the trust placed in a witness.

This is where I think fuzzy logic can help because it is developing concepts that offer an approximation to reality—the reality of pervasive imprecision, uncertainty and partiality of truth. Those are exactly the problems that fact finders encounter in trials. There would mostly be no need for a trial if there were precision, certainty and full truth. Fuzzy logic may not determine whether Witness A or Witness B, or either, is telling the truth, but it might provide a framework for discussion about the degrees of reliability of trust that a fact finder has in a witness. I suspect it may have much to say about the systemic application of a most fuzzy concept—reasonable doubt.

The reasonable doubt standard is a single, objective and exacting standard of proof. It is not the same as a proof of probability, and it is not like subjective standards of care that we apply in important everyday situations. It is not proof to an absolute certainty. It is not proof beyond *any* doubt, nor is it an imaginary or frivolous doubt. It is based on reason and common sense, and not on sympathy or prejudice (*R. v. Lifchus*, 1997). Proof beyond reasonable doubt falls much closer to absolute certainty than to proof on a balance of probabilities (*R. v. Starr*, 2001).

It is especially at this level, at the systems level, that fuzzy logic may enrich our dialogue and study. For example, given the fuzziness of the application of a standard like *reasonable doubt*, is it not highly likely that different fact finders will end up at different degree points along the range of 0.0–1.0? Given such vagaries among fact finders, the outcome of a trial may vary according to the particular fact finder. This systemic indeterminacy is recognized (Polya, 1988), but not fully confronted as an issue.

In this connection, the insights provided by psychologists in the judicial workshops (Seniuk & Yuille, 1996) become even more important than we realized at the beginning of our project. We can see now that credibility assessment of witnesses is not simply a matter of technique and training. Given the complexity of assessing credibility, and given the legal discretion afforded fact finders in those determinations, that exercise in itself will be fuzzy in many cases. Add to that the fuzziness of the application of the standard of proof of reasonable doubt, and the systemic fuzziness in the common law trial may be significant. This is where fuzzy logic analysis provides a new lens through which to consider the implications of this indeterminacy. The following charts are typical of fuzzy logic analysis. Figure 2.1 shows an example of student grades as set out on a crisp, traditional chart. We define the range of marks, 0–59, for a student we rate as *poor*, 60–84 for *good* and 85–100 for *excellent*. The lines are fixed. If you have a score of 58, you are given a *poor* rating, despite the fact that your colleague, who only got 2 more marks than you, is rated as *good*. That student gets the same *good* rating as the student who is almost *excellent* at the 84 level.

Greater precision can be provided through the exact grade, but when the rating of students is at the verbal level, such as poor or excellent, that precision is lost. The ratings in a criminal trial are almost all at the imprecise verbal level—you are either guilty or not guilty. Although criminal proof is not a matter of probabilities (*R. v. Lifchus*, 1997), commentators often define proof beyond a reasonable doubt as proof above 95%, but not necessarily absolute certainty (see Fig. 2.2). The civil standard of proof is proof on a balance of probabilities, which is taken to mean the asserter's case is proven to above 50% (see Fig. 2.3).

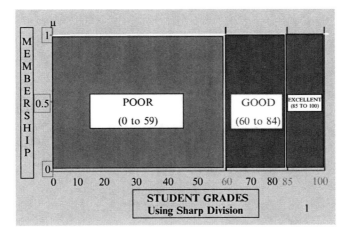

Fig. 2.1 Example of fuzzy logic analysis using sharp division for student grades

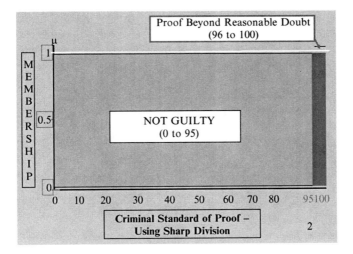

Fig. 2.2 Example of fuzzy logic analysis using sharp division for criminal standard of proof

Such comparisons to probabilities are misleading when discussing human cognitive actions such as determining guilt or liability. Probabilities have to do with physical events. For example, drawing one card randomly from a full deck allows one to state the probability of drawing any particular card. But assessments of evidence and the making of judgments are human, cognitive actions. So, proof beyond reasonable doubt is not proof between 95 and 100%—it is simply a very high degree of proof. That is a fuzzy concept.

By either standard of proof, once the determination of proof is made, a crisp line is drawn. You are either guilty or not guilty. You are either civilly liable or you are not liable. But such crispness must be illusory in some cases because there is a

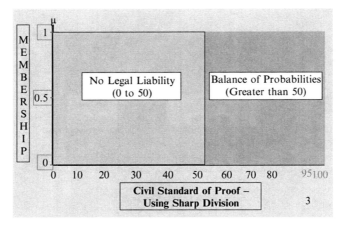

Fig. 2.3 Example of fuzzy logic analysis using sharp division for civil standard of proof

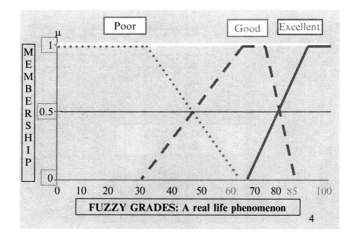

Fig. 2.4 Example of fuzzy logic analysis without sharp division for student grades

subjective element in making these determinations of criminal guilt or civil liability. In addition, such determinations are affected by the *context* of the case and the evidence. And as indicated earlier, modern evidence scholarship acknowledges the cognitive role played by the *experience and predilections* of a particular fact finder. Whenever we say that reasonable people might disagree with the determination, we are conceding that there is fuzziness about it.

Considerations such as these are all matters that fuzzy logic tries to come to grips with. In the example of the student grade, instead of drawing a crisp line, fuzzy logic would try to capture the slow, smooth and gradual progression within the sets of *poor, good* and *excellent*. In Fig. 2.4, we can see how one such graph might look, although the choice of graph style is itself subjective and fuzzy. The key concept in the fuzzy logic chart is that the categories of *poor, good and excellent* can overlap.

You can be both a *poor* and a *good* student at the same time. Instead of drawing crisp lines at "60" and "85," fuzzy logic treats the three categories as sets with ranges of membership in each.

The way to interpret such a graph is to view the green line with long dashes for *good* students as indicating that anyone at a mark of 60 and over has full membership of 1.0 in the *good* category. But, in addition, it tells us that those on the upward slope who would have been excluded from the *good* category in a crisp line are seen to be members of the set to varying degrees. For example, someone with a mark of 40 is a member of the *good* set to a degree of about 0.25. At the same time, someone on the downward slope of the green-dashed line is still a full member of the *good* category to a degree of 1.0, but they are also now members of the *excellent* set to varying degrees. For example, someone on the green-dashed line with a mark of 80 is totally a *good* student, but that student is also a member of the set of *excellent* students to a lesser degree, by about 0.5 on this graph. And while someone with a mark of 25 on their exam is fully within the set of *poor* students to a degree of 1.0, someone with a mark of 58 would only be a member of the *poor* student set to a degree of about 0.1 and, more importantly, would now be considered a member of the set of *good* students to a degree of 0.9.

Judges are experienced in dealing with such fuzzy sets when it comes to matters such as sentencing. For the same charge, different offenders might receive significantly different sentences (see Fig. 2.5). That is because, as fuzzy logic recognizes, each case is contextual and unique to its circumstances and experience. The offenders and their circumstances may differ, and so too might the circumstances or the harm intended or caused of the particular offence. And not unlike the example of student grades, sentencing is also exact—18 months for example—but people might differ over whether such a sentence was in the *light* or *moderate* set.

Other areas of judicial adjudication, however, are fuzzy without the underlying crispness that specific sentences provide—for example, the more fundamental issue of whether someone committed the offence at all, an issue that relates to credibility. Although the legal definition of the offence will be a crisp definition, the necessary finding of facts, often based on the credibility of a witness, or the matching of particular facts to the definition can be fuzzy. In actual practice, we, of course, make crisp conclusions—either guilty or not guilty—and make no use of fuzzy logic's insight of gradation and partial membership. Fuzzy logic reveals the uncertainty behind our picture of crispness and certainty, and it also provides a framework within which we can explore issues of uncertainty in a more precise manner. How far could one go in applying this framework?

It would be unsafe and unacceptable to recognize gradations or degrees of guilt, as in Fig. 2.6, for example, when considering whether someone was guilty of an offence beyond a reasonable doubt. That would be a slippery slope that is fraught with danger. Before we dare to allow the state to punish citizens, centuries of experience across different civilizations and continents has shown the necessity of maintaining the strict application of burdens of proof and high standards of crisp proof.

At the same time, real trial experience encounters the public frustration with such safe and crisp outcomes in the face of fuzzy and festering human and communal

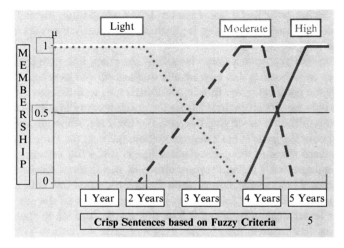

Fig. 2.5 Example of fuzzy logic analysis for criminal sentencing: crisp sentences for fuzzy criteria

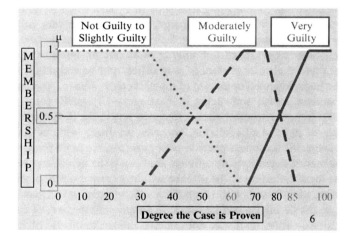

Fig. 2.6 Example of fuzzy logic analysis for degree of proof and guilt decision

relationship problems. Should there or could there be a finding other than "guilty" or "not guilty?" Could there be a category, for now call it "finding X", that somehow revealed the fuzziness and the uncertainty of exactly who did what, but yet recognized a community's ability, short of punishment, to respond to this "finding X," as in Fig. 2.7?

Could the prosecution have proven its case to a degree of 0.7 and the accused raised a reasonable doubt to a degree 0.3? We are able to deal in such gradations once the threshold has been crossed and the accused proven guilty beyond a reasonable doubt. Are there not some steps, albeit not a criminal sentence, that we

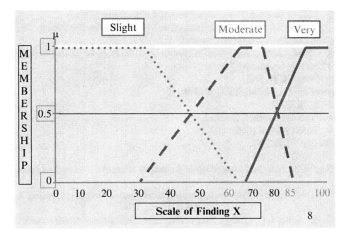

Fig. 2.7 Example of fuzzy logic analysis for "finding X"

could take when the proof does not cross the threshold of full membership of 1.0, but is definitely at membership level of 0.8? Another related question is whether we could apply the same gradation to the credibility of a witness, who might be quite believable, but how do you know for sure? In law, you apply the standard of reasonable doubt to questions of credibility, the same standard as applied to the test of criminal proof (*R. v. J.H.S.*, 2008). I know the answer in law would be to fear that such gradations will become a slippery slope with dangerous consequences. Hopefully, however, it can be safely discussed without leading us down any slippery slopes in the way demeanour evidence has apparently lead us for many, many years.

Acknowledgment Thanks to Dr. Madan M. Gupta, University of Saskatchewan, College of Engineering, for explaining fuzzy logic and for guiding the development of the fuzzy logic charts.

References

Allen, R. J. (1994a). Burdens of proof, uncertainty and ambiguity in modern legal discourse. *Harvard Journal of Law and Public Policy, 17,* 627–646.
Allen, R. J. (1994b). Factual ambiguity and a theory of evidence. *Northwestern Law Review, 88,* 604–640.
Allen, R. J., & Seniuk, G. T. G. (1997). Two puzzles of juridical proof. *Canadian Bar Review, 76,* 65.
Anderson, T., & Twinning, W. (1991). *Analysis of evidence.* London: George Weidenfeld and Nicholson.
Ding, H., & Gupta, M. M. (2000). Competitive and cooperative adaptive reasoning with fuzzy causal knowledge. *Journal of Intelligent and Fuzzy Systems, 9,* 191–196.
Ekman, P. (1992). *Telling lies.* New York: W.W. Norton.

Frank, J. (1949). *Courts on trial*. Princeton: Princeton University Press.
Kaufmann, A., & Gupta, M. M. (1985). *Introduction to fuzzy arithmetic: Theory and applications*. New York: Van Nostrand Reinhold Company Inc.
Polya, G. (1988). *Mathematics and plausible reasoning: Patterns of plausible inference* (Vol. 2). Princeton: Princeton University Press.
R. v. *B. (K.G.)* (1948) 7 C.R. 342.
R. v. *Belland and Phillips*, (1987) 2 S.C.R. 398.
R. v. *J.H.S.*, (2008) SCC 30.
R. v. *Lifchus* (1997) 5 C.R. (5th) 1 S.C.C.
R. v. *Mackenzie* (1993) 18 C.R. (4th) 133.
R. v. *Presley*, (1948) 7 C.R. 342.
R. v. *Starr* (2001) 36 C.R. (5th) 1.
Seniuk, G. T. G. (1992). Judicial fact-finding and a theory of credit. *Saskatchewan Law Review, 56*, 79.
Seniuk, G. T. G. (1994). Judicial fact-finding and contradictory witnesses. *Criminal Law Quarterly, 37*, 70.
Seniuk, G. T. G., & Yuille, J. C. (1996). *Fact finding and the judiciary*. Saskatoon: Commonwealth of Learning.
Zadeh, L. A. (2004). *Fuzzy logic systems: Origin, concepts, and trends*. Hong Kong: Paper presented at the Web Intelligence Consortium.

Part II
Investigative Interviewing

Chapter 3
The Investigation and Investigative Interviewing of Benefit Fraud Suspects in the UK: Historical and Contemporary Perspectives

Dave Walsh and Ray Bull

Introduction

Investigative interviewing in England and Wales has undergone transformation over the last 20 years or so as a result of (1) interviewers being trained in an interviewing framework; (2) the effects of legislation; and (3) the mandatory recording of interviews with all suspects (and those witnesses defined as vulnerable). Interviews that have been audio or video recorded have sometimes allowed the opportunity for later examination by either investigation professionals (e.g., senior officers) or researchers. As such, the number of studies of actual interviewing performance has grown. Almost all of these studies have examined the professional practice of police officers (e.g., Baldwin, 1993; Clarke & Milne, 2001; Griffiths & Milne, 2006; Moston, Stephenson, & Williamson, 1992; Oxburgh, Williamson, & Ost, 2006; Soukara, Bull, Vrij, Turner, & Cherryman, 2009). This is, perhaps, understandable since the police deal with most (and most serious) crimes. However, this approach has led to a gap in the knowledge of what happens in the growing number of interviews conducted by government agencies around the world that are also responsible for detecting and prosecuting criminal activity within their particular jurisdictions.

In the United Kingdom (UK), it is highly probable that, outside of the police, no other organizations interview suspects as regularly as those involved in the investigation of social security benefit fraud, where it is estimated that at least 120,000 interviews are conducted each year (Walsh, 2011). Over 400 local authorities (LAs) in the UK, in addition to a central government department (i.e., Department for Work and Pensions, 2010 [DWP]), administer social security benefits and investigate benefit fraud. The DWP employs approximately 3,250

D. Walsh (✉)
University of Derby, Derby, UK
e-mail: d.walsh@derby.ac.uk

R. Bull
University of Leicester, Leicester, UK

fraud investigation staff along with a further 2,000 personnel being employed in the range of LAs (Smith, Button, Johnston, & Frimpong, 2011). In this chapter, after the types of benefit fraud are defined, we examined, first from an historical perspective and then, later, from a more contemporary viewpoint, the performance of benefit fraud investigators when undertaking the investigative interviewing of suspected benefit fraudsters.

When compared to the wide range of crimes that the police investigate, benefit fraud is a relatively homogeneous matter, largely concerning the incorrect disclosure of personal circumstances. An example includes the unemployed deliberately failing to declare that they were undertaking work (or that they had substantial savings) as they knew that such declarations would reduce their social security benefit entitlements. Another example would be the case of a lone parent claiming social security benefits on the basis that there was no other household income, who concealed the matter that he/she was now living together with someone as husband and wife. Overstating or feigning the extent of one's reckoned disability is yet another form of benefit fraud. LAs also investigate landlords who either charge rent for their fictitious tenants (or continue to claim for those tenants who have moved on) or are colluding with tenants in claiming for rent that are in excess of that actually being paid (Smith et al., 2011). Benefit fraud is by no means a concern for the UK alone. Schneider and Enste (2002), for example, report that large shadow economies exist in both Austria and Germany, resulting in both abuse of the social security system and nonpayment of income tax. Other countries confronted with similar problems include Australia, Canada, France, Ireland, the Netherlands, New Zealand, and the USA (National Audit Office [NAO] 2006).

Despite the geographical breadth of social security fraud, little is known about either how the crime is investigated or, indeed, the motivations or attitudes of benefit fraudsters. In regard to the latter, Rowlingson, Whyley, Newburn, and Berthoud (1997) did find that many of those who admitted to committing benefit fraud knew it was illegal but (paradoxically) did not view themselves as criminals. This belief may stem from the view that benefit fraud can often be the result of perceived financial need (Katungi, Neale, & Barbour, 2006). Another study found that it was not uncommon for fraudsters to believe their illicit activity would go undetected and were most surprised when the authorities asked them to attend an interview concerning their committed fraud (SPARK, 2004). This finding may suggest that there is little preparedness by benefit fraudsters for the consequences of their actions. That said, Kapardis (2010) argues that fraudsters present at interviews as recalcitrant. This attitude, if true, may be possibly due to benefit fraud suspects' own beliefs that they have not committed any crime or what they did was justified through financial desperation. Further, although elsewhere (e.g., Porter & Yuille, 1995, 1996; Porter, Yuille, & Birt, 2001) it has been argued that criminals, in general, engage in deception and manipulation, Kapardis conjectures that the matter that fraudsters lied to commit their frauds may mean that they are also adept at lying in interviews conducted by the investigating authorities. O'Neal (2001) reinforces this viewpoint, stating that fraudsters provide an increased challenge for law enforcement as particularly competent and intelligent liars.

Benefit fraud investigators have exuded confidence in the belief that they can stop when suspects are lying, identifying nonverbal behaviors such as gaze aversion, fidgeting and hesitation as "indicators" of deceit (Walsh & Bull, 2011; Walsh & Milne, 2007). Similar confidence levels, later revealed to be overstated, have been found with police officers (DePaulo & Pfeifer, 1986; Mann, Vrij, & Bull, 2004). Mann et al. (also Akehurst, Köhnken, Vrij, & Bull, 1996; Strömwall, Granhag, & Hartwig, 2004) found this frequent inability to detect lies due to inaccurate beliefs (such as those found in the above studies of benefit fraud investigators) concerning what were cues to deception. Studies have regularly found that people often perform at no better than could be expected by chance when they rely on nonverbal signals to detect deception (Colwell, Hiscock-Anisman, & Fede, this volume; Feeley & Young, 1998; Porter, Woodworth, & Birt, 2000; ten Brinke & Porter, this volume).

In interviews with suspects, benefit fraud investigators are trained to gather information in interviews with suspects to inform the investigation (Walsh, 2002, 2011). However, they may also be aiming to identify deceptive behavior of suspects based on these (and other) untrustworthy behavioral indicators, many of whom they already suspect of being guilty (Walsh & Bull, 2011; Walsh & Milne, 2007). This level of assumption of guilt may be as a result of the way that benefit fraud tends to be investigated. Generally, it is known that interviews with benefit fraud suspects are often the culmination of the investigative process, conducted only after investigators have gathered sufficient evidence that supports and reinforces their own beliefs that the suspect has committed offences.

In more general criminal investigative contexts, Ormerod, Barrett, and Taylor (2008) argue that early commitment to a specific hypothesis (such as deciding that the suspect is guilty) can have highly negative consequences on the subsequent investigation, where investigators either fail to pursue lines of enquiry or pursue ineffective lines of enquiry. Thus, Ormerod et al. state that, unless multiple hypotheses are generated during an investigation (including those that retain the notion that the suspect is innocent), this investigative mindset may lead to distortions of objective information that merely correspond to existing, but possibly inaccurate, beliefs, being an intrinsic part of cognitive processes (Ask & Granhag, 2005). Such biases towards guilt may lead to benefit fraud investigators being confident prior to the interview that the suspect is guilty (Shawyer, 2009; Walsh & Bull, 2011; Walsh & Milne, 2007). Existing belief in the guilt of suspects may well also influence interviewing behavior, resulting in a confirmation bias during the interview as interviewers attempt to confirm their beliefs (Savage & Milne, 2007). The presence of organizational and personal targets associated with positive case outcomes (i.e., those that relate to establishing that an offence appears to have been committed) may only serve to distort this behavior further. In such contexts, there is less personal stake in investigators believing that the suspect is innocent. Moreover, Walsh and Bull found a tendency for interviews conducted by benefit fraud investigators to possess a confession orientation, despite this explicitly not being the aim of the interview model in which they are trained. It is thought that such approaches are a result of implicit beliefs held by investigators that decisions made concerning the outcome of the cases are more likely to be in favor of, say, a prosecution if a confession has been made in the interview (Walsh, 2002).

Historical Approaches to the Investigation of Benefit Fraud Suspects

As has been noted, little research exists concerning the practices of investigators employed in combating abuses of welfare systems. This is particularly the case in the UK where prosecuting benefit fraudsters was, up until the early 1980s, deemed to be the appropriate method of dealing with those who were believed to have committed offences. As with the police in this era, little was known about the interviewing practices of benefit fraud investigators. At this time, all interviews with criminal suspects were conducted under procedures known as the Judges'Rules, which merely required interviewers to produce a written summary report of the interview as soon as practicable after the interview had concluded. Thus, as many interviews were conducted with suspects who were not legally represented, interviewers were frequently the sole presenters of what was said in the interview (Bryan, 1997). In regard to benefit fraud, two developments had a major influence on benefit fraud investigations in the 1980s. Firstly, legislation in England and Wales was introduced that revised the approach and procedures concerning interviews with suspects. Secondly, government efficiency measures at this time designed to reduce the financial burdens of the public services meant that there was a move away from prosecuting benefit fraudsters. Each is examined in turn below.

The Police and Criminal Evidence Act (1984) was brought about as a result of concerns with miscarriages of justice as a result of the interviewing techniques of police officers and their apparent disregard for the rights of suspects. In studies conducted for the Royal Commission on Criminal Procedure (RCCP), which led to the introduction of PACE, it was found that the police usage of manipulative and persuasive tactics was prevalent (Irving, 1980; Softley, Brown, Forde, Mair, & Moxon, 1980). Examples of these tactics included the police (1) pretending to have more evidence than they actually had; (2) pointing out the futility of denial and the "benefits" of confession; (3) minimizing the seriousness of the offence; and (4) manipulating the suspect's self esteem (Milne & Bull, 1999). While, as Redlich and Meissner (2009) acknowledge, such tactics can lead to the guilty confessing, these interviewing techniques may also lead to innocent suspects making false confessions (see Gudjonsson, 2003, for a review).

PACE, along with its associated compulsory Codes of Practice, provided the framework by which any investigators (i.e., not just the police) undertook interviews with suspects if their case were to be later considered for criminal proceedings. Briefly, the legislation required interviewers to inform suspects of their legal rights before any questioning took place. Specifically, any interview conducted under PACE was to be prefaced by the interviewing officer informing the suspect of their legal position in relation to what evidence they provided in the interview, the implication of remaining silent in response to questions, and their right to legal representation in the interview.

The legislation also necessitated all those interviewing criminal suspects to fully record, initially (i.e., when PACE was first introduced) on a written contemporaneous

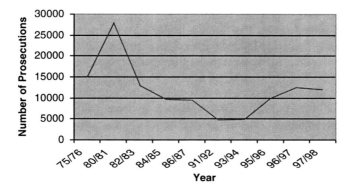

Fig. 3.1 Social Security Prosecutions in the UK 1975–1998 (Source: Benefits Agency Security Branch, 1999)

basis, and then later (i.e., from 1986), by audio-taping, the exchanges that occurred during the interview. These measures provided forms of assurance to the suspect that they knew fully the implications of any statements made, before making them, while the interview record was reckoned to supply some safeguard, for example, that the interviewer's questioning was neither oppressive nor inducing to admissions. PACE therefore supplied the legal imposition on investigating agencies to ensure that suspects are treated fairly when undergoing questioning about possible criminal offences.

The second major change that impacted upon the way that benefit fraud was investigated was prompted by governmental initiatives to reduce public expenditure. In regard to social security benefits, the changes meant introducing measures argued to help in restraining and reducing fast growing social security expenditure on benefits themselves, as well as undertaking to (1) investigate more suspected fraud cases; and (2) where fraud was thought to have been uncovered, to deal with it more swiftly (and in a less costly way) than would otherwise happened had the case been prosecuted. Both of these steps meant that fewer people were prosecuted each year during the 1980s and 1990s, as can be seen from Fig. 3.1. Instead, the emphasis was for benefit fraud investigators to terminate benefit claims, often without much consideration as to whether there had been any past fraud. As a result, during the 1980s, as Fig. 3.1 demonstrates, a considerable reduction in the number of prosecutions occurred (Barker, Watchman, & Rowan-Robertson, 1990).

The revised approach in the 1980s to combating social security fraud and abuse included investigators employing interviewing procedures that were not as tightly governed as those necessarily conducted under PACE guidelines, e.g., as there was no intention to prosecute. It was in this period that a number of small studies, although not examining specifically the interviewing performance of benefit fraud investigators, voiced concerns over their practices. In one such study, Moore (1981) examined social security fraud investigation strategies, reporting concerns regarding the standards of investigation when investigation outcomes other than criminal prosecutions were chosen by investigators. Moore found that, in practice, benefit claims were often reinstated when welfare rights organizations challenged the activities of investigators. His findings reflected concern over the lower level of legal safeguards involving informal interviews, resulting in "negotiated settlements" such as benefit claim withdrawal rather than prosecution.

Loveland (1989), in his study of LA benefit fraud investigations, found a divergence of practice not only between different LAs but also among investigators in the same LA. Loveland noted that investigators saw claim withdrawal by suspects as a "victory." Furthermore, for investigators, threats of prosecution were seen as favored and acceptable forms of bluff, as was a warning of continued investigation, should the suspect not agree to a termination of the benefit claim.

In another study, a report by the charity, the National Association for the Care and Resettlement of Offenders (1986), noted that, during the 1980s and 1990s, there was a more proactive approach to benefit fraud investigation. Rather than teams responding to allegations made by the public about possible benefit fraud, investigation teams examined what was claimed to be "at risk" cases (e.g., those who had been claiming benefit for a period of time without making requests for extra single payments for essential items such as clothing and bedding). The belief was that such benefit claimants would have to be receiving income from elsewhere if they had not resorted to claiming for these extra needed items. This unscientific and guilt presumptuous base for investigation, selected wholly on case characteristics rather than any genuine suspicions, led to some controversial practices with benefit claimants being interviewed without any apparent firm evidence of wrongdoing, seemingly at random. Examples of interviewer practice were persuasion, coercion, bluff, negotiation, and threats of prosecution if benefit claims were not withdrawn (Barker et al., 1990; NACRO, 1986; Smith, 1985). These activities occurred despite the absence of any supportive evidence of wrongdoing had the case been put to proof in the courts (Dingwall & Harding, 1998). Undue pressure and harassment by these specialist teams also emerged with allegations of (1) interview rooms being locked until agreement to terminate claims had been reached; (2) deals being entered into if the claim was terminated; and (3) interviewees' benefit payment books being torn up in front of them (e.g., as if to show them their claim was now terminated, regardless of any protestations of innocence; Smith, 1985).

Smith (1985) also noted that official procedural guidance in 1981 appeared to condone hard and soft interrogation methods: "If two officers are involved in the interview, leave one to concentrate on understanding the claimant's circumstances and problems while the other concentrates on safeguarding public funds" (Hansard, as cited in Smith, 1985, p. 139).

Investigations undertaken with the sole aim of terminating claims were carried out outside of the criminal justice system, requiring the (i.e., lesser) civil burden of proof, which would be based on the balance of probabilities rather than the criminal one of beyond a reasonable doubt. As such, investigations requiring this lower test of evidential proof required less rigorous evidence gathering. Further, as these particular investigations would not normally enter the process of criminal law, being more usually conducted under administrative than criminal procedures, interviews with suspects were not generally conducted under PACE guidelines. Official figures illustrate the frequency of these less formal investigations. In 1989–1990, for example, UK government statistics showed that around 86,000 investigations had resulted in a withdrawal of the benefit claim while, during the same period, less than 10,000 prosecutions were conducted (Benefits Agency Security Branch, 1999; Department of Employment, 1991).

To an extent, such policies and procedures enacted by benefit fraud investigation teams were far from opposed by public opinion at that time. Public attitudes across the whole socio-economic spectrum towards certain benefit claimants (i.e., the unemployed and lone parents—those most likely to be investigated) were largely pejorative (Deacon, 1978), being seen as feckless, workshy or criminal (Fitzpatrick, 1999; Whiteley, 1981); they were labelled as the "undeserving poor" (Lister, 2004; McKeever, 1999; Sainsbury, 2003; Taylor-Gooby, 1985), or more bluntly, "scroungers" (Cook, 2006; Deacon, 1980; Golding & Middleton, 1982; Lister, 1991; Moore, 1981). Rowlingson et al. (1997) also found that the public tended to believe that most benefit claimants were fraudsters. Loveland (1989) provided conjecture as to whether official attitudes conspired to view a disregarding of any rights of benefit fraud suspects as legitimate. That is, suspects, presumed guilty of "fiddling" the benefit system and stealing "our" money, were viewed as the very worst of a very bad lot. Consequently, they merited little respect when under investigation or when being interviewed (e.g., a basic right they had forfeited when "choosing" to first to claim and then defraud "us"). Espousals from the then Conservative government in Britain hardly discouraged these stereotyped views to flourish (Lilley, 1992). As benefit fraud investigators are also drawn from the general population, Hill (1969) argued that it could have been reasonably assumed that they too held these prejudices.

Guilt presumption has been shown to have adverse consequences upon interviewers' behavior (see Yarbrough, Hervé, & Harms, this volume). Kassin, Goldstein, and Savitsky (2003) found that interviewers who held preexisting beliefs about the guilt of suspects asked questions in mock interviews with suspects geared towards confirming these beliefs, while undertaking interviewing strategies that were more coercive, being conducted to obtain a confession. Kassin et al. highlight the dangers of such coercive tactics in persuading innocent suspects to falsely confess. In contrast, Holmberg and Christianson (2002), and Kebbell, Hurren, and Mazerolle (2006) both found that convicted offenders, who confessed to their crimes, stated that their interviewers were open-minded. It would seem from the above that there is a disparity between what interviewers consider as appropriate strategies for uncovering what they believe to be the truth concerning suspects' presumed guilt and those where actual guilty suspects will more willingly tell the truth.

The majority of benefit investigations during the latter part of the 1980s and early 1990s, as has been noted, were largely carried outside of formal criminal justice procedures and without measures that had been introduced to protect the rights of suspects. From the first author's knowledge, records of interviews conducted outside the provisions were file notes and statements composed by the interviewing investigator, which harked back to the period before PACE was introduced. Even in those interviews that eventually led to prosecution, the practice of contemporaneously written note-taking persisted until around 1997 when audio-taped interviewing of interviews with benefit fraud suspects became normal practice. Accordingly, there continued to be little opportunity to examine the interviewing skills or techniques. This is in contrast with the police who had audiotape recorded interviews with suspects since the mid 1980s (Milne & Bull, 1999).

The presence of tapes as records of police interviews had led to several independent analyses being conducted (e.g., Baldwin, 1993; Moston et al., 1992). These studies found that the manipulation and persuasion, evident in those studies before PACE was introduced, was no longer apparent in interviews with suspects [note: similar findings were reported by Irving and McKenzie (1989), who observed police interviews]. However, revealed in both Baldwin's and Moston et al.'s large scale studies were the presence of approaches by interviewers, characterized by (1) an accusatorial stance; (2) failures to build rapport with, or gather any account from, suspects; and (3) in the face of denials, many officers appeared to be unaware of what else they could do and, as such, the interview generally subsided to closure.

These findings suggested that, although PACE had restricted the conduct of certain unethical practices (i.e., compared to the situation prior to its implementation), police officers had not been advised (or trained) in what they could do to help professionalize their interviewing practice. In contrast, most benefit fraud investigations in the early 1990s continued to be conducted without the aim of prosecution. As a direct result of this organizational strategy, it appeared that those investigating these offences could continue to both disregard PACE and to use unsavory practices since the termination of benefit claims was viewed as a "satisfactory" (and expected) means of resolving the vast majority of fraud investigations. Thus, tension was built between (1) benefit fraud investigation targets and the practices required to meet them, and (2) the intentions of PACE that sought to safeguard suspects against such practices.

Training Police Officers to Interview

The lack of interview training or guidance for police officers noted above meant that police officers were already facing a tension. On the one hand, they were expected to detect crimes and prosecute criminals (who denied offences of which they had been accused). On the other hand, they were now to conduct interviews in a fair but robust manner, which was a departure from the interviewing styles that had been practised before the introduction of PACE (Irving, 1980). The resulting unsatisfactory interviewing performance, found in the studies that examined police interviews at the turn of the 1990s (e.g., Baldwin, 1993; Moston et al., 1992) led to an introduction of an interviewing framework that would be soon implemented throughout police forces in England and Wales, (entitled the PEACE model; Milne & Bull, 1999).

PEACE is advocated as an ethical and fair approach to interviewing (Milne & Bull, 1999), and is a mnemonic acronym which provides a structure for the recommended five stages of the interview framework—(1) *Preparation and Planning* before the interview (this task includes the thorough collection and, then, assembling of evidence, considering any rebuttals and alibis that may be offered by the suspect and undertaking, if necessary, further evidence gathering to deal with them, and ensuring that it is understood what legal points need to be proven for the offence to be considered as one that may well have occurred); (2) *E*ngaging and *E*xplaining to the suspect the purpose of the interview and their rights therein; (3) asking for an *A*ccount from the suspect (and clarifying and challenging when necessary, and is the phase where evidence should be disclosed) before (4) bringing the interview to *C*losure; and, thereafter, (5) *E*valuating the interview to ascertain where any improvements could be made. Evaluation concerns both self and subordinate evaluation, although inconsistent approaches to this task have been found in a number of studies (largely believed to be caused by a lack of senior management guidance) (Clarke & Milne, 2001; Walsh & Bull, 2011; Walsh & Milne, 2007). The model is not necessarily a linear one. For example, when undertaking a final summary in the Closure phase, an interviewer may identify an opportunity to resume questioning if it is identified (e.g., after summarizing what had been said in the interview) that further clarification of the suspect's account is needed.

Initial evaluations of officers trained in the PEACE model were positive. For example, officers who had been trained were assessed as having improved communication skills both immediately following training and 6 months afterwards, when compared to a control group of untrained officers (McGurk, Carr, & McGurk, 1993). Indeed, further evaluations using similar scales of measurement built around the recommended PEACE framework of skills, although still noting several flaws in officers' interviewing performance (e.g., such as in preparation, rapport building, summarizing, developing topics, challenging, and closure skills) suggested a trend towards better interviewing styles than that which was present before the introduction of the PEACE model (see Clarke & Milne, 2001; Griffiths, 2008; Soukara et al., 2009). These studies particularly noted the absence of unethical interviewing techniques and the increased efforts to obtain a full account from suspects by way of open and probing questions.

The introduction of the PEACE model represented the first standardized approach in the UK towards training police officers in the discipline of investigative interviewing of suspects. Previously, police officers had been trained in a haphazard and unstructured way, for example, by way of sitting in with more experienced officers (Milne & Bull, 1999). Further, no literature had been published that guided police officers in England and Wales (and others responsible for investigating offences in that country) as to how to interview suspects. One exception to this scarcity of published material was that of a serving British police officer (i.e., Walkley, 1987). However, his recommendation to persist in the manipulation of suspects who were presumed to be guilty had been quickly discarded by the police in England and Wales, as it was soon recognized by senior police officers how at odds Walkley's approach was with the aims of PACE. Walkley's recommended approach was heavily influenced by the Reid model (see Inbau, Reid, & Buckley, 1986; Inbau, Reid, Buckley, & Jayne, 2013). The confession-centred Reid model, still used extensively to train investigators in the USA and Canada, advocated, amongst other tactics to be used by interrogators, the use of (1) maximization (e.g., stating that the evidence against them was greater than it actually was or stating that the consequences of not confessing would be serious); (2) minimization (e.g., underplaying the seriousness of the offence or excusing the motivations); or (3) stating situational futility (i.e., officers telling suspects that they were guilty so they should confess).

Inbau et al. (2013) declare that their Reid model should only be used with guilty suspects, although such assumptions of guilt were to be derived from a preceding interview before the interrogation proper (i.e., known as the Behavioral Analysis Interview or BAI). In the BAI, it is advocated that interpretations of verbal and nonverbal responses provide confidence if suspects are lying about their guilt. Recent studies have consistently found that (1) such indications were unreliable channels in identifying liars and (2) that police officers (whether trained in the Reid model or otherwise) are often no better than chance in detecting whether people are telling either truth or lies when based on such signals, regardless of their expressed confidence in their own ability to detect lies (see ten Brinke & Porter, present volume; see Vrij, 2008, for a comprehensive review). Additionally, those investigators undertaking the Reid model have rarely been scrutinized concerning the effectiveness of their interviewing performance in the way that the police recently have in England and Wales. King and Snook (2009), however, observed 44 interviews conducted by police officers in Canada, finding that many of them used many components of the Reid model. King and Snook also found that, when that model was undertaken along with, what was described by the authors as a coercive style, there was a positive association with confessions by suspects (but see Bull & Soukara; 2010; Holmberg & Christianson, 2002).

It has also been argued elsewhere that the very approaches that the Reid model advocates may lead to the likelihood of some suspects confessing to crimes that they did not commit (see Gudjonsson, 2003). The Reid model, which, as Perillo and Kassin (2011) assert, "increases the anxiety associated with denial while reducing the anxiety of confession" raises concerns (p. 327). Memon, Vrij, and Bull (2003) argue that trickery and deceit, inherent to the Reid model, make false confessions more likely and that the method is unethical because it includes lying to suspects. Memon et al. also assert that the model is heavily reliant on using nonverbal cues to deception that have been found to be unreliable (DePaulo & Pfeifer, 1986; Köhnken, 1987; Vrij & Mann, 2001). It is, perhaps, unsurprising that Walkley's (1987) model was ignored by the police since it was these very techniques that were effectively being discouraged by the introduction of PACE.

Training Benefit Fraud Investigators to Interview

Unlike the police, Walkley's (1987) recommended approach to interviewing suspects was not similarly discouraged in benefit fraud investigations. Indeed, it is the first author's knowledge that Walkley's model formed the backbone of their advanced

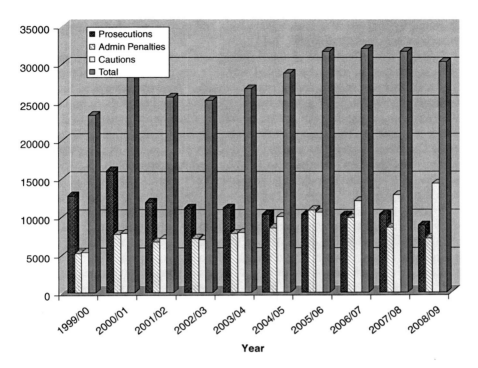

Fig. 3.2 Numbers sanctioned nationally for benefit fraud by the DWP 1999–2009; Source: Cook (2006); DWP (2010)

interviewing training courses in the early 1990s. However, the British Government began to concede that an approach to tackling benefit fraud predicated upon claim termination rather than prosecution had not made any real impact upon the level of benefit fraud (Benefits Agency, 1995). In response, a strategy strongly tilted towards an increased examination of retrospective wrongdoing was to be introduced (Department of Social Security, 1998). A new range of sanctions were initiated that not only included prosecutions, but also cautions and administrative penalties (for lesser serious cases). Cases considered for these new sanctions would, however, still have to be of a prosecutable standard. That is, regardless of whether the intention was to prosecute, those cases would be expected to be of a similar standard in terms of investigation procedures and evidence of guilt as those cases that proceeded to court. This revised approach led to an increase during the next 10 years of the numbers sanctioned (and thus interviewed) by the DWP when compared to the previous performance regime in much of the 1980s and 1990s (see Fig. 3.2).

At the same time as this introduction of the sanctions, a national roll-out of training in the PEACE model commenced for DWP and LA investigators. The PEACE interview training course (i.e., designed for both investigation managers and their investigators) initially lasted for 5 days and contained theory and discussion followed by two simulated interviews (Walsh, 2002). More recently, training is now delivered by a blend of e-learning methods and course attendance (when mock interviews are conducted; Walsh, 2011).

LAs and the performance of their investigators during the mid-1990s had come to be scrutinized in an unprecedented way. For example, the Audit Commission (i.e., a British government authority that examines performance across the public services) reported in 1997 that an over-emphasis existed upon the termination of claims from a current date rather than examining fraud retrospectively which could lead to prosecution. This attention towards benefit claim termination reported by the Audit Commission was illustrated in their findings where, nationally, less than 1,000 prosecutions had been undertaken in 1996 by the LAs compared to 150,000 claims terminated. It was also found that more than half of those LAs studied had not prosecuted anyone at all.

In 1999, a further Audit Commission report detailing progress since their 1997 study still showed a patchy response nationally to the investigation of fraud by LAs and that training of investigators was reckoned to be inadequate in 60% of LAs, as it largely consisted of observing more experienced investigators. The 1999 report also noted that around one-third of LAs still did not pursue overpayment of benefit and, thereby, prosecutions were being apparently content to terminate current claims, despite such concerns being highlighted in their earlier 1997 report.

The later report did find, however, increases, though slight, in the number of prosecutions undertaken; that said, some LAs seemingly still possessed no prosecution policy. The consequence of such an approach was that prosecutions remained relatively exiguous. Since 2002, however, various central government funding mechanisms for LAs have been regeared to encourage retrospective investigation of wrongdoing of those suspected of fraud against LAs. The effect of these changes has led to further increased levels of prosecution and the other sanctions. Similar to the change in performance indicators in the DWP in 1999, Fig. 3.3 illustrates that the number of sanctions (and, therefore, interviews with suspects under PACE) has grown hugely as a result (National Audit Office, 2003).

Audits of LA performance in their anti-fraud activity were also undertaken between 1998 and 2008 by a central government organization (and part of the DWP) called the Benefit Fraud Inspectorate (BFI). Reporting to the Secretary of State for Work and Pensions, the BFI, before their disbandment, played a key role in identifying good practices in counter-fraud activity both in the DWP and the LAs. The Inspectorate conducted 267 inspections into LA fraud operations across the UK from 1998 to 2008 covering almost half of the 440 LAs in the UK (e.g., including repeat visits to certain LAs; http://www.dwp.gov.uk).

A review of these 267 inspections undertaken by Walsh (2011) suggested concern by the BFI regarding the standard of certain selected key areas of performance. Specifically, this review found that 77% of BFI reports showed concern largely relating to the lack of attention to the PEACE model. The BFI reported that their inspections of investigative standards found many investigators conducting unsatisfactory questioning of suspects (such as tending to ask closed questions or making statements as to what they thought suspects had done or knew, but little time was spent on gathering information or probing of given accounts as the PEACE model

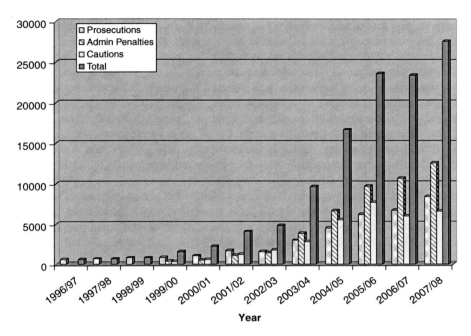

Fig. 3.3 Sanctions completed by LAs from 1996–1997 to 2007–2008; Sources: Audit Commission (1997; 1999); NAO (2003); DWP (2010)

prescribes). The BFI suggested these shortfalls were likely due to a lack of thoroughness in interview planning and preparation by investigators (again, as the PEACE model recommends). Concerns were also expressed in 64% of the BFI reports in regard to the matter that training had not been given to staff. Thus, the BFI felt that investigators were ill-equipped with the necessary skills to carry out interviews. Where training had been delivered, the BFI generally found that it had not been undertaken in any systematic fashion but merely consisted of job shadowing more experienced DWP or LA investigators. After examining the BFI reports year by year, however, the twin effects of their critical reports on the LAs alongside the take-up of training in the PEACE model may have been the reason why, in 2007, 21% of reports showed concerns by the BFI concerning the training of LA investigators compared to 91% of reports in 1999. A lesser, but still dramatic, decrease was also found in terms of the number of reports where the BFI assessed in their inspections that interviewing performance was still less than satisfactory (97% in 1999; 47% in 2007). Nevertheless, even after training it seemed that half of the interviews examined by the BFI were still assessed as unsatisfactory. Walsh and Milne (2008) found in their study of DWP interviewing performance that many trained investigators also performed no better than their untrained counterparts.

The reasons why training does not have the desired effect of uplifting performance is not clear. However, Walsh and Milne (2007) found that almost all untrained investigators believed that they were already skilled at interviewing. This finding may suggest that most investigators attended the PEACE training course believing that the course could teach them little as they were already expert. This view is reinforced by Walsh and Milne's further finding that investigation managers believed that many investigators (after attending the training course) reverted back to their previous interviewing techniques. It is believed that amongst the reasons why this return occurred is because investigation managers received training in the PEACE model only once almost all investigators had been trained (Walsh & Milne, 2007). Thus, they might well have been unaware of what investigators were actually expected to do following training in the new model. It was also found in this study that both trained and untrained investigators very rarely received feedback on their own interviewing performance from their managers. As a result, the important element of supervision in ensuring that lessons learned in the training room are reinforced in the field (so that skill levels do increase) was conspicuously absent in the implementation of the PEACE model in the area of benefit fraud investigation (Lamb, Sternberg, Orbach, Esplin & Mitchell, 2002a; Lamb et al., 2002b).

Examining Benefit Fraud Investigators' Practice and Beliefs

The problem of mediocre interviewing performance of benefit fraud interviews was not just the domain of LAs. Walsh and Milne (2008) conducted a study of 99 interviews conducted by DWP investigators with suspects during the period 1999–2001. Around half of the interviews involved investigators who were untrained in the PEACE model. In this study, using a measurement scale that had been modified from Clarke and Milne (2001), Walsh and Milne found concerns with the standard of skills in particular regard to the lack of preparation, rapport, summarizing, and challenging the suspect's account [also see Shawyer (2009) for another study of DWP interviewers that also found indifferent skill levels]. The closing of interviews effectively was also found to be very weak in Walsh and Milne's study. The importance of effectively undertaking these (and other) tasks, as prescribed by the PEACE model, was found in Walsh and Bull's (2010a) study where effective performance was revealed to be associated with interviews which yielded fully tested denials and confessions from suspects. In brief, good interviewing performance appears to be connected with good interviewing outcomes. However, both Walsh and Milne and Shawyer conducted their studies during the time that the DWP was undergoing the large scale retraining in the PEACE model. It may have been, therefore, that investigators were still yet to fully absorb the effects of their training into everyday practice.

Walsh and Milne's (2008) study revealed that the trained investigators significantly performed better at certain tasks when compared to their untrained colleagues. This was particularly noted regarding (1) actively encouraging the suspect to talk freely; (2) developing topics for further discussion; (3) exploring information received from the suspect; (4) dealing with difficulties in the interview; and (5) the use of pauses and silences. However, Walsh and Milne found that training was not significantly associated with better interviewing behaviors in many of the skills required for effective interviewing (e.g., rapport building, summarizing, and communication skills; see Yarbrough et al., this volume). As noted earlier, Walsh and Milne (2007) argued that any lack of improvement after training may be due to (1) investigator attitudes as to whether the training could teach them anything, as they felt already skilled as interviewers; (2) a reversion to their "tried and trusted" prior interviewing techniques following training; and (3) a lack of effective supervision of interviews. In regard to the latter matter, the BFI also found, amongst their inspections, many LA investigation managers failing to provide adequate supervision.

Many of the interviews in the study by Walsh and Milne (2008) were found to cover relatively simple matters where the suspects were clearly naïve of such investigative interviews, appearing not to have personally experienced them before. The suspects also often seemed not particularly recalcitrant, confessing to the crimes with little or no urging from interviewers. Many cases also involved evidence that was incontrovertible and, where the size of the fraud was, at most, modest, having not been carried out with any significant amounts of ingenuity by suspects (for example, the fraud was easily detected following basic enquiries with no steps taken by suspects to "cover their tracks"). Although this might be seen as a typical sample of benefit fraud cases, it hardly presented a true measure of the fraud investigators' skills where they are most likely to be tested (e.g., in the more challenging interviews such as those involving more complex frauds and/or resistant suspects). Paradoxically, the mediocre interviewer performance found by Walsh and Milne to be present in such "easy" cases might be due to the simplicity of these cases. Interviewers may come to expect that they require little exertion of effort to gain a confession from often contrite suspects and (because of the weight of the evidence) demonstrate that fraud had occurred.

Several studies have also examined the attitudes and beliefs of benefit fraud investigation personnel themselves concerning what constitutes skilled interviewing (Shawyer, 2009; Walsh & Milne, 2007). Walsh and Bull (2011) found that there was a strong level of support for the PEACE model; however, this backing has not been universal, with some professionals advocating that it is not always appropriate for benefit fraud interviews. Walsh and Bull found that those not endorsing the model believed that "other models worked just as well" (p. 139), although no such training has been provided in alternative models. Indeed, Walsh and Bull (2010a) found that those interviewers who did not apply the skills associated with the PEACE model were those less likely to obtain a comprehensive account from suspects, including fully tested confessions. Walsh and Bull (2011; see also Shawyer, 2009; Walsh & Milne, 2007) also found that investigators in these surveys stated that they possessed an ability to detect truth-tellers and liars (which they said they largely identified through observing a range of nonverbal behaviors). How skilled interviewers actually were at detecting deception or truth via nonverbal indicators was not tested in these various studies. Investigators, however, have received no training in the task of reading "body language." Neither is such practice part of the PEACE model. It has already been noted in the relevant literature that such signals, on their own, have tended to be found as unreliable in their prediction (see Vrij,

2008, for a review; also see Seniuk, present volume) and that professionals using such indicators as a means of detecting either truth or lies perform generally poorly (Mann et al., 2004).

The above notwithstanding, almost half of the respondents in Walsh and Bull's (2011) study declared that they did not rely on behavioral signals to detect deception or truth telling. Instead, they stated that they either compared the suspect's account to the gathered evidence or identified if there were any contradictions in that account as a more reliable means (in line with the aims of the PEACE model). If true (in practice), this finding represents a more positive approach by investigators as it suggests that any conclusion as to the veracity of the suspect's account is based on more concrete foundations than those based solely on nonverbal (and unreliable) predictors.

Recurring high levels of guilt presumption have also been found in attitudinal studies of benefit fraud staff. Shawyer and Milne (2009) noted that, perhaps the nature of fraud investigations (e.g., where investigational evidence is gathered and incrementally built up, sometimes over several months before interviews take place with suspects), may lead to a position that filters out doubts concerning innocence while factoring in opinions of guilt. The concerning risks attendant to an interviewing strategy that is predicated on the unwavering belief in the suspect's presumed guilt has been exposed in prior studies (e.g., Hill, Memon, & McGeorge, 2008; Kassin et al., 2003). Both these studies found that, when there was a preexisting presumption of guilt, interviewers sought to ask questions that confirmed this belief and attempted to gain compliance (and a confession) rather than adopt an information gathering approach in order to reliable and comprehensive accounts. This is significant since the latter aim is the very keystone of the PEACE model (and, for that matter, the Step-Wise Interview—see Yuille, Hunter, Joffe, & Zaparniuk, 1993).

Self-report studies, notoriously, are maligned by the fact that whatever is reported by participants does not always necessarily reflect reality. Our study of benefit fraud professionals' beliefs (Walsh & Bull, 2011) was later found to be no different. This survey found that fraud investigators appeared to understand the meaning of those tasks that are required to undertake interviewing of suspects, as prescribed by the PEACE model. They also stated that they conducted these tasks frequently. Once these findings were then compared to our field study of actual interviewing performance (Walsh & Bull, 2010b), a picture emerged that showed that the distance between perception of practice and actuality was large. We examined 142 interviews that had been conducted by both DWP and LA investigators, most having been conducted during the period 2004–2007 (i.e., once the PEACE training had undergone sufficient time to be embedded into everyday practice). This study of professional skills in practice deliberately avoided the random sample that Walsh and Milne (2008) examined, where many of the interviews were found to involve the less complex frauds and more cooperative suspects. It was found that this earlier sample tended to inhibit the ability to assess the full range of interviewers' skills. Instead, the sample of 142 interviews in Walsh and Bull's (2010b) study was deliberately skewed towards the more demanding of interviews, i.e., those that involved frauds that were more challenging to investigate (identified either through the complexity of the suspected fraudulent activity and/or those interviews that involved suspects that were resistant to admitting any offences, regardless as to whether they were actually innocent or otherwise).

Walsh and Bull (2010b), using a instrument of measurement that had evolved from prior studies (e.g., Bull & Cherryman, 1995; Clarke & Milne, 2001; McGurk et al., 1993), found a general mediocrity in these more testing circumstances with only around 10% of those interviews assessed as skilled ones. Many investigators were found to be ill-prepared for denials, through a suspected lack of planning ahead of interviews. Walsh and Bull (2010a) found that, in cases where planning was assessed as having been clearly undertaken more thoroughly, investigators were more ready to deal with such refutations of wrongdoing. Walsh and Bull (2010b) also found a regular occurrence of investigators failing to build or maintain rapport. In our later study (Walsh & Bull, 2012a) an association was found between, what the authors assessed as, skilled demonstrations of rapport and suspects providing full accounts. Walsh and Bull (2010b) found that almost all investigators tended to rush through the closure stage in an apparent haste to leave the interview room. This latter scenario was often found to occur where interviewers, having attempted to gain a confession and failed to do so, withdrew without taking any of the steps that they had earlier acknowledged were the important components of this closure phase, e.g., such as advising suspects what would happen next or undertaking final interview summaries (Walsh & Bull, 2011; Walsh & Milne, 2007). As such, it remained unclear whether suspects were aware of what had occurred in the interview and, for example, where suspects had denied allegations, opportunities (gained through providing a summary of the interview) were felt to have been missed in potentially identifying any inconsistencies in suspects' accounts which could have then led to further lines of questioning.

Differences between beliefs found in Walsh and Bull's (2011) study and those practices found in our (2010b) study occurred in several other interviewing tasks where confidence had been expressed in their frequent regularity only to be found extremely rarely utilized (e.g., advising suspects of the purpose of the interview and then advising that the interview was their chance to provide their own account; periodic summarizing, and thoroughly ensuring suspects understood their rights in the interview). The chasm between what is seen in practice and what is believed by practitioners to occur leads to the question as to how accurately the fifth component of the PEACE model (i.e., the task of evaluation) is being undertaken, both in benefit fraud and in any other investigative interviewing contexts.

Although studies of PEACE interviews have largely examined what can be observed in practice, there has been little examination of what has been frequently described as the demanding nature of either third party evaluation or self-evaluation (Alicke & Sedikides, 2009; Argyris & Schön, 1978; Dunning, Health, & Suls, 2004; Sedikides, Campbell, Reeder, & Elliot, 2002; Sedikides & Gregg, 2003, 2008). In this regard, it is argued that professionals might justifiably feel maligned by the lack of research that has thus far been conducted concerning the task of conducting evaluations either within, or following the interview. More studies may well have assisted professionals in recognizing the challenges of undertaking accurate evaluation and helped towards finding solutions. Much the same might be said of the first component of PEACE—preparation—where research has tended to see only the product of good planning (or the lack of it) and have neither sufficiently examined what constitutes good practice in this preinterview activity nor how investigators make decisions during investigations that can influence their later interviews with suspects (Ask & Alison, 2010; Ormerod et al., 2008) In regard to evaluation, our study of benefit fraud professionals' beliefs (Walsh & Bull, 2011) found no consistency concerning how this task was undertaken by those who have management responsibility for the performance of investigators. Regardless of job role, no respondents in the survey identified that evaluation is also to be undertaken during the interview as well as afterwards.

Griffiths (2008), in his study of police interviews, refers to certain tasks as being complex and demanding on interviewer skills (e.g., topic development, challenging and probing given accounts for further detail), which he tended to assess in his study of police officers as being less skilfully performed. In our study (Walsh & Bull, 2010b), tasks that demanded high level skills (but were also found to be often ineptly performed) included (1) evidence disclosure tactics; (2) topic development; (3) accurate summaries; (4) positive challenges when appropriate; (5) applications of questioning strategies; and (6) examples of an appropriate interview structure. One suggested reason for this "poor" performance of these particular (and inter-related) skills might be due to those already noted concerning ineffective supervision (which Walsh and Bull, 2011 found as still present). Another might be due to what Griffiths terms as, "skills erosion," where he found that police officers' skill levels declined over periods of time. Since most benefit fraud investigators do not undergo refresher training, it is thought that the "poor" performance revealed in Walsh and Bull's (2010b) study may also be attributed to the same phenomenon.

It would seem that, from Walsh and Bull's (2010b) study, although interviewers did not act oppressively when interviewing suspects, case complexity and resistance from suspects were factors often present in interviews with benefit fraud suspects that were not undertaken skilfully. The causes of such poor performance might be deeply rooted. That is, the legacy of the interviewing practices that predated the PEACE model, chronicled deliberately at some length earlier in the present chapter, might be still be influencing interviewing styles. Why these influences still persist is a matter of conjecture. Unethical practices seem to have largely disappeared in the UK, regardless of whether the police or other agencies are the interviewers (Soukara et al., 2009; Walsh & Bull, 2010b). However, variable standards of interviewing continue (Clarke & Milne, 2001; Griffiths, 2008; Walsh & Bull, 2010b).

In terms of benefit fraud, another reason that poor performance appears to persist might be that, up until 2006, DWP interviewers continued to conduct both criminal and administrative procedural interviews within their caseload. That is, cases investigated under the formal criminal process were subject to stricter rules concerning evidence gathering and tape-recorded interviews with suspects, and where the burden of proof of wrongdoing was (and remains) at a higher threshold than those investigations conducted as a civil matter. The latter type of investigations were characterized by an absence of evidence, considered by investigators as unlikely to be obtained without an undue exertion of effort that would not prove worthwhile when perceiving the slim chances of obtaining sufficient evidence to achieve a sanction. In such investigations, the dearth of evidence may mean that an investigator adopts a "negotiation" stance in interviews in order to obtain a suspect's agreement to claim termination. It is not suggested that the aggressive tactics found in studies conducted prior to the introduction of the PEACE model (and reported earlier in this chapter) continued to be undertaken by investigators. However, these interviews (in contrast to the "criminal procedure" ones) were (1) not recorded; (2) largely unmonitored by any third party in the absence of any contemporaneous record; (3) often dependent upon gaining suspects' compliance to yield a result of accepted wrongdoing and claim termination; and (4) not regulated by PACE. Thus, suspects could continue to be subjected to unethical interviewing practices, as noted in studies cited earlier in this chapter when sanctions were not the chosen method of case disposal and where the safeguards provided by PACE were absent.

LA investigators still conduct both types of interviews. Walsh (2002) argued that such different types of interviews were a cause of such mediocrity found in interviewing performance. Many officers were not believed sufficiently agile to adapt between those interviews with suspects in the less serious "compliance focussed" administrative cases that sought their agreement (but were ones that rarely had any evidence of wrongdoing) and those "criminal procedure" interviews, conducted after a more thorough investigation and where evidence had been gathered, that demonstrated whether criminality had occurred to the satisfaction of the courts, if necessary (also see Shawyer, 2009; Walsh & Bull, 2010b; Walsh & Milne, 2008). A cause of the frequent poor performance in the criminal interviews found in these studies may be partly due to a migration of an investigation mindset in administrative cases. For example, little preparation is encouraged in the less serious investigations (in contrast to the PEACE model that should be the framework for criminal interviews), being reliant on the compliant nature of the suspect for a case to be resolved. In the more serious criminal cases, such compliance may not be as forthcoming as suspects may recognize they have more at stake. Walsh and Bull's study of criminal interviews found that many investigators did not perform skilfully when faced with resistance from suspects.

Walsh (2002) recommended that the caseload be bisected so that certain investigators undertook the criminal procedure interviews (conducted under PACE) and others conducted the administrative procedure interviews. In 2006, this split between the two procedural areas was undertaken so that the DWP's fraud investigators now only conduct criminal interviews under PACE. To our knowledge, no research has been conducted on interviews undertaken by the DWP following the implementation of this initiative to determine whether there has been any subsequent increase in interviewing skills of fraud investigators.

Conclusion

Before the advent of PACE, and, indeed, the PEACE model, fraud investigations in the UK were characterized as ones that were undertaken unfairly and with scant regard for the rights of suspects. Studies suggested that interviewers tended to be oppressive, being focussed upon gaining confessions from suspects who, as benefit claimants, were viewed almost universally in a pejorative way. The introduction of the PEACE model along with tape-recording and undertaking of interviews in line with PACE seems to have enabled a culture change so that the unethical practices have largely disappeared (in tape-recorded interviews, at any rate). However, a consistent finding from studies examining the interviewing skills of benefit fraud investigators is that performance remains unremarkable. Walsh and Bull (2011), however, did find in our survey of benefit fraud investigation professionals an acknowledgement that the tasks that were required to fulfil the PEACE model did represent skilled interviewing, displaying awareness of the meaning of these tasks and claiming (albeit inaccurately, when compared to studies of actual interviews) that their undertaking was common practice.

The PEACE model, when undertaken either in a satisfactory or skilled manner, does appear to be associated with outcomes that Walsh and Bull (2010a) described as being more desirable (e.g., such as those where a comprehensive account is obtained) regardless of whether a denial or an admission is received and where either is examined thoroughly for its veracity. Concerns voiced by professionals in Shawyer (2009) that the model is unsuitable for many of the interviews that benefit fraud investigators deal with may be true. In reinforcing these concerns, Walsh and Milne (2008) found interviews tended to be characterized by simply conceived frauds that were solved relatively easily, and were typified by both incontrovertible evidence and contrite suspects. In these circumstances, it may be the PEACE model may not be the only one that resolves the investigation. Indeed, it is possible, such was the willingness of suspects to admit their wrongdoing with minimal prompting from investigators, that these interviews, regardless of how (and how well) they are conducted may have yielded similar results. Nevertheless, it is argued that it is not until interviews actually take place do investigators know whether suspects will be so compliant. As such, excellent practice is to plan ahead as if suspects will be resistant, whether because of their innocence or in an attempt evade responsibility for their crimes. It has been seen that, when interviews are more demanding, they are often undertaken poorly (Walsh & Bull, 2010b). Further, it is in these particular interviews that it was found that, when the PEACE model was conducted poorly, there was less likely to be an association with obtaining a comprehensive (and comprehensively tested) account (Walsh & Bull, 2010a).

In October 2010, The British Government announced that benefit fraud investigation is to be incorporated into a single fraud investigation service which examines all benefit frauds (i.e., including those currently investigated separately by either the DWP or the LAs), together with those tax credit frauds that are, at present, investigated by another government department (DWP/Her Majesties' Revenue and

Customs, 2010). When this initiative is combined with the increasing amounts of information and evidence gathered from a range of sources as a product of either increased data mining and sharing, enacting more powerful legislation or increasingly smarter government IT systems, it may mean that fraud investigations may delve into areas hitherto inhibited by a lack of information, evidence or regulatory powers. It will certainly mean that more sophisticated criminal investigations will become the norm. As such, the need for investigators to be able to undertake more complex and serious investigations will increase and, since the stakes will in turn generally be higher, the number of resistant suspects can be expected to be more prevalent.

The requirement for fraud investigators to be equipped with interviewing skills to meet these challenges is self evident in this context. Skilled interviewing of fraud suspects will never be more essential to organizational success. Regardless of how skilfully any prior benefit fraud investigation may have been conducted and what evidence has been yielded, it is likely that the interview with the suspect will remain most pivotal in deciding the outcome of the investigation. The suspects' responses to questions put to them by interviewers will strongly indicate if benefit fraud has occurred. Continued research is therefore vital to inform practitioners what skilled interviewing looks like so that it shapes training and, in turn, practice. Walsh and Bull (2012b), for example, have examined what tactics are particularly associated with overcoming suspects' denials where the evidence strongly suggests guilt. This study revealed that skilful and more regular employment of key tasks (such as disclosing evidence, summarizing regularly, emphasizing contradictions in the suspects account) when coupled with skillful and more constant attitudinal displays (e.g., being openminded and communicative) are associated with increased shifts towards confession from those suspects who initially denied the offence. Organizations such as those examined in this chapter undertake a primary role, which is the provision of welfare. As such, decisions to prosecute individuals suspected of abusing the system may be aided by a confession *ethically obtained* as it may well lessen the risk of prosecuting innocent (and possibly vulnerable) service users.

In sum, it would seem, on the one hand, that the manipulative and coercive practices found in studies during the 1980s have now disappeared from interviews with benefit fraud suspects, although some remnants of the guilt bias towards suspects still appears to linger. On the other hand, the skilled interviewing that will be required in the new era remains largely an elusive concept outside the police service. It is crucial that senior management in the new organization recognize, understand and act upon that fact. It has been shown in this chapter that, in the UK, the examination of interviews with suspected criminals conducted by nonpolice agencies prompt concerns regarding skill levels. Nevertheless, it might be argued that, by such transparency (e.g., by the taping of interviews with suspects and the preparedness to share this data with researchers), at least there is a growing awareness of these actual skill levels. However, as was noted, dealing with the challenge of benefit fraud is not a UK question alone. International collaboration has benefited the developing research on police interviews (see for example, the activities of the International Investigative Interviewing Research Group). Similar trans-national collaborations by agencies such as those covered in this chapter that tackle benefit fraud (and other nonpolice organizations as well) will likely identify similar positive opportunities to enhance interviewing professionalism across the world.

References

Akehurst, L., Köhnken, G., Vrij, A., & Bull, R. (1996). Layperson's and police officer's beliefs regarding deceptive behaviour. *Applied Cognitive Psychology, 10*, 461–471.
Alicke, M., & Sedikides, C. (2009). Self-enhancement and self-protection: What they are and what they do. *European Review of Social Psychology, 20*, 1–48.
Argyris, C., & Schön, D. (1978). *Organizational learning: A theory in action perspective.* New York: Addison-Wesley.
Ask, K., & Alison, L. (2010). Investigators' decision making. In P. A. Granhag (Ed.), *Forensic psychology in context* (pp. 35–55). Cullompton: Willan.
Ask, K., & Granhag, P. A. (2005). Motivational sources of confirmation bias in criminal investigations: The need for cognitive closure. *Journal of Investigative Psychology and Offender Profiling, 2*, 43–63.
Audit Commission. (1997). *Department of social security: Measures to combat housing benefit fraud.* London: National Audit Office.
Audit Commission. (1999). *Fraud and lodging: Progress in tackling fraud and error in housing benefit.* London: Audit Commission.
Baldwin, J. (1993). Police interview techniques: Establishing truth or proof? *British Journal of Criminology, 33*, 325–351.
Barker, C., Watchman, P., & Rowan-Robertson, J. (1990). Social security abuse. *Journal of Social Policy and Administration, 24*, 104–119.
Benefits Agency. (1995). *Five year programme against fraud and abuse.* London: Her Majesty's Stationery Office.
Benefit Fraud Inspectorate. Reports of BFI inspections available at http://www.dwp.gov.uk/publications/bfi/bfi-reports.asp accessed on numerous occasions from November, 2004 to February, 2010.
Benefits Agency Security Branch. (1999). *Annual Report.*
Bryan, I. (1997). *Interrogation and confession: A study of progress, process and practice.* Aldershot: Ashgate.
Bull, R., & Cherryman, J. (1995). *Helping to identify skills gaps in specialist investigative interviewing.* London: Home Office Police Department.
Bull, R., & Soukara, S. (2010). Four studies of what really happens in police interviews. In G. D. Lassiter & C. A. Meissner (Eds.), *Police interrogations and false confessions: Current research, practice, and policy recommendations* (pp. 81–95). Washington: American Psychological Association.
Clarke, C. & Milne, R. (2001). *National evaluation of the PEACE investigative interviewing course.* Report no: PRAS/149. London: The Home Office.
Colwell, K., Hiscock-Anisman, & Fede, J. (2013). Assessment criteria indicative of deception (ACID): An example of the new paradigm of differential recall enhancement. In B.S. Cooper, D. Griesel, & M. Ternes (Eds.), *Applied issues in investigative interviewing, eyewitness memory and credibility assessment* (pp. 259–292). New York: Springer.
Cook, D. (2006). *Criminal and social justice.* London: Sage.
Deacon, A. (1978). The scrounging controversy: Public attitudes towards the unemployed in contemporary Britain. *Journal of Social Policy and Administration, 12*, 120–135.
Deacon, A. (1980) *Spivs, drones and other scroungers.* New Society, 28 February.
Department of Social Security. (1998). *Beating fraud is everyone's business.* London: The Stationery Office.

Department for Work and Pensions/Her Majesties' Revenue and Customs. (2010). *Tackling fraud and error in the benefit and tax credits systems*. London: Department of Work and Pensions.

Department of Employment. (1991). *Progress on tackling fraud and abuse*. London: Her Majesty's Stationery Office.

DePaulo, B. M., & Pfeifer, R. L. (1986). On the job experience and skill at detecting deception. *Journal of Applied Social Psychology, 16*, 249–267.

Dingwall, G., & Harding, C. (1998). *Diversion in the criminal process*. London: Sweet & Maxwell.

Dunning, D., Health, C., & Suls, J. M. (2004). Flawed self-assessment. *Psychological Science in the Public Interest, 5*, 69–106.

Feeley, T. H., & Young, M. J. (1998). Humans as lie detectors: Some more second thoughts. *Communication Quarterly, 46*, 109–126.

Fitzpatrick, A. (1999). *Freedom and security: An introduction to the basic income debate*. Basingstoke: Macmillan.

Golding, P., & Middleton, S. (1982). *Images of welfare: Press and public attitudes to welfare*. Oxford: Blackwell.

Griffiths A. (2008). *An examination into the efficacy of police advanced investigative interview training*. Unpublished Ph.D. thesis. University of Portsmouth.

Griffiths, A., & Milne, R. (2006). Will it all end in tiers? Police interviews with suspects in Britain. In T. Williamson (Ed.), *Investigative interviewing: Rights, research and regulation* (pp. 167–189). Cullompton: Willan.

Gudjonsson, G. H. (2003). *The psychology of interrogations and confessions: A handbook*. Chichester: Wiley.

Hill, C., Memon, A., & McGeorge, P. (2008). The role of confirmation bias in suspect interviews: A systematic evaluation. *Legal and Criminological Psychology, 13*, 357–371.

Hill, M. (1969). The exercise of discretion in the National Assistance Board. *Public Administration, 47*, 75–90.

Holmberg, U., & Christianson, S. (2002). Murderers' and sexual offenders' experiences of police interviews and their inclination to admit or deny crimes. *Behavioural Sciences & The Law, 20*, 31–45.

Inbau, F. E., Reid, J., & Buckley, J. P. (1986). *Criminal interrogations and confessions* (2nd ed.). Baltimore: Williams & Wilkins.

Inbau, F. E., Reid, J., Buckley, J. P., & Jayne, B. C. (2013). *Criminal interrogations and confessions* (5th ed.). Burlington: Jones and Bartlett.

Irving, B. (1980). *Police interrogation. A case study of current practice*, Research Study No. 2, London: HMSO.

Irving, B., & McKenzie, I. (1989). *Police interrogation: The effects of PACE 1984*. London: Police Foundation.

Kapardis, A. (2010). *Psychology and law: A critical introduction. (3rd edition)*. Cambridge: Cambridge University Press.

Kassin, S. M., Goldstein, C. J., & Savitsky, K. (2003). Behavioural confirmation in the interrogation room: On the dangers of presuming guilt. *Law and Human Behavior, 27*, 187–203.

Katungi, D., Neale, E., & Barbour, A. (2006). *Need not greed: Informal paid work*. Bristol: Joseph Rowntree Foundation and Policy Press.

Kebbell, M.R., Hurren, E., & Mazerolle, P. (2006). *An investigation into the effective and ethical interviewing of suspected sex offenders*. Report to the Criminological Research Council and Crime and Misconduct Commission. Brisbane, Australia: Griffith University.

Köhnken, G. (1987). Training police officers to detect deceptive eyewitness statements. Does it work? *Social Behaviour, 2*, 1–17.

King, L., & Snook, B. (2009). Peering inside the Canadian interrogation room: An examination of the Reid model of interrogation, influence tactics, and coercive strategies. *Criminal Justice and Behavior, 36*, 674–694.

Lamb, M. E., Sternberg, K. J., Orbach, Y., Esplin, P. W., & Mitchell, S. (2002). Is ongoing feedback necessary to maintain the quality of investigative interviews with allegedly abused children? *Applied Developmental Science, 6*, 35–41.

Lamb, M. E., Sternberg, K. J., Orbach, Y., Hershkowitz, I., Horowitz, D., & Esplin, P. W. (2002). The effects of intensive training and ongoing supervision on the quality of investigative interviews with alleged sex abuse victims. *Applied Developmental Science, 6*, 114–125.

Lilley, P. (1992). *Untitled speech as minister for social security.* Paper presented at the British annual Conservative Party conference, Brighton, UK.

Lister, R. (1991). Social security in the 1980s. *Social Policy and Administration, 25*, 91–107.

Lister, R. (2004). *Poverty.* Bristol: Policy Press.

Loveland, I. (1989). The micro-politics of welfare rights: The interpretation and application of the cohabitation rule in the Housing Benefit scheme. *Journal of Social Welfare Law, 11*, 23–42.

Mann, S., Vrij, A., & Bull, R. (2004). Detecting true lies: Police officers' ability to detect suspects' lies. *Journal of Applied Psychology, 89*, 137–149.

McGurk, B.J., Carr, M.J., & McGurk D. (1993). *Investigative interviewing courses for police officers: An evaluation.* Police Research Group Paper No. 4, London: Home Office.

McKeever, G. (1999). Fighting fraud: An evaluation of the government's social security fraud strategy. *Journal of Social Welfare and Family Law, 21*(4), 357–371.

Memon, A., Vrij, A., & Bull, R. (2003). *Psychology and law: Truthfulness, accuracy and credibility* (3rd ed.). Chichester: Wiley.

Milne, R., & Bull, R. (1999). *Investigative interviewing: Psychology and practice.* Chichester: Wiley.

Moore, P. (1981). Scroungermania at the DHSS. *New Society,* January 22.

Moston, S., Stephenson, G. M., & Williamson, T. (1992). The effects of case characteristics on suspect behaviour during police questioning. *British Journal of Criminology, 32*, 23–40.

National Association for the Care and Resettlement of Offenders. (1986). *Enforcement of the law relating to social security.* London: Author.

National Audit Office. (2003). *Department for work and pensions: Tackling benefit fraud.* Report by the Comptroller and Auditor General. HC393, Session 2002–2003. London: The Stationery Office.

National Audit Office. (2006). *International benchmark of fraud and error in social security systems.* Report by the Comptroller and Auditor General. HC 1387 Session 2005–2006. London: The Stationery Office.

O'Neal, S. (2001). Interviewing self-confident con artists. *FBI Law Enforcement Bulletin, 70*, 16–21.

Ormerod, T. C., Barrett, E. C., & Taylor, P. J. (2008). Investigative sense-making in criminal contexts. In J. M. C. Schraagen, L. Militello, T. Ormerod, & R. Lipshitz (Eds.), *Naturalistic decision making and macrocognition* (pp. 81–98). Aldershot: Ashgate.

Oxburgh, G. E., Williamson, T., & Ost, J. (2006). Police officers' use of negative emotional language during child sexual abuse investigations. *International Journal of Investigative Psychology and Offender Profiling, 3*, 35–45.

Perillo, J. T., & Kassin, S. M. (2011). Inside interrogation: The lie, the bluff, and false confessions. *Law and Human Behavior, 35*, 327–337.

Police and Criminal Evidence Act 1984. (1999). *6th Impression.* London: The Stationery Office.

Porter, S., Woodworth, M., & Birt, A. (2000). Truth, lies, and videotape: An investigation of the ability of federal parole officers to detect deception. *Law and Human Behavior, 24*, 643–658.

Porter, S., & Yuille, J. C. (1995). Credibility assessment of criminal suspects through statement analysis. *Psychology, Crime, and Law, 1*, 319–331.

Porter, S., & Yuille, J. C. (1996). The language of deceit: An investigation of the verbal clues to deception in the interrogation context. *Law and Human Behavior, 20*, 443–458.

Porter, S., Yuille, J. C., & Birt, A. R. (2001). The discrimination of deceitful, mistaken, and real memories for emotional events. In R. Roesch, R. Carrado, & R. Dempster (Eds.), *Psychology in the courts: International advances in knowledge* (pp. 253–270). London: Routledge.

Redlich, A. D., & Meissner, C. A. (2009). Techniques and controversies in the interrogation of suspects: The artful practice versus the scientific study. In J. L. Skeem, K. Douglas, & S. Lilienfeld (Eds.), *Psychological science in the courtroom: Controversies and consensus* (pp. 124–148). New York: Guilford Press.

Rowlingson, K., Whyley, C., Newburn, T., & Berthoud, R. (1997). *Social security fraud: The role of penalties*. London: HMSO: The Stationery Office.

Sainsbury, R. (2003). Understanding social security fraud. In J. Millar (Ed.), *Understanding social security* (pp. 277–295). Bristol: Policy Press.

Savage, S., & Milne, R. (2007). Miscarriages of justice: The role of the investigative process. In T. Newburn, T. Williamson, & A. Wright (Eds.), *Handbook of criminal investigation* (pp. 610–627). Cullompton: Willan.

Schneider, F., & Enste, D. H. (2002). *The shadow economy: An international survey*. Cambridge: Cambridge University Press.

Sedikides, C., & Gregg, A. P. (2003). Portraits of the self. In M. A. Hogg & J. Cooper (Eds.), *Sage handbook of social psychology* (pp. 110–138). London: Sage Publications.

Sedikides, C., & Gregg, A. P. (2008). Self-enhancement: Food for thought. *Perspectives on Psychological Science, 3*, 102–116.

Sedikides, C., Campbell, W. K., Reeder, G., & Elliot, A. J. (2002). The self in relationships: Whether, how, and when close others put the self in its place. In W. Stroebe & M. Hewstone (Eds.), *European Review of Social Psychology* (Vol. 12, pp. 237–265). Chichester: Wiley.

Shawyer, A. (2009). *Investigative interviewing: Interviewing counter fraud and deception*. Unpublished Ph.D. thesis, University of Portsmouth.

Shawyer, A. & Milne, R. (2009) *Investigative interviewing: Investigation, counter-fraud and behaviour*. Paper presented at the 2nd International Investigative Interviewing Research Group Conference, University of Teesside.

Smith, G., Button, M., Johnston, L., & Frimpong, K. (2011). *Studying fraud as white collar crime*. Basingstoke: Palgrave Macmillan.

Smith, R. (1985). Who's fiddling: Fraud and abuse. In S. Ward (Ed.), *DHSS in crisis* (pp. 130–146). London: CPAG.

Softley, P., Brown, D., Forde, B., Mair, G., & Moxon, D. (1980). *Police interrogation: An observational study in four police stations* (p. 61). London: HMSO, Home Office Research Study No.

Soukara, S., Bull, R., Vrij, A., Turner, M., & Cherryman, J. (2009). What really happens in police interviews with suspects?: Tactics and confessions. *Psychology, Crime and Law, 15*, 493–506.

SPARK Research. (2004). *A review of the DWP benefit fraud sanctions scheme*. In-house Report 149. London: Department of Work and Pensions.

Strömwall, L. A., Granhag, P. A., & Hartwig, M. (2004). Practitioners' beliefs about deception. In P. A. Granhag & L. A. Stromwall (Eds.), *The detection of deception in forensic contexts* (pp. 229–250). Cambridge: Cambridge University Press.

Taylor-Gooby, P. (1985). *Public opinion, ideology and the welfare state*. London: Routledge Kegan Paul.

Vrij, A. (2008). *Detecting lies and deceit: Pitfalls and opportunities*. Chichester: Wiley.

Vrij, A., & Mann, S. (2001). Who killed my relative? Police officers' ability to detect real-life high stake lies. *Psychology, Crime and Law, 7*, 119–132.

Walkley, J. (1987). *Police interrogation: A handbook for investigators*. London: Police Review Publication.

Walsh, D. (2002). *An analysis and evaluation of the standards of investigative interviews conducted by benefit fraud investigators*. Unpublished MSc Dissertation. University of Portsmouth.

Walsh, D. (2011). *Towards a framework of interviewing fraud suspects*. Unpublished Ph.D. thesis. University of Leicester.

Walsh, D., & Bull, R. (2010a). The interviewing of suspects by non-police agencies: What's effective? What is effective! *Legal and Criminological Psychology, 15*, 305–321.

Walsh, D., & Bull, R. (2010b). Interviewing suspects of fraud: An analysis of interviewing skills. *Journal of Psychiatry and Law, 38*, 99–135.

Walsh, D., & Bull, R. (2011). Benefit fraud investigative interviewing: A self-report study of investigation professionals' beliefs concerning practice. *Journal of Investigative Psychology and Offender Profiling, 8*, 131–148.

Walsh, D., & Bull, R. (2012a). How do interviewers attempt to overcome suspects' denials? *Psychiatry, Psychology, and Law, 19*, 151–168.

Walsh, D., & Bull, R. (2012b). Examining rapport in investigative interviews with suspects: Does its building and maintenance work? *Journal of Police and Criminal Psychology, 27*, 73–84.

Walsh, D., & Milne, R. (2007). Giving PEACE a chance. *Public Administration, 85*(3), 525–540.

Walsh, D., & Milne, R. (2008). Keeping the P.E.A.C.E.? An Analysis of the taped interview performance of benefit fraud investigators within the DWP. *Legal and Criminological Psychology, 13*, 39–57.

Whiteley, P. (1981). Public opinion and the demand for social welfare in Britain. *Journal of Social Policy, 10*, 453–475.

Yuille, J. C., Hunter, R., Joffe, R., & Zaparniuk, J. (1993). Interviewing children in sexual abuse cases. In G. S. Goodman & B. L. Bottoms (Eds.), *Child victims, child witnesses: Understanding and improving children's testimony* (pp. 95–115). New York: Guilford Press.

Chapter 4
The Sins of Interviewing: Errors Made by Investigative Interviewers and Suggestions for Redress

John Yarbrough, Hugues F. Hervé, and Robert Harms

Introduction

Interviewing is the essence of law enforcement. The goal of an effective interview, be it with a victim, witness, informant, or suspect, is to elicit complete and accurate information. Of course, the gathering of complete and accurate information is not unique to law enforcement. Psychologists and psychiatrists rely on fact-finding interviews to—among other activities—diagnose and treat mental illness, assess malingering, and determine risk of violence. The retail loss prevention and other industries use investigative interviews to gather data to identify, neutralize, assess, and prevent thefts and frauds (see Walsh & Bull, this volume). Leaders of countries and politicians rely on accurate information to make geopolitical and economic decisions and to navigate diplomatic relationships. The gathering of intelligence has always been critical to the military in times of both peace and war. In other words, many important decisions are made on a daily basis that depends on information gathered by people through interviews.

The importance of interviewing notwithstanding, most professionals receive little training in effective interviewing (e.g., fact finding, reading people, and evaluating truthfulness); and the training that is provided is too often based on anecdotal experience and faulty concepts, assumptions, theories, and/or research findings based on inadequate or simplistic methodologies. As a result, interviewers are frequently left with an erroneous or simplistic view of human behavior when trying to design an

J. Yarbrough (✉) • R. Harms
Los Angeles County Sheriff's Department,
Los Angeles, USA
e-mail: johnyarbro@npgcable.com

H.F. Hervé
The Forensic Alliance,
British Columbia, Canada
e-mail: hherve@theforensicalliance.com

interview strategy or evaluate the credibility of statements. These realities were the experiences of the first and third authors, two veterans of the law enforcement profession. Despite having over 55 years of combined experience, the first and third authors admittedly received little quality training in effective interviewing. It was not until they started to make connections with other professionals—forensic psychiatrists, research psychologists, specially trained law enforcement agents, etc.—that the realization of the number of errors being made during interviews became apparent (e.g., by themselves, by others within law enforcement, and by professionals from other disciplines tasked with conducting investigative interviews). These collaborative efforts led to another important revelation: academics/researchers were making significant errors as well. These errors likely contaminated the training and therefore the work of front line staff (note: identifying the errors made by academics is outside the scope of this chapter. See Colwell, Hiscock-Anisman, & Fede, this volume, for further information; also see Hervé, Cooper, & Yuille, 2007).

This chapter examines the "Sins of Interviewing" that were identified as a result of the collaboration between law enforcement professionals, mental health professionals, and academics. The "Sins of Interviewing" were originally developed by the first author. The list of "sins" started with a few and grew over time through experience and recommendations from mentors or associates, and all have since found empirical support. Fifteen sins are currently listed and they all have one variable in common: they detract from achieving the goal of an effective interview. That is, the goal of finding the truth—whatever it might be—and why the person believes it to be the truth. The 15 sins are not meant to be an exhaustive list, and the sins are not meant to be mutually exclusive. The listed sins simply reflect the most common errors committed by interviewers. The following describes these 15 sins and their causes, as well as practical solutions for overcoming them.

Sin Number 1: Imposing the "Me" Theory of Personality

The "me" theory is based on the concept that many of us believe that how we see the world, how we make decisions, or how we behave is necessarily the same for all other human beings (Cooper, Hervé, & Yuille, 2009; Ekman, 2009). Clearly, this is not the case. Humans have variability in genetic expression, life experiences, and sociocultural backgrounds that impact thinking, feeling, and behavior. Despite the heterogeneous nature of human beings, we nevertheless often rely on the "me" theory to try to understand the people around us. This may be due to the fact that the "me" theory provides us with a simple, automatic heuristic for making sense of other people and their actions (Stanovich, 2009). That is, it is much easier (i.e., it requires less mental effort or cognitive load) to make interpretations based on one's own viewpoints and experiences than to gather relevant data and test multiple hypotheses to make an informed decision about the person under scrutiny. The end result is a predisposition to make quick (or automatic) and simplistic interpretations about other people based on our own belief system and experiences.

Obviously, relying on the "me" theory to make sense of other people has its limitations. First, it often leads to erroneous judgements about the thoughts, feelings and/or actions of others (Cooper et al., 2009; Ekman, 2009). This is especially true when trying to apply the "me" theory to people who are markedly different from us, such as individuals from different cultures or subgroups, with psychiatric problems, and/or with developmental delays. Second, when it leads to correct judgements, it typically reinforces poor interviewing skills (e.g., using automatic thought processes rather than critical thinking skills; believing that the behavior you share in common with the interviewee is a reliable sign of deception; e.g., Stanovich, 2009). In fact, when the "me" theory leads to a correct interpretation, it tells us more that the person being evaluated is similar to us than anything about our interpretation and related assumptions.

Not surprisingly, police officers, like everyone else, are not immune to the influence of the "me" theory. That is, it is not uncommon in law enforcement to see or hear interviewers relying on their own personal beliefs and assumptions as a way of judging truthfulness during an investigative interview. For example, an officer who averts his/her eye gaze (i.e., looks away) when lying may wrongly believe that anyone who looks away when making a statement must be lying. Consequently, the truth teller who looks away to collect his/her thoughts could be wrongfully labelled as deceptive, while the liar who maintains eye contact throughout his/her statement could be wrongfully deemed as honest.

The "me" theory can also impact how an interviewer interprets verbal content. When an interviewee tells a story that contains elements that contradict the interviewer's preconceived assumptions about offending or offenders, our experience suggests that the interviewer is prone to disbelieve that statement. For example, during the investigation of a serial offender who had committed multiple residential sexual assaults in a small town in the southern United States, one of the victims reported that, after being sexually assaulted, the offender sat on the bed and asked her where she went to high school. After she answered him, the offender told her that he had attended the same school and asked if "Mr. Johnson" was still the principal. Why would the offender say that? Surely, he must have known that this would be a clue to his identity. An investigative interviewer following the "me" theory could have dismissed this victim's statement as untruthful because s/he (i.e., the investigative interviewer) simply could not believe that an offender would make such a mistake. In this case, after the offender was identified, the school's records confirmed that he had told the victim the truth. He had indeed attended the same high school as the victim and "Mr. Johnson" was the principal at that time.

The "me" theory may also be responsible, at least in part, for the development of questionable interviewing practices. For example, a popular assumption in the field of interviewing in the last century was that innocent people do not confess to offences they did not commit (Drizin & Leo, 2004; Kassin, Drizin et al., 2010). We now know that this assumption is erroneous and that there are numerous reasons why innocent people may falsely confess to crimes (Gudjonsson, Sigurdsson, Sigfusdottir, & Asgeirsdottir, 2008; Kassin, Appleby, & Perillo, 2010). It is possible that this assumption was developed in the context of the "me" theory: since there is absolutely no way "I" would ever confess to something "I" did not do, anyone who confesses to a crime must be guilty of that crime. Unfortunately, this assumption has created a context in which some investigative interviewers have felt justified in using whatever means necessary to gain a confession.

The take home message is: *"Don't use your personal views to judge other people's behavior."* This statement was, in fact, one of the first training messages the first author learned from his mentor, Dr. Bennett Blum, a forensic psychiatrist. As Dr. Blum explained, attempting to answer the question "why would the offender do that" from a perspective other than that particular offender presupposes that both the interviewer and the offender share similar values, ethics, experiences, and behavioral traits. This is normally not the case. Irrespective of who is being interviewed, the best defence against the "me" theory is knowledge. The more the interviewer knows about the people s/he is dealing with and the topic under investigation (e.g., violent crimes, fraud, and terrorism), the easier it will be for the interviewer to consider other hypotheses—hypotheses that take into account the perspective of the interviewee and the context in which the offence took place.

Sin Number 2: Misunderstanding Memory

The second "sin" of interviewing relates to the lack of understanding that many law enforcement personnel have about memory. This is surprising given the importance of memory to police work (see Hervé, Cooper, & Yuille, this volume). By definition, the goal of an investigative interview is to mine the interviewee's memory (i.e., the truth as s/he knows it). This holds true irrespective of whether the interviewee is a victim, witness, informant, or suspect. In many cases, particularly in child sexual abuse contexts, the victim's memory is often the only evidence that an alleged crime has been committed (Daylen, van Tongeren Harvey, & O'Toole, 2006). Therefore, the importance of understanding how memory works cannot be overstated. In fact, it could be argued that investigators should treat offence-related memories as part of the crime scene (M. St. Yves, personal communication, December 19th, 2011). Would crime scene investigators (CSIs) be sent to a scene without any understanding of evidence collection? Would CSIs be allowed to contaminate the crime scene or only collect part of the evidence? The answers here are easy: no. Yet, investigative interviewers are often not held to the same standards with respect to collecting memory-based evidence.

The following provides the main properties/characteristics of memory that all investigative interviewers should know, as well as some of the common sins committed by memory-uninformed interviewers (for further details, see Hervé et al., this volume; Hervé et al., 2007; Schacter, 1996, 2001; Yuille & Daylen, 1998).

First, memory for personally experienced events is reconstructive, not reproductive (Schacter, 1996). That is, we do not have an exact video recording of past events stored in our brains that we can freely play back at any time. If we did, we would have totally accurate recall but we would likely eventually run out of storage space for new memories. Instead, we only encode or store information that is important to us and reconstruct our memories piece by piece in a manner consistent with the cues that elicited or triggered them. The good news about this method is that we do not have any storage issues. The bad news is that this process is imperfect and prone to error (Hervé et al., 2007; Schacter, 1996, 2001). By imperfect, we mean that memory is incomplete because individuals simply cannot pay attention to everything of investigative importance (e.g., to the behaviors of all present during a crime). By prone to error, we mean that, each time a memory is recalled and, therefore, reconstructed, it is susceptible to being distorted by a host of factors. As Schacter (2001) notes, "in the process of reconstruction we add on feelings, beliefs, or even knowledge we obtained after the experience" (p. 9).

The knowledge that can distort one's memory need not be self-generated; in reality, it is often suggested by others, including interviewers. For example, when a witness to an event spontaneously recalls the details of an event or is interviewed and asked to recall the details of an event, the resulting product becomes a reconstruction of the stored parts and pieces of the memory being elicited, not a single reproduction of the memory. When the memory is reconstructed and verbalized, the quality and quantity of the actual memory becomes vulnerable to influences from external sources, such as the questions posed or information supplied to the witness that was not part of his/her original memory. Thereafter, this newly reconstructed memory is restored, only to be reconstructed and influenced again when the witness is re-interviewed at a later time (Hervé et al., 2007; Schacter, 1996).

Despite the fact that memory is reconstructive in nature and, therefore, incomplete and error prone, many inexperienced and experienced interviewers continue to believe that memory is like a video recording. As a result, they become frustrated when the results of an interview are not as expected (e.g., when a witness does not provide a smooth, linear "play back" of everything that happened during the offence). Many also fail to understand the malleable nature of memory and, therefore, the impact their own questions will have on the interviewee's memory, a sin further discussed below.

Second, our memory is best for events of personal significance (Christianson, 1992; Schacter, 1996). While most experiences are quickly forgotten because they are routine, mundane, or unimportant, events of personal significance, either positive or negative, may be retained for months or even years (see Connolly & Price, this volume; Fisher, Vrij, & Leins, this volume; Hervé et al., this volume). This may be due to several factors, including the fact that events of personal significance are, by their very nature, emotional events and emotions serve as powerful memory cues. Furthermore, events of personal significance are more likely to be retold or discussed over and over again, a process that is known to reinforce memory (Hervé et al., 2007; Schacter, 2001).

One error made by improperly trained interviewers is in defining what is significant from their own perspective (i.e., according to the "me" theory) or from the perspective of the investigation (e.g., what evidence is "needed" to catch and convict the suspect), rather than from the perspective of the interviewee (i.e., what s/he found to be especially significant and, therefore, memorable). A victim of fraud, for example, may not know that s/he was being defrauded (i.e., at the time the fraud was being committed) and, therefore, may have little to no memory of the event (i.e., as it was not originally encoded as memorable; Tollestrup, Turtle, & Yuille, 1994). The longer the time between this type of event and its recall, the more likely it will be forgotten (e.g., in part or in whole). Unfortunately, a well-meaning interviewer may wrongly assume that the victim should recall the incident and consequently pressure the victim to provide information related to the fraud—information that is likely to be inaccurate and, therefore, lead the investigation down the wrong path.

Another error that novice and improperly trained interviewers sometimes make is changing topics when an interviewee becomes emotional during a retelling. This typically reflects the interviewer's discomfort dealing with emotional subjects and, unfortunately, serves to disrupt the reconstruction of memory. Emotions are a powerful cue to memory and, therefore, can serve to elicit important offence-related details. As such, the interviewer should allow the interviewee to express his/her emotions while providing their narrative. Of course, if a victim or witness becomes overwhelmed by their emotions (i.e., cries uncontrollably or is so angry or agitated that communication is disrupted), it would be appropriate to temporarily change topics (Hervé et al., 2007; Morrison, 2008).

Third, memory is not a discreet entity. Rather, it is a set of processes. There are, in fact, different types of processes and different types of memories, including the following (Schacter, 1996, 2001): (1) Procedural memory (i.e., memory for psychomotor functioning, such as walking, sexual behavior, etc.); (2) Semantic memory (i.e., memory for general knowledge, such as math, physics, chemistry, geography, etc.); (3) Narrative memory (i.e., memory for personally experienced events, such as committing violence or being the victim of violence); (4) Script memory (i.e., memory for routine events, such as our typical morning routine); and (5) Prospective memory (i.e., memory for future events, such as going to a hockey game).

Narrative memory (also referred to as episodic or autobiographical memory; Schacter, 1996, 2001) is typically the type of memory at the focus of most investigations. It may be about a single event at a single location, such as witnessing a car accident or a bank robbery; or it may be about a series of events, such as multiple meetings and discussions among conspirators to commit some type of action. In the latter case, multiple locations, multiple dates, multiple participants, and multiple acts could be involved and recalled. The second most likely type of memory to surface during an investigation is a script memory.[1] We develop scripts for routine events, such as our typical drive to work or our typical family dinner. Likewise, some victims and offenders may develop scripts for repeated acts of violence that they interpret as routine (e.g., repeated acts of sexual or domestic violence; see Hervé et al., this volume; Paz-Alonso, Ogle, & Goodman, this volume). Remember

---

[1] This is not to say that the other types of memories do not surface during an investigation. For example, a serial sex offender may spontaneously show how he tied up his victims, thereby displaying procedural memory.

not to fall prey to the "me" theory when it comes to the definition of routine. It is not what you believe to be routine, but what the interviewee believes to be routine.

The distinction between a narrative and script memory is often lost on improperly trained interviewers. However, the distinction is crucial. With all other factors being equal, the quality and quantity of information within a narrative memory will be greater than that in a script memory (Schacter, 1996, 2001). For example, a victim who was sexually assaulted on one occasion may provide a great deal of information about the offender (e.g., what he was wearing, his approach behavior, and what he was saying), the offence (e.g., sequence of events, particular behaviors), and the location of the assault (e.g., place, time, and other contextual details) because of the uniqueness of the event. In contrast, a victim of repeated sexual assaults by the same perpetrator in the same context may only provide generalities about the offence script or how it "usually" happened because of the routine nature of these events (e.g., he used to come into my room at night, usually after drinking beer; he would start by turning off the light and taking my panties off). If the interviewer falsely believes that s/he is dealing with a narrative memory when, in fact, s/he is facing a script, s/he may become frustrated by the lack of details provided by the interviewee and perhaps become suspicious. Under this circumstance, the improperly trained interviewer may be at risk of asking leading or suggestive questions and, therefore, of contaminating the victim's memory. Instead, when dealing with a script memory, it is best to simply ask the interviewee how the offending typically occurred. Once the script is known, it may be possible to get information about a particular episode by asking if there was a time when the offending unfolded in a different manner (e.g., when an act of domestic violence is interrupted by the unexpected presence of a child; when a sexual offence of a child is interrupted by the non-offending parent unexpectedly returning home). This is called a script violation (Schacter, 1996, 2001). Script violations are significant departures from how events typically unfold and, therefore, are memorable. The interviewer can use script violations to cue memory for a particular episode by asking the interviewee if s/he recalls anything more about the particular incident in which the script was violated. This process can be repeated until no further script violations and/or episodes come to mind.

Fourth, narrative memory is often piecemeal (i.e., only parts and pieces of the actual event are recalled; Hervé et al., 2007; Loftus, 1979; Schacter, 1996, 2001). As noted above, when an event is unfolding, a witness cannot pay attention to every facet of the event, and different witnesses may focus on different parts of the event. Later, when recalling the event, the witness may fill in the holes in his/her memory with information that makes the memory seem complete but may, in fact, be inaccurate (Yuille, 2007). Filling in the gaps is typical of social interactions and often relies on our semantic memory or our scripts. In other words, if a witness did not see a particular act during an event (e.g., the perpetrator's car swerve prior to hitting the victim), that witness might still assume that the particular act occurred (i.e., the car swerved prior to impact) based on his/her general knowledge and/or typical experiences with similar events (i.e., motor vehicle accidents). While an improperly trained interviewer would likely not stop (and may even sometimes encourage) witnesses to fill in the gaps, properly trained interviewers know to instruct witnesses to only report on what they saw and heard (Fisher & Geiselman, 1992; Hervé et al., 2007). Another effective way to avoid having a witness fill in the gaps is to first find out what s/he was paying attention to and then only ask questions about this information. Remember that many cooperative witnesses will provide information when questioned by officers, irrespective if they actually have a memory for what is being asked.

Fifth, memory is not formed in a vacuum. The memory for a significant event will have been surrounded by the memories for a whole array of relatively irrelevant events and experiences (e.g., from the perspective of the interviewer) that took place before, during, or after the event under investigation (Fisher & Geiselman, 1992; Schacter, 1996, 2001). The event in question may also trigger memories for other completely unrelated events (Hervé et al., 2007). It is not uncommon for improperly trained interviewers to become frustrated when interviewees provide such information rather than focus on the details of the event under question (e.g., an alleged offence), which may lead the interviewer to interrupt the interviewee. This is a mistake for three reasons. First, this may negatively impact rapport, a sin discussed below. Second, this may disrupt the reconstructive process underway. Since memory is cued, personally significant but seemingly irrelevant details may assist in the reconstructive process of memory for the event in question. Third, since memory is cued, the emergence of "irrelevant" information during an investigative interview in which "relevant" information is also provided adds credibility to the witness' statement (see Griesel, Ternes, Schraml, Cooper, & Yuille, this volume; Hervé et al., 2007; Yuille, 1990). In contrast, when such "irrelevant" information surfaces in the absence of any significant "relevant" information, the credibility of the witness' statement is diminished. A related issue is that memory of an event is a process in which some, if not all, of the five human senses are involved (Fisher & Geiselman, 1992). Information is obtained and stored through sight, smell, hearing, taste, and tactile experience. While these senses do not equally contribute to memory encoding, those senses that were involved in the formation of the memory may serve as important cues for later recall. An interviewer can help the interviewee exhaust his/her memory by cueing the interviewee to recall what s/he saw, smelled, heard, tasted and/or touched to elicit further event-related details (Yuille, Cooper, & Hervé, in press).

Sixth, memory reconstruction is impacted by several cognitive processes. Knowing these can help interviewers better understand why narrative memories are often imperfect and prone to error. It also helps them to avoid pursuing lines of question that may contaminate their witness' memory. Schacter (2001) describes seven cognitive/memory processes (i.e., "the seven sins of memory") that all interviewers should know: transience, absent-mindedness, blocking, misattribution, suggestibility, bias, and persistence.[2] Transience, absent-mindedness and blocking are sins of omission: the inability to recall a particular piece of information. Misattribution, suggestibility, bias and persistence are sins of commission: some

---

[2] Although these are called "sins of memory," Schacter (2001) points to the fact that these processes have both advantages and disadvantages when it comes to memory formation and retention.

memory is present but it is either inaccurate or intrusive (e.g., unwanted). Each of these sins of memory and how they may impact an investigative interview are described below.[3]

1. Transience refers to the decay of memory over time. This is the process behind normal forgetting. While a witness may have a detailed memory of an offence minutes after its occurrence, his/her memory may decay over time. This is why it is important to interview witnesses as quickly as possible following an event. We note that the memory "may" be prone to decay; that is, in some cases, a witness may have a remarkable memory for an event (i.e., a memory that evidences a great deal of detail, accuracy, and consistency over time; see Yuille & Daylen, 1998). This may be due to, for example, frequent recollection of the event or to the nature of event (see persistence below for further details). Another important characteristic of transience is that different types of information may decay at different rates. In general, irrelevant or peripheral information (e.g., other witnesses) will decay at a faster rate than relevant or central information (e.g., what the perpetrator was doing; Christianson, 1992). Again, it is important to not fall prey to the "me" theory: what is peripheral and what is central information is in the eye of the beholder (see Hervé et al., 2007, this volume).

2. Absent-mindedness "involves a breakdown at the interface between attention and memory" (Schacter, 2001, p. 4). As noted above, witnesses simply cannot focus on everything that happens in their environment. Absent-mindedness may also occur at the time of recall. In this case, the witness may focus only on some aspects of his/her memory and, therefore, not provide a full account of what s/he remembers. For example, a victim may only report on what she believes to be most important: the sexual assault. She may not, however, spontaneously provide information regarding how the offender gained access to her (e.g., grooming behavior) and/or what happened thereafter (e.g., how and where the ejaculate was disposed of). It is the job of the interviewer to cue these additional details.

3. Blocking refers to an inability to recall what one wants to and/or should recall. In this case, the witness may try to recall something that is in memory but is simply unable to retrieve it. Blocking may be involved in cases of dissociative amnesia (i.e., the inability to recall all or parts of a traumatic event; American Psychiatric Association [APA], 2000). While issues concerning assessing the credibility of amnesia in victims, witnesses and offenders are beyond the scope of this chapter, it is important to note that a good understanding of memory is crucial to this task (see Hervé et al., this volume; Hervé et al., 2007; Porter, Birt, Yuille, & Hervé, 2001). There are two other types of blocking that are relevant to the interviewing context: retrieval inhibition and active forgetting. The former refers to the finding that selectively recalling certain events or parts of events can interfere with (or inhibit) the recall of the non-remembered information (Schacter, 2001). This occurs when, for example, a victim or witness is

---

[3] Schacter (2001) provides further insight into the various causes and consequences of these sins, as well as ways to minimize their influence.

questioned selectively about only certain aspects of the event in question (e.g., an offence) at the exclusion of other aspects of the event. Over time, the information that was not canvased may become more difficult to elicit. Active (or directed) forgetting occurs when a person consciously avoids cues that could elicit a memory (Yuille & Daylen, 1998). Although little is known about this phenomenon, it is a strategy reported by some victims of trauma. In cases of both retrieval inhibition and active forgetting, the end result is the weakening of the cues available to access a memory. While an improperly trained interviewer may become frustrated and leading when facing situations in which blocking occurs, the well trained investigator will know of and utilize memory enhancing techniques to overcome blocking (e.g., the Cognitive Interview; Fisher & Geiselman, 1992; see Colwell et al., this volume). A knowledgeable and experienced interviewer will also know that spontaneous expressions of poor memory may be a clue to credibility (see Griesel et al., this volume; Yuille, 1990). A good understanding of memory helps the interviewer to differentiate likely true claims of poor memory from potentially false claims made to avoid discussing a particular topic.
4. Misattribution occurs when a person recalls aspects of an event correctly but misattributes the source (or origin) of the memory (Schacter, 2001). For example, a bystander may believe s/he saw what the offender was wearing when, in fact, this information was provided by another witness. Alternatively, a witness may misattribute seeing someone during the event in question (e.g., an offence) when, in fact, s/he had seen him/her at some other time or place. In other words, interviewees may "have sketchy recollections of the precise details of previous experiences—when and where they encountered a person or object" (Schacter, 2001, p. 93). According to Schacter, "A strong sense of general familiarity, together with an absence of specific recollections, adds up to a lethal recipe for misattribution" (p. 97). Fortunately, misattribution can be minimized by encouraging interviewees to only report what they specifically remember and by discouraging guessing and/or filling the gaps. Misattribution also points to the importance of both investigating the source of memories and corroborating this information. Otherwise, interviewers may risk focusing on false leads, including focusing on the wrong "suspect."
5. Suggestibility refers to the fact that memory can be contaminated by other people via leading questions, comments, or suggestions, or from misleading information from other sources (e.g., written materials, pictures, the media). Children and the developmentally delayed are especially susceptive to suggestions (Drizin & Leo, 2004; Yuille et al., in press). Remember that memory is reconstructive and incomplete. Accordingly, each time a memory is reconstructed, it can be influenced by leading or suggestive questions or comments (Bruck, Ceci, & Hembrooke, 1998), particularly for information that was not encoded and/or that was affected by transience or blocking (Hervé et al., 2007). It is imperative that interviewers avoid leading/suggestive questions (see Sin Number 9 below). The role of the interviewer should be to cue memory, not lead it. Suggestibility is also the reason why it is important to separate witnesses to an event as quickly as

possible. Otherwise, they may discuss their personal experiences and contaminate each other's memories.
6. Bias reflects memory contamination of another kind, most notably that which is self-imposed. Our current knowledge and beliefs exert powerful influences on how we remember our past. In essence, our current thoughts, beliefs, and emotions serve as filters through which we interpret and potentially rewrite our past. "The result can be a skewed rending of a specific incident, or even of an extended period of our lives, which says more about how we feel *now* than about what happened *then*" (Schacter, 2001, p. 5; italics in the original). The properly trained interviewer will know this and, therefore, focus on eliciting facts (e.g., who did what to whom) and stay clear of (or at least place less weight on) subjective interpretations of past events. The properly trained interviewer will also know the significant influence of stereotypes on interviewees (Brewer & Wells, 2011).
7. In the present context, persistence relates to the repeated recall of events/memories that we do not want to remember. Persistent memories are typically associated with experiences that the interviewee deems stressful/traumatic in nature and are, therefore, experienced as negative and intrusive. Although typically discussed in relation to victims and witnesses, it is important to note that offenders can be traumatized by their own offences and, therefore, experience persistence (Cooper, Cuttler, Dell, & Yuille, 2006; Pollock, 1999). This process accounts for why some interviewees have remarkable memories. When interviewing someone who experiences such intrusive, persistent memories, it would be important to monitor his/her emotional state. By definition, these memories are about traumatic events and their recollection could re-traumatize the individual. While a detailed review of trauma and memory is outside the scope of this chapter, it is important to note that trauma can have a variety of effects on memory, from amnesia to remarkable memories (see Hervé et al., this volume; Hervé et al., 2007; Yuille & Daylen, 1998).

Seventh, in light of the above discussion on memory, it should now be clear that memory for past events should evidence variability over time, with memory for peripheral information being more variable than for central information (Conway, 1997; Erdelyi & Kleinbard, 1978; Fisher et al., this volume). Yet, many improperly trained interviewers wrongly believe that memory should remain consistent over time and, consequently, view any deviations as a sign of deception. The reconstructive nature of memory in combination with the various sins of memory generally do not allow for perfect recollections from one time to another, although there are some exceptions to this (e.g., when an individual has retold the event numerous times or s/he experiences memory persistence; Hervé et al., 2007). When there are no deviations from one retelling to another, then the memory should be viewed with suspicion as this may reflect rote memory (i.e., memorizing a story, such as when making a false claim of victimization or a false alibi; Yuille, 1990). This raises another important topic to canvas during an interview: the history of the person's memory. This concerns how many times has the person thought about, dreamt about, written and/or discussed his/her memory for the event under investigation, as well as what kind of questions that were asked of him/her during retellings (Hervé et al., 2007). This information may help the interviewer sift facts from fiction. Gaining the history of the interviewee's memory is especially important in the investigative interviewing context.

Finally, all investigative interviewers should be familiar with the Undeutsch hypothesis, which stipulates that the quality and quantity of memories for personally experienced events differ from the quality and quantity of fabricated events (Undeutsch, 1989). This is why probing poorly prepared false accounts typically results in little to no additional details. Simply put, the person making a false claim cannot pull from memory the amount or type of details that are typical of personally experienced events. The Undeutsch hypothesis led to the development of Criteria-Based Content Analysis (CBCA), a tool that, in essence, translated what is known about memory into a set of specific criteria associated with truth telling (see Colwell et al., this volume; Griesel et al., this volume; Vrij, 2005; Yuille, 1990). This tool is one of the most validated methods for assessing credibility (Colwell, Hiscock, & Memon, 2002; Lamb et al., 1997; Ruby & Brigham, 1997; Steller, 1989; Steller & Koehnken, 1989; Vrij, 2005).

As the above discussion demonstrates, the more one knows about memory, the easier it is to elicit it and the easier it is to assess its credibility. In contrast, the less one knows about memory, the easier it is to contaminate it and/or the more likely one is to fail to elicit information crucial to the event in question.

Sin Number 3: Misunderstanding Lying and Truth Telling

As with the previous sin, the third "sin" of interviewing reflects the lack of understanding that many interviewers have about the nature and characteristics of lying and truth telling (Akehurst, Kohnken, Vrij, & Bull, 1996; Vrij, 2004). Indeed, even though most people believe that they can accurately identify deception, research with professionals from various backgrounds (e.g., judges, lawyers, psychologists, and police) has shown that most people do no better than chance when trying to distinguish truth from lies in a standard laboratory task (Colwell et al., this volume; Ekman & O'Sullivan, 1991; Porter, Woodworth, & Birt, 2000; ten Brinke & Porter, this volume). This is especially problematic in the investigative interviewing context given that assessing the credibility of statements from victims, witnesses, informants, and suspects is central to the investigative process. The bottom line is that, to effectively assess credibility, interviewers need to understand what the truth looks like, what clues to lies looks like and how to assess these variables in their day-to-day work (Cooper et al., 2009; Ekman, 2009; Griesel et al., this volume; Porter & ten Brinke, 2010; Seniuk, this volume; Vrij, 2000; Yuille, 1989).

The "truth" is whatever information the person being interviewed believes to be true (Cooper et al., 2009; Ekman, 2009). Can a person who is being interviewed give information that is not true and yet not be lying? The answer, of course, is yes.

Every day, many people provide false and erroneous information to others, information that they believe is true but, in fact, is not. As noted above, one's memory is fallible for a variety of reasons. Accordingly, it is important to understand that false information can be supplied quite innocently during an interview. For example, the interviewee may believe that some tidbit of information is correct and report it honestly, yet the information may ultimately prove to be false. Because the individual "believes" the information, s/he will not experience any of the emotional and/or cognitive consequences typically associated with lying (Cooper et al., 2009; Ekman, 2009; Undeutsch, 1989). This is why it is important to understand the nature of memory, to cue memory and not lead it, and to stop interviewees from filling in the gaps.

A "lie" is whatever information the person being interviewed intentionally reports as truthful but knows to be false (Cooper et al., 2009; Ekman, 2009). While there are many contexts in which lying is of little consequence and/or acceptable (e.g., lying to your partner about a surprise birthday party; deception in laboratory research), this is not the case in the investigative interviewing context. This is important to note because "high stake" lies are likely to have more significant emotional and/or cognitive consequences for individuals than "low stake" lies (Frank & Ekman, 1997; O'Sullivan, this volume; Porter & ten Brinke, 2010; ten Brinke & Porter, this volume).

People lie about a variety of issues (DePaulo, Kashey, Kirkendol, Wyer & Epstein, 1996; Ekman, 2009; Ford, 2006; Hancock & Woodworth, this volume; Spidel, Hervé, Greaves, Cooper, & Hare, 2003). An emotional lie is an intentional misrepresentation of one's true emotional state. The suspect who states—with a red face, clenched teeth, and abrupt tone—that he "WASN'T ANGRY" at his missing spouse is an example. An opinion lie is an intentional misrepresentation of the true opinion held by the liar. A chronic spousal abuser who states, "It's wrong to hit women," is an example. Another example would be the suspect who, after being asked "What should happen to someone who committed this type of crime," timidly states, "I…I think that an apology and treatment would best serve everyone." A factual lie is a false denial of a fact, action, or experience or a false assertion of a fact, action, or experience, such as a false alibi or a false claim of victimization. An intent lie is a denial of an intention to do something in the future or a false claim that the liar will not do something in the future. Claims such as "I would never lie to you" have been made many times by many liars. National security professionals are especially concerned with intent lies—e.g., the terrorist who falsely claims that he/she is entering the country to attend a local auto show.

There are several methods used by interviewees to intentionally mislead interviewers (Ekman, 2009; Ford, 2006). The two most common are concealment (i.e., leaving out true information) and falsification (i.e., presenting false information as if it were true). This is why witnesses are asked in court, "Do you swear to tell the truth, the whole truth, and nothing but the truth?" This oath implies that there are several ways that misleading information can be supplied by a witness to the trier of fact (i.e., judge or jury). Not only could a liar intentionally misstate a fact ("…the truth"), but they could intentionally withhold truthful information ("…the whole truth"), or they could also mix a lie in with a lot of truth ("...and nothing but the truth"). Although various methods of lying exist, experience suggests that simply withholding truthful information is the method most used by successful liars. The reason for this is simple: it is much easier to say nothing than to invent a story. This is why it is often what is not said or what is skipped over that is often most revealing. When inventing, the liar has to create a credible story (e.g., an alibi) and then remember the false information in case the topic resurfaces later in the interview or in a subsequent interview. Moreover, if the lie is particularly complicated, there is a lot to remember the next time the same lie is told. This is why asking an interviewee who you suspect of lying via falsification to repeat his/her story can be a useful tool in assessing his/her credibility.

While certain types of lies may be easier to detect than others (e.g., emotional lie vs. factual lie; falsification vs. concealment), it is important to understand that the business of evaluating truthfulness is complex (Colwell et al., this volume; Ekman, 2009; Griesel & Yuille, 2007; O'Sullivan, this volume; ten Brinke & Porter, this volume; Vrij, 2000). The main reason for this is that there are no emotional, cognitive, behavioral and/or physiological signs that a person displays when lying that s/he does not also display under other circumstances (e.g., when stressed). That is, both truth-telling and lying have emotional and/or cognitive consequences (Cooper et al., 2009; Yuille, 1989). When telling the truth, the emotional and cognitive responses tend to be consistent with the content of the story and/or contextual demands. For example, the truthful witness who is being interviewed shortly after a robbery may display heightened emotional arousal stemming from his/her recent experience, while the truthful victim may display offence-related fear that has yet to dissipate. Over time, however, these emotions may no longer be present unless, for example, the event continues to have psychological impact. The person of interest who is, in fact, innocent may display stress, anxiety, or fear simply because s/he is being wrongly suspected of a crime, and this may be heightened if the interviewer uses an accusatory or challenging approach rather than an open-minded method. The truthful person may also show increased mental effort (or cognitive load) when telling his/her story because s/he is eager to provide as much detail as possible. However, when asked open-ended questions about his/her experience, the truthful person will generally display relatively mild cognitive load because s/he has an actual memory to rely on when answering questions.

In contrast, the liar's emotional and cognitive consequences tend to be inconsistent with the content of the story and/or contextual demands (Cooper et al., 2009). As noted above, it is not uncommon for a suspect to claim that he has no anger/animosity towards a victim but nevertheless display signs of anger. In addition, the act of lying can trigger an emotion itself (Ekman, 2009). For many, lying produces some internal emotions, such as the fear of being caught or guilt over deceiving someone. However, not everyone experiences negative emotions when lying. Some people, psychopaths, for example, habitually lie and can actually experience a thrill at the thought that they are fooling the interviewer (Hare, 1998; Spidel et al., 2003). This is known as duping delight (Ekman, 2009). With all other variables being equal, lying also requires greater mental effort than truth telling (Colwell et al., this volume). A police officer conducting a routine roadside stop should have cause for concern if, for example, the driver stumbles or takes time to answer a question that s/he should know automatically, such as his/her name or birth date. Following a line of questioning, making up a plausible story and keeping one's story straight all requires more effort than simply telling the truth.

Knowing that truths and lies have emotional and cognitive responses is important but such represents only part of the process of evaluating truthfulness. How does someone know what someone else is feeling or thinking? While this is difficult to achieve with any certainty—hence why the business of evaluating truthfulness is complex—the good news is that the emotional and cognitive consequences associated with truth telling and lying tend to be displayed in behavior (Cooper et al., 2009; Ekman, 2009; Vrij & Granhag, 2007; Yuille, 1989). This is referred to as "leakage." Leakage can be observed in a variety of behavioral channels, including the face, the body, in voice quality, verbal style, and in verbal content (Ekman, 2009; Ekman, O'Sullivan, Friesen, & Scherer, 1991; Horowitz, 1991; Porter & Yuille, 1996; ten Brinke & Porter, in press; ten Brinke, Porter & Baker, in press). Most of the time, when someone is telling the truth, his/her behaviors will be evidence that corroborates his/her claims and/or apparent emotional and cognitive load. In contrast, when someone is lying, his/her behaviors may betray him/her.

Leakage related to lying can be observed in two fashions: from a change in baseline and/or in light of inconsistencies across behavioral channels (Cooper et al., 2009; Ekman, 2009; Griesel & Yuille, 2007). Baseline refers to how someone typically behaves when telling the truth. With a good grasp of the interviewee's baseline behavior, the interviewer may then spot deviations from this baseline when discussing topics of importance. For example, the interviewee may suddenly evidence a change in posture, voice pitch and/or speech mannerisms (e.g., pauses or filled pauses) when asked about his whereabouts concerning a crime in question. This is the easiest way to identify leakage. Spotting inconsistencies takes more practice and skill but is also more revealing. Inconsistencies in behavioral channels, by definition, mean that the person is communicating different messages. For example, a person may say yes but nod no, or may shrug their shoulders when "confidently" verbally denying any wrongdoing.

Once leakage has been identified, it is the interviewer's job to explore, via effective interviewing techniques, its cause(s) (Cooper et al., 2009; Yuille, 1989). Here lies another important point to understand about leakage. Emotional leakage by an interviewee only tells the interviewer that an emotion has occurred; it does not tell the interviewer the cause of that emotion (Ekman, 2009, 2003). Similarly, seeing signs of cognitive load only tells the interviewer that the interviewee is exerting greater mental effort than is expected given the question or task (Cooper et al., 2009). It is therefore crucial that interviewers not label leakage as a sign of deception. That decision is simply premature. Instead, the interviewer should note the information as it is important; that is, it is a "hot spot" (i.e., a clue to importance) to be further investigated (Cooper et al., 2009). Otherwise, errors that could have been avoided will be made.

Wrongly judging a truth to be deception can have devastating consequences. The consequences of disbelieving the truth are exemplified by the phenomenon of false confessions (Drizin & Leo, 2004; Gudjonsson et al., 2008). However, this is not the only example. Did a co-conspirator warn authorities of a pending hijacked airliner attack on the World Trade Center on September 11, 2011 and was the co-conspirator judged to be a lying? Wrongly believing the lie can also have dramatic consequences, particularly when the purpose of the interview is to determine some future activity. In 1938, British Prime Minister Chamberlain interviewed Hitler and erroneously believed that Hitler was telling the truth about his peaceful intentions in parts of Czechoslovakia. History proved this to be a significant lie.

To summarize, while there are many other factors that influence our ability to differentiate truths from lies (see Cooper et al., 2009; Ekman, 2009; Vrij, 2004; Vrij, Granhag, & Mann, 2010), evaluating truthfulness depends primarily on a good understanding of the nature and types of lies and of the psychology of truth telling and lying, and on skills in identifying, assessing, and interpreting behavioral leakage. Evaluating truthfulness should not be viewed as a single event or decision (i.e., deciding if person is being truthful or not) but rather as a process in which behavior is identified, hypotheses are generated, more questions are asked to test these hypotheses, and conclusions are data driven and logical.

Sin Number 4: Making the Pinocchio Error

Sin numbers 4–6 are by-products of Sin number 3: misunderstanding lying and truth telling. Making the Pinocchio error occurs when someone believes that there is a universal sign for lying: a specific type of leakage that always means a person is lying (Ekman, 2009). This belief is propagated by a variety of factors, including erroneous theoretical perspectives (e.g., that looking up and to the left is associated with lying based on the theory of neuro-linguistic programming; see Mann et al., 2012), the mislabelling of signs of stress as signs of deception (e.g., as suggested by the developers of the voice stress analyser; see Damphousse, 2008), simplistic portrayals in the media, and/or by well-meaning senior interviewers who were taught to believe in this myth (Ekman, 2009; Ford, 2006). The bottom line is that there is no emotional, cognitive and/or physiological response in humans that equates to Pinocchio's nose growing. Research has consistently failed to find a single clue that means someone is lying across all people in all situations. In fact, it could be argued that there is greater variability than consistency when it comes to signs of deception across people (Cooper et al., 2009). In the same way that the presence of a particular clue does not guarantee a lie, the absence of a particular clue does not mean someone is truthful.

Sin Number 5: Making the Othello Error

The Othello error occurs when a displayed emotion is wrongly interpreted as evidence of lying (Ekman, 2009). Othello was a character in Shakespeare's play, *Othello* and was led to believe that his wife, Desdemona, had been unfaithful. This was not true. However, when he confronted her with the accusation of infidelity, she was frightened because she knew how jealous he was. In fact, Othello had already killed the man he suspected was her lover, so she knew how dangerous his anger was and how hopeless was her situation. Nevertheless, Othello misinterpreted his wife's fear as evidence of her guilt, as opposed to her legitimate fear of being disbelieved. Remember that, when an interviewer sees an emotion, all the interviewer knows is that the emotion occurred (Cooper et al., 2009; Ekman, 2003). If an interviewee feels physically threatened, s/he may "leak" fear that could easily be misinterpreted as a clue to lying. For example, when a gang member who is corroborating with police shows fear, is this detection apprehension or fear of retaliation from fellow gang members? The Othello error cautions interviewers against relying too heavily on reactions/answers to specific questions as a sign of deception or guilt. The effective interviewer will note this as a hot spot to be probed further during the interview (Cooper et al., 2009).

Sin Number 6: Making the Idiosyncrasy Error

The idiosyncrasy error reflects the failure to consider individual differences when interpreting the behaviors of others (Ekman, 2009). There are a number of culturally dictated behaviors and idiosyncratic behavioral habits that are commonly misinterpreted as indications of deception but, in reality, have little meaning as hot spots without some understanding of the baseline rate of these behaviors (Cooper et al., 2009). For example, some people never or rarely make eye contact; some people rub their noses a lot; some people frequently move their eyebrows; and so on. When a behavior is culturally sanctioned and/or habitual, its occurrence tells us little with regard to deception detection. For example, avoiding eye contact does not represent a hot spot during an interview if the person usually avoids eye contact. In this case, a more telling hot spot would be intimidating eye contact as such is inconsistent with the person's culture and baseline behavior.

The lesson here is that any leakage should be interpreted in relation to the person's baseline (Cooper et al., 2009; Ekman, 2009). The reasons behind individual behaviors are multifaceted and, among other factors, influenced by culture. For example, some cultures, such as certain Aboriginal or Asian cultures, tend to avoid eye contact, especially when talking with strangers or authority figures (McCarthy, Lee, Itakura, & Muir, 2006). However, experience suggests that some of these well-known culturally dictated behaviors are changing just as the world is changing. It may be that world-wide instant communication, such as e-mail communication or the availability of films on the Internet is breaking down these traditions. What we have always believed to be traditionally true may or may not be true any longer. This is another reason that no matter what you might assume about a person given his/her background (including culture), the best way to avoid errors is to compare the individuals' behavior to his/her baseline (Cooper et al., 2009).

Sin Number 7: Not Being Self-Aware

One of the biggest impediments to effective interviewing is interviewer bias (Vrij, 2000, 2004). That interviewers are susceptible to bias should not be a surprise in that all interviewers have one thing in common: they are human. Like other humans, they are subject to likes and dislikes, prejudices and fears, and personality traits that can bias their approach to the investigation and/or to the manner in which they interview others. While an effective interviewer will know his/her biases and attempt to minimize their impact, an ineffective interviewer unknowingly allows his/her biases to contaminate the investigation and/or interview.

There are three important points to remember when it comes to biases. First, biases affect the way we think about a particular subject, person or behavior (Blanchette & Richards, 2010; Morrison, 2008; Schacter, 2001; Stanovich, 2009). That is, biases reflect erroneous thoughts/beliefs. For example, as explained under Sin number 1, the "Me" Theory of Personality, interviewers often use their own thoughts, behaviors, and assumptions as a way of assessing the actions of victims, witnesses, informants, or suspects, or to judge the truthfulness of an interviewee's statement. Through improper training, an interviewer may also believe in a one-size-fits-all (or cookie-cutter) approach to interviewing. This type of approach "assumes" that all types of interviewees will respond identically to one interviewing style. This is too simplistic. Special populations, such as children, the developmentally delayed and the mentally ill, for example, require tailored approaches that take into account their unique characteristics (Gudjonsson & Joyce, 2011; Williamson, 2006; Yuille, 1988, 2007; Yuille et al., in press). For example, it is not uncommon for interviewers facing a suspect who is denying any wrongdoing to employ behavioral observations questions (i.e., questions based on the assumption that guilty and innocent individuals will respond differently; e.g., "What do you think should happen to someone who committed such a crime?"; e.g., Inbau, Reid, Buckley, & Jayne, 2001). While such questions may lead to important insights into the suspect, these insights are simply hot spots that need to be validated through further questioning, not conclusions with respect to guilt or deception. Remember that there is no Pinocchio response, and there are many reasons why someone may show hot spots to such questions. An innocent developmentally delayed suspect, for example, may have difficulty comprehending and, therefore, answering such questions, which should not be confused as a sign of guilt. Thus, the skilled interviewer will always remember that effective interviewing requires a person-centered approach in which the interviewee's behaviors are interpreted from the interviewee's perspective rather than from the interviewers or in relation to other victims, witnesses, informants and/or suspects.

Second, biases are learned and, therefore, the product of our experiences (e.g., family, social, cultural, professional, and/or training influences; Schacter, 2001; Stanovich, 2009). Within the investigative interviewing context, there are three major sources of biases (i.e., one internal and two external) that any interviewer should guard against. The first has to do with the interviewer's "gut instincts." With experience, interviewers understandably develop intuitions or instincts about people and their behaviors. If these intuitions are based on faulty assumptions (e.g., certain erroneous clues to lying; see above), then they will lead to errors more often than not (Cooper et al., 2009). If the interviewer's gut instinct motivates him/her to follow up on one lead over others, then it only serves to blind him/her to other leads/possibilities and, therefore, increases the chance of errors. An effective interviewer will consider his/her gut instinct but not to the exclusion of other possibilities.

The second source of bias stems from the belief that the goal of a suspect interview is to seek a confession rather than the truth (Drizin & Leo, 2004; Gudjonsson et al., 2008; Kassin, Drizin, et al., 2010). This predisposes the interviewer to feel justified in using whatever means necessary to get a confession, and to pay little attention to the dangers of this approach, particularly as it relates to false confessions. The unbiased interviewer does not seek a confession but rather focuses on fact finding (Yuille, 1988; Yuille et al., in press). The goal is to find the truth, whatever it might be, and why the person believes it to be the truth. When facing a deceptive suspect, for example, the goal is to provide every opportunity for the suspect to provide a truthful account and, if this fails, to examine the deceptive account in enough depth as to elicit information that can then be discredited as part of the investigation. The goal is to provide the trier of fact with enough information to make a judgment. The third major source of bias stems from the suspicious context within which investigative interviewers operate (Ekman, 2009; Kassin, Drizin et al., 2010). The more suspicious the interviewer, the more s/he expects to be told a lie and, conversely, the less s/he expects to be told the truth. S/he will have a lower rate of believing a lie but a higher rate of not believing the truth. This is another factor that contributes to false confessions (Drizin & Leo, 2004; Gudjonsson et al., 2008; Kassin, Appleby, et al., 2010). In contrast, the more trusting the interviewer, the more s/he expects to be told the truth and, conversely, the less s/he expects to be told a lie. The overly trusting interviewer will have a lower rate of not believing the truth but also a higher rate of believing a lie. This bias likely plays an impact in, for example, believing false claims of victimization. Obviously, the optimum combination is believing truth-tellers and disbelieving liars. The best way to achieve this is to keep an open mind and evaluate each case on its own merits.

Third, the stronger our bias, the more impact it will have on our actions (Blanchette & Richards, 2010; Schacter, 2001; Stanovich, 2009). The conviction with which we hold our biases will partly be influenced by our personality. Most notably, a bias may be strengthened by self-generated pressures to catch a suspect or identify the liar to, for example, prove to others how good we are. This is when the interviewer runs the risk of misinterpreting a hot spot as a sign of deception. The more our ego is involved in our work, the less effective we will be as our search for and analysis of hot spots will be a pursuit to prove our ego right (i.e., our pre-conceived notions). When ego is involved, we tend to avoid seeking any information that could damage the ego (i.e., evidence against the ego-driven beliefs/conclusions), leading to a self-fulfilling prophecy. This is what occurs, for example, when one only tries to prove his/her gut instincts at the exclusion of other possibilities.

The strength of biases can also be affected by external pressures. For example, the extent to which our beliefs, assumptions and behaviors are supported within the context in which they operate is key in determining their strength. This is why it is often so difficult to stand up against what the larger group is doing or saying. Another external factor is the pressure placed upon the interviewer by their supervisor, team and/or the public (often via the media) to find a suspect and, consequently, identify the liar from the people of interest. As a result, the interviewer is predisposed to assume that at least one interviewee in the group is "guilty" of whatever is being investigated. This will bias the guilt—or confession—seeking interviewer to only look for "signs" of deceit at the exclusion of "signs" of truthfulness. This is problematic given that there are no clear signs of deceit. Consequently, this may result in a situation in which the truth teller is wrongly suspected of lying, such as when a highly cooperative interviewee withholds information or shades the information in a more favorable light—a situation not uncommonly encountered in investigative interviews. Finally, and not unrelated to the above, it is important to note that emotions can also add saliency to our biases, stereotypes and prejudices (Blanchette & Richards, 2010). For example, the nature of the investigation (e.g., the sexual assault and murder of local children) can trigger emotions (e.g., anger, sadness, frustration) in even the most experienced of interviewers, and the characteristics of interviewees can add to these emotions (e.g., a person of interest with a dislikeable demeanor). Interviewers will vary in how much and how long emotions affect them. For example, some interviewers are quick to anger but then mellow almost immediately, while other interviewers are slow to anger but then remain angry for long periods of time (Ekman, 2003). Successful interviewers are probably more self-aware of these traits and, therefore, are more controlling of these emotions rather than letting their emotions dictate their behavior during the interview.

Sin Number 8: Not Considering Multiple Explanations

It is a common trap for any interviewer, experienced or not, to "know" what must have occurred and then set out to prove it. Magically, after the premature judgment has been made, much of the information that is gathered during the interview seems to support that judgment, even if the judgment was wrong. Jumping to conclusions is a consequence of being biased and this sin of interviewing emerges because the interviewer fails to maintain an open mind (Cooper et al., 2009; Kassin, Drizin et al., 2010; Vrij, 2004; Yuille, 1988). Yuille has repeatedly testified on this issue in both Canadian and American courts, and commonly informs the triers of fact something to the effect of the following: the biggest single impediment to effective interviewing is when the interviewer has a single hypothesis about the fact pattern that he or she is dealing with. In contrast to that, the most effective approach to investigative interviewing is the alternative hypothesis method, where the interviewer entertains several alternative explanations as the interview/investigation unfolds. This way, the investigator is not blinded by one hypothesis. When there is only one hypothesis, there is a tendency to exaggerate the evidence that is consistent with it and minimize the evidence that is inconsistent. Keeping an open mind through multiple hypotheses testing reduces that problem.

Erroneous results are often produced when the interviewer assumes that any information provided by the interviewee that does not fit with the interviewer's single hypothesis must be false and, therefore, a lie. When this sin is being committed, the interview questions are generally worded in a biased fashion and the answers are generally interpreted in a manner favorable to the interviewer's biased hypothesis (Drizin & Leo, 2004; Kassin, Appleby, et al., 2010). Usually, this is not an intentionally malicious act. The "self-fulfilling prophecy" is the inevitable consequence of not keeping an open mind. Interviewers may also jump to the conclusion that an interviewee who lies about something or withholds information is guilty when the reason for this behavior may be something else altogether. For example, a woman being interviewed about her murdered husband may lie about her whereabouts not because she had something do to with his death but because she was having an affair. The interviewer who is locked into only one hypothesis will likely erroneously interpret her efforts to conceal the affair as a sign of guilt in the murder. This is why interviewers are encouraged to consider behavioral leakage a hot spot rather than a sign of deception or guilt. Remember that a hot spot may occur for a variety of reasons, of which lying is only one possibility. It may turn out that the interviewee has lied, but the process by which that conclusion has been reached should include identifying the hot spot, entertaining alternate hypotheses for the hot spot, probing the different alternate hypotheses about the hot spot with a variety of questions, considering other evidence in the case, and then making a decision (Cooper et al., 2009). Considering multiple hypotheses for what we see and hear during an interview will go a long way to neutralizing interviewer biases and reducing errors in disbelieving the truth and believing the lie.

Sin Number 9: Not Planning Ahead

We have all heard the following edict: "A plan…even a bad plan … is better than no plan at all." Yet, it is not uncommon for an interviewer facing a heavy caseload to forgo planning an interview due to time management issues. Unfortunately, going into the interview without much preparation often leaves the interviewer frustrated that the interview produced very little information of value.

Properly planning an interview should include seeking knowledge about the topic under investigation, knowledge about the interviewee, and preparing for the interview itself (Cooper et al., 2009; Yuille, 2007). Case-specific knowledge not only ensures that the interviewer will canvas all topics of investigative value (e.g., all alleged events of abuse) but it also facilitates the business of evaluating truthfulness. If, for example, the interviewer has reviewed the victim and witness statements, the interviewer will then be better prepared to identify details provided by a suspect that are inconsistent with this information. This information may also assist in making sense of the memory patterns evidenced during the interview (see Hervé et al., this volume; Hervé et al., 2007). Knowing about the particular case may also inform interview strategies. For example, if there is information to suggest that an offence was out of character (i.e., ego-dystonic in nature) and may have been committed due to external pressure (e.g., a substance abuser committing an offence to repay his dealer; a woman committing fraud for her domestically abusive husband), then tactics relying on guilt (or remorse) or providing a justifiable rationale for the offence (e.g., you were coerced by your husband and simply had no options) might prove fruitful. In contrast, if the offence appeared to be internally and ego-driven (i.e., ego-syntonic in nature), then strategies that play on the offender's ego might be warranted. More generic knowledge about offence patterns is also useful. For example, knowing that seductive paedophiles engage in grooming behavior, enables the interviewer to seek information regarding grooming (e.g., the victim reports that he was first approached at the local swimming pool and was offered help by the offender regarding learning how to dive), information which may lead to other potential victims. Similarly, knowing that, in some cases of reported domestic partner abuse, the female is the actual perpetrator allows the interviewer to keep an open mind and identify false claims of victimizations by women and true claims of innocence by men.

Gathering knowledge about the interviewee also has numerous benefits (Bull, 2010; Christianson, 2007; Morrison, 2008; Williamson, 2006; Yuille, 2007). For example, the more we know about the person we are about to interview, the less likely we will engage in the "me" theory or other biases, contaminate memory, and misinterpret innocuous hot spots as signs of deception, and the better we will be at developing relevant alternative hypothesis, at cuing memory, and at tailoring our interviews (Cooper et al., 2009; Hervé et al., 2007). Indeed, while there are general principles that apply across all interviews, the bottom line is that each interviewee is unique and should be treated as such.

There are five general domains to canvas when seeking background information about an interviewee. First, it is important to understand the cognitive abilities of the interviewee (Gudjonsson & Joyce, 2011; Yuille et al., in press). Cognitive abilities may be age related (e.g., children vs. adolescents vs. adults vs. the elderly), or due to neurocognitive abnormalities (e.g., the developmental delayed, the brain injured). Cognitive abilities affect memory, understanding of concepts, and suggestibility, and dictate the complexity of questions that can be used (e.g., concrete vs. abstract language, word difficulty, sentence length). Someone with intellectual functioning deficits, for example, could have a limited understanding of the concepts covered during behavioral observation questions. Without knowing this, an interviewer could misinterpret this person's limited and simplistic response as a sign of guilt, particularly if the interviewee also shows stress (i.e., simple confusion at being interviewed rather than detection apprehension). Similarly, there are certain interviewing techniques, such as the Cognitive Interview and other memory enhancement techniques, that may be inappropriate for use in the cognitively limited or impaired (Fisher & Geiselman, 1992; Geiselman, 1999). Failure to know this could lead one to misinterpret the limited usefulness of these tools in eliciting additional information as a sign of guilt.

Second, preparation should include gaining knowledge of the interviewee's personality. While a detailed review of personality theory and research is outside the scope of this chapter, it is important to remember that everyone has behavioral characteristics and traits that define his/her personality. These traits are likely to be most salient under times of stress (e.g., during an offence and criminal investigation) and these traits can affect memory, suggestibility, disclosure motivation, and/or interview dynamics (Blair et al., 1995; Drizin & Leo, 2004; Hervé et al., 2007; Kassin, Drizin et al., 2010). Some people, for example, are prone to being depressed versus happy, manipulative versus honest, trusting versus suspicious, selfless versus self-centered, and/or socially conscious vs. socially inappropriate/unaware. Designing the interview according to these traits will most likely result in a more productive interview. Consider, for example, the Unabomber who mailed packages containing explosives to a variety of victims. The victims were killed or wounded by the explosion that resulted from opening the packages. When the Unabomber was finally identified and arrested, he reportedly lived a Spartan-like existence in the state of Montana, alone in a shed without electricity or running water because of his personality. Not many of us would want to live that kind of life but apparently he did. Knowing this, the interviewer would probably prepare an interview plan differently than if the Unabomber were a more social person (i.e., reduce the amount of people involved; take time to identify topics of interest to develop rapport; etc.). As another example, consider interviewing the late Theodore Bundy, who was convicted and executed by the State of Florida for sexually sadistic murders committed in various US states. Bundy was reportedly a very self-centered, intelligent, and charismatic individual. Knowing this, the interviewer would probably prepare an interview plan that would have anticipated Bundy's self-centeredness, and his attempts to manipulate the interviewer and control the interview. An interview with someone like Bundy could easily take a long time to conduct. The sage advice, "give him enough rope and he'll hang himself," would be very applicable in this situation.

Knowing the personality style of interviewees has the added advantage of helping the interviewer be more effective with respect to evaluating truthfulness (Cooper et al., 2009). As mentioned previously, the ability to detect and correctly interpret hot spots depends on a good understanding of the person's baseline behavior, and an understanding of what may lead to deviations from baseline. Baseline is, in part, determined by the person's personality. An interviewee who tends to be suspicious and distrustful of others will, for example, behave differently than an interviewee who tends to be extremely manipulative and self-centered (e.g., introverted, reserved, and cautious versus extroverted, gregarious, and superficially cooperative). Similarly, a depressed and suspicious individual will interpret their life experiences differently than a very happy and trusting individual (e.g., negative and pessimistic vs. overly positive and optimistic). As per the memory sin of "bias," these interpretations may eventually become reality to these individuals (Schacter, 2001), a sin of memory that should not be confused with a sign of deception. Remember that interviewees often give away lies by unintentionally changing *their* behavior from *their* baseline.

Third, the interviewer should assess if the interviewee has any mental health issues that may complicate the interview. While a review of mental health issues and how they impact the interview is beyond the scope of this chapter, there are some general principles that are worth mentioning. First, individuals with serious mental health problems, by and large, react poorly to stress. Interviewing them in a stress-free manner and environment is, therefore, especially important with this group, and stress-inducing tactics are counter-indicated. Second, as seen in problems of personality, mental health symptoms may cause an interviewee to have a unique (if not odd) interpretation of the world (Hervé et al., 2007). This may be most evident within, for example, the statement of a psychotic individual (e.g., someone who has lost touch with reality and who may have experienced visual and auditory hallucinations). Focusing on facts as opposed to interpretations can serve to reduce the contaminating influences of this effect and make such individuals more reliable witnesses than would otherwise be the case. That is, interviewers should not be distracted by a schizophrenic's belief that s/he was abducted by five "aliens" but rather focus on investigating how five individuals took him in a vehicle and assaulted him. Other points to consider when working with the mentally ill are their medication regime and compliance. Knowing the side effects of medications and medication schedules can help the interviewer schedule an interview when the interviewee will be at his/her best.

Fourth, the interviewer should learn about the physical state of the interviewee and prepare accordingly. If the interviewee is taking medication or has limited physical stamina, the interview should be scheduled to take this into account. Similarly, if the interviewee has some form of disability, the interview context should be adjusted accordingly (e.g., providing comfortable seating and appropriate breaks; ensuring easy access to the interview room and bathrooms). As well, the interviewer should seek information regarding the interviewee's cultural background (Cooper et al., 2009). While there is little research on the impact of culture on interviews, experience suggests that culture may influence what someone is willing to share (and to whom), their response to authority figures (including deception appropriateness), and their sensitivity to particular interpersonal behaviors and/or contexts. The bottom line is that this information may be useful in developing rapport—which is discussed below, in understanding the person's baseline, in interpreting hot spots and in developing interview strategies (e.g., culturally appropriate forms of rationalization).

One of the simplest ways to learn about the interviewee and his/her baseline presentation is to contact the interviewers who have conducted interviews of the same person in the past. As the edict goes, "the best predictor of future behavior is past behavior." However, in other cases, determining the background of the interviewee can be a very complex process, requiring considerable time—even days, consulting with various behavioral experts, conducting background interviews of friends, associates, or co-workers of the interviewee, and researching other sources such as prior written reports about the interviewee and the interviewee's arrest and driving records.

While other demands may limit how much background information about the case, topic, and person may be collected, the interviewer should always take time to prepare for the interview itself (Yuille, 2007; Yuille et al., in press). As noted above, it is recommended that interviews be scheduled at a time when the interviewee is likely to be at his/her best (i.e., most alert and stable). Given memory transience, the shorter the time frame between the event of interest and the interview the better (i.e., with respect to memory). Indeed, Fisher and Geiselman (1992) recommend that, if an interviewee is reasonably calm, seems capable of following instructions, and can perform intensive memory retrieval operations, the interview should be conducted as soon as possible after the event in question. If, however, the interviewee is extremely anxious, has difficulty following even simple instructions, and appears incapable of doing intensive memory retrieval, it is better to postpone the interview to a later date. Planning where the interview is to take place is also important. While the actual interview location may be determined by circumstances (e.g., the first responder taking a statement at the scene of the crime), the interviewer's primary concern should be a location where there will be the fewest distractions. Not only can distractions disrupt the memory flow, they often negatively impact rapport building, the next sin reviewed.

Sin Number 10: Not Establishing Rapport

Rapport refers to the connection, harmony, confidence, or trust between the interviewer and interviewee (Yuille et al., in press). There is probably no other activity that can potentially influence the success of an interview to the same degree as establishing rapport (see Colwell et al., this volume). Positive rapport encourages people to talk and to talk honestly, including about topics they would otherwise not have talked about (Morrison, 2008). Taking time to establish rapport further permits the interviewer the opportunity to establish a baseline and, therefore, contributes to evaluating truthfulness (Cooper et al., 2009). Conversely, the failure to establish or maintain rapport can potentially jeopardize an interview. For example, an otherwise cooperative victim or witness may be put off and leave out crucial pieces of information, an informant may fail to report crime-related information, and a suspect may never feel comfortable enough to unload his burden onto the shoulders of the interviewer. If the interviewee reacts to the inability of the interviewer to establish rapport, his/her feelings may leak out and could potentially be misinterpreted as a sign of guilt. Moreover, if the interviewee is chronically stressed by the inability of the interviewer to establish rapport, the associated stress-related leakage could serve to mask more subtle hot spots elicited by offence-related questions. The importance of establishing rapport cannot be overstated.

Rapport can be established at the beginning of the interview by inquiring as to the interviewee's welfare and background, and by attending to his/her basic needs. Often, common events, experiences will be discovered during the preparation step or early in rapport building that both the interviewer and interviewee share.

Discussing children, jobs or places lived are examples. Rapport should be maintained throughout the interview and can be strengthened at any point during the interview by again inquiring about the interviewee's welfare or comfort. Furthermore, complimenting the interviewee as to their performance or ability to communicate often enhances positive rapport. This includes thanking suspects for their disclosure(s). Rapport can be further supported at the end of the interview when the interviewer provides the interviewee with contact information and informs him/her of the next step in the investigation. Infrequently, establishing rapport may be the only activity that takes place in the first few interviews. This may be because the interviewee is highly suspicious of the interviewer's intentions, because the interviewee is too traumatized to comfortably talk about what happened, or due to some other factors. For example, experience suggests that, while establishing rapport with prisoners of war takes a long time, the effort occasionally pays unexpected positive results.

The problem that many improperly trained interviewers have with establishing and maintaining rapport is that it requires time and patience. Interviewers are frequently pressured to conduct interviews quickly and efficiently in order to move on to other pending interviews or to conduct other phases of an investigation. This is unfortunate because it often forces the interviewer to rush into the essence of the interview (i.e., asking questions about the event in question) without first establishing positive rapport with the interviewee. At other times, interviewers fail to recognize the value of rapport building and only superficially attend to it. Again, they rush through this part of the interview to get to what they believe is the crucial part of the interview: talking about the event in question (e.g., the offence). This effect is further intensified when one is simply focused on seeking a confession.

Another feature of rapport is that it cannot be faked. If the interviewer has any biases or prejudices towards the interviewee, these are likely to leak out in his/her behavior. Just as the interviewer is reading the interviewee, the interviewee is reading the interviewer. Accordingly, these biases are likely to disrupt (if not prevent) rapport building and unnecessarily complicate the interview. Another roadblock to rapport building is the interviewer's ego. The bottom line is that no one is liked by everyone and, consequently, an effective interviewer will know when to remove him/herself from the interview in favor of another interviewer who may have the right characteristics to build rapport with a particular interviewee.

Sin Number 11: Not Actively Observing and Listening

Crucial information can be missed when one is distracted. Indeed, lies often succeed because the recipient of the lie was not paying attention (Cooper et al., 2009; Ekman, 2009). Unfortunately, there are many personal and professional demands that make distraction a reality within the interview context. An interviewer who is having problems at home or facing other personal problems will likely be distracted. Failure to attend to basic needs, such as food and sleep, can reduce our attentional capabilities. Acute and chronic pain further reduces our concentration, and some medications have known effects on attention and concentration. An interviewer facing a seemingly unmanageable case load or external pressures to find the suspect or identify the liar will likely be distracted. During the interview, the interviewer may be distracted by thinking about what question to ask next. This scenario is especially likely in novice interviewers and/or when the interviewer failed to prepare for the interview. The interviewer who is busy writing notes is, by definition, distracted. As well, the biased interviewer will also be distracted. His/her prejudices will likely surface into consciousness and, therefore, take away from limited attentional resources. The confession-seeking interviewer will be focused on navigating the interview to elicit a confession rather than focused on the here and now. The bottom line is that, the more one has on one's mind, the more likely one is to be distracted; and the more one is distracted, the less attention one has for the task at hand. Remember that attention is limited. This situation also sets the context by which corners are cut and poor interviewing techniques thrive (e.g., biases and not establishing rapport). For these reasons, distraction is the nemesis of the effective interviewer.

While distractions within the investigative context cannot be fully removed, their impact can be minimized by active listening and observing (Cooper et al., 2009; Ekman, 2009; Yuille et al., in press), the key word being "active." By active, we mean the degree of concentration (or effort) the interviewer puts into paying attention to what is said and done by the interviewee. Actively observing refers to watching for the interviewee's baseline behaviors in the face and body when developing rapport, and to being attentive to deviations or hot spots when more sensitive topics are discussed. Actively listening refers to paying attention to the interviewee's baseline use of language early in the interview (e.g., voice characteristics, verbal style, and verbal content), and to actively identify verbal hot spots during the more sensitive part of the interview. Often, it is what is left unsaid that is most revealing.

Actively observing and actively listening are difficult to do at the same time. Even for the very experienced and properly trained interviewer, many audio and visual behaviors of the interviewee will be missed. This is one of the many advantages of recording interviews: the interviewer can later view the recording at a time when s/he is less distracted. Recording also allows for a more accurate account of what transpired in the interview, including what the interviewee reported. Indeed, note taking, particularly when conducted retrospectively following the interview, typically results in key information being left out, most notably information that is inconsistent with the interviewer's primary hypothesis (Lamb, Orbach, Sternberg, Hershkowitz, & Horowitz, 2000). Should recording not be possible, the interviewer is encouraged to actively listen and observe what is being said and done, and to document this information when the interviewee pauses between questions. Paraphrasing these findings back to the interviewee (when appropriate) to allow for corrections can reduce the chance that information inconsistent with the interviewer's primary hypothesis was inadvertently left out of the paraphrased summary.

Sin Number 12: Phrasing the Question Wrongly

One of the most frequent sins of interviewing is the improper phrasing of questions (Kassin, Drizin et al., 2010; Morrison, 2008). This may be due, at least in part, to the fact that questions asked in the investigative interviewing context differ drastically from questions asked in the social context. The former requires a fact-finding mindset that avoids contaminating the interviewee's memory and/or distorting his/her self-report. These factors are not present in the social context which consequently promotes bad habits (e.g., phrasing questions to get a desirable answer or a story rather than just facts).

Within the investigative interviewing context, poorly phrased questions can have several unwanted consequences. Questions that are poorly worded can influence or contaminate how the interviewee answers the question, which itself may contaminate the interviewee's memory, or simply confuse the interviewee (Gudjonsson et al., 2008; Hervé et al., 2007; Schacter, 2001). At best, this reduces rapport and, at worst, it may serve as grounds to dismiss the case. An improperly worded question can also contain information that reveals what the interviewer already knows or, in some cases, does not know. Giving away your position is never a good plan. It matters not whether the questions are used in an interview (i.e., generally a non-confrontational solicitation of information from a cooperative interviewee) or an interrogation (i.e., generally a search for truthful or incriminating information from a reluctant or hostile interviewee)—the effects of a poorly worded question are the same. In order to recognize how often improperly worded questions are used in an interview, the interviewer should record the interview and then review the tape at a later date, critically listening for those questions that were confusing, leading, or otherwise supplied information to the interviewee, as well as the impact of such questions on the interviewee's self-report.

One example of a commonly asked but poorly worded question is a closed-ended question. A close-ended question can only be answered with "yes, no or I don't know." For example, "Did you have anything to do with the murder of Joe?" is a close-ended question. The problem with this question is that it typically fails to elicit a multiple word response. Remember that lies of concealment are easier to get away with than lies of falsification. That is, it is easier to lie with only one simple word than with having to create a multiple-word response that contains false or misleading information. Accordingly, a better question would be an open-ended question; that is, a question that requires a multiple word response, such as "What do you remember about the past 24 h?" Avoiding (or at least minimizing) close-ended questions accomplishes one interview goal: challenging the interviewee to supply information without much prompting by the interviewer.

Another common mistake occurs when the answer to the question is suggested in the wording of the question (Bruck et al., 1998; Kassin, Drizin et al., 2010). "Do you live at 125 Main Street?" is an example of a close-ended leading (or suggestive) question. A better question would be, "What is your home address?" Open-ended suggestive questions are less obvious but as problematic. For example, asking a witness, "What was the color of the car?" presumes that s/he knows that information. The problem is that a cooperative interviewee might answer this to be helpful despite not having a clear recollection of the car's color. In such cases, the color s/he provides may become part of his/her memory and, therefore, contaminate his/her recollection. It is, consequently, important to avoid suggesting qualities of objects, places or people in a question. A better question would be, "What do you remember about the car?" Suggestions can also occur via nonverbal communication by, for example, the emphasis placed on a particular question via the emotional tone in which the question was posed.

Another example of a poorly worded question is a compound question (Yuille, 2007; Yuille et al., in press). At times, compound questions occur when the actual question is preceded by a lengthy, often confusing preamble. The wording often reveals the questioner's opinions or knowledge and it may also influence the answer. Extreme examples of the use of compound questions can be seen during televised American Senate investigations in which the Senators make lengthy political speeches that ultimately lead to a question. At other times, compound questions take the form of multiple questions being asked at once (e.g., How satisfied are you with your job? Do you like the pay, your coworkers…are you happy with your duties?). This may serve to confuse the interviewee, particularly those with limited cognitive abilities, or allow the sophisticated manipulator to choose which question to answer. It also may confuse the interviewer who may be unsure which question is being answered. A better prompt would be, "Tell me about your job." This gives the interviewee the chance to spontaneously discuss his/her views about his/her job, and permits the interviewer to actively listen and observe for hot spots which may dictate which follow up topics to query (e.g., "Tell me more about your coworkers.").

Another example of a poorly worded question is a multiple choice question (Yuille, 2007; Yuille et al., in press). An example would be, "Did you go somewhere on your vacation or did you stay at home or what?" A better prompt would be, "You said you went on vacation. Please tell me everything you remember about that." As with leading questions, multiple choice questions makes it easier to lie when the questions contain the answer (see Colwell et al., this volume). All the liar has to do is select one of the choices. Recall taking tests in school. Which type of question challenged you the most: a question that required composing two or three paragraphs or a multiple-choice question that required picking an answer from four or five choices? Accordingly, multiple choice questions should be used sparingly (if at all). If used, it is good practice to come back to that question later in the interview and provide the choices in a different order. This is especially important when working with suggestible or cognitively impaired individuals as such individuals may simply pick a choice because of its order, not its content.

Another consideration with respect to phrasing questions has to do with words that solicit, words that command, and words that connote detail. Words that solicit are best used early in an interview, as they politely request that the interviewee answer questions. These include such words as *"please," "can you," "would you,"* etc. For example, the interviewer might say, "Please tell me what happened on the way to the forum." Words that command are best used later in an interview. Words that command are less polite and, in effect, order the interviewee to provide information. For example, words that command are words such as *"Tell me"* or *"describe,"* as when prompting the interviewee, *"Tell me everything that happened when you arrived home yesterday."* Words that connote detail can be used throughout the interview, as they simply request the interviewee to be detailed and exact in his/her account. For example, you may prompt a witness with, *"tell me specifically…"* or *"describe in detail…"*

Overall, effective interviewing is characterized by the use of open-ended and non-leading questions. When querying a topic (e.g., an offence), broad open-ended questions are asked to prompt a spontaneous and detailed account. More specific open-ended w-h questions can then be asked as needed (e.g., what, when, where), followed by more specific questions if warranted. The more questions asked, however, the greater the chance for contamination and misinformation.

Sin Number 13: Timing the Question Wrongly

There are a number of ways that an interviewer can disrupt the tempo of an interview, cause the interviewee to forget to report vital information, or put the interviewee on the defensive by the timing of his/her questions. One of the most common examples of this sin is when the interviewer interrupts the interviewee (Fisher & Geiselman, 1992; Williamson, 2006; Yuille, 1988, 2007). Interrupting any interviewee, deceptive or cooperative, is problematic more often than not. In many cases, an interviewer, after having established rapport, introduces the topic under investigation with a great opening statement, such as "Please describe everything that you can recall about the robbery yesterday." The mistake occurs when the interviewer quickly interrupts the interviewee with a second question. For example, the interviewer may stop the narrative and ask about specific characteristics of the perpetrator. With the cooperative interviewee, the interruption can disrupt the reconstructive process of memory and, therefore, result in less information being provided or key details being left out. The interruption can also be confusing and distracting to the interviewee, which may reduce rapport and/or implicitly communicate to the interviewee that the interviewer has an agenda that is not necessarily to get the interviewee's detailed account of what s/he knows. By definition, an interruption indicates that the interviewer was thinking of another line of questioning rather than actively paying attention to what was being said.

With the deceptive interviewee, the interruption can actually make it harder to identify the lie (Cooper et al., 2009). As Napoleon stated, "Never interrupt your enemy when he is making a mistake." While it is not a good idea to view the interviewee as an enemy (as this has obvious biasing effects and is counterproductive to rapport building), interviewers should refrain from interrupting an interviewee who may be "hanging himself" with a series of subtle deceptions, outright lies, or other distortions of the truth. In addition to reducing the potential for hot spots, interruptions may telegraph the interviewer's suspicions, thereby allowing the deceptive individual to adjust his strategy and/or provide him/her more time to prepare a story. A far better strategy is to remain silent while the interviewee answers the question. This should be followed by a pause, as this may motivate the interviewee to resume talking and, therefore, add even more information. Silence between questions also allows the interviewer to think about the wording of the next question, or think about a strategy change, or make notes. Thereafter, another open-ended question should be asked, and the process repeated. Encouraging the interviewee to do most of the talking is desirable and often helps in the task to differentiate the truth teller from the liar.

Another common error is committed when a specific aspect of the interviewee's narrative becomes the central issue of a disproportionate number of questions. Repeatedly asking about that specific aspect teaches the interviewee that the aspect in question is very important. Suppose, for example, that the interviewee witnessed a robbery committed by two suspects and the witness describes the suspects as two males. If the interviewer believes that the second suspect was in fact a female, the interviewer may then repeatedly ask the interviewee about the description of the second suspect, thereby telegraphing his/her suspicions. The interviewer may eventually even ask, "Are you sure you saw two males?" This may very likely cause the interviewee to question his/her memory, if not taint it. As noted above, telegraphing your beliefs to interviewees early in the interview only serves to help them better prepare for more difficult aspects of the interview to come. A better approach is to allow the deceptive interviewee to continue his/her deception uninterrupted. Later in the interview (i.e., when the interviewer has elicited and tested enough hot spots and, therefore, gathered evidence against the lie(s)), the interviewer can ask questions to clarify inconsistencies or to challenge the interviewee's account (Yuille et al., in press). Indeed, while clarification questions are important, they are best left to the end of the interview and asked in a non-leading and non-suggestive manner (see PEACE model introduced by Walsh & Bull, this volume). When challenging an interviewee's account (e.g., if credibility of the account is in question), one tactic is to point out contradictions in his/her statement or between his/her statement and other evidence or sources of information.

Poorly timed questions are also commonly seen when the subject matter being discussed is multifaceted or otherwise complicated (e.g., multiple offences; multiple perpetrators; multiple parts to one offence). In such cases, the improperly trained or overwhelmed interviewer may ask a series of questions that jump from one topic to another, rather than exhausting the memory for one topic before moving on to the next. Suppose, for example, that the interviewee is questioned about his/her activities on a certain day and reports four separate activities. Asking a few questions about the first activity, a few questions about the fourth and then asking a few more questions about the first activity can cause confusion in both the interviewer and interviewee. This may result in the interviewer forgetting to follow-up on key information and/or may cause the interviewee to forget to mention some important detail. These problems can be avoided by preparing for the interview and/or identifying and labelling the different parts, and then exhausting the memory for each.

Sometimes a good question may be asked at the wrong time. Interviewers who ask the "why" question too early in the interview can cause the interviewee to become defensive and, consequently, to edit the remainder of his/her statement in order to justify their actions. Imagine, for example, interviewing a victim about a sexual assault she suffered as she was leaving work late at night and walking to her car parked in a secluded parking lot. If she is asked why she parked her car where she did, suggesting that this contributed to her vulnerability, she may become defensive about that decision and edit her answers to justify her decision to park her car where she did. Now imagine if the victim was asked at the beginning of the interview why she didn't try to fiercely fight off the rapist. The same holds true for offenders. Some offenders simply do not know why they do what they do (B. Pitt-Payne, personal communication, Fall, 2011), and asking them the "why" question may serve to highlight their lack of insight and, therefore, threaten rapport.

The best way to learn about the timing of questions and their impact is to record interviews. The interviewer who audio or video records his/her interviews can review them at a later date and critically listen for those questions that were timed in such a way as to cause confusion, cause the interviewee to forget to report critical information, or cause the interviewee to become defensive. At times, this exercise may lead the interviewer to learn how poorly timed questions ended up confusing him/herself to the extent that crucial pieces of information or hot spots were not properly followed up.

Sin Number 14: Misunderstanding Coercion

History is filled with descriptions of torture tactics, from "the rack" to "the rubber hose." Defining some of these tactics as "torture" is often self-evident. But there are other, less brutal tactics that are designed to manipulate the interrogated person psychologically. Tactics such as exposure to loud sounds, prolonged isolation in extreme ambient environments, and degrading techniques are but a few. These are considered abusive in nature and are increasingly being shunned by the public, various professional groups and the courts (Drizin & Leo, 2004; Kassin, Appleby, et al., 2010; Kassin, Drizin et al., 2010). There are, however, other less abusive techniques that also aim to manipulate the interviewee who is being interrogated. These are viewed as coercive in that they are likely to render a confession that is not the product of the interviewee's free will regardless of whether free will was actually actively overcome (Gudjonsson et al., 2008). Coercive tactics include manipulation and deception (e.g., falsely claiming that evidence exists when it does not) and the failure to consider important individual difference factors (e.g., the limited cognitive abilities of the interviewee). Coercive tactics have been implicated in false confessions and the legal acceptability of these tactics depends on local policies (e.g., Canadian laws do not allow for the use of false evidence during interrogations that some other jurisdictions permit).

There are two major concerns with the use of coercive techniques. First, the probability is strong that memory, both in terms of content and accuracy, will be adversely affected in direct proportion to the amount/severity of the coercive techniques that are employed (Hervé et al., 2007). The second concern relates to the possibility that the individual being interviewed or interrogated may not have engaged in the suspected activity or may not possess the knowledge being sought (Drizin & Leo, 2004; Kassin, Drizin et al., 2010). This is not a statement of fact but a constant reminder that the purpose of the interview is to develop as much accurate information as possible from the interviewee without presupposing that the interviewee must know anything about what actually happened. By adopting this attitude, the interviewer is much more likely to consider alternate investigative hypotheses, ask more open-ended questions, allow the interviewee more narrative latitude, avoid coercive and unethical tactics, and consider lesser explanations for false or misleading information. In fact, this attitude forces the interviewer to work diligently at developing the information necessary to make accurate judgments about the interviewee. In contrast, the use of torture and other coercive or unethical tactics, by definition, presupposes that the individual has the information and that it is just a matter of breaking his or her will to withhold it.

Sin Number 15: Not Corroborating Information

The final sin of interviewing reviewed in this chapter occurs when the interviewer fails to corroborate the information gained in the interview (Drizin & Leo, 2004). As noted above, the "truth" is whatever the interviewee believes to be true and there are a host of reasons why this "truth" may be historically wrong. It is, therefore, always important to find out why the interviewee believes the information to be true. It then becomes the responsibility of the interviewer to conduct a follow-up investigation to determine whether or not the information can be corroborated. Only then will the interviewer know for sure that what was said by the interviewee was, in fact, true or not. Corroborating statements would go a long way to reducing incidences of wrongful convictions due to false confessions and/or false claims of victimization (Kassin, Drizin et al., 2010; Marin, 2012).

Conclusion

This chapter covers 15 sins of interviewing that have been identified through practical experience and the collaboration between law enforcement professionals and academics/researchers. This chapter also provided practical suggestions for overcoming these sins. The first three sins are arguably the cardinal sins of interviewing in that they account for the development and/or maintenance of the remaining 12 sins. Avoiding these cardinal sins would, therefore, go a long way towards promoting effective interviewing skills. It seems only reasonable to assume that, if some of the major mistakes associated with the practice and research of interviewing could be identified and, therefore, avoided, the result would be more effective interviews and more complete and accurate information.

Many of these sins reflect insufficient or improper training, and point to the need for scientifically based training in investigative interviewing that is both practical and delivered in a way that maximizes learning and generalizing of skills to the real world. Arguably, the most effective training is developed through collaborative efforts between law enforcement professionals and academics, and delivered by subject matter experts who are also qualified instructors that can effectively communicate, demonstrate, and convey the training content. For now, the reader is reminded that the probability of conducting a successful interview that results in accurate information is enhanced when the following steps are followed:

1. Be **A**ware of the personality characteristics, traits, and background of the interviewer and the interviewee;
2. Determine the **B**aseline behavior of the interviewee;
3. Watch for **C**hanges in the interviewee's behavior during the interview;
4. Actively listen and watch for **D**iscrepancies between the interviewee's behavior and the verbal content of the statements;
5. Be willing to **E**ngage and challenge the interviewee when deception possibly occurs; and,
6. Conduct a **F**ollow-up investigation to corroborate the interviewee's statements.

Acknowledgements The authors are grateful to Susan Kim, Barry Cooper, Dorothee Griesel, and Marguerite Ternes for their helpful comments on earlier drafts of this chapter.

References

Akehurst, L., Kohnken, G., Vrij, A., & Bull, R. (1996). Lay persons' and police officers' beliefs regarding deceptive behavior. *Applied Cognitive Psychology, 10*, 461–471.
American Psychiatric Association. (2000). *Diagnostic and statistical manual of mental disorders* (4th ed., Text Revision). Washington, DC: Author.
Blair, R. J. R., Sellars, C., Strickland, I., Clark, F., Williams, A. O., Smith, M., et al. (1995). Emotion attributions in the psychopath. *Personality and Individual Differences, 19*, 431–437.
Blanchette, I., & Richards, A. (2010). The influence of affect on higher level cognition: A review of research on interpretation, judgement, decision making and reasoning. *Cognition and Emotion, 24*(4), 561–595.
Brewer, N., & Wells, G. L. (2011). Eyewitness identification. *Current Directions in Psychological Science, 20*(1), 24–27.
Bruck, M., Ceci, S. J., & Hembrooke, H. (1998). Reliability and credibility of young children's reports: From research to policy and practice. *The American Psychologist, 53*, 136–151.

Bull, R. (2010). The investigative interviewing of children and other vulnerable witnesses: Psychological research and working/professional practice. *Legal and Criminological Psychology, 15*(1), 5–23.

Christianson, S.-A. (1992). Emotional stress and eyewitness memory: A critical review. *Psychological Bulletin, 112*, 284–309.

Christianson, S.-A. (2007). *Offenders' memories of violent crimes*. Chichester, England: John Wiley and Sons.

Colwell, K., Hiscock, C. K., & Memon, A. (2002). Interviewing techniques and the assessment of statement credibility. *Applied Cognitive Psychology, 16*, 287–300.

Conway, M. A. (1997). Introduction: What are memories? In M. A. Conway (Ed.), *Recovered memories and false memories* (pp. 1–22). Oxford: Oxford University Press.

Cooper, B. S., Cuttler, C., Dell, P., & Yuille, J. C. (2006). Dissociation and amnesia: A study with male offenders. *International Journal of Forensic Psychology, 1*(3), 69–83.

Cooper, B. S., Hervé, H., & Yuille, J. C. (2009). Evaluating truthfulness: Detecting truths and lies in forensic contexts. In R. Bull, T. Valentine, & T. Williamson (Eds.), *Handbook of psychology of investigative interviewing* (pp. 301–328). Chichester, England: Wiley-Blackwell.

Damphousse, K. (2008). Voice stress analysis: Only 15 percent of lies about drug use detected in field test. *National Institute of Justice Journal*, 259. Retrieved from http://www.nij.gov/journals/259/voice-stress-analysis.htm.

Daylen, J., van Tongeren Harvey, W., & O'Toole, D. (2006). *Trauma, trials, and transformation: Guiding sexual assault victims through the legal system and beyond*. Toronto, Ontario: Irwin Law Inc.

DePaulo, B. M., Kashey, D. A., Kirkendol, S. E., Wyer, M. M., & Epstein, J. A. (1996). Lying in everyday life. *Journal of Personality and Social Psychology, 70*, 979–995.

Drizin, S. A., & Leo, R. A. (2004). The problem of false confessions in the post-DNA world. *North Carolina Law Review, 82*, 891–1007.

Ekman, P. (2003). *Emotions revealed: Recognizing faces and feeling to improve communication and emotional life*. New York: Henry Holt and Company.

Ekman, P. (2009). *Telling lies: Clues to deceit in the marketplace, politics, and marriage*. New York: Norton.

Ekman, P., & O'Sullivan, M. (1991). Who can catch a liar? *The American Psychologist, 46*, 913–920.

Ekman, P., O'Sullivan, M., Friesen, W. V., & Scherer, K. R. (1991). Face, voice, and body in detecting deceit. *Journal of Nonverbal Behavior, 15*, 125–135.

Erdelyi, M. H., & Kleinbard, J. (1978). Has Ebbinghaus decayed with time? The growth of recall (hypernesia) over days. *Journal of Experimental Psychology: Human Learning and Memory, 4*, 275–289.

Fisher, R. P., & Geiselman, R. E. (1992). *Memory-enhancing techniques for investigative interviewing: The cognitive interview*. Springfield, IL: Charles C Thomas.

Ford, E. B. (2006). Lie detection: Historical, neuropsychiatric and legal dimensions. *Internal Journal of Law and Psychiatry, 29*, 159–177.

Frank, M. G., & Ekman, P. (1997). The ability to detect deceit generalizes across different types of high-stake lies. *Journal of Personality and Social Psychology, 72*(6), 1429–1439.

Geiselman, R. E. (1999). Commentary on recent research with the cognitive interview. *Psychology, Crime & Law, 5*(1–2), 197–202.

Griesel, D., & Yuille, J. C. (2007). Credibility assessment in eyewitness memory. In M. P. Toglia, J. D. Read, D. F. Ross, & R. C. L. Lindsay (Eds.), *Handbook of eyewitness psychology* (Memory for events, Vol. I, pp. 339–370). Mahwah, NJ: Lawrence Erlbaum.

Gudjonsson, G. H., & Joyce, T. (2011). Interviewing adults with intellectual disabilities. *Advances in Mental Health and Intellectual Disabilities, 5*(2), 16–21.

Gudjonsson, G. H., Sigurdsson, J. F., Sigfusdottir, I. D., & Asgeirsdottir, B. B. (2008). False confessions and individual differences: The importance of victimization among youth. *Personality and Individual Differences, 45*(8), 801–805.

Hare, R. D. (1998). *Without conscience: The disturbing world of the Psychopaths Among Us*. New York, NY: Guilford Press.

Hervé, H., Cooper, B. S., & Yuille, J. C. (2007). Memory formation in offenders: Perspectives from a biopsychosocial theory of eyewitness memory. In S. A. Christianson (Ed.), *Offenders' memories of violent crimes* (pp. 37–74). Chichester, England: John Wiley and Sons.

Horowitz, S. W. (1991). Empirical support for statement validity assessment. *Behavioral Assessment, 13*, 293–313.

Inbau, F. E., Reid, J. E., Buckley, J. P., & Jayne, B. C. (2001). *Criminal interrogation and confessions* (4th ed.). Gaithersberg, MD: Aspen.

Kassin, S. M., Appleby, S. C., & Perillo, J. T. (2010). Interviewing suspects: Practice, science, and future directions. *Legal and Criminological Psychology, 15*, 39–55.

Kassin, S. M., Drizin, S. A., Grisso, T., Gudjonsson, G. H., Leo, R. A., & Redlich, A. D. (2010). Police-induced confessions: Risk factors and recommendations. *Law and Human Behaviour, 34*, 3–38.

Lamb, M. E., Orbach, Y., Sternberg, K. J., Hershkowitz, I., & Horowitz, D. (2000). Accuracy of investigators' verbatim notes of their forensic interviews with alleged child abuse victims. *Law and Human Behavior, 24*(6), 699–708.

Lamb, M. E., Sternberg, K. J., Esplin, P. W., Hershkowitz, I., Orbach, Y., & Hovav, M. (1997). Criterion-based content analysis: A field validation study. *Child Abuse & Neglect, 21*(3), 255–264.

Loftus, E. F. (1979). *Eyewitness testimony*. Cambridge, MA: Harvard University Press.

Mann, S., Vrij, A., Nasholm, E., Warmelink, L., Leal, S., & Forrester, D. (2012). The direction of deception: Neuro-linguistic programming as a lie detection tool. *Journal of Police and Criminal Psychology*. doi:10.1007/s11896-011-9097-8. ISSN: 1936-6469.

Marin, R. J. (2012). *Admissibility of statements: Recent developments*. Paper presented at the RCMP conference, Surrey, BC.

McCarthy, A., Lee, K., Itakura, S., & Muir, D. W. (2006). Cultural display rules drive eye gaze during thinking. *Journal of Cross-Cultural Psychology, 37*, 717–722.

Morrison, J. (2008). *The first interview* (3rd ed.). New York, NY: The Guilford Press.

Pollock, P. H. (1999). When the killer suffers: Post-traumatic stress reactions following homicide. *Legal and Criminological Psychology, 4*, 185–202.

Porter, S., Birt, A. R., Yuille, J. C., & Hervé, H. F. (2001). Memory for murder: A psychological perspective on dissociative amnesia in forensic contexts. *International Journal of Law and Psychiatry, 24*, 23–42.

Porter, S., & ten Brinke, L. (2010). The truth about lies: What works in detecting high-stakes deception? *Legal and Criminological Psychology, 15*, 57–75.

Porter, S., Woodworth, M., & Birt, A. R. (2000). Truth, lies and videotape: An investigation of the ability of federal parole officers to detect deception. *Law and Human Behavior, 24*, 643–658.

Porter, S., & Yuille, J. C. (1996). The language of deceit: An investigation of the verbal clues to deception in the interrogation context. *Law and Human Behavior, 20*, 442–458.

Ruby, C. L., & Brigham, J. C. (1997). The usefulness of the Criteria-Based Content Analysis technique in distinguishing between truthful and fabricated allegations: A critical review. *Psychology, Public Policy, and Law, 3*(4), 705–737.

Schacter, D. L. (1996). *Searching for memory*. New York: Basic Books.

Schacter, D. L. (2001). *The seven sins of memory: How the mind forgets and remembers*. New York: Houghton Mifflin Company.

Spidel, A., Hervé, H. F., Greaves, C., Cooper, B. S., & Hare, R. D. (2003). Psychopathy and deceptive motivations in young offenders. In M. Vanderhallen, G. Vervaeke, P. J. Van Koppen, & J. Goethals (Eds.), *Much ado about crime: Chapters on psychology and law* (pp. 287–299). Brussel: Politeia.

Stanovich, K. E. (2009). *What intelligence tests miss: The psychology of rational thought*. New Haven, CT: Yale University Press.

Steller, M. (1989). Recent developments in statement analysis. In J. C. Yuille (Ed.), *Credibility assessment* (pp. 135–154). Dordrecht: Kluwer.

Steller, M., & Koehnken, G. (1989). Criteria-based statement analysis: Credibility assessment of children's testimonies in sexual abuse cases. In D. C. Raskin (Ed.), *Psychological methods in criminal investigation and evidence* (pp. 217–245). New York: Springer.

ten Brinke, L. & Porter, S. (in press). Cry me a river: Identifying the behavioural consequences of extremely high-stakes interpersonal deception. *Law and Human Behavior.*

ten Brinke, L., Porter, S., & Baker, A. (in press). Darwin the detective: Observable facial muscle contractions reveal emotional high-stakes lies. *Evolution and Human Behavior.*

Tollestrup, P. A., Turtle, J. W., & Yuille, J. C. (1994). Actual victims and witnesses to robbery and fraud: An archival analysis. In D. Ross, D. Read, & S. Ceci (Eds.), *Adult eyewitness testimony: Current trends and developments* (pp. 144–162). New York: Press syndicate of the University of Cambridge.

Undeutsch, U. (1989). The development of statement reality analysis. In J. C. Yuille (Ed.), *Credibility assessment* (pp. 101–120). Dordrecht: Kluwer.

Vrij, A. (2000). *Detecting lies and deceit: The psychology of lying and the implications for professional practice.* Chichester: Wiley.

Vrij, A. (2004). Why professionals fail to catch liars and how they can improve. *Legal and Criminological Psychology, 9*, 159–181.

Vrij, A. (2005). Criteria-based content analysis: A qualitative review of the first 37 studies. *Psychology, Public Policy, and Law, 11*(1), 3–41.

Vrij, A., & Granhag, P. A. (2007). Interviewing to detect deception. In S. A. Christianson (Ed.), *Offenders' memories of violent crimes* (pp. 279–304). Chichester: John Wiley & Sons.

Vrij, A., Granhag, P. A., & Mann, S. (2010). Good liars. *The Journal of Psychiatry and Law, 38*, 77–98.

Williamson, T. (2006). *Investigative interviewing: Rights, research, and regulation.* Portland, OR: Willan Publishing.

Yuille, J. C. (1988). The systematic assessment of children's testimony. *Canadian Psychology, 29*(3), 247–262.

Yuille, J. C. (1989). *Credibility assessment.* Dordrecht: Kluwer.

Yuille, J. C. (1990). *Use of the criteria based content analysis.* Vancouver, BC: University of British Columbia [Unpublished manuscript].

Yuille, J. C. (2007). *Adult interview guidelines.* [Unpublished manuscript].

Yuille, J. C., Cooper, B. S., & Hervé H. F. (in press). The step-wise guidelines for child interviews: The new generation. In M. Casonato & Pfafflin (Eds.), *Handbook of pedosexuality and forensic science.*

Yuille, J. C., & Daylen, J. (1998). The impact of traumatic events on eyewitness memory. In C. Thompson, D. Herman, D. Read, D. Bruce, D. Payne, & M. Toglia (Eds.), *Eyewitness memory: Theoretical and applied perspectives* (pp. 155–178). Mahwah, New Jersey: Lawrence Erlbaum Associates.

Part III
Eyewitness Memory

Chapter 5
Biopsychosocial Perspectives on Memory Variability in Eyewitnesses

Hugues F. Hervé, Barry S. Cooper, and John C. Yuille

Introduction

Eyewitness memory has evolved into an umbrella term to account for the memory of criminal actions witnessed by victims, bystanders, and committed by perpetrators. Encompassed by the narrative memory of a crime as well as recognition memory for the perpetrator, eyewitness memory plays an important role in the criminal justice process—from the initial investigative interview by law enforcement to the assessment of credibility by the triers of fact. In an effort to assist criminal justice

---

The authors are grateful to Kristin Kendrick, Dr. Dorothee Griesel, Dr. Marguerite Ternes, Dr. Caroline Greaves, and Dr. Sven Christianson for their helpful comments on earlier drafts of this chapter. Separate parts of this chapter were presented at the Canadian Psychological Association's 2002 Annual Convention, the Society for Applied Research on Memory and Cognition's 2003 Conference, and the Society for the Scientific Study of Psychopathy's 2005 Conference. This chapter is a partial reproduction of a previous chapter (Hervé, Cooper, & Yuille, 2007), and permission to reprint the tables and figures has been received. Please address all correspondence concerning this chapter to: Hugues Hervé, Ph.D. at hherve@theforensicalliance.com.

H.F. Hervé (✉)
The Forensic Alliance, Port Moody, BC, Canada
e-mail: hherve@theforensicalliance.com

B.S. Cooper
The Forensic Alliance, Vancouver, BC, Canada

University of British Columbia-Okanagan, Kelowna, BC, Canada

University of British Columbia, Vancouver, BC, Canada

Simon Fraser University, Burnaby, BC, Canada

Forensic Psychiatric Hospital, Port Coquitlam, BC, Canada

J.C. Yuille
The Forensic Alliance, Salt Spring Island, BC, Canada

University of British Columbia, Vancouver, BC, Canada

system professionals, researchers—mostly psychologists—have empirically investigated the variables associated with eyewitness memory for over 100 years (e.g., Stern, 1904). In fact, thousands of studies have been conducted in the area, making the study of eyewitness memory one of the largest subfields in the area of forensic psychology. The impressive quantity of literature is, however, daunting in nature when one attempts to make sense of the discrepant empirical findings. Indeed, consistent with clinical-forensic experience, the results from eyewitness research indicate that different witnesses to the same criminal event can produce widely variable memory patterns. Without a unifying evidence-informed model to explain the different memory patterns observed, criminal justice professionals are faced with a difficult task when attempting to makes sense out of the variable nature of eyewitness memory.

In this chapter, the different eyewitness memory patterns observed in research and clinical-forensic practice are reviewed. Additionally, perspectives from our biopsychosocial model of eyewitness memory are offered to assist in explaining this memory variability. Parts of this model were previously disseminated to explain memory formation in offenders in response to their own criminal actions (see Hervé, Cooper, & Yuille, 2007). However, the model was developed with a larger scope in mind—to explain the memory patterns in all types of eyewitnesses, including victims and bystanders, the focus of the present chapter. In the following sections, certain underlying assumptions are discussed, including the nature of crime (i.e., the stimulus event) and the multidimensional nature of emotion. Thereafter, memory patterns are reviewed and central aspects of the biopsychosocial model are presented. Following a summary of biopsychosocial predictions, this chapter concludes with a few implications for investigative interviewing, researching eyewitness memory, assessing credibility, and providing expert testimony.

The Nature of Crime: The Stimulus Event

To understand eyewitness memory, one must first be knowledgeable about the events that provide the stimulus for subsequent remembering. Indeed, eyewitness memory does not exist without a crime. Although a complete review of criminal acts is beyond the scope of this chapter, certain basic features are noteworthy. First, there are three basic conditions that must exist in order for a crime to be committed: (1) the offender must be motivated to act (i.e., with or without ill intent); (2) the offender must overcome internal inhibitors; and (3) the offender must overcome external inhibitors (Hervé, Cooper, & Yuille, 2012). In addition, when offences are interpersonal in nature, often, the offender must also overcome the victim's resistance. These factors are relevant to the present focus, as they may exert an impact on aspects of the to-be-remembered event as well as on the resultant memory for said event. For example, criminal motivation (e.g., instrumental vs. reactive) has been shown to affect perpetrators' memory for violent crimes (Cooper & Yuille, 2007). Similarly, factors that are used to overcome inhibitors (e.g., intoxicants) may have their own impact on eyewitness memory (Read, Yuille, & Tollestrup, 1992; Yuille, Tollestrup, Marxsen, Porter, & Hervé, 1998). How the victim's resistance was overcome is not only relevant to the criminal investigation but can also have various effects on the victim (i.e., from no effect to a traumatic effect; Cooper, Kennedy, & Yuille, 2004; Griesel & Yuille, 2012) that may also influence memory formation. Indeed, research has shown that post-traumatic stress disorder (PTSD), a disorder not uncommonly experienced by individuals exposed to crime/trauma, has complex effects on memory (Klein, Caspi, & Gil, 2003; Southwick, Morgan, Nicolaou, & Charney, 1997).

Second, offences can vary in terms of the number of to-be-remembered events, with some events lasting only seconds and others lasting hours or days (e.g., robbery vs. unlawful confinement, respectively); some offences consist of only one act while others involve several (e.g., assault vs. stalking, abduction and sexual assault, respectively); and some offences involve a limited number of people while others involve numerous perpetrators, victims and bystanders (e.g., a sexual assault vs. a terrorist act, respectively). No doubt, these characteristics have memory consequences that should be considered in combination in light of the dynamic nature of crimes. Third, different offences induce different levels of stress/trauma[1] in those involved. While some offences, such as frauds, induce little-to-no stress in individuals (e.g., at the time of the fraud), more intrusive and violent offences are known to trigger a great deal of stress/trauma in victims and/or bystanders and perpetrators (Darves-Bornoz, Pierre, Lepine, Degiovanni, & Gaillard, 1998; Griesel, Cooper, & Yuille, 2004; Griesel & Yuille, 2012; Pollock, 1999). Finally, prior criminal experience impacts how individuals respond to a particular criminal act. As they gain experience, some perpetrators are likely to become increasingly comfortable conducting a particular form of crime, which may serve to reduce the stress associated with that behavior. Moreover, victims and bystanders of crime can either be sensitized or desensitized by prior criminal acts (see Connolly & Price, present volume). As discussed below, the emotional impact of criminal acts on those involved is central to memory formation and, therefore, needs to be clearly understood when investigating eyewitness memory.

Multidimensional Nature of Emotion

As with others, we assume that eyewitness memory is partly mediated by the witnesses' emotional response at the time of the experienced event and/or upon subsequent recall (Christianson, 1992). However, we assume that this emotional response

---

[1] For the purposes of the present chapter, we accept, in part, the following definition of trauma provided by the American Psychiatric Association (APA, 2000): "actual or threatened death or serious injury, or a threat to the physical integrity of self and others" (p. 467). In our view, trauma is related not only to the nature of the event (e.g., threat to life or limb) but to the traits and states of the eyewitness as well.

is more complex than previously proposed. While previous theories and theorists have utilized a unidimensional view of emotions (e.g., Easterbrook, 1959; Yerkes & Dodson, 1908), we have adopted a multidimensional perspective. Most theorists of emotional processing agree that emotional experiences depend on two correlated, yet independent mechanisms: a biological system that mediates arousal responses to emotional events (e.g., crimes) and a cognitive-interpretative system that evaluates the significance of emotional events (Charland, 1997; Power & Dalgleish, 1999). It is believed that each system, when activated, continuously feeds back information to the other system. Within this framework, arousal refers to the physiological activity produced by the autonomic nervous system (ANS; Critchley, 2005). The arousal, which is non-specific (i.e., does not differentiate between emotions), solely sets the quantitative specifications for emotional life. In other words, arousal alone does not produce an emotional response (e.g., Bockheler, 1995; Schachter, 1971; but see Levenson, 1988, 1992). The arousal must be perceived as emotional in nature rather than being solely due to physiological activation (Russell, 1989). The autonomic arousal, however, serves to prepare us, at the physiological level, for action, while concurrently signalling the mental organization for attention, alertness, and scanning of the environment—all variables that are likely to have an impact on eyewitness memory.

The cognitive-interpretative system performs a meaning analysis of the emotional (e.g., criminal) event (Mandler, 1984). Mediated by the central nervous system, this mechanism ascribes the particular quality (e.g., pleasant vs. unpleasant) of the felt emotion which, in turn, serves to either decrease or increase subsequent ANS arousal (i.e., the cognitive-interpretive system has either a physiological activating or deactivating effect; Russell, 2003). Although these meaning analyses may be influenced by arousal, they are primarily set by the general situation and cognitive state of the eyewitness, factors that could also affect eyewitness memory. It is the joint product of both of these systems—arousal and meaning analysis—which construct emotions as currently defined. As noted by Mandler, "arousal provides the intensity of the emotional state, and cognition provides its quality" (p. 119). It thus follows that, since affect mediates responses to traumatic/stressful events (e.g., crimes), eyewitness memory research should consider the impact of each of these systems, both in isolation and in combination, and how these may differ across individuals and/or situations. As discussed below, an eyewitness' sensitivity to arousal—reflecting both autonomic and interpretive components—is a major factor used to explain memory variability.

The Reconstructive and Variable Nature of Eyewitness Memory

Eyewitness memory research conducted over the past century has provided a firm foundation underlying two general principles of memory. First, memory is not reproductive but reconstructive in nature (Schacter, 1996; Yarbrough, Hervé, & Harms, present volume). This holds true whether the to-be-remembered event is a stressful/traumatic crime or a positive experience. Because memory is reconstructive, the account of an event will usually differ across retellings. Although the gist of an account of an event can remain largely unaltered, it is usually the case that, upon retellings, new details are added and old details are omitted (Erdelyi & Kleinbard, 1978). As Conway (1997) suggested, this is thought to occur because "memory construction is mediated by control processes which vary from one recall to the next and use different cues to probe autobiographical knowledge on different occasions of retrieval" (pp. 4–5). Presumably, the more efficient the control processes and/or the greater the number of available cues, the more detailed the memory will be from one account to the next. Note, however, that increased memory detail does not necessarily translate to accurate recall.

Second, as indicated above, it is clear from the eyewitness literature and clinical-forensic experience that witnesses to events display a variety of memory patterns. Indeed, the following ten memory patterns have thus far been identified (Hervé et al. 2007; Yuille & Daylen, 1998): normal forgetting, active forgetting, dissociative amnesia, state dependent memory, red out, remarkable memory, script memory, dissociative memory with either an external or internal focus, and created memory. These patterns are descriptions of consistent forms of eyewitness recall, in terms of both quality and quantity, representing a mixture of processes (e.g., forgetting, anger) and products of processes (e.g., red out) and, as such, can co-occur. The first five (i.e., normal forgetting, active forgetting, dissociative amnesia, state-dependent memory [SDM] and red out) concern different patterns of memory loss. Remarkable memories and script memories, in contrast, are patterns associated with long-term retention. Dissociative memories reflect event-related processes (e.g., dissociation) that affect the quality of memory. Finally, created memories are a product of suggestion, not of events and, therefore, affect quality. The evidence supporting these patterns is reviewed below followed by biopsychosocial explanations to explain the variability.

Normal Forgetting

Normal forgetting occurs for routine, everyday events, such as driving to work or shopping (Yuille & Daylen, 1998). When such a routine experience occurs, the memory is initially good but, barring any unexpected event of impact, a loss of memory detail over time usually transpires. Normal forgetting is the pattern of memory that has been routinely examined with the analogue (e.g., simulation) method of eyewitness memory. In these studies, the modal stimuli are crime simulations (e.g., videos of criminal acts). Most people forget many aspects of events viewed in the laboratory, especially those of a peripheral nature (e.g., Loftus & Burns, 1982). Actual victims of fraud also exhibit normal forgetting as, at the time of a typical fraud, the victim is usually unaware that a crime is being committed (Tollestrup, Turtle, & Yuille, 1994). The mundane nature of the event (e.g., a normal transaction) likely results in relatively superficial encoding that is susceptible to both erosion (e.g., via transience; Schacter, 2001; Yarbrough et al., present volume) and distortions (e.g., source confusion; Deffenbacher, Bornstein, & Penrod, 2006). Normal forgetting may also apply to some aspects of a stressful/traumatic event such as a violent crime. Although such events of impact may lead to a remarkable memory (see below) of the central details, the peripheral details may be recalled immediately but forgotten with the passage of time.

Active Forgetting

As with normal forgetting, active forgetting concerns memory loss; however, this pattern is a consequence of a conscious attempt to forget an event (Yuille & Daylen, 1998). It involves avoiding recalling the event and such may reduce the details available to memory. Conversely, active forgetting may lead to memory enhancement as avoiding a memory of an experience has been empirically demonstrated to be related to having intrusive memories of that experience (Cooper, 2005). Active forgetting and normal forgetting differ, as the precipitating events that lead to active forgetting are typically emotional events (e.g., crimes) while those that lead to normal forgetting are typically routine events.

Dissociative Amnesia

Dissociative amnesia, the inability to recall all or part of an event of impact (APA, 2000), such as a crime, is the result of poorly understood processes. The amnesia may develop at the time of the event or after some delay and may be circumscribed or selective (Yuille & Daylen, 1998). This type of amnesia is psychologically based, not the product organic processes (e.g., brain damage; intoxicants; Caine & Lyness, 2000). Dissociative amnesia is thought to be resistant to state specific effects unlike amnesia resulting from state-dependent processes (see below). Studies of abused victims (e.g., Christianson & Nilsson, 1989; Darves-Bornoz, 1997; Mechanic, Resick, & Griffin, 1998), combat veterans (Southwick et al., 1997), and survivors of natural disasters (Koopman, Classen, & Spiegel, 1994) have produced this pattern of memory, although it occurs rarely.

As with active forgetting, dissociative amnesia is distinguished from normal forgetting as the precipitating event is one that the person should recall (e.g., an event of personal significance such as a crime)—this pattern of memory is associated with stressful/traumatic experiences as opposed to routine events that are subjected to normal forgetting. Although normal forgetting can lead to a permanent loss of memory, clinical-forensic experience suggests that dissociative amnesia can reverse itself, typically in the presence of a potent event-related cue. In such cases, the memory typically comes flooding back.

State-Dependent Memory

SDM refers to the finding that we are better able to remember an event when tested in the same state (e.g., physical environment) in which we experienced the event (e.g., Godden & Baddeley, 1975; Goodwin, Powell, Bremer, Hoine, & Stern, 1969). In addition to our physical environment, statement-dependent memory is affected by a variety of stimuli such as odours, music, and internal states (e.g., Eich, 1987, 1995; Reisberg, 1997). Thus, memory suffers if the context between encoding and retrieval is discrepant and, conversely, memory is facilitated when the context is similar across encoding and retrieval. Given, in part, the unique nature of criminal events, it is only reasonable to assume that state-dependent effects may occur. Presumably, reinstating the state the individual experienced while experiencing an offence could lead to memory retrieval, be it in part or in whole. There are, in fact, clinical examples of individuals recalling past traumas when facing new stressful/traumatic situations (i.e., a similar emotional state), as well as when being returned to the scene of a crime (i.e., a similar cognitive/experiential state). The Cognitive Interview (Fisher & Geiselman, 1992) capitalizes on SDM effects by virtue of the context reinstatement step, which is used to increase memory (note: this is also used as an enhancement step with the Step-Wise Interview, adapted for adults; Cooper, Hervé, & Yuille, 2012).

Red Out

This pattern is of concern when a witness' emotional state during an event becomes altered by extreme negative valence (e.g., anger). In fact, it has been suggested that it is possible to become so enraged that a different state of consciousness is attained (Swihart, Yuille, & Porter, 1999). In this state of "catathymia" (Dutton & Yamini, 1995), or in a "red out" the perpetrator is thought to act in a rigid, derealized manner, and is later amnesic for the violent act committed. The acts leading up to and following the violent incident are, however, thought to be available in memory. Thus, in a red out, amnesia is circumscribed to only the violent aspects of the incident. This is consistent with various understandings of some forms of amnesia (Guttmacher, 1960; O'Connell, 1960; Tanay, 1969). Indeed, strong emotions can contribute to amnesia, an effect that occurs irrespective of intoxication (Parwatikar, Holcomb, & Menninger, 1985). There are, in fact, many instances of domestic violence where the offender has claimed amnesia for a battering incident, and in some instances for a murder, in the absence of alcohol ingestion (Dutton, 1995). While many of these cases could be construed as examples of malingered amnesia in an attempt to lessen or divert criminal responsibility (Hervé & Cooper, 2008), there are cases in which the offender admitted responsibility and provided a detailed memory for certain reprehensible acts such as necrophilia but claimed amnesia for less-shocking criminal actions such as multiple stabbings (Porter, Birt, Yuille, & Hervé, 2001).

The biopsychosocial basis for red outs is not entirely clear. Red outs may be a unique case of dissociative amnesia. More likely, red outs may occur as an extreme form of a SDM effect and, if state dependent, it follows that the memory may be retrievable. Such is only likely to occur if the person experiences the same state of rage that was exhibited during the original incident. While theoretically appealing and supported by anecdotal evidence (Cooper & Yuille, 2007), ethical restrictions rightfully preclude researchers and practitioners from returning offenders' mental states to the time that they committed acts of rage-induced violence.

Although thought to be restricted to the perpetrator context, in theory, red outs may occur in victims and witnesses to crimes as well. That is, it could be the case that a victim becomes so enraged by his/her victimization as to experience a red out. However, to date, there is no anecdotal or empirical evidence to support the red out pattern in those other than perpetrators of violent crime.

Remarkable Memories

Precipitated by events of impact, remarkable memories are vivid, detailed, and generally accurate recollections retained over long intervals (Leitch, 1948; Terr, 1991; Yuille & Daylen, 1998). Remarkable memories (RM) may be maintained via repeated recall, either to others or to oneself (Scrivner & Safer, 1988). Events leading to this pattern of memory are unique and consequential and occur in the context of high arousal and either positive or negative valence (Cooper, Hervé, & Yuille, 2003). As an example, in the first field study of actual eyewitness memory, Yuille and Cutshall (1986) demonstrated that witnesses to a shooting were detailed and highly accurate in their accounts, with little loss of accuracy over a period of months. Other field studies of witnesses to and victims of actual crime (e.g., Cutshall & Yuille, 1989; Griesel & Yuille, 2012; Odinot, Wolters, & van Koppen, 2009), as well as victims of disasters (Thompson, Morton, & Fraser, 1997), have replicated this memory pattern.

Laboratory-based methodologies are, for ethical reasons, unable to evoke remarkable memories as the stimuli used cannot produce extreme stress or trauma. Yet, findings from analogue research, which generally reflect the normal forgetting pattern, have been generalized to explain the memory consequences of experiencing events of impact (e.g., Loftus, 2012). Expert witnesses have testified in court that the pattern of recall found in analogue studies applies to a sexual assault victim, or a witness to a murder, or a witness to another type of violent criminal event (Cooper, Hervé, & Yuille, 2010). For instance, in a 1995 International Criminal Tribunal, a psychologist testified about analogue research regarding the effects of stress on memory, and the weapon focus effect. Without noting the limitations of the research (e.g., ecological validity), she extended the findings from the laboratory to the field, reporting that the research examined "the effects of extreme stress or the effects of experiencing something very violent or the effects of experiencing an event that involves a weapon" (p. 604; *Tribunal* vs. *Anto Furundzija*). Participants in analogue research, however, do not *experience* extreme stress or *experience* something very violent. Rather, they view stimuli under the conditions of low stress. Unfortunately, this mixing of "apples and oranges" has produced confusion in the field (Yuille, Ternes, & Cooper, 2010).

Clearly not all events of impact lead to remarkable memories. Indeed, as indicated above, there are many examples of victims of crime developing the opposite pattern—dissociative amnesia. How do situations of high stress/arousal lead to poor memory in one witness and excellent memory in another? We believe this state of affairs is explained by the complex effects of stress/trauma on memory (Yuille & Tollestrup, 1992), effects that have biopsychosocial underpinnings (Yuille & Cooper, 2012; see below).

Script Memory

A script memory (SM) reflects a blending together of similar episodes into one's script (Ceci & Bruck, 1993). We all have scripts. For example, a script of our childhood birthday parties could involve our parents having our friends gather, receive presents, and eat birthday cake, etc. There are also script memories of repeated crimes (e.g., childhood sexual abuse, domestic violence; see Paz-Alonso, Ogle, & Goodman, present volume). Indeed, it is not uncommon for victims of repeated abuse to have a general recollection of "what used to happen" (King & Yuille, 1987). The repeated episodes of abuse may become blended together into a script unless a specific action deviated from the general way the abuse "used to" transpire—a script violation (see Yarbrough et al., present volume). Script memories are distinguished from narrative memories of specific events by a distinctive linguistic presentation style—script memories are usually recalled in a generalized manner with the use of tense-less verbs (Nelson & Gruendel, 1981). For example, in a study of memory for violence in sex trade workers, a few of the participants had script memories for the repeated sexual abuse they suffered as children—invariably, their memories for the abuse commenced with the phrase "he used to" (Cooper, 1999). Script memories, particularly script violations, may be retained for long periods of time, unlike memories that have been subjected to normal forgetting (Yuille & Daylen, 1998).

Dissociative Memories

The study of dissociation—a psychological response to trauma—and its cognitive impact has a rich clinical history (Janet, 1920; van der Kolk, 1996; van der Kolk & van der Hart, 1989). The general premise is that normally integrated mental processes such as memory and emotions can be separated through the process of dissociation (APA, 2000; Cardeña, 1994; Holtgraves & Stockdale, 1997). An individual who dissociates during an event may experience symptoms of depersonalization ("I do not seem real") and/or derealization ("the world does not seem real"; Marmar & Weiss, 1994); the event may appear to unfold very slow or very fast, and the person might experience the event as an "out of body experience" (Cooper, Kennedy, & Yuille, 2001). Research indicates that a variety of events may lead to a dissociative response including physical and sexual abuse (Chu & Dill, 1990; Darves-Bornoz, 1997; Dunmore, Clark, & Ehlers, 1999; Herman, 1996; Spiegel & Cardeña, 1991), natural disasters (Koopman et al., 1994), torture (Weisaeth, 1989), and combat (Marmar et al., 1994). It is thought that dissociation renders the initial psychological impact of the event less intense (Chu, 1998; Spiegel, 1993).

Research and clinical experience suggest that a witness to a crime who dissociates during the event may focus on aspects of the event or on aspects of his/her response to the event or a combination of both (Yuille & Daylen, 1998). These two styles are discussed below.

Dissociative Memory: External focus

When an eyewitness dissociates during a criminal experience and has an external focus, they may view the event from a field or observer perspective (Schacter, 1996; Yuille & Daylen, 1998). In terms of the latter, the eyewitness may perceive an event as would an external observer (e.g., akin to an out of body experience) either at the time of the event and/or upon recall (Nigro & Neisser, 1983; *R v. Stephens*, 2000; Robinson & Swanson, 1993; Spiegel, 1993). Such alteration in perception/memory involves the "observer" viewing the event and themselves from a detached, alternative viewpoint (e.g., Hillman, 1981), arguably serving the function of "depersonalizing" an experience/memory (Terry & Barwick, 1995; van der Kolk, McFarlane, & Weisaeth, 1996). The validity of observer perspectives notwithstanding (Cooper, Cuttler, Dell, & Yuille, 2006; Cooper, Yuille, & Kennedy, 2002), the veracity of the observer memories remains unknown; no research has examined the accuracy of observer perspectives/memories in actual eyewitnesses. The triers of fact would surely welcome research on the accuracy of memories of criminal events experienced from observer perspectives, an area in need of empirical attention.

Dissociative Memory: Internal focus

This pattern occurs when an eyewitness dissociates during a crime and takes an internal focus. That is, eyewitnesses may focus internally on their emotions or on their physiological processes. For example, in one study, an eyewitness to a stabbing who dissociated during the experience stated the following, "I just remember being scared ... thinking that something else may happen but not knowing what"; he had no memory for the event, per se (Cooper et al., 2003). Scant attention has been devoted to understanding this phenomenon, although it is likely the case that an internal focus results in the encoding of little event-related information but significant subjective information (Yuille & Daylen, 1998). Indeed, clinical anecdotes suggest that some individuals dissociate into fantasy when facing traumatic/criminal experiences. For example, some victims of repeated child sexual abuse have reported using a number of strategies to cope with their sexual abuse, including dissociating, isolating their affect, and daydreaming in order to mentally escape the reality of their abuse (Darlington, 1996). Irrespective of one's internal focus (e.g., emotions vs. thoughts), dissociating away from the event of impact appears to serve a protective factor (e.g., enables one to subjectively avoid the traumatic/criminal event, thereby decreasing the acute affective intensity/subjective distress).

Created Memory

This pattern concerns a false/illusory memory, which research suggests is typically developed through suggestive influence in both victims (Lindsay & Read, 1994; Loftus, 1993; Loftus & Pickrell, 1995; Porter, Yuille, & Lehman, 1999) and offenders (e.g., false confessions; Gudjonsson, 1992; Ofshe, 1992). It seems clear from the literature that people can be led to believe that they have experienced events that did not actually transpire, the consequences of which could be severe (Bala, 1996; Brown, Scheflin & Hammond, 1997; Lazo, 1995; Leo, 1998; Loftus, 2012; Vella, 1998). Research suggests that it is the combination of individual difference variables and situational factors that facilitates the creation of a false memory. For the person with a false memory, this includes having both an introverted and dissociative personality, and being repeatedly interviewed by an extroverted authority figure with the use of questionable techniques (e.g., guided imagery, suggestion; Porter, Birt, & Yuille, 2000). It is clear that more research needs to be conducted before any firm conclusions can be made concerning the variables that influence the development of a created memory (CM).

Summary of Memory Patterns

The aforementioned review demonstrates that eyewitness memory is a highly variable phenomenon—some eyewitnesses have poor memory for their experiences while others have excellent memory; still others may have a memory pattern in between such polar opposites. The above memory patterns are not mutually exclusive (Yuille & Daylen, 1998). For instance, an eyewitness to a murder may have a remarkable memory for the central details of the event but show normal forgetting for peripheral aspects of the event (Yuille & Cutshall, 1986). Conversely, a victim of a sexual assault may have dissociative amnesia for the sexual component of his/her experience (Christianson & Nilsson, 1989) but demonstrate a remarkable memory for the events that led up to the attack. In addition, the list of memory patterns is not thought to be exhaustive of all possible eyewitness memory outcomes. Clearly, other patterns could be added via the consideration of other influences. For example, intoxication at the time of an event could lead to SDM or organic-induced memory impairment (Goodwin, 1995; Goodwin, Crane, & Guze, 1969; Goodwin, Powell et al., 1969). Biopsychosocial moderating and mediating influences are, in fact, thought to impact the above patterns and are, therefore, expanded upon below.

Perspectives from a Biopsychosocial Model of Eyewitness Memory

Why does one eyewitness to a criminal event have a remarkable memory for his/her experience while another eyewitness to the same event develops dissociative amnesia? This question led us to develop a biopsychosocial model of eyewitness memory to assist in explaining eyewitness memory variability (see Hervé et al. 2007). A review of the literature indicates that the quality and quantity of crime-related memories are significantly influenced by an eyewitness' emotional response to the event, which reflects the interaction between characteristics of the eyewitness and of the event (Yuille & Daylen, 1998). In our view, emotional reactions reflect both physiological and psychological processes. It is proposed that eyewitness memory variability results from individual differences in both of these processes, differences stemming from specific and interacting biopsychosocial factors. As seen in Fig. 5.1 below, these factors are considered in terms of how they predispose an eyewitness to respond to an event (i.e., predisposing factors), how they affect an eyewitness during the event (i.e., precipitating factors), and how they affect the retention of the eyewitness' memory after the event (i.e., perpetuating factors). Although the entire biopsychosocial model is not outlined, examples of each of these factors are considered below.

Predisposing Factors

Predisposing factors concern the innate traits (e.g., personality characteristics) or prior experiences that influence how an eyewitness would typically respond to a criminal event (see Fig. 5.1). Theoretically, these factors lay the foundation for memory formation (Hervé et al. 2007). As illustrated below, we have divided predisposing (as well as precipitating and perpetuating) factors into biological, psychological, and social influences. This knowledge can be used to make predictions about the quality and quantity of memory that any given eyewitness should exhibit.

Biological Variables

Arousal sensitivity is a major factor mediating individuals' emotional responses to events of impact such as crimes/traumas (Blascovich, 1990, 1992; Feldman, 1995) and, as such, is a major factor accounting for individuals' memories for these experiences. Individuals vary in their sensitivity to arousal, with some individuals

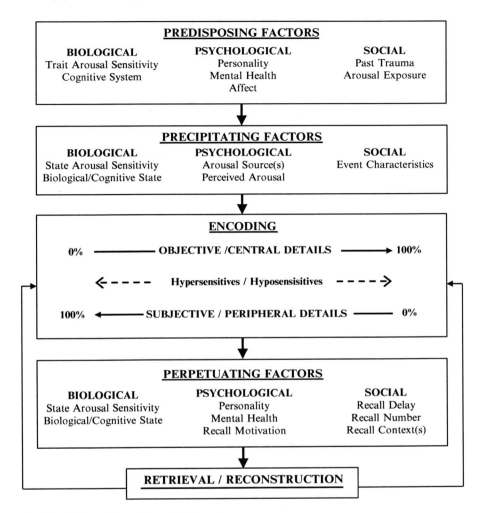

Fig. 5.1 A biopsychosocial model of eyewitness memory

focusing more strongly on autonomic arousal vs. their cognitive-interpretation of that arousal (Mandler, 1984). Arousal sensitivity can be viewed as a dimension, with hyposensitive individuals (i.e., those with low baseline levels of arousal such as psychopaths) and hypersensitive individuals (i.e., those with high baseline levels of arousal such as individuals with borderline personality disorder) defining the end points, and most individuals falling somewhere in between (see Fig. 5.2 below; Cooper, Hervé, & Yuille, 2007; Ellis, 1987).

It is thought that arousal sensitivity sets the threshold at which context-elicited arousal would be perceived as traumatic (e.g., high in arousal and extremely unpleasant). Table 5.1 (see below) provides a truncated illustration of how arousal affects

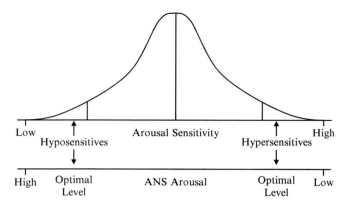

Fig. 5.2 Theoretical distribution of ANS arousal sensitivity and consequent optimal arousal levels

hyposensitive and hypersensitive individuals. As the Table suggests, hypersensitive individuals are likely to experience arousing events as traumatic at lower levels of arousal than would hyposensitive individuals (i.e., the same situation can lead to different levels of perceived arousal in different types of individuals). Although *trait* arousal sensitivity is theoretically resistant to long-term change, there are a number of factors that could affect arousal *state* sensitivity such as the level of threat an eyewitness is exposed to and/or acute substance abuse. These factors could functionally render individuals either hypersensitive or hyposensitive within a specific event.

The memory consequences of eyewitness' arousal sensitivity are multi-faceted. First, an eyewitness' sensitivity to arousal should dictate the point in time during arousal augmentation at which they would experience arousal-mediated attentional problems and, thus, memory distortions. As illustrated in Table 5.1, hypersensitive eyewitnesses should demonstrate memory distortions at an earlier point in time during arousal augmentation than hyposensitive individuals. Following this logic, during criminal/traumatic events, hypersensitive eyewitnesses are more likely than hyposensitive eyewitnesses to display serious memory distortions such as dissociative amnesia. Conversely, hyposensitive eyewitnesses are more likely than hypersensitive eyewitnesses to have vivid and detailed recollections of criminal/traumatic events (Cooper et al., 2007).

Second, individuals with different sensitivities to arousal should focus on different parts of an emotional event (Blascovich, 1990, 1992). Theoretically, hypersensitive eyewitnesses should focus more on their level of perceived arousal, while hyposensitive eyewitnesses should focus on their interpretation of such arousal and therefore on the emotion-evoking event (Mandler, 1984). Accordingly, during a criminal/traumatic event, hypersensitive eyewitnesses are likely to focus on internal (e.g., somesthetic) cues over external (e.g., environmental) cues and the opposite would transpire for hyposensitive eyewitnesses (see Fig. 5.3).

Table 5.1 Hypothetical arousal perception and arousal-mediated effects on attention, memory, and suggestibility based on trait arousal sensitivity and intensity of event-related arousal

Event-related arousal effects	Hypersensitive	Hyposensitive
Extremely low		
Perceived arousal	Very low/Uncomfortable	Extremely low/Intolerable
Attentional bias	External > Internal	External <<< Internal
External[a]	Central > Peripheral	Peripheral
Internal[b]	Cognitive > Sensory	Cognitive <<< Sensory
Memory distortions	RM/AF > NF/SM > DM(EF)/SDM (NF/SM)[d]	DM(IF)/SDM > RM/AF (NF/SM)[d]
Suggestibility[c]	Mild/Internal	Extreme/External
Very low		
Perceived arousal	Low/Comfortable	Extremely low/Distressing
Attentional bias	External = Internal	External « Internal
External[a]	Central = Peripheral	Central « Peripheral
Internal[b]	Cognitive = Sensory	Cognitive « Sensory
Memory distortions	NF/SM	RM/AF/DM(IF)/SDM (NF/SM)[d]
Suggestibility[c]	None[e]	Moderate/External
Low		
Perceived arousal	Medium/Optimal	Very low/Uncomfortable
Attentional bias	External ≤ Internal	External < Internal
External[a]	Central ≤ Peripheral	Central < Peripheral
Internal[b]	Cognitive < Sensory	Cognitive < Sensory
Memory distortions	RM/NF/SM	RM/AF > NF/SM > DM(IF)/SDM (NF/SM)[d]
Suggestibility[c]	Mild/External	Mild/External
Medium		
Arousal perception	High/Uncomfortable	Low/Comfortable
Attentional bias	External < Internal	External = Internal
External[a]	Central < Peripheral	Central = Peripheral
Internal[b]	Cognitive « Sensory	Cognitive = Sensory
Memory distortions	RM/AF > NF/SM > DM(IF)/SDM (NF/SM)[d]	NF/SM
Suggestibility[c]	Moderate/External	None[e]
High		
Perceived arousal	Very high/Traumatic	Medium/Optimal
Attentional bias	External « Internal	External ≥ Internal
External[a]	Central « Peripheral	Central ≥ Peripheral
Internal[b]	Cognitive <<< Sensory	Cognitive > Sensory
Memory distortions	RM/AF/DM(IF)/SDM(RO) (NF/SM)[d]	RM/NF/SM
Suggestibility[c]	High/External	Mild/Internal
Very high		
Perceived arousal	Extremely high/Unbearable	High/Uncomfortable
Attentional bias	External <<< Internal	External > Internal
External[a]	Peripheral	Central > Peripheral

(continued)

Table 5.1 (continued)

Event-related arousal effects	Hypersensitive	Hyposensitive
Internal[b]	Cognitive <<< Sensory	Cognitive » Sensory
Memory distortions	DM(IF)/SDM(RO) > RM/AF (NF/SM)[d]	RM/AF > NF/SM > DM(EF)/SDM (NF/SM)[d]
Suggestibility[c] Extremely high	Extreme/External	Moderate/Internal
Perceived arousal	Extremely high/Debilitating	Very high to extremely high/Traumatic to Debilitating
Attentional bias	Internal	External » Internal to Internal
External[a]	N/A	Central » Peripheral to Central
Internal[b]	Sensory	Cognitive >>> Sensory to Sensory
Memory distortions	DA	DM(EF)/SDM(RO) ≥ RM/AF (NF/SM)[d] to DA
Suggestibility[c]	Extreme/External	High to Extreme/Internal to External

NF normal forgetting; *AF* active forgetting; *DA* dissociative amnesia; *RM* remarkable memory; *SDM* state-dependent memory; *RO* red out; *SM* script memory; *DM* dissociative memory
[a]Central and peripheral information objectively defined
[b]Cognitive and sensory information of environmentally elicited affective response
[c]Refers to both susceptibility level and type, the latter stemming from attentional bias—created memory not specified as reflects post encoding psychosocial factors
[d]Occurs only if individual, due to personal history, habituated to event
[e]While increasingly likely over time, suggestibility not provided as reflects state more than trait effects

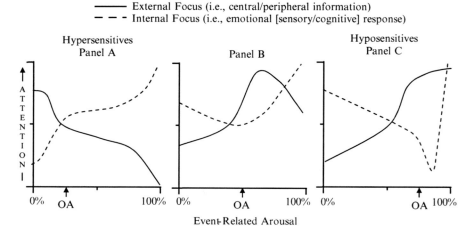

Fig. 5.3 Theorized orientation response (external vs. internal attentional focus) based on event-related arousal and arousal sensitivity (OA = optimal arousal)

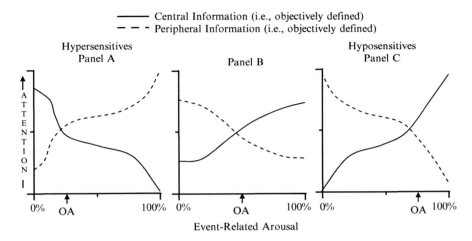

Fig. 5.4 Theorized external orientation response (central vs. peripheral attentional focus) based on event-related arousal and arousal sensitivity (*OA* optimal arousal)

Consistent with the above theoretical speculations, it has been shown that individuals have a tendency to be either emotion-focused (e.g., pleasure-focused) or arousal-focused when evaluating either their own emotional reactions, with the former having an affective response strongly based on the interpretation of the emotional event itself and the latter having an affective response strongly based on their reactions to an emotional event (Feldman, 1995). Taken together, one would expect hyposensitive eyewitnesses to have more cognitively based memories (e.g., autobiographical/narrative) and hypersensitive eyewitnesses to have more physiologically based (i.e., emotional-sensory) memories for criminal/traumatic events (Hervé et al. 2007). With augmentations in perceived arousal, hypersensitive eyewitnesses—who are likely to view moderate-to-intense arousal as aversive—should increasingly focus internally while concurrently avoiding the arousal-eliciting source (see Table 5.1 and Fig. 5.3). Any attention focused externally is likely geared towards decreasing the intensity of the situation (e.g., by locating an escape route). This reaction is consistent to a phobic individual who, although peripherally aware of a phobic stimuli (e.g., an insect), searches for a way to escape the situation in order to decrease his/her anxiety (Thorpe & Salkovskis, 1998). In contrast to hypersensitive eyewitnesses, arousal augmentations in hyposensitive eyewitnesses should lead them to increasingly focus externally on the arousal-eliciting source and away from their internal states (see Table 5.1 and Fig. 5.3). This reaction is akin to that of experienced law enforcement personnel who, for example, although vaguely aware of his/her internal state during an armed stand-off, primarily focuses his/her attention on the perpetrator. Consequently, hyposensitive individuals should generally make better eyewitnesses than hypersensitive individuals (Cooper et al., 2007). Relative to the latter, the former are likely to recall information that is crucial to the investigative process (i.e., who did what to who; see Fig. 5.4).

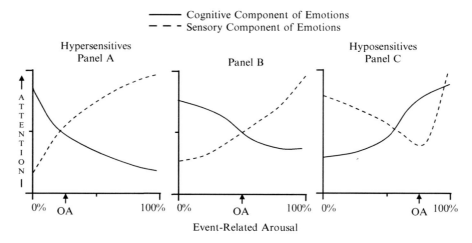

Fig. 5.5 Theorized internal orientation response (cognitive vs. sensory attentional focus) based on event-related arousal and arousal sensitivity (*OA* optimal arousal)

The above differences between hyposensitive and hypersensitive eyewitnesses notwithstanding, intense levels of arousal are likely to result in a potent ANS reaction irrespective of an individual's trait arousal sensitivity. Thus, at such high intensity levels, all eyewitnesses are likely to recall, at least in part, their sensory experiences (see Fig. 5.5). That is, arousal intensity should be strongly associated with somesthetic memories, albeit more strongly so with hypersensitive eyewitnesses than hyposensitive eyewitnesses. In support of this view, van der Kolk and Fisler (1995) provided examples of patients who could recall their emotions related to their traumatic experience without remembering the actual experiences. For example, they discussed a victim of sexual assault who became agitated when brought back to the scene of her attack without an explicit recollection of the actual sexual assault.

Given its impact on orientation/attention, memory processes and motivation (e.g., fight vs. flight), arousal sensitivity is proposed to be the single most important individual difference factor influencing eyewitness memory. Indeed, the majority of the mediating/moderating variables reviewed below are likely to exert effects on memory either upon or as a result of one's trait arousal sensitivity.

As with arousal sensitivity, neurocognitive functioning is an innate characteristic with implications for memory formation. Not only will neurocognitive functioning impact the emotional processing of an eyewitness by delineating the meaning analysis of the criminal/traumatic event, but it may also separately impact the stages of memory. For example, attentional and working memory functioning are likely to impact encoding quantity; and spatial and language functioning are likely to impact encoding quality. Memory functioning and processing speed should impact storage, and executive and language functioning should impact the quantity and quality of retrieval (Hervé et al. 2007). Impairments in any of these neurocognitive domains, coupled with ANS stimulation in the context of witnessing a crime, may disrupt mental processing. Therefore, understanding an eyewitness' neurocognitive strengths and weaknesses, is crucial to the understanding of the eyewitness' memory capabilities. Indeed, neurocognitively impaired eyewitnesses have been found to recall memories with less quantity in comparison to those without neurocognitive deficits (Ternes & Yuille, 2008).

Psychological Variables

Psychologically, emotions are regulated by a cognitive interpretative system. As reviewed above, while arousal sensitivity guides attention, the cognitive system primarily interprets the attended-to information and, therefore, sets the quality of emotional/traumatic events such as crimes. Throughout development, individuals learn to emotionally differentiate objects, situations, and people (Mandler, 1984). New emotional events are then interpreted in light of both their current characteristics (e.g., valence, threat, duration, type) and one's lifelong emotional learning history (e.g., current interpretations reflect, in part, the sum of past interpretations of similar events). Given the developmental nature of this system, mental ability (e.g., neurocognitive impairments/strengths), personality, specific traits (e.g., arousal sensitivity, cognitive distortions), and more transient psychological factors (e.g., Axis I disorders, substance use) are thought to exert an influence. These factors are believed to add unique, idiosyncratic cognitive filters through which events are interpreted, as well as to expose different individuals to different emotional events, thereby setting the parameters of one's emotional learning environments/history. For example, hypersensitive eyewitnesses, who are emotionally motivated to avoid arousal, are likely to be quick to label events as either good (e.g., low arousing) or bad (e.g., high arousing)—that is, along a valence dimension. In contrast, hyposensitive eyewitnesses, who seek out and focus upon arousing events, are likely to interpret events as either arousing or not—that is, along an arousal continuum. These labels should then be reflected within eyewitnesses' statements. For example, a hyposensitive bystander, when asked to describe how he felt when witnessing an assault, is likely to report how energized and excited the event made him/her feel. In contrast, a hypersensitive bystander faced with the same situation may report how scared s/he was and describe the incident as "awful."

Personality is another predisposing psychological factor that should be considered in eyewitness research and practice, especially given its theoretical connection to arousal sensitivity (Deffenbacher, Bornstein, Penrod, & McGorty, 2004; Ellis, 1987; Eysenck, 1967; Hervé & Hare, 1998). Indeed, personality delineates what information is encoded (e.g., Christianson et al., 1996) and mediates post-encoding distortions (e.g., Porter et al., 1999, 2000). Moreover, an individual's meaning analysis of a particular event will be affected, in part, by an individual's personality (e.g., Blair et al., 1995). In terms of non-pathological personalities, introverted individuals are likely to be more sensitive to traumatic/criminal experiences than are extroverted individuals, as the former are more sensitive to arousal than the latter (Zuckerman, 1979). As such, the introverted eyewitness is likely to feel more threatened under stress than the extrovert, a factor that is likely to affect the quantity and quality of his/her eyewitness memory (see Bothwell, Brigham, & Pigott, 1987 regarding the memory performance of "neurotics" vs. "stables"). Indeed, although both the introverted eyewitness and the extroverted eyewitness may recall a specific crime as arousing, the introvert is likely to recall it as more unpleasant than the extrovert, a point that has obvious memory consequences. It should be noted that these personality-related differences are likely exaggerated when considering pathological personalities, personalities that are frequently encountered within the forensic arena in which eyewitness researchers and clinicians practice (Christianson et al., 1996). For example, the psychopath, who is theoretically the most arousal hyposensitive of all eyewitnesses (Blackburn, 1979; Hare, 1965; Hervé & Hare, 1998), is likely to feel little traumatic arousal. Preliminary research suggests that psychopaths have better memories than nonpsychopaths arguably due to differences in arousal sensitivity (Cooper et al., 2007).

An individual's psychiatric history is also a predisposing eyewitness memory factor. Indeed, psychiatric problems are likely to affect eyewitness' arousal sensitivity and their interpretative abilities. For example, eyewitnesses with anxiety disorders are likely to be highly sensitive to arousal fluctuations during events of impact. That is, some Axis I disorders may serve to delineate the intensity of emotional responses during crimes, a point with important memory implications (Hervé et al. 2007). Unfortunately, little is known regarding the influence of Axis I disorders on eyewitness memory, a point in need of research. In addition to helping expand our knowledge regarding the processes affecting memory, such information could also be used as an index of arousal sensitivity (e.g., one would expect anxiety disorders to be over-represented in hypersensitive eyewitnesses).

Social Variables

In addition to biological and psychological factors, a variety of predisposing social variables could impact eyewitness memory. Although arousal sensitivity, viewed as a trait, is by definition, resistant to change, it can theoretically alter due to experience (Mandler, 1984). Indeed, an eyewitness' history of victimization may affect his/her state arousal sensitivity for similar future events via sensitization. That is, past experiences with trauma/crime may have important consequences in terms of how future traumas/crimes are experienced and remembered (Porter, 1996; Terr, 1991; van der Kolk, van der Hart, & Marmar, 1996).

The direction of the sensitization (e.g., negative vs. positive) depends on the type of events previously experienced. One the one hand, the experience of past crimes of a traumatic nature (e.g., events that are highly arousing and unpleasant) may sensitize eyewitnesses in such a manner that future crimes are experienced as relatively more disturbing. This view is reflected, in part, in the symptom formulation of PTSD

(APA, 2000). A defining feature of PTSD is hyperarousal/hypervigilance (van der Kolk, 1997), a symptom consistently reported by veterans and victims of crime (Cooper et al., 2004; Darves-Bornoz, 1997; Darves-Bornoz et al., 1998; Griesel & Yuille, 2012; O'Toole, Marshall, Schureck, & Dobson, 1999; Op den Velde et al., 1996). The end result is that such individuals, when faced with subsequent crimes/traumas, can functionally become hypersensitive eyewitnesses, irrespective of their trait arousal sensitivity. However, this effect may dissipate if the experienced event, although objectively of high intensity, is subjectively experienced as relatively benign (i.e., as compared to the intensity of the previous crime/trauma).

On the other hand, past experiences with highly arousing, but non-traumatic situations are likely to desensitize eyewitnesses to the effects of arousal. That is, a history of experiencing non-traumatic arousal may decrease an eyewitness' arousal sensitivity for future events (i.e., creating a state of hyposensitivity). For example, an individual who regularly participates in extreme sports (e.g., sky diving, cliff jumping) and/or is an avid consumer of arousal inducing intoxicants (e.g., amphetamines) may habituate to the effects of arousal over time. At the very least, they are likely to label the arousal inducing event as more positive in valence than someone who has not habituated (Bockheler, 1995). Such cognitive interpretations of emotional events are important, as perceptions of valence have been shown to affect eyewitness memory, independent of perceptions of arousal (Cooper, 2005).

Precipitating Factors

Precipitating factors concern variables at play during the to-be-remembered event and include the type of event itself (e.g., event of impact/personal significance vs. mundane event). As Fig. 5.1 suggests, the effects of precipitating factors are influenced by the foundation laid by predisposing factors (Hervé et al. 2007).

Biological Variables

In terms of physiological arousal, emotional reactions should, in part, delineate the content of eyewitness memory. Arousal physiologically prepares the eyewitness to deal with the event (e.g., flight, fight or freeze). Obviously, a victim of a crime who fights will have different recollections than a victim who freezes or flees the scene. Theoretically, this response is likely mediated by arousal sensitivity. While the hypersensitive eyewitness is likely to become extremely uncomfortable by crime-induced arousal, the hyposensitive eyewitness is less likely to be affected by such stimulation; in certain cases, the hyposensitive eyewitness may even enjoy the situation or at least perceive it as less negative (Cooper, 2005). For example, consider how individuals respond to a sky diving experience: the hypersensitive sky diver is likely to feel highly aroused and terrified while the hyposensitive is likely to feel aroused and excited. Of course, this effect may be mediated by variables that affect one's state sensitivity such as substance use (e.g., alcohol and amphetamines have dampening and stimulating ANS effects, respectively) and experience (e.g., novice vs. experienced sky diver; see Bockheler, 1995). Clearly, this distinction has important behavioral consequences and, therefore, memory consequences. While the hypersensitive eyewitness is likely to seek a quick escape (i.e., a flight response) from a crime, the hyposensitive eyewitness, in his/her search for stimulation, is likely to confront the situation (i.e., fight response) and focus his/her attention on the event proper. The hypersensitive eyewitness' memory is likely to contain, in addition to significant somesthetic information, a greater amount of peripheral information, reflecting a flight response (e.g., a focus on an escape route and possible obstacles; a focus on bystanders and their reactions), than central information (e.g., a focus on the perpetrator and his/her actions). In contrast, the hyposensitive eyewitness' memory may reflect his/her strong focus on the situation at hand and, therefore, will likely contain a great deal of both peripheral (e.g., the fight response and objects that may facilitate such a response) and central information (e.g., perpetrator, accomplice and weapon information). Accordingly, researchers/investigators are urged to consider how high levels of arousal and arousal sensitivity interact when examining the effects of stress/crime on eyewitness memory. It is suggested that investigative interviews primarily use open-ended questions and examine what the eyewitness focused on during the crime (see Yarbrough et al., present volume).

All variables considered equal, criminal events should cue an ANS response that guides the eyewitness' attention towards the source of the arousal. As such, the source of the arousal should be given priority over arousal-irrelevant information in the processing stream, thereby resulting in greater memory for arousal-relevant, as compared to arousal-irrelevant information. In support of this hypothesis, research has found emotional stress to evoke an orientating response, where the emotional event is allocated the most attention in a quick and efficient fashion (Burke, Heuer, & Reisberg, 1992; Christianson & Loftus, 1990; Deffenbacher et al., 2004). For example, Christianson and Loftus (1991) had participants view slides of either neutral or emotionally unpleasant events and showed that participants remembered more of the central details, as opposed to peripheral details, when the slides were emotionally laden. Others have found that central information, both spatially and temporally, is remembered better than peripheral information, and that theme-related information is better remembered than theme-unrelated information (e.g., Safer, Christianson, Autry, & Osterland, 1998; see Christianson, 1992, for a review). This attention-related effect is also found in the eyewitness literature that has utilized archival and field methods, thus helping to bridge the gap between laboratory and field studies. For example, Christianson and Hubinette (1993) examined witness' and victims' memories of post office robberies and found that the recollections concerning the robbery's central details (e.g., regarding action, weapon, and clothing details) were more consistent with police reports than their recollection of peripheral information (e.g., regarding the date, time, and descriptions of other people). Similarly, mock witnesses exposed to simulated crimes in which a weapon was involved have been found to quite clearly remember details regarding the weapon used, while having poorer memories for other details, such as the hair colour, height, or clothes of the mock assailant (e.g., Kramer, Buckhout, & Eugenio, 1990; Loftus, Loftus, & Messo, 1987; O'Rourke, Penrod, Cutler, & Stuve, 1989; Pickel, 1998, 1999; note, however, that this analogue weapon focus has not been conclusively demonstrated with actual eyewitnesses—see Behrman & Davey, 2001; Cooper, Kennedy, Hervé, & Yuille, 2002; Griesel & Yuille, 2012; Tollestrup et al., 1994; Valentine, Pickering, & Darling, 2003). Thus, the arousal elicited by certain events, irrespective of its intensity, has the effect of narrowing one's attention on the central details of the scene as Easterbrook's (1959) theory suggests. These arousal-mediated attention effects seem adaptive. Indeed, quickly changing one's attention from a relatively neutral act (e.g., feeding) to an emotionally laden one (e.g., the presence of a predator) or from irrelevant (e.g., the price of fruit) to relevant (e.g., the sight of a gun) information has obvious survival value.

Psychological Variables

While arousal sensitivity and other genetic/biological factors may delineate what information is allocated attentional resources during a criminal event, evaluative cognitions define the quality of the event. As such, to understand memory for crime, one should be knowledgeable about how cognitive styles and distortions affect thoughts and memories. Although several different evaluative dimensions have been suggested (e.g., Larsen & Diener, 1992; Watson, Clark, & Tellegen, 1988), valence and arousal (i.e., defined cognitively, not biologically) have received the most empirical support across age groups, cultures, and gender (Bradley & Greenwald, 1992; Russell, 1989; Russell & Bullock, 1985, 1986; Smith & Ellsworth, 1985). Given this consistency, Russell (1980) noted that, although both components are necessary for an emotional evaluation, neither alone is sufficient (also see Mandler, 1984). As suggested above, individuals differ in regards to how much weight they place on one dimension over another (Blascovich, 1990, 1992; Feldman, 1995), with hypersensitive individuals and hyposensitive individuals being more concerned with valence and arousal, respectively (see Fig. 5.5). These emotive cognitive differences, in turn, are then likely to be reflected in the quality of memory, with the recall of hypersensitive eyewitness reflecting valence over arousal and the recall of hyposensitive eyewitnesses showing the opposite pattern.

In addition to emotive variability in cognitive processing, a number of psychological and predisposing processes (see above) are known to influence cognition, each of which may help to explain the variable nature of eyewitness memory. As noted by Mandler (1984), while the pre-programmed ANS reactions are resistant to change, the cognitively based reactions, being rooted in one's autobiographical past, are likely to be highly idiosyncratic and dynamic. These reactions, or evaluative cognitions, mirror a learned response. They become associated with emotional/criminal events via classical conditioning, thereby turning the neutral into the emotional. There are, for example, objects (e.g., a gun) and events (e.g., banking) that are initially neutral in connotation but may become—through classical conditioning—actual ANS releasers. Such classical conditioning, in turn, is dependent on the types of events experienced, as well as on the fashion in which these experiences are evaluated—both of which are dependent, in part, on personality and mental health. An in-depth psychological profile of eyewitnesses/interviewees could therefore help shed some light on these apparent idiosyncratic responses (see Yarbrough et al., present volume). As noted above, introverted and extroverted individuals are likely to seek out different types of events and, hence, experience different conditioning paradigms. Similarly, the cognitive distortions of schizophrenics, as an example, are likely to result in memory distortions unlike any seen in non-schizophrenics. Accordingly, it is suggested that laboratory models of memory for trauma/crime would gain external validity by using trauma/crime-specific stimuli (i.e., specific to the participant at hand), rather than general threat stimuli (e.g., Clifford & Hollin, 1981), a method effectively used in the study of anxiety disorders and memory (see Radomsky & Rachman, 1999, 2001; Radomsky, Rachman, & Hammond, 2001).

Another precipitating psychological variable is the type of event the eyewitness experiences (e.g., whether the eyewitness interprets the event as stressful, irrespective of the "objective" nature of the event). In fact, the study of this issue has been the subject of a large amount of research attention, although researchers have often confounded event type with event interpretation. Researchers have examined the effects of event type on eyewitness memory in analogue laboratory research by exposing mock eyewitnesses to different levels of stress or arousal or by varying the type of event they view (e.g., violent vs. nonviolent; stressful vs. non-stressful), typically via slides or videos and less commonly through staged events. Early research on this topic led to the conclusion that high levels of stress/arousal had debilitating effects on eyewitness memory (see Deffenbacher, 1983; also see Deffenbacher et al., 2004). Seemingly at odds with the results of laboratory research are the results of field studies of actual eyewitnesses which demonstrated that eyewitnesses can be detailed and accurate in their accounts of events experienced under high stress (Cutshall & Yuille, 1989; Yuille & Cutshall, 1986). In attempt to explain these divergent findings, Christianson (1992), via a critical review of the literature, showed that the effects of stress/arousal on memory is complex and depends on a number of variables (e.g., what dependent variables researchers examine and highlight—e.g., central vs. peripheral details). Indeed, as the above review of memory patterns suggests, stress/arousal has complex effects on eyewitness memory with some witnesses displaying good memory and other eyewitnesses displaying poor memory (Yuille & Daylen, 1998).

An excellent example of the complex effects of arousal/stress on memory is the results of the study by Morgan et al. (2004). The researchers capitalized on a US military survival school where the participants, mock prisoners of war (POW), were sleep and food deprived before being faced with "interrogation stress." All participants were subjected to both high and low interrogation stress conditions which encompassed being interrogated for 40 min by an interrogator in the presence of a guard—the only difference between the conditions concerned the presence of "physical confrontation" by the guard in the high stress condition.

Twenty-four hours after their mock interrogations, the participants were asked to identify their interrogator from a lineup or photospread. The results indicated that 42–50% of the participants performed better in their mock eyewitness identifications in the low stress condition in comparison to the high stress condition. Results such as these have led many to argue that high levels of stress negatively impact eyewitness memory (e.g., Deffenbacher et al., 2004) and that eyewitness are prone to make identification errors (e.g., Loftus, 2012). What should be highlighted, however, is that 42–45% of the participants performed equally poorly or equally well across the stress conditions, and that 8–13% of the participants actually performed better in the high stress condition in comparison to the low stress condition. That is, the results confirm that stress/arousal has complex effects on memory: some participants performed better under conditions of low stress and some participants performed better under conditions of high stress. It is possible that biopsychosocial factors (e.g., arousal sensitivity), independent of the type of event, can, in part, account for these findings. Indeed, it may be the case that the participants who performed better in the low stress than high stress condition were relatively hypersensitive to arousal and those participants who performed better in the high stress condition than the low stress condition were relatively hyposensitive to arousal (Morgan, personal communication, February, 2011). Clearly, future research that assesses for such individual difference variables in the context of multi-method approaches (e.g., laboratory, archival, field) is needed to assist in disentangling the complex effects of the type of event (e.g., high stress vs. low stress) experienced on eyewitness memory (Hervé et al. 2007; Yuille, 1993; Yuille et al., 2010).

Social Variables

In addition to precipitating biological and psychological factors, precipitating social variables are thought to influence eyewitness memory. The context at encoding, for example, is likely to impact eyewitness memory as it should delineate the intensity and quality of the accompanying affective response and assist in defining the subjective meaning ascribed to events. As noted above, an emotional response encompasses both physiological and cognitive components, and the relative contribution of each response to the overall emotional experience is likely to depend, at least in part, on the nature of the situation (e.g., a laboratory vs. a field setting). On the one hand, most laboratory studies and other neutral settings are not likely to present mock witnesses with highly arousing situations, forcing participants to evaluate yet not experience emotional material. On the other hand, emotional settings, such as those seen in field research, represent highly arousing contexts that are generally evaluated and experienced as emotional in nature (Yuille, present volume). Thus, while the quality attached to memories of videos and slides (e.g., as seen in laboratory paradigms) reflect only cognitive processes, the quality attached to memories of criminal events (e.g., as seen in field research) reflects both ANS and cognitive functions, suggesting that the quality of memories for benign as opposed to significant events differ, at the very least, in degree (Hervé et al. 2007).

Context also affects the meaning assigned to particular events. For example, in terms of personal safety, some research has found victims and injured victims to report less crime-related information than witnesses and non-injured victims, respectively (e.g., Christianson & Hubinette, 1993; Kuehn, 1974). This suggests that the level of personal involvement within a criminal event can have significant effects on eyewitness memory. Distinguishing between emotional events that are life threatening (i.e., with personal consequences) and those that are not (i.e., without personal consequences) is thus encouraged in future research. It seems logical to predict that highly arousing events which place eyewitnesses in dangerous positions (e.g., being a victim) would evoke deeper and more personal sensations/cognitions than those that, although highly arousing, do not suggest imminent danger (e.g., witnessing a crime from across the street). The field would benefit from understanding the memory consequences of these different situations.

Perpetuating Factors

Perpetuating factors concern variables that effect memory after it has been formed. Considering the reconstructive nature of memory, eyewitness memory is susceptible to influences each time it is recalled (e.g., in thoughts, conversations, interviews).

Biological Variables

In addition to playing a role as both a predisposing and a precipitating factor, arousal sensitivity is also a significant perpetuating factor in light of its impact on decay (Hervé et al. 2007). Decay refers to the natural memory process of time-based forgetting, a process that usually occurs when memories are not given any subsequent attention (i.e., not recalled). Research indicates that certain memories are more resistant to decay than others, with affectively benign memories decaying at a faster rate than affectively loaded memories (Christianson, 1989; Cutshall & Yuille, 1989; Thompson et al., 1997; Yuille & Cutshall, 1986). Such findings highlight the central role of affect in decay, suggesting that arousal sensitivity, given its impact on emotions, should also influence decay. Specifically, one's arousal sensitivity (with all other variables being equal) should delineate the intensity of the affective load attached to memory, with hypersensitive eyewitnesses having a greater affective load attached to their memories for criminal events than hyposensitive eyewitnesses. Consequently, one would expect the memories of hyposensitive eyewitnesses to be more resistant to decay than the memories of hypersensitive eyewitnesses. However, this effect should not be considered in isolation, especially since hypersensitive and hyposensitive eyewitnesses are likely to differ in terms of how motivated they are to recall such events. As hypersensitive and hyposensitive individuals differ in behavioral motivation (Ellis, 1987), with the former motivated to avoid and the latter to seek out arousing situations, it follows that hypersensitive eyewitnesses are relatively more likely to avoid thinking about their past criminal experiences and hyposensitive eyewitnesses are relatively more likely to actively seek out an audience to share their memories. Thus, recall-related memory decay should be facilitated in hypersensitive eyewitnesses and impeded in hyposensitive eyewitnesses.

The above notwithstanding, repeated recall should have different effects on the memories of hypersensitive vs. hyposensitive eyewitnesses. On the one hand, hypersensitive eyewitnesses, given their internal affective focus, will, theoretically, focus their thoughts on what transpired within their own systems during their past criminal experience. As such, repeated recall should strengthen their memory trace for crime-related sensory information leaving, however, event-related information vulnerable to decay (Hervé et al. 2007). On the other hand, hyposensitive eyewitnesses, given their external affective focus, will, in theory, focus their thoughts on the event proper. Therefore, repeated recall should strengthen their memory trace for event-related information, with decay affecting subjective information.

Psychological Variables

As perpetuating factors, psychological variables are likely to exert their memory impact on when, why, and how recall occurs (Hervé et al. 2007). For example, eyewitnesses may be motivated to distort their memories of their criminal experiences for a variety of reasons. Indeed, a sexual assault victim may consciously leave out some aspect(s) of his/her experience when telling his/her partner. Others might consciously distort their experiences to either ensure that they are taken seriously or as a form of retaliation against the perpetrator, as seen when victims/witnesses exaggerate their memories. Unfortunately, such distortions, given the reconstructive nature of memory, may become memory reality (i.e., historical vs. narrative truth; Hyman & Loftus, 1997; Nash, 1994), thereby distorting the veracity of the eyewitness account upon further recall.

In addition to motivation, there are other psychological variables that may intervene between encoding and recall that may affect one's memory for traumatic/criminal events. For example, traumatized individuals need to make sense of their experience, recalling and reconstructing the event as they see fit until they can safely integrate it within their own worldview. This process is related, in part, to one's personality makeup and, depending on the specific personality, different memory distortions may therefore emerge. Given the impact that affect has upon memory, affective state/reactions during recall should also delineate the quality and quantity of eyewitness memories. As noted above, one's dominant affective style will affect what type of information is given the most attention, irrespective if this occurs at encoding or at recall. In addition, affect can also serve as a memory cue, as seen in mood-dependent research (see above). Finally, affect, with its influence on ANS arousal, has a host of influences on cognitive mechanisms (see above), each of which has predictable memory consequences.

As suggested above, the development of PTSD may also impact eyewitness memory. Intrusions of the precipitating event of impact (Horowitz, Wilner, & Alvarez, 1979), in combination with arousal sensitivity, may be responsible for the phenomena of hypernesia (i.e., better than normal memory; Scrivner & Safer, 1988). Repeated recollections of crimes in the form of flashbacks and/or nightmares are typically accompanied by significant physiological arousal (APA, 2000). In the hypersensitive eyewitness, such added arousal may be overwhelming. As a result, the individual may actively try to forget the experience (i.e., push the memory out of mind whenever it arises) and avoid anything that may remind him/her of the event (another feature of PTSD). Active forgetting may be successful in reducing the amount of unpleasant details available to memory and, in its extreme, may lead to dissociative amnesia. With a hyposensitive eyewitness, the added arousal, while likely unpleasant given its negative source (i.e., past crime), might never become unbearable. As such, every recollection may be accompanied with a manageable level of arousal that could serve to enhance memory and, therefore, progressively leads to hypernesia (Scrivner & Safer, 1988) or a remarkable memory (Yuille & Daylen, 1998).

Social Variables

The recall context will impact what type of information is sought from eyewitnesses and, therefore, what is recalled upon retrieval. For example, investigative interviews, in which the motivation is to elicit an account of an alleged crime (see Walsh & Bull, present volume; Yuille, Marxsen, & Cooper, 1999), are likely to be focused primarily on event-related information (see Yarbrough et al., present volume). In contrast, while some overlap exists, therapeutic encounters, in which the motivation is successful treatment, are likely equally focused on event- and sensory-related information, if not more so on the latter than the former. A consequence is that each type of context likely solidifies different types of memories, leaving other memories vulnerable to the effects of decay and/or suggestibility.

The manner in which the information is elicited from eyewitnesses should also be considered. For example, a substantial body of research highlights the negative impact of leading/suggestive questions/interviews on eyewitness memory (see Bruck, Ceci, & Hembrooke, 1998; Ceci & Bruck, 1993; Hyman & Loftus, 1997; Memon, Holley, Wark, Bull, & Kohnken, 1996; Wells & Turtle, 1987). In addition to jeopardizing criminal investigations, leading questions/interviews can facilitate memory distortions. Indeed, several investigators have been able to implant false trauma-like memories (Loftus, 2012; Loftus & Pickrell, 1995; Porter et al., 1999), highlighting the malleable nature of memory. Leading questions/interviews may lead to memory distortions, which may subsequently be perceived as reality (Nash, 1994), spoiling memory accuracy.

Social factors could also impact eyewitnesses when faced with making identifications at lineups (Wells et al., 1998). Laboratory researchers have suggested that non-blind lineup administrators could unknowingly cue the eyewitness as to the police suspect's position in the lineup (Dysart, Lawson, & Rainey, 2011), possibly leading to false identifications. Further, laboratory research has examined the post-identification feedback effect, the results of which suggest that confirming or disconfirming feedback by mock lineup administrators can distort mock eyewitness' confidence ratings of their identifications (Douglass & Steblay, 2006; Semmler, Brewer, & Wells, 2004; Wells, Olson, & Charman, 2003). These and other lineup effects, however, have not been sufficiently tested in real world settings (but see Wright & Skagerberg, 2007), suggesting caution in their interpretation and applicability to actual eyewitnesses (Yuille, present volume; Yuille & Cooper, 2012; Yuille et al., 2010). Indeed, it has been shown that effects found in the laboratory may not translate to the field—in fact, sometimes, the effects found in the real world are opposite to those found in the laboratory (Mitchell, 2012). Nevertheless, if lineup effects are sufficiently tested in archival and field studies and if the results conform to the results of controlled laboratory experiments, some of the findings may be impacted by issues concerning suggestibility (e.g., a biased lineup or a suggestive lineup administrator could arguably be akin to a suggestive interview—with negative recognition and recall consequences, respectively).

The type of information an eyewitness is suggestible to may depend on his/her arousal sensitivity. Take the extreme example of dissociation—dissociative experiences are likely to disrupt the encoding of event-related information in hypersensitive eyewitnesses and of sensory-related information in hyposensitive eyewitnesses. Accordingly, while the hypersensitive eyewitness, given his/her access to sensory information, would be suggestible to event-related information, the hyposensitive eyewitness, given his/her relatively intact event-related information, is more likely to be suggestible to sensory- than to event-related information. Consequently, interviewers should be aware of the possibility that interviewees may not have access to "everything" that transpired during their criminal experiences, a point with important practical implications (see Yarbrough et al., present volume). For example, eyewitnesses without a complete narrative of their experience may, in attempts to make sense of what happened to them or others, latch on to the "explanations" given to them. That is, such individuals are likely to be very suggestible, which, if not paid attention to, could lead to serious memory distortions (Yuille & Daylen, 1998).

Biopsychosocial Predictions of Eyewitness Memory Variability

The aforementioned review suggests that the memory variability reported within and across the eyewitness memory literature stems from a host of predisposing, precipitating, and perpetuating individual differences variables that impact a multi-dimensional affective response that influence each stage of memory (see Fig. 5.1). At the encoding/storage stages, the type, quality, and quantity of an eyewitness'

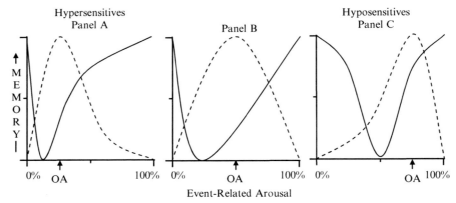

Fig. 5.6 The theorized relationship between memory (quality and quantity) and emotions based on a multidimensional model of emotions (cognitive and physiological components), event-related arousal, and arousal sensitivity (*OA* optimal arousal)

memory should be highly dependent on his/her emotional state (see Fig. 5.6). Initially, criminal events should initiate an ANS arousal response that serves to prepare and orient the eyewitness. As such, trait and/or state arousal sensitivity, a physiologically based function that moderates ANS reactions, should delineate both the rate at which a particular eyewitness will succumb to arousal-mediated effects and the type of information given attentional and, therefore, memory preference. On the one hand, hypersensitive eyewitnesses should fall prey to arousal-induced memory distortions at a relatively faster rate than hyposensitive eyewitnesses, distortions in which internal (e.g., sensory) information is increasingly given memory priority over external (e.g., narrative) information, with objectively central information deteriorating at a faster rate than peripheral information (see Table 5.1; and Figs. 5.3 and 5.4). On the other hand, hyposensitive eyewitnesses should show memory distortions at a relatively slower rate and increasingly focus on external information, most notably that which is objectively central to the event, at the detriment of internal and, later in the arousal stream, peripherally external information (see Table 5.1; and Figs. 5.3 and 5.4).

Concurrently, cognitive evaluations, which are psychological in nature, should assign the quality of the experience in question, which itself should reflect one's personal history, personality, and physiological (e.g., sober vs. inebriated vs. high) and affective states, the latter of which being closely tied to the nature of the criminal event (i.e., danger level; e.g., witness vs. victim). While positive (i.e., safety) evaluations, which hyposensitive eyewitnesses are most likely to have, will lead to an ANS dampening effect, negative (i.e., threat) evaluations, which are more characteristic of hypersensitive eyewitnesses, should serve to further excite the ANS. These cognitively moderated ANS reactions should then feedback into the interpretative system, thereby leading to an event-related affective reaction. Once complete, this affective response should become associated with the event in question, thereby setting the stage for storing the experience into long-term memory (LTM).

Although an eyewitness' arousal sensitivity should delineate the type of crime-related information allocated attention (e.g., internal vs. external), it is the affective load of the event that should predominantly dictate how well (i.e., in terms of type, quality, and quantity) and for how long a memory will be recalled (see Table 5.1). Indeed, affective load should have two memory consequences. First, emotions should add significance to events of impact and, as such, should increase the saliency (or quality) of memory traces, thereby making them easier to recall than events of less personal significance (Christianson, 1989, 1992; Thompson et al., 1997). Second, emotions should add information value to memories. That is, they increase the size (or quantity) of the memory by accelerating information transfer from short-term memory (STM) to LTM. As such, emotional memories (e.g., of crimes) should be sensitive to a number of triggers (i.e., emotional and non-emotional) and therefore more susceptible to free/cued recall than emotionally neutral memories. Given that recall serves to enhance memory, one should expect emotional memories (e.g., of crimes) to be remembered for longer periods of time than memories of neutral events. More generally, the affective load—adding quality and quantity to the memory—should serve to minimize (or protect against) memory decay. Objectively significant events that are subjectively interpreted as relatively benign (e.g., as low-to-moderate in intensity) should decay at a faster rate than those interpreted as significant (i.e., as moderate-to-high intensity). That is, with all other variables being equal, mundane events should evidence normal forgetting, while events of impact should be remembered quite well and for long periods of time (i.e., particularly if rehearsed), thereby leading to remarkable memories.

Based on differences in trait arousal sensitivity, remarkable memory patterns for criminal/traumatic events should be more common in hyposensitive eyewitnesses than in hypersensitive eyewitnesses given that the former is likely to make a less (and the latter a more) catastrophic interpretation of the situation at hand (see Figs. 5.3 and 5.4). When a hypersensitive develops a remarkable memory, his/her memory is likely to decay at a relatively faster rate than the remarkable memory of a hyposensitive eyewitness because the hypersensitive, in his/her attempt to avoid stimulation, is not as likely to be self-motivated to think/talk about the experience that led to the remarkable memory. Contextual variables are also likely to affect the development of these memory patterns via cognitively moderated affective reactions. Indeed, certain types of events are likely to be interpreted as more significant than others (e.g., being defrauded vs. robbed at gun point) and, therefore, will be differentially resistant to memory decay (e.g., fraud events leading to normal forgetting and an armed robbery to a remarkable memory).

As arousal approaches an eyewitness' trauma threshold (see Figs. 5.3 and 5.4), significantly negative event-related interpretations are likely to occur (i.e., traumatic interpretations). Such interpretations, given their ANS excitatory effects, could lead to post-traumatic responses, the addition of which could have at least two memory consequences. On the one hand, eyewitnesses may attempt to actively avoid thinking of the event proper (i.e., a cardinal symptom of PTSD; APA, 2000). If successful, this conscious attempt at forgetting could result in fewer memory triggers for the "feared" event and, therefore, lead to a loss of memory detail (i.e., decay) over time, resulting in active forgetting (Yuille & Daylen, 1998). On the other hand and somewhat paradoxically, a PTSD response may lead to intrusive thoughts about the event proper (another defining feature of PTSD; Cooper, 2005). In this situation, the central information of the event would be unconsciously and repeatedly recalled, thereby leading to hypernesia (Scrivner & Safer, 1988)—another pathway to remarkable memories. Arousal sensitivity would decree at which point in the arousal stream eyewitnesses would be impacted by these effects, with hypersensitive eyewitnesses showing these memory patterns at subjectively lower intensity levels and across a wider range of arousal levels than hyposensitive eyewitnesses. It should be noted that the impact of intrusive thoughts, flashbacks and nightmares on memory veracity remains unknown and, therefore, is in need of research.

At a certain point in the arousal stream (i.e., as arousal surpasses the trauma threshold) affective load should also exert its impact on memory processes thereby leading to significant distortions. Although initially benefiting memory storage by making information transfer (IT) more efficient, emotional intensity eventually leads to memory decay by overloading STM resources. At this point, certain pieces of event-related information should be given priority. It is expected that, shortly after surpassing the eyewitness' trauma threshold, sensory information will be given LTM priority in hypersensitives and narrative information will be given priority in hyposensitives. The resulting loss in narrative and sensory information, respectively, could lead to further PTSD symptom formation. The loss of external information in hypersensitive eyewitnesses could be associated with feelings of derealization as reality (i.e., the external world) would become increasingly overshadowed by fantasy (i.e., the internal world). In contrast, the loss of sensory information that hyposensitive eyewitnesses experience could result in feelings of depersonalisation, reflecting the fact that one is losing him/herself in the event at hand (i.e., external world) and, therefore, loses touch with one's own sense of self (i.e., internal world).

As the aforementioned effect increases in magnitude, certain predictable memory consequences should ensue. At their most extreme, derealization and depersonalization during encoding/storage should result in dissociative memories (DM), with hypersensitive eyewitnesses and hyposensitive eyewitnesses being more likely to take an internal and external (or observer) perspective, respectively. Consequently, hyposensitive eyewitnesses who display an observer perspective would remain valuable eyewitnesses, while hypersensitive eyewitnesses who escaped into fantasy would be relatively unhelpful in the investigative process. However, with further increases in perceived arousal, some eyewitnesses—expectedly over represented on the hypersensitivity spectrum—may be rendered relatively amnesic for the event in question. That is, they would be susceptible to the development of dissociative amnesia.

Unbearable (e.g., traumatic) arousal could also take on a subjectively unique quality (i.e., one that has never previously been experienced), which could serve to explain the development of state-dependent memories, as well as red outs (Cooper & Yuille, 2007; Swihart et al., 1999). Events may be ascribed unique affective loads for several reasons. First, given that cognitive interpretations depend, in part, on one's affective conditioning history, events of extreme intensity would, by definition, be unique. It is expected that hypersensitive eyewitnesses, given their relatively limited arousal history, would be more affected by this intensity than hyposensitive eyewitnesses. Second, specific contextual cues could also result in the creation of unique emotional experiences by reflecting a large discrepancy between pre- and post-crime affective states (e.g., from an extremely pleasant and relatively un-aroused state to a highly negative and intense state; see Russell, 1980). If such an emotional change has never been experienced in the past, then, by definition, it would be interpreted as unique. Although hyposensitive eyewitnesses are arousal seekers, they typically seek arousal in a controlled fashion (i.e., their sensation seeking occurs gradually rather than abruptly) and, consequently, should be as susceptible to this process as hypersensitive eyewitnesses. Third, idiosyncratic filters stemming from specific cognitive distortions (e.g., related to psychopathology or personality disorder) could also lead to unique interpretations. Aside from the ANS inhibitory and excitatory effects, arousal sensitivity should not be a factor in this regard. Finally, given that criminal events of high intensity may serve to cue past emotional memories, competition for attentional and, therefore, memory resources may occur. If the criminal event in question is given attentional/memory priority and if the affective load of the event in question is then combined at the encoding/storage stages with that of the past memory, one would expect the resulting event-related memory to be unique. Unlike other more circumscribed memories, it would reflect a specific emotional combination—a combination that has likely never been previously experienced. Both of these emotional states would then have to be present for retrieval to be successful. For successful retrieval, interviewers would have to attempt to figure out which mechanism led to the state-dependent effects. Presumably, such effects would occur earlier in the arousal stream and over a larger arousal range in hypersensitive eyewitnesses than in hyposensitive eyewitnesses (see Figs. 5.3 and 5.4).

The cueing of past memories by current criminal events could have other memory consequences as well. Barring any other factors and assuming that the current arousing/criminal situations trigger memories of past similar events, the resulting memory impact should depend on the influence of the cued memory upon ANS function via affective feedback mechanisms. If the current situation triggers a memory of a past similar situation with relatively little adverse consequences, the feedback mechanisms would have a dampening effect on the ANS, thereby signalling to the eyewitness that the current situation is less dangerous/significant than would otherwise be the case (i.e., if no memory cueing had occurred). This process may help to explain the development of some script memories. Take, for example, cases of repeated child sexual abuse. The first time the event occurs, the child would have no way of knowing its outcome and, therefore, the resulting memory may be of significance. If the child escapes relatively unharmed, it is possible that s/he learns that the event is not to be as feared as initially thought. Accordingly, the next time s/he is assaulted by the same assailant, who would serve as a memory cue, the child may interpret the event as relatively less significant. With successive assaults, the child may then habituate to the affective load, rendering successive events less and less subjectively disturbing and, therefore, less and less important in terms of memory allocation—a script memory may result (note: the child would not necessarily need to interpret the event as benign for a script memory to develop). Obviously, there are other types of repeated events that may lead to the development of a script memory (e.g., being the victim of serial robberies or domestic assault). Irrespective of the type of event, the end result may be that the eyewitness ends up developing a script memory regarding what "generally" happened to him/her. Significant departures from the script, however, would likely be of memory significance and, therefore, better recalled (see Yarbrough et al., present volume).

The above notwithstanding, if the current situation triggers a traumatic memory and, therefore, a heightened ANS reaction, then other memory distortions reflecting dissociative processes are expected. For example, the current event may trigger a "flashback" of a past traumatic event, resulting in the formation of a memory that reflects a combination of events (i.e., the flashback and the current situation). In extreme cases, this process could lead to total amnesia for the event at hand (i.e., the dissociative process bars encoding/storage), leaving the eyewitness only able to report about peripheral information (e.g., events that preceded and followed the actual offence). This process suggests that the "red out" phenomenon might reflect not only a state-dependent mechanism (i.e., event-related rage states of a unique affective load) but also dissociative processes (i.e., event-unrelated rage states that are allocated attentional priority; e.g., past jealous episodes).

As previously discussed, memory for criminal/traumatic events can take many forms and any one memory can be characterized by several patterns reflecting different processes occurring at different points in the formation of the memory. For example, one victim of repeated childhood sexual abuse recalled that she "used to" climb up the bedroom wall and enter the red light on the ceiling and "watch" what was happening to the "little girl" (i.e., Cooper, 1999). In this case, the victim described a script memory for abuse from the perspective of an observer. Once the victim took on an observer perspective, this process was repeated in subsequent abuse incidents, leading to the formation of a script. Such a strategy is arguably defensive in nature and is used to depersonalize an experience/memory (Cooper, Kennedy et al., 2002). Similarly, it is not uncommon for eyewitness to have remarkable memories for events that led to and followed an offence, with dissociative memories or amnesia for the event proper.

In addition to the encoding and storage stages of memory, distortions can occur at the retrieval stage, reflecting, for example, recall motivation and retrieval methods. Recall motivation is an important variable to consider when interpreting the validity of eyewitnesses' statements. There are many reasons, for example, that a victim would distort (e.g., embellish, minimize) his/her account of a criminal experience to law enforcement (e.g., fear or protection of perpetrator). These motivations are likely to be accompanied with their own emotional connotations, which could serve to further influence/contaminate memory. Indeed, distortions, irrespective of their motives, could, with time, take on a memory dominant role and, therefore, become reality. Just as active forgetting can lead to memory decay, active confabulation can lead to (false) memory strengthening.

In terms of retrieval mechanisms, the use of leading and suggestive questions by investigative interviewers could lead to false/created memories for event-related information that was either not encoded or poorly encoded in the first place. That memory decays with time suggests a positive correlation between retrieval delay and suggestibility. The impact of questionable interviewing techniques is proposed to be much more significant, in terms of the investigative processes, for hypersensitive eyewitnesses than hyposensitive eyewitnesses. The former, having likely focused internally and, therefore, having little event-related information available, would be suggestible to information of most relevance: objectively central information. In contrast, the latter should be resistant to event-related suggestibility in that it is specifically this knowledge that s/he has at his/her disposal. S/he might, however, be suggestible to peripheral information and explanations regarding how s/he should have experienced the event in question. Arousal sensitivity would further dictate that hypersensitive eyewitnesses become suggestible at lower arousal levels and across a wider range of arousal levels than hyposensitive eyewitnesses (see Figs. 5.3 and 5.4).

Implications

Although certain aspects of our biopsychosocial model of eyewitness memory (Hervé et al. 2007) have been put to the empirical test (e.g., Cooper et al., 2007; Cooper & Yuille, 2007; Griesel, 2008), clearly more research is needed. We suggest that a combination of methods (i.e., laboratory, archival, and field research) be used to study eyewitness memory (also see Paz-Alonso et al., present volume; Yuille, 1993) and to assess and refine our theoretical underpinnings and predictions. At the very least, we suggest that researchers and practitioners pay more attention to individual and situational differences and how they relate to eyewitness memory. Indeed, as reviewed throughout this chapter, there a host of biopsychosocial variables that influence the quality, quantity, and veracity of eyewitness memory. Whether in research or practice, we suggest that investigators assess for predisposing factors (e.g., arousal sensitivity, psychiatric history, neurocognitive impairments), precipitating factors (e.g., state dissociation, arousal, affect, substance use, nature of event), and perpetuating factors (e.g., previous recall attempts, the recall context, types of questions asked, PTSD symptoms) in mock and actual eyewitnesses to be in a better position to explain the observed memory processes and patterns. As detailed above, each of these factors should impact eyewitness memory directly and indirectly and individually and collectively.

Until more research has been conducted on eyewitness memory in general and on our theory in particular, this model of eyewitness memory should be used with caution. As others have suggested (see Yarbrough et al., present volume), effective interviewing (e.g., of witnesses to crimes) is impacted by the investigative interviewer's knowledge of memory processes and patterns. A biopsychosocial basis for understanding these issues would no doubt assist investigative interviews in becoming more effective. For example, knowing that the use of leading/suggestive questions/interviews could negatively impact eyewitness memory would help interviewers avoid such tactics and ask better, memory-compatible questions. Moreover, knowing that different types of eyewitnesses are more or less susceptible to arousal mediated memory distortions should assist interviewers in making sense of the memory patterns they receive from eyewitnesses. Indeed, assessing the credibility of an account of a crime is heavily dependent on effective interviewing and knowledge of how memory works (see Colwell, Hiscock-Anisman, & Fede, present volume; Griesel, Ternes, Schraml, Cooper, & Yuille, present volume; ten Brinke & Porter, present volume). The pattern of memory that a witness displays should be predictable based on the Hervé et al. (2007) model, with deviations explained within the context of the mediating/moderating variables described throughout this chapter. Otherwise, the credibility of the witness' account should be questioned.

In terms of expert testimony on eyewitness memory issues, it seems clear that eyewitness memory for criminal events is a complex phenomenon mediated by a number of biopsychosocial variables. Simplistic statements by expert witnesses about the negative effects of stress/arousal on memory, for example, are unwarranted (Cooper et al., 2010; Griesel & Yuille, 2012; Yuille et al., 2010; Yuille & Cooper, 2012). Experts would be in a better position to assist the triers of fact if expert testimony—based on laboratory, archival and field research—is evidence based, balanced, and limitations to expert opinions are highlighted, not minimized. This would promote the role of being a true friend of the court.

References

American Psychiatric Association. (2000). *Diagnostic and statistical manual of mental disorders* (Rev.4th ed., Text Revision), Washington, DC: Author.

Bala, N. (1996). False memory 'syndrome': Backlash or *bona fide* defense? *Queens Law Journal, 21*, 423–456.

Behrman, B. W., & Davey, S. L. (2001). Eyewitness identification in actual criminal cases: An archival analysis. *Law and Human Behavior, 25*(5), 475–491.

Blackburn, R. (1979). Cortical and autonomic arousal in primary and secondary psychopaths. *Psychophysiology, 16*(2), 143–150.

Blair, R. J. R., Sellars, C., Strickland, I., Clark, F., Williams, A. O., Smith, M., & Jones, L. (1995). Emotion attributions in the psychopath. *Personality and Individual Differences, 19*(4), 431–437.

Blascovich, J. (1990). Individual differences in physiological arousal and perceptions of arousal: Missing links between Jamesian notions of arousal-based behaviours. *Personality & Social Psychology Bulletin, 16*, 665–675.

Blascovich, J. (1992). A biopsychosocial approach to arousal regulation. *Journal of Social and Clinical Psychology, 11*, 213–237.

Bockheler, J. F. N. (1995). Parachuting: Fear or excitement- A matter of experience. *European Review of Applied Psychology, 45*(2), 83–91.

Bothwell, R. K., Brigham, J. C., & Pigott, M. A. (1987). An exploratory study of personality differences in eyewitness memory. *Journal of Social Behavior and Personality, 2*, 335–343.

Bradley, M. M., & Greenwald, M. K. (1992). Remembering pictures: Pleasure and arousal in memory. *Journal of Experimental Psychology: Learning, Memory, and Cognition, 8*(2), 379–390.

Brown, D., Scheflin, A. W., & Hammond, D. C. (1997). *Memory, trauma treatment, and the law.* New York, NY: W.W. Norton.

Bruck, M., Ceci, S. J., & Hembrooke, H. (1998). Reliability and credibility of young children's reports: From research to policy and practice. *American Psychologist, 53*(2), 136–151.

Burke, A., Heuer, F., & Reisberg, D. (1992). Remembering emotional events. *Memory & Cognition, 20,* 277–290.

Caine, E. D., & Lyness, J. M. (2000). Delirium, dementia, and amnestic and other cognitive disorders. In B. J. Sadock & V. A. Sadock (Eds.), *Comprehensive textbook of psychiatry* (7th Edition, Vol. 1, pp. 854–923). Philadelphia, PA: Lippincott Williams & Wilkins.

Cardeña, E. (1994). The domain of dissociation. In S. J. Lynn & J. W. Rhue (Eds.), *Dissociation: Clinical and theoretical perspectives* (pp. 15–31). New York, NY: The Guilford press.

Ceci, S. J., & Bruck, M. (1993). Suggestibility of the child witness: A historical review and synthesis. *Psychological Bulletin, 113*(3), 403–439.

Charland, L. C. (1997). Reconciling cognitive and perceptual theories of emotion: A representational proposal. *Philosophy of Science, 64*(4), 555–579.

Christianson, S.-A. (1989). Flashbulb memories: Special, but not so special. *Memory & Cognition, 17*(4), 435–443.

Christianson, S.-A. (1992). Emotional stress and eyewitness memory: A critical review. *Psychological Bulletin, 112*(2), 284–309.

Christianson, S.-A., & Hubinette, B. (1993). Hands up! A study of witness' emotional reactions and memories with bank robberies. *Applied Cognitive Psychology, 7,* 365–379.

Christianson, S.-A., & Loftus, E. F. (1990). Some characteristics of people's traumatic memories. *Bulletin of the Psychonomic Society, 28,* 195–198.

Christianson, S.-A., & Loftus, E. F. (1991). Remembering emotional events: The fate of detailed information. *Cognition & Emotion, 5,* 81–108.

Christianson, S.-A., & Nilsson, L. (1989). Hysterical amnesia: A case of aversively motivated isolation of memory. In T. Archer & L. Nilsson (Eds.), *Aversion, avoidance and anxiety: Perspectives on aversively motivated behavior* (pp. 289–310). Hillsdale, NJ: Lawrence Erlbaum.

Christianson, S.-A., Forth, A. E., Hare, R. D., Strachan, C., Lidberg, L., & Lars-Hakan, T. (1996). Remembering details of emotional events: A comparison between psychopathic and nonpsychopathic offenders. *Personality and Individual Differences, 20*(4), 437–443.

Chu, J. A. (1998). Dissociative symptomatology in adult patients with histories of childhood physical and sexual abuse. In C. R. Bremner & C. R. Marmar (Eds.), *Trauma, memory and dissociation* (pp. 179–203). Washington, DC: American Psychiatric Press.

Chu, J. A., & Dill, D. L. (1990). Dissociative symptoms in relation to childhood physical and sexual abuse. *The American Journal of Psychiatry, 147*(7), 887–892.

Clifford, B. R., & Hollin, C. R. (1981). Effects of the type of incident and the number of perpetrators on eyewitness memory. *Journal of Applied Psychology, 66*(3), 364–370.

Conway, M. A. (1997). Introduction: What are memories? In M. A. Conway (Ed.), *Recovered memories and false memories* (pp. 1–22). Oxford: Oxford University Press.

Cooper, B. S. (1999). *Post-traumatic stress and dissociative autobiographical memories: Overview and exploratory study in a sample of prostitutes.* Unpublished Master's thesis. University of British Columbia, Vancouver, BC.

Cooper, B. S. (2005). *Memory for mayhem.* Dissertation Abstracts International.

Cooper, B. S., Cuttler, C., Dell, P., & Yuille, J. C. (2006). Dissociation and amnesia: A study with male offenders. *International Journal of Forensic Psychology, 1*(3), 69–83.

Cooper, B. S., Hervé, H. F., & Yuille, J. C. (2003). *Canadian violent offenders' memories for crimes and traumas.* Paper presented at the Society for Applied Research on Memory and Cognition's conference, Aberdeen, Scotland.

Cooper, B. S., Hervé, H. F., & Yuille, J. C. (2007). Psychopathy and memory for violence. *International Journal of Forensic Mental Health, 6*(2), 123–135.

Cooper, B. S., Hervé, H. F., & Yuille, J. C. (2010). *Memory on trial: Expert testimony by psychologists.* Paper presented at the International Association of Forensic Mental Health Services conference, Vancouver, BC.

Cooper, B. S., Hervé, H. F., & Yuille, J. C. (2012). *Supervising and managing sex offenders: An introduction to effective interviewing and evaluating truthfulness.* Invited presentation. Association for the Treatment of Sexual Abusers, Mid-Atlantic Region Chapter, Harrisburg, PN.

Cooper, B. S., Kennedy, M. A., Hervé, H. F., & Yuille, J. C. (2002). Weapon focus in sexual assault memories of prostitutes. *International Journal of Law and Psychiatry, 25,* 181–191.

Cooper, B. S., Kennedy, M. A., & Yuille, J. C. (2001). Dissociation and sexual trauma in prostitutes: Variability of responses. *Journal of Trauma & Dissociation, 2*(2), 27–36.

Cooper, B. S., Kennedy, M. A., & Yuille, J. C. (2004). Traumatic stress in prostitutes: A within-subject comparison of PTSD symptom levels across sexual and non-sexual traumatic experiences. *Journal of Trauma Practice, 3*(1), 51–70.

Cooper, B. S., & Yuille, J. C. (2007). Offenders' memories for instrumental and reactive violence. In S.-A. Christianson (Ed.), *Offenders' memories of violent crimes* (pp. 75–97). Chichester, England: John Wiley and Sons.

Cooper, B. S., Yuille, J. C., & Kennedy, M. A. (2002). Divergent perspectives in prostitutes' autobiographical memories: Trauma and dissociation. *Journal of Trauma & Dissociation, 3*(3), 75–95.

Critchley, H. G. (2005). Neural mechanisms of autonomic, affective, and cognitive integration. *The Journal of Comparative Neurology, 493,* 154–166.

Cutshall, J. L., & Yuille, J. C. (1989). Field studies of eyewitness memory of actual crimes. In D. C. Raskin (Ed.), *Psychological methods in criminal investigation and evidence* (pp. 97–124). New York, NY: Springer.

Darlington, Y. (1996). Escape as a response to childhood sexual abuse. *Journal of Childhood Sexual Abuse, 5*(3), 77–93.

Darves-Bornoz, J. M. (1997). Rape-related psychotraumatic syndromes. *European Journal of Obstetrics, Gynecology, and Reproductive Biology, 71,* 59–65.

Darves-Bornoz, J. M., Pierre, F., Lepine, J. P., Degiovanni, A., & Gaillard, P. (1998). Screening for psychologically traumatized rape victims. *European Journal of Obstetrics, Gynecology, and Reproductive Biology, 77,* 71–75.

Deffenbacher, K. A. (1983). The influence of arousal on reliability of testimony. In S. M. A. Lloyd-Bostock & B. R. Clifford (Eds.), *Evaluating witness evidence* (pp. 235–251). Chichester: Wiley.

Deffenbacher, K. A., Bornstein, B. H., Penrod, S. D., & McGorty, E. K. (2004). A meta-analytic review of the effects of high stress on eyewitness memory. *Law and Human Behavior, 28*(6), 687–706.

Deffenbacher, K. A., Bornstein, B. H., & Penrod, S. D. (2006). Mugshot exposure effects: Retroactive interference, mugshot commitment, source confusion and unconscious transference. *Law and Human Behavior, 30*(3), 287–307.

Douglass, A. B., & Steblay, N. (2006). Memory distortion in eyewitnesses: A meta-analysis of the post-identification feedback effect. *Applied Cognitive Psychology, 20,* 859–869.

Dunmore, E., Clark, D. M., & Ehlers, A. (1999). Cognitive factors involved in the onset and maintenance of posttraumatic stress disorder (PTSD) after physical or sexual assault. *Behavior Research and Therapy, 37,* 809–829.

Dutton, D. G. (1995). *The batterer.* New York, NY: Basic Books.

Dutton, D. G., & Yamini, S. (1995). Adolescent parricide: An integration of social cognitive theory and clinical views of projective-introjective cycling. *The American Journal of Orthopsychiatry, 65*(1), 39–47.

Dysart, J. E., Lawson, V. Z., & Rainey, A. (2011). Blind lineup administration as a prophylactic against the post-identification feedback effect. *Law and Human Behavior.* doi:10.1037/h0093921.

Easterbrook, J. A. (1959). The effect of emotion on cue utilization and the organization of behavior. *Psychological Review, 66*(3), 183–201.

Eich, E. (1987). Theoretical issues in state dependent memory. In H. L. Roediger & F. I. M. Craik (Eds.), *Varieties of memory and consciousness: Essays in honour of Endel Tulving* (pp. 331–354). Hillsdale, NJ: Lawrence Erlbaum.

Eich, E. (1995). Searching for mood dependent memory. *Psychological Science, 6*, 67–75.
Ellis, L. (1987). Relationship of criminality and psychopathy with eight other apparent behavioral manifestations of sub-optimal arousal. *Personality and Individual Differences, 8*(6), 905–925.
Erdelyi, M. H., & Kleinbard, J. (1978). Has Ebbinghaus decayed with time? The growth of recall (hypernesia) over days. *Journal of Experimental Psychology: Human Learning and Memory, 4*(4), 275–289.
Eysenck, M. W. (1967). *The biological basis of personality*. Springfield, IL: Thomas.
Feldman, L. A. (1995). Valence focus and arousal focus: Individual differences in the structure of affective experience. *Journal of Personality and Social Psychology, 69*(1), 150–166.
Fisher, R. P., & Geiselman, R. E. (1992). *Memory-enhancing techniques for investigative interviewing: The cognitive interview*. Springfield, IL: Charles C. Thomas.
Godden, D. R., & Baddeley, A. D. (1975). Context-dependent memory in two natural environments: On land and underwater. *British Journal of Psychology, 66*, 325–332.
Goodwin, D. W. (1995). Alcohol amnesia. *Addiction, 90*(3), 315–317.
Goodwin, D. W., Crane, J. B., & Guze, S. B. (1969). Alcohol "blackouts": A review and clinical study of 100 alcoholics. *The American Journal of Psychiatry, 162*(2), 77–84.
Goodwin, D. W., Powell, B., Bremer, D., Hoine, H., & Stern, J. (1969). Alcohol and recall: State-dependent effects in man. *Science, 163*, 1358–1360.
Griesel, D. (2008). *An investigation of trauma and its cognitive and emotional consequences in prostituted victims of sexual crimes*. Unpublished doctoral dissertation. University of British Columbia, Vancouver, BC.
Griesel, D., & Yuille, J. C. (2012). Sex trade workers' narratives of sexual violence: A field investigation. *Memory*. doi:10.1080/09658211.2012.654797.
Griesel, D., Cooper, B. S., & Yuille, J. C. (2004). *Victims of trauma and perpetrators of violent crime: The development of PTSD symptoms in male violent offenders*. Paper presented at the 4th Annual Conference of the International Association of Forensic Mental Health Services, Stockholm, Sweden.
Gudjonsson, G. H. (1992). The psychology of false confessions and ways to improve the system. *Expert Evidence, 1*(2), 49–53.
Guttmacher, M. S. (1960). *The mind of the murderer*. New York, NY: Farrar, Straus and Cudahy.
Hare, R. D. (1965). Psychopathy, fear arousal and anticipated pain. *Psychological Reports, 16*, 499–502.
Herman, J. L. (1996). Crime and memory. In C. B. Strozier & M. Flynn (Eds.), *Trauma and self* (pp. 3–17). London: Rowman & Littlefield publishers, Inc.
Hervé, H. F. & Cooper, B. S. (2008). *Who us? A biopsychosocial model for assessing malingering*. Paper presented at the Canadian Psychological Association's conference, Halifax, NS.
Hervé, H. F., Cooper, B. S., & Yuille, J. C. (2007). Memory formation in offenders: Perspectives from a biopsychosocial theory of eyewitness memory. In S.-A. Christianson (Ed.), *Offenders' memories of violent crimes* (pp. 37–74). Chichester: Wiley.
Hervé, H. F., Cooper, B. S., & Yuille, J. C. (2012). *Extreme behaviours in the workplace: A multidisciplinary approach to threat assessment and management*. Presented at the Unique Perspectives on Workplace Violence Workshop, Vancouver, BC.
Hervé, H. F., & Hare, R. D. (1998). *Psychopathy: A deficit in multidimensional emotional processing*. Paper presented at the Biennial Meeting of the American Psychology-Law Society, Los Angeles, CA.
Hillman, R. G. (1981). The psychopathology of being held hostage. *The American Journal of Psychiatry, 138*(9), 1193–1197.
Holtgraves, T., & Stockdale, G. (1997). The assessment of dissociative experiences in a non-clinical population: Reliability, validity, and factor structure of the dissociative experiences scale. *Personality and Individual Differences, 22*(5), 669–706.
Horowitz, M. J., Wilner, H., & Alvarez, W. (1979). Impact of Events Scale: A measure of subjective distress. *Psychosomatic Medicine, 41*(3), 209–218.
Hyman, I. E., Jr., & Loftus, E. F. (1997). Some people recover memories of childhood trauma that never really happened. In P. S. Appelbaum, L. A. Uyehara, & M. R. Elin (Eds.), *Trauma and memory: Clinical and legal controversies* (pp. 3–23). New York, NY: Oxford University Press.
International Criminal Tribunal for the former Yugoslavia vs. Anto Furundzija. (1995). Case number: IT-95-17/1-T. http://www.un.org/icty/transel17-1/980622ed.htm.

Janet, P. (1920). The major symptoms of hysteria. *Fifteen lectures Given in the Medical School of Harvard University* (Lecture II, Monoideic Somambulisms, pp. 22–43). New York, NY: Macmillan.

King, M. A., & Yuille, J. C. (1987). Suggestibility and the child witness. In S. J. Ceci, M. P. Toglia, & D. F. Ross (Eds.), *Children's eyewitness memory* (pp. 24–35). New York, NY: Springer.

Klein, E., Caspi, Y., & Gil, S. (2003). The relation between memory of the traumatic event and PTSD: Evidence from studies of traumatic brain injury. *Canadian Journal of Psychiatry, 48*(1), 28–33.

Koopman, C., Classen, C., & Spiegel, D. A. (1994). Predictors of posttraumatic stress symptoms among survivors of the Oakland/Berkeley, Calif., firestorm. *The American Journal of Psychiatry, 151*(6), 888–894.

Kramer, T. H., Buckhout, R., & Eugenio, P. (1990). Weapon focus, arousal, and eyewitness memory. *Law and Human Behavior, 14*(2), 167–184.

Kuehn, L. L. (1974). Looking down a gun barrel: Person perception and violent crime. *Perceptual and Motor Skills, 39*, 1159–1164.

Larsen, R. J., & Diener, E. (1992). Affect intensity as an individual difference characteristic: A review. *Journal of Research in Personality, 21*, 1–39.

Lazo, J. (1995). True or false: Expert testimony on repressed memory. *Loyola of Los Angeles Law Review, 28*(3–4), 1345–1414.

Leitch, A. (1948). Notes on amnesia in crime for the general practitioner. *The Medical Press, 26*, 459–463.

Leo, R. A. (1998). The social and legal construction of repressed memory. *Law & Social Inquiry, 22*, 653–694.

Levenson, R. W. (1988). Emotion and the autonomic nervous system: A prospectus for research on autonomic specificity. In H. L. Wagner (Ed.), *Social psychophysiology and emotions: Theory and clinical applications* (pp. 17–42). Chichester: John Wiley & Sons.

Levenson, R. W. (1992). Autonomic nervous system differences among emotions. *Psychological Science, 3*(1), 23–27.

Lindsay, D. S., & Read, J. D. (1994). Psychotherapy and memories of childhood sexual abuse: A cognitive perspective. *Applied Cognitive Psychology, 8*, 281–338.

Loftus, E. F. (1993). The reality of repressed memories. *American Psychologist, 48*, 518–537.

Loftus, E. F. (2012). *Illusions of memory*. Invited presentation: Simon Fraser University, Vancouver, British Columbia, Canada.

Loftus, E. F., & Burns, T. (1982). Mental shock can produce retrograde amnesia. *Memory & Cognition, 10*(4), 318–323.

Loftus, E. F., Loftus, G. R., & Messo, J. (1987). Some facts about "weapon focus." *Law and Human Behavior, 11*(1), 55–62.

Loftus, E. F., & Pickrell, J. E. (1995). The formation of false memories. *Psychiatric Annals, 25*, 720–725.

Mandler, G. (1984). *Mind and body*. New York, NY: Norton.

Marmar, C. R. & Weiss, D. S. (1994). *Peritraumatic dissociative experiences questionnaire—Rater version*. Received from authors.

Marmar, C. R., Weiss, D. S., Schlenger, W. E., Fairbank, J. A., Jordan, B. K., Kulka, R. A., & Hough, R. L. (1994). Peritraumatic dissociation and posttraumatic stress in male Vietnam theater veterans. *The American Journal of Psychiatry, 151*(6), 902–907.

Mechanic, M. B., Resick, P. A., & Griffin, M. G. (1998). A comparison of normal forgetting, psychopathology, and information-processing models of reported amnesia for recent sexual trauma. *Journal of Consulting and Clinical Psychology, 66*(6), 948–957.

Memon, A., Holley, A., Wark, L., Bull, R., & Kohnken, G. (1996). Reducing suggestibility in child witness interviews. *Applied Cognitive Psychology, 10*, 503–518.

Mitchell, G. (2012). Revisiting the truth or triviality: The external validity of research in the laboratory. *Perspectives on Psychological Science, 7*(2), 109–117.

Morgan, C. A., III, Hazlett, G., Doran, A., Garrett, S., Hoyt, G., Thomas, P., Baranoski, M., & Southwick, S. M. (2004). Accuracy of eyewitness memory for persons encountered during exposure to highly intense stress. *International Journal of Law and Psychiatry, 27*, 265–279.

Nash, M. R. (1994). Memory distortion and sexual trauma: The problem of false negatives and false positives. *The International Journal of Clinical and Experimental Hypnosis, XLII*(4), 346–362.
Nelson, K., & Gruendel, J. (1981). Generalized event representations: Basic building blocks of cognitive development. In A. Brown & M. Lamb (Eds.), *Advances in developmental psychology* (pp. 131–158). Hillsdale: Erlbaum.
Nigro, G., & Neisser, U. (1983). Point of view in personal memories. *Cognitive Psychology, 15*, 467–482.
O'Connell, B. A. (1960). Amnesia and homicide: A study of 50 murderers. *British Journal of Delinquency, 10*, 262–276.
O'Rourke, T. E., Penrod, S. D., Cutler, B. L., & Stuve, T. E. (1989). The external validity of eyewitness identification research: Generalizing across subject populations. *Law and Human Behavior, 13*(4), 385–395.
O'Toole, B. I., Marshall, R. P., Schureck, R. J., & Dobson, M. (1999). Combat, dissociation, and posttraumatic stress disorder in Australian Vietnam veterans. *Journal of Traumatic Stress, 12*(4), 625–640.
Odinot, G., Wolters, G., & van Koppen, P. J. (2009). Eyewitness memory of a supermarket robbery: A case study of accuracy and confidence after 3 months. *Law and Human Behavior, 33*(6), 506–514.
Ofshe, R. O. (1992). Inadvertent hypnosis during interrogation: False confession due to dissociative state; Mis-identified multiple personality and the satanic cult hypothesis. *The International Journal of Clinical and Experimental Hypnosis, XL*(3), 125–156.
Op den Velde, W., Aarts, P. G. H., Falger, P. R. J., Hovens, J. E., Frey-Wouters, E., & Van Duijn, H. (1996). Prevalence and course of posttraumatic stress disorder in Dutch veterans of the civilian resistance during World War II: An overview. *Psychological Reports, 78*, 519–529.
Parwatikar, S. D., Holcomb, W. R., & Menninger, K. A. (1985). The detection of malingered amnesia in accused murderers. *The Bulletin of the American Academy of Psychiatry and the Law, 13*(1), 97–103.
Pickel, K. L. (1998). Unusualness and threat as possible causes of "weapon focus." *Memory, 6*(3), 277–295.
Pickel, K. L. (1999). The influence of context on the "weapon focus" effect. *Law and Human Behavior, 23*(3), 299–311.
Pollock, P. H. (1999). When the killer suffers: Post-traumatic stress reactions following homicide. *Legal and Criminological Psychology, 4*, 185–202.
Porter, S. (1996). Without conscience or without active conscious? The etiology of psychopathy revisited. *Aggression and Violent Behavior, 1*(2), 179–189.
Porter, S., Birt, A. R., & Yuille, J. C. (2000). Negotiating false memories: Influence of interviewer and rememberer characteristics on memory distortion. *Psychological Science, 11*(6), 507–510.
Porter, S., Birt, A. R., Yuille, J. C., & Hervé, H. F. (2001). Memory for murder: A psychological perspective on dissociative amnesia in legal contexts. *International Journal of Law and Psychiatry, 24*, 23–42.
Porter, S., Yuille, J. C., & Lehman, D. L. (1999). The nature of real, implanted, and fabricated memories for emotional childhood events: Implications for the recovered memory debate. *Law and Human Behavior, 23*(5), 517–537.
Power, M. J., & Dalgleish, T. (1999). Two routes to emotion: Some implications of multi-level theories of emotion for therapeutic practice. *Behavioural and Cognitive Psychotherapy, 27*, 129–141.
R v. Stephens (2000). No. CC990312 S.C.B.C.
Radomsky, A. S., & Rachman, S. (1999). Memory bias in obsessive-compulsive disorder (OCD). *Behaviour Research and Therapy, 37*(7), 605–618.
Radomsky, A. S., & Rachman, S. (2001). *The use of words and other meaningless stimuli in OCD memory research*. Vancouver, BC. Paper presented at the World Congress of Behavioural and Cognitive Psychotherapies.
Radomsky, A. S., Rachman, S., & Hammond, D. (2001). Memory bias, confidence and responsibility in compulsive checking. *Behaviour Research and Therapy, 39*(7), 813–822.

Read, J. D., Yuille, J. C., & Tollestrup, P. (1992). Recollections of a robbery: Effects of arousal and alcohol upon recall and person identification. *Law and Human Behavior, 16*, 425–446.

Reisberg, D. (1997). *Cognition: Exploring the science of the mind*. London: W.W. Norton & Company.

Robinson, J. A., & Swanson, K. L. (1993). Field and observer modes of remembering. *Memory, 1*(3), 169–184.

Russell, J. A. (1980). A circumplex model of affect. *Journal of Personality and Social Psychology, 39*(6), 1161–1178.

Russell, J. A. (1989). Measures of emotion. In R. Plutchik & H. Kellerman (Eds.), *Emotion: Theory, research, and experience* (pp. 83–111). Toronto, ON: Academic.

Russell, J. A. (2003). Core affect and the psychological construction of emotion. *Psychological Review, 110*(1), 145–172.

Russell, J. A., & Bullock, M. (1985). Multidimensional scaling of emotional facial expressions: Similarity from preschoolers to adults. *Journal of Personality and Social Psychology, 38*, 1290–1298.

Russell, J. A., & Bullock, M. (1986). Fussy concepts and the perception of emotion in facial expressions. *Social Cognition, 4*, 309–341.

Safer, M. A., Christianson, S., Autry, M. W., & Osterland, K. (1998). Tunnel memory for traumatic events. *Applied Cognitive Psychology, 12*, 99–117.

Schachter, S. (1971). *Emotion, obesity, and crime*. New York, NY: Academic.

Schacter, D. L. (1996). *Searching for memory*. New York, NY: Basic Books.

Schacter, D. L. (2001). *The seven sins of memory: How the mind forgets and remembers*. New York, NY: Houghton Mifflin Company.

Scrivner, E., & Safer, M. A. (1988). Eyewitnesses show hypernesia for details about a violent event. *Journal of Applied Psychology, 73*(3), 371–377.

Semmler, C., Brewer, N., & Wells, G. L. (2004). Effects of postidentification feedback on eyewitness identification and nonidentification confidence. *Journal of Applied Psychology, 89*(2), 334–346.

Smith, C. A., & Ellsworth, P. C. (1985). Patterns of cognitive appraisal in emotion. *Journal of Personality and Social Psychology, 48*, 813–838.

Southwick, S. M., Morgan, C. A., III, Nicolaou, A. L., & Charney, D. S. (1997). Consistency of memory for combat-related traumatic events in veterans of operation desert storm. *The American Journal of Psychiatry, 154*(2), 173–177.

Spiegel, D. (1993). Dissociation and trauma. In D. Spiegel, R. P. Kluft, R. J. Loewenstein, J. C. Nemiah, F. W. Putman, & M. Steinberg (Eds.), *Dissociative disorders: A clinical review* (pp. 117–131). Lutherville, MD: Sidran Press.

Spiegel, D., & Cardeña, E. (1991). Disintegrated experience: The dissociative disorders revisited. *Journal of Abnormal Psychology, 100*(3), 366–378.

Stern, W. (1904). Realistic experiments. Wirklichkeitsversuche, *Beitrage zur Psychology der Aussage, 2*(1), 1–31 (Translation by U. Neisser and reprinted in U. Neisser & I.E. Hyman, Jr. (Eds.), *Memory observed: Remembering in natural contexts* (2nd ed.), (2000). New York, NY: Worth)".

Swihart, G., Yuille, J. C., & Porter, S. (1999). The role of state dependent memory in "red outs." *International Journal of Law and Psychiatry, 125*, 199–212.

Tanay, E. (1969). Psychiatric study of homicide. *The American Journal of Psychiatry, 125*(9), 1252–1258.

Ternes, M., & Yuille, J. C. (2008). Eyewitness memory and eyewitness identification performance in adults with intellectual disabilities. *Journal of Applied Research in Intellectual Disabilities, 21*(6), 519–531.

Terr, L. C. (1991). Childhood traumas: An outline and overview. *The American Journal of Psychiatry, 148*(1), 10–20.

Terry, W. S., & Barwick, E. C. (1995). Observer versus field memories in repressive, low anxious, and obsessive-compulsive subjects. *Imagination, Cognition, and Personality, 15*(2), 159–169.

Thompson, J., Morton, J., & Fraser, L. (1997). Memories for the marchioness. *Memory, 5*(5), 615–638.

Thorpe, S. J., & Salkovskis, P. M. (1998). Selective attention to real phobic and safety stimuli. *Behavioral Research and Therapy, 36*, 471–481.

Tollestrup, P. A., Turtle, J. W., & Yuille, J. C. (1994). Actual victims and witnesses to robbery and fraud: An archival analysis. In D. Ross, D. Read, & S. Ceci (Eds.), *Adult eyewitness testimony: Current trends and developments* (pp. 144–160). New York, NY: Press syndicate of the University of Cambridge.

Valentine, T., Pickering, A., & Darling, S. (2003). Characteristics of eyewitness identifications that predict the outcome of real lineups. *Applied Cognitive Psychology, 17*(8), 969–993.

van der Kolk, B. A. (1996). Trauma and memory. In B. A. van der Kolk, A. C. McFarlane, & L. Weisaeth (Eds.), *Traumatic stress: The effects of overwhelming experience on mind, body, and society* (pp. 279–302). New York, NY: Guilford Press.

van der Kolk, B. A. (1997). The psychobiology of posttraumatic stress disorder. *The Journal of Clinical Psychiatry, 58*, 16–22.

van der Kolk, B. A., & Fisler, R. (1995). Dissociation and the fragmentary nature of traumatic memories: Overview and exploratory study. *Journal of Traumatic Stress, 8*(4), 505–525.

van der Kolk, B. A., McFarlane, A. C., & Weisaeth, L. (1996). *Traumatic stress: The effects of overwhelming experience on mind, body, and society*. New York, NY: Guilford Press.

van der Kolk, B. A., & van der Hart, O. (1989). Pierre Janet and the breakdown of adaptation in psychological trauma. *The American Journal of Psychiatry, 146*(12), 1530–1540.

van der Kolk, B. A., van der Hart, O., & Marmar, C. R. (1996). Dissociation and information processing in posttraumatic stress disorder. In B. A. van der Kolk, A. C. McFarlane, & L. Weisaeth (Eds.), *Traumatic stress: The effects of overwhelming experience on mind, body, and society* (pp. 303–327). New York, NY: Guilford Press.

Vella, S. M. (1998). Recovered traumatic memory in historical childhood sexual abuse cases: Credibility on trial. *UBC Law Review, 55*(set 3), 91–125.

Watson, D., Clark, L. A., & Tellegen, A. (1988). Development and validation of brief measures of positive and negative affect: The PANAS scales. *Journal of Personality and Social Psychology, 54*(6), 1063–1070.

Weisaeth, L. (1989). Torture of a Norwegians ship's crew: The torture, stress reactions and psychiatric after-effects. *Acta Psychiatrica Scandinavica, 80*(355), 63–72.

Wells, G. L., Olson, E. A., & Charman, S. D. (2003). Distorted retrospective eyewitness reports as functions feedback and delay. *Journal of Experimental Psychology. Applied, 9*(1), 42–52.

Wells, G. L., Small, M., Penrod, S., Malpass, R. S., Fulero, S. M., & Brimacombe, C. A. E. (1998). Eyewitness identification procedures: Recommendations for lineups and photospreads. *Law and Human Behaviour, 22*, 1–39.

Wells, G. L., & Turtle, J. W. (1987). Eyewitness testimony research: Current knowledge and emergent controversies. *Canadian Journal of Behavioral Sciences, 19*(4), 363–388.

Wright, D. B., & Skagerberg, E. M. (2007). Post-identification feedback affects real eyewitnesses. *Psychological Science, 18*, 172–178.

Yerkes, R. M., & Dodson, J. D. (1908). The relation of strength of stimulus to rapidity of habit-information. *Journal of Comparative Neurological Psychology, 18*, 459–482.

Yuille, J. C. (1993). We must study forensic eyewitnesses to know about them. *American Psychologist, 48*(5), 572–573.

Yuille, J. C., & Cooper, B. S. (2012). Challenging the eyewitness expert. In D. Faust & J. Ziskin (Eds.), *Coping with psychiatric and psychological testimony*, 6th Edition (pp. 685–695). New York, NY: Oxford University Press.

Yuille, J. C., & Cutshall, J. L. (1986). A case study of eyewitness memory of a crime. *Journal of Applied Psychology, 71*(2), 291–301.

Yuille, J. C., & Daylen, J. (1998). The impact of traumatic events on eyewitness memory. In C. Thompson, D. Herman, D. Read, D. Bruce, D. Payne, & M. Toglia (Eds.), *Eyewitness memory: Theoretical and applied perspectives* (pp. 155–178). Mahwah, NJ: Lawrence Erlbaum.

Yuille, J. C., Marxsen, D., & Cooper, B. S. (1999). Training investigative interviewers: Adherence to the spirit, as well as to the letter. *International Journal of Law and Psychiatry, 22*(3), 323–336.

Yuille, J. C., Ternes, M., & Cooper, B. S. (2010). Expert testimony on laboratory witnesses. *Journal of Forensic Psychology Practice, 10*(3), 238–251.

Yuille, J. C., & Tollestrup, P. A. (1992). A model of the diverse effects of emotion on eyewitness memory. In S.-A. Christianson (Ed.), *The handbook of emotion and memory: Research and theory* (pp. 201–215). Hillsdale, NJ: Lawrence Erlbaum.

Yuille, J. C., Tollestrup, P. A., Marxsen, D., Porter, S., & Hervé, H. F. (1998). An exploration on the effects of marijuana on eyewitness memory. *International Journal of Law and Psychiatry, 21*(1), 117–128.

Zuckerman, M. (1979). *Sensation seeking: Beyond the optimal level of arousal.* London: Wiley.

Chapter 6
Children's Memory in "Scientific Case Studies" of Child Sexual Abuse: A Review

Pedro M. Paz-Alonso, Christin M. Ogle, and Gail S. Goodman

Introduction

Yuille and Cutshall (1986) published a landmark study of adults' eyewitness memory. A tragic shooting in front of a gun shop—killing one person and seriously injuring a second—occurred before the startled eyes of 21 witnesses, varying in age from 15 to 32 years. After the shooting, the witnesses were interviewed by the police and then, fortunately, a subset of them later agreed to be interviewed by the research team. In this way, the witnesses' memory was evaluated up to 5 months after the event. Yuille and Cutshall concluded that:

> "The witnesses were very accurate in their accounts, and there was little change in amount or accuracy of recall over 5 months. However, some aspects of colour memory, and age, height, and weight estimations were found to be subject to error. The eyewitnesses resisted leading questions, and their stress level at the time of the event appeared to have no negative effects on subsequent memory. The results differ from the pattern of many laboratory studies of eyewitness memory and point to the need for field research of this type to evaluate the generalizability of laboratory experiments" (p. 291).

At that point in history, fascinating case studies concerning human memory had been written for centuries. What was so special about Yuille and Cutshall's (1986) research, however, was the excellent documentation of the shooting incident against which to evaluate the accuracy of the witnesses' memory. These findings flew in the face of laboratory researchers who emphasized the inaccuracies of eyewitness

---

P.M. Paz-Alonso
University of California, Davis, CA, USA

Basque Center on Cognition, Brain and Language (BCBL), San Sebastián, Spain

C.M. Ogle
Duke University, Durham, NC, USA

G.S. Goodman (✉)
University of California, Davis, CA, USA
e-mail: ggoodman@ucdavis.edu

accounts (see Yuille, present volume). Moreover, the research laid important groundwork for a new research paradigm, one we have called "the scientific case study" paradigm (Bidrose & Goodman, 2000). As applied to eyewitness testimony, this paradigm requires that researchers have at least some "ground truth" documentation of what actually occurred in a criminal or abusive event.

Years ago, Yuille and Cutshall published an important paper on the accuracy of adults' eyewitness memory of a real crime. In the present chapter, we extend that approach by reviewing studies on the accuracy of children's memories of sexual abuse. In these "scientific case studies" documented evidence (e.g., photographs) of abusive events existed permitting researchers to determine the accuracy of the child victims' statements. In our review, the main characteristics of the abusive events and the types of documentation are detailed, followed by a description of the findings regarding the accuracy and completeness of the children's memory reports. Second, we review recent case study research on false reports of child sexual abuse. Third, limitations and advantages of scientific case studies are discussed, followed by an integrative overview of more traditional methodology (e.g., laboratory studies) used to examine children's memory for stressful, inappropriate, and/or traumatic events. Findings from such research are compared to those from scientific case studies of children's memory of child sexual abuse[1]. Finally, we review research evidence derived from these various approaches in regard to the effects of cognitive and social factors on children's memory for emotional, stressful, and traumatic events.

It should be noted that a subset of the studies reviewed profited from use of standardized child forensic interview protocols that were inspired by Yuille's Step-Wise Interview (Yuille, Hunter, Joffe, & Zaparniuk, 1993). Table 6.1 shows the main characteristics of the scientific case studies of CSA reviewed in this chapter. As can be seen from this table, the characteristics of the abusive events examined to date are heterogeneous, including, for example: single (Leander, Christianson, & Granhag, 2007; Leander, Granhag, & Christianson, 2005) and repetitive (Bidrose & Goodman, 2000; Orbach & Lamb, 1999) sexual encounters; sexual behaviors ranging from obscene phone calls (Leander et al., 2005) to genital touch (Leander et al., 2007) and penetration (Bidrose & Goodman, 2000); and intrafamilial (Orbach & Lamb, 1999) and extrafamilial (Bidrose & Goodman, 2000; Leander et al., 2005, 2007; Leander, Christianson, & Granhag, 2008) abuse cases. The extent of trauma resulting from this range of sexual encounters also likely varied considerably (Alexander et al., 2005; Clancy, 2009).

---

[1] Scientific cases studies of CSA can be considered a type of field research. However, compared to some other field-based approaches where researchers can design materials to test individuals' memory in regard to target events, scientific case studies of CSA typically examine existent legal reports in relation to documented evidence of the abusive events to draw conclusions about victims' memories of stressful, inappropriate, and/or traumatic experiences. For ease of communication, in this chapter, we distinguish scientific case studies from other forms of field research. We therefore use the terms "scientific case studies" and "field research" to designate separate approaches.

Table 6.1 Main characteristics of scientific case studies of CSA

Study	N and Gender	Age at abuse/ Disclosure	Sexual abuse or trauma type	Sexual acts[a]	Number of incidents	Duration of incident(s)	Delay to interview	Corroboration	Records examined
Cederborg et al. (2007)	10 boys	3.1–1.1 years/ 4.8–12.6 years	Extrafamilial (50%) Intrafamilial (50%)	Masturbation (70%) Oral (50%) and anal (40%) penetration	1–40	Variable	1.2–2.2 years	Videotapes	Victims' testimony Videotapes
Terr (1988)	20 (55% girls)	0.5–4.8 years /0.4–12 years older	Intra/Extrafamilial (30%) Accidents (25%) Abductions (20%) Witness Accidents (15%) Others (10%)	Child pornography Penetration	Repetitive Single (65%)	Variable	Variable	Injuries Confessions Photographs Eyewitnesses	Police Reports Photos Psychotherapy
Bidrose and Goodman (2000)	4 girls	8–15 years/ 0.2–1.2 years older	Extrafamilial (100%)	28 types of sexual acts, including intercourse and oral contact	6–49	2–14 months	Variable per victim, but short	Photographs Audiotape	Audiotapes Photographs
Orbach and Lamb (1999)	1 girl	11 years/13 years	Intrafamilial (100%)	Not specified	Repetitive	2 years	2–17 days after last abusive experience	Audiotape Confessions	Audiotape of last abusive experience Testimony of victim's sister

(continued)

Table 6.1 (continued)

Study	N and Gender	Age at abuse/ Disclosure	Sexual abuse or trauma type	Sexual acts[a]	Number of incidents	Duration of incident(s)	Delay to interview	Corroboration	Records examined
Leander et al. (2007)	8 (75% girls)	3–10 years/ 1–3 days (63%) 3.5–5.5 years (27%) older	Extrafamilial (100%) Abduction (25%)	Genital touch (100%) Attempted penetration (63%)	1	Short	1–3 days (5 cases) 3.5–5.5 years (3 cases)	Photographs Suspect's records Medical records Confession	Photos Confession Victims' testimony
Leander (2010)	27 (81% girls)	NA/5–17 years	Extrafamilial (15%) Intrafamilial (85%)	Genital touch (40%) Masturbation (30%) Anal, oral, vaginal penetration (30%)	Repetitive Single (44%)	Years (37%) Less than a year (63%)	1–3 days (56%) <1 year (37%) >1 year (7%)	Videotapes Pictures	Police interviews
Sjöberg and Lindblad (2002)	10 (10% girls)	Group $M=5.6$ years/ Group $M=6.9$ years	Extrafamilial (80%) Intrafamilial (20%)	Anal, oral, vaginal penetration Forced urination, defecation	1–60	3–23 months	3–23 months (police investigation)	Videotapes Pictures	Videotapes Police interviews

Study	N	Age	Relationship	Type of act	Number of acts	Duration	Time to disclosure	Source of information
Leander et al. (2005)	64 (80% girls)	8–16 years /0.1–1.9 years older	Extrafamilial (100%)	Obscene phone calls	1	Short	1–21 months after calls	Computer records Confession Victims' testimony Suspect records
Leander et al. (2008)	68 girls	11–19 years/ 12–19 years	Extrafamilial (100%)	Sexual recordings, On- and off-line meetings (40% engaged sexual acts)	1–74	1 week to 1 year	1–17 months	Computer records Computer chats Victims' testimony

[a]The percentages sum to over 100% because sexual acts in this study were reported based on the total number of children who suffer each of the sexual acts

Scientific Case Studies of Child Sexual Abuse

Research on CSA cases has been instrumental for understanding children's memory for traumatic events (see Connolly & Price, present volume). Outcomes from this research generally suggest that children can accurately recall traumatic experiences even after long delays; however, a certain percentage of individuals may fail to disclose their traumatic experiences, which may be due to such factors as young age, forgetting, lack of rehearsal (e.g., defensive avoidance), guilt, and/or embarrassment (e.g., Goodman-Brown, Edelstein, Goodman, Jones, & Gordon, 2003; Saywitz, Goodman, Nicholas, & Moan, 1991; Williams, 1994). Moreover, it is known from other research that memories for stressful and traumatic events are not indelible (e.g., Goodman et al., 2003; Williams, 1994), nor immune to distortion (Bruck, Ceci, Francoeur, & Barr, 1995), and memory inaccuracies may persist over time (London, Bruck, & Melnyk, 2009; Terr, 1983).

One important issue examined within case studies of CSA is whether abuse is disclosed by the child during forensic interviews. Factors that influence disclosure of abuse are of interest to researchers who aim to determine the optimal method of obtaining legally relevant information from suspected victims of child abuse (see Yarbrough, Hervé, & Harms, present volume). Investigations of the determinants of disclosure in scientific case studies reveal that nondisclosure may be influenced by social-emotional and memory-related factors, as well as by specific characteristics of the abuse. Next, we review several of these studies.

In a multi-victim case of CSA, Cederborg, Lamb, and Laurell (2007) compared the details provided in forensic interviews of ten child victims to evidence from 116 videotapes of the abuse experiences. Although six of the ten children were judged to have experienced abuse severe enough to be memorable, some children minimized the abuse, and others refused to admit that abuse occurred. Examination of police interviews, investigation records, and court files revealed that the children's *relationship to the perpetrator* may have been an important factor in determining why the severely abused children denied their experiences. Consistent with research indicating that children may be more reluctant to disclose when closely related to the perpetrator (DiPietro, Runyan, & Frederickson, 1997), three of the severely abused children were relatives of the accused, and three were cared for by him at a daycare centre or at the children's home. Similarly, *fear of reprisal and pacts of secrecy* may have influenced children's lack of disclosure: three of the ten severely abused children were also at risk of being punished by the perpetrator if the abuse was disclosed, and four were instructed to keep the abusive events secret. Moreover, three of the children who also failed to disclose in this study may have feared disbelief due to *lack of parental support*, which is consistent with research suggesting that lack of parental support has a detrimental effect on children's accounts of trauma (e.g., Goodman, Quas, Batterman-Faunce, Riddlesberger, & Kuhn, 1994). Finally, one child's reluctance to disclose may have been primarily related to *feelings of guilt, shame, and responsibility* for the abusive events, as has been documented in past studies (e.g., Goodman-Brown et al., 2003). Combinations of these factors were also likely at play (e.g., fear of reprisal and feelings of guilt or shame). The four children who experienced abuse described as "not severe" were unable to remember specific details of their abuse. However, failure to disclose abuse in these cases was likely, in part, due to the young age of the children at the time of the incidents, which may have affected the ability of these children to understand, encode, and retrieve memories of the events. Although the researchers' analysis of the reasons for the children's lack of disclosure was based, in part, on inference after considering the various case factors, the analysis was also informed by the children's statements. For example, a child who had been repeatedly abused between the ages of 4–11 years of age stated during the police interview that he "did not dare tell" and "was afraid" (p. 169).

Factors that influence disclosure of abuse, such as age, may also affect the accuracy and completeness of children's memory for abuse. Terr (1988) examined verbal memories and "behavioral memories" of early traumas experienced prior to the age of five. Behavioral memories were defined as children's behaviors and affects that may be related to abuse experiences, such as post-traumatic play and reenactment, personality changes, and trauma-specific fears. Memories of traumatic events were obtained from 20 children during clinical interviews conducted as part of psychological treatment. Although the degree of external documentation of the traumatic events varied, corroborative evidence of trauma was obtained from photographs, police records, clinical reports, and confessions, and was used to assess the accuracy and completeness of memory reports. Events were classified as *short* (i.e., less than 15 min in duration) or *long*, and as *single* or *repeated*. Verbal memories, reported by 15 out of 20 children, were rated as *full* (i.e., when compared to corroborating evidence, the child's report was complete), *spotty* (i.e., the child provided a partial or vague report of the event), or *absent* (i.e., the child could not remember the event). Although the types of traumatic events examined by Terr varied (e.g., CSA, death of a parent or sibling, and dog bites), because CSA was included, we describe the findings here.

Of the 11 children younger than 36 months of age when the traumatic event occurred, only two reported *full* memories. In comparison, six of the nine children over 36 months of age at the time of the event demonstrated full verbal recall. In general, long events were less well-remembered (i.e., *spotty*) than short events, and repeated events, such as recurrent sexual abuse, were less well-remembered than single events: four reports of repeated events were coded as *spotty*, three were *absent*, and no repeated event was coded as a *full* memory. Regarding memory accuracy, ten children reported accurate verbal memories. The gist of the remaining five verbal reports was accurate compared to the documentation, but the reports also contained details inconsistent with the corroborating evidence. For the children who recalled the event, no relations were found between memory accuracy and children's age, event duration, event repetition, IQ, family stability, whether an adult family member was present during the event, or the reported willingness of the family to discuss the traumatic event.

Results from these two studies suggest that abuse disclosure may be influenced by child factors, such as age, in addition to socio-emotional factors (e.g., feelings of shame or responsibility) and abuse characteristics, such as relationship to the perpetrator (see also Sas, Hatch, Malla, Dick, & Hurley, 1993, for similar findings). The studies also suggest that children are often quite accurate in their reports of abuse; although, if the abuse occurred when children were quite young, memory gaps may result.

In the studies reviewed so far, researchers did not attempt quantitative analysis of the data. Instead, they relied on qualitative methodology. Next, we review scientific case studies of CSA from which quantitative analyses were conducted. These quantitative scientific case studies arguably represent an advance over the qualitative research, providing a more objective means to examine how real-life traumatic events may be represented in memory. In these studies, researchers scored victims' memory accuracy and completeness in relation to the photographic, video, and/or audio records of the actual abusive experiences (e.g., Bidrose & Goodman, 2000; Leander et al., 2005, 2007, 2008). At present, relatively few quantitative scientific case studies of CSA exist, but the numbers are growing.

In a study concerning a "sex ring," Bidrose and Goodman (2000) examined a large number of records regarding the abuse of four preadolescent and teenage girls (i.e., 8–15 years of age). In this case, an ageing paraplegic man confined to a wheel chair and four other men (e.g., some as old as 80 years) were sexually molesting, prostituting, photographing, and audiotaping repeated assaults of the victims. To examine memory accuracy, hundreds of photographs and audio recordings of the sexual assaults, confiscated by the police, were compared to statements made by the girls in police interviews and legal depositions. Overall, 78.9% of the victims' allegations were supported by the documentation. Specifically, using the photographs and audio recordings as "ground truth," a total of 85.6% of the alleged sexual acts, 82.5% of the alleged preparatory acts, and 42.9% of the alleged coercive acts were reported accurately by the children. Of interest, there were no significant age differences associated with the children's accuracy about the sexual acts. With respect to memory errors, victims showed a relatively high number of omissions (i.e., 39%), 36.9% of which were for sexual acts and 31.8% for coercive events.[2] However, the proportion of unsupportive allegations or commission errors (i.e., 21.1%) was relatively low compared to omission errors. Moreover, over half of the unsupported sexual allegations were of acts considered highly likely to have occurred, but not certain to have taken place given they were not recorded on tape or documented by photographs. These findings indicate that children can provide accurate, detailed, and reliable testimony (although perhaps not completely free of error) about their victimization (see discussion of remarkable memories by Hervé, Cooper, & Yuille, present volume). In this way, the findings are comparable to Yuille and Cutshall's (1986) study regarding 13 witnesses' memory of a shooting, in which 84.6% of the descriptive details provided in the witnesses' allegations was determined to be accurate.

---

[2] Omission errors may reflect forgetting, lack of realization of the information's importance or relevance, temporary inability of retrieval, or conscious decisions not to report certain information for motivational reasons (e.g., embarrassment).

Memory accuracy for a single incident of CSA was examined in Orbach and Lamb's (1999) study. Although the female victim suffered repeated CSA over the course of 2 years from the ages of 11–13, audio-recorded documentation was only available for the last abusive incident. The perpetrator was the victim's maternal grandfather, and the abuse took place in the victim's home, where the perpetrator also lived. The victim was 13 years of age at the time of disclosure, but the mother reported that the victim made allegations of abuse 17 months earlier. In this study, accuracy of the victim's memory was assessed by comparing information provided during the victim's forensic interview with the audio recording of the last abusive incident. The victim had surreptitiously audio recorded the event. Using a quantitative measure (i.e., number of informative details) and qualitative content analysis that compared central versus peripheral information, Orbach and Lamb found that the victim provided a total of 189 informative details during the forensic interview. Ninety-six details (50.8%) were corroborated by the audio recording, and 94 of the corroborated details (97.9%) were classified as central details defined as plot-related details that specifically concerned sexual events. Approximately 88% of the non-corroborated details were descriptions of actions that could not be verified. Sixty-eight details (36%) reported by the victim were confirmed by the perpetrator, one detail was contradicted by the perpetrator, and the remaining details were unaddressed by the perpetrator. The victim's sister, who witnessed the context leading up to the abuse incident, confirmed 24 out of 32 (75%) contextual details. Again, although memory is rarely perfect, these results suggest that the victim was able to provide a fairly accurate and complete account following the last abusive incident.

In a scientific case study involving sexual assaults of eight 3–10-year-old children (i.e., six girls and two boys; $M=5.8$ years), Leander et al. (2007) compared victims' reports to the perpetrator's photographs of the sex crimes. The CSA was committed by a single man who abducted the children, one at a time, to buildings or other locations, where he sexually assaulted them (e.g., attempted penetration), each on a single day. He was a stranger to the children and, based on his own account and that of the children, he did not threaten them and did not tell the children to keep the incidents secret. In addition to the photographs and the confession, medical and police information was also available. Parents, day care workers, siblings, and other relevant individuals were interviewed. The children's accounts to the police, provided 1 day to 5.5 years after the assaults, were compared to such documentation. Based on the perpetrator's reports and the documentation of the cases, children provided considerable detail during police interviews about what preceded the sexual assaults, indicating they remembered the incident. However, five children failed to provide any information about the sexual assault itself, and one child reported very little sexual information. Only two of the eight children gave detailed reports of the sexual acts. Overall, 7.6% of the information reported concerned sexual activities, and on 97 occasions, the children denied or expressed reluctance to talk about the sexual acts, with the 3–5-year-olds expressing the most denial and the fewest number of total details. Despite the limited completeness, the researchers concluded that "the children's reports (in all cases)" were "in very good agreement with the documentation of the abuse" (p. 125). These results indicate that children may be reluctant to report sexual abuse not only in cases of intrafamilial abuse, as one might expect, but also in cases of extrafamilial abuse. Leander et al. (2007) concluded that age and socio-emotional factors, such as shame, embarrassment, fear of negative consequences of disclosure, and/or perceived responsibility, may underlie children's delayed disclosure, denial, and omission errors (Goodman-Brown et al., 2003; Leander, 2010; Leander et al., 2008; Sjöberg & Lindblad, 2002).

In another study by Leander (2010), police interviews with 27 sexually abused children and adolescents (5–17-years-olds, $M=10.63$ years; 22 girls) were analyzed in relation to documentation (e.g., film, photographs) showing that the abuse had occurred in 23 of these cases. The abusive experiences included genital touch, masturbation, and sexual intercourse. In 63% of the cases, the duration of the events was less than 1 year; 44% of the cases involved a single or a few abusive episodes. The time interval between the last abusive event and police interview was less than a year in 93% of the cases and ranged from 1 to 3 days in 56% of the cases.

In the first interview with the police, most of the children were highly avoidant of discussing the sexual incidents, and they frequently denied the abusive acts (i.e., verified acts). Information provided by them about the sexual abuse consisted of details about neutral information; only one in ten details actually concerned sexual information. Children's age at disclosure, the type of abusive acts, the victims' relationship to the perpetrator, and the frequency of abuse were not associated with the amount of sensitive or sexually related information provided by the children in their reports. However, children showed a substantial increase in information given in repeated interviews, providing twice as much new sexually related information at the second and third interviews relative to the first interview. An opposite pattern was found for avoidance and denials, in that children were more likely to avoid and deny during the first interview than during subsequent interviews. Findings from this study suggest that, although sexually abused children may be reluctant to report sexual information, being interviewed on more than one occasion may help them relate more information about their sexual experiences (see Connolly & Price, present volume; La Rooy, Katz, Malloy, & Lamb, 2010; Yarbrough et al., present volume).

Sjöberg and Lindblad (2002) investigated factors influencing children's disclosure of sexual abuse in a case in which a man abused ten children who were either his stepchildren or known by him from his work at day care centres. Abusive acts included anal, oral, and/or vaginal penetration and forced urination/defecation. In this study, police interviews of the abused children were compared to videotapes ($n = 103$) of the sexual abuse incidents; the videotapes were confiscated from the perpetrator's home. The children made no spontaneous abuse disclosures prior to the police interviews. The frequency of abuse per child ranged from 1 to 60 incidents, with four children having experienced only a single abusive episode. The children were on average 5.6 ($SD=2.4$) years of age at the time of the last abuse incident, and 6.9 ($SD=2.4$) years of age at the time of the police questioning. Interview narratives were coded for victims' denials of abuse and details elicited in response to leading questions, as well as interviewers' accusatory statements and confrontational utterances, some of which may suggest the child was intentionally withholding information. Interview narratives and videotapes were also coded for severity of abuse (0 = no disclosure; 1 = low severity, such as sexually suggestive talk, kissing; 12 = extreme severity, such as bondage).

Comparison of the children's interviews with the videotapes of the abuse incidents revealed that all reports of abuse behaviors were documented on videotape (i.e., there were no sexual acts falsely reported). The abuse disclosed by children during interviews was rated as significantly less severe ($M = 2.7$, $SD = 3.8$, range = 0–10) than the ratings of abuse incidents captured on videotape ($M = 6.9$, $SD = 3.8$, range = 4–11), suggesting that the children tended to minimize or underreport their abuse experiences. Indeed, five children, including the child who suffered the greatest number of abuse incidents ($n = 60$) and received the highest abuse severity rating based on the videotapes, failed to disclose abuse during the police interviews. Four children (i.e., three disclosing, one non-disclosing) stated that they did not want to tell. Although abuse disclosure and children's reports were not considered in relation to victim age or victim relationship to the perpetrator, the study suggests that children generally showed a relatively high number of omission errors, even in the face of leading questions and accusatory statements made by interviewers.

Additional scientific case studies further underscore children's hesitancy to report sexual experiences. Memories for obscene phone calls involving 64 8–16-year-olds (51 girls and 13 boys; $M = 11.9$ years) were examined in Leander et al.'s (2005) study. A man posing as a university researcher located the child victims through newspaper ads regarding bicycles for sale. He called the children saying he was from the university and was conducting a study. The questions quickly turned to sexual matters (e.g., "Do you like to masturbate?" "Have you ever had sex with an adult?"). The perpetrator maintained detailed computer records of his phone conversations with the children. Once authorities were notified, police questioned the children, following a standardized interview protocol, which involved asking several free recall questions, 18 open-ended questions, and 8 closed questions. Audio recordings of the children's police interviews, which took place 1–21 months after the obscene phone calls, were compared to the documentation. Although children's reports were quite accurate overall, the children reported a greater amount of correct information in response to questions about neutral topics (89%; e.g., "He asked about my age") than about sensitive questions (83%; e.g., "He wanted to know if I had kissed anyone") and questions of a sexual nature (76%; e.g., "He asked if I had had sex with an adult"). Of interest, children's age was not related to memory accuracy and completeness. Also, longer retention intervals between the phone calls and the forensic interview negatively influenced the completeness, but not the accuracy, of children's reports (see discussion of transience by Yarbrough et al., present volume). Results from this study suggest that, although children were able to report highly accurate and complete neutral information, indicating that they remembered the phone calls, they may have consciously omitted some of the sensitive and sexual information related to the abuse experience.

The high-profile "Alexandria case" in Sweden led Leander et al. (2008) to conduct a scientific case study of children's memory for Internet-initiated sexual activities. This dramatic case involved a man who presented himself on the Internet as a woman named "Alexandria" who worked for a model/escort agency (see the use of Internet deception by Hancock & Woodworth, present volume). "Alexandria" asked 68 preadolescent and adolescent girls (11–19-years-olds; $M = 15.13$ years) to provide personal information, facial photos, and nude photos; to engage in Web shows while performing sex acts; and to meet with a client (the man himself) for sex. The duration of the girls' contact with "Alexandria" ranged from 1 week to 12 months, and the time interval between the last contacts with "Alexandria" to police interviews ranged from 1 to 17 months.

Documentation of the online sexual abuse consisted of detailed computer chat-logs. The girls' audio-recorded statements made during police interviews were evaluated against the computer chat-log records. During police interviews, a large number of suggestive questions were asked referring to the documented evidence. Regarding the off-line abuse incidents, 32 girls actually met with the man, and 27 of them engaged in sex with him. When questioned, 81% of the 27 girls disclosed sexual intercourse. Regarding online acts, for the less severe acts (e.g., providing personal information, discussing sex), the victims reported 72% and omitted 28% of the acts. For the more severe acts (e.g., nude photos, Web strip shows), the victims reported 49% and omitted/denied 51% of the acts. Results suggest that victims were generally accurate in their reports. In fact, the authors reported that, as far as they could determine, "the victims gave no false reports about on- or off-line acts (i.e., acts that could not be supported by the verification material)" (p. 1270). However, they were more hesitant to disclose online sexual acts severe in nature. Disclosure may have been influenced by feelings of shame and embarrassment: it may be particularly embarrassing to have engaged in acts like online sex shows—acts that could potentially be viewed by many others—compared to talking about sex or even engaging in sexual acts privately. Of interest, 29 of the victims denied the online sex acts even when the interviewers made clear they had the documentation, and despite a massive media campaign to ensure that the victims realized there were other victims. The level of distress was so great that some of the girls were suicidal after the incidents. Age, abuse duration, and time interval between the last contact and the police interview did not predict victims' memory accuracy, memory completeness, denials, and unsupported allegations.

Taken together, results from scientific case studies strongly suggest that children are able to provide largely accurate testimony about personal episodes of sexual abuse. Moreover, these studies often indicated that children's accuracy was not necessarily affected by age (Bidrose & Goodman, 2000; Leander et al., 2005, 2007, 2008) or by the time interval between the last abusive contact and the forensic interview, although the report may be less complete if it is delayed (Leander et al., 2005, 2007, 2008). Moreover, children's accounts about their own victimization did not include high levels of commission errors (e.g., Bidrose & Goodman, 2000; Orbach & Lamb, 1999; Sjöberg & Lindblad, 2002), mirroring evidence from laboratory research (e.g., Saywitz et al., 1991). Omission errors, however, were relatively frequent. Of interest, the children's reports seemed to be less complete for sensitive and abuse-related information than for neutral information (e.g., Bidrose & Goodman, 2000; Leander, 2010; Leander et al., 2005, 2007, 2008). For instance, Leander et al. (2008) found that child victims omitted or denied 51% of the severe online sexual acts, but only 28% of the less severe online activities. Similarly, children showed a high proportion of omission errors, a large number of denials, and great reluctance to talk about sexual activities in Leander et al.'s (2007) study.

The potentially chilling effect of child victims' feelings of fear, shame, embarrassment, and/or guilt has been suggested as an explanation for children's omission of a considerably greater amount of sensitive compared to neutral information (e.g., Leander, 2010; Leander et al., 2008; Sjöberg & Lindblad, 2002). Additionally, in Leander et al.'s (2007) study, the number of omission errors was influenced by age, with the youngest children producing more such errors than the older children (age ranged from 3- to 10-year-old at the time of the events and of the forensic interviews). This result contrasts with findings from other scientific case studies failing to find significant decreases in the proportion of omission errors or denials with age (Bidrose & Goodman, 2000; Leander et al., 2005, 2008). Nevertheless, the scientific case studies reviewed here that did not find age-related changes in omission errors usually included children older in age at the time of the abusive events and the forensic interviews (i.e., 8–19-year-olds). Thus, cognitive limitations, such as in language capacity, memory retrieval strategies, and understanding of the abusive acts, may have contributed to the youngest children's greater difficulty in expressing and reporting relevant information during the forensic interviews (e.g., see Sjöberg & Lindblad, 2002; Yarbrough et al., present volume).

Two other factors that can potentially influence omission errors in children's reports about personal episodes of sexual abuse are the retention interval between the abusive events and the forensic interview and the number of interviews. With respect to retention interval, findings from the scientific case studies reviewed here are mixed; some studies showed no effects of delay interval on children's omissions (time intervals ranging from 1 to 17 months; Leander et al., 2008), whereas other studies revealed a negative influence of delay interval (time intervals ranging from 1 to 21 months) in testimony completeness (Leander et al., 2005). Regarding the number of forensic interviews, Leander's (2010) study underlined that omission errors and denials were high in the first interviewing session, and that the second and third interviews doubled the amount of new sensitive information reported by the victim relative to the first interview (see also Goodman & Quas, 2008; La Rooy et al., 2010).

Finally, results from scientific case studies appear to be consistent, suggesting that children can be quite accurate in their reports of abuse when the abuse has actually occurred. Moreover, the studies confirm that abuse disclosure and abuse memory are both influenced by child and interview factors.

False Reports of Child Sexual Abuse

So far, we have reviewed studies in which CSA clearly occurred. Scientific case studies, by definition, require documentation of ground truth. However, even when perpetrators record their assaults and the ground truth evidence is potentially available for scientific analysis, it is still quite difficult for researchers to obtain such documentation and to conduct the corresponding studies. The cooperation of authorities (e.g., police, courts) is typically required to obtain the documentation, and the materials must be held in strict confidence, under court order. In cases when a child makes a false report of CSA, it can be even more difficult to obtain documentation of what actually took place (see Griesel, Ternes, Schraml, Cooper, & Yuille, present volume).

One research project that approximates a scientific case study of a false report was published by Hershkowitz (2001). This case study of a sexual abuse allegation elicited in response to leading questions demonstrates children's potential susceptibility to false reports following accusatory interview contexts and suggestive questioning by a parent (see Yarbrough et al., present volume). The case involved a 10-year-old female who claimed to have been surprised in the woods by a man who then exposed his genitals. Thus, if true, a prosecutable crime did indeed occur. Fearing punishment from her mother for taking a forbidden path through the woods home from school, the child did not report her experiences until 1 week after the alleged event. When the child did disclose, because she was crying, the mother instructed the child to nod affirmatively in response to her questions, rather than requiring the child to provide a free narrative of the event. The child nodded affirmatively to all questions posed, including those related to being touched on the genitals. When the mother inspected the child's genitals, she mistakenly thought she saw male pubic hair and called the police. During the police interview, the child reported forceful penetration. However, forensic examination revealed no signs of penetration, and no evidence was found at the scene. That night, the child recanted her allegation and explained that she went along with her mother's questioning to end the investigation sooner.

For the research study, the medical examination results, the child's recantation, evidence from the crime scene, and the mother's description of the initial parent–child conversation were analyzed using an independent case facts scale to determine the plausibility of the alleged abuse (Horowitz et al., 1995). The credibility of the child's account was assessed using Criterion-Based Content Analysis (CBCA; Raskin & Esplin, 1991; Yuille, 1988), a controversial method designed to assess how likely it is that specific statements are event-based (see Colwell, Hiscock-Anisman, & Fede, present volume; Griesel et al., present volume). Some research using CBCA suggests that descriptions of true and plausible events are richer in CBCA criteria compared to descriptions of false and implausible events (but see Buck, Warren, Betman, & Brigham, 2002; Pezdek et al., 2004; Rassin, 2000). Analyses of the plausibility of the child's allegation using an independent case facts scale suggested that the event was unlikely to have occurred. Moreover, comparison of the details provided in the initial statement and the later recantation revealed that the child may have fabricated 22.5% ($n=25$) of the details. According to this analysis, although the majority (77.5%) of the details provided in both the initial statement and final recantation ($n=111$) were truthful, they represented her genuine experiences of another event. Moreover, no evidence of the CSA event was discovered by medical or forensic investigations.

The credibility of the event as assessed by CBCA failed to detect the implausibility of the child's allegations; seven out of 14 CBCA criteria of credibility were present in the child's statement. CBCA may have failed to detect the implausibility of the event if the child's allegation involved genuine memory of an experienced event with fabricated details added, rather than a false report of a nonexperienced event (see Griesel et al., present volume).

This case study highlights the possibility that children may at times acquiesce to authority figures upon whom they depend physically and emotionally. Children's ignorance of the consequences of false allegations, fear of negative consequences, and misperceptions of interview rules may contribute to false reports and suggestibility. The research also demonstrates the difficulty of conducting a scientific case study of children's false reports. If a video or audio recording of a child's nonabusive experiences were somehow made and then the child produced a false report of CSA about that experience, a true scientific case study of a false report could, in principle, be conducted.

In fact, two such false reports were captured in a recent study of children whose memory for their kindergarten inoculations were examined (Larson et al., 2009). The children were videotaped at the doctor's office while a nurse gave them their shots and then, days later, the children were suggestively interviewed. Of the nearly 90 children questioned, two 4-year-old boys (i.e., about 2%) made explicit false reports of sexual acts with the nurse. One of the boys showed highly sexualized behavior generally. Although this research did not involve cases that were being investigated by the police and, although it was part of an analogue study rather than a case study, it shows that, at times, false reports of sexual abuse can be investigated by researchers.

In the next section, we review some of the disadvantages of scientific case studies of CSA. Delineation of these limitations helps set the stage for discussing the possible effects of cognitive and social factors on children's testimony in scientific case studies, on the one hand, and such effects in laboratory and field-based studies, on the other hand—a topic we address in the last section of the present chapter.

Limitations of Scientific Case Studies of Child Sexual Abuse

Scientific case study research affords the opportunity to examine memory for stressful, inappropriate, and/or traumatic childhood experiences in relation to several cognitive, emotional, and social outcomes. Scientific case study research holds its most unique value in its ability to offer insight into the associations between trauma and memory as they operate within real cases of child abuse, as opposed to the analogue situations (e.g., medical procedures) often examined in other types of field and laboratory research. Case studies that rely on independent documentation of abuse can also bolster the generalizability of experimental findings by replicating results from laboratory studies under ecologically valid conditions, thereby further contributing to the scientific literature on trauma on memory. Scientific case studies of CSA may also advance the theoretical understanding of emotional outcomes for child victims. Overall, such studies aid researchers in investigating applied and theoretical issues related to trauma (see Hervé et al., present volume; Yuille, present volume).

Although scientific sexual abuse case studies are emotionally gripping and socially consequential, a critique of the quality of the science behind such research is important to consider before drawing firm conclusions about the effects of such factors as emotion, stress, and trauma, or even just inappropriate experiences, on children's memory. One of the main methodological limitations of these studies is the difficulty of obtaining *complete* objective records of the abuse events. Most CSA cases occur in private, and later the child's word is often pitted against that of the accused. Recordings are invaluable for evaluating children's later memory reports but, in many of the scientific case studies, only a subset of the assaults was recorded.

As mentioned earlier, a second limitation is the difficulty of studying false reports of CSA. The difficulty in identifying false reports with certainty in case study research prevents scientists from examining differences in children's true vs. false reports as well as reports in which children falsely elaborate upon events that did occur (but see Hershkowitz, 2001; Larson et al., 2009). Third, even when corroborative evidence of the abuse is available, the relation between variables cannot be isolated or controlled as in experimental research. Also, researchers cannot randomly assign children to groups; for instance, having a group that experiences trauma and a group that does not. Random assignment is crucial for drawing causal inferences.

Fourth, a small number of children at each age may experience the events. Moreover, the events may differ considerably in their nature (e.g., abuse duration, abusive acts), in the investigation process (e.g., time delay to disclosure, type of forensic interview), and in the emotional consequences for each child (e.g., feelings of fear, embarrassment). When using scientific case study methodology, the typically small number of children at each age and the heterogeneity of the individual cases make it difficult to conduct truly *developmental*, sound research on the effects of stress and trauma on memory. Finally, the lack of generally accepted scientific methods of coding characteristics of abuse and related outcomes in scientific case study research makes comparisons across studies problematic. Such factors can preclude replication of experimental findings. Despite these limitations, scientific case studies can serve as a basis for more rigorous experimental investigation of important issues.

In the next section, we review evidence from laboratory and field research regarding the effects of several cognitive and social factors on children's memory for emotional, stressful, and traumatic events. An integrative overview of what is known from scientific case studies of CSA, field approaches, and laboratory research can shed further light on our understanding of trauma and memory development.

Laboratory and Field Research on Children's Memory and Emotion: An Integrative Overview

Research on emotion, stress, trauma, and memory development has concerned a variety of events and relied upon several different methodological procedures to examine children's memory. Whereas laboratory research has investigated children's memories for relatively mild emotional materials (e.g., Howe, 2007), field research has taken advantage of naturally occurring, real-life stressful and traumatic occurrences, such as natural disasters (e.g., Ackil, Van Abbema, & Bauer, 2003), shocking public events (e.g., Pillemer, 1992), emergency room procedures (e.g., Peterson & Whalen, 2001), stressful medical experiences (e.g., Goodman et al., 1994; Quas et al., 1999), violent events (e.g., Pynoos & Nader, 1989), and acts of CSA (e.g., Alexander et al., 2005).

In *laboratory research,* the study of children's emotional memories has primarily relied on negative word lists and stories (e.g., Bartlett, Burleson, & Santrock, 1982; Davidson & Jergovic, 1996; Davidson, Luo, & Burden, 2001; Forgas, Burnham, & Trimboli, 1988; Goodman et al., 2011; Moradi, Taghavi, Neshat-Doost, Yule, & Dalgleish, 2000; Neshat-Doost, Taghavi, Moradi, Yule, & Dalgleish, 1998), or videotaped or staged events where children watch but do not directly experience a somewhat stressful incident (e.g., Bugental, Blue, Cortez, Fleck, & Rodriguez, 1992; Poole & White, 1991; Roebers & Schneider, 2002; Roebers, Schwartz, & Neumann, 2005). Overall, these studies have shown that emotional and distinct material is better remembered than neutral material, and that children's memory is often quite accurate but also susceptible to forgetting, inaccuracies, and distortion. However, one frequent methodological problem in such research is that the stimuli do not evoke the level of emotion and trauma involved in actual cases of CSA. Moreover, when studies include a control group that views neutral material and an experimental group that views more emotional material, the stimuli typically differ not only in emotional valence, but also in content, resulting in a potentially important confound.

In *field research*, the study of natural disasters, violent events, and events that may give rise to "flashbulb" memories has constituted a useful approach for investigating the effects of stressful and traumatic experiences on children's memory. Flashbulb memories are believed to form as a result of single, public, distinctive events that are unexpected and that are charged with emotional content and personal relevance (for developmental flashbulb memory studies, see Pillemer, 1992; Terr, Bloch, Michel, & Shi, 1996; Warren & Swartwood, 1992; Winograd & Killinger, 1983). For instance, Terr et al. (1996) examined children's memories of the Challenger explosion and found that those who watched the event (i.e., high-involvement group) produced more clear, consistent, and detailed accounts about the explosion itself and their surrounding personal circumstances (e.g., personal placement, incidents, other people present) than those who just heard about the event (i.e., low-involvement group), at both 5–7-week and 14-month retention intervals.

In a similar study, Bahrick, Parker, Fivush, and Levitt (1998) examined the memories of 3- and 4-year-old children who experienced Hurricane Andrew, a strong storm that devastated the Florida coast in 1992. Although all children provided detailed accounts of the disaster when interviewed a few weeks after the event, children who experienced moderate to high levels of stress recalled more than those in the low stress group, as determined by a scale designed to objectify the degree of storm exposure.

Using methodology similar to that in scientific case studies of CSA, some researchers have examined children's memories of public reports of an event and compared memory accounts across repeated questionings. In one example, Terr (1981) examined 5–14-year-old victims' memories of the Chowchilla school-bus kidnapping, and found that children exhibited vivid memories of the experience immediately, and retained accurate memory for the gist of the incident 1 and 5 years after the kidnapping (Terr, 1983; see also Pynoos & Eth, 1984; Pynoos & Nader, 1989).

Overall, evidence from research on these forms of stressful events suggests that detailed memories of highly salient and personally consequential experiences in childhood are relatively well retained over long periods of time (e.g., 6 years, Fivush, Sales, Goldberg, Bahrick, & Parker, 2004), and can remain vivid into adulthood (e.g., Berntsen & Rubin, 2006; Reviere & Bakeman, 2001; Winograd & Killinger, 1983), as long as the children are not too young (e.g., 1- or 2-year-olds) when the events occurred. Moreover, because public events are often involved in these studies, children and adults may have opportunities to discuss their experiences socially, which may help explain the endurance of these memories in some instances (e.g., Fivush et al., 2004). Nevertheless, it is important to note that even with high personal involvement and strong emotion during the incident, these traumatic memories are not immune to inaccuracies in children (e.g., Terr et al., 1996), as well as in adults (e.g., Neisser & Harsch, 1992; Nourkova, Bernstein, & Loftus, 2004; Pezdek, 2003; Yuille & Cutshall, 1986). As we saw from our review of scientific case studies of CSA, children can misunderstand some details of stressful events, such as certain acts, dates, times, and durations of the events and incorporate these inaccuracies consistently into their memory reports (e.g., Cederborg et al., 2007; Sjöberg & Lindblad, 2002; Terr, 1983).

Another field-based research approach to investigating children's memory for stressful experiences has been to use medical procedures as target events in analogue studies. Typically, medical procedures are salient personal experiences that can elicit distress. Memory researchers take advantage of that fact to study memory for mildly stressful (e.g., well-child checkups) to highly stressful (e.g., emergency room visits, surgery, cancer treatments) medical procedures (Baker-Ward, Gordon, Ornstein, Larus, & Clubb, 1993; Burgwyn-Bailes, Baker-Ward, Gordon, & Ornstein, 2001; Chen, Zeltzer, Craske, & Katz, 2000; Goodman, Hirschman, Hepps, & Rudy, 1991; Goodman, Quas, Batterman-Faunce, Riddlesberger & Kuhn, 1997; Melinder et al., 2010; Peterson & Bell, 1996; Shrimpton, Oates, & Hayes, 1998). Evidence from studies using medical procedures involving genital touch is of special relevance to the present review because these events offer the opportunity to produce situations, feelings, and information that is usually of concern in CSA investigations.

One painful and potentially embarrassing procedure involving genital penetration is Voiding Cystourethrogram Fluoroscopy (VCUG; e.g., Goodman et al., 1997; Merritt, Ornstein, & Spicker, 1994; Quas et al., 1999; Salmon, Price, & Pereira, 2002). Results from studies examining children's memory for VCUG reveal that, although young children can accurately report details of the procedure, more distressed children tend to report fewer details in free recall (Merritt et al., 1994). Moreover, VCUG studies have also shown that, when presented with specific or misleading questions, older children are more accurate and less suggestible than younger children (see Sjöberg & Lindhom, 2005, for a review).

These results are consistent with findings from scientific cases studies of CSA in suggesting that even young children can accurately report information about stressful personal experiences and that completeness of children's accounts may be affected by age, the distress experienced during the events, and the eliciting utterances used during the interview. Despite the heterogeneity of the events studied, the laboratory and field approaches have been vital in shedding light on the cognitive and social factors influencing children's memory for emotional experiences. This knowledge can help us understand the accumulating evidence from scientific case studies of CSA. Next, findings from laboratory and field research are compared to findings from scientific case studies of CSA with respect to some of the main cognitive and social factors examined by these research approaches.

Regarding cognitive-related factors, *age* is a crucial variable in predicting memory of emotional stimuli and past experiences (for reviews, see Baker-Ward, Gordon, & Ornstein, 2001; Cordon, Pipe, Sayfan, Melinder, & Goodman, 2004; Peterson, 2002). Clear developmental trends have emerged, suggesting that, compared to older children (i.e., school-aged), younger children (i.e., preschoolers) tend to produce a larger number of omission errors, and provide less-detailed and less-complete, as well as less-consistent reports of emotional (e.g., Pillemer, Picariello, & Pruett, 1994) and stressful events (Ghetti, Goodman, Eisen, Qin, & Davis, 2002; Merritt et al., 1994). These results fit relatively well with findings from scientific case studies with respect to memory completeness or the amount of information provided in children's reports (e.g., Leander et al., 2007). However, in contrast to most laboratory-based evidence of age-related increases in memory accuracy (e.g., Brady, Poole, Warren, & Jones, 1999), our review of scientific case studies of CSA showed that accuracy was generally not influenced by children's age, at least within the age ranges tested (e.g., Bidrose & Goodman, 2000; Leander, 2010; Leander et al., 2008). Nevertheless, there is also a large body of evidence from field-based research, indicating that even young children can be fairly accurate in their reports of salient and personally relevant information (e.g., Pipe et al., 1997; Saywitz et al., 1991).

Overall, age-related improvements in memory are likely determined in part by age-related increases in knowledge base and processing speed (Howe, 2011), the ability to use memory strategies (e.g., Schneider & Pressley, 1997), and engagement of source monitoring processes (e.g., Bright-Paul, Jarrold, & Wright, 2005; Johnson, Hashtroudi, & Lindsay, 1993; Poole & Lindsay, 2002), as well as decreases in forgetting rates (e.g., Bauer, Wenner, Dropik, & Wewerka, 2000; Brainerd, Reyna, Howe, & Kingma, 1990). The development of certain aspects of executive functioning during preschool and early childhood, such as inhibitory control and theory of mind, partially predicts children's eyewitness memory and suggestibility (e.g., Alexander, Quas, & Goodman, 2002; Bright-Paul, Jarrold, & Wright, 2008; Roberts & Powell, 2005). Moreover, consistent with dual process models of memory, recent evidence shows differential developmental trajectories in children's recollection and familiarity, with recollection still developing during adolescence, and familiarity reaching a more stationary level around 6–8 years of age (Ghetti & Angelini, 2008).

Another important factor that influences memory completeness, accuracy, and consistency is the *retention interval* or time *delay* to disclosure. However, results from laboratory and field-based research concerning children's accuracy for emotional stimuli following extended delays (e.g., 1–12 years) are mixed. On the one hand, children may experience significant memory decay and provide less complete reports after long delays (e.g., Goodman, Batterman-Faunce, Schaaf, & Kenney, 2002). On the other hand, those experiences associated with more emotional intensity and salience tend to be forgotten less (see Cordon et al., 2004, for a review) and can be relatively well-retained even after extended periods of time (Alexander et al., 2005; Brainerd & Poole, 1997; Burgwyn-Bailes et al., 2001; Peterson, 1999; Peterson & Whalen, 2001). The scientific case studies of CSA reviewed in the present chapter did not necessarily show that delay to disclosure affected children's memory accuracy about their personal victimization (Leander et al., 2005, 2007, 2008). However, in some cases, longer time delays to disclosure were associated with a higher number of omission errors (Leander et al., 2005). Overall, results suggest that children may forget aspects of distant experiences, but the proportion of information remembered can be remarkably accurate and detailed even years after the occurrence of stressful events (e.g., Hudson & Fivush, 1991; Van Abbema & Bauer, 2005). However, infantile amnesia (i.e., forgetting of experiences from infancy and very early childhood) occurs even for real-life traumatic events such as CSA (Terr, 1988).

The *distinctiveness* and *personal relevance* of an event may be important—and often intertwined—predictors of children's ability to consistently and accurately report past experiences. Distinctive events are characterized by a violation of one's expectations and are unique relative to one's other experiences and knowledge (e.g., Howe, 1997, 2000). Distinctiveness may help individuals to discriminate between highly similar memory traces, as well as help to reduce interference from other information in memory (e.g., Ghetti, Qin, & Goodman, 2002; Howe, 2006). Children may find "unusual" characteristics of an event to be emotionally arousing or attention grabbing. Although both non-traumatic and highly emotional events can be distinctive, traumatic events are often relatively more unique and personally salient and perhaps, therefore, are recalled with greater vividness over short and long retention intervals than less emotional experiences (Ackil et al., 2003; Berliner, Hyman, Thomas, & Fitzgerald, 2003; Cordon et al., 2004; but see Goodman, Quas, & Ogle, 2010). This also applies to the traumatic events examined in scientific case studies of CSA. Although these events are experiences of clear personal relevance, their degree of distinctiveness may vary depending on several characteristics of the abuse, such as duration, repetition, and severity. After repeated exposure, sexually abused children may no longer view abusive events as distinctive, and gist or script memory may result in a blending of experiences in memory (see Connolly & Price, present volume; Hervé et al., present volume; Nelson, 1993). Moreover, evaluation of event or stimulus characteristics as distinctive can change with an individual's increasing age and may vary over time (e.g., Howe, Courage, Vernescu, & Hunt, 2000). For example, an event that may be unique for a child may not be unique to an adult (e.g., Howe, 2006). Changes in distinctiveness may also occur for traumatic events irrespective of age. The fact that even young children can report these experiences quite accurately also suggests that these personally significant events lead to superior encoding and rehearsal, especially in regard to their central details (Westmacott & Moscovitch, 2003).

Another related factor examined by experimental research is *personal involvement* in an experience. Individuals who directly experience an event often report more accurate and detailed memory accounts than those who merely witness the event (e.g., Lindberg, Jones, McComas, & Thomas, 2001; Roebers, Gelhaar, & Schneider, 2004; Rudy & Goodman, 1991; Thierry & Spence, 2004; van Giezen, Arensman, Spinhoven, & Wolters, 2005). In certain cases of severe trauma, however, children who observe a highly stressful or traumatic event (e.g., sexual, physical, or emotional abuse of a family member) may encode and retain memories in a way that is similar to those who directly experience it (Johnson, Greenhoot, Glisky, & McCloskey, 2005; see Howe, 1997, for a review).

Parenting variables such as parent–child interaction, parenting styles, and parental responsiveness play a critical role in children's memories for emotional and stressful experiences (Burch, Austin, & Bauer, 2004; Chae, Ogle, & Goodman, 2009; Clarke-Stewart, Malloy, & Allhusen, 2004; Fivush & Vasudeva, 2002; Reese, Haden, & Fivush, 1993; Wareham & Salmon, 2006). Parent–child interactions provide an opportunity for rehearsal and reactivation of event details that may help maintain and strengthen memory traces (e.g., Howe, Courage, & Bryant-Brown, 1993), thus reducing the effects of memory decay, while enhancing long-term retention. When parents avoid discussion of emotional events, this may contribute to forgetting or memory errors (e.g., Chae, Goodman, & Edelstein, 2011; Goodman et al., 1994). For example, children who received maternal support after disclosure of CSA provided more accurate reports of their maltreatment experiences years after the abuse reportedly ended, compared to those who did not (e.g., Alexander et al., 2005). In contrast, children expecting negative reactions from their parents exhibited decreased willingness to disclose sexual abuse, as well as decreased opportunity for overt rehearsal of event details that can contribute to memory maintenance (Hershkowitz, Lanes, & Lamb, 2007). Nevertheless, overt rehearsal and conversations with others, including parents, may also lead to false reports if misinformation is included in these interactions or in repeated questioning about an event (e.g., Howe et al., 1993; Poole & Lindsay, 2001). Similarly, an interviewer's style and the interview context may profoundly affect children's disclosures and the information they provide regarding abusive acts (e.g., Hershkowitz, 2001).

Finally, and related to the above, children's and parents' *attachment* (Bowlby, 1980) may influence children's reactions to and memory for emotional, stressful, and traumatic events (e.g., Chae et al., 2009, 2011; Goodman et al., 1997; Goodman & Quas, 1997). Children who form avoidant attachment styles may use strategies that interfere with memory encoding and storage of distressing information so as not to have their attachment systems activated (Alexander et al., 2002; Dykas, Ehrlich, & Cassidy, 2011). For instance, survivors of CSA who self-report a more avoidant attachment orientation, and who do not receive maternal support following disclosure, may be unlikely to discuss their trauma with others (e.g., Edelstein et al., 2005).

In sum, laboratory and field studies have been instrumental for examining effects of stress and trauma on memory and its development, as well as for determining the influence of cognitive and social factors on memory outcomes. The extant evidence indicates that even young children can be accurate in their reports of these experiences, but omission errors are relatively common, and commission errors and false reports can occur. Overall, findings from experimental research appear to resemble the results from scientific case studies of CSA in important ways, highlighting the importance of combining different and complementary methodologies to shed further light on a phenomenon—children's memory for stressful and traumatic events—that cannot be entirely addressed using a single approach.

Conclusion

Scientific case study findings correspond well to those of laboratory and field research, with the possible exceptions that there may be less forgetting of central information over time and more omission errors of core information in the former than in the latter. This correspondence is important in validating the results of laboratory and field research with studies that are unquestionably high in external validity (see ten Brinke & Porter, present volume).

One of the important findings of the extant scientific case studies is that children who have suffered sexual abuse produce eyewitness memory reports high in accuracy but incomplete in detail, and that this relation is exacerbated by young age, likely due, at least in part, to such factors as limited understanding of the abuse experience and of the legal context, along with underdeveloped language capabilities, knowledge base, and memory retrieval skills. Moreover, victims' feelings of shame, embarrassment, fear, and guilt about sexual abuse likely contribute to incomplete reports, as indicated by a tendency of child victims to omit significant detail about the sexual acts or in some cases, to deny the sexual acts completely despite clear documentation that the abuse was experienced. These feelings are difficult to elicit in controlled laboratory studies and yet may have a powerful effect on children's eyewitness reports in CSA cases. Being able to capture the effects of such emotions on children's reports is one advantage of scientific case studies.

False reports and suggestibility are particularly difficult to examine in scientific case study research. Evidence from laboratory and field research shows that memory for highly stressful experiences is not indelible and that, compared to older children, younger children can be more susceptible to inaccuracies under accusatory interview contexts and with the use of leading and misleading questions (e.g., Ceci & Bruck, 1993; Schaaf, Alexander, & Goodman, 2008; but see Quas et al., 2007). Such age trends are likely inherent in actual CSA investigations as well. However, it is typically quite difficult in actual cases of CSA to prove—scientifically—that a CSA report is false. Even, for example, when children give fantastic claims that cannot be true, that does not prove that CSA did not occur (Dalenberg, 1996). Future scientific case studies should attempt to tackle this difficult but important issue.

The lack of ability to manipulate independent variables and the lack of opportunity to employ random assignment in scientific case studies limits researchers—for example, by precluding researchers from examining in a controlled fashion the causal influence of cognitive and social factors that may affect children's memory accuracy and suggestibility. This is another significant but unavoidable problem. Nevertheless, much can be learned from such research, with more controlled scientific studies also being conducted to examine causal effects, as possible. Expansion of scientific case study research into the realm of CSA rests squarely on the initial contributions that Yuille and Cutshall (1986) made to the science of eyewitness memory.

Acknowledgement The authors were supported by a Juan de la Cierva and Consolider-Ingenio 2010 (CSD2008-00048) grant from the Spanish Ministry of Innovation and Science to Pedro Paz-Alonso, by a National Institute on Aging grant to Christin Ogle (5T32 AG000029-35), and by a National Science Foundation grant to Gail Goodman (Grant #0545413). Any opinions, findings, and conclusions or recommendations expressed are those of the authors and do not necessarily reflect the views of the National Science Foundation or other agencies. We thank Dr. Kathy Pezdek for past support of scientific case study research. Address correspondence to Dr. Gail S. Goodman, Department of Psychology, University of California, 1 Shields Avenue, Davis 95616 USA (ggoodman@ucdavis.edu).

References

Ackil, J. K., Van Abbema, D. L., & Bauer, P. J. (2003). After the storm: Enduring differences in mother-child recollections of traumatic and nontraumatic events. *Journal of Experimental Child Psychology, 84*, 286–309.

Alexander, K. W., Quas, J. A., Ghetti, S., Goodman, G. S., Edelstein, R. S., Redlich, A. D., ... Jones, D. P. H. (2005). Traumatic impact predicts long-term memory for documented child sexual abuse. *Psychological Science, 16*, 33–40.

Alexander, K. W., Quas, J. A., & Goodman, G. S. (2002). Theoretical advances in understanding children's memory for distressing events: The role of attachment. *Developmental Review, 22*, 490–519.
Bahrick, L. E., Parker, J. F., Fivush, R., & Levitt, M. (1998). The effects of stress on young children's memory for a natural disaster. *Journal of Experimental Psychology. Applied, 4*, 308–331.
Baker-Ward, L., Gordon, B. N., & Ornstein, P. A. (2001). Children's testimony: A review of research on memory for past experiences. *Clinical Child and Family Psychology, 4*, 157–181.
Baker-Ward, L., Gordon, B. N., Ornstein, P. A., Larus, D. M., & Clubb, P. A. (1993). Young children's long-term retention of a pediatric examination. *Child Development, 64*, 1519–1533.
Bartlett, J. C., Burleson, G., & Santrock, J. W. (1982). Emotional mood and memory in young children. *Journal of Experimental Child Psychology, 34*, 59–76.
Bauer, P. J., Wenner, J. A., Dropik, P. L., & Wewerka, S. S. (2000). Parameters of remembering and forgetting in the transition from infancy to early childhood. *Monographs of the Society for Research in Child Development, 65*, 1–213.
Berliner, L., Hyman, I., Thomas, A., & Fitzgerald, M. (2003). Children's memory for traumatic and positive experiences. *Journal of Traumatic Stress, 16*, 229–236.
Berntsen, D., & Rubin, D. C. (2006). Flashbulb memories and posttraumatic stress reactions across the life span: Age-related effects of the German occupation of Denmark during World War II. *Psychology and Aging, 21*, 127–139.
Bidrose, S., & Goodman, G. S. (2000). Testimony and evidence: A scientific case study of memory for child sexual abuse. *Applied Cognitive Psychology, 14*(3), 197–213.
Bowlby, J. (1980). *Attachment and loss: Sadness and depression* (Vol. III). New York: Basic Books.
Brady, M. S., Poole, D. A., Warren, A. R., & Jones, H. R. (1999). Young children's responses to yes-no questions: Patterns and problems. *Applied Developmental Science, 3*, 47–57.
Brainerd, C. J., & Poole, D. A. (1997). Long-term survival of children's false memories: A review. *Learning and Individual Differences, 9*, 125–151.
Brainerd, C. J., Reyna, V. F., Howe, M. L., & Kingma, J. (1990). The development of forgetting and reminiscence. *Monographs of the Society for Research in Child Development, 55*, 1–109.
Bright-Paul, A., Jarrold, C., & Wright, D. B. (2005). Age-appropriate cues facilitate source-monitoring and reduce suggestibility in 3- to 7-year-olds. *Cognitive Development, 20*, 1–18.
Bright-Paul, A., Jarrold, C., & Wright, D. B. (2008). Theory-of-mind development influences suggestibility and source monitoring. *Developmental Psychology, 44*, 1055–1068.
Bruck, M., Ceci, S. J., Francoeur, E., & Barr, R. (1995). "I hardly cried when I got my shot": Influencing children's reports about a visit to their pediatrician. *Child Development, 66*, 193–208.
Buck, J., Warren, A., Betman, S., & Brigham, J. (2002). Age differences in Criteria-Based Content Analysis scores in typical child sexual abuse interviews. *Journal of Applied Developmental Psychology, 23*, 267–283.
Bugental, D. B., Blue, J., Cortez, V., Fleck, K., & Rodriguez, A. (1992). Influences of witnessed affect on information processing in children. *Child Development, 63*, 774–786.
Burch, M. M., Austin, J., & Bauer, P. J. (2004). Understanding the emotional past: Relations between parent and child contributions in emotionally negative and nonnegative events. *Journal of Experimental Child Psychology, 89*, 276–297.
Burgwyn-Bailes, E., Baker-Ward, L., Gordon, B. N., & Ornstein, P. A. (2001). Children's memory for emergency medical treatment after one year: The impact of individual difference variables on recall and suggestibility. *Applied Cognitive Psychology, 15*, S25–S48.
Ceci, S. J., & Bruck, M. (1993). Suggestibility of the child witness: A historical review and synthesis. *Psychological Bulletin, 113*, 403–439.
Cederborg, A., Lamb, M. E., & Laurell, O. (2007). Delay of disclosure, minimization, and denial of abuse when the evidence is unambiguous: A multivictim case. In M. Pipe, M. E. Lamb, Y. Orbach, & A. Cederborg (Eds.), *Child sexual abuse: Disclosure, delay, and denial* (pp. 159–173). Lawrence: Mahwah, NJ.

Chae, Y., Goodman, G. S., & Edelstein, R. S. (2011). The development of autobiographical memory from an attachment perspective: The special role of negative events. *Advances in Child Development and Behavior, 40*, 1–49. New York: Academic Press.

Chae, Y., Ogle, C. M., & Goodman, G. S. (2009). Remembering negative childhood experiences: An attachment theory perspective. In J. Quas & R. Fivush (Eds.), *Emotion and memory in development: Biological, cognitive, and social considerations* (pp. 3–27). New York: Oxford University Press.

Chen, E., Zeltzer, L. K., Craske, M. G., & Katz, E. R. (2000). Children's memories for painful cancer treatment procedures: Implications for distress. *Child Development, 71*, 933–947.

Clancy, S. (2009). *The trauma myth*. New York: Basic Books.

Clarke-Stewart, K. A., Malloy, L. C., & Allhusen, V. D. (2004). Verbal ability, self-control, and close relationships with parents protect children against misleading suggestions. *Applied Cognitive Psychology, 18*, 1037–1058.

Cordon, I. M., Pipe, M.-E., Sayfan, L., Melinder, A., & Goodman, G. S. (2004). Memory for traumatic experiences in early childhood. *Developmental Review, 24*, 101–132.

Dalenberg, C. J. (1996). Fantastic elements in child disclosure of abuse. *APSAC Advisor, 9*(1), 5–6.

Davidson, D., & Jergovic, D. (1996). Children's memory for atypical actions in script-based stories: An examination of the disruption effect. *Journal of Experimental Child Psychology, 61*, 134–152.

Davidson, D., Luo, Z., & Burden, M. J. (2001). Children's recall of emotional behaviours, emotional labels, and nonemotional behaviors: Does emotion enhance memory? *Cognition and Emotion, 15*, 1–26.

DiPietro, E. K., Runyan, D. K., & Fredrickson, D. D. (1997). Predictors of disclosure during medical evaluation for suspected sexual abuse. *Journal of Child Sexual Abuse, 6*, 133–142.

Dykas, M. J., Ehrlich, K. B., & Cassidy, J. (2011). Links between attachment and social information processing: Examination of intergenerational processes. *Advances in Child Development and Behavior, 40*, 51–94.

Edelstein, R. S., Ghetti, S., Quas, J. A., Goodman, G. S., Alexander, K. W., Redlich, A. D., & Cordon, I. M. (2005). Individual differences in emotional memory: Adult attachment and long-term memory for child sexual abuse. *Personality and Social Psychology Bulletin, 31*(11), 1537–1548.

Fivush, R., Sales, J. M., Goldberg, A., Bahrick, L., & Parker, J. (2004). Weathering the storm: Children's long-term recall of Hurricane Andrew. *Memory, 12*, 104–118.

Fivush, R., & Vasudeva, A. (2002). Remembering to relate: Socioemotional correlates of mother-child reminiscing. *Journal of Cognition and Development, 3*, 73–90.

Forgas, J. P., Burnham, D. K., & Trimboli, C. (1988). Mood, memory, and social judgments in children. *Journal of Personality and Social Psychology, 54*, 697–703.

Ghetti, S., & Angelini, L. (2008). The development of recollection and familiarity in childhood and adolescence: Evidence from the dual-process signal detection model. *Child Development, 79*, 339–358.

Ghetti, S., Goodman, G. S., Eisen, M. L., Qin, J., & Davis, S. L. (2002). Consistency in reports of sexual and physical abuse. *Child Abuse & Neglect, 26*, 977–995.

Ghetti, S., Qin, J., & Goodman, G. S. (2002). False memories in children and adults: Age, distinctiveness, and subjective experience. *Developmental Psychology, 38*, 705–718.

Goodman, G. S., Batterman-Faunce, J. M., Schaaf, J. M., & Kenney, R. (2002). Nearly 4 years after an event: Children's eyewitness memory and adults' perception of children's accuracy. *Child Abuse & Neglect, 26*, 849–884.

Goodman, G. S., Ghetti, S., Quas, J. A., Edelstein, R. S., Alexander, K. W., Redlich, A. D., & Jones, D. P. H. (2003). A prospective study of memory for child sexual abuse: New findings relevant to the repressed-memory controversy. *Psychological Science, 14*, 113–118.

Goodman, G. S., Hirschman, J. E., Hepps, D., & Rudy, L. (1991). Children's memory for stressful events. *Merrill-Palmer Quarterly, 37*, 109–157.

Goodman, G. S., Ogle, C. M., Block, S. D., Harris, L., Larsen, R., Augusti, E.-M., …Urquiza, A. (2011). False memory for trauma-related DRM lists in adolescents and adults with histories of child sexual abuse. *Development and Psychopathology, 23*, 423–438.

Goodman, G. S., & Quas, J. A. (1997). Trauma and memory: Individual differences in children's recounting of a stressful experience. In N. L. Stein, P. A. Ornstein, B. Tversky, & C. Brainerd (Eds.), *Memory for everyday and emotional events* (pp. 267–294). Mahwah, NJ: Lawrence Erlbaum.

Goodman, G. S., & Quas, J. A. (2008). It's when and how, not just how many: Repeated interviews and children's memory. *Current Directions in Psychology, 17*, 386–390.

Goodman, G. S., Quas, J. A., Batterman-Faunce, J. M., Riddlesberger, M. M., & Kuhn, J. (1994). Predictors of accurate and inaccurate memories of traumatic events experienced in childhood. *Consciousness and Cognition, 3*, 269–294.

Goodman, G. S., Quas, J. A., Batterman-Faunce, J. M., Riddlesberger, M. M., & Kuhn, J. (1997). Children's reactions and memory for a stressful event: Influences of age, anatomical dolls, knowledge, and parental attachment. *Applied Developmental Science, 1*, 54–75.

Goodman, G. S., Quas, J. A., & Ogle, C. M. (2010). Childhood trauma and memory. *Annual Review of Psychology, 61*, 325–351.

Goodman-Brown, T. B., Edelstein, R. S., Goodman, G. S., Jones, D. P. H., & Gordon, D. S. (2003). Why children tell: A model of children's disclosure of sexual abuse. *Child Abuse & Neglect, 27*, 525–540.

Hershkowitz, I. (2001). A case study of child sexual false allegation. *Child Abuse & Neglect, 25*, 1397–1411.

Hershkowitz, I., Lanes, O., & Lamb, M. E. (2007). Exploring the disclosure of child sexual abuse with alleged victims and their parents. *Child Abuse & Neglect, 31*, 111–123.

Horowitz, S. W., Lamb, M. E., Esplin, P. W., Boychuck, T. D., Reiter-Lavery, L., & Krispin, O. (1995). Establishing ground truth in studies of child sexual abuse. *Expert Evidence, 42*, 42–51.

Howe, M. L. (1997). Children's memory for traumatic experiences. *Learning and Individual Differences, 9*, 153–174.

Howe, M. L. (2000). *The fate of early memories: Developmental science and the retention of childhood experiences.* Washington, DC: American Psychological Association.

Howe, M. L. (2006). Developmental invariance in distinctiveness effects in memory. *Developmental Psychology, 42*, 1193–1205.

Howe, M. L. (2007). Children's emotional false memories. *Psychological Science, 18*, 856–860.

Howe, M. L. (2011). *The nature of early memory: An adaptive theory of the genesis and development of memory.* New York: Oxford University Press.

Howe, M. L., Courage, M. L., & Bryant-Brown, L. (1993). Reinstating children's memories. *Developmental Psychology, 26*, 292–303.

Howe, M. L., Courage, M. L., Vernescu, R., & Hunt, M. (2000). Distinctiveness effects in children's long-term retention. *Developmental Psychology, 36*, 778–792.

Hudson, J. A., & Fivush, R. (1991). As time goes by: Sixth graders remember a kindergarten experience. *Applied Cognitive Psychology, 5*, 347–360.

Johnson, R. J., Greenhoot, A. F., Glisky, E., & McCloskey, L. A. (2005). The relations among abuse, depression, and adolescents' autobiographical memory. *Journal of Clinical Child and Adolescent Psychology, 4*, 235–247.

Johnson, M. K., Hashtroudi, S., & Lindsay, D. S. (1993). Source monitoring. *Psychological Bulletin, 114*, 3–28.

La Rooy, D., Katz, C., Malloy, L. C., & Lamb, M. E. (2010). Do we need to rethink guidance on repeated interviews? *Psychology, Public Policy, and Law, 16*, 373–392.

Larson, R., Chae, Y., Augusti, E. M., Alley, D., Hansen, R., & Goodman, G. S. (2009). Children's use of body drawings to recall a stressful event. In M. Bruck, & M. E. Lamb, (Chairs), *Children's memories and reports of touching events.* Symposium presented at the Association of Psychological Science, San Francisco, CA.

Leander, L. (2010). Police interviews with child sexual abuse victims: Patterns of reporting, avoidance and denial. *Child Abuse & Neglect, 34*, 192–205.

Leander, L., Christianson, S. Å., & Granhag, P. A. (2007). A sexual abuse case study: Children's memories and reports. *Psychiatry, Psychology, and Law, 14*(1), 120–129.

Leander, L., Christianson, S. Å., & Granhag, P. A. (2008). Internet-initiated sexual abuse: Adolescent victims' reports about on- and off-line sexual activities. *Applied Cognitive Psychology, 22*, 1260–1274.

Leander, L., Granhag, P. A., & Christianson, S. Å. (2005). Children exposed to obscene phone calls: What they remember and tell. *Child Abuse & Neglect, 29*, 871–888.

Lindberg, M. A., Jones, S., McComas, L. M., & Thomas, S. W. (2001). Similarities and differences in eyewitness testimonies of children who directly versus vicariously experience stress. *Journal of Genetic Psychology, 162*, 314–333.

London, K., Bruck, M., & Melnyk, L. (2009). Post-event information affects children's autobiographical memory after one year. *Law and Human Behavior, 33*, 344–355.

Melinder, A., Alexander, K., Cho, Y., Goodman, G. S., Thoresen, C., & Lonnum, K. (2010). Children's eyewitness memory: A comparison of two interviewing strategies as realized by forensic professionals. *Journal of Experimental Child Psychology, 105*, 156–177.

Merritt, K. A., Ornstein, P. A., & Spicker, B. (1994). Children's memory for a salient medical procedure: Implications for testimony. *Pediatrics, 94*, 17–23.

Moradi, A. R., Taghavi, M. R., Neshat-Doost, H. T., Yule, W., & Dalgleish, T. (2000). Memory bias for emotional information in children and adolescents with posttraumatic stress disorder: A preliminary study. *Journal of Anxiety Disorders, 14*, 521–534.

Neisser, U., & Harsch, N. (1992). Phantom flashbulbs: False recollections of hearing the news about challenger. In E. Winograd & U. Neisser (Eds.), *Affect and accuracy in recall: Studies of "flashbulb" memories* (Emory symposia in cognition, Vol. 4, pp. 9–31). New York: Cambridge University Press.

Nelson, K. (1993). The psychological and social origins of autobiographical memory. *Psychological Science, 4*, 7–14.

Neshat-Doost, H. T., Taghavi, M. R., Moradi, A. R., Yule, W., & Dalgleish, T. (1998). Memory for emotional trait adjectives in clinically depressed youth. *Journal of Abnormal Psychology, 107*, 642–650.

Nourkova, V., Bernstein, D. M., & Loftus, E. F. (2004). Altering traumatic memory. *Cognition & Emotion, 18*, 575–585.

Orbach, Y., & Lamb, M. E. (1999). Assessing the accuracy of a child's account of sexual abuse: A case study. *Child Abuse & Neglect, 23*, 91–98.

Peterson, C. (1999). Children's memory for medical emergencies: 2 years later. *Developmental Psychology, 35*, 1493–1506.

Peterson, C. (2002). Children's long-term memory for autobiographical events. *Developmental Review, 22*, 370–402.

Peterson, C., & Bell, M. (1996). Children's memory for traumatic injury. *Child Development, 67*, 3045–3070.

Peterson, C., & Whalen, N. (2001). Five years later: Children's memory for medical emergencies. *Applied Cognitive Psychology, 15*, S7–S24.

Pezdek, K. (2003). Event memory and autobiographical memory for the events of September 11, 2001. *Applied Cognitive Psychology, 17*, 1033–1045.

Pezdek, K., Morrow, A., Blandon-Gitlin, I., Goodman, G. S., Quas, J. A., Saywitz, K. J., … Brodie, L. (2004). Detecting deception in children: Event familiarity affects Criterion-Based Content Analysis ratings. *Journal of Applied Psychology, 89*, 119–126.

Pillemer, D. B. (1992). Preschool children's memories of personal circumstances: The fire alarm study. In E. Winograd & U. Neisser (Eds.), *Affect and accuracy in recall: Studies of "flashbulb" memories* (pp. 121–137). New York: Cambridge University Press.

Pillemer, D. B., Picariello, M. L., & Pruett, J. C. (1994). Very long term memories of a salient preschool event. *Journal of Applied Cognitive Psychology, 8*, 95–106.

Pipe, M.-E., Goodman, G. S., Quas, J., Bidrose, S., Ablin, D., & Craw, S. (1997). Remembering early experiences during childhood. In J. D. Read & D. S. Lindsay (Eds.), *Recollections of trauma: Scientific evidence and clinical practice* (pp. 417–423). New York: Plenum.

Poole, D. A., & Lindsay, D. S. (2001). Children's eyewitness reports after exposure to misinformation from parents. *Journal of Experimental Child Psychology: Applied, 7*, 27–50.

Poole, D. A., & Lindsay, D. S. (2002). Reducing child witnesses' false reports of misinformation from parents. *Journal of Experimental Child Psychology, 81*, 117–140.

Poole, D. A., & White, L. T. (1991). Effects of question repetition on the eyewitness testimony of children and adults. *Developmental Psychology, 27*, 975–986.

Pynoos, R. S., & Eth, S. (1984). The child as witness to homicide. *Journal of Social Issues, 40*, 87–108.

Pynoos, R. S., & Nader, K. (1989). Children's memory and proximity to violence. *Journal of the American Academy of Child and Adolescent Psychiatry, 28*, 236–241.

Quas, J. A., Goodman, G. S., Bidrose, S., Pipe, M.-E., Craw, S., & Ablin, D. (1999). Emotion and memory: Children's long-term remembering, forgetting, and suggestibility. *Journal of Experimental Child Psychology, 72*, 235–270.

Quas, J. A., Malloy, L. C., Melinder, A., Goodman, G. S., D'Mello, M., & Schaaf, J. (2007). Developmental differences in the effects of repeated interviews and interviewer bias on young children's event memory and false reports. *Developmental Psychology, 43*, 823–837.

Raskin, D. C., & Esplin, P. W. (1991). *Assessment of children's statements of sexual abuse.* Washington, DC: APA.

Rassin, E. (2000). Criterion based content analysis: The less scientific road to truth. *Expert Evidence, 7*, 265–278.

Reese, E., Haden, C. A., & Fivush, R. (1993). Mother-child conversations about the past: Relationships of style and memory over time. *Cognitive Development, 8*, 403–430.

Reviere, S. L., & Bakeman, R. (2001). The effects of early trauma on autobiographical memory and schematic self-representation. *Applied Cognitive Psychology, 15*, 89–100.

Roberts, K. P., & Powell, M. B. (2005). The relation between inhibitory control and children's eyewitness memory. *Applied Cognitive Psychology, 19*, 1003–1018.

Roebers, C. M., Gelhaar, T., & Schneider, W. (2004). "It's magic!" The effects of presentation modality on children's event memory, suggestibility, and confidence judgments. *Journal of Experimental Child Psychology, 87*, 320–335.

Roebers, C. M., & Schneider, W. (2002). Stability and consistency of children's event recall. *Cognitive Development, 17*, 1085–1103.

Roebers, C. M., Schwartz, S., & Neumann, R. (2005). Social influence and children's event recall and suggestibility. *The European Journal of Developmental Psychology, 2*, 47–69.

Rudy, L., & Goodman, G. S. (1991). Effects of participation on children's reports: Implications for children's testimony. *Developmental Psychology, 27*, 527–538.

Salmon, K., Price, J., & Pereira, J. K. (2002). Factors associated with young children's long-term recall of an invasive medical procedure: A preliminary investigation. *Developmental and Behavioral Pediatrics, 23*, 347–352.

Sas, D. L., Hatch, A., Malla, S., Dick, T., & Hurley, P. (1993). *Three years after the verdict: A longitudinal study of the social and psychological adjustment of child witnesses referred to the child witness project.* London, Canada: London Family Court Clinic.

Saywitz, K. J., Goodman, G. S., Nicholas, E., & Moan, S. F. (1991). Children's memories of a physical examination involving genital touch: Implications for reports of child sexual abuse. *Journal of Consulting and Clinical Psychology, 59*, 682–691.

Schaaf, J., Alexander, K., & Goodman, G. S. (2008). Predictors of children's true disclosure and false memory. *Journal of Experimental Child Psychology, 100*, 157–185.

Schneider, W., & Pressley, M. (1997). *Memory development between two and twenty* (2nd ed.). Mahwah, NJ: Lawrence Erlbaum Associates.

Shrimpton, S., Oates, K., & Hayes, S. (1998). Children's memory of events: Effects of stress, age, time delay and location of interview. *Applied Cognitive Psychology, 12*, 133–143.

Sjöberg, R. L., & Lindblad, F. (2002). Limited disclosure of sexual abuse in children whose experiences were documented by videotape. *The American Journal of Psychiatry, 159*, 312–314.

Sjöberg, R. L., & Lindhom, T. (2005). A systematic review of age-related errors in children's memories for voiding cystourethrograms (VCUG). *European Child & Adolescent Psychiatry, 14*, 104–105.

Terr, L. C. (1981). Psychic trauma in children: Observations following the Chowchilla school-bus kidnapping. *The American Journal of Psychiatry, 138*, 14–19.

Terr, L. C. (1983). Chowchilla revisited: The effects of psychic trauma four years after a school-bus kidnapping. *The American Journal of Psychiatry, 140*, 1543–1550.

Terr, L. C. (1988). What happens to early memories of trauma? A study of twenty children under age five at the time of documents events. *Journal of the American Academy of Child and Adolescent Psychiatric, 27*, 96–104.

Terr, L. C., Bloch, D. A., Michel, B. A., & Shi, H. (1996). Children's memories in the wake of Challenger. *The American Journal of Psychiatry, 153*, 618–625.

Thierry, K. L., & Spence, M. J. (2004). A real-life event enhances the accuracy of preschoolers' recall. *Applied Cognitive Psychology, 18*, 297–309.

Van Abbema, D. L., & Bauer, P. J. (2005). Autobiographical memory in middle childhood: Recollections of the recent and distant past. *Memory, 13*, 829–845.

van Giezen, A. E., Arensman, E., Spinhoven, P., & Wolters, G. (2005). Consistency of memory for emotionally arousing events: A review of prospective and experimental studies. *Clinical Psychology Review, 25*, 935–953.

Wareham, P., & Salmon, K. (2006). Mother-child reminiscing about everyday experiences: Implications for psychological interventions in the preschool years. *Clinical Psychology Review, 26*, 535–554.

Warren, A. R., & Swartwood, J. N. (1992). Developmental issues in flashbulb memory research: Children recall the challenger event. In E. Winograd & U. Neisser (Eds.), *Affect and accuracy in recall: Studies of "flashbulb" memories* (pp. 95–120). New York: Cambridge University Press.

Westmacott, R., & Moscovitch, M. (2003). The contribution of autobiographical significance to semantic memory. *Memory and Cognition, 31*, 761–774.

Williams, L. M. (1994). Recall of childhood trauma: A prospective study of women's memories of child sexual abuse. *Journal of Consulting and Clinical Psychology, 62*, 1167–1176.

Winograd, E., & Killinger, W. A. (1983). Relating age at encoding in early childhood to adult recall: Development of flashbulb memories. *Journal of Experimental Psychology. General, 112*, 413–422.

Yuille, J. C. (1988). *Credibility assessment*. Dordrecht, Netherlands: Kluwer.

Yuille, J. C., & Cutshall, J. L. (1986). A case study of eyewitness memory of a crime. *Journal of Applied Psychology, 71*, 291–301.

Yuille, J. C., Hunter, R., Joffe, R., & Zaparniuk, J. (1993). Interviewing children in sexual abuse cases. In G. S. Goodman & B. L. Bottoms (Eds.), *Child victims, child witnesses: Understanding and improving testimony* (pp. 95–115). New York: Guilford Press.

Chapter 7
Does Testimonial Inconsistency Indicate Memory Inaccuracy and Deception? Beliefs, Empirical Research, and Theory

Ronald P. Fisher, Aldert Vrij, and Drew A. Leins

Introduction

When eyewitnesses and criminal suspects change their sworn testimony, their credibility is challenged, either because inconsistent testimony is a sign that people have poor memories or because they are deceptive and "can't keep their story straight." As reviewed below, inconsistency is the most often cited reason for discrediting others (e.g., Brewer, Potter, Fisher, Bond, & Lusczc, 1999; Granhag & Strömwall, 2000; Strömwall, Granhag, & Jonsson, 2003) and is often the attack point for impeaching witnesses in the courtroom. But is it justifiable? In support of this approach, research on memory warns us that changes in recollection may be the product of contamination from sources such as misleading questions, which could distort memory (Loftus, 1975; see Yarbrough, Hervé, & Harms, this volume). However, one can imagine just the opposite pattern: in an effort to sound truthful, good liars often simply repeat whatever they said earlier and, so, they may be more, not less, consistent than truth-tellers (Vrij, Granhag, & Mann, 2010). Perhaps the true meaning of inconsistency is not so obvious.

This chapter examines the role of inconsistency in memory and deception from a variety of perspectives. After showing that both experts and novices regularly use inconsistency to infer people's mental state—either a faulty memory or deception—we examine the scientific evidence itself: in fact, is inconsistency a valid predictor of inaccurate recollection or deception? Finally, we speculate about the psychological processes that underlie inconsistency and present a tentative framework to understand the phenomenon of inconsistency.

R.P. Fisher (✉) • D.A. Leins
Florida International University, Miami, FL, USA
e-mail: fisherr@fiu.edu

A. Vrij
University of Portsmouth, Portsmouth, UK

Inconsistency as a Predictor of Memory Inaccuracy

Inconsistency in the Legal Framework

Research examining the question of inconsistency as a predictor of memory accuracy has been conducted using survey and experimental methodology. Brewer and Burke (2002), Brewer and Hupfeld (2004), and Brewer et al. (1999) have surveyed lay people, police, attorneys, and judges, asking them to indicate how predictive of memory inaccuracy are various eyewitness behaviors, including: (a) inconsistency with previous statements, (b) too little confidence in testimony, (c) testimony not in chronological order, and (d) exaggeration of circumstances (see also Leippe, Manion, & Romanczyk, 1992). Invariably, the most predictive measure of perceived eyewitness inaccuracy was inconsistent testimony. In parallel with this survey research, others have conducted experimental research to see whether mock jurors assigned differential credibility to experimental witnesses who provided consistent versus inconsistent testimony (Berman & Cutler, 1996; Lindsay, Lim, Marando, & Cully, 1986). In these studies, participants observed or read transcripts of a simulated trial in which some witnesses responded consistently across testimony and other witnesses contradicted their earlier statements. Participants then rendered several decisions to reflect their credibility in the witnesses. The typical finding, which mirrors the survey research, is that participants judged inconsistent witnesses to be less credible than consistent witnesses.

Dependence on consistency of eyewitness reporting has made its way into law school training and the courtroom itself. Books written by expert litigators encourage attorneys to monitor, or even create, inconsistencies in (their opponents') eyewitnesses' testimonies for the purpose of impeaching them. Glissan (1991) recommends: "A true inconsistency can effectively destroy a witness, and sometimes a whole case … If you find a true inconsistency, or if you can manufacture one, then use the deposition of previous evidence to sheet it home" (p. 108). Finally, the law itself, in the form of judicial instructions, directs jurors to attend to inconsistencies within witness statements. A standard (U.S.) federal instruction on witness credibility directs jurors to attend to whether "the witness testified inconsistently while on the witness stand, or if the witness said or did something, or failed to say or do something, at any other time that is inconsistent with what the witness said while testifying" (Committee on Pattern Jury Instructions of the District Judges Association, 2005). In short, just about everyone involved in a legal investigation (e.g., police, defense and prosecuting attorneys, judges) believes that inconsistent testimony is a sign of inaccurate recollection (see Connolly & Price, this volume).

We can understand why attorneys would argue that eyewitnesses who testify inconsistently should be impeached. If attorneys take as their goal to convince the judge or jury that their side of the argument is correct and, if the judge or jury believes that inconsistent testimony is an indicator of having a weak memory, then, not surprisingly, attorneys will play into that belief and highlight those instances in which the opposing eyewitness provided inconsistent testimony. From the scientific perspective, however, we are not so concerned about convincing others but whether *in fact* inconsistent testimony is a valid predictor of an eyewitness' inaccurate memory. Is it the case, as most people seem to believe, that inconsistent eyewitnesses are much less accurate than consistent eyewitnesses?

Scientific Research on Inconsistency

Prior to 1970, there were relatively few studies about the (in)consistency of memory with repeated testing (for reviews, see Erdelyi, 1996; Payne, 1987). Most theories of memory were concerned with recollection at the (one) time of testing, and the science of memory had little to say about how memory for individual items might change over repeated testing. More recently, researchers have become interested in the (in)stability of recollection. Much of this research emanates from the field of autobiographical memory, where researchers have sometimes tested people repeatedly for earlier real-life experiences (see Connolly & Price, this volume). These studies generally show that, although many of our repeated recollections are stable, there are some instances of change, either in the form of (a) direct contradictions of earlier claims, (b) new recollections that did not appear on earlier tests, or (c) old recollections dropping out from later reports. This occurs for conventional autobiographical experiences and also for highly arousing or flashbulb memories (see Paz-Alonso, Ogle, & Goodman, this volume). One historically noteworthy finding was reported by Wagenaar and Groeneweg (1990) who compared Holocaust survivors' memories of their imprisonment experience when tested initially in the mid-1940s and again in the mid-1980s. In general, most recollections, and especially of central events and actions, were reported consistently over time, although some details—typically non-central, context-defining elements (e.g., dates and specific locations of objects)—were reported inconsistently. A related study was reported by Fisher, Falkner, Trevisan, and McCauley (2000), who described people's recollections of typical activities (e.g., visiting friends, playing sports, doing laundry). People were tested initially in 1960, as part of an epidemiological survey, and again in 1995 as part of a psychological study of long-term recall. In general, people provided similar answers about their activities across the 35-year interval (e.g., whether they engaged in the activity or not), although there were some inconsistencies about frequency (e.g., whether they did the activity once per week or less often). Finally, a few studies have examined flashbulb-memory kinds of experience (e.g., political assassinations, terrorist activities) and, again, central experiences (e.g., whether the World Trade Center was destroyed, or whether President Kennedy was assassinated) are reported consistently, whereas peripheral details of the learning experience (e.g., in which location or from which source one learned about the experience) are sometimes reported inconsistently (e.g., Pezdek, 2003).

These naturalistic studies of autobiographical memory show some instances of inconsistency—which some may consider surprising, given the importance of these events. However, because they are naturalistic events and not experimenter-created, we do not know whether the recollections are historically accurate (e.g., whether the Holocaust inmate was actually beaten at one prison camp or another; whether the participant heard about Kennedy's assassination from a friend or from a teacher). In order to determine if inconsistency is predictive of accuracy, we must turn to laboratory studies, where we know exactly what occurred, and hence we can measure accuracy in addition to consistency.

Experimental Testing

We describe here a series of laboratory experiments that converge on the relation between consistency and accuracy of eyewitness recall. Each of the experiments followed the same general plan. Experimental witnesses (e.g., usually college students) either watched a videotape of a simulated crime (i.e., robbery or homicide) or observed a live, innocuous event or a staged confrontation between two people. The witnesses were then interviewed twice to assess their memories of the observed event. The first interview occurred shortly after observing the event (i.e., within 30 min), and the second interview occurred after a delay of up to 2 weeks. The interviewers' questions were either open-ended (e.g., Describe the robber) or closed: cued recall (e.g., what color was the robber's hair?), multiple choice (e.g., what color was the robber's hair: blond, black, or brown?), or true/false (e.g., the robber's hair was brown: true or false?). The witnesses were sometimes encouraged to be very certain before volunteering an answer, sometimes encouraged to guess, and sometimes not provided any explicit instructions about certainty.

We compared each witness' statements across the two interviews and categorized them as one of four types: consistent (i.e., same answer at Time 1 and Time 2, e.g., *robber was clean shaven* at Time 1, and *robber was clean shaven* at Time 2), contradiction (i.e., contradictory answers at Time1 [*clean shaven*] and Time 2 [*bearded*]), reminiscent (i.e., no answer at Time 1, but witness provided an answer at Time 2 [*clean shaven*]), and forgotten (i.e., witness provided an answer at Time 1 [*clean shaven*] but no answer at Time 2). We then calculated the accuracy of each of the four response categories in addition to the accuracy of the entire testimony. Accuracy was calculated separately at Time 1 and Time 2 by dividing the number of correct statements by the total number of statements reported. For instance, if at Time 1, a witness made eight correct statements (i.e., out of ten total statements), then his or her accuracy rate at Time 1 was 0.8 (8/10).

Two corollaries of the common belief that inconsistent recall is predictive of memory inaccuracy are examined here. First, individual statements that are reported inconsistently should be less accurate than those reported consistently. Second, witnesses who make more inconsistent statements should be generally less accurate than witnesses who make fewer inconsistent statements.

Inaccuracy of Inconsistent Statements

In all of our experiments, the accuracy rate of contradictory statements was low (Brock, Fisher, & Cutler, 1999; Fisher & Patterson, 2004; Gilbert & Fisher, 2006). For instance, in Gilbert and Fisher, the accuracy rate of contradictory statements was 0.49 (i.e., averaged across Time 1 and Time 2); by comparison, the accuracy rate of consistent answers was 0.95. At some level, this should be obvious, since, if a witness gives contradictory answers (e.g., clean shaven & bearded) then at least one of those answers must be wrong—which sets the upper level of accuracy at 0.50. By contrast, if people's recollections are generally accurate, then consistent statements, which constitute the bulk of most reports, will be very accurate. Experimental testing, therefore, supports the common belief that contradictory statements are relatively inaccurate.

What about other forms of inconsistent recollections, forgotten, and reminiscent items? In Gilbert and Fisher (2006), forgotten and reminiscent items were recalled almost as accurately (i.e., 0.93 and 0.87, respectively) as consistent items (i.e., 0.95; see La Rooy, Pipe, & Murray, 2005 for comparable findings with child witnesses, although note some studies in which reminiscent answers were less accurate: see Brock, Fisher, & Cutler, 1999; La Rooy, Lamb, & Pipe, 2008). The high accuracy of reminiscent items is particularly interesting, as it violates the commonly held belief that memory gets worse with the passage of time—and hence is often challenged in the courtroom (see Hervé, Cooper, & Yuille, this volume). If nothing else, these results suggest that we need to distinguish between different kinds of inconsistency. Only contradictory statements are grossly less accurate than consistent recollections. Forgotten and reminiscent statements, although somewhat less accurate than consistent statements, may be generally accurate.

Inconsistent Versus Consistent Witnesses

Although contradictory statements were considerably less accurate than consistent statements, inconsistency's ability to predict accuracy changed when the same data set was analyzed at the level of the individual witness. That is, *witnesses* who made many contradictory statements were not much less accurate than witnesses who made no or only a few contradictory statements. To examine the role of inconsistency at the witness level, we scored each witness in terms of the consistency of his/her recall (i.e., the proportion of all statements that were contradictory) and the accuracy of his/her recall (i.e., the proportion of all statements that were accurate). Across the various conditions of the experiments, the correlations between inconsistency and accuracy were relatively low (i.e., the Pearson correlation coefficients were generally between 0.00 and 0.35; Brewer et al., 1999; Fisher & Cutler, 1995; Fisher & Patterson, 2004; Gilbert & Fisher, 2006). Inconsistent witnesses were almost as accurate as consistent witnesses. Furthermore, this pattern held whether the inconsistencies occurred on material or peripheral aspects of the crime (Carbone & Fisher, 2011).

There is an apparent conundrum here: contradictory statements are much less accurate than consistent statements, yet witnesses who make many contradictory statements are almost as accurate as witnesses who make none or a few contradictory statements. We believe that this conundrum can be explained by the idea that the various components of a complex event (e.g., a crime) are processed nearly independently of one another. That is, accuracy of memory for one component of a complex event tells us very little about accuracy of memory for other components of the event (see Hervé et al., this volume). Thus, if a specific statement (e.g., facial hair) is believed to be inaccurate, because the witness contradicted her/himself, this tells us very little or nothing about the accuracy of the remainder of the testimony (e.g., description of gun). To test this idea, we conducted several experiments in which witnesses attempted to describe the various components of complex events. We then measured the relationships between accuracy levels for each of these various components. For example, Brewer et al. (1999) classified the recall of witnesses to a bank robbery into five different dimensions—offender description, offender actions, bystander description, bystander actions, and objects—and found no meaningful relationships between accuracy on one dimension and that on any other. Other studies have replicated this finding (e.g., Fisher et al., 2000; Mitchell, Haw, & Fisher, 2003). It is not surprising, therefore, that inaccurate recollection for a few, isolated parts of a crime (e.g., as inferred by contradictory statements) cannot predict the accuracy of the witness's overall testimony. That is, inconsistency of recollection informs us about the *specific statement* that is reported inconsistently, but it tells us little or nothing about the accuracy of the *rest of the witness's testimony*.

We believe that this pattern, of the independence across elements of a complex event, is critical as it exposes the weakness of a common courtroom tactic. Specifically, attorneys will often demonstrate that one specific statement with an eyewitness's testimony is incorrect, either because the statement is inconsistent with an earlier statement or because other, reliable evidence contradicts the eyewitness's statement (e.g., the eyewitness claims that she heard two gunshots, but the police found four bullet casings.). After demonstrating that the eyewitness was wrong about one element, the attorney then generalizes to the entire testimony, based on the assumption that memory for one element of the case is indicative of memory for all other elements of the case. Instead, our data show that extrapolating across elements is unfounded, and that the safer argument is to challenge only those specific statements that are inconsistent or otherwise shown to be incorrect.

A Framework for Understanding Inconsistency

The previous section reflected a purely empirical approach, but was not informed very well by cognitive theory. In order to make progress in understanding why inconsistency is or is not predictive of accuracy, we must first gain a better understanding of the psychological processes underlying the phenomenon of inconsistency itself. Therefore, an initial framework around which to understand inconsistency is presented here. This is not so much a formal theory as a general framework for thinking about the phenomenon of inconsistency.

The unifying principle within our framework is that *something* must change from the earlier test (T1) to the later retest (T2) to account for inconsistent recollection. Specifically, what changes from T1 to T2? We offer various candidates about what might change from T1 to T2, and then we leave it to the reader to develop these ideas more thoroughly. The candidates for change are the three components of memory (e.g., following Tulving, 1983): the *mental representation* of the event to be remembered (i.e., the "memory trace"), the *retrieval* processes that activate the mental representation, and *metacognition* (i.e., monitoring and controlling one's memory). We assume that (a) recollection is the product of activating or retrieving a memory of the to-be-recalled event or related knowledge, and (b) this product is monitored for confidence, so that a response is produced only if the assessed confidence level is above some criterion (Koriat & Goldsmith, 1996).

Underlying Mental Representation

The underlying mental representation may change over time, because (a) the eyewitness is exposed to some new information between T1 and T2 (e.g., either via communicating with other eyewitnesses, exposure to the media, or interviewers providing information via leading questions, [e.g., Gabbert, Memon, & Allen, 2003; Loftus, 1975]; see Yarbrough et al., this volume), or (b) there are systematic or random changes in the relative accessibility of events from T1 to T2, so that events that were relatively accessible at T1 may be less accessible at T2 (e.g., the different forgetting rates of gist and verbatim information; Brainerd & Reyna, 1993), or (c) the various events are rehearsed unequally, so that frequently rehearsed events become more accessible and infrequently rehearsed events become less accessible (see Hervé et al., this volume).

Retrieval Processes

The retrieval processes applied to the underlying mental representations may change over time. One kind of change may be global (e.g., shifting from reproductive to reconstructive recall). Reproductive recall refers to searching for the mental record of the specific to-be-remembered event (e.g., what I ate for breakfast this morning); reconstructive recall refers to constructing a memory from a schema or related set of knowledge (e.g., using my knowledge of what I usually eat for breakfast to calculate or construct what I probably ate for breakfast today; see discussion of script memories by Connolly & Price, this volume; Hervé et al., this volume; Paz-Alonso et al., this volume; Ogle, & Goodman, this volume). A second kind of change may reflect the specific retrieval cues available at T1 and T2. These changes may be brought about by changes in the wording of specific questions asked at T1 and T2, or even in the general style of interviewing as, for example, greater reliance on broad open-ended questions or on narrow, closed questions (see Yarbrough et al., this volume).

Metacognition

Eyewitnesses' thoughts about their own recollections or the goal of the interview may change over time. For instance, an eyewitness might adopt a more lenient output criterion at T1 and a more stringent output criterion at T2, or vice versa. These changes may manifest themselves with fewer or more "I don't know" responses, which may, in turn, alter the relative frequency of omission and commission errors (Evans, 2011). Such changes might reflect different interview contexts (e.g., police station vs. courtroom) or different instructions by the interviewers (e.g., to be complete or to be certain). Given these various candidates for the elements or processes that may change between T1 and T2, what are the implications for whether inconsistencies are predictive of accuracy? We organize these predictions along the three areas of change: underlying representation, retrieval processes, and metacognition.

Analysis by Components

If the underlying representation has changed because the eyewitness is exposed to new facts, then T2 recollection accuracy will depend on the validity of these new facts. They may be correct (e.g., if acquired from another, unbiased eyewitness who had a good view of the critical event) or incorrect (e.g., if acquired from a biased source, for instance, the opposing party's attorney or an investigator whose goal may be to introduce an error into the eyewitness' recollection). Although this approach is sound theoretically, in most realistic situations, it will be difficult to know who or what was the source of the newly exposed facts. Eyewitnesses may be exposed to many new sources and, given people's limitations to monitor the source of their knowledge (Johnson, Hashtroudi, & Lindsay, 1993), the validity of the newly exposed information is likely not to be known.

If the underlying representation changes because of differential forgetting or rehearsing, then T2 accuracy will depend on whether correct items are less or more likely to be forgotten or rehearsed than incorrect items. We cannot think of any a priori reason why incorrect recollections might be more likely to be rehearsed than correct recollections.

If the retrieval process, which is likely to be driven by the interviewer's question, has changed from T1 to T2, then it is important to know the specific questions that were posed to the eyewitness at T1 and T2. In general, open-ended questions yield more accurate recollections than closed questions (Fisher & Patterson, 2004). The difficulty in most investigations will be to know what questions were asked.

Interviewers (and eyewitnesses) are unlikely to remember the exact form of their own questions (Warren & Woodall, 1999). Tape recordings and videotapes should, therefore, contribute substantially to inferring the nature of the question posed and, hence, the likelihood of new recollections being correct (see Yarbrough et al., this volume).

Eyewitnesses' metacognitive processes, whether they use a lenient or stringent output criterion, may vary over time, perhaps influenced by interviewers encouraging or discouraging them to guess. Again, an audio or video record of the interview will be helpful to know whether interviewers encouraged eyewitnesses to be certain (high accuracy) or to guess (low accuracy) when responding.

In overview, whether inconsistent testimony is an indicator of memory inaccuracy depends theoretically on (a) which of the various psychological processes are responsible for the inconsistency, and (b) how the engaged psychological processes are related to recall accuracy. Furthermore, we should distinguish between different forms of inconsistency: direct contradictions, adding new information in a later interview (i.e., reminiscence), or forgetting earlier stated information. Presumably other factors are also involved. Put simply, the matter is not as simple as many believe.

Inconsistency as a Predictor of Deception

We turn now to the second area within the law in which inconsistent reporting leads observers to draw inferences about the respondent, viz., whether he/she is lying. Again, we ask (a) whether people use inconsistency to infer deception, and (b) in fact, how valid is inconsistency as a predictor of deception?

Beliefs About Inconsistency

Parallel to the research showing that inconsistency influences observers' beliefs about eyewitness memory, research also shows that inconsistency influences observers' beliefs about eyewitnesses' veracity. This follows from both informal and formal surveys and from controlled laboratory experiments. A casual search through the Internet shows that many investigators and training agencies believe that inconsistency within a suspect's interview is a reliable cue to deception. The same belief is found in more formal print (e.g., interrogations manuals; Shuy, 1998; Zulawski & Wicklander, 1993). A survey of police officers about their experiences conducting sexual assault investigations found that inconsistency of reporting was the most commonly mentioned cue to detect deception (Greuel, 1992, as reported by Strömwall & Granhag, 2003). Similarly, Strömwall and Granhag asked experienced police officers, prosecutors, and judges to indicate their beliefs about signs of deception.

Eighty-two percent of the police officers, 72 % of the prosecutors, and 74 % of the judges indicated that truth-tellers' stories will be more consistent than liars' stories. In short, most people, irrespective of their professional experience, believe that inconsistency is an indicator of deception.

In addition to these surveys, Granhag, Strömwall, and their colleagues conducted several controlled laboratory studies to examine how observers relied on their beliefs about inconsistency (i.e., the consistency heuristic) to decide whether suspects were being deceptive (e.g., Granhag & Strömwall, 2000). In one study, Granhag and Strömwall (2001) showed a simulated crime to 24 witnesses and then interviewed each laboratory witness three times (i.e., after 3 hours, 4 days, and 11 days). Half of the witnesses were instructed to be truthful when describing the "crime" and half of the witnesses were asked to lie such that the victim was the perpetrator. These interviews were videotaped and shown to 144 observers who were asked to determine which of the witnesses were truthful and which were deceptive, and to justify their judgments. The most commonly reported justification of the deception judgments was inconsistency of the witness's story across repeated tellings. The same findings were observed when adults judged the veracity of children who had been interviewed twice (Strömwall & Granhag, 2005).

Strömwall et al. (2003) extended the earlier study to examine consistency in a novel fashion (i.e., consistency across two respondents) in addition to the earlier tested measure (i.e., consistency within one respondent on repeated interviews). In this innovative study, 10 pairs of people ate lunch at a restaurant and then returned to the laboratory to describe truthfully their lunch-time activities. Another matched group of 10 pairs of people did not go to lunch at the restaurant, but were asked to fabricate a lie that they had gone to lunch. All 40 people (i.e., 10 pairs of truth-tellers and 10 pairs of liars) were then interviewed about their truthful or fabricated lunch-time experiences. Videotape recordings of these interviews were then shown to 120 observers who decided which respondents were truthful and which were deceptive. The results show that observers depended on consistency both across respondents and, also, within each respondent, across time.

In short, lay people and experts within the fields of law enforcement and security strongly believe that inconsistent reporting, both across and within respondents, is grounds for doubting the veracity of the respondent.

Scientific Evidence Relating Consistency and Deception

As was the case with inconsistency as an indicator of poor memory, relatively little research has been conducted to examine whether inconsistency, in fact, is predictive of deception. This is odd, given that observers rely on inconsistency more than any other cue when multiple statements are available (Strömwall et al., 2003). We suspect that there is a paucity of research examining inconsistency as a predictor of deception and poor memory because such research is resource-demanding: the researcher must interview each respondent twice, compare the responses given at the two or more interviews, and then calculate the observed relationship between inconsistency and deception. Nevertheless, there are enough studies now, mainly from the labs of two teams of researchers (i.e., Granhag & Strömwall; Vrij & Fisher), that we can establish some general patterns.

Most of the laboratory studies examining the empirical relation between consistency and deception follow the same general procedure. Truth-telling participants (e.g., typically college students) are instructed to go to a specified location and engage in an activity (e.g., go to a restaurant and eat; go to a laboratory room and perform a specific task), whereas liars do not go to the specified location and do not participate in the activity. Liars typically spend a comparable amount of time thinking about such an activity. Truth-tellers and liars are then interviewed shortly thereafter by someone who is blind to the respondents' experimental condition. Truth-tellers are instructed to describe the event they participated in; liars are instructed to try to convince the interviewer that they actually participated in the event. After an interval of time following this first interview (i.e., Int-1), which might range from a few minutes to several days, the participants are interviewed a second time (i.e., Int-2) about the same event. The participants' responses on the two interviews are then compared and scored for consistency to determine whether the consistency score differs for liars and truth-tellers, as would be predicted by the consistency heuristic. In some variants of this procedure, the participants do the activities in pairs and both participants are interviewed (i.e., individually), so that consistency may be measured by comparing one member of the pair's responses to those of the other pair member.

Two distinct patterns emerge from these studies: in those studies conducted by Granhag and Strömwall, liars generated equivalent amounts or slightly fewer inconsistencies than did truth-tellers, whereas, in those studies conducted by Vrij and Fisher, liars produced more inconsistencies than did truth-tellers. We believe that the critical differences between the two sets of studies reflect (a) the participants' preparations for the interview, (b) the questions that the interviewers posed at the interview, and (c) the similarity of the questions at Int-1 and Int-2. In the Granhag/Strömwall studies, (a) the liars were given time to rehearse their stories prior to the interview whereas the truth-tellers did not have time to rehearse, (b) the interviewers asked the participants to describe in general what happened during the target activity (e.g., What did you do when you went to the restaurant?), and (c) the same questions were usually asked at Int-1 and Int-2. By comparison, in the Vrij/Fisher studies, (a) both the liars and the truth-tellers had time to prepare for the interview, (b) the questions asked about non-central aspects of the activity (e.g., Where was the waiter standing relative to your companion?), and (c) different questions were asked at Int-1 and Int-2. Why should it matter if (a) the participants have time to prepare for the interview, (b) the interviewer asks about the core activity or about a non-central detail, and (c) the questions asked at Int-1 and Int-2 are the same or different? We believe that two simple factors can account for the results: liars and truth-tellers (a) prepare differently and (b) use different retrieval strategies for the interview. These differences are expanded upon below, as they are critical to understanding the diverse patterns of results.

Differential Preparation

In preparation for the interview, liars are more likely than truth-tellers to rehearse their answers. As a result of this pre-interview rehearsal, liars are prepared to describe their (fabricated) story; however, they are prepared to narrate a response only to the questions that they anticipated, which is likely to be about the central activity. By contrast, truth-tellers do not prepare thoroughly for their interview, because they have less reason to think that the investigator will disbelieve them (Hartwig, Granhag, & Strömwall, 2007). Instead, truth-tellers rely on their being able to recall the critical event, which they can retrieve on command, to convince the interviewer of their veracity. We examine this explanation by (a) showing that liars do rehearse more than truth-tellers in preparing for the interview, and (b) exploring the implications of this differential rehearsal.

In a recent study in our lab, truthful participants were asked to go to the campus bookstore and engage in specific tasks, and then later to describe their activities (Cahill, Fisher, & Rivard, 2011). Liars did not go to the bookstore, but were asked to convince an interviewer that, in fact, they had gone to the bookstore. Prior to participating in the interview, the liars and truth-tellers were given 5 min to sit in a waiting room that was filled with a book of cartoons. The liars and truth-tellers were told that they could rehearse in preparation for the interview or they could read through the book of cartoons (and rate the cartoons for humor) or do whatever they wished prior to the interview. We assumed that, if the participants were preoccupied with rehearsing their fabricated story, they would not be enticed to look at the cartoons, whereas if they were not concerned about being believed, they would not bother rehearsing and would look at the cartoons. In support of the differential preparation hypothesis, liars read (rated) fewer cartoons than did the truth-tellers. Liars, compared to truth-tellers, were also more likely to tell the experimenter that they rehearsed in preparation for the interview.

As a result of liars rehearsing their stories more than truth-tellers, liars are better prepared than truth-tellers to tell their story during the interview—but only if the interviewer asks them questions that are compatible with how they rehearsed. Prompts such as "tell me what happened [at the critical time period],"— the types of prompts/questions used by Granhag and Strömwall—are likely to be compatible with the liars' rehearsal and, hence, are answered easily by the liars. Asking the same question on a later interview again allows liars to rely on their rehearsed story a second time and, not surprisingly, to generate the same stories on both occasions. Given that Granhag and Strömwall asked their participants questions that they could easily anticipate and likely rehearsed, it is not surprising that Granhag and Strömwall found that liars were as or more consistent than truth-tellers.

In a slightly different version of this study, Granhag, Strömwall, and Jonsson (2003) tested participants in pairs, as if two people had committed a crime together and were being interviewed (i.e., individually) about their earlier activity. Again, Granhag and colleagues gave the pairs of liars time (i.e., 30 min) to prepare for the interview. Given the time to prepare, liars were able to provide similar stories when asked the same easily anticipated questions/prompts: "tell me what happened [at the critical time period]." Once again, when liars can anticipate the interview question, they can rehearse before the interview and, as a result, their responses will match one another's and they will be consistent across time.

In comparison to the Granhag/Strömwall studies, where the interviewer asked easily anticipated questions, the studies conducted by Vrij, Fisher, and their colleagues posed questions that were not easily anticipated. For example, in Vrij et al. (2009), pairs of truth-telling participants went to and ate at a restaurant, whereas pairs of liars did not go to the restaurant but attempted to convince the interviewer that they did. They were then interviewed (i.e., individually), but the questions were difficult to anticipate, because they were specific and addressed non-central aspects of the activity (e.g., in relation to the front door and where you sat, where were the closest diners?). Not surprisingly, given the lack of opportunity to prepare answers to these questions, liars often contradicted one another as compared to truth-tellers, whose responses tended to corroborate one another. In a related set of studies, Leins, Fisher, Vrij, and Mann (2011) asked truth-telling participants to go to a designated room and engage in a set of activities (e.g., turn on the radio, untie the shoes). The participants were then interviewed twice with questions that they did not anticipate (e.g., where was the radio relative to the location of the shoes?). After answering such questions, the participants were then asked to draw a sketch of the room, placing within the sketch the various objects that they had named. Again, such a request was not anticipated, as confirmed by a post-experimental debriefing of the participants. The results replicated Vrij et al.'s earlier finding: when participants cannot anticipate the interview questions, liars contradict themselves more than truth-tellers. In summary, whether liars are less consistent than truth-tellers, as most people believe, or are equally or more consistent than truth-tellers, depends in part on whether they can anticipate the interviewer's questions (see Colwell, Hiscock-Anisman, & Fede, this volume).

Different Retrieval Strategies

Granhag and Strömwall (1999) postulated that liars adopt a different answering strategy than truth-tellers, because liars are more concerned that others will find out that they are lying. Hence, if liars believe that inconsistency is characteristic of lying, they will try to answer consistently across interviews. If they are successful in providing the same answer on both interviews, they may fool the investigator into thinking they are truthful, which ultimately is the goal of lying. In attempting to answer consistently, liars may, therefore, use the strategy of remembering what they said at the first interview and then repeating the same answer on the second interview (Granhag & Strömwall, 1999). By comparison, truth-tellers are likely to assume that, if they simply describe their truthful experience, the truth will "shine through" and they will be believed (Hartwig et al., 2007). Truth-tellers should, therefore, adopt the strategy of simply retrieving from memory their original experience and reconstructing it each time they are asked. The difference between the repeat (liars) and reconstruct (truth-tellers) strategies should be observable by focusing on the similarity of the questions at Int-1 and Int-2. Liars should find it easier to implement the response-repetition strategy if the questions at Int-2 are similar to those at Int-1. By comparison, truth-tellers, who always try to recall the original experience, should be relatively uninfluenced by the similarity of the questions across the two interviews. We should, therefore, predict that liars will be more influenced than truth-tellers by the similarity of the questions from Int-1 to Int-2. Specifically, liars should respond less consistently as the questions change from Int-1 to Int-2, whereas truth-tellers' consistency should not be influenced by the similarity of questions from Int-1 to Int-2.

Leins, Fisher, and Vrij (2012) examined this question-similarity hypothesis by asking liars and truth-tellers either the same questions or different questions on two interviews. In their study, the participants were interviewed twice. Half were required to use the same mode of responding on the two interviews (i.e., recall verbally at both Int-1 and Int-2, or draw a sketch at both Int-1 and Int-2) and half were required to use a different mode of responding on the two interviews (i.e., recall verbally at Int-1 but draw a sketch at Int-2, or vice versa). The experimenter then scored the two interviews to see if the participants responded consistently or not. For example, if the participant indicated that the shoes were to the left of the radio on both interviews, this response was scored as consistent; but, if the participant indicated that the shoes were to the left of the radio on Int-1, but to the right of the radio on Int-2, this was scored as an inconsistent response. The results supported our hypothesis: truth-tellers' responses were highly consistent whether they answered in the same mode on both interviews (i.e., verbal/verbal or sketch/sketch) or in different modes (i.e., verbal/sketch or sketch/verbal), whereas liars were much more consistent if the modes of responding were the same than if they differed.

In overview, whether liars in experimental studies are more inconsistent than truth-tellers seems to depend heavily on the nature of the interviewer's questions. If interviewers ask questions that liars can anticipate and, therefore, prepare for, then liars will answer consistently, because liars have rehearsed their answer. Similarly, if interviewers ask the same questions on succeeding interviews, liars will also respond consistently, but for a different reason: they will be able to recall their answers from the earlier interview. Two important principles follow from these conclusions: first, when interviewing suspects, or others who might be motivated to lie, investigators should (a) anticipate how deceptive respondents prepare for the interview and then ask questions that are unexpected, and (b) avoid asking the same questions on consecutive interviews. Second, and more in keeping with the theme of this chapter, no simple rule can be applied universally to categorize people as liars or truth-tellers based on the consistency of their responses (see ten Brinke & Porter, this volume). Rather, we need to understand the cognitive and social processes that account for consistent and inconsistent recollections, and how these processes may differ for liars and truth-tellers.

Summary and Practical Implications

We have noted several findings in this chapter, including: (a) some forms of inconsistency (i.e., contradictions) are much more indicative of memory inaccuracy than other forms (e.g., forgetting and reminiscence), (b) inconsistency is more predictive of memory inaccuracy at the level of the individual statement than at the level of the witness's entire testimony, and (c) liars are more inconsistent than truth-tellers, but only when the questions are unanticipated. These findings not only advance our theoretical understanding, but they also have practical implications for investigators and the legal system. A few implications are as follows. First, witnesses who testify in court and reveal information they had not described in an earlier deposition should not reflexively be badgered about their "newly found" information (e.g., as if they had been fed the new facts by someone else), as such reminiscences are common and often accurate. Second, if eyewitnesses contradict themselves when reporting some facts, interviewers should continue to probe these eyewitnesses for additional information, as the contradictions (i.e., low accuracy items) may not be predictive of the eyewitness's ability to remember other facts. Third, before interviewing a suspect, interviewers should try to think as if they were the suspect, duplicating how the suspect might prepare for the interview, and then ask questions that the suspect probably did not anticipate. We leave it to the reader to derive other practical implications.

Conclusion

Despite people's reliance on inconsistency as a means to infer the inaccuracy or deception of others' reports, controlled laboratory tests show that inconsistency is not as predictive as we might expect. Rather, the behavioral patterns appear to reflect complex underlying cognitive and social processes. We can take two approaches in response to these findings. One approach is to abandon relying on inconsistency to assess memory and deception. That approach seems to have limited utility since, (a) under some conditions, inconsistency is predictive of inaccuracy and deception, and (b) we need to rely on some indicators to assess others' reports, and it is not obvious what behaviors we would substitute for inconsistency (see Vrij & Granhag, 2012, for an assessment of some of these alternatives). A second approach is to understand better the nature of inconsistency so that we are more sensitive to its subtlety, why it is a good indicator of memory inaccuracy and deception sometimes but not at other times. That approach seems to have more promise. We have tried here to hint at some of the cognitive and social processes that underlie inconsistency. We trust that other researchers will advance our knowledge beyond the elementary notions presented here.

References

Berman, G. L., & Cutler, B. L. (1996). Effects of inconsistencies in eyewitness testimony on mock-juror decision making. *Journal of Applied Psychology, 81*, 170–177.

Brainerd, C. J., & Reyna, V. F. (1993). Memory independence and memory interference in cognitive development. *Psychological Review, 100*, 42–67.

Brewer, N., & Burke, A. (2002). Effects of testimonial inconsistencies and eyewitness confidence on mock-juror judgments. *Law and Human Behavior, 26*, 353–364.

Brewer, N., & Hupfeld, R. M. (2004). Effects of testimonial inconsistencies and witness group identity on mock-juror judgments. *Journal of Applied Social Psychology, 34*, 493–513.

Brewer, N., Potter, R., Fisher, R. P., Bond, N., & Lusczc, M. A. (1999). Beliefs and data on the relationship between consistency and accuracy of eyewitness testimony. *Applied Cognitive Psychology, 13*, 297–313.

Brock, P., Fisher, R. P., & Cutler, B. L. (1999). Examining the cognitive interview in a double-test paradigm. *Psychology, Crime & Law, 5*, 29–45.

Cahill, B.S., Fisher, R.P., & Rivard, J.J. (2011). *Catching liars with cartoons*. Paper presented at the meeting of the American Psychology-Law Society, Miami, Florida.

Carbone, J. & Fisher, R.P. (2011). *Inconsistency on the witness stand*. Paper presented at the meeting of the American Psychology-Law Society, Miami, Florida.

Committee on Pattern Jury Instructions of the District Judges Association (2005). *Sixth circuit criminal pattern jury instructions*.

Erdelyi, M. H. (1996). *The recovery of unconscious memories: Hypermnesia and reminiscence*. Chicago: University of Chicago Press.

Evans, J. R. (2011). Eyewitness memory: Balancing the accuracy, precision, and quantity of information. *Applied Cognitive Psychology, 25*, 501–508.

Fisher, R. P., & Cutler, B. L. (1995). The relation between consistency and accuracy of eyewitness testimony. In G. Davies, S. Lloyd-Bostock, M. McMurran, & C. Wilson (Eds.), *Law and criminal justice: International developments in research and practice*. Berlin: De Gruyter.

Fisher, R. P., Falkner, K. L., Trevisan, M., & McCauley, M. R. (2000). Adapting the Cognitive Interview to enhance long term (35 years) recall of physical activities. *Journal of Applied Psychology, 85*, 180–189.

Fisher, R.P. & Patterson, T. (2004). *The relationship between consistency and accuracy of eyewitness memory*. Paper presented at 45th Annual Meeting of the Psychnomic Society, Minneapolis, Minnesota.

Gabbert, F., Memon, A., & Allen, K. (2003). Memory conformity: Can eyewitnesses influence each other's memories for an event? *Applied Cognitive Psychology, 17*, 533–543.

Gilbert, J. A. E., & Fisher, R. P. (2006). The effects of varied retrieval cues on reminiscence in eyewitness memory. *Applied Cognitive Psychology, 20*, 723–739.

Glissan, J. L. (1991). *Cross-examination: Practice and procedure*. Sydney: Butterworths.

Granhag, P. A., & Strömwall, L. A. (1999). Repeated interrogations: Stretching the deception detection paradigm. *Expert Evidence, 7*, 163–174.

Granhag, P. A., & Strömwall, L. A. (2000). Deception detection: Examining the consistency heuristic. In C. M. Breur, M. M. Kommer, J. F. Nijboer, & J. M. Reintjes (Eds.), *New trends in criminal investigation and evidence* (Vol. 2, pp. 309–321). Antwerpen: Intresentia.

Granhag, P. A., & Strömwall, L. A. (2001). Deception detection based on repeated interrogations. *Legal and Criminological Psychology, 6*, 85–101.

Granhag, P. A., Strömwall, L. A., & Jonsson, A.-C. (2003). Partners in crime: How liars in collusion betray themselves. *Journal of Applied Social Psychology, 33*, 848–868.

Hartwig, M., Granhag, P. A., & Strömwall, L. (2007). Guilty and innocent suspects' strategies during police interrogations. *Psychology, Crime and Law, 13*, 213–227.

Johnson, M. K., Hashtroudi, S., & Lindsay, D. S. (1993). Source monitoring. *Psychological Bulletin, 114*, 3–28.

Koriat, A., & Goldsmith, M. (1996). Monitoring and control processes in the strategic manipulation of memory accuracy. *Psychological Review, 103*, 490–517.

La Rooy, D., Lamb, M. E., & Pipe, M.-E. (2008). Repeated interviewing: A critical evaluation of the risks and potential benefits. In K. Kuehnle & M. Connell (Eds.), *Child sexual abuse: Research, evaluation, and testimony for the courts*. Hoboken: Wiley.

La Rooy, D., Pipe, M.-E., & Murray, J. E. (2005). Reminiscence and hypermnesia in children's eyewitness memory. *Journal of Experimental Child Psychology, 90*, 235–254.

Leins, D., Fisher, R. P., & Vrij, A. (2012). Drawing on liars' lack of cognitive flexibility: detecting deception through varying report modes. *Applied Cognitive Psychology, 26*, 601–607.

Leins, D., Fisher, R. P., Vrij, A., & Mann, S. (2011). Using sketch-drawing to induce inconsistency in liars. *Legal and Criminological Psychology, 16*, 253–265.

Leippe, M. R., Manion, A. P., & Romanczyk, A. (1992). Eyewitness persuasion: How and how well do fact finders judge the accuracy of adults' and children's memory reports? *Journal of Personality and Social Psychology, 63*, 181–197.

Lindsay, R. C. L., Lim, R., Marando, L., & Cully, D. (1986). Mock-juror evaluations of eyewitness testimony: A test of metamemory hypotheses. *Journal of Applied Social Psychology, 16*, 447–459.

Loftus, E. (1975). Leading questions and the eyewitness report. *Cognitive Psychology, 7*, 550–572.

Mitchell, T., Haw, R., & Fisher, R. P. (2003). *Eyewitness accuracy: Can accuracy for one statement be predictive of more 'global' accuracy?* Paper presented at European Psych-Law Society. Edinburgh.

Payne, D. (1987). Hypermnesia and reminiscence in recall: A historical and empirical review. *Psychological Bulletin, 101*, 5–27.

Pezdek, K. (2003). Event memory and autobiographical memory for the events of September 11, 2001. *Applied Cognitive Psychology, 17*, 1033–1045.

Shuy, R. (1998). *The language of confession, interrogation and deception*. Thousand Oaks: Sage Publications.

Strömwall, L. A., & Granhag, P. A. (2003). How to detect deception? Arresting the beliefs of police officers, prosecutors and judges. *Psychology, Crime & Law, 9*, 19–36.

Strömwall, L. A., & Granhag, P. A. (2005). Children's repeated lies and truths: Effects on adult's judgments and Reality Monitoring scores. *Psychiatry, Psychology & Law, 12*, 345–356.

Strömwall, L. A., Granhag, P. A., & Jonsson, A.-C. (2003). Deception among pairs: "Let's say we had lunch and hope they will swallow it!". *Psychology, Crime & Law, 9*, 109–124.

Tulving, E. (1983). *Elements of episodic memory*. Oxford: Clarendon.

Vrij, A., & Granhag, P-A. (2012). Eliciting cues to deception and truth: What matters are the questions asked. *Journal of Applied Research in Memory and Cognition, 1*, 110–117.

Vrij, A., Leal, S., Granhag, P. A., Mann, S., Fisher, R. P., Hillman, J., & Sperry, K. (2009). Outsmarting the Liars: The benefit of asking unanticipated questions. *Law and Human Behavior, 33*, 159–166.

Wagenaar, W. A., & Groeneweg, J. (1990). The memory of concentration camp survivors. *Applied Cognitive Psychology, 4*, 77–87.

Warren, A. R., & Woodall, C. E. (1999). The reliability of hearsay testimony: How well do interviewers recall their interviews with children? *Psychology, Public Policy, and Law, 5*, 355–371.

Zulawski, D. E., & Wicklander, D. E. (1993). *Practical aspects of interview and interrogation*. New York: CRC Press.

Chapter 8
Repeated Interviews About Repeated Trauma from the Distant Past: A Study of Report Consistency

Deborah A. Connolly and Heather L. Price

Testing our beliefs about memory for crimes with participants who have memories for crimes is an essential component of research that is meant to be applied outside of the laboratory (e.g., Yuille, Ternes, & Cooper, 2010). This is a challenge, not just because it is difficult to locate and recruit participants with memories for crimes, but because the research is messy: often there is no control group, base truth is not known, and random assignment is impossible (see Paz-Alonso, Ogle, & Goodman, this volume). Notwithstanding these difficulties, applied work is essential if we are to have an impact (see Yuille, present volume). In this spirit, we describe a study in which a woman who reported having been a victim of five armed bank robberies in Montreal, Canada in the 1970s and who recalled the experiences on three separate occasions. First, we explain why this work was undertaken.

In most Common law jurisdictions (e.g., Canada, England, Australia, New Zealand), there are no Statutes of Limitations on most criminal offences. This means that a criminal offence can be prosecuted any time, even decades after it was committed. Predictably, very long delays have a myriad of legal and psychological implications that complicate effective prosecutions. Although most criminal prosecutions are not delayed by years or decades, for at least one type of criminal offence, child sexual abuse (CSA), a lengthy delay to prosecution is common. This is because most child victims of sexual assault do not report the offence immediately and it has been estimated that up to one-third of such victims do not report the offence until adulthood (London, Bruck, Ceci, Shuman, 2005).

Since the early to mid-1990s, in most Common law jurisdictions, there has been a dramatic increase in criminal prosecutions of CSA that is alleged to have happened in the distant past (Connolly & Read, 2006). Delayed prosecutions of CSA is

D.A. Connolly (✉)
Simon Fraser University, 8888 University Drive, Burnaby, BC, Canada
e-mail: debc@sfu.ca

H.L. Price
University of Regina, 3737 Wascana Parkway, Regina, SK, Canada

"now a thriving legal industry," stated Madam Justice Southin of the British Columbia Court of Appeal (*R.* v. *R.* [*J.W.*], 2001, at Para. 26). The Select Committee on Home Affairs in the United Kingdom indicated "[i]n the last 5 years, 34 of the 43 police forces in England and Wales have been involved in investigations into allegations of child abuse in children's homes and other institutions. All of the allegations relate to historical abuse, said to have occurred several years—often decades—ago" (Home Affairs Committee, 2002, p. 1). There are several characteristics of these cases that make them particularly challenging to adjudicate: the alleged crime occurred a long time ago (e.g., sometimes decades earlier), often repeatedly, and cases often rest on perceptions of credibility (Connolly & Read, 2003; Seniuk, present volume; ten Brinke & Porter, present volume).

In this chapter, the relatively sparse research on long-term autobiographical memory for repeated events is reviewed. Although we had hoped to confine our review to long-term autobiographical memory for instances of repeated trauma, the paucity of such research made it impossible to restrict our analysis in this way. Our literature review, therefore, includes a focus on long-term autobiographical memory for general characteristics of repeated events and a discussion of the only two studies we were able to find on long-term memory for instances of repeated events. Because base truth was not known in these studies, the focus of the research is not on accuracy; most commonly, it is on report consistency. Given the prominence of report consistency in these studies, and given our interest in the forensic applications of the work, the context for this literature review is the effect of report inconsistencies on perceptions of credibility (also see Fisher, Vrij, & Leins, this volume). Next, we describe two new studies. In the first study, a woman (Beth) described, on three separate occasions, each of the five times she was a victim of an armed robbery, all of which occurred in the 1970s. Our analyses of her reports focus on the number of details reported, report consistency, and the extent to which details cluster across interviews. In the second study, we examined the perceived credibility of Beth's reports as evaluated by research participants. We conclude with a discussion of possible forensic implications of the nature of reports such as the ones provided by Beth.

Report Consistency and Perceived Credibility

When a case proceeds to criminal court, key witnesses are interviewed at least three times: during the police investigation, during the preliminary inquiry, and at trial. One consequence of multiple interviews is that reports may be inconsistent across interviews (see Fisher et al., this volume). Inconsistent reports can have unfortunate consequences, particularly when the outcome of the legal case rests on perceptions of credibility. The results of several laboratory-based studies converge on the conclusion that an inconsistent witness is seen as less credible than a consistent witness. Brewer, Potter, Fisher, Bond, and Lusczcz (1999) found that, among ten possible indicators of inaccurate testimony, undergraduate students rated inconsistencies with previous statements as the strongest indicator of perceived inaccuracy (see also Conte, Sorenson, Fogarty, & Rosa, 1991; Fisher et al., this volume). Berman, Narby, and Cutler (1995) as well as Berman and Cutler (1996) found that, compared to a consistent report, an inconsistent report was judged to be less credible and the case was less likely to end with a conviction.[1] A similar conclusion comes from studies of reports of victimization as assessed by lay persons and by judges. In Desmarais' (2009) study, participants evaluated the credibility of a complainant who reported intimate partner abuse on two separate occasions; the two accounts were either consistent or they were inconsistent. Credibility ratings were lower when the reports were inconsistent than when they were consistent. Connolly, Price, and Gordon (2010) studied judicial reasons in criminal cases that rested, largely, on perceived credibility of the parties. Judicial comments concerning inconsistencies were more frequent in cases that ended in acquittals than in cases that ended in convictions. Based on laboratory studies as well as studies of reports of victimization, we find that, generally, reports that are inconsistent are judged to be less credible than reports that are consistent. Malloy and Lamb (2010) point out that this conclusion is supportable when evaluating statements of witnesses; however, it is not supportable when evaluating statements of accused persons, where an inconsistent confession is often viewed as accurate. In this chapter, our interest is in statements of witnesses.

Of importance, the empirical literature evidences only a weak (negative) relation between inconsistencies and actual accuracy (Brewer et al., 1999; Fisher & Cutler, 1995; Fisher et al., this volume). In other words, a person may be both inconsistent and accurate across interviews. In a particularly striking demonstration of this, Yuille and Cutshall (1986) interviewed 13 eyewitnesses to an actual robbery wherein the storeowner was seriously injured and the robber was killed. The eyewitnesses had been interviewed by police immediately after the incident and again 4–5 months later by the researchers. Both interviews began with free recall, followed by specific prompts intended to clarify information and to solicit additional information. Sixty percent of the information provided to the researchers had not been reported to the police and the new information had an average accuracy rate of over 80% (note: some questions were asked by the researchers that were not asked or considered relevant by the police—e.g., description of the dead thief who was present at the scene).

The reminiscence effect provides an explanation for the aforementioned findings. When an event is recounted multiple times, new correct information may emerge and previously reported information may be omitted—a reminiscence effect (Anderson, Cohen, & Taylor, 2000; Turtle & Yuille, 1994). Accounts of the reminiscence effect presume a stimulus sampling model in which any given recall attempt samples some amount of finite information within the memory

---

[1] Brewer and Burke (2002) found that confidence mediated the relationship between inconsistencies and perceived credibility such that inconsistencies in a very high- or very low-confident witness had no effect on perceived credibility. However, we were not concerned with extreme levels of witness confidence in this chapter but conclude that inconsistencies are an important predictor of perceived credibility.

representation for an event (e.g., Conway & Pleydell-Pearce, 2000; Read & Connolly, 2007). Inconsistencies in reported units of information result from accessing different features of the memory representation, as well as the varying availability of cues that elicit retrieval of particular units of information. According to this model, inconsistencies are more common for peripheral than central details because central details are more likely to be recalled during each retrieval attempt. Indeed, when researchers measured inconsistencies in both central and peripheral details, participants were more inconsistent in their reports of the latter than the former (Read & Connolly, 2007). However, as is clear from the literature reviewed below, reporting of central details can also be inconsistent across reports (e.g., the presence and frequency of experienced wartime stressors; the presence of childhood physical and sexual abuse; witnessing a murder while detained in a concentration camp).

Most of the research on report inconsistencies has concerned repeated interviews about a unique event. For a couple of reasons, we are concerned, in this chapter, with inconsistencies in multiple reports of repeated events.[2] For our purposes, repeated events are defined as a series of similar events that "go together." First, as described in the introduction of this chapter, some crimes routinely occur repeatedly (e.g., child abuse, domestic violence, criminal harassment) and witnesses/victims of those crimes are likely to be interviewed repeatedly. Based on an analysis of 2,064 delayed complaints of CSA, Connolly and Read (2006) reported that 68% of the complaints involved allegations of repeated sexual abuse. Second, when recalling an instance of a repeated event, there are at least two ways that reports could be inconsistent: sampling different details from the same instance and sampling details from different instances. This may have important implications for the type of inconsistency observed across interviews. When each recall attempt samples a slightly different subset of details from the *same* instance (or from a unique event), new correct information is recalled and old correct information is omitted. The reports are inconsistent in the sense that each provides somewhat different details (e.g., the culprit had brown hair during one recall attempt and the culprit had brown eyes during another recall attempt); however, they are not contradictory; both reports could be accurate descriptions of the same event. That said, when each recall attempt samples a different subset of details from different instances, inconsistencies could be contradictory (e.g., the assault happened in the living room during one recall attempt and it happened at the cabin during another recall attempt); the reports cannot be describing the same event. Arguably, the detrimental effect on credibility will be larger when the inconsistencies are contradictions than when they are not (Fisher, Brewer, & Mitchell, 2009).

---

[2] There is an extensive literature on repeated reports of Flashbulb Memories - memory for one's personal circumstances when learning of a shocking event. We do not review that literature here because it is unlikely to be the subject of forensic investigation. In addition, Pezdek (2003) argued that memory for details of a shocking event and one's personal circumstances of learning of the shocking event may be experienced and processed differently.

Repeated Interviews About Repeated Autobiographical Events

The relatively few studies that are available concerning repeated interviews about repeated events can be organized into two groups: reports of wartime stressors and reports of childhood abuse/stressors. These studies are briefly described in Table 8.1. As is clear from this table, even when the events are central and life-threatening, there were substantial inconsistencies across reports. Of importance, in these studies, participants were asked to describe the repeated event *generally*, to report the presence or absence of particular kinds of details during *any* of the instances, and/or to provide frequency estimates. However, this is not likely to be the information elicited in a forensic interview. When a legal case proceeds to trial, a principle of fundamental justice requires that the charge be specific enough for the accused to raise a defense (i.e., the sufficiency principle; *R* v. *B.[G.]*, 1990). This means that complainants must report specific details of the alleged offence and, if the alleged offence occurred repeatedly, it may mean that specific details of a particular instance or a subset of instances of the offence must be reported. Guadagno, Powell, and Wright (2006) found that failure to recall some specific details about a particular occurrence of the alleged abuse may terminate an investigation. As Bifulco, Brown, Lillie, and Jarvis (1997) argued, concordance on the overall presence of adversity does not speak to concordance on the details of incidents of adversity. As illustrated in Table 8.1, researchers have reported moderate to low report consistency when the target information concerned general characteristics of repeated events. Given that particular instances are more difficult to retrieve and are more likely to be confused, we would not be surprised if consistency on details of particular instances was very low indeed.

We have only been able to locate two studies in which researchers studied repeated interviews concerning particular details of past instances of a repeated event; in neither study was actual consistency reported. However, a conclusion that can reasonably be drawn from both studies is that, when asked to report details of a particular instance of a repeated event, a substantial number of inconsistencies are expected. In one study, John Dean's testimony concerning his memories of discussions with then-President Nixon 9 months earlier was compared with recordings of those same meetings (Neisser, 1981). Much, but not all, of what Dean said was consistent with the gist of the conversations; however, he often attributed statements to the wrong meeting. In a study by Wagenaar and Groeneweg (1990), similar effects were found when reports of profound and personally threatening events were described. Reports from prisoners of Camp Erika, a Nazi Concentration Camp, that were taken during a war crimes trial between 1984 and 1987 were compared with reports made during an investigation of Camp Erika between 1943 and 1947. There was a high level of agreement between witnesses concerning general facts (e.g., conditions, general treatment, routines, meals); however, particular details were easily confused with different instances and, in some cases, missing from one of the reports. In summary, inconsistencies across reports of general characteristics of repeated events are common and have

Table 8.1 Inconsistencies in repeated reports of trauma

Event	Participants	Focus of the interview	Time between interviews	Measure of inconsistencies
Wartime Stressors				
Herlihy, Scragg, and Turner (2002)	Asylum seekers	Trauma	3–32 weeks	100% of participants were inconsistent on some details
Spinhoven, Bean, and Eurelings-Bontekoe (2006)	Asylum seekers	Trauma	12 months	86.4% of participants were inconsistent on some details
King et al. (2000)	Gulf War Veterans	Wartime stressors	18–24 months	91% of participants were inconsistent in their estimates of frequency of wartimes stressors
Roemer, Litz, Orsillo, Ehlich, and Friedman (1998)	Soldiers who served in Somalia	Peacekeeping stressors	12–36 months	Correlation between responses across interviews was 0.66
Southwick, Morgan, Nicolaou, and Charney (1997)	Operation Desert Storm veterans	Combat experiences	24 months	88% of participants changed at least one response across interviews
Engelhard, van den Hout, and McNally (2008)	Dutch soldiers in Iraq	Wartime stressors	8 months	80% of participants changed at least one answer across interviews
Child Abuse/Stress				
Offer, Kaiz, Howard, and Bennett (2000)	High-school students	Typical teenage experiences	34 years	For only 3 of 28 questions concordance between responses was higher than chance
Femina, Yeager, and Lewis (1990)	Formerly incarcerated youth	Child abuse	9 years	38% of participants gave information in the second interview that was discrepant with information given in the first interview
Fergusson, Horwood, and Woodward (2000)	Birth cohort	Child abuse	3 years	50% of those who reported child abuse in interview 1 failed to report it in interview 2
Cournoyer and Rohner (1996)	Community sample	Parental acceptance questionnaire	7 years	The correlation between responses was 0.62

been observed in reports of general characteristics of repeated events. Based on these two studies that were not specifically designed to study repeated reports of particular instances of repeated events, we also expect that central and peripheral details of particular instances of a repeated event that are intensely personally threatening may also be very inconsistent across reports. This hypothesis is drawn from these two studies and theory about how repeated events are organized in memory.[3]

One consequence of experiencing an event repeatedly is that details of particular instances become difficult to access (Connolly & Lindsay, 2001; Connolly & Price, 2006; Farrar & Goodman, 1990, 1992; Fivush, 1984; Means & Loftus, 1991; Pearse, Powell, & Thomson, 2003; Price & Connolly, 2004) and, when accessed, they are easily confused (Powell & Roberts, 2002; Powell, Roberts, Ceci, & Hembrook, 1999; Price & Connolly, 2004). Script theory has been used to explain these phenomena (see Hervé, Cooper, & Yuille, present volume; Yarbrough, Hervé, & Harms, present volume). A script is a cognitive representation of what usually happens during a routine and it provides expectations about what will occur during future instances (Abelson, 1981; Nelson, 1986). When an event recurs, it is not likely to recur in precisely the same way: some details will remain the same and others will vary. Event details that vary are said to be represented at a general level (e.g., each instance of abuse begins with "comforting" words) with an associated list of *options* (e.g., the particular words that have been spoken in the past such as "we can go to the movies tonight," "this is how I show you how much I care," "after this, I will give you a drink from my special stash of vodka," "it won't hurt," and" I will take you shopping when we are done"; Fivush, 1984; Nelson & Gruendel, 1986; Slackman & Nelson, 1984). Because, according to script theory, options are not tightly associated with particular instances (Connolly & Price, 2006; Nelson, 1986; Powell & Thompson, 1997), one is often confused about what happened during each instance. Therefore, both within and across reports of a particular instance of the repeated offence, details from instances that are not under investigation, could be misattributed to instance(s) that are under investigation (Gordon, Connolly, Banipal, & Price, 2006). Further, the particular non-target instance from which details are reported may change within and across reports. Suppose there were five instances of abuse, but only the last one, when the perpetrator said "I will take you shopping when we are done", was the subject of a criminal charge. During two different interviews, the witness may misattribute details from instance two (e.g., when he said "this is how I show you how much I care") and instance three (e.g., when he said "after this, I will give you a drink from my special stash of vodka") to the last instance. This would lead to inconsistent reports that could jeopardize the perceived credibility of the report.

We specifically stated that multiple interviews about an instance of a repeated event *could* lead to contradictory reports. This is because we don't yet know if

---

[3] We cite research involving child samples because, as just discussed, there is a paucity of research on adults' memories of instances of repeated events.

some details associated with repeated events are grouped or clustered such that certain details are always reported together, regardless of whether the group, or "cluster," is attributed to different instances across reports. To return to the example introduced above, suppose that the "comforting" words, "I will take you shopping when we are done", and, "the time it happened just before I went to a school dance", are clustered such that the complainant believes both details occurred during the same instance (whether or not both details actually occurred together). The complainant may always report the two details together, but may attribute them to different instances across reports (e.g., the 2006 incident in one interview and the time she was 15, in 2004, in another interview). Most of the research with adults on "clustering" has been concerned with whether entire events tend to go together in autobiographical memory (e.g., Brown, 2005; Brown & Schopflocher, 1998; Burt, Kemp, & Conway, 2003; Odegard, Lampinen, & Wirth-Beaumont, 2004). In the current research, we ask whether *details* associated with instances tend to cluster together.

In the developmental literature, there is some evidence that, over time, details become less tightly associated with particular instances and, perhaps, with each other. For example, Powell and Thompson (1997) reported that, when children were asked to recall a target instance of a repeated event after 1 week, intrusions from related non-target instances were temporally closer to the target instance than when children were interviewed 6 weeks after the target instance. This suggests that the links between details fade over time setting the stage for reports that contain contradictory details. Of course, this research concerned a child population and, in the current study, we are concerned with an adult.

In the next section, two studies are described that were conducted to explore inconsistencies across three interviews with a woman who, as a bank administrator, reported that she had been a victim of five armed bank robberies in the early 1970s. We studied the amount of information reported about each robbery, report consistency, consistency of assignment of details to robberies, and the extent to which details were reported together. In Study 2, we investigated perceived credibility of her reports.

Study 1

Method

Procedure

During a class on Autobiographical Memory and the Law, a student (Beth) reported to the Instructor that she had been a victim of five armed robberies in Montréal, Canada in the early 1970s, about 25 years earlier. The Instructor had been studying autobiographical memory for repeated events and was interested in Beth's recollections of each robbery. Beth agreed to be interviewed on three separate occasions: April of 1999, January of 2004, and August of 2004. During each interview, Beth reported as many details as she could about each of the five robberies except that, during Interview 2, Beth ran out of time before the fifth could be discussed. Interviews were scheduled far enough apart that it was unlikely that the second or third Interviews would be based on Beth's memory of the previous interview (s) (see Dill, Chu, Grob, & Eisen, 1991; Fry, Rozewicz, & Crisp, 1996; Martin, Anderson, Romans, Mullen, & O'Shea, 1993). Each robbery was described in a great deal of detail and each was described as exceptionally traumatic and shocking. To illustrate, following are a few of Beth's descriptions of the robberies (for the three descriptions of Robbery 3, see the Appendix):

> They force people to get on the floor and they scream and they do all kinds of things. Um, and that's kind of how it comes back to me and the thing that comes back to me the most, um, when I try to think about it, um, is the feeling, the feeling of just sheer, um, panic, sheer fear, um ..., kind of if you would see your child kind of driving off a cliff, or something and ... you know, that kind of just hopelessness, fear, um, that icy hand around your heart (Interview 1, p. 1).
>
> [W]hat had happened at, you know, in that case was, um, a fellow who had walked in, um, not even sunglasses on, like had just walked in, um, the guard was leaning up against the check cashing, you know, desk, where people write out their things. The guy came over, walked over like he was gonna write a thing, took a gun out and shot the guard. And as he did that, um, another four, you know, I say four, four or five, probably just four, then the door opened, then they all came in, then they kind of did their thing (Interview 1, p. 17).
>
> The guy's, you know, screaming, like, 'SHUT UP!' You know, blah, blah. And for whatever reason in this particular hold up ... taking the change containers and throwing them on the ground. So of course, the change was going everywhere. So, of course, we're under this (table), so change is going. And they were yelling, like in French, "you bunch of thieves, we're going to kill you all" (Interview 1, p. 13).

According to Beth, each robbery was very carefully timed so that the robbers were out of the bank in 2 min. This, Beth stated, maximized the amount of cash the robbers obtained and minimized the possibility that they would be in the bank when the police arrived. Arguably, then, each robbery contained roughly the same amount of information.

The interviews were conducted in accordance with Yuille's Step-Wise Interview guidelines (Yuille, Hunter, Joffe, & Zaparniuk, 1993) to encourage and assist Beth to report as much as she could about each robbery. The interviews began with an open-ended prompt such as "Tell me everything that you can remember about the first Robbery" followed by encouragement to recall more, "What happened next?" or "Can you recall something else about that Robbery?" Specific prompts for information Beth had already reported were used occasionally (e.g., "You said that the robbers were wearing black clothes; can you tell me more about that?"). When Beth reported a detail without attributing it to a particular Robbery, she was asked to think about which Robbery contained that detail. When Beth appeared to have exhausted her memory for a particular Robbery, she was asked to report all she could recall about the next one. Each interview lasted approximately 3 h and was audiotaped and transcribed verbatim.

Coding

As with many studies of long-term autobiographical memory, base truth was not known. Official records of events that had occurred decades earlier were not available. More to the point, however, even if we had found official records of the robberies, the kind of information that Beth reported would not have been documented (e.g., "I flew down the stairs," "After the Robbery, we went across the street to drink," and "The customer in the bank could only remember the smell of floor wax") in anything other than, perhaps, a personal diary. As reported in many of the studies described above, we examined amount of information reported and consistency across reports.

Units of information. Each interview was parsed into units of information. A unit of information was a sentence or phrase that was independent of all other units of information and all information in the unit logically went together. For example, "There was a large clerk who got stuck under the desk and the table had to be taken apart to free her" was coded as one unit because all of the information goes together; logically, it could not be parsed according to the coding scheme. However, "One robber was standing at the doorway with a sawed-off shotgun while another yelled 'you bunch of thieves, we are going to kill you all'" was coded as two units because they could logically occur separately. We used this strategy because we did not want to assign a positive consistency score to propositions that were causally or logically connected.

Units of information were identified as either general (e.g., "it always happened this way," "they always wore masks," and "they always carried guns") or specific (e.g., units of information that were specific to a robbery; "when they left the bank they sprayed the back wall with bullets" and "he put a gun to my face and said 'I told you to get on the floor!'"). Using consensus coding on Interview 1, two coders agreed on the parsing of units of information. Based on independent coding of Interview 2, intercoder agreement was 80%. One person coded Interview 3 into units of information. One-hundred and 31 units of information were identified.

Assignment of units of information to robberies. All specific units of information were assigned to one of the five Robberies. As we expected, Beth did not always assign details to the same Robbery; when Beth was inconsistent in her attribution of a detail to a Robbery, assignment was undertaken by the researchers. A detail was deemed to "belong" to a Robbery if Beth attributed it to the same one in two of the three interviews. If Beth assigned a unit to different robberies in each interview, it was deemed to "belong" to the Robbery it was assigned to first (note: this occurred only seven times). Consensus coding on Interview 1 was used to assign units of information to robberies. Intercoder agreement based on independent coding of Interview 2 was 94%. As indicated above, one person assigned units of information from Interview 3.

Overall consistency. Each unit of information was given a consistency score. A score of 0 was assigned if the unit of information was reported once, a score of 1 if the unit of information was reported twice, and a score of 2 if it was reported in all 3 interviews. To maximize consistency, credit was given if one detail was unambiguously the same detail as reported in a different interview (see also Christianson & Engelberg, 1999). For example "the branch got held up so often" is equivalent to "this was known as the 'hold up branch'" and "I jumped from the top stair" is the same as "I flew down the stairs." This scoring was independent of assignment of units of information to robberies. That is, if a detail was reported three times, but attributed to a different robbery during each interview, it would still receive an overall consistency score of 2.

Consistency of assignment of units of information to robberies. Each unit of information was given a *consistency* of assignment score: a score of 0 was given if the unit of information was assigned to a particular Robbery only once, a score of 1 if it was assigned to the same Robbery twice, and a score of 2 if the unit of information was assigned to the same Robbery in all three interviews. A low consistency score could occur if units of information tended to be assigned to different robberies or if units of information tended to be mentioned only one or two times (i.e., but always assigned to the same Robbery). To account for this, we also computed an *inconsistency* of assignment score. A score of 0 was assigned if the detail was attributed to the same Robbery each time the detail was reported, a score of 1 if it was attributed to two different robberies across interviews, and an inconsistency score of 2 if it was attributed to three different robberies. Thus, if, across the three interviews, Beth assigned a detail to Robberies 3, 4, and 3, it was given an inconsistency score of 1 for Robberies 3 and 4 and a consistency score of 1 for Robbery 3. If, across the three interviews, Beth assigned a detail to Robberies 2 or 3 (i.e., she could not commit to one of these two options), 3 and 4, it was given an inconsistency score of 2 for Robberies 2, 3, and 4 and a consistency score of 1 for Robbery 3.

In summary, a low consistency score combined with a low inconsistency score indicates a tendency to report units of information in only one or two interviews. A low consistency score combined with a high inconsistency score demonstrates that the detail was reported in multiple interviews but assigned to different robberies.

Results

Amount of Information

The total number of units deemed to belong to Robberies 1, 2, 3, 4, 5, and general units of information were 26, 14, 19, 7, 25, and 37, respectively (note: three units of information could not be assigned to a robbery and could not be considered "general"). As can be seen in Fig. 8.1 below, there was an advantage, in terms of the number of units of information reported for Robberies 1 and 5, despite the arguably equal amount of information available for each robbery. Recall that Beth reported that each robbery was timed by the robbers to take exactly 2 min—just less than the amount of time it took the police to arrive.

Overall Consistency

Did Beth consistently report units of information, regardless of whether she attributed them to the same Robbery during each interview? Because Robbery 5 was reported only twice and because each Robbery had a different number of units of information, raw consistency scores would be misleading. Therefore, we computed a percentage consistency score. We multiplied the total number of units of information deemed to belong to Robberies 1–4 and "general" by two (note: Beth described Robberies 1–4 three times so she could obtain a score of 2 on each unit of information) and the total number of units attributed to Robbery 5 by one (note: Beth described Robbery 5 twice so the maximum score for each of these units of information was one). This provided a total possible consistency score of 231 [$(103 \times 2) + (25 \times 1)$]. The total actual consistency score was 116: 40 units of information were reported in all three interviews, 39 were reported in two interviews, and 49 units of information were reported once. Therefore, the overall percentage consistency was 50.22% (i.e., 116/231). We also computed a consistency score for units of information deemed to belong to Robberies 1 through 5 and general units of information. As can be seen in Fig. 8.2 below, the advantage is for Robberies 1 and 3.

There are two ways to obtain a high consistency score: if memory for the Robbery was very clear or if it was a kind of "default" Robbery. A particular Robbery may be a default if the Robbery details were attributed to Beth not remembering when something happened (e.g., if Beth remembered that one time the back of the bank was sprayed with bullets but she could not remember when that happened, she might always attribute it to the same default Robbery—say Robbery 3). In the former case, units of information should be consistently assigned to the same Robbery because Beth feels she has a clear memory of it. In the latter case, consistency of assignment of units to the "default" Robbery is not expected to be as high because Beth does not have clear recollection of it. To partially disentangle these two possibilities, we analyzed consistency of assignment scores.

Consistency of Assignment of Units of Information to Robberies

For each Robbery, we assigned a consistency of assignment score and an inconsistency of assignment score because each score alone is ambiguous. We then computed the percentage of the total possible consistency and inconsistency of assignment scores for each Robbery.

From Fig. 8.3 above, it is clear that the advantage is in Robberies 1 and 5; Beth was far more consistent than inconsistent in her assignment of units of information to these Robberies. However, Beth was far more inconsistent than consistent in her

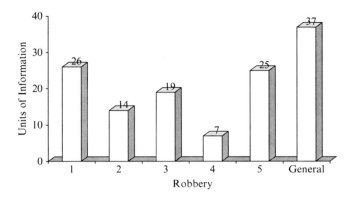

Fig. 8.1 Number of units of information reported for each Robbery

assignment of units of information to Robberies 2 and 3. We did not weigh heavily the consistency or inconsistency of assignment of units of information to Robbery 4 because only seven units of information were assigned to it.

Clustering

It is possible to have a low consistency of assignment score and a high inconsistency of assignment score, but still keep units of information together. For example, Beth could know that units of information 1–10 always happened together, but assign the units of information to different Robberies during Interviews 1, 2, and 3. In this analysis, we measured whether units of information clustered together, independent of their assignment to Robberies. To measure clustering, we used the Adjusted Rand Index (Yeung & Ruzzo, 2001). This is a measure, corrected for chance, of the degree to which units of information cluster together across two interviews. In other words, regardless of whether units of information are assigned to the same Robbery across interviews, the Adjusted Rand Index is a measure of the extent to which units of information were reported together. The analyses involved developing a contingency table for each pair of interviews with Robberies 1, 2, 3, 4, and 5 represented in both rows and columns. Because Interview 2 contained information about Robberies 1–4 only, the contingency tables for Interviews 1 and 2 and for Interviews 2 and 3 were 4×4, while the contingency table for Interviews 1 and 3 was 5×5. Using the formula reported in Yeung and Ruzzo, an Adjusted Rand Index was computed for each pair of interviews. The Adjusted Rand Index has a range of 0–1 with a score of 0 representing no clustering and a score of 1 representing perfect clustering (i.e., units of information are always kept together). The Adjusted Rand Index for Interviews 1 and 2, 1 and 3, and 2 and 3 were 0.73, 0.75, and 0.67, respectively.

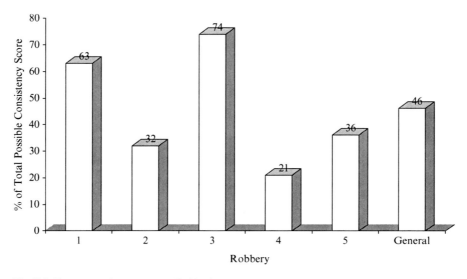

Fig. 8.2 Report consistency across Robberies

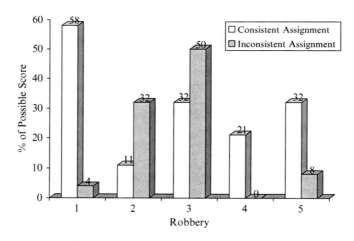

Fig. 8.3 Consistency and inconsistency of assignment of units of information to Robberies

Discussion

The overall consistency of reports of units of information was moderate: almost 60% of the units of information were reported in more than one interview, but the pattern across reports of different Robberies was uneven. Consistency scores were high for Robbery 1 and lower for Robberies 2, 3, 4, and 5. Moreover, inconsistency scores were high for Robberies 2 and 3, and low for Robberies 1 and 5. Indeed, when one looks at the three reports for Robberies 2 and 3, one would not know that Beth was discussing the same Robbery (see the Appendix for the three abbreviated descriptions of the third Robbery). This pattern suggests that Beth had a reasonably good idea of what she believed occurred during Robbery 1 (i.e., high consistent assignment score), what she believed did not occur during Robberies 1 and 5 (i.e., low inconsistent assignment scores), and she was much more confused about Robberies 2 and 3 (i.e., higher inconsistent than consistent assignment scores). This summary is consistent with the distribution of units of information deemed to belong to each Robbery: Beth reported more units of information about Robberies 1 and 5 than Robberies 2, 3, and 4.

Although the present results are too preliminary to draw compelling conclusions, it is interesting that the level of consistency observed here is roughly equivalent to other studies of report consistency involving reports of more mundane events. For example, in Anderson et al. (2000), participants were asked to select any two memories from their past and to describe them on two separate occasions. About half of the facts reported at Time 2 were also reported at Time 1 and this did not vary as a function of the emotionality of the memory. Talarico and Rubin (2003) asked participants to report, on two separate occasions, how they heard about the terrorist attack on September 11, 2001 and about an ordinary event from the same period. When the delay between interviews was 224 days, approximately two thirds of the details were classified as consistent, and this pattern was the same for reports of the terrorist attack and the ordinary event.

In our estimation, the degree of clustering was moderate. Although some details were consistently reported as occurring together (i.e., whether or not they were assigned to the same Robbery), we found evidence that a substantial number of units of information were not consistently connected to either a Robbery or other details.

Given differences in consistency across reports, we predicted that credibility ratings would be higher for descriptions of Robberies 1 and 5 than Robberies 2, 3, and 4. In Study 2, undergraduate students were randomly assigned to read the three (or two in the case of Robbery 5) verbatim accounts of one of the five Robberies and to answer a series of questions concerning the credibility of the account.

Study 2

Method

Participants

One-hundred and nine undergraduate students participated in this study (M age = 22.63 years; $SD = 5.71$ years). Participants received either course credit or \$5 for their participation. Most participants ($N=67$) reported that English was their first language. Of those participants who did not speak English as a first language, the average number of years they spoke English was 11.01 ($SD=5.10$).

Materials

Based on verbatim transcripts of the interviews with Beth, three descriptions of each of the first four Robberies and two descriptions of the fifth Robbery were compiled to create five sets of descriptions, one description set for each Robbery. The description sets were developed directly from verbatim transcripts and contained the precise language, including hesitations, pauses, and corrections that were present in Beth's verbal description of the Robberies; however, off-topic content was omitted. Beth was a very animated and conversational interviewee; there was a lot of off-topic discussion. In our judgment, to include this text in the description sets would have been distracting and tiring for the participants. The number of words in each of the description sets presented to participants was 5,552; 3,563; 4,296; 2,669; and 3,237 for Robberies 1, 2, 3, 4, and 5, respectively. The description sets were presented in temporal order, with the first interview (i.e., April 1999) presented first. An abbreviated version of one of the description sets is in the Appendix. Participants were randomly assigned to read one of the five sets of descriptions and to rate Beth's credibility. We decided not to provide all description sets to each participant for two reasons. First, we did not want participants to make relative judgments of credibility (e.g., which Robbery do they believe actually happened). Second, each description set was very lengthy and we were concerned about participant fatigue. Other than the transcripts, participants had no information about Beth.

Credibility questionnaire. Participants were asked to rate, on 6-point scales from (1) not at all to (6) very, Beth's honesty (i.e., one question about honesty, one about truthfulness, and one about how likely it was that the witness fabricated the report), her cognitive competence (i.e., one question about intelligence and two questions about the witness' accuracy), her overall credibility (i.e., one question about credibility and one about believability), her consistency, confidence, likeability, and suggestibility (see Connolly, Gagnon, & Lavoie, 2008; Connolly, Price, Lavoie, & Gordon, 2008). Overall credibility is thought to be comprised of honesty and cognitive competence (Bottoms, 1993). In the present study, these constructs were measured using the questions reported by Ross, Jurden, Lindsay, and Keeney (2003) as well as Leippe, Manion, and Romanczyk (1992). Questions about consistency (Berman & Cutler, 1996; Brewer et al., 1999; Conte et al., 1991), confidence (Cutler, Penrod, & Stuve, 1988; Lindsay, Wells, & O'Connor, 1989; Luus & Wells, 1994), likeability (Leippe et al., 1992), and suggestibility (Castelli, Goodman, & Ghetti, 2005; Tubb, Wood, & Hosch, 1999) have been shown to predict perceptions of credibility and were included in the questionnaire. Two random orders of questions were generated, and half of the participants were randomly assigned to receive each order. Following the questions about credibility, participants were asked to provide some demographic information.

Recognition task. To ensure that participants had read and understood the transcript, they completed a recognition test of details presented in the description set to which they were assigned. Participants were provided with a list of ten details (e.g., the robbers shot the guard): five of the details were *present* in their description set, and five of the details were not present but were drawn from Beth's descriptions of other robberies. For each detail, participants were asked to indicate whether or not that particular detail was present. Response options were: sure it was *present*, probably *present* but not really sure, probably *not present* but not really sure, or sure it was *not present*. "Sure" and "probably" responses were combined to form total "correct" and "incorrect" responses. Participants with fewer than seven (of 10) correct responses were omitted. Ten participants were excluded based on this criterion.

Design and Procedure

Participants were told that they would read all three (or two, in the case of Robbery 5) reports of a woman who was interviewed three times about something that may or may not have happened, in this case a Robbery. They were instructed that the transcripts would be followed by a series of questions related to the credibility of the statement and about their own memory of the reports. After completing the credibility questionnaire and recognition task, participants were debriefed and received course credit or $5.

Results

With the exception of ratings of suggestibility, measures of credibility were moderately to highly correlated (see Table 8.2 below). One-way ANOVAs revealed reliable effects of Robbery on ratings of: accuracy, $F(4, 104) = 3.32$, $p = .01$; credibility, $F(4, 104) = 3.01$, $p = .02$; consistency, $F(4, 104) = 5.70$, $p = .00$; and suggestibility, $F(4, 104) = 2.64$, $p = .04$; and a marginally reliable main effect on honesty, $F(4, 102) = 2.03$, $p = .10$. Mean ratings on all measures are presented in Table 8.3 (see below). Tukey's post hoc tests were used to investigate differences. Alpha was set at 0.05. Beth was rated more honest in her reports of Robbery 1 compared to Robbery 4. She was rated more accurate for Robberies 1 and 2 than Robbery 4 and more credible and more honest for Robbery 1 than Robbery 4. Beth was rated more consistent for Robbery 1 than Robbery 2 or 4 (note: the latter two did not differ from each other) and for Robbery 5 than Robbery 4. Finally, Beth was rated more suggestible in her report of Robbery 2 than 4.

Discussion

We predicted that more consistent reports would be judged to be more credible than less consistent reports. In accord with this, reports of Robbery 1 were considered more accurate, more honest, and more credible than reports of Robbery 4. However, credibility judgments of Robbery 1 did not differ from those of Robberies 2 or 3.

Table 8.2 Correlations between ratings of credibility

	Accuracy	Honesty	Overall credibility	Consistency	Confidence	Likeable
Accuracy						
Honesty	0.49[a]					
Overall credibility	0.70[a]	0.67[a]				
Consistency	0.60[a]	0.44[a]	0.63[a]			
Confidence	0.30[a]	0.24[a]	0.30[a]	0.19[a]		
Likeable	0.33[a]	0.24[a]	0.39[a]	0.19[a]	0.26[a]	
Suggestible	0.06	0.21[a]	0.13	0.08	0.22[a]	0.23

[a]denotes a significant correlation at the 0.05 level

Table 8.3 Mean rating (SDs in parentheses) for each robbery

	Robbery 1	Robbery 2	Robbery 3	Robbery 4	Robbery 5
Honest	4.23 (0.095)	3.86 (1.03)	3.84 (1.04)	3.40 (0.81)	3.72 (1.09)
Accurate	3.27 (0.72)	3.17 (0.55)	2.92 (0.74)	2.56 (0.72)	2.87 (0.87)
Credible	3.50 (1.07)	3.17 (1.00)	3.14 (0.95)	2.47 (0.70)	2.98 (1.24)
Consistent	3.74 (1.39)	2.52 (1.12)	2.86 (1.15)	2.19 (1.12)	3.33 (1.28)
Suggestible	4.04 (1.26)	4.30 (1.15)	4.12 (1.11)	3.24 (1.09)	3.95 (1.24)
Confident	3.43 (1.44)	3.43 (1.08)	2.67 (0.79)	3.00 (1.34)	2.86 (1.19)
Likeable	3.22 (1.31)	3.43 (1.16)	3.14 (1.35)	3.00 (0.89)	2.90 (1.09)

In addition, our hypothesis that Robbery 5 would also be seen as more credible than Robberies 2, 3, and 4 was not supported. Given the empirical evidence that (in)consistency is one of the strongest predictors of perceived credibility, this was surprising. Importantly, the pattern of results cannot be explained by differences in *perceptions* of consistency because participants were sensitive to actual variations in report consistency. That is, participants gave higher consistency ratings to the two Robberies that, in fact, were most consistent (Robberies 1 and 5) than to the Robberies that were least consistent (Robberies 2 and 4). The actual consistency score for Robbery 3 was intermediate, as was the rating of perceived consistency.

General Discussion

To more fully understand memory for crime, field studies are important (see Paz-Alonso, Ogle, & Goodman, present volume). The careful recording of crime victims' recollections, though lacking in experimental control, provides crucial insight into "real-world" memory (Yuille, present volume). In the present work, our interviewee reported that she was the victim of five exceptionally violent bank Robberies. We studied how Beth's statements of repeated trauma from the distant past were repeatedly reported (i.e., Study 1) and how credible her reports were judged to be (i.e., Study 2).

Consistent with our expectations based on laboratory work, the first and last Robberies were remembered best, both in terms of the number of units of information reported and the relationship between consistent and inconsistent assignment of units of information to Robberies. Indeed, for Robberies 2 and 3, assignment of details was far more inconsistent than consistent. This observed advantage for the first and last Robberies is consistent with research on memory for instances in a series of benign play sessions with children. Powell, Thomson, and Ceci (2003) found that, following a short delay between the last event in a sequence of six similar events and a memory test, there was a reporting advantage for the first and last instances. In Study 1, we demonstrated a similar phenomenon with a sequence of traumatic events, the last of which reportedly occurred more than 20 years before the first interview.

The observed pattern looks much like a recency and primacy effect. This effect has been studied most commonly in the context of word lists, with words at the beginning and end of the list recalled best. One explanation for the effect is that items at the beginning of the list benefit from more attention and rehearsal, while items at the end of the list benefit from less retroactive interference and a shorter delay to test (for a review of this and other explanations, see Friedman, 1993; Oberauer, 2003). Whether this explains the effects observed with complex autobiographical events is an empirical question. However, based on Beth's subjective assessment of her experience, there is at least one alternative explanation that relates uniquely to the first and last instances in the sequence and rests on the notion of a reporting advantage for events that are experienced as distinctive, either because the event is unusual or because the person's subjective reaction to it is powerful (Edery-Halpern & Nachson, 2004; Howe, 2000; Yuille & Cutshall, 1986; Yuille & Daylen, 1998). The first instance may be recalled well because it is distinct, never having occurred before and, therefore, commands a lot of attention. The last instance may be recalled well because something caused the sequence to terminate. Beth reported that the first Robbery was the most traumatic because it was so profoundly shocking; she had never experienced anything like it before. The last Robbery was distinct because her reaction was so intense that she felt she could not endure another Robbery; she and her husband left Montréal shortly thereafter. This explanation is consistent with the biopsychosocial theory that posits that a person's memory for an event is a function, in part, of the meaning assigned by the individual (Hervé, Cooper, & Yuille, 2007; Hervé et al., present volume).

There are at least two other reasons to treat the ostensible primacy and recency effects as preliminary. First, because we do not have an independent measure of truth, we cannot be sure that Beth's reports of Robberies 1 and 5 really are details of the first and last Robberies. Second, Beth was asked to report details of Robberies 1–5, in that order. It is possible that she assigned the most memorable details to Robberies 1 and 5 because she assumed they would be the most memorable or because that is a natural output strategy. In future research, it may be instructive to allow an interviewee to determine the order in which instances of a repeated event are reported or to counterbalance output order.

Given the damaging effect of report inconsistencies on perceptions of credibility (Berman et al., 1995; Berman & Cutler, 1996; Brewer et al., 1999; Connolly et al., 2010; Fisher et al., present volume) and the extent of inconsistencies in Beth's reports, we were intrigued by how these reports may be perceived by those likely to evaluate such evidence in the criminal justice system—potential jurors. Thus, in Study 2, we examined perceptions of credibility of Beth's reports of the Robberies. Beth's description of the first Robbery was superior to her descriptions of the other Robberies on several dimensions including number of details, overall consistency, consistency of assignment to Robberies, and inconsistency of assignment to Robberies. This advantage was expressed in higher credibility ratings, at least compared to ratings given to Robbery 4. This is in line with our hypothesis and with the literature that low consistency scores are associated with low ratings of credibility (Berman et al., 1995; Berman & Cutler, 1996; Brewer et al., 1999; Conte et al., 1991). However, the overall pattern of data suggests that consistency alone does not tell the entire story. Note that consistency ratings of Robbery 2 were lower than consistency ratings of Robbery 4, but only Robbery 4 was judged to be less credible than Robbery 1. Moreover, in spite of the lower consistency ratings of Robbery 2 relative to Robbery 4, accuracy ratings for Robbery 2 were higher than accuracy Ratings for Robbery 4. Also, the actual consistency of Robbery 5 was second only to Robbery 1, yet only perceived consistency distinguished Robbery 5 from Robbery 4. Thus, there was something else about the reports of Robbery 4 that negatively impacted participant evaluations.

The most salient difference between reports of Robbery 4 and all of the others is that Robbery 4 contained the fewest number of independent units of information. Although there were also relatively few details provided in the reports of Robberies 2 and 3, the most dramatic decrease was seen in the report of Robbery 4. This paucity of details in the reports of Robbery 4 may have contributed independently or interactively with consistency to influence credibility scores (see Griesel, Ternes, Schraml, Cooper, & Yuille, present volume, for a discussion of appropriate amount of detail). Bell and Loftus (1989) found that a more detailed report was judged by mock jurors to be more credible than a less detailed report (see also Colwell, Hiscock-Anisman, & Fede, present volume; but see Borckardt, Sprohge, & Nash, 2003). We have some preliminary evidence to support this possibility. Participants in the present study were asked to provide three reasons for their judgments of credibility. Two independent coders categorized the reasons and agreed that the top two reasons were consistency and memory for details. Indeed, these two reasons represented 46% of all responses.

Limitations

Limitations of Study 1 are first discussed, followed by limitations of Study 2. First, Beth may have recalled what she had reported in a previous interview when reporting details of the Robberies in Interviews 2 and 3. If Beth had relied on her prior recollections, we would have expected high consistency and low inconsistency scores. Because we did not observe unusually high scores on these measures, we are somewhat confident that, during each interview, Beth reported what she recalled about the Robberies rather than what she recalled having previously reported. Second, we do not know what actually happened during any of the Robberies. Our primary research interest, however, was how she repeatedly reported the Robberies and how those multiple reports might influence perceived credibility. After all, when a trier of fact hears reports of an event, ground truth is not known but it is assessed based on characteristics of the report (see Seniuk, present volume). Finally, with only one participant, individual factors may have influenced the findings. Indeed, Beth was an exceptionally articulate woman, a characteristic that may have influenced consistency scores.

Study 2 was a perceived credibility study that involved undergraduate students rather than a more representative sample of participants from the community. Although we support replication of these data with a community sample, use of undergraduates as mock jurors is not uncommon and may not be unrepresentative. Based on a meta-analysis, Bornstein (1999) found few differences between undergraduates and community member mock jurors. Indeed, in only 5 of 26 studies that directly compared students and non-students were there differences in mock jury behavior.

In Study 2, mock jurors read a verbatim account from Beth. They did not have the advantage of observing her demeanor as would have been possible with a videotape or live presentation. Although the use of demeanor evidence by lay persons to assess credibility may not assist with correct judgments, it is used (e.g., Golding, Fryman, Marshall, & Yozwiak, 2003; Regan & Baker, 1998). Although we acknowledge some limitations based on mode of presentation, the fact that demeanor was not present in Study 2 to interfere with ratings of credibility may be seen as a strength. Finally, in the current study, we employed a between-subjects design; participants read about one Robbery only. In her descriptions of one Robbery, Beth often made reference to other Robberies and so we are confident that all participants knew that Beth was reporting one Robbery from a series of similar Robberies. However, allowing participants to read Beth's reports of each Robbery may have helped them to place the events into a more complete context which may, in turn, have affected ratings of credibility. Finally, as discussed above, the transcripts represent a single person's multiple reports of repeated traumatic events. It is important to replicate these findings with other multiple reports of repeated events.

Conclusion

Increasingly, courts are hearing evidence from persons who allege having been repeatedly victimized in the distant past (Connolly & Read, 2006). These allegations raise a myriad of challenges for those involved in the legal system. Given the sufficiency principle that requires a charge be specific enough for the accused to raise a defense, one issue that arises is which of the multiple instances of the alleged offence should be probed to elicit the most complete report. Given the results of Study 1, our preliminary conclusion is that, relative to the middle instances, the first and last instances may be more detailed than the middle instances. The first and last may also be more consistent and less inconsistent. Each of these characteristics is associated with perceptions of credibility and, as such, is very forensically relevant.

The study of memory for trauma in a naturalistic context is critical for understanding and interpreting witness evidence (see Paz-Alonso et al., present volume; Yuille, present volume). This approach, spearheaded by Yuille and Cutshall (1986) and others, has added invaluable perspective to controlled laboratory experiments.

Acknowledgments This research was supported by a SSHRC operating grant to the first author and an NSERC PGS-D grant to the second author. We extend a special thanks to "Beth" who spent hours with us describing her experiences.

Appendix: Abbreviated Description of Robbery 3 Across Three Interviews

Interview 1. The bank thought it would be a good idea to have armed guards in the bank. At the beginning of this Robbery, a totally unmasked robber entered the bank and shot the guard.

When the robbers arrived, I jumped down three stairs. I remember saying "Everyone get down." The hardware store clerk who was in the bank at the time said that, when he was told to hit the floor, he did and all he remembers is the smell of the wax. A few days later, when he saw me in the hardware store, he kissed me and hugged me and told me how brave I was. On their way out, they sprayed the back of the bank with bullets. When we closed the doors, one customer broke open the liquor that he had just bought. It was 2 pm when everything was over. We told head office that we could not reopen, but when they said they would send in another team, we decided it would be too much trouble and we returned to work. After this one, I bought my husband skis with the danger pay. Later, when my husband and I were skiing, I saw a man with a mask on and I screamed and passed out (Transcripts).

Interview 2. We were short staffed that day. There was a bad snowstorm and I had to call in a teller who was very pregnant. Just when she arrived, the robbers burst in. Just after the robbers entered the bank, a teller was frantically and obviously trying to find her alarm button. I pulled the pregnant teller under the desk and tried to comfort her but she was screaming. The robber put a gun to our face and said "I told you to shut her up." That is when she yelled back at him and he left. With a gun, one of the robbers took a teller to the back of the bank to open the vault. She could never remember her combination and so we were convinced that we were all dead. Well, she remembered and had the vault open in no time. I remember helping others in the bank, getting them off the floor. Later, when my husband and I were skiing, I saw a man with a mask on and I screamed and passed out (Transcripts).

Interview 3. The bank thought it would be a good idea to have armed guards in the bank. There was a bad snowstorm and I had to call in a teller who was very pregnant. Just when she arrived, the robbers burst in. At the beginning of this Robbery, a totally unmasked robber entered the bank and shot the guard. Just after the robbers entered the bank, a teller was frantically and obviously trying to find her alarm button. When the alarm was activated, you could hear the video recorder come on. I pulled the pregnant teller under the desk and tried to comfort her but she was screaming. The robber put a gun to our face and said "I told you to shut her up." That is when she yelled back at him and he left. After this one, I bought my husband skis with the danger pay. Later, when my husband and I were skiing, I saw a man with a mask on and I screamed and passed out (Transcripts).

References

Abelson, R. P. (1981). Psychological status of script concept. *American Psychologist, 36*, 715–729.

Anderson, S. J., Cohen, G., & Taylor, S. (2000). Rewriting the past: Some factors affecting the variability of personal memories. *Applied Cognitive Psychology, 14*, 435–454.

Bell, B. E., & Loftus, E. F. (1989). Trivial persuasion in the courtroom: The power of (a few) minor details. *Journal of Personality and Social Psychology, 56*, 669–679.

Berman, G. L., & Cutler, B. L. (1996). Effects of inconsistencies in eyewitness testimony and mock-juror judgements. *Journal of Applied Psychology, 81*, 170–177.

Berman, G. L., Narby, D. J., & Cutler, B. L. (1995). Effects of inconsistent eyewitness statements on mock-jurors' evaluations of the eyewitness, perceptions of defendant culpability and verdicts. *Law and Human Behavior, 19*, 79–88.

Bifulco, A., Brown, G. W., Lillie, A., & Jarvis, J. (1997). Memories of childhood neglect and abuse: Corroboration in a series of sisters. *Journal of Child Psychology and Psychiatry, 38*, 365–374.

Borckardt, J. J., Sprohge, E., & Nash, M. (2003). Effects of the inclusion and refutation of peripheral details on eyewitness credibility. *Journal of Applied Social Psychology, 33*, 2187–2197.

Bornstein, B. H. (1999). The ecological validity of jury simulations: Is the jury still out? *Law and Human Behavior, 23*, 75–91.

Bottoms, B. L. (1993). Individual differences in perceptions of child sexual assault victims. In G. S. Goodman & B. L. Bottoms (Eds.), *Child victims, child witnesses: Understanding and improving testimony* (pp. 229–261). New York: Guilford Press.

Brewer, N., & Burke, A. (2002). Effects of testimonial inconsistencies and eyewitness confidence on mock-juror judgments. *Law and Human Behavior, 26*, 353–364.

Brewer, N., Potter, B., Fisher, R. P., Bond, N., & Lusczcz, M. A. (1999). Beliefs and data on the relationships between consistency and accuracy on eyewitness testimony. *Applied Cognitive Psychology, 13*, 297–313.

Brown, N. R. (2005). On the prevalence of event clusters in autobiographical memory. *Social Cognition, 23*, 35–69.

Brown, N. R., & Schopflocher, D. (1998). Event clusters: An organization of personal events in autobiographical memory. *Psychological Science, 9*, 470–475.

Burt, C. D. B., Kemp, S., & Conway, M. A. (2003). Themes, events, and episodes in autobiographical memory. *Memory & Cognition, 31*, 317–325.

Castelli, P., Goodman, G. S., & Ghetti, S. (2005). Effects of interview style and witness age on perceptions of children's credibility in sexual abuse cases. *Journal of Applied Social Psychology, 35*, 297–319.

Christianson, S.-A., & Engelberg, E. (1999). Memory and emotional consistency: The MS Estonia ferry disaster. *Memory, 7*, 471–482.

Connolly, D. A., Gagnon, N., & Lavoie, J. A. (2008). The effect of a judicial declaration of competence on the perceived credibility of children and defendants. *Legal and Criminological Psychology, 13*, 257–277.

Connolly, D. A., & Lindsay, D. S. (2001). The influence of suggestions on children's reports of a unique experience versus an instance of a repeated experience. *Applied Cognitive Psychology, 15*, 205–223.

Connolly, D. A., & Price, H. L. (2006). Children's suggestibility for an instance of a repeated event versus a unique event: The effect of degree of association between variable options. *Journal of Experimental Child Psychology, 93*, 207–223.

Connolly, D. A., Price, H. L., & Gordon, H. M. (2010). Judicial decision-making in timely and delayed prosecutions of child sexual abuse: A study of honesty and cognitive ability in assessments of credibility. *Psychology, Public Policy, and Law, 16*, 177–199.

Connolly, D. A., Price, H. L., Lavoie, J. A., & Gordon, H. M. (2008). Perceptions and predictors of children's credibility of a unique event and an instance of a repeated event. *Law and Human Behavior, 32*, 92–112.

Connolly, D. A., & Read, J. D. (2003). Remembering historical child sexual abuse. *Criminal Law Quarterly, 47*, 438–480.

Connolly, D. A., & Read, J. D. (2006). Delayed prosecutions of historic child sexual abuse: Analyses of 2064 Canadian criminal complaints. *Law and Human Behavior, 30*, 409–434.

Conte, J. R., Sorenson, E., Fogarty, L., & Rosa, J. D. (1991). Evaluating children's reports of sexual abuse: Results from a survey of professionals. *The American Journal of Orthopsychiatry, 78*, 428–437.

Conway, M. A., & Pleydell-Pearce, C. W. (2000). The construction of autobiographical memories in the self-memory system. *Psychological Review, 107*, 261–288.

Cournoyer, D. E., & Rohner, R. P. (1996). Reliability of retrospective reports of perceived maternal acceptance-rejection in childhood. *Psychological Reports, 78*, 147–150.

Cutler, B., Penrod, S., & Stuve, T. (1988). Juror decision making in eyewitness identification cases. *Law and Human Behavior, 12*, 41–55.

Desmarais, S. L. (2009). Examining report content and social categorization to understand consistency effects on credibility. *Law and Human Behavior, 33*, 470–480.

Dill, D. L., Chu, J. A., Grob, M. C., & Eisen, S. V. (1991). The reliability of abuse history reports: A comparison of two inquiry formats. *Comprehensive Psychiatry, 32*, 166–169.

Edery-Halpern, G., & Nachson, I. (2004). Distinctiveness in flashbulb memory: Comparative analysis of five terrorist attacks. *Memory, 12*, 147–157.

Engelhard, I. M., van den Hout, M. A., & McNally, R. J. (2008). Memory consistency for traumatic events in Dutch soldiers deployed in Iraq. *Memory, 16*, 3–9.

Farrar, M. J., & Goodman, G. S. (1990). Developmental differences in the relation between scripts and episodic memory: Do they exist? In R. Fivush & J. A. Hudson (Eds.), *Knowing and remembering in young children* (pp. 30–64). New York: Cambridge University Press.

Farrar, M. J., & Goodman, G. S. (1992). Developmental changes in event memory. *Child Development, 63*, 173–187.

Femina, D. D., Yeager, C. A., & Lewis, D. O. (1990). Child abuse: Adolescent records vs. adult recall. *Child Abuse & Neglect, 14*, 227–231.

Fergusson, D. M., Horwood, L. J., & Woodward, L. J. (2000). The stability of child abuse reports: A longitudinal study of the behavioural reporting of young adults. *Psychological Medicine, 30*, 529–544.

Fisher, R. P., Brewer, N., & Mitchell, G. (2009). The relation between consistency and accuracy of eyewitness testimony: Legal versus cognitive explanations. In R. Bull, T. Valentine, &

T. Williamson (Eds.), *Handbook of psychology of investigative interviewing: Current developments and future directions* (pp. 121–136). Chichester, UK: Wiley-Blackwell.

Fisher, R. P., & Cutler, B. L. (1995). The relation between consistency and accuracy of eyewitness testimony. In G. Davies, S. Lloyd-Bostock, M. McMurran, & C. Wilson (Eds.), *Law and criminal justice: International developments in research and practice*. Berlin: De Gruyter.

Fivush, R. (1984). Learning about school: The development of kindergartner's school script. *Child Development, 55*, 1697–1709.

Friedman, W. J. (1993). Memory for the time of past events. *Psychological Bulletin, 113*, 44–66.

Fry, R. P. W., Rozewicz, L. M., & Crisp, A. H. (1996). Interviewing for sexual abuse: Reliability and effect of interviewer gender. *Child Abuse & Neglect, 20*, 725–729.

Golding, J. M., Fryman, H. M., Marshall, D. F., & Yozwiak, J. A. (2003). Big girls don't cry: the effect of child witness demeanor on juror decisions in a child sexual abuse trial. *Child Abuse & Neglect, 27*, 1311–1321.

Gordon, H. M., Connolly, D. A., Banipal, R., & Price, H. L. (2006). *Repeated interviews: The consistency of children's reports of an instance of a repeated event*. Paper presented at the meeting of the American Psychology-Law Society, St. Petersburg, Florida, USA.

Guadagno, B. L., Powell, M. B., & Wright, R. (2006). Police officers' and legal professionals' perceptions regarding how children are, and should be, questioned about repeated abuse. *Psychiatry, Psychology and Law, 13*, 251–260.

Herlihy, J., Scragg, P., & Turner, S. (2002). Discrepancies in autobiographical memories-implications for the assessment of asylum seekers: Repeated interview study. *British Medical Journal, 324*, 324–327.

Hervé, H. F., Cooper, B. S., & Yuille, J. C. (2007). Memory formation in offenders: Perspectives from a biopsychosocial model of eyewitness memory. In S. A. Christianson (Ed.), *Offenders' memories of violent crimes* (pp. 38–74). West Sussex, England: John Wiley & Sons.

Home Affairs Committee. (2002). *The conduct of investigations into past cases of abuse in children's homes: Fourth report of session 2001-02*. Retrieved from, 22 April, 2008, http://www.publications.parliament.uk/pa/cm200102/cmselect/cmhaff/cmhaff.htm.

Howe, M. L. (2000). *Fate of early memories: Developmental science and the retention of childhood experiences*. Washington, DC: American Psychological Association.

King, D. W., King, L. A., Erickson, D. J., Huang, M. T., Sharkansky, E. J., & Wolfe, J. (2000). Posttraumatic stress disorder and retrospectively reported stressor exposure: A longitudinal prediction model. *Journal of Abnormal Psychology, 109*, 624–633.

Leippe, M. R., Manion, A. P., & Romanczyk, A. (1992). Eyewitness persuasion: How and how well do fact finders judge the accuracy of adults' and children's memory reports? *Journal of Personality and Social Psychology, 63*, 181–197.

Lindsay, R. C. L., Wells, G. L., & O'Connor, F. (1989). Mock juror belief of accurate and inaccurate witnesses: A replication. *Law and Human Behavior, 13*, 333–340.

London, K., Bruck, M., Ceci, S. J., & Shuman, D. W. (2005). Disclosure of child sexual abuse: What does the research tell us about the ways that children tell? *Psychology, Public Policy, and Law, 11*, 194–226.

Luus, C. A. E., & Wells, G. L. (1994). The malleability of eyewitness confidence: Co-witness and perseverance effects. *Journal of Applied Psychology, 79*, 714–724.

Malloy, L. C., & Lamb, M. E. (2010). Biases in judging victims and suspects whose statements are inconsistent. *Law and Human Behavior, 34*, 46–48.

Martin, J., Anderson, J., Romans, S., Mullen, P., & O'Shea, M. (1993). Asking about child sexual abuse: Methodological implications of a two stage survey. *Child Abuse & Neglect, 17*, 383–392.

Means, B., & Loftus, E. F. (1991). When personal memory repeats itself: Decomposing memories for recurring events. *Applied Cognitive Psychology, 5*, 297–318.

Neisser, U. (1981). John Dean's memory: A case study. *Cognition, 9*, 1–22.

Nelson, K. (1986). *Event knowledge: Structure and function in development*. Hillside NJ: Erlbaum.

Nelson, K., & Gruendel, J. (1986). Children's scripts. In K. Nelson (Ed.), *Event knowledge: Structure and function in development* (pp. 21–46). Hillside, NJ: Erlbaum.

Oberauer, K. (2003). Understanding serial position curves in short-term recognition and recall. *Journal of Memory and Language, 49*, 469–483.

Odegard, T., Lampinen, J. M., & Wirth-Beaumont, E. T. (2004). Organization and retrieval: The generation of event clusters. *Memory, 12*, 685–695.

Offer, D., Kaiz, M., Howard, K. I., & Bennett, E. S. (2000). The altering of reported experiences. *Journal of the American Academy of Child and Adolescent Psychiatry, 39*, 735–742.

Pearse, S. L., Powell, M. B., & Thomson, D. M. (2003). The effect of contextual cues on children's ability to remember an occurrence of a repeated event. *Legal and Criminological Psychology, 8*, 39–50.

Pezdek, K. (2003). Event memory and autobiographical memory for the events of September 11, 2001. *Applied Cognitive Psychology, 17*, 1033–1045.

Powell, M. B., & Roberts, K. P. (2002). The effect of repeated experience on children's suggestibility across two question types. *Applied Cognitive Psychology, 16*, 367–386.

Powell, M. B., Roberts, K. P., Ceci, S. J., & Hembrooke, H. (1999). The effects of repeated experience on children's suggestibility. *Developmental Psychology, 35*, 1462–1477.

Powell, M. B., & Thompson, D. M. (1997). Contrasting memory for temporal-source and memory for content in children's discrimination of repeated events. *Applied Cognitive Psychology, 11*, 339–360.

Powell, M. B., Thomson, D. M., & Ceci, S. J. (2003). Children's memory of recurring events: Is the first event always the best remembered? *Applied Cognitive Psychology, 17*, 127–146.

Price, H. L., & Connolly, D. A. (2004). Event frequency and children's suggestibility: A study of cued recall responses. *Applied Cognitive Psychology, 18*, 809–821.

R. v. B.(G.). (1990). 2 S.C.R. 30.

R. v. R.(J.W.). (2001). 151 C.C.C. (3d) 236.

Read, J. D., & Connolly, D. A. (2007). The effects of delay on long-term memory for witnessed events. In M. P. Toglia, J. D. Read, D. F. Ross, & R. C. L. Lindsay (Eds.), *Handbook of eyewitness psychology: Volume 1: Memory for events* (pp. 117–155). Mahway, NJ: Lawrence Erlbaum Associates Inc.

Regan, P. C., & Baker, S. J. (1998). The impact of child witness demeanor on perceived credibility and trial outcome in sexual abuse cases. *Journal of Family Violence, 13*, 187–195.

Roemer, L., Litz, B. T., Orsillo, S. M., Ehlich, P. J., & Friedman, M. J. (1998). Increases in retrospective accounts of war-zone exposure over time: The role of PTSD symptom severity. *Journal of Traumatic Stress, 11*, 597–605.

Ross, D. F., Jurden, F. H., Lindsay, R. C. L., & Keeney, J. M. (2003). Replication and limitations of a two-factor model of child witness credibility. *Journal of Applied Social Psychology, 33*, 418–431.

Slackman, E., & Nelson, K. (1984). Acquisition of an unfamiliar script in story form by young children. *Child Development, 55*, 329–340.

Southwick, S. M., Morgan, C. A., Nicolaou, A. L., & Charney, D. S. (1997). Consistency of memory for combat-related traumatic events in veterans of Operation Desert Storm. *The American Journal of Psychiatry, 154*, 173–177.

Spinhoven, P., Bean, T., & Eurelings-Bontekoe, L. (2006). Inconsistencies in the self-report of traumatic experiences by unaccompanied refugee minors. *Journal of Traumatic Stress, 19*, 663–673.

Talarico, J. M., & Rubin, D. C. (2003). Confidence, not consistency, characterizes autobiographical memory. *Psychological Science, 14*, 455–461.

Tubb, V. A., Wood, J. M., & Hosch, H. M. (1999). Effects of suggestive interviewing and indirect evidence on child credibility in a sexual abuse case. *Journal of Applied Social Psychology, 29*, 1111–1127.

Turtle, J. W., & Yuille, J. C. (1994). Lost but not forgotten: Repeated eyewitness recall leads to reminiscence but not hypermnesia. *Journal of Applied Psychology, 79*, 260–271.

Wagenaar, W. A., & Groeneweg, J. (1990). The memory of concentration camp survivors. *Applied Cognitive Psychology, 4*, 77–87.

Yeung, K.Y. & Ruzzo, W.L. (2001). *Details of the adjusted rand index and clustering algorithms.* Supplement to the paper "An empirical study of principal component analysis for clustering gene expression data." Retrieved from, 16 April, 2008, http://faculty.washington.edu/kayee/pca/supp.pdf.

Yuille, J. C., & Cutshall, J. L. (1986). A case study of an eyewitness memory of a crime. *Journal of Applied Psychology, 71*, 291–301.

Yuille, J. C., & Daylen, J. (1998). The impact of traumatic events on eyewitness memory. In C. P. Thompson, D. J. Herrmann, J. Read, D. Bruce, D. Payne, & M. Toglia (Eds.), *Eyewitness memory: Theoretical and applied perspectives* (pp. 155–178). Mahwah, NJ: Lawrence Erlbaum Associates.

Yuille, J. C., Hunter, R., Joffe, R., & Zaparniuk, J. (1993). Interviewing children in sexual abuse cases. In G. S. Goodman & B. L. Bottoms (Eds.), *Child victims, child witnesses: Understanding and improving testimony* (pp. 95–115). New York, NY: Guilford Press.

Yuille, J. C., Ternes, M., & Cooper, B. S. (2010). Expert testimony on laboratory witnesses. *Journal of Forensic Psychology Practice, 10*, 238–251.

Part IV
Credibility Assessment

Chapter 9
Discovering Deceit: Applying Laboratory and Field Research in the Search for Truthful and Deceptive Behavior

Leanne ten Brinke and Stephen Porter

Introduction

"Science is the captain, and practice the soldiers"—Leonardo da Vinci

da Vinci's sage observation may be conceptualized as a guide for applied researchers; the most meaningful psychological research addresses an interesting topic with both basic and applied relevance. Once identified, the phenomenon of interest should be studied both in the lab—offering a high level of internal validity—and in the "field", lacking experimental control but offering more realism, and not rushing to scientific judgment based on or the other (Yuille, 1996, present volume). Subsequently, converging empirical findings from the lab and field should be responsibly applied in the legal context (e.g., Paz-Alonso, Ogle, & Goodman, present volume; Yuille, 1989). One program of research exemplifying these principles is outlined in this chapter: detecting deception.

A key role of judges and jurors at trial is to decide whether various witnesses are lying or telling the truth (see Seniuk, present volume). But is it possible to determine accurately whether a witness is providing an honest and accurate version of events, an unintentionally mistaken memory, or lying through his/her teeth? This issue is not trivial; in an adversarial system, most trials feature contradictory testimony by witnesses (see Connolly & Price, present volume; also see Fisher, Vrij, & Leins, present volume, for research focusing on contradictory statements within witnesses). In increasingly common "he said, she said" cases, there is little or no evidence other than conflicting stories told by a complainant and defendant, and decision-making is guided almost entirely by credibility assessments (e.g., Porter, Campbell, Birt & Woodworth, 2003). For example, the judge in the Air India mass murder case (*R. v. Malik & Bagri*, 2005) concluded that the case was reduced to a credibility contest: "… the determination of

L. ten Brinke (✉) • S. Porter
Haas School of Business, UC Berkeley, Berkeley, CA, USA
University of British Columbia, Kelowna, BC, Canada
e-mail: leannetenbrinke@berkeley.edu

guilt devolves to the weighing of the credibility of a number of witnesses who testified in these proceedings (para. 5)." In fact, we would argue that credibility assessment is the "bread and butter" task for judges and juries in all trials. Our research team has been interested in both the behaviors that are actually associated with deception, and the manner in which others (such as judges) assess credibility.

Deception is an important and common aspect of human social interaction present in much of interpersonal interaction. People confess to using deceit in 14% of emails, 27% of face-to-face interactions, and 37% of phone calls (Hancock, 2007; Hancock & Woodworth, present volume), and lie on average about twice a day (DePaulo, Kashy, Kirkendol, Wyer, & Epstein, 1996). Although most everyday lies do not carry heavy consequences, deception in the interview room, courtroom, or parole hearing holds enormous consequences at both the individual and societal level. Despite the widespread use of deception, it is notoriously difficult to detect; when asked to determine whether another person is lying, most people, including police officers and judges perform at or only slightly better than chance (e.g., Bond & DePaulo, 2006; Ekman & O'Sullivan, 1991). Despite empirical findings that deception detection is a difficult task laden with errors, people are typically confident in their ability to spot a liar and consider it to be a simple assessment (e.g., Vrij, 2000).

Demonstrating the difficulty of this task and the major misconceptions concerning deceptive behavior, Porter, Woodworth, and Birt (2000) found that Canadian federal parole officers performed significantly below chance at detecting deception in videotaped speakers. Such a low rate of accuracy strongly suggests that these professionals were *actively* attending to misleading cues and making mistakes. Fortunately, empirically based training methods that provide professionals with reliable verbal and nonverbal cues to deception, gathered from decades of research on deceptive behavior (for a meta-analytic review, see DePaulo et al., 2003), have been shown to be at least modestly successful (see Colwell, Hiscock-Anisman, & Fede, present volume). The same federal parole officers who detected deception below chance increased their accuracy to 76.7% after a 2-day training program (Porter et al., 2000). With advances in knowledge of deception through laboratory and field studies, there is a reason to believe that empirically validated training could achieve even greater success in the near future.

Deception Detection by Police

The consequences of the failed identification of concealed and falsified information are enormous in many contexts, including suspect interviews, customs agencies, airport security, and the courtroom (e.g., Porter & ten Brinke, 2008). For example, the failure to detect deception by a suspect who denies his or her involvement in a crime might allow a prolific offender to return to society and continue to victimize innocent people. Alternatively, an innocent suspect who is thought to be lying might be wrongfully convicted (see Yarbrough, Hervé, & Harms, present volume). In their daily interactions with citizens, police officers' ability to detect deception serves as a "front line" defence in the prevention of false allegations and the prosecution of guilty parties. Given that many police officers receive some form of deception detection training (most commonly in the Reid technique; Inbau, Reid, Buckley, & Jayne, 2001) and encounter potentially deceptive individuals on a daily basis, one might expect that they would be especially skilled in this task. However, research suggests that police officers perform no better than lay persons in deception detection tasks; like the average person, police tend to "flip a coin" when making assessments of credibility (e.g., Bond & DePaulo, 2006; Ekman & O'Sullivan, 1991; Garrido, Masip, & Herrero, 2004).

Although many deception detection tasks employed in research thus far appear "artificial" (e.g., use of university student participants, low motivation lies; see O'Sullivan, present volume) for police officers, similar levels of accuracy have been replicated in more ecologically valid tasks (Vrij & Mann, 2001). In missing persons cases, relatives are often considered persons of interest despite their attempts to assist police and aid in the search for their lost relative. Real-life, high-stakes lies occur when those that make emotional pleas to the public for information about their missing loved ones are later uncovered as the murderer themselves (e.g., Michael White of Alberta, Canada, who claimed his pregnant wife went missing after he brutally murdered her and dumped her body in the woods). Vrij and Mann (2001) had police officers view such footage and asked them to assess the sincerity of the emotional pleas. Similar to laboratory-based studies, these findings suggested that police officers were unable to detect deceit in this context above the level of chance and, while those with interviewing experience were more confident in their judgments, they were no more accurate than less experienced officers. However, police officers may be better at detecting deceit in an investigative interview. Mann, Vrij, and Bull (2004a) asked police officers to classify the veracity of videotaped segments of real-life suspect interviews, and found accuracy to be around 65%, significantly greater than chance. As such, some laboratory-based assessments of deception detection skill may underestimate real-world accuracy. Despite this possible underestimation of their accuracy, there remains a high level of error and a need for more accurate assessments.

Perhaps as a consequence of their line of work, police officers tend to show a deception bias—labelling more (i.e., guilty and innocent) individuals as liars than what would be expected by chance or in comparison with a layperson (Garrido, Masip, & Herrero, 2004). Meissner and Kassin (2002) found that training and prior experience increased the likelihood of believing a speaker was being deceitful. Further, training and prior experience can inflate confidence in one's ability to detect deceit (DePaulo & Pfeifer, 1986). For example, experimental training for a group of student participants in the popular (but largely unvalidated) Reid technique (Inbau et al., 2001) actually resulted in poorer performances in detecting deceit than their untrained counterparts (Kassin & Fong, 1999). Despite the decrease in performance, trained students were significantly more confident in their assessments, signalling trouble for officers trained in this manner.

Training in the Reid technique, in particular, may impair the ability to detect deception, given that it does not endorse appropriate attention to empirically substantiated cues (in fact, quite the opposite; see Walsh & Bull, present volume). Vrij, Mann, and Fisher (2006) conducted the first empirical test of the Reid recommendations for detecting deceit in a behavior analysis interview (BAI), as described by Inbau et al. (2001). While Reid and colleagues suggest that lies will be accompanied by nervous behaviors associated with discomfort, they fail to account for the importance of impression management. In Vrij et al.'s (2001) study, deceptive participants exhibited behaviors opposite of those predicted by the BAI, while genuine participants appeared nervous and uncomfortable, providing an explanation for the decrease in accuracy reported by Kassin and Fong (1999). Thus, the convergence of evidence from laboratory and applied studies suggests that attempts to enhance deception detection skills with empirically valid practices among police officers would be a worthwhile endeavour (see Griesel, Ternes, Schraml, Cooper, & Yuille, present volume).

Deception Detection in the Courtroom

After the initial investigation and credibility determination by police, a subsequent step on the proverbial path to justice occurs in the courtroom where the determination of an individual's credibility is of utmost importance to rulings of guilt and innocence. How does a judge or juror decide whether a witness is providing an honest and accurate recollection of events, an unintentionally mistaken memory, or intentionally providing a false account? As indicated above, this issue is not trivial; in an adversarial legal system such as Canada's, most trials feature contradictory testimony. In many cases, conflicting testimony by witnesses represents the only evidence available, and determinations of guilt or innocence are guided almost entirely by credibility assessment. Thus, we suggest that the determination of an individual's credibility is a fundamental task for judges and juries with weighty consequences (see Seniuk, present volume). The assessment of credibility is made more difficult when historical offenses are brought to trial, particularly in countries such as Canada with no statute of limitations.

Given the central role of credibility assessment in judicial decision-making, it is important to examine the manner in which it is viewed and approached by the court. A review of rulings on the matter clearly points to the predominant view that credibility assessment is a straightforward matter, best undertaken with the use of "common sense." In *R. v. Marquard* (1993), the Canadian Supreme Court concluded that the determination of the honesty is *common sense*: "Credibility is a matter within the competence of lay people. Ordinary people draw conclusions about whether someone is lying or telling the truth on a daily basis" (p. 248). Similarly, in *R. v. Francois* (1994), Justice McLachlin stated: "In the end, the jury must decide whether it believes the witness' story in whole or in part. That determination turns ... on the demeanour of the witness and the common sense of the jury" (see Seniuk, present volume, for a discussion of demeanour evidence).

This common sense argument advocated by Canada's highest court is incompatible with the empirically-based conclusion that credibility assessment is a highly complex and often unreliable task (e.g., Bond & DePaulo, 2006; Vrij, 2000). At a 2005 judicial education conference in which the second author gave a workshop on credibility assessment, 16 Canadian judges completed questionnaires (e.g., at baseline) regarding their beliefs about verbal, vocal, and nonverbal behaviors as they might relate to deception (Porter & ten Brinke, 2009). For all questions, the judges' responses about directional differences in valid cues were highly variable (e.g., often evenly or near evenly split among possible responses), suggesting a complete lack of consensus about deceptive cues. For example, six judges believed that liars provide more details that truth-tellers, three judges believed the opposite, two did not believe there was a difference in level of detail, and five did not know if there was a relationship between amount of detail and veracity. Further, the judges expressed a high level of confidence in their ability to detect deception (Porter & ten Brinke, 2008). However, judges, as with police officers and laypersons, perform around the level of chance in judging the credibility of videotaped speakers (Ekman & O'Sullivan, 1991).

While it is not possible to know the frequency of mistakes concerning credibility in the courtroom, recent wrongful convictions suggest that credibility assessment is a highly fallible process and by no means a matter of mere common sense. Such cases also highlight the gravity of the consequences of flawed credibility assessments. In a 2001 inquiry into Thomas Sophonow's wrongful conviction for the murder of Barbara Stoppel, Justice Cory concluded that the testimony of "honest, right-thinking (but inaccurate) witnesses" and "smooth and convincing liars" contribute to false convictions (e.g., Wilson, 2003).

Cues to Deception

Despite the evidence that judges, police officers, and laypersons apply strategies that disallow effective credibility assessments, effective strategies may exist. Three primary theories have emerged to predict cues to deception: the content complexity, attempted control, and emotional approaches (e.g., Porter & Yuille, 1995; Vrij, 2000, 2008). Content complexity (Vrij, 2008) suggests that lying is more cognitively difficult than telling the truth and will, therefore, result in measurable differences such as shorter stories, repetitions to avoid contradictions, and a neglect of body language (see Colwell et al., present volume). Alternatively, the attempted control approach (Vrij, 2008) suggests that liars channel considerable effort into behaving normally. However, it is not possible for liars to consciously replicate all aspects of behavior that occur naturally during truthful discussion, leading to overly rigid or suspiciously smooth behavior. Finally, the emotional approach (Vrij, 2008) predicts that deception is accompanied by guilt, fear, and excitement reflected in patterns of nervous behavior. Although no single cue signals deceit (see Yarbrough et al., present volume), a large body of literature has highlighted a variety of verbal, behavioral, and facial cues to deception (see Colwell et al., present volume; Griesel et al., present volume; O'Sullivan, present volume). In a 2003 meta-analysis of 120 independent samples, DePaulo et al. (2003) found support for elements of each of these theories: liars provided fewer details, spent less time talking, told less plausible stories, used fewer illustrators, and appeared more nervous than truth tellers. While this synthesis provided a concise summary of relevant cues to deception, it should be noted that, of the 120 samples included, 101 were studies in which students served as participants in artificial situations. As such, an examination of deceptive cues within forensically relevant populations and settings is needed.

There are reasons to believe that criminal offenders may behave differently when engaging in deception. First, criminals likely have greater practice in (forensically-relevant) deception than the average individual—maintaining lies about their criminal involvement for years or decades (e.g., Porter & Woodworth, 2007). Given this extensive experience with deceit, it is not surprising that criminals report more realistic beliefs about deceptive behavior and consider the task to require less effort when compared to students' responses on the same survey (Granhag, Andersson, Strömwall, & Hartwig, 2004). Further, criminals are able to capitalize on their knowledge of deception, outperforming students on deception detection tasks (Hartwig, Granhag, Strömwall, & Andersson, 2004). However, to date, few studies have examined the deceptive behavior of offender samples. An examination by Porter, Doucette, Earle, and MacNeil (2008) had offenders and students tell genuine and deceptive autobiographical stories and compared deceptive behavior across the samples. As suspected, some differences emerged: offenders engaged in more self-manipulations and less smiling during deception. It was theorized that these behavioral differences were attempts on behalf of the offenders to appear credible and distract listeners from their speech content. Vrij and colleagues have conducted increasingly relevant studies of deceptive behavior during real-world interrogations in which suspects were known to have lied. Results suggest that cues associated with nervousness do not differentiate between genuine and deceptive statements in this context; however, suspects engaged in longer pauses and blinked less frequently when lying (Mann, Vrij, & Bull, 2004b). Thus, while research has highlighted some potentially valuable cues to deception, field studies suggest that additional research is warranted to understand which of those cues are most useful in applied settings.

A complementary approach to detecting deception is the baseline method, in which behavioral cues associated with deceit are compared during known truthful statements and potentially deceptive statements. Given that cognitively controllable behaviors (e.g., illustrator use) may increase or decrease during deception, according to individual differences (e.g., experience with deception in criminal contexts; impression management skills), using each person as their own basis for comparison may enhance our ability to detect aberrant—potentially deceitful—behavior (Vrij, 2008). Indeed, in a recent study by the authors, the baseline approach revealed emotional, verbal, and nonverbal behavior differences in genuine vs. deceptive accounts of remorse (ten Brinke, MacDonald, Porter, & O'Connor, 2012).

The difficulty of detecting deception and the ability of liars, particularly offenders, to engage in impression management techniques has prompted researchers to search for less controllable cues to deceit. One such proposed channel is facial expressions of emotion. Some research has suggested that genuine and deceptive emotional expressions can be differentiated by the trained observer. While deceivers can easily mimic the up-turned mouth involved in a smile, it is more difficult to mimic the muscular activity around the eyes (i.e., produced by the *orbicularis oculi*) associated with genuine happiness (Ekman, Davidson, & Friesen, 1990). Darwin (1872) posited that certain, uncontrollable facial muscles may be responsible for leakage of true emotion during deceptive emotional expressions. Borrowing from Darwin's observation is Ekman's famous proposal that, when an emotion is concealed, the true emotion may be revealed through a "micro-expression"—a brief but complete facial expression—which reveal the felt emotion during emotional concealment and is usually suppressed within 1/5–1/25th of a second (e.g., Ekman, 1992). Despite the popularity of both suggestions, neither supposition had received direct, empirical examination until a recent study by Porter and ten Brinke (2008). Participants viewed disgusting, sad, frightening, happy, and neutral images, responding to each with a genuine or deceptive (i.e., simulated, neutralized, or masked) expression. Each 1/30th-second frame of the expression (i.e., 104,550 frames in 697 expressions) was analyzed for the presence of universal emotional expressions (i.e., micro-expressions, and longer-lasting emotional expressions that revealed feelings inconsistent with the intended emotional display). Relative to genuine emotions, masked emotions contained more inconsistent expressions and a higher blink rate. Inconsistent expressions were more frequent and longer in falsified negative emotions than in happiness expressions. "Ekman micro-expressions" occurred rarely—in 2% of expressions (e.g., including during genuine expressions in which participants responded to an emotional image with a congruent emotional facial expression)—and were expressed in the upper or lower face only. However, the leakage of longer lasting inconsistent emotions was difficult for participants to control—such expressions lasted slightly longer than a second, on average. As might be expected based on previous deception detection studies, judges of the veracity of these facial expression performed at or only slightly above the level of chance. Emotional leakage can reveal deception in other laboratory based tasks too; in a mock crime study, Jo (2010) found that deceptive participants (i.e., who denied stealing $100) revealed their guilty knowledge via fearful and asymmetric facial expressions. In sum, these results suggest that, given the appropriate knowledge regarding accurate cues to facial deceit, a careful analysis of the face might provide an important avenue for the detection of deception.

The utility of emotional facial analysis in applied settings requires research. Addressing this need, the current authors (ten Brinke & Porter, 2011; ten Brinke, Porter, & Baker, 2012) utilized a similar frame-by-frame approach to analyze videos of perhaps one of the highest stakes deception scenarios—those in which relatives (e.g., honest, innocent vs. deceptive killers) publicly plead for the return of their loved ones. Further, verbal, nonverbal, and linguistic cues to deception were examined in this high-stakes emotional setting. As in any "field" study, one challenge has been the establishment of ground truth (see Paz-Alonso et al., present volume; Yuille, present volume). In cases labelled as deceptive, we selected cases in which the individuals were later convicted of the crime based on persuasive physical (e.g., DNA) or other powerful evidence (e.g., being caught on video). In contrast, innocent individuals were labelled as such if they were either never suspected of involvement or cleared of any involvement, and another individual was convicted of the crime. Analyses reveal that deceptive pleaders are more likely to show emotional expressions of happiness and surprise, and are less likely to display the signs of sadness/distress that pervade genuine pleas. Deceptive pleaders also provided shorter pleas (i.e., fewer words) and used more tentative language, avoiding commitment to their lies. Importantly, however, this work suggests that facial cues to deception may be a useful cue to deceit in high-stakes applied settings.

Dangerous Decisions: Why People Fail to Detect Deceit in Forensic Settings

Despite the presence of verbal, behavioral and facial cues, and recent advances in the scientific understanding of deception (see O'Sullivan, present volume), our attempts to detect deception remain an inaccurate endeavour (e.g., Bond & DePaulo, 2006). Our Dangerous Decisions Theory (DDT; Porter & ten Brinke, 2009) offers a model outlining the psychological processes involved in arriving at an evaluation of credibility, from which we can deduce the pitfalls and promises of deception detection. This model suggests that inaccurate assessments of credibility are a product of reliance on intuition, incorrect cues, and overconfidence leading to tunnel vision in decision-making (see Yarbrough et al., present volume).

According to DDT (Porter & ten Brinke, 2009), interpersonal judgments of trustworthiness occur almost instantaneously upon seeing an individual's face. Trustworthiness is an evaluation of interpersonal threat based on signs of dominance/strength (i.e., masculinity) and anger on a stranger's face (Porter, ten Brinke & Mathesius, 2012). The process of judging another person's trustworthiness is associated with increased activity in the primitive brain areas, especially the amygdala, indicating the presence of a "threat" in the environment. The expediency of this process was demonstrated by Willis and Todorov (2006) who had participants view images of strangers' faces for 100 ms, 500 ms, 1 s, or unlimited time, and evaluate trustworthiness. While confidence in judgment accuracy increased with time, the judgments themselves remained virtually unchanged from the initial brief exposure. Judgments made after only 100 ms of exposure had the greatest impact for ratings of trustworthiness, indicating their instantaneous and enduring nature. Applied to legal contexts, we hypothesize that an investigator, judge, or juror makes a similar intuitive evaluation of the general trustworthiness of a suspect/defendant, complainant, or other witness immediately upon seeing his/her face for the first time and that this initial impression can impair one's ability to objectively examine the credibility of a witness's statement.

While these assessments appear to form rapidly, their accuracy remains a key issue. As Willis and Todorov (2006) appear to assume, perhaps these automatic judgments of a stranger's trustworthiness based on his/her face are accurate.

However, this assumption lacks support, given that the actual trustworthiness of the target faces presented in their study were unknown. For example, there is considerable variability in trustworthiness ratings assigned to a common face by different observers, suggesting that at least some assessors are inaccurate (Adolphs, 2002). But just how unreliable might the process be? If intuitive judgments of trustworthiness have any validity, the discrimination of faces of untrustworthy, dangerous individuals from relatively virtuous, trustworthy individuals should be possible. Research by Porter, England, Juodis, and ten Brinke (2008) examined the accuracy of such instantaneous assessments of trustworthiness. Participants viewed 34 faces, comprising Nobel Peace Prize recipients/humanitarians and America's Most Wanted criminals, and rated the trustworthiness of each. Subsequently, they were informed about the two groups and estimated group membership. Initial judgments of untrustworthy faces were less accurate (i.e., mean accuracy of 48.8%) than those of trustworthy faces (i.e., mean accuracy of 62.67%), potentially reflecting a trustworthy bias. However, when asked to assess group membership, judgment accuracy was slightly above chance for both target types. Despite the small amount of information available to participants (i.e., still facial image only), it appears that intuition plays a small facilitative role in trustworthiness judgments, but that errors are common. Further research suggests that these evaluations of trustworthiness may be impaired by a reliance on erroneous facial features. Facial features (unjustifiably) associated with perceived honesty include "babyfacedness", symmetry, and attractiveness (Bull, 2006; Bull & Vine, 2003; Zebrowitz, Voinescu, & Collins, 1996). Because the initial assessment occurs largely outside of our conscious awareness, it may strike the observer as "intuition".

A reliance on intuitive feelings about the credibility of claims in court is a commonly cited strategy by judges (see *R. v. Mervyn*, 2003; *R. v. Roble*, 2004; *R. v. S. [R.D.]*, 1997). Judges may determine the extent to which the testimony held a "ring of truth" by relying on their intuition or "gut instinct" (see Seniuk, present volume) In *R. v. Lifchus* (1997), Justice Cory noted: "it may be that the juror is unable to point to the precise aspect of the witness's demeanour which was found to be suspicious ... A juror should not be made to feel that the overall, perhaps intangible, effect of a witness's demeanour cannot be taken into consideration in the assessment of credibility". Such intuitive assessments appear to be actively encouraged in the courtroom. However, there is no evidence that the use of intuition is a valid tool for evaluating credibility. In fact, contrary to Justice Cory's suggestion, Porter et al. (2000) found that a self-reported reliance on intuition was related to lower accuracy in detecting deception. Thus, intuitive judgments of the defendant, complainant, or witness's face may play a role in an investigator, judge, or jury's initial assessment of credibility, determining guilt or innocence before due process begins.

The DDT suggests that this rapid process of trustworthiness assessment was initially intended to assess the "danger" to the observer in the evolutionary past (Porter & ten Brinke, 2009; Todorov, 2008). However, in the modern legal context, the impression leads to biased (or dangerous) decisions concerning the target. The initial, powerful impression of a defendant's trustworthiness in the courtroom has an enduring and powerful subconscious influence on the manner in which new information concerning the target is assimilated by investigators, judges, and jurors. Specifically, the initial intuitive evaluation will influence subsequent inferences concerning the suspect/defendant (or other witness) by making decision-making about him/her increasingly irrational (Kahneman & Tversky, 1982). Decisions also will be influenced by an individual observer's experience and personal schemas about deceptive behavior and heuristics for detecting lies (see Yarbrough et al., present volume). Thus, there will be individual differences in decision-making (as is witnessed on many juries) and judgments often will be unreliable. Ensuing inferences about the suspect/defendant will be rationalized by the decision-maker through his/her beliefs about dishonest behavior.

Recent surveys of judges' beliefs about deceptive behavior have highlighted the inconsistent and erroneous nature of individually held heuristics about deceptive behavior, incorrectly informing their assessments of credibility. Porter and ten Brinke's (2008) survey of 16 Canadian judges found that beliefs were both highly variable, and did not conform to empirical knowledge about deception. Similarly, Strömwall and Granhag (2003) found that legal professionals (e.g., including trial judges and police officers) in Sweden often held false beliefs about deception, such as the notion that lying is associated with gaze aversion and fidgeting. These beliefs conform to the false stereotypes held by laypersons in countries all over the world (Akehurst, Köhnken, Vrij, & Bull, 1996; Bond & Atoum, 2000; DePaulo et al., 2003; Global Deception Research Team, 2006). Studies have repeatedly shown that observers rely too heavily upon emotion-based, stereotypical signs of guilt (e.g., "shifty eyes" and nervous gestures), over empirically based cues to deception (e.g., decrease in illustrator use and sparsely detailed accounts) (e.g., DePaulo et al., 2003; Mann et al., 2004b; Strömwall & Granhag, 2003; Vrij, 2004).

As predicted by the DDT, the combination of intuition and erroneous beliefs about deception may generate a non-critical, "tunnel vision" assimilation of potentially ambiguous or contradictory evidence to support initial assessments. In a study of criminal investigators, Ask and Granhag (2007) found strong support for "asymmetrical skepticism"—the tendency to be more skeptical about evidence that runs counter to one's prior belief than confirming evidence. Kassin, Goldstein, and Savitsky (2003) found that investigators who presumed guilt asked more guilt-presumptive questions and exerted more pressure in order to obtain a confession than did investigators without such bias (see Walsh & Bull, present volume; Yarbrough et al., present volume). Thus, holding preconceived notions about the guilt of a suspect (or a defendant) results in a tendency to seek confirmation for this belief (Meissner & Kassin, 2004). Further, initial beliefs can persevere even in the face of major disconfirming evidence (e.g., Ross, Lepper, & Hubbard, 1975). Such a bias towards maintaining initial beliefs is of particular concern with police officers who, as discussed earlier, seem to exhibit a bias towards the presumption of guilt (Meissner & Kassin, 2002). For example, a guilt-biased officer may engage in confirmatory hypothesis testing, perceiving signs of deceit in the suspect's behavior and resorting to coercive interrogation techniques to elicit a confession (Meissner & Kassin, 2004). While it is not clear whether judges and/or jurors hold a particular "guilty" or "innocent" bias, they may subscribe to their early (unreliable) assessment of trustworthiness, influencing the interpretation of evidence to come.

It should be noted that most legal decision makers probably are genuine in their efforts to make the correct decisions concerning credibility. However, this motivation may be detrimental to the goal; high motivation can exacerbate the level of bias in decisions about credibility. Porter, McCabe, Woodworth, and Peace (2007) identified a *motivational impairment* effect such that a high level of motivation in a deception detection task was negatively associated with accuracy (also see Ask & Granhag, 2007). Similarly, with other types of judgment tasks, high motivation facilitates performance for easy tasks, but impairs it for difficult ones (Pelham & Neter, 1995). A high level of motivation, coupled with the complexity of credibility assessment, may serve to increase the power of the initial perception of trustworthiness and create tunnel vision decision-making. To use a courtroom example, a judge upon seeing a defendant—who is innocent and generally honest—may instantaneously assess his face as being untrustworthy based on certain physical characteristics. Although the judge is determined to be objective in evaluating credibility, the damage may already be done. Evidence in favor of the defendant's credibility is undervalued, while information suggestive of lying and guilt is emphasized (Porter, Gustaw & ten Brinke, 2010). When the defendant acts nervously on the stand and emotionally denies his guilt, the judge concludes that his/her nervousness is a sign of lying and the emotional display represents "crocodile tears", thus confirming the bias held by the observer. As such, a fundamental attribution error takes place—the emotional display is considered to reflect the deceptive nature of the defendant while other hypotheses and potential situational explanations for this display are discounted (Jones & Harris, 1967).

Exemplifying the DDT phenomenon, the influence of biases was evident in the inconsistent assessments of wrongly convicted Steven Truscott, who was recently exonerated for a 1957 murder in Canada. His facial response to his guilty verdict was reported widely in the press at the time of his conviction (Sher, 2007). The lead detective in the case, Inspector Graham, noted that Truscott looked like a "lying, sexual deviant" upon their first meeting, was highly confident in Truscott's guilt and saw that his "eyes were filled with anger, not fear" as the judge announced that he would be hanged for the crime. Interestingly, (presumably less-biased) journalists described the same reaction in a remarkably different light: "his eyes filled with tears, Steven Truscott gasped in the dock" and "the boy simply turned pale". This dramatic example further highlights the necessity of objectivity when evaluating demeanour.

A recent study examined the validity of the DDT proposed by Porter and ten Brinke (2009) with a laboratory, mock jury approach. Porter, Gustaw and ten Brinke (2010) presented participants with two vignettes describing (extremely violent or petty) crimes accompanied by a photo of the supposed defendant, previously rated by a group of pilot participants as trustworthy or untrustworthy. Verdicts were rendered with the presentation of each of five "ambiguous" pieces of evidence, five increasingly incriminating and, subsequently, one piece of exonerating evidence for each case. Results of this study were strongly supportive of the DDT model;

participants required fewer pieces of evidence before finding a defendant previously rated as appearing untrustworthy guilty of a severe crime (i.e., murder). Thus, when the pictured defendant was initially assessed as an untrustworthy individual, participants required less supporting information to come to a determination of guilt beyond a reasonable doubt. Further, the pieces of evidence that participants relied upon to convict untrustworthy defendants were qualitatively less incriminating than information needed to convict a trustworthy individual. Thus, ambiguous evidence was interpreted as incriminating beyond a reasonable doubt for untrustworthy, but not trustworthy defendants. Perhaps even stronger support for DDT was the manner in which participants assimilated exonerating evidence about the photographed defendant. While 84% of participants agreed that exonerating information suggested that the trustworthy defendant was innocent, only 42% of participants felt that the same information was sufficient to exonerate the untrustworthy looking defendant of the same murder scenario. Thus, it appears as though assessments of trustworthiness based on the face play a major role in the assimilation of subsequent evidence about that individual. We plan to test the model, in a similar paradigm, with images of real-life wrongly (and rightly) convicted individuals. If this field-based study provides additional support of DDT, we might be able to suggest that these wrongly convicted individuals were unfortunate to appear untrustworthy at the time of their trial and this intuitive assessment slanted the judge or jury's assimilation of evidence against them, ultimately resulting in their incarceration and a dramatic miscarriage of justice.

As described poignantly by William Mullins-Johnson, wrongly convicted of the sexual assault and murder of his niece in 1994, the beginning of tunnel vision can be the end of a fair trial. He noted that his prosecution was like, "the train left the station and there was no stopping it" (CBC Radio, 2007). Tunnel vision originating from incorrect intuitive judgments can be reflected in patterns found in ultimate judicial decisions. For example, baby-faced individuals, generally considered trustworthy based on their facial features, received more lenient judicial outcomes than mature-faced individuals and, within a population of African American prisoners, those with more Afrocentric facial features received harsher sentences for comparable crimes (Blair, Judd, & Chapleau, 2004; Zebrowitz & McDonald, 1991). Additionally, attractive defendants are more likely to be found not guilty, dealt shorter sentences, and considered less dangerous in Canadian Dangerous Offender hearings than unattractive individuals (e.g., Bull & Rumsey, 1988; Downs & Lyons, 1991; Esses & Webster, 1988). The DDT would suggest that these facial characteristics influenced the initial assessment of trustworthiness made by judges and jurors. From that first impression forward, all evidence was slanted in the mind of the decision-maker to fit the initial assessment and thus, resulted in biased verdicts. In general, these findings highlight the importance of future research examining conscious strategies (e.g., awareness of human biases, multiple hypothesis testing) and individual differences (e.g., need for cognition; Reinhard, 2010) that mitigate tunnel vision (see Yarbrough et al., present volume). These findings may be integrated into future credibility assessment training programs and can potentially reduce biased legal decisions resulting from defendant/complainant appearance.

Towards the Truth: Empirically Valid Training

If the natural pitfalls outlined by DDT are correct, miscarriages of justice may result from a series of dangerous decisions concerning a defendant's credibility, a process initiated by an unreliable initial impression and maintained by a biased interpretation of evidence. It is possible that this situation can be rectified to some degree through relevant, empirical education for society's decision-makers (see Porter & ten Brinke, 2009). First, the myths that credibility assessment is a common sense matter and that intuition is a useful tool in this context must be dispelled. While this notion is strong within the Canadian court system, research illustrates the difficulty of this task. Holding onto the idea that credibility assessment requires only common sense, only serves to increase the tunnel vision and overconfidence flowing from DDT—contributing to miscarriages of justice. Further, decision-makers need to be aware of the instantaneous nature of trustworthiness judgments and accept their unreliability. Second, the common reliance on misleading aspects of demeanour and behavior by police, judges, and juries/laypersons alike (Global Deception Research Team, 2006; Porter & ten Brinke, 2009; Vrij, Mann & Fisher, 2006) must be combated. It has been previously shown that this approach can improve credibility assessment. Porter et al. (2000) demonstrated that a workshop for parole officers held over the course of 2 days led to a marked improvement in their deception detection ability (from 40.4% to 76.7% accuracy; see Colwell et al., present volume). Training consisted of myth dissolution, wherein common, inaccurate beliefs about deception were combated. Previous beliefs were then replaced with empirically valid knowledge about cues to deception. New knowledge was then put into action with testing, practice assessments, and performance feedback. Importantly, participants were also encouraged to critically examine their decision-making with colleagues in order to reduce "tunnel vision" decision-making (Porter et al., 2007). That is, having decision-makers think more critically about their decision-making, in general, could reduce the strength of biases present in the assimilation of evidence stage of the DDT framework.

A more recent training program delivered by the second author to workers' compensation staff incorporated education about behavioral, verbal, as well as the most recent findings about facial indices of deception. Similarly to the approach described in Porter et al. (2000), this training involved myth dissolution, information provision, and practice judgments. Despite the abbreviated length of this training program (i.e., 3 hours as opposed to 2 days), this approach was successful at significantly increasing participants' ability to detect deception in both videotaped narratives and emotional expressions. After only a short training session, the ability to discriminate genuine and deceptive facial expressions rose from 56% to 63%, while the ability to detect deceit in videotaped narratives rose from 46% to 58% (Porter, Juodis, ten Brinke, Klein, & Wilson, 2010). Thus, providing empirically based training to legal decision-makers holds promise for increasing deception detection accuracy and reducing miscarriages of justice (see also Cooper, Hervé, & Yuille, 2009).

In addition to the information at hand, judges and juries should follow several guidelines, as outlined by Porter et al. (2003), when assessing the credibility of testimony for out-right deception and distorted memories. First, the context in which the complaint was made may signal the presence of deception or the possibility for inaccurate memory of events. Leading interviews or interrogations may distort the recollection of events, or deception may occur in situations where the individual is in a position to (directly or indirectly) gain from making a false complaint. Secondly, an individual's account of the event in question should remain relatively consistent over time. Although some decay in memory is expected, inconsistencies in major details suggest the presence of deception or a distortion of memory. Finally, corroboration of the alleged event adds credibility to testimony and, as such, should remain a priority. Given past successes, it appears that workshops outlining such recommendations are an effective means of educating trial judges and peace officers about credibility assessment.

Conclusions

When investigators decide whom to charge and judges and juries formulate decisions of guilt and innocence, they must rely heavily on the evidence provided by witnesses who are deemed credible. However, a recent inquiry into the wrongful conviction of Thomas Sophonow has highlighted the difficulty of credibility assessment (Wilson, 2003), despite the Canadian Supreme Court's contention that it can be achieved through common sense. As highlighted by laboratory and field studies, police officers and judges, like the layperson, are susceptible to unconscious biases and hold false beliefs about assessing demeanour. However, that is not to say that behavioral cues to deception do not exist. Empirically guided education, training, and a critical approach to the challenges of detecting deceit are necessary to improve credibility assessment in the interrogation room and courtroom. In general, we contend that theoretically driven psychological science using diverse methodologies in diverse contexts can lead to accurate conclusions and the responsible application of research in an improved legal system.

References

Adolphs, R. (2002). Trust in the brain. *Nature Neuroscience, 5*, 8–9.
Akehurst, L., Köhnken, G., Vrij, A., & Bull, R. (1996). Lay persons' and police officers' beliefs regarding deceptive behaviour. *Applied Cognitive Psychology, 10*, 461–471.
Ask, K., & Granhag, P. A. (2007). Motivational bias in criminal investigators' judgments of witness reliability. *Journal of Applied Social Psychology, 37*, 561–591.
Blair, I. V., Judd, C. M., & Chapleau, K. M. (2004). The influence of afrocentric facial features in criminal sentencing. *Psychological Science, 15*, 674–679.
Bond, C. F., & Atoum, A. O. (2000). International deception. *Personality and Social Psychology Bulletin, 26*, 385–395.

Bond, C. F., & DePaulo, B. M. (2006). Accuracy of deception judgments. *Personality and Social Psychology Review, 10*, 214–234.

Bull, P. (2006). Detecting lies and deceit: The psychology of lying and the implications for professional practice. *Journal of Community & Applied Social Psychology, 16*, 166–167.

Bull, R., & Rumsey, N. (1988). *The social psychology of facial appearance.* London: Springer-Verlag Publishing.

Bull, R., & Vine, M. (2003). *Attractive people tell the truth: Can you believe it?* Poster presented at the Annual Conference of the European Association of Psychology and Law, Edinburgh, Scotland.

CBC Radio. (2007). *As it happens: William Mullins-Johnson.* Retrieved from www.cbc.ca.

Cooper, B. S., Hervé, H. F., & Yuille, J. C. (2009). Evaluating truthfulness: Detecting truths and lies in forensic contexts. In R. Bull, T. Valentine, & T. Williamson (Eds.), *Handbook of the psychology of investigative interviewing* (pp. 301–328). Chichester, UK: Wiley-Blackwell.

Darwin, C. (1872). *The expression of the emotions in man and animals.* Chicago: University of Chicago Press.

DePaulo, B. M., Kashy, D. A., Kirkendol, S. E., Wyer, M. M., & Epstein, J. A. (1996). Lying in everyday life. *Journal of Personality and Social Psychology, 74*, 63–79.

DePaulo, B. M., Lindsay, J. J., Malone, B. E., Muhlenbruck, L., Charlton, K., & Cooper, H. (2003). Cues to deception. *Psychological Bulletin, 129*, 74–118.

DePaulo, B. M., & Pfeifer, R. L. (1986). On-the-job experience and skill at detecting deception. *Journal of Applied Social Psychology, 16*, 249–267.

Downs, A. C., & Lyons, P. M. (1991). Natural observations of the links between attractiveness and initial legal judgments. *Personality and Social Psychology Bulletin, 17*, 541–547.

Ekman, P. (1992). *Telling lies: Clues to deceit in the marketplace, politics, and marriage.* New York: Norton.

Ekman, P., Davidson, R. J., & Friesen, W. V. (1990). The Duchenne smile: Emotional expression and brain physiology: II. *Journal of Personality and Social Psychology, 58*, 342–353.

Ekman, P., & O'Sullivan, M. (1991). Who can catch a liar? *American Psychologist, 46*, 913–920.

Esses, V. M., & Webster, C. D. (1988). Physical attractiveness, dangerousness, and the Canadian Criminal Code. *Journal of Applied Social Psychology, 18*, 1017–1031.

Garrido, E., Masip, J., & Herrero, C. (2004). Police officers' credibility judgments: Accuracy and estimated ability. *International Journal of Psychology, 39*, 254–275.

Global Deception Research Team. (2006). A world of lies. *Journal of Cross-Cultural Psychology, 37*, 60–74.

Granhag, P. A., Andersson, L. O., Strömwall, L. A., & Hartwig, M. (2004). Imprisoned knowledge: Criminal' beliefs about deception. *Legal and Criminological Psychology, 9*, 103–119.

Hancock, J. T. (2007). Digital deception: When, where and how people lie online. In K. McKenna, T. Postmes, U. Reips, & A. N. Joinson (Eds.), *Oxford Handbook of Internet Psychology* (pp. 287–301). Oxford: Oxford University Press.

Hartwig, M., Granhag, P. A., Strömwall, L. A., & Andersson, L. O. (2004). Suspicious minds: Criminals' ability to detect deception. *Psychology, Crime & Law, 10*, 83–94.

Inbau, F. E., Reid, J. E., Buckley, J. P., & Jayne, B. C. (2001). *Criminal interrogation and confessions* (4th ed.). Gaithersburg, Maryland: Aspen Publishers.

Jo, E. (2010). *The effects of question types on diagnostic cues to deception.* Paper presented at the Annual Conference of the American Psychology-Law Society. Vancouver, BC, Canada.

Jones, E. E., & Harris, V. A. (1967). The attribution of attitudes. *Journal of Experimental Social Psychology, 3*, 1–24.

Kahneman, D., & Tversky, A. (1982). The psychology of preferences. *Scientific American, 246*, 160–173.

Kassin, S. M., & Fong, C. T. (1999). "I'm Innocent!": Effects of training on judgments of truth and deception in the interrogation room. *Law and Human Behavior, 23*, 499–516.

Kassin, S. M., Goldstein, C. C., & Savitsky, K. (2003). Behavioral confirmation in the interrogation room: On the dangers of presuming guilt. *Law and Human Behavior, 27*, 187–203.

Mann, S., Vrij, A., & Bull, R. (2004a). Detecting true lies: Police officers' ability to detect deceit. *Journal of Applied Psychology, 89*, 137–149.

Mann, S., Vrij, A., & Bull, R. (2004b). Suspects, lies, and videotape: An analysis of authentic high-stake liars. *Law and Human Behavior, 26*, 365–376.
Meissner, C. A., & Kassin, S. M. (2002). "He's guilty!": Investigator bias in judgments of truth and deception. *Law and Human Behavior, 26*, 469–480.
Meissner, C. A., & Kassin, S. M. (2004). "You're guilty, so just confess!" Cognitive and confirmational biases in the interrogation room. In G. D. Lassiter (Ed.), *Interrogations, Confessions, and Entrapment* (pp. 85–106). New York: Kluwer.
Pelham, B. W., & Neter, E. (1995). The effect of motivation of judgment depends on the difficulty of the judgment. *Journal of Personality and Social Psychology, 64*, 581–594.
Porter, S., Campbell, M. A., Birt, A., & Woodworth, M. (2003). "He said, she said": A psychological perspective on historical memory evidence in the courtroom. *Canadian Psychology, 44*, 190–206.
Porter, S., Doucette, N., Earle, J., & MacNeil, B. (2008). 'Half the world knows not how the other half lies': Investigation of cues to deception exhibited by criminal offenders and non-offenders. *Legal and Criminological Psychology, 13*, 27–38.
Porter, S., England, L., Juodis, M., ten Brinke, L., & Wilson, K. (2008). Is the face a window to the soul? Investigation of the validity of intuitive judgments of the trustworthiness of human faces. *Canadian Journal of Behavioural Science, 40*, 171–177.
Porter, S., Gustaw, C., & ten Brinke, L. (2010). Dangerous decisions: The impact of first impressions of trustworthiness on the evaluation of legal evidence and defendant culpability. *Psychology Crime & Law, 16*, 477–491.
Porter, S., Juodis, M., ten Brinke, L., Klein, R., & Wilson, K. (2010). Evaluation of a brief deception detection training program. *Journal of Forensic Psychiatry & Psychology, 21*, 66–76.
Porter, S., McCabe, S., Woodworth, M., & Peace, K. A. (2007). "Genius is 1% inspiration and 99% perspiration"…or is it? An investigation of the effects of motivation and feedback on deception detection. *Legal and Criminological Psychology, 12*, 297–309.
Porter, S., & ten Brinke, L. (2008). Reading between the lies: Identifying concealed and falsified emotions in universal facial expressions. *Psychological Science, 19*, 508–514.
Porter, S., & ten Brinke, L. (2009). Dangerous decisions: A theoretical framework for understanding how judges assess credibility in the courtroom. *Legal and Criminological Psychology, 14*, 119–134.
Porter, S., ten Brinke, L., & Mathesius, J. (2012, under review). *Why do bad boys get the girls? Investigation of the facial characteristics associated with perceived trustworthiness in male faces.*
Porter, S., & Woodworth, M. (2007). I'm sorry I did it … but he started it: A comparison of the official and self-reported homicide descriptions of psychopath and non-psychopaths. *Law and Human Behavior, 31*, 91–107.
Porter, S., Woodworth, M., & Birt, A. R. (2000). Truth, lies, and videotape: An investigation of the ability of federal parole officers to detect deception. *Law and Human Behavior, 24*, 643–658.
Porter, S., & Yuille, J. C. (1995). Credibility assessment of criminal suspects through statement analysis. *Psychology, Crime & Law, 1*, 319–331.
R. v. Francois, (1994) 2 S.C.R. 827.
R. v. Lifchus, (1997) 3 S.C.R. 320.
R. v. Malik & Bagri, (2005) B.C.S.C. 350.
R. v. Marquard, (1993) 4 S.C.R. 223.
R. v. Mervyn, (2003) Y.K.T.C. 34.
R. v. Roble, (2004) CanLII 23106 (ON C.A.).
R. v. S. [R.D.] (1997) 3 S.C.R.
Reinhard, M.-A. (2010). Need for cognition and the process of lie detection. *Journal of Experimental Social Psychology, 46*, 961–971.
Ross, L., Lepper, M. R., & Hubbard, M. (1975). Perseverance in self-perception and social perception: Biased attribution processes in the debriefing paradigm. *Journal of Personality and Social Psychology, 32*, 880–892.
Sher, J. (2007). 'Hanged by the neck until you are dead.' *The Globe and Mail*, p. F3.

Strömwall, L. A., & Granhag, P. A. (2003). How to detect deception? Arresting the beliefs of police officers, prosecutors and judges. *Psychology, Crime & Law, 9*, 19–36.

ten Brinke, L., MacDonald, S., & Porter, S. (2012). Crocodile tears: Facial, verbal and body language behaviours associated with genuine and fabricated remorse. *Law and Human Behavior, 36*, 51–59.

ten Brinke, L., & Porter, S. (2011, in press). Cry me a river: Identifying the behavioural consequences of extremely high-stakes interpersonal deception. *Law and Human Behavior.*

ten Brinke, L., Porter, S., & Baker, A. (2012). Darwin the detective: Observable facial muscle contractions reveal emotional high-stakes lies. *Evolution and Human Behavior, 33*, 411–416.

Todorov, A (2008). Evaluating faces on trustworthiness: An extension of systems for recognition of emotional signaling approach/avoidance behaviors. *Annals of the New York Academy of Sciences, 1124*, 208–224.

Vrij, A. (2000). *Detecting lies and deceit: The psychology of lying and the implications for professional practice.* Chichester, England: Wiley.

Vrij, A. (2004). Why professionals fail to catch liars and how they can improve. *Legal and Criminological Psychology, 9*, 159–181.

Vrij, A. (2008). *Detecting lies and deceit: Pitfalls and opportunities.* Chichester, England: Wiley.

Vrij, A., & Mann, S. (2001). Who killed my relative? Police officers' ability to detect real-life high-stake lies. *Psychology, Crime & Law, 7*, 119–132.

Vrij, A., Mann, S., & Fisher, R. P. (2006). An empirical test of the behaviour analysis interview. *Law and Human Behavior, 30*, 329–435.

Willis, J., & Todorov, A. (2006). First impressions: Making up your mind after a 100-ms exposure to a face. *Psychological Science, 17*, 592–598.

Wilson, P.J. (2003). Wrongful convictions: Lessons learned from the Sophonow Public Inquiry. *Canadian Police College.*

Yuille, J. C. (1989). *Credibility assessment.* Dordrecht, The Netherlands: Kluwer Academic Press.

Yuille, J. C. (1996). A guide and a challenge for the application of psychology. *Contemporary Psychology, 41*, 154–155.

Zebrowitz, L. A., & McDonald, S. M. (1991). The impact of litigants' baby-facedness and attractiveness on adjudications in small claims courts. *Law and Human Behavior, 15*, 603–623.

Zebrowitz, L. A., Voinescu, L., & Collins, M. A. (1996). 'Wide-eyed' and 'crooked-faced': Determinants of perceived and real honesty across the life span. *Personality and Social Psychology Bulletin, 22*, 1258–1269.

Chapter 10
Is *Le Mot Juste*? The Contexualization of Words by Expert Lie Detectors

Maureen O'Sullivan

Some of the chapters in this book discuss the ways in which language samples can be analyzed to determine credibility (e.g., Colwell, Hiscock-Anisman, & Fede, this volume; Griesel, Ternes, Schraml, Cooper, & Yuille, this volume). This chapter illustrates how expert lie detectors use information from a single word in discerning the truthfulness of others. These illustrations were obtained from in-depth interviews with highly accurate lie detectors (O'Sullivan & Ekman, 2004) who received scores of 80% or more on at least two of three different lie detection tests. The three tests were not easy, since average scores on the measures are close to 50%. Although the base rate occurrence of such expert lie detectors varies from group to group, the expert lie detectors in this analysis are at least two standard deviations above the mean in their lie detection abilities. For example, using the criterion described, no expert lie detector has been found among college students, although thousands have been examined. Although there are now a sufficient number of experts ($n = 50$) to aggregate their responses and compare them with their matched controls, another value of the project[1] is the opportunity to compare the description of the lie detection enterprise that results from the efforts of a single expert with the contributions to knowledge made by scores of scientists using a wide variety of methodologies. A brief review of these methodologies is offered in order to situate the kind of information obtained from individual interviews in the broader research endeavor. This review is, of necessity, cursory. Many subtle distinctions are disregarded in the effort to describe briefly each approach.

---

[1] Editorial note: "The project" refers to the "Truth Wizard Project"- O'Sullivan and Ekman's research project that sought to identify expert lie detectors, who obtained highly accurate scores on at least two of three videotaped lie detection tasks.

M. O'Sullivan (✉)
University of San Francisco, San Francisco, CA, USA

Five Ways in Which the Contribution of Language to Lie Detection has Been Studied

Some research has focused on the content of speech to determine whether language alone can provide clues to deception, or, alternately, to assess the relative importance of language in the detection of deception. At least five different methods of addressing these questions can be discriminated: (1) language analysis of honest and deceptive verbal content alone (e.g., based on transcripts or other written documents); (2) behavioral measurement of verbal and nonverbal behaviors in honest and deceptive videotaped or audiotaped materials; (3) comparison of communication channels (e.g., verbal or nonverbal) to determine which is more effective in accurate lie detection; (4) statistical models of how individuals use different clues in making summary judgments of honest and deceptive individuals; and (5) soliciting and analyzing the reasons people give for deciding that someone is lying or telling the truth. A variety of approaches may be further distinguished within each of these five research paradigms but, except for the last paradigm (i.e., soliciting reasons for the truth vs. lie decision), those distinctions are ignored in the present chapter.

(1) Verbal Content Analysis

Within the research tradition of language analysis based on written materials, several different approaches to the analysis of an entire statement have been used, for example, Criteria-Based Content Analysis (Porter & Yuille, 1995; Steller & Koehnken, 1989; Undeutsch, 1982) and Reality Monitoring (Masip, Sporer, Garrido, & Herrero, 2005). Although each of these methods varies in both the speech qualities it deems to be most important and the objectivity with which the analysis of the materials can be completed, they share the belief that a substantial amount of language is necessary to assess credibility based on factors such as the immediacy of the language used, the quantity and quality of details provided, the consistency or coherence of the account, and its spontaneity (see Colwell et al., this volume; Griesel et al., this volume). These judgments are usually global, based on a complete story or account.

A somewhat different language-only approach is provided by Pennebaker and his colleagues (Newman, Pennebaker, Berry, & Richards, 2003). Their approach proceeds from the premise that word counts alone can provide a means of differentiating honest and lying communications (also see Hancock & Woodworth, this volume). Unlike the other theories mentioned above, in which the meaning of the statement and the overall coherence or consistency of the story is central to the final determination of truthfulness, the Pennebaker approach proposes that a sufficiently sophisticated analysis of parts of speech and combinations of words can provide a competing method of language-only lie detection. Computer-generated word counts, independent of the overall content of the story or other written communication, and various statistical models such as logistic regression and Latent Semantic Analysis (Campbell

& Pennebaker, 2003) are used to differentiate lying and truthful and more or less traumatic communications (Cohn, Mehl, & Pennebaker, 2004). The appeal of the method is its efficiency (e.g., computer counts rather than people assessment) and the counter-intuitive use of pronouns and other parts of speech to distinguish communications varying in truthfulness and/or emotionality. For example, although different kinds of lies resulted in somewhat different language styles, across five studies, "… deceptive communications were characterized by fewer first-person singular pronouns, fewer third person pronouns, more negative emotion words, fewer exclusive words, and more motion verbs" (Newman et al., 2003, p. 670).

Obviously, the use of fewer first person singular pronouns and fewer motion words is consistent with the lessened immediacy of a statement suggested by the Undeutsch Hypothesis[2] (Undeutsch, 1982) and Criteria-Based Content Analysis (Yuille, 1989). What differs is the method of obtaining this information and the loss of the "gist" of the communication.

Although most language-only techniques suggest that both the individual words used and the context within which they occur contain information that can be used to distinguish truth and deception, they differ in terms of the source of the materials they analyze. While many language-only assessment methods attempt to determine the credibility of actual suspect or witness statements made for forensic purposes, the Pennebaker group has tended to use truthful and deceptive materials produced in the laboratory or obtained from non-forensic sources. There is some evidence that different clues are available in different kinds of lies: high stakes vs. low stakes (Ekman, 2001), emotional vs. nonemotional (Warren, 2007), lies about facts vs. lies about feelings (O'Sullivan, 2008), sanctioned vs. unsanctioned lies (Feeley & deTurck, 1998), more vs. less complex lies (Vrij & Heaven, 1999), as well as the relationship between the liar and lie catcher (Burgoon, Buller, White, Afifi, & Buslig, 1999; Ekman, 2001). Differences in these variables as well as interest in and experience with those kinds of lies may also affect the accuracy of those seeking to uncover them (see ten Brinke & Porter, this volume).

(2) Behavioral Measurement of Verbal and Nonverbal Behaviors

Although no researcher interested in the accurate detection of deception would disregard the importance of verbal clues, some researchers have thought a more complete picture of honest vs. deceptive communication results from the simultaneous analysis of both verbal and nonverbal behaviors. So, a second approach to the question of the relative importance of language in deception detection can be seen in the scores of articles in which researchers have actually measured both nonverbal behaviors such as facial expressions, hand gestures, and body postures (Ekman &

---

[2] Editorial note: The Undeutsch hypothesis states that statements based on experienced events differ in quantity and quality from fictitious accounts.

Friesen, 1969; Ekman, Friesen, & O'Sullivan, 1988; Granhag & Strömwall, 2002; Porter, Doucette, Woodworth, Earle, & MacNeil, 2008) as well as vocal quality (e.g., pitch; Ekman, O'Sullivan, Friesen, & Scherer, 1991; Rockwell, Buller, & Burgoon, 1997) and verbal characteristics (e.g., number of words, content, detail; Kraut, 1978; Vrij, Akehurst, Soukara, & Bull, 2006). This literature has produced many widely varying conclusions. The reasons for these inconsistencies are many. The kinds of lies sampled reflect the entire continuum of ecological validity. Some of the lies are high stakes, causing significant behavioral changes in the liars and truth tellers. Others are trivial lies of politeness or courtesy which may have insufficient emotional or cognitive arousal to result in behavior. The liars and truth tellers studied include paroled felons (Bond, 2008), convicted murderers, or crime suspects (Vrij & Mann, 2001), while others use college students or children (Feldman & Jenkins, 1979; Vrij et al., 2006). The degree of sophistication and/or objectivity of the behavioral measures used are also highly variable. Some researchers merely ask observers to make Likert ratings as to whether a particular behavior, such as a smile, has occurred. Other researchers count the frequency of occurrence of any smile-like behavior while, still others, use muscle movement coding systems (Ekman & Friesen, 1978) that distinguish whether or not a very subtle movement has occurred around the eye (i.e., as a result of the *orbicularis oculi* muscle firing) simultaneously with the movement of the smiling typical lip corner raise occasioned by the action of the *zygomatic major*.

Since 2000, several meta-analyses of these studies have been provided (Aamodt & Custer, 2006; DePaulo et al., 2003; Sporer & Schwandt, 2006; Sporer & Schwandt, 2007). These summaries are very useful compendia, but they provide little but a rough guide to the relevant verbal and nonverbal behaviors that distinguish honest and deceptive behavior. By summing over such disparate methodologies, subtle differences that are very useful in real-world interviewing and in real-world assessments of the honesty of a particular individual may be lost. Nonetheless, despite the confusing variation provided by a plethora of lie types, subjects, and measurement methods, DePaulo et al. reported many variables which had significant d's (i.e., a behavior discriminated honest and deceptive samples significantly, either across several studies or so strongly in a single study that its effect was not eradicated in the meta-analysis). Even examining only those effect sizes (i.e., d's) of 0.50 or above (i.e., consistent with a moderate effect), objectively measured verbal and vocal behaviors were identified that consistently differentiated honest and deceptive samples. The value of such meta-analyses is that they demonstrate the replicability of clues, both verbal and nonverbal, across many kinds of lie detection materials. They also demonstrate that at least some lie detection materials have significant clues to deception in them.

The above is important because a continuing bias in the field of lie detection accuracy research is the lack of lie detection accuracy of most of the subjects studied. Bond and DePaulo (2006) reported a mean accuracy of 54.3% over 20,000 subjects and, although they summarized that result as "mean lie-truth discrimination abilities are nontrivial, with ... a d of roughly 0.40 ... an effect that is at roughly the 60th percentile in size, relative to others that have been meta-analyzed by social psychologists" (p. 214), they then went on to claim that, although there is evidence of reliable observer truth bias and target demeanor credibility, there is no evidence for any lie detection accuracy (Bond & DePaulo, 2008).[3] O'Sullivan (2008), however, questioned their conclusions on theoretical, methodological, and empirical grounds.

Ekman (2001) has long argued that many lie detection scenarios used in determining accuracy are too low stakes to provide the cognitive and/or emotional clues necessary to produce discernible clues to deception. O'Sullivan (2008) reiterated this observation and argued that, in addition, most of the 20,000 subjects surveyed in the aforementioned meta-analysis were college students with little life experience, feedback, or motivation to support accurate lie detection in the low stakes lies provided in most studies.

(3) Modality Dissection

In the studies just reviewed, the relative importance of different kinds of verbal and nonverbal behaviors was examined through a direct measurement of the liars' and truth tellers' behaviors and a frequency count of whether a particular kind of behavior occurred or not was provided. Of course, only those behaviors which researchers chose to measure were included in the analyses. Behavioral measurement, of necessity, reflects the interests and expertise of the people doing the often costly and always tedious behavioral analyses. But whether real-life observers actually attend to the clues that researchers so laboriously assess is another question. The naive observer and the sophisticated scientist may have non-overlapping sets of clues to which they attend. A cognitive scientist, steeped in the knowledge of the fallibility of human memory, will judge admitted lack of memory as more believable than claimed total recall; the untutored observer may come to the opposite conclusion. Similarly, a facial expression expert might use rapidly occurring signs of emotion, i.e., microexpressions (Ekman, 2003), as clues to suppressed or repressed emotion that might be related to lying, but most observers may neither perceive such clues nor be able to interpret them accurately.

This difficulty was addressed in a third type of analysis which sought to determine the relative importance of one kind of communication compared with another by limiting the information that observers are given and examining the accuracy of the judgments they make under each of the different viewing or listening conditions. DePaulo, Rosenthal, Eisenstat, Rogers, and Finkestein (1978), for example, showed observers lie detection scenarios in three formats: video alone, audio alone, or combined audio and video information (i.e., the usual audiovisual format). They found

---

[3] Editorial note: Bond and DePaulo (2008) suggest that there is very little variation in individuals' ability to detect deception, that detection accuracy ranges no more widely than would be expected by chance, and that the most accurate judges are no more accurate than a stochastic mechanism would produce.

a video primacy effect, with those judgments based on the video only being more accurate than those made from the audio material. DePaulo, Lanier, and Davis (1983), however, showed observers verbal only (i.e., transcript), audio only (i.e., verbal and audio), visual only, and the complete audiovisual recording. Lies told by more motivated senders were more readily detected with more information, that is, in the audio and the audiovisual conditions. Visual only and verbal only conditions were not associated with deception detectability.

A variant of the above paradigm is the attempt to study experimentally the discrepancy between different channels of communication. The overall lack of coherence or consistency of a statement is a frequently reported characteristic of statements judged to be less credible in the forensic context (see Connolly & Price, this volume; Fisher, Vrij, & Leins, this volume). In the nonverbal area, many theorists (Bugental, Kaswan, & Love, 1970) have suggested that the perception of verbal/nonverbal discrepancies is one of the more important clues in accurate lie detection. As is discussed at the end of this chapter, that is certainly an important characteristic of the lie detection strategies of the "truth wizards," but they are sensitive not only to verbal/nonverbal discrepancies, but also to discrepancies concerning demographic characteristics of the liar or truth teller—age, race, social class, gender, personality type, interpersonal style, and many other variables that differ among individuals.

(4) Processes Involved in Judging Others as Deceptive

O'Sullivan (2005) has argued that discerning the truthfulness of others is a particular example of the more general ability referred to as empathic accuracy (Ickes, 1993), understanding others (Funder, 1999), social-emotional intelligence (Mayer, Salovey, & Caruso, 2002), interpersonal and intrapersonal intelligence (Gardner, 1993) and behavioral cognition (O'Sullivan & Guilford, 1975). In addition to the differences in variance provided by the different kinds of lies examined (discussed above), the processes involved in accurate lie detection probably involve more than merely the perception and interpretation of lie-related clues. The finding (Warren, 2007) that individuals with greater sensitivity to subtle facial expressions of emotion are more accurate in detecting emotional lies but not non-emotional ones is consistent with this view. Similarly, O'Sullivan reports (2008) that, among expert lie detectors, police professionals are significantly better than therapists in detecting lies about a theft, but significantly less accurate in detecting lies about feelings (see Table 10.1).

Years of research on social cognition (Fiske, 1992) suggests that judgments of honesty or deceptiveness, like all judgments made under uncertainty, will be characterized by the cognitive biases and heuristics that mark other kinds of social assessments. A well-known bias in lie detection studies is the truth bias (Zuckerman, DeFrank, Hall, Larrance, & Rosenthal, 1979) in which observers have reliable tendencies (Bond & DePaulo, 2008) to call people honest, regardless of the base rate

Table 10.1 Lie detection accuracy in percentages for "truth wizard" police professionals and therapists

Expert Group	N	Lie scenario					
		Opinion		Crime		Emotion	
		Mean	S.D.	Mean	S.D.	Mean	S.D.
Police	18	88	3	88	8	69	15
Therapists/Psychologists	10	89	.3	61	15	82	12

or actual honesty of the people they are judging (i.e., even if told that about half the people they will see are lying, many judges will rate 70% or more of the targets as honest). Ekman (2001) and Meissner and Kassin (2002) have reported a deceptive bias among police professionals, in which their tendency is to presume that those they are interviewing are deceptive, even when they have been instructed that is not the case (see Yarbrough, Hervé, & Harms, this volume).

The mere act of labeling someone as a liar also seems to be problematic, although this "accusatory reluctance" (O'Sullivan, 2003) may be circumvented by changes in how the judgment of honesty is obtained. DePaulo (1998) found that observers, who were only at chance in labeling targets as deceptive, obtained significantly higher accuracy rates if they were asked to characterize the targets as comfortable or uncomfortable. Similarly, Mann and Vrij (2006) found that observers were more accurate if they were asked to categorize liars and truth tellers as "thinking hard" rather than "lying vs. truthful."

O'Sullivan (2003) demonstrated that observers' fundamental attribution (Ross & Nisbett, 1991) about someone based on a 1-sec still photograph of him was significantly correlated with their later judgment of that man's truthfulness in a 1-min interview. She called this the "boy-who-cried-wolf" effect because the effect was much stronger for those initially judged as untrustworthy. Although observers would sometimes judge a person rated as trustworthy on the basis of a photograph as lying in an interview, they rarely rated someone they thought to be an untrustworthy person as telling the truth.

These above noted studies suggest that the processes involved in judging whether someone is lying or telling the truth are complex ones and only a little work has been done to untangle the processes involved. Two different approaches have been reported.

Ekman, Friesen, O'Sullivan, and Scherer (1980) obtained personality/trait judgments of young women videotaped describing their feelings truthfully or lying about them. In earlier research, it had been found that observers were only at chance in their judgments of the women's veracity. Various groups of observers were shown the same 15 women in different formats: speech only, face only, body only and total audio visual recording. About half of the women were lying, although the observers were not told that deception was involved. Each of the women was rated on 14 seven-point bipolar scales such as outgoing-inhibited and calm-agitated. The ratings of the observer group which saw and heard the entire audiovisual record was used as the criterion and the ratings of the other three groups were regressed against them. These multiple regression analyses were conducted separately for the truthful nurses and the deceptive ones. Two different judgment strategies were found. If the target nurses were telling the truth, different channels were more highly correlated with the total criterion judgment depending on what the trait was. For example, in the honest condition, ratings from the face-only and speech-only conditions were both correlated with total judgments of outgoingness, sociability and expressivity. Body ratings were more often correlated with total judgments of calmness, stability and relaxation. However, these same judges, when judging the deceptive nurses, tended to use only the verbal channel. That is, the ratings made on the basis of the voice only were most highly correlated with the total audio visual criterion (note: the same judges made the ratings of both the honest and deceptive nurses).

The above study presented the entire audio channel to the observers, so it was not clear whether judges were attending to the content of speech or vocal quality, or both. In a follow-up study, O'Sullivan, Ekman, Friesen, and Scherer (1985) had one group of judges read the transcripts of the interviews; a second group heard an audio tape which had been content filtered. This retained the rhythm and cadence of speech, but removed the meaning of the words spoken. The ratings of the full speech group from the earlier study were used as the criterion, and the ratings based on the transcript and the content-filtered speech was used as the predictors. When the women were lying, ratings based on the transcript alone were significantly more highly correlated with the ratings based on the complete speech recording than those made based on content filtered speech. In the honest interviews (i.e., with the same women), observers showed the opposite pattern, attending significantly more frequently to vocal quality.

These two noted studies are important because they suggest that, although observers are loath to label someone as a liar, they process the behavioral and verbal information produced by liars and truth tellers differently. And despite the many studies and folk wisdom about the importance of attending to discrepancies in information, the results of these studies are consistent with the social cognition finding that most people are cognitively lazy (Fiske, 1992) and may attempt to solve discrepancies by attending to the channel for which the target is most responsible—her words.

Heinrich and Borkenau (1998) proceeded from a different premise in attempting to understand the cognitive strategies used by lie catchers in understanding others. They hypothesized that the human default option in social judgments is to assess the overall character of an individual. They demonstrated that ratings of the Agreeableness of the individual (i.e., measured by a four item scale based on the Big Five model of personality, and containing a rating on scrupulousness vs. unscrupulousness) were significantly correlated with ratings of deceptiveness, but not with other personality factors such as Extraversion, Neuroticism and Openness. They argued that overall judgments of character are more predictive of more behaviors than particularized truthfulness assessments (also see ten Brinke & Porter, this volume). Their results are consistent with those reported by O'Sullivan (2003) but, while they emphasized the observer's assessment of personality characteristics, O'Sullivan conceptualized this relationship between trait judgments of trustworthiness and state judgments of honesty as an example of the fundamental attribution error.

(5) Beliefs About Clues to Deception

A fifth type of study has tried to evaluate the relative importance of verbal and nonverbal behaviors by asking people to report what they believe the clues to lying to be or to describe how they arrived at their judgment of someone as truthful or deceptive. The kinds of reasons solicited, and the kinds of studies used to examine them can be categorized into four groups: The General Belief Group, The Expert Belief Group, The Free Response to Item Group and the Personal Remembered Lie Group.

The General Belief Group includes early work by Zuckerman and Driver (1985) and more recent work by Bond and Rao (2004) who asked individuals what they believe to be important clues to deception. This literature suggests that eye gaze aversion is widely believed to be a useful clue to deception, although laboratory evidence suggests that some liars actually increase their eye gaze when lying (Zuckerman & Driver). DePaulo et al. (2003) concluded that increased eye gaze aversion may occur when lying about something one is ashamed of, but not in other circumstances. Park, Levine, Harms, and, Ferrara (2002) had students rate the importance of 11 behaviors on a seven-point scale. The behaviors included eye contact; plausibility or consistency of verbal statements; body movements such as fidgeting, speech fluency or disfluency, "intuition" or "gut feeling"; consistency of verbal statements; nervous nonverbal behaviors (i.e., other than body movements); random guessing; facial expressions; consistency of nonverbal behavior; and content of verbal statements. Unlike the earlier Zuckerman and DePaulo studies, the Park et al. students reported speech fluency and the plausibility and content of verbal statements to be the more important behaviors in detecting deception.

A second group of studies (i.e., The Expert Belief Group) compared the beliefs about clues to deception of various lie detector professionals. Vrij and Semin (1996) contrasted the ratings made by prisoners, students and police professionals of the importance of 16 behaviors studied previously or reported in the experimental literature. These included: gaze behavior, smiling, head movements, trunk movements, shifting positions, foot/leg movements, gestures, self-touches, hand and finger movements, shoulder shrugs, response length, speech rate, latency period, ah-filled pauses, non-ah speech disturbances and pitch of voice. Although differences were found between students and police professionals in gestures and shoulder shrugs, with police officers finding them more important than the college students did, the more significant differences were between the prisoners and the other two groups with the prisoners reporting many more behaviors to be unimportant in lie detection.

Strömwell and Granhag (2003) asked judges, prosecutors and police about the importance to lie detection of two verbal clues to deception (i.e., number of details and consistency) and three nonverbal behaviors (i.e., gaze aversion, pitch of voice and body movements) using the same four-point scale as Vrij and Semin (1996). They found that judges believed that verbal content clues were more reliable than nonverbal clues significantly more frequently than police officers did. Police were more likely to view nonverbal behavior as more reliable. Hartwig, Granhag, Strömwall, and Vrij (2004) contrasted the ratings given by police officers following an interrogation they performed vs. one they watched on videotape. Seven kinds of verbal clues were rated: completeness of the statement, confidence in the statement, consistency, details, plausibility, whether the story seemed rehearsed, and general clarity of the statement. The nonverbal clues assessed were: body movements, general behavioral trustworthiness, gaze aversion and nervousness. When rating the use of verbal vs. nonverbal cues, police rated verbal cue usage as significantly greater. When the percentage of time that individual police interviewers or observers actually used any of the seven different cues was used as a measure, a somewhat different pattern was found. General behavioral credibility was cited 24% of the time by interrogators and 16% of the time by observers. Observers cited body movements 20% of the time and general nervousness 15% of the time. Statement plausibility and general statement credibility were each cited 12% of the time. The other cues were all mentioned fewer than 9% of the time. A limitation of all these studies, whether using students or lie detection professionals as respondents, is that the respondents were presented with a predetermined and limited number of clues selected by the experimenters.

A third group of studies (i.e., The Free Response to Item Group) is exemplified by Ekman and O'Sullivan (1991) who contrasted the kinds of reasons accurate vs. inaccurate observers produced after their decisions on two different lie detection items (note: the observers were classified on the basis of whether they were accurate on a particular item, not on their overall accuracy). After deciding whether a particular individual was lying or telling the truth, the observers wrote down their reasons after each item. Every different reason provided was classified as verbal or nonverbal. Ekman and O'Sullivan found that, when observers got an item correct, they were more likely to report using nonverbal clues or a combination of verbal and nonverbal behaviors to make their decision. Those observers who were inaccurate on the item reported using only verbal clues. The kind of lie used in this study, however, was one in which the targets were lying about the emotions they were feeling as they watched an extremely upsetting film. A recent study by Warren (2007) suggests that sensitivity to nonverbal behavior is relevant to the detection of emotional lies but is uncorrelated with non-emotional lies. This report of different clues being used in making different kinds of inferences is consistent with research on empathic accuracy by Hall and Mast (2007). They found that verbal clues contributed the most to accuracy when thoughts were being inferred, but that visual nonverbal clues contributed more to inferring feelings.

Using a videotaped deception scenario in which people lied or told the truth about strongly held opinions, so that both feelings and thoughts were involved, Soohoo and O'Sullivan (2001) hypothesized that accurate and inaccurate judges would be more likely to use different strategies with different items. Using the written reasons given by 65 college students for correct or incorrect answers to two items, they demonstrated that accurate judges used different clues in the two items they got correct, whereas the inaccurate judges tended to use the same kind of clue (i.e., verbal vs. nonverbal) regardless of the relevance of those clues in the items they were judging.

A fourth and quite different approach to the verbal reporting of reasons for detecting deception is the Personal Remembered Lie approach examined by Park, Levine, McCornack, Morrison, and Ferrara (2002) in which they asked subjects to recall a lie that they had discovered in their own life; they then asked them how they discovered that lie. The authors argue that, with this paradigm, the results obtained are strikingly different from those obtained by research in the General Belief, Expert Belief or Free Response to Item approaches. When people reported how they detected a lie in their own life, the more important variables were physical evidence, confirmation by a third party, or the liar confessing the truth. Verbal and nonverbal behaviors of the sort studied by social scientists were rarely reported. Obviously, a personal recollected lie is more likely to be a serious one, which might have required a higher degree of certainty before being acknowledged.

In all of the studies reviewed, with the exception of Ekman and O'Sullivan (1991) and Soohoo and O'Sullivan (2001), the reasons were obtained from college students or police officers of no special lie detection ability. The last methodology to be considered is a variant of the Free Response to Item approach in which highly expert lie detectors are interviewed using a think aloud procedure to determine the emotional and cognitive processes they use in arriving at their correct decisions. Sample responses were chosen to illustrate how some of these experts use single words contextualized by their understanding of the individual and/or of their knowledge of what usual methods of discourse sound like.

The think aloud protocol was developed by Chase and Simon (1988) for their analysis of expert chess players. Since then, it has been widely used to study expertise in many different areas (Ericcson, 1996; Ericcson & Simon, 1998). Recently, Bond (2008) and O'Sullivan (2007; 2008) have used different versions of this technique to examine lie detection expertise. O'Sullivan has been doing research for the last 5 years on a group of extremely rare expert lie detectors (i.e., "truth wizards"), now totaling 50, who obtained highly accurate scores on at least two of three videotaped lie detection tasks. Although the study is ongoing, preliminary evidence suggests that any approach that groups reasons across items may not be the most useful, at least to understand how a truth wizard uses verbal material to assess truthfulness of a given individual. As Kraut (1978) noted: "A danger in research on impression management and on the detection of lying is to treat verbal and nonverbal cues associated with deception as if they were analogous to cues associated with emotion, and, thereby, underestimate the importance of the context in providing them with meanings" (p. 389).

"Truth wizards" are very sensitive to incongruities in communication, but this need not be between communication channels only (e.g., face vs. words). Many kinds of inconsistencies are attended to, including changes in the use of particular words within a statement and inconsistencies between what the person's overall appearance or manner suggests and what she is saying at a particular moment. What expert lie detectors seem to do when presented with videotaped material and asked to judge whether the person shown is lying or telling the truth is to contextualize the individual, to make sense of what it is that particular person is doing and saying in that particular situation. This takes into account the quality of the interview, the relationship with the interviewer (Burgoon et al., 1999), the interactive style of the liar or truth teller and a host of other factors (see Griesel et al., this volume). Even individual words are given great weight.

Following are verbatim examples of this assessment of the "rightness" of words (*le mot juste*) from interviews done with some of the expert lie detectors (note: each "truth wizard" was also matched with a control who participated in the same kind of interviews). The "truth wizards" and their controls had already seen the following three lie detection videos since their responses to them (i.e., whether each individual was lying or telling the truth) were the bases for their identification as "truth wizards" or controls. The three lies included one about a strongly held opinion and another about stealing money. Both of these lies involved a significant cash reward and a threatened punishment (for more details, see Frank & Ekman, 1997). The third lie showed women lying or telling the truth about their feelings as they watched either a distressing surgical film or pleasant nature films. The subjects were nursing students motivated by a letter from the Dean of their school and the belief that their ability to control their emotional display was important to their professional success (see Ekman et al., 1988 for more details).

In the "debriefing" think aloud part of the study, each expert watched the video again and was encouraged to say whatever came into his or her mind (e.g., what she thought about the person she was looking at; what ideas went through her mind; what feelings she experienced, etc.). The interviewer adapted her style to maximize the quantity and quality of the verbal output provided by each expert. If an expert preferred to watch the entire interview before commenting, or wanted to go back and forth in the tape, that is what was done. If the expert made a movement or a sound or a facial expression, the interviewer would stop the tape and ask about it (e.g., "you just had a little smile on your face. What was that about?"; "When she said 'I am enjoying it', you cocked your head to the side. What were you thinking?"). At the end of each item, if the expert had not commented on a striking behavior that most observers mentioned, the interviewer would inquire about it (e.g., "Many people comment on the way he moves his eyebrows. What did you think about that?"). All 30 items were reviewed in this manner. The interviews took from 2 to 4 h to complete and were transcribed by one individual and checked by a second. What follows are a selection of comments made by expert lie detectors that illustrate the way in which they interpret single words.

The first expert to discuss is also the youngest involved in The Truth Wizard Project. Abigail was a 26 year old third year law student when she was identified as an expert lie detector. During the debriefing of one of the crime video items, she watched an interview with a young Asian man whom most observers think is telling the truth about whether he stole $50 (i.e., a great deal of money in 1995 when the experiment was conducted). Most people were positively impressed by his consistent and unwavering eye contact with the interviewer as well as by the lack of hesitation with which he answered the questions he was asked about whether he took the money. But Abigail was struck by the sound of a single word. She said:

"Did you hear how he said 'money?' ... it was soft, and special, not at all like how he said the other words in the interview. Money is important to him. So when he says he doesn't need the money, I don't believe him." She went on to elaborate that needing money was not the issue for him; he just really liked money. It gave him pleasure.

Pennebaker and others (e.g., Newman et al., 2003) have written about the importance of pronoun use. The research methods used in those studies, however, depend on an objective counting of the frequency of occurrence of such parts of speech. Many of the expert lie detectors, particularly those in legal professions, such as law enforcement personnel or arbitrators, pay attention not only to pronouns but to the context of the statement in which the pronouns occur. Although most of the "truth wizards" attend to both verbal and nonverbal behaviors, one of them depends almost exclusively on language.

Daniel is a well-known arbitrator. His language analysis, however, is contextualized by his astute assessment of the kind of person speaking: his intelligence, education, personality, social class, etc. In response to a young man saying that he did not support the death penalty, when he actually did, Daniel said:

> I don't (remember) what the question was, but (the man in the interview) answered it, 'I don't think *they* should be executed', which, whatever the question ... is an odd way to put it. 'I don't think *people* should be executed,' 'I don't think *criminals* should be executed,' but the use of the term, *they* is interesting. Not conclusive, but interesting ... it suggests ... a depersonalization, an alienation (that I want to pay more attention to) ...

Here is what Daniel had to say about another young man who was also lying about his belief in the death penalty:

> There were places in the conversation, (where) ... he was kind of tentative ... where I would not expect him to (be) ... He talks quickly and without interruption at times, when I would expect him to be hesitant. He's looking directly at the interviewer, holding his gaze for a significant amount of time. But he's also looking down ... from time to time. His facial expression is not a natural facial expression ... the sequence is not right between what he's saying, how fast he's saying it, how his eyes are looking, how he's carrying his facial expression. So, I don't believe this guy.

All human beings have expectations of social behavior that they use to evaluate the information that occurs in their relationships with others. Daniel explicitly refers to it in his explanation of his thought processes. Other expert lie detectors do the same thing.

Linda is a retired FBI agent whose interest in language is suggested by her license plate, "lemotjust." She noticed that a young man who was telling the truth when he said he supported the death penalty for murderers focused on the victims, rather than the murderer. Linda said:

> See, and then he goes into 'before they kill someone' (else) ... it's personal ... personal responsibility to him.

About another young man who was lying about his opinion, Linda said:

> He probably would have rather had (the answer) be a yes or no, (but he is asked) 'What is your position?', so he has to say more than he thought he was going to have to say, so ... he has to think about what his answer's going to be ... he has to labor to get this opinion out because I don't think he believes it.

Abigail concluded that money was important to the speaker she was watching on a videotape because of the softness and carefulness with which he said the word. Based on that combination of speech-quality-perception and the inference from it that money was important, she did not believe him when, later in the interview, he said money was not important to him. Daniel had a template in his mind about how and when a tentative statement is made and how and when a strongly-held one is. He does not merely make an overall conclusion about a statement, but considers its constituent parts, sequence by sequence, weighing the plausibility of each component (note: his process is not unlike that suggested by Criteria-Based Content Analysis [CBCA; Griesel et al., this volume; Steller & Koehnken, 1989] and other language only methods. The added value, however, is the understanding of the uniqueness of the individual producing the words).

Another expert, Julian, is a law professor with a Ph.D. in counseling psychology. He was struck by the use of a particular word, but also checked to see whether it was consistent with other aspects of the truth teller's behavior. In explaining why he thought the man was telling the truth about his opinion he said:

> I'd say the biggest thing on him was that he says, 'hypocritical.' It was a big word, it describes his argument well, he said it so forcefully, and his head supported it.

In these two sentences, Julian illustrates observations consistent with findings from many research areas. He notes the consistency of the word with the argument; he notes that the word is unusual ("a big word"), that it was said forcefully, and that his head movements were consistent with it. He had already commented that the man looked intellectual, so his acceptance of the argument was also based on his assessment of the personality of that individual.

An expert lie detector, Liam, is an internal investigator for the Bureau of Prisons. He illustrates how expert lie detectors not only listen to single words, such as "no" but also observe the accompanying nonverbal behaviors and the consistency over the time of the interview (i.e., 1 min in this instance) of the pairing of verbal and nonverbal behavior. Liam said:

> ... the first 'no,' he was sort of, you know, 'Of course I'm not lying,' it was ... a downward smirk. And then the last 'no,' it was ... an astonishment, his eyes ... went up ... I'd say he was lying.

What Liam was attending to was the combination of the content of speech with a variety of emotional states or motives (i.e., smirks vs. astonishment) and the inconsistency over the course of the interview of those feelings. The experts almost always commented on their uncertainty, noting that the inconsistency could arise from several factors, only one of which was deception. They would then run through a variety of alternative explanations and, only after ruling those out, would they settle on deception as the more likely explanation.

The scientific method demands replicable operationalization. This assumes that many samples can reasonably be coalesced. This assumption has led to the many valuable findings resulting from the studies briefly reviewed under the first four classifications discussed above: language only, measurement of language and non-language behaviors, accuracy determination under limited information conditions, and various models of impression formation, including those involving lie detection. The intensive analysis of the decision making processes of expert observers has been used in other arenas as well (Ericcson, 1996). Although most studies of expertise examine physicians, engineers, chess players and the like, Ceci and Liker (1986) examined a horse race handicapper.

Ceci and Liker (1986) provided a lengthy transcript of the thinking processes of a single highly successful handicapper and suggested that his talent combined both quantitative and qualitative aspects. The information from a general data base (e.g., previous record of the horse's speed) was qualified by knowledge of moderating variables—track condition, competition, jockey, weather, etc. They argued that this more individualized database will vary from handicapper to handicapper and will reflect their personalized knowledge. This personalized knowledge is more like the kinds of information possessed by individual therapists and artists. So, while science is necessary to support our understanding of the general processes involved in lying and lie detection, studies of the individualization, the contextualization of the decisions made by particular kinds of lie detectors are also needed.

Some beginning information in support of the above view has been reported originally by O'Sullivan and Ekman (2004) and, in more detail, using more experts by O'Sullivan (2008). The latter report contrasted the means and standard deviations on the three different lie detection scenarios explained above (e.g., opinion about death penalty, crime [e.g., stealing money] and emotion [e.g., feelings while watching pleasant vs. medical film]) obtained by 18 police professionals who had been identified as "truth wizards," as well as the corresponding information on the same three tests by ten expert lie detector therapists or psychologists. These means and standard deviations are listed in Table 10.1 (see above).

All six mean scores are significantly different from chance (50%). There was no significant difference between the police and the therapists on the opinion test since that test was used as the screening measure (note: to be considered for The Truth Wizard Project, potential experts needed to obtain scores of 80 or 90% on the opinion scenario). The opinion lie is the easiest for most examinees, since the items contain many verbal and nonverbal clues to deceit. The pattern of scores on the crime and emotion lies, however, was quite different for the two professional groups. For the police professionals, their accuracy on the crime items was significantly greater than their accuracy on the emotion lie items ($t[17] = 5.52, p < 0.000$). It is both not surprising, as well as reassuring, that police observers have significantly greater lie detection accuracy on lies concerning a crime (i.e., theft of a significant amount of money) than they do for lies concerning emotional reactions to films. This accuracy pattern makes sense and is mirrored by a complementary accuracy pattern obtained by the expert lie detectors who are therapists and psychologists. Comparing the therapists' crime and emotion detection accuracy scores with those of the police officers shown in Table 10.1 in a repeated measures ANOVA indicated a significant interaction between profession and test accuracy ($F[1, 26] = 31.407, p < 0.000$). Although some police officers and therapists were highly accurate on all three measures, overall, the police were significantly more accurate on the crime scenario and the therapists were significantly more accurate on the emotion scenario. This finding suggests that, while it is likely that there are some generalized lie detection accuracy processes (e.g., based perhaps on cues such as those discovered in the science-based paradigms discussed earlier), there are also profession-specific, and perhaps, liar specific and expert specific clues to deception. The acquisition of that more specific knowledge base is probably acquired only through individual experience, feedback and motivation to master a particular kind of lie detection.

The idiographic analysis provided by the dissection of the cognitive and emotional processes used by expert lie detectors amplifies rather than contradicts laboratory research findings based on the examination of groups of examinees. All of the verbal, vocal and nonverbal clues to deception reported in the literature were used by one or more of the expert lie detectors. In addition, however, they reported scores of other behaviors that have not been analyzed in the literature: specific kinds of head rotations, nostril flaring, neck blushing, particular patterns of eye movements and, as has been illustrated here, a more nuanced interpretation of language than most language-only methods of deceptive communication ordinarily use.

In addition, the grounding of the "truth wizards'" interpretation of the behavior relevant to lie detection in their understanding of the kind of person showing that behavior is crucial. Heinrich and Borkenau (1998) argued that, in judging deception, most people make overall trait assessments of other people (also see ten Brinke & Porter, this volume). Both the experts and their controls certainly did that. What differentiated them from one another, however, was that the experts had more accurate, complex and far-reaching person perceptions and, although they often started their assessment with a global interpretation of the person, they considered alternative interpretations as they proceeded to watch the interviews (see Griesel et al., this volume). Matched controls, who were not accurate lie detectors, tended not to question their first impression and to ignore the implication of inconsistencies, even when they perceived them.

A difficulty in most experimental research of lie detection accuracy is that we study the pack, rather than the leader; the tribe, rather than Moses. This is appropriate if we are interested in the processes underlying the lie detection of insufficiently accurate observers. If we want to understand how people who actually can detect deception do so, then other subject groups in addition to non-randomly selected college students need to be examined (see a related argument for the study of eyewitness memory by Yuille, this volume). Studies of expertise may lack generalizability (Bond & DePaulo, 2008), but they offer superior guidance in terms of training for improvement and clarification of existing knowledge.

References

Aamodt, M. G., & Custer, H. (2006). Who can best catch a liar? A meta-analysis of individual differences in detecting deception. *The Forensic Examiner, 25*, 6–11.
Bond, C. F., Jr., & DePaulo, B. M. (2006). Accuracy of deception judgments. *Personality and Social Psychology Review, 10*, 214–234.

Bond, C. F., Jr., & DePaulo, B. M. (2008). Individual differences in judging deception: Accuracy and bias. *Psychological Bulletin, 134*, 477–492.
Bond, C. F., Jr., & Rao, S. R. (2004). Mendacity in a mobile world. In P. A. Granhag & L. Stromwall (Eds.), *The detection of deception in forensic contexts* (pp. 127–147). NY: Cambridge University Press.
Bond, G. D. (2008). Deception detection expertise. *Law and Human Behavior, 4*, 339–351.
Bugental, D., Kaswan, J., & Love, L. (1970). Perceptions of contradictory meanings conveyed by verbal and nonverbal channels. *Journal of Personality and Social Psychology, 16*, 647–655.
Burgoon, J. K., Buller, D. B., White, C. H., Afifi, W., & Buslig, A. L. S. (1999). The role of conversational involvement in deceptive interpersonal interactions. *Personality and Social Psychology Bulletin, 25*(6), 669–685.
Campbell, R. S., & Pennebaker, J. (2003). The secret life of pronouns: Flexibility in writing style and physical health. *Psychological Science, 14*(1), 60–65.
Ceci, S. J., & Liker, J. K. (1986). A day at the races: A study of IQ, expertise, and cognitive complexity. *Journal of Experimental Psychology. General, 115*(3), 255–266.
Chase, W. G., & Simon, H. A. (1988). The mind's eye in chess. In A. M. Collins & E. E. Smith (Eds.), *Readings in cognitive science: A perspective from psychology and artificial intelligence* (pp. 461–494). San Mateo, CA: Morgan Kaufmann.
Cohn, M. A., Mehl, M. R., & Pennebaker, J. W. (2004). Linguistic markers of psychological change surrounding September 11, 2001. *Psychological Science, 15*(10), 687–693.
DePaulo, B.M. (1998). *Deceiving and detecting deceit: Insights and oversights from the first several hundred studies*. Invited address. Washington, DC: American Psychological Society.
DePaulo, B. M., Lanier, K., & Davis, T. (1983). Detecting the deceit of the motivated liar. *Journal of Personality and Social Psychology, 45*, 1096–1103.
DePaulo, B. M., Lindsay, J. J., Malone, B. E., Muhlenbruck, L., Charlton, K., & Cooper, H. (2003). Cues to deception. *Psychological Bulletin, 129*(1), 74–118.
DePaulo, B. M., Rosenthal, R., Eisenstat, R. A., Rogers, P. L., & Finkelstein, S. (1978). Decoding discrepant nonverbal cues. *Journal of Personality and Social Psychology, 36*(3), 313–323.
Ekman, P. (2001). *Telling lies: Clues to deceit in the marketplace, politics, and marriage* (3rd ed.). New York: W.W. Norton.
Ekman, P. (2003). *Emotions revealed*. New York: Holt.
Ekman, P., & Friesen, W. V. (1969). The repertoire of nonverbal behavior: Categories, origins, usage, and coding. *Semiotica, 1*, 49–98.
Ekman, P., & Friesen, W. V. (1978). *Facial action coding system*. Palo Alto, CA: Consulting Psychologists Press.
Ekman, P., Friesen, W. V., & O'Sullivan, M. (1988). Smiles when lying. *Journal of Personality and Social Psychology, 54*(3), 414–420.
Ekman, P., Friesen, W. V., O'Sullivan, M., & Scherer, K. R. (1980). Relative importance of face, body, and speech in judgments of personality and affect. *Journal of Personality and Social Psychology, 38*(2), 270–277.
Ekman, P., & O'Sullivan, M. (1991). Who can catch a liar? *American Psychologist, 46*(9), 913–920.
Ekman, P., O'Sullivan, M., Friesen, W. V., & Scherer, K. (1991). Invited article: Face, voice and body in detecting deceit. *Journal of Nonverbal Behavior, 15*(2), 125–135.
Ericcson, K. A. (1996). The acquisition of expert performance: An introduction to some of the issues. In K. A. Ericsson (Ed.), *The road to excellence: The acquisition of expert performance in the arts and sciences, sports, and games* (pp. 1–50). Hillsdale, NJ: Lawrence Erlbaum.
Ericcson, K. A., & Simon, H. A. (1998). How to study thinking in everyday life: Contrasting think-aloud protocols with descriptions and explanations of thinking. *Mind, Culture and Activity, 5*(3), 178–186.
Feeley, T. H., & deTurck, M. A. (1998). The behavioral correlates of sanctioned and unsanctioned deceptive communication. *Journal of Nonverbal Behavior, 22*(3), 189–204.
Feldman, R. S., & Jenkins, L. (1979). Detection of deception in adults and children via facial expressions. *Child Development, 50*(2), 350–355.

Fiske, S. T. (1992). Thinking is for doing: Portraits of social cognition from Daguerreotype to laserphoto. *Journal of Personality and Social Psychology, 63*(6), 877–889.

Frank, M. G., & Ekman, P. (1997). The ability to detect deceit generalizes across different types of high-stake lies. *Journal of Personality and Social Psychology, 72*(6), 1429–1439.

Funder, D. (1999). *Personality judgment: A realistic approach to person perception*. San Diego: Academic.

Gardner, H. (1993). *Frames of mind: The theory of multiple intelligences*. New York: Perseus.

Granhag, P. A., & Strömwall, L. A. (2002). Repeated interrogations: Verbal and non-verbal cues to deception. *Applied Cognitive Psychology, 16*, 243–257.

Hall, J. A., & Mast, M. S. (2007). Sources of accuracy in the empathic accuracy paradigm. *Emotion, 7*(2), 438–446.

Hartwig, M., Granhag, P. A., Strömwall, L. A., & Vrij, A. (2004). Police officers' lie detection accuracy: Interrogating freely versus observing video. *Police Quarterly, 7*(4), 429–436.

Heinrich, C. U., & Borkenau, P. (1998). Deception and deception detection: The role of cross-modal inconsistency. *Journal of Personality, 66*(5), 687–712.

Ickes, W. (1993). Empathic accuracy. *Journal of Personality, 61*, 587–610.

Kraut, R. (1978). Verbal and nonverbal cues in the perception of lying. *Journal of Personality and Social Psychology, 36*(4), 380–391.

Mann, S. A., & Vrij, A. (2006). Police officers' judgments of veracity, tenseness, cognitive load and attempted behavioral control in real-life police interviews. *Psychology, Crime & Law, 12*(3), 307–319.

Masip, J., Sporer, S. L., Garrido, E., & Herrero, C. (2005). The detection of deception with the reality monitoring approach: A review of the empirical evidence. *Psychology, Crime & Law, 11*(1), 99–122.

Mayer, J. D., Salovey, P., & Caruso, D. (2002). *Mayer-Salovey-Caruso emotional intelligence test, user's manual*. Toronto, Canada: Multi-Health Systems.

Meissner, C. A., & Kassin, S. M. (2002). "He's guilty!": Investigator bias in judgments of truth and deception. *Law and Human Behavior, 26*(5), 469–480.

Newman, M. L., Pennebaker, J. W., Berry, D. S., & Richards, J. M. (2003). Lying words: Predicting deception from linguistic styles. *Personality and Social Psychology Bulletin, 29*(5), 665–675.

O'Sullivan, M. (2003). The fundamental attribution error in detecting deception: The boy-who-cried-wolf effect. *Personality and Social Psychology Bulletin, 29*(10), 1316–1327.

O'Sullivan, M. (2005). Emotional intelligence and detecting deception. Why most people can't "read" others, but a few can. In R. Riggio & R. Feldman (Eds.), *Applications of nonverbal communication* (pp. 215–253). Mahwah, NJ: Erlbaum.

O'Sullivan, M. (2007). Unicorns or Tiger Woods: Are lie detection experts myths or realities? A response to on lie detection wizards by Bond and Uysal. *Law and Human Behavior, 31*, 117–123.

O'Sullivan, M. (2008). Homeruns and humbugs: Comment on Bond and DePaulo (2008). *Psychological Bulletin, 134*, 493–497.

O'Sullivan, M., & Ekman, P. (2004). The wizards of deception detection. In P. A. Granhag & L. Stromwell (Eds.), *Detecting deception in forensic contexts* (pp. 269–286). Cambridge, UK: Cambridge University Press.

O'Sullivan, M., Ekman, P., Friesen, W., & Scherer, K. R. (1985). What you say and how you say it: The contribution of speech content and voice quality to judgments of others. *Journal of Personality and Social Psychology, 48*(1), 54–62.

O'Sullivan, M., & Guilford, J. P. (1975). Six factors of behavioral cognition: Understanding other people. *Journal of Educational Measurement, 12*(4), 255–271.

Park, E. S., Levine, T. R., Harms, C. M., & Ferrara, M. H. (2002). Group and individual accuracy in deception detection. *Communication Research Reports, 19*(2), 99–106.

Park, H. S., Levine, T. R., McCornack, S. A., Morrison, K., & Ferrara, M. (2002). How people really detect lies. *Communication Monographs, 69*(2), 144–157.

Porter, S., Doucette, N. L., Woodworth, M., Earle, J., & MacNeil, B. (2008). Halfe the world knows not how the other halfe lies: Investigation of verbal and non-verbal signs of deception exhibited by criminal offenders and non-offenders. *Legal and Criminological Psychology, 13,* 27–38.

Porter, S., & Yuille, J. C. (1995). Credibility assessment of criminal suspects through statement analysis. *Psychology, Crime & Law, 1,* 1–13.

Rockwell, P., Buller, D. B., & Burgoon, J. K. (1997). The voice of deceit: Refining and expanding cues to deception. *Communication Research Reports, 14,* 451–459.

Ross, L., & Nisbett, R. E. (1991). *The person and the situation: Perspectives of social psychology.* New York: McGraw-Hill.

Soohoo, T., & O'Sullivan, M. (2001). *Lie detection: Decision reasons and accuracy.* Poster presented at the annual meeting of the Society for Personality and Social Psychology, San Antonio, TX.

Sporer, S. L., & Schwandt, B. (2006). Paraverbal indicators of deception: A meta-analytic synthesis. *Applied Cognitive Psychology, 20,* 421–446.

Sporer, S. L., & Schwandt, B. (2007). Moderators of nonverbal indicators of deception: A meta-analytic synthesis. *Psychology, Public Policy, and Law, 13*(1), 1–34.

Steller, M., & Koehnken, G. (1989). Criteria-based statement analysis. In D. C. Raskin (Ed.), *Psychological methods in criminal investigation and evidence* (pp. 217–245). New York, NY: Springer Publishing.

Strömwell, L. A., & Granhag, P. A. (2003). How to detect deception? Arresting the beliefs of police officers, prosecutors and judges. *Psychology, Crime & Law, 9,* 19–36.

Undeutsch, U. (1982). Statement reality analysis. In A. Trankell (Ed.), *Reconstructing the past: The role of psychologists in criminal trials* (pp. 27–56). Stockholm: Norsted & Sons.

Vrij, A., Akehurst, L., Soukara, S., & Bull, R. (2006). Detecting deceit via analyses of verbal and nonverbal children and adults. *Human Communication Research, 30,* 8–41.

Vrij, A., & Heaven, S. (1999). Vocal and verbal indicators of deception as a function of lie complexity. *Psychology, Crime & Law, 5*(3), 203–215.

Vrij, A., & Mann, S. (2001). Telling and detecting lies in a high-stake situation: The case of a convicted murderer. *Applied Cognitive Psychology, 15,* 187–203.

Vrij, A., & Semin, G. R. (1996). Lie experts' beliefs about nonverbal indicators of deception. *Journal of Nonverbal Behavior, 20*(1), 65–80.

Warren, G. (2007). *The development of a deception detection task: The importance of emotion.* Paper presented at the Annual Conference of the Division of Forensic Psychology, British Psychological Society, University of York, UK.

Yuille, J. C. (1989). *Credibility assessment.* The Netherlands: Kluwer.

Zuckerman, M., DeFrank, R. S., Hall, J. A., Larrance, D. T., & Rosenthal, R. (1979). Facial and vocal cues of deception and honesty. *Journal of Experimental Social Psychology, 15,* 378–396.

Zuckerman, M., & Driver, R. E. (1985). Telling lies: Verbal and nonverbal correlates of deception. In W. A. Siegman & S. Feldstein (Eds.), *Multichannel integration of nonverbal behavior* (pp. 129–147). Hillsdale, NJ: Erlbaum.

Chapter 11
Assessment Criteria Indicative of Deception: An Example of the New Paradigm of Differential Recall Enhancement

Kevin Colwell, Cheryl Hiscock-Anisman, and Jacquelyn Fede

The present chapter details the historical and conceptual evolution of a new paradigm in statement analysis that has developed over the past 20 years. There has been an increasing awareness of the importance of interviewing designed to facilitate the detection of deception as a necessary component of statement analysis (Colwell, Hiscock, & Memon, 2002; Hartwig & Bond, 2011; Hernández-Fernaud & Alonso-Quecuty, 1997; Koehnken, Schimossek, Ascherman, & Hofer, 1995; Vrij, Fisher, Mann, & Leal, 2006). Subsequently, the work of multiple researchers has created a zeitgeist that has nurtured and informed the development of this new paradigm. This chapter begins by providing a quick overview of the various lines of research that comprise this paradigm. Attention is then given to credibility assessment and statement content criteria that discriminate honest from deceptive responding. Then, the focus is on strategies of impression management and the subjective experience of respondents during an investigative interview. This sets the stage for a discussion of investigative interviewing structure and techniques that facilitate the detection of deception through the process of Differential Recall Enhancement (DRE: Colwell et al., 2012). Finally, this chapter considers in detail an approach to interviewing and assessment that is representative of the new paradigm.

The New Paradigm

In the past two decades, there has been a shift to focus on the importance of interviewing to detect deception as being the most important aspect of statement analysis (Hartwig & Bond, 2011). Without effective interviewing, there are few reliable

K. Colwell (✉) • J. Fede
Department of Psychology, Southern Connecticut State University,
501 Crescent St., New Haven, CT, 06515 USA
e-mail: colwellk2@southernct.edu

C. Hiscock-Anisman
The National University,
La Jolla, CA, 92037 USA

differences between honest and deceptive responding. With effective interviewing and an awareness of critical content criteria, the differences between honest and deceptive responding are maximized and readily apparent. This work can be traced back to independent studies done comparing the Step-Wise Interview (SI: Zaparniuk, Yuille, & Taylor, 1995) to the Cognitive Interview (CI: Fisher, Geiselman, & Amador, 1989) or the SI, CI, and Reality Interview (Colwell, 1997). The first of these studies noted that adult memory for events is so complex, in general, that effective credibility assessment will require the use of interviewing that enhances differences between honest and deceptive responding (Koehnken et al., 1995). The second went on to state that the relationship between question type and content criteria should be closely studied (Colwell, 1997), with the intent of using techniques that take advantage of the increased cognitive and interpersonal demands placed upon deceivers (Colwell et al., 2002). In recent years, there has been a proliferation of research based upon these ideas. There has been the *cognitive load* hypothesis (Vrij et al., 2006), which builds upon the early work by focusing upon the specific CI technique of reverse-order recall to magnify differences between honest and deceptive responding. Similarly, unanticipated questions have been shown to increase cognitive load (Vrij et al., 2009). In the same vein, there has been study of the manner and timing of disclosure of evidence during an investigation to facilitate the detection of deception (Dando & Bull, 2011; Hartwig, Granhag, Strömwall, & Kronkvist, 2006). The oldest and most integrated set of techniques that represent this paradigm is assessment criteria indicative of deception (ACID: Colwell, Hiscock-Anisman, Memon, Taylor, & Prewett, 2008). All of these approaches share a goal of enhancing recall for honest respondents while making deception more difficult for deceivers, and thereby magnifying the differences between the two. This is the essence of DRE – to help honest respondents while making deception more difficult and more obvious.

Credibility Assessment

The process of statement analysis refers to the use of content criteria in the analysis of a statement taken from an investigative interview. This process involves a properly conducted interview, content analysis of the resulting statement, and careful analysis of all available case data. This is drastically different from interrogation, which is neither ethically permissible for psychologists in the United States nor designed as an investigative tool. Statement analysis, first and foremost, seeks to obtain accurate and useful information from victims, witnesses, and suspects. In other words, it is primarily an investigative tool. Secondarily, statement analysis seeks to provide a mechanism for assessing the credibility of the information obtained. Credibility assessment determines whether a statement possesses the characteristics associated with accurate recall for an experienced event. It is related to detecting deception, but there are some specific differences. Credibility assessment is a form of truth confirmation. It seeks to provide a mechanism for weighing the various sources of information presented to an investigator or to a trier of fact.

Especially in the legal systems derived from British Common Law (e.g., Australia, US, Canada, United Kingdom), whether a statement is honest or deceptive is a decision for the trier of fact (e.g., judge, jury, magistrate; see Seniuk, present volume). It also provides a mechanism for investigators to determine what additional information must be gathered. This last application is the primary role for the type of credibility assessment described in the present chapter.

Memory and Credibility Assessment

Criteria-Based Content Analysis

The oldest, most researched, and prototypical approach to statement analysis is Criteria-Based Content Analysis (CBCA; Vrij, 2005). This system was first devised for use with allegations of child sexual abuse in Germany, and it has been used as part of court-mandated assessments since the 1950s (Undeutsch, 1954). The underlying premise of CBCA is that systematic differences exist between statements derived from memory for a real event and statements derived from imagination or fabrication. This has been referred to as the *Undeutsch hypothesis* (Porter & Yuille, 1995; also see O'Sullivan, present volume). There has been debate in the field as to the total number and application of CBCA criteria. However, it is generally accepted that CBCA comprises at least 19 content criteria, the presence of which increases the likelihood that a statement is true (Zaparniuk et al., 1995). CBCA is a form of credibility assessment – higher numbers of the criteria do not indicate honesty per se but rather increase the likelihood that the statement is derived from genuine experience, that is, it is more likely to be honest (see Griesel, Ternes, Schraml, Cooper, & Yuille; present volume). Under certain circumstances, a single criterion could suffice for the statement to be deemed credible.

CBCA was designed to evaluate statements from children regarding alleged abuse. For this reason, a number of the criteria are not relevant to all statements. Because the present work focuses on interviewing and credibility assessment in general, we limit our discussion to the portion of CBCA that applies to all memories for events, not just to alleged victims' memories for child abuse.

The presence of the first three criteria of CBCA is considered to be necessary in order for a statement to be judged as credible, and these are the three that apply to memories for all events. These criteria include: coherence (sometimes referred to as logical structure), sufficient detail (sometimes referred to as appropriate amount of detail), and spontaneous reproduction (sometimes referred to as unstructured production; Zaparniuk et al., 1995). Coherence (or logical structure) refers to the various portions of a statement that consistently hold together and agree with one another. It also deals with whether the events described in a statement are possible given the basic limitations of time and space. Therefore, a statement that contains serious contradictions, or one that is simply physically impossible, would not be rated as coherent. In contrast, a statement in which all of the portions describe the same basic event in the same basic manner, and which restricts itself to limitations imposed by time and space, would be rated as coherent (Colwell et al., 2002). This criterion is especially important in the assessment of children's statements. Children often accidentally release sensitive information which contradicts information they have previously stated (Williams et al., 2012). Coherence has been found to have some utility with adults (Colwell et al., 2002). However, this criterion should be applied carefully to adult statements. For example, one study found that honest men are more likely to provide incoherent statements than are deceptive women (Suckle-Nelson et al., 2010).

Sufficient detail is a statement characteristic that addresses the rich amount of sensory information that can be provided by a cooperative witness who is reporting an event he or she experienced. Credible statements tend to contain a copious amount of detail and are rich in visual, spatial, and auditory information (Vrij, 2005). Determining the amount of detail that is sufficient is a subjective judgment made by the rater, and it is based upon experience and training. There are issues with training, reliability, and confounds due to age and language (Blandon-Gitlin, Pezdek, Lindsay, & Hagen, 2009; Blandon-Gitlin, Pezdek, Rogers, & Brodie, 2005). Therefore, this criterion assesses a vital aspect of credibility, but there are problems with its current application.

One major limitation of the sufficient detail criterion comes from the manner in which CBCA is scored. Therefore, this limitation will apply to all CBCA criteria, but is considered here. In CBCA scoring, the criteria are scored as *present* or *absent*, and they are scored so that, if they appear anywhere in a statement, they are counted as, "present" for that statement. This type of scoring loses the rich information that can be gained by matching the type of question asked with resulting content criteria (Colwell et al., 2002). This dichotomous scoring reduces the extent to which variability is possible and negatively affects the psychometric properties of the criteria; that is, it reduces the reliability and potential validity. The scoring of a statement as a whole minimizes the role of the all-important effects of interviewing and the requisite understanding of how memory operates. That is, different questions lead to different statement characteristics, and it is important to link questioning strategy to content criteria to achieve optimal results (Colwell et al.).

Spontaneous reproduction (or unstructured production) is a statement characteristic that addresses the offhand and unplanned nature of honest responding (Zaparniuk et al., 1995). This characteristic emerges for two reasons. First, honest respondents are aware of their honesty and might believe that other people can see this sense of honesty. So, they are not concerned with telling a scripted narrative from start to finish, and are free to provide information as they remember it (Colwell, Hiscock-Anisman, Memon, Yaeger, & Michlik, 2006; Hines et al., 2010). The second reason has to do with the automatic nature of memory. The process of interviewing, when carried out correctly, leads to the recall of additional information (see Yarbrough, Hervé, & Harms, present volume). Therefore, a person who is engaged in honest responding will provide a certain amount of detail in response to an initial question. If additional questions are asked, especially questions using mnemonics, then the honest respondent should have a significant amount of additional information become available due to spreading activation and cue-dependent recall (Colwell et al., 2008; Fisher et al., 1989; Memon, Fraser, Colwell, Odino, & Mastroberadino, 2009; Memon, Meissner, & Fraser, 2010). In short, honest responding during an investigative interview leads to a positive-feedback system. The act of remembering provides new cues, which in turn lead to even more remembering.

Table 11.1 contains an overview of CBCA studies and their findings regarding sufficient detail and spontaneous reproduction, as these are the two criteria that appear to be the most promising indicators of credibility across a range of ages and with both genders. Coherence is not considered in this table due to potential misapplication with adults (Suckle-Nelson et al., 2010).

Although there has been some promise in CBCA research, there are many problems that hinder its application in North America. For example, CBCA is confounded by age, familiarity with the type of event, and language capacity (Blandon-Gitlin et al., 2009, 2005; Vrij, Akehurst, Soukara, & Bull, 2002). Therefore, the system of adult credibility assessment presented here pulled from the theory underlying CBCA but was forced to consider other perspectives related to memory in order to avoid the pitfalls described above (dichotomous scoring, confounds with age, gender, and, uncertain rules for when a statement should be labeled, "credible," or, "not credible").

Reality Monitoring

Johnson and Raye (1981) posited that memories for experienced events will have more external-sensorial information and more contextual information than will memories derived from imagination or fabrication. The method of assessment based on that hypothesis, labeled Reality Monitoring (RM), initially appeared to be promising. Indeed, numerous studies found a direct relationship between the amount of sensory detail and the credibility of a statement (Masip, Sporer, Garrido, & Herrero, 2005). RM assessments have been used to assess the credibility of intrapersonal memories and interpersonal statements. In the first case, a person assesses his or her own memory and, in the second, an external rater typically reads a transcript from a statement and rates it. The ratings have been done according to Likert-type scales or by tallying the amount of individual details related to sensorial, contextual, and internal cognitive processes. These Likert-type and the detail tally assessments, despite apparent differences, are actually assessing the same constructs and perform with the same level of accuracy (Memon et al., 2009).

In general, RM-based techniques have led to accuracy rates in the 80% range when predicting statements as honest or deceptive (Masip et al., 2005). The original hypothesis of RM, when applied to interpersonal deception, also posited that deceptive statements will have more details derived from internal sources, such as cognitive operations, imagination, fabrication, associated memories for previous events, etc. Unfortunately, this hypothesis has not been supported (Memon et al., 2009;

Table 11.1 Studies considering the relationship of sufficient detail and spontaneous reproduction to credibility

Citation	Sufficient detail	Spontaneous reproduction
Akehurst, Koehnken, and Hofer (1995)	Increase	No relationship
Blandon-Gitlin et al. (2009)		
Experiment 1	Increase	No relationship
Experiment 2	No relationship	Increase
Boychuk (1991)	Increase	Increase
Esplin, Boychuk, and Raskin (1988)	Increase	Increase
Hofer, Akehurst, and Metzger (1996)	Increase	No relationship
Koehnken et al. (1995)	Increase	Increase
Lamb, Sternberg, Esplin, and Hershkowitz (1997)	Increase	Increase
Landry and Brigham (1992)	Increase	*
Porter and Yuille (1996)	Increase	No relationship
Ruby and Brigham (1998)	No relationship	Decrease
Steller, Wellershaus, and Wolf (1988)	Increase	*
Vrij et al. (2002)	Increase	*
Vrij, Edward, Roberts, and Bull (2000)		
Experiment 1	No relationship	*
Experiment 2	Increase	No relationship
Winkel and Vrij (1995)	Increase	Increase
Zaparniuk et al. (1995)	No relationship	Increase
Totals	13 increase	7 increase
	4 no relationship	4 no relationship: 1 decrease

Note: An asterisk (*) indicates that no data was available for this study

Memon, Omerod, & Dando, 2012). Furthermore, there are a number of problems with the measurement of RM that hinder its forensic application (e.g., lack of consistent definitions, poor reliability, no accepted decision criteria, confoundedness with the emotional valence of an event; Memon et al., 2012).

What, then, was the reason for the initial success of RM-based assessments? RM appeared to be promising because, during an investigative interview, honest respondents often provide more overall detail than do deceptive respondents. This increase in detail allows for classification at higher-than-chance rates. Because the overall amount of detail in a statement, (especially under appropriate interviewing circumstances) is correlated with the credibility of a statement, it often appeared that the assessment of RM could provide an effective mechanism of credibility assessment (Colwell, Hiscock-Anisman, Memon, Rachel, & Colwell, 2007). However, the increase in detail was not due specifically to the reasons posited by RM theory. Honest statements do have more sensory details in many circumstances, but deceptive statements do not have more details from cognitive operations, previous memories, or other internal sources (Colwell et al., 2007). Finally, and to restate the central lesson of this chapter, no content criterion ought to be considered in the absence of the interviewing technique used to elicit the statement (Colwell et al., 2002).

Honest respondents may provide more detail, or they may provide less, depending upon the question posed (Memon et al., 2009).

Impression Management and Credibility Assessment: Subjective Clues

Credibility assessment must take into account subjective indicators of deception (i.e., those behaviors that people believe to be indicative of honesty or deception) as well as objective indicators of deception (i.e., those behaviors that truly are indicative of honesty or deception). This is due to the central fact that deceivers are aware of their deception and take steps to hide this. Deception during an investigative interview is a pragmatic enterprise where deceivers must avoid the disclosure of sensitive information, avoid making obvious contradictions in their statements, and generally appear honest and cooperative. They must present sufficient information to satisfy their interviewer while withholding or changing any information that could lead to their detection (Colwell & Sjerven, 2005; Hines et al., 2010; Porter & Yuille, 1996). Therefore, a complete approach to interviewing and credibility assessment needs to account for the effort that is being made by the respondent to avoid detection and to look honest. Knowing what people think is indicative of deception, and where people are exerting effort provides important information for crafting a system of interviewing and assessment. Most important are discrepancies between what is thought to be indicative of credibility and what truly is indicative of credibility. This allows the assessor to judge credibility without worrying about the effects of motivation or preparation. Often, in fact, motivation and preparation can make deception detection easier because the effort expended by motivated deceivers leads to predictable changes in their behavior, whereas motivation does not have the same effects on honest respondents (Colwell et al., 2002, 2007).

One of the best ways to determine how honest and deceptive respondents attempt to present honestly during an investigative interview is to ask them. In a series of studies, Hiscock-Anisman et al. (2012) did exactly this. College students either committed or witnessed a theft, or either told the truth or lied about an autobiographical memory, and then underwent an investigative interview. Several hundred students from universities across the US have been assessed. The demographic and socio-economic characteristics of these samples are quite varied, including one set of students who spoke Chinese and had their data translated into English for assessment. Table 11.2 provides a summary of the strategy data provided across all of these different studies. These studies generally involved the chance to win up to $200.00 for successfully convincing an interviewer that one was honest. This level of motivation is consistent with a large number of situations, but it does not match the extreme consequences of some investigative situations. However, the vast literature on the relationship between performance and anxiety is clear on the point that people do not develop and demonstrate new skills when under high stress. They simply continue to use the strategies they have already learned, with a decrease in skill level as the anxiety or consequences move from moderate to high. Students are motivated at a moderate level and, in fact, it is difficult to find non-motivated student volunteers. Therefore, the information obtained from the assessment of students, despite the doubts of many investigators, provides a very good insight into honesty and deception during investigative interviews (Colwell et al., 2002).

One important finding from the above data is that deceivers tried hard not to make mistakes in their stories, and they incorporated some specific strategies in doing so. Deceivers were generally concerned about making certain that they did not do anything that would draw attention to their story, such as to present any inconsistencies or to make overt mistakes. They also developed and practiced their stories in advance of the interview. They believed that this is a useful approach, to 'stay on script', in order not to provide any information that might implicate them. This approach also allowed the deceivers to feel better prepared to answer questions based upon the fabricated script rather than upon the real event in question. Deceivers wanted to make sure that they presented both verbal and nonverbal information in a controlled way. They believed that, if they manage the information, they would be less likely viewed with suspicion. Deceivers also believed that it is important to be seen as cooperative as possible and to avoid drawing attention to themselves. This was done by appearing calm and sincere and by acting certain about the information presented. Strategies such as appearing relaxed, appearing self-assured, and providing direct eye contact were viewed as important approaches to avoid being caught. Overall, deceivers in this study wanted to provide a relatively short, carefully phrased description and to appear confident while doing so. Many strategies which were listed by deceptive respondents were also listed by honest respondents. In other words, there was considerable overlap between the intended behavior of honest and deceptive respondents during an investigative interview. However, it is possible to elicit differences between the two groups through careful, strategic interviewing. The data from this large, multi-site and multi-ethnic sample is also consistent with two previous studies on this same topic (Colwell, Hiscock-Anisman, et al., 2006; Hines et al., 2010).

Perhaps the most important finding from research regarding subjective strategies of deception is the mismatch between perceived and genuine cues to credibility or deception (see ten Brinke & Porter, present volume). The following information comes from Table 11.2 as well as from a previous series of studies (Colwell, Hiscock-Anisman, et al., 2006; Hines et al., 2010). More than 75% of respondents have a wrong understanding of the relationship between the amount of detail in a statement and the credibility of that statement. Only one participant across all samples correctly mentioned that adding information as the interview progressed was indicative of credibility. In contrast to these perceptions, the most powerful predictor of honest responding in our research, given appropriate interviewing, is the addition of new details following an initial description. Similarly, deceptive statements

Table 11.2 Strategies of impression management for honest and deceptive participants ($N=320$)

Strategy to appear credible	Honest % ($n=175$)	Deceptive % ($n=145$)	t	p
Details not mentioned	38	49	0.26	0.79
Details mentioned, direction not specified[a]	15	15	0.03	0.98
Complete detail	32	26	0.91	0.36
Minimal detail	9	10	−0.22	0.82
Calm and confident	28	35	−1.20	0.24
Coherent and consistent	8	41	−1.60	0.01
Thoughts and emotions[b]	17	9	1.80	0.08
Eye contact	7	17	−2.30	0.02
Accuracy of details provided	11	52	1.20	0.01
Honest about non-event details	11	14	0.18	0.50
Tone of voice	4	3	0.58	0.78
Convincing or plausible	2	0	1.60	0.12
Believe it yourself	4	3	0.64	0.52
Spontaneous (credible)	1	0	1.10	0.27
Not Spontaneous	3	3	−0.11	0.91
Other	4	4	−0.05	0.96

[a] These participants mentioned that statements should have detail but they did not say whether a high or a low degree of detail gave the appearance of credibility
[b] These participants indicated that one should describe either what one was thinking or what one was feeling during the target event in order to appear credible

become obvious because they are shorter and more carefully phrased. This means that, to the extent that participants have insight into their own behavior, they are focusing their efforts in the wrong areas. This mismatch between perceived and genuine cues, and the resulting misplaced effort, minimizes the benefits of planning and motivation. In fact, it is likely that planning and motivation have a paradoxical effect, leading to increased ability to detect deception through appropriate interviewing and assessment. A similar situation has long been observed in the symptom validity approach to the assessment of malingering (Colwell & Sjerven, 2005; Hiscock & Hiscock, 1989).[1]

---

[1] In the symptom-validity approach to malingering, respondents who are motivated often perform worse-than-chance on two-alternative, forced-choice tests.

Impression Management and Credibility Assessment: Objective Clues

The Lie Script

One primary goal of impression management during an investigative interview is to provide a story that does not include any information that could lead to detection (for deceivers) and to provide a narrative that does not have any major contradictions (for deceivers and honest respondents, alike). Most honest respondents tend to believe that their honesty is transparent, whereas most deceptive respondents believe that they must plan ahead and prepare in order to appear honest (Hartwig & Doering, 2009). This preparation is often the development of a fictitious account of the target event. This account, rather than a memory for a real event, is used to provide information to investigators. In this way, a deceiver can avoid sensitive information, can give the appearance of cooperation, and can provide a story that is coherent and well phrased. This strategy was originally termed *superficial encoding* (Porter & Yuille, 1995), and it is currently referred to in the literature as the use of a *lie script* (Colwell, Hiscock-Anisman, et al., 2006). Regardless of the term used to describe it, this strategy has two components: the creation and rehearsal of a lie script to replace the target memory, and the inhibition of the target memory during the interview (note: even when people are lying to claim that they have done things they did not, they have a memory for what they really did during that time period, and they must inhibit this memory and replace it with their lie script). In regard to the first component, some research has demonstrated that deceptive responses during an investigative interview are often shorter, are more carefully phrased, and contain less unique detail than honest responses (Colwell et al., 2007; Suckle-Nelson et al., 2010). In regard to the second component, some brain-imaging studies suggest that there is a significant amount of activity in inhibitory cortical centers during the act of deception, suggesting that many deceivers expend mental effort to inhibit their memory for the target event (Karim et al., 2010). This need to inhibit the memory for the original event for successful deception has important implications for investigative interviewing and is discussed at length in that section below.

The use of a lie script to avoid detection (e.g., due to accidental disclosure of sensitive information or to contradictions in one's story) seems to develop between childhood and adolescence. These were among the most common mistakes that children made when attempting deception in previous research. Williams et al. (2012) found that between 20% and 30% of children, between the ages of 8 and 12, who were lying about taking a wallet during a scavenger hunt either accidentally disclosed sensitive information or gave a story with major contradictions. These children typically either mentioned the wallet when they should not have, or changed their story midway through the interview. Such deceptions are obvious. As adults, we have learned this lesson well and, therefore, focus a great deal of our attention on avoiding the release of sensitive information or on not contradicting ourselves (Suckle-Nelson et al., 2010). This often is taken so far that many deceivers believe that making changes to their story or admitting that they could be mistaken is actually indicative of deception. Again, the use of a short script helps the deceiver with his or her task. Also, providing essentially the same script to each question asked is common (Colwell, Hiscock-Anisman, et al., 2006; Hines et al., 2010).

There is one significant result of using a lie script that has implications for investigative interviewing and credibility assessment. The act of rehearsing a script and then answering questions based upon that script (rather than upon the original memory) results in a loss or change of information in the original memory. In other words, the act of deception may change one's memory for an event (Colwell, Hiscock-Anisman, Corbett, et al., 2011). People who are lying to say that they did something that they did not actually do may come to believe that they did this thing, while those lying to omit an action that they actually committed may come to believe that they did not do this thing. The implications of this may be profound. The act of holding suspects for long-term interrogation may not only be unethical but also fruitless. Rehearsing a deception appears to be akin to imagination inflation (Loftus & Palmer, 1974) and may preclude later access to accurate information. Therefore, a person who spends a period of time carefully rehearsing a lie to fool interrogators may never be able to remember accurately the true information that is sought by those interrogators. Not only will many suspects lie to escape captivity, but those who may eventually desire to tell the truth are likely unable to provide accurate information after their period of internment. Additionally, holding innocent people for long periods of time, especially in conditions that promote anxiety, could lead to continued rehearsal. This continued rehearsal of their honest statements could make these honest statements become more rigid and cause them to appear more like deceptive statements. Long-term confinement can mask differences between honesty and deception and may render a person relatively useless as a potential source of information.

Appearing Calm and Cooperative

The secondary goal of impression management, on behalf of deceivers, is arguably to attempt to appear calm and cooperative. A well-spoken, confident response is considered to be a clue to honesty (Colwell, Hiscock-Anisman, et al., 2006; Hines et al., 2010). To the untrained observer, a short and carefully phrased script facilitates this sort of responding. Having a script that excludes any information that could lead to detection allows the deceptive respondent to be less anxious than he or she would be if forced to create the lie during the interview. In addition, a clear and well-organized response conveys the impression of credibility and certainty. The deceptive respondent is then able to appear confident. In previous research, this confidence has been described in two related manners – one deals with lack of anxiety, as in, "calm and confident," and the other deals with a metacognitive assessment, as in, "certain about the correctness of their statement." It is arguably vital to convey both variations of confidence if one is to appear credible according to the average person (as well as to law enforcement; Colwell, Miller, Miller, & Lyons, 2006).

Careful phrasing can be measured by the type-token ratio (TTR), which is a ratio of the unique words in a statement to the total number of words in a statement. For example, the sentence "One small step for man, one giant leap for mankind," has a TTR of 0.8. There are eight unique words in the statement and ten total words. As people speak more carefully, they tend to speak with a wider range of their vocabulary in order to look intelligent and helpful, and they tend to provide fewer total words to avoid the possibility of making a mistake. Both of these tendencies cause the TTR of deceptive respondents to be higher than the TTR of honest respondents during an investigative interview (Colwell et al., 2002). Honest statements tend to be long and not-so-careful, whereas deceptive statements tend to be short and careful. Along the same lines, deceivers are less likely to admit that they could have been mistaken than are honest respondents. This finding is also consistent with the motivational criteria from CBCA, most specifically, "admitting lack of memory" (Griesel et al., present volume; Zaparniuk et al., 1995). Unfortunately, like any other cue, willingness to admit error is not diagnostic by itself. Approximately one sixth of deceivers will admit they could have been mistaken, whereas approximately one third of honest respondents will admit to such potential error (Colwell et al., 2008). The application of this criterion parallels the larger state of affairs in investigative interviewing and credibility assessment. No single criterion is indicative of honesty or deception, and there must always be a careful consideration given to (1) other aspects of a statement, and (2) all other available case data. A significant amount of hardship and mistaken decision making could have been avoided if investigators had always realized that a single criterion (e.g., looking up and to the right or to the left) is not indicative of honesty or deception (Scheck, Neufeld, & Dwyer, 2001).

Summary

In sum, research has shown that most deceptive statements tend to be shorter, to be less detailed, to be more carefully phrased, to contain more contradictions or sensitive disclosures (especially in children), and to be less likely to contain admissions of possible mistakes. Research targeting the subjective perceptions of those engaged in an investigative interview has shown that honest respondents believe that their honesty should be transparent; therefore, they do not expend as much effort in managing their appearance. In contrast, deceivers work to manage their appearance by creating and rehearsing a short script to avoid incrimination and to appear cooperative. While responding, deceivers attempt to avoid sensitive disclosures, contradictions, or anything that would create questions regarding their credibility, such as changing their story, admitting mistakes, or appearing anxious. Taken together, this indicates that the act of deception is a more difficult and planned act than that of honest responding. Honest respondents are free to access their memory for the original event, whereas deceivers must constantly control information and attempt to stick to their rehearsed lie script. Therefore, honest respondents have fewer demands placed upon them and are able to benefit from the positive-feedback nature of recall, whereas deceivers are under significant cognitive demands and are not able to benefit from the positive-feedback nature of recall.

It is now possible to provide an integrated approach to content criteria and credibility. Often, honest statements during an investigative interview are more detailed, and they tend to have more words and more unique details added after the first telling of the story. The fact that there is more overall detail relates in part to vividness, and the fact that more words and more unique details are added after the free recall relates in part to spontaneity (Colwell et al., 2007). This is because honest recall is an automatic process that forms a positive-feedback mechanism. The act of remembering leads to the recall of new information, which can then be used as recall cues for even more information. The result is more and more information from honest respondents as an interview progresses. In contrast, deceptive statements are often less detailed, and they have significantly fewer words and details added after their initial free recall. This is because most deceivers believe that adding new words and details after free recall causes suspicion in interviewers (Colwell, Hiscock-Anisman, et al., 2006; Hines et al., 2010). Another reason that fewer new words and details are added by deceivers after an initial free recall is that deceivers are focusing their effort on providing careful phrasing and on tracking their own statements, and there is too much cognitive demand required to track their previous statements and to sufficiently elaborate a statement they are currently making (Colwell et al., 2002, 2007). They are working to avoid disclosing sensitive information, making contradictions, or any other behaviors that could lead to a loss of credibility (e.g., lack of eye contact, admission of possible mistakes). The result is often less overall detail and a dearth of additional detail from deceivers throughout the interview.

The aforementioned sometimes explains the existence of systematic differences between honest and deceptive responding regarding a witnessed or experienced event. However, all of these differences are predicated upon appropriate interviewing, and no system of credibility assessment will ever exist without careful consideration to interviewing. A good interviewer must obtain unbiased information from honest respondents while exploiting the differences between honest and deceptive responding to facilitate the detection of deception. In other words, interviews are needed that facilitate honest recall while hindering and highlighting attempts to control information and to impression manage.

Investigative Interviewing

The goals of an investigative interview are (1) to maximize the amount of information obtained, (2) to minimize contamination of memory, (3) to generate statements that can be used in credibility assessment and (4) to maintain the integrity of the investigative process (Yuille, Hunter, Joffe, & Zaparniuk, 1993). These goals are listed in order of importance. This means that the primary consideration during an investigation is to interview in a manner that obtains maximal accurate information from an honest respondent. Only after a framework has been developed that does this can an investigator or researcher attempt to implement strategies to discriminate honesty from deception. Detecting deception is pointless unless one first has created a mechanism to support honesty. To reiterate, an investigative interview is primarily a mechanism to gather information. Judging the veracity of that information is only meaningful to the extent that the information has been obtained in a manner that protected the memory of honest respondents.

There are a number of investigative interviews in existence. The Step-Wise Interview (SI; Zaparniuk et al., 1995; Colwell et al., 2002), for example, was created by Yuille for systematic assessment of statements and protection of memory. There is some research evidence to indicate that the SI does not work as well as the Cognitive Interview (CI; Fisher et al., 1989) and the Reality Interview (RI; Colwell et al., 2002) in the detection of deception, but is a very good assessment tool for obtaining statements where accuracy of information is paramount. Further research is necessary to determine the relative ability of the SI, CI, and RI in detecting deception. The SI is an excellent interviewing strategy when accuracy of information is paramount and detection of deception is not the goal (Colwell et al., 2002). No interview is appropriate for all situations. The SI is best for those situations where accuracy of information obtained is the most important consideration. The CI is best for those situations where maximizing the amount of information obtained is the most important consideration. Finally, the RI is best for those situations in which detecting deception is the most important consideration. The SI and the CI can be used to detect deception, but this is not their primary reason for existing. Similarly, the RI elicits accurate information from honest respondents, but the reason this interview exists is to facilitate the detection of deception. It is up to the interviewer to choose the most appropriate interview for each situation (Colwell et al., 2002).

The CI (Fisher et al., 1989; Memon, Meissner, et al., 2010; Memon, Zaragoza, Clifford & Kidd, 2010) is the oldest of the three and provided the basis for the RI (Colwell et al., 2002).[2] An early and important step of any investigative interview is the development of rapport (Walsh & Bull, present volume; Yarbrough et al., present volume; Yuille et al., 1993). Without rapport, it will not be possible to obtain complete and accurate information from an honest witness, thereby making the investigation less fruitful overall and hindering any attempts to detect deception (Colwell et al., 2002, 2007, 2008; Vallano & Compo, 2011).

The actual investigation portion of the interviewing begins with the elicitation of a free narrative. This allows for an honest person to provide information with as little potential for contamination as possible, and it has some valuable consequences for deceivers which are explained later. Following the free narrative, an interviewer can use mnemonics to enhance the respondent's recall for the event (Table 11.3).

---

[2] The Reality Interview was called the Inferential Interview in its original article (Colwell et al., 2002). However, many readers thought that *inferential* meant *untrained*, in that the group *inferred* their own style of interviewing. This was not correct, and the name was changed to avoid later confusion.

Table 11.3 Script for Reality Interview as used with students suspected of stealing an exam key

Recall task	Phrase from recall task	Interview portion for scoring[a]
Baseline and rapport	Last meal	Not scored
	First day of semester	
Free recall	Please describe, in as much detail as possible, everything that happened in Room 212	Free recall
Mental reinstatement of context	Think about and include all sights, sounds, smells, emotions, thoughts, or anything else from the time of the event	Mnemonics
Forced-choice Block 1	If a police officer had been present, would he have noticed something wrong?	Not scored
	Was a crime committed?	
	Did anyone speak with an accent?	
Recall from other perspective	If someone else had been in the room, what would they have seen?	Mnemonics
Forced-choice Block 2	Did anyone intend to harm anyone else?	Not scored
	Was this an act of violence?	
	Were there any weapons in the event?	
Reverse order recall	Beginning with the last, and ending with the first, please describe the entire event in reverse order	Mnemonics
Forced-choice Block 3	Did you notice anything unusual about the room?	Question C scored Yes or No
	Would anyone think that you did something you weren't supposed to while in the room?	
	Do you think that you could have been mistaken about anything you have said so far?	
Recall entire event	Please describe, in as much detail as possible, everything that happened in Room 212	Mnemonics

[a]The segment of the interview will later be used to guide scoring. Information from the open-ended questions is divided into that information obtained during Free Recall and information obtained during the Mnemonics. This allows for isolation of the recall enhancement effects of the Mnemonics

This approach is a direct form of the CI, and the field is grateful to the seminal research done by Fisher, Geiselman, and, later, Memon on this topic. Following the use of mnemonics, the respondent is asked to provide his or her description one last time. This last task, "Tell me everything again, and provide everything you remember even if you think it is irrelevant," can be considered a mnemonic in its own right. The basic structure of the RI is shown in Table 11.3. This table shows the script for the RI and how dependent variables are broken down as being elicited either by the free recall or by the mnemonics.

Interpersonal Dynamics and Recall Enhancement

As indicated above, an important early step of an investigative interview is the development of rapport. Sometimes, rapport requires the demonstration of empathy. It is important to mention that it is ethically questionable to demonstrate empathy in many forensic settings (Melton, Petrila, Poytherss, & Slobogin, 2007). Empathy is a powerful tool that should be used only when one is acting in a manner that is beneficial to the person being assessed. This means that empathy is acceptable during an investigative interview, where the goal is to gain information to ascertain what happened. Empathy is not acceptable during an interrogation, where the goal is to get a person to confess to a crime (Buckley, 2006). This is standard training for those in forensic psychology (Melton et al., 2007), but it is not something that appears to be widely known among investigators or psychologists who train investigators (Inbau, Reid, Buckley, & Jayne, 2004). In fact, participation in interrogation is not ethical for psychologists. Psychologists are to "do no harm" and are not to engage in activities that diminish the overall perception of psychology as a field. Psychologists who study investigative interviewing must walk a fine line and would do well to remember the drastic difference between interrogation and investigation. The safest approach is to develop rapport without the use of empathy. After all, empathy is necessary in therapy, but it is not necessary for an investigation.

The strength of rapport between the interviewer and the respondent is a primary factor in determining the amount and quality of information obtained during an investigative interview (Vallano & Compo, 2011). Most respondents need to be comfortable and to feel safe with the interviewer. Importantly, there must be a *transfer of control* to the respondent. This means that the respondents are taught that, in some respects, they are to lead the interview and to proceed at their own pace. They are instructed to take as much time as necessary to prepare a response, and they are informed that the interview process is meant to facilitate their responding. It is not meant to be a question-and-answer session controlled by the interviewer. To do this properly, it is good practice to have the respondent describe a couple of neutral events prior to discussion of the target event. In this way, the interviewer can teach the respondent about the process of the interview and what his or her responsibilities are. These descriptions also provide an opportunity to increase rapport. They have been considered as baselines for verbal behavior, but this is questionable as the sample of behavior obtained from a neutral event might be different from a sample of behavior obtained regarding the target event in an investigation (Colwell et al., 2007).[3] If done properly, the respondent will feel as comfortable as possible and will be aware that it is his or her responsibility to lead the interview (Colwell et al., 2002; Memon, Meissner, et al., 2010). This provides honest respondents with an environment that maximizes the utility of the mnemon-

---

[3] This chapter is concerned with verbal behavior, and this statement regarding difficulties in obtaining baselines during recall of innocuous events only applies to verbal behavior, and not to nonverbal behavior.

ics, and it creates for deceptive respondents an environment that highlights their attempts at control of information and impression management (Colwell et al., 2008; Suckle-Nelson et al., 2010).

Mnemonics and Recall Enhancement

A mnemonic is a memory aid. There are two general types of mnemonics: those that assist with encoding and those that assist with recall. Most witnesses and victims do not have advanced warning that they are about to experience something that will need to be remembered. Therefore, the mnemonics that aid in encoding are of minimal use to investigative interviewers. However, mnemonics that assist with recall are a tremendous asset to the investigative interviewer. The mnemonics used to enhance recall are based upon the principles of encoding specificity and spreading activation. Encoding specificity is the principle that any stimulus that was encoded at the time of a target event can serve as a retrieval cue for the memory of the target event (Fisher et al., 1989). Spreading activation is the notion that recalling parts of a target memory enhance one's ability to recall the remainder of that memory. Activation of one area of a memory network can facilitate the activation of other areas of that network. Practically, this means that the act of recall can become a positive-feedback system (Colwell et al., 2007).

The mnemonics used in the interview techniques discussed in this chapter are taken directly from early CI research. The first mnemonic to be used with the CI is *mental reinstatement of context* (Colwell et al., 2002; Fisher et al., 1989). This is an image-based technique in which the interviewer asks the respondent to think back to the time of the original event. The respondent is instructed to think of details from each sensory modality, as well as to describe his or her thoughts and feelings. He or she is also told to report everything even if he or she does not think it is important (another mnemonic). This is critical to the outcome of an interview. The mental reinstatement of context mnemonic can protect a respondent against subsequent contamination of memory (e.g., the "Geiselman effect"; Verkampt & Ginet, 2010). This could serve to partially inoculate against later misinformation and protects the memory trace (Memon, Zaragoza, et al., 2010). The second specific mnemonic is *recall from another perspective*. This attempts to get beyond the filtering effects of a respondent's schema for the target event. The respondent is asked, for example, to imagine if someone else had been in the room or to describe the event as someone else would have seen it. The third specific mnemonic is *reverse-order recall*. This is quite difficult for respondents but is very useful, especially for the detection of deception (Colwell et al., 2007, 2008, 2012; Vrij et al., 2006). Respondents are literally asked to describe the entire event but to begin with the end and end with the beginning. Finally, respondents are asked to retell the entire event, one last time.

In the context of an investigative interview, a mnemonic is a memory enhancement strategy used at the time of recall (Fisher et al., 1989). There is an interaction between mnemonics and honesty vs. deception that is vital to interviewing that facilitates the detection of deception. Honest respondents are free to think about and completely report the target memory. Deceptive respondents are not, and instead must focus on their lie script. Because of this, honest respondents benefit from mnemonics to a higher degree than deceptive respondents (Colwell et al., 2002, 2007, 2008). Mnemonics, in general, lead to recall enhancement, but there is a difference in the recall enhancement for honest respondents compared to deceptive respondents. The variables that help honest people remember actually make the act of reporting and impression management more difficult for deceptive respondents. Mnemonics help honest respondents and hinder deceptive respondents; stated another way, mnemonics lead to DRE (Colwell et al., 2012).

Differential Recall Enhancement

The central lesson of the authors' last 16 years of research is: mnemonics and forced-choice questions enhance the reporting of honest respondents, allowing them to provide longer, more detailed, and spontaneously structured statements. These same mnemonics and forced-choice questions make responding more difficult for deceptive respondents, causing them to provide shorter, less detailed, and less spontaneously structured statements. There are two reasons for this DRE. First, a properly administered interview helps honest respondents to remember and to provide statements with a significant amount of additional words and details. Second, the same interview causes deceptive respondents to work harder and to rely more on their short, carefully phrased lie scripts (Ansarra et al., 2011; Colwell et al., 2002, 2007; Suckle-Nelson et al., 2010). Concretely, this DRE is manifested as the presentation of new information as a result of the mnemonics. Accordingly, the information provided during an investigative interview can essentially be divided into two phases – information provided prior to the use of mnemonics and additional information provided as a result of the mnemonics. In the CI and RI, this division is described as Free Recall (i.e., information presented before the mnemonics) and Mnemonics (i.e., additional information provided as a result of the mnemonics). Therefore, DRE can be highlighted by assessing the information provided during Free Recall vs. the information provided during the Mnemonics (Colwell et al., 2008, 2012).

DRE depends on a proper interview structure, appropriate mnemonics, and the operationalization of criteria suggestive of honesty or deception in a manner that takes advantage of this structure and content. Specifically, to take advantage of DRE, one must (1) obtain an original free narrative, (2) proceed with mnemonics and associated tasks, and finally, (3) perform a content analysis of the information derived with dependent variables divided across the free recall and mnemonics sections of the interview (see "Interview Portion for Scoring" column in Table 11.3). An effective exercise to demonstrate the DRE effect is to analyze the data obtained from an investigative interview in two ways. First, consider all of the information provided as a whole; that is, simply examine the content criteria of interest and calculate an average

Table 11.4 Accuracy of decisions assessing whole statement versus assessing free recall and mnemonics separately: Improvement from considering the DRE effect of the interview

	Accuracy of decisions (%)		
Citation	Whole statement	Free recall vs. mnemonics	Improvement to highlight DRE
Colwell et al. (2002)			
Transcribed verbal accounts from CI and RI	68.6	92.4	23.8
Colwell et al. (2007) Experiment 1			
Hand-written statements from RI	67.5	81.0	13.5
Colwell et al. (2007) Experiment 2			
Transcribed verbal accounts from RI	67.5	95.0	27.5
Colwell et al. (2008)			
Transcribed verbal accounts from RI	63.7	86.8	23.1
Suckle-Nelson et al. (2010)			
Transcribed verbal accounts from RI, males	76.5	88.3	11.8
Transcribed verbal accounts from RI, females	79.5	89.8	10.3
Average			18.3

value for the entire description. Second, take the same description, but examine the information obtained as a function of when it was first provided. Calculate a value for each content criterion based upon the free recall portion of the interview, and calculate a second value for each content criterion based upon the mnemonics portion of the interview. This gives the ability to assess the information provided at free recall, and then assess any new information that was provided as a result of the mnemonics. This second approach highlights the differential effects of the mnemonics for honest and deceptive respondents (i.e., highlights DRE). As seen in Table 11.4, based on our previous research, the second approach yielded an increase in the ability of the statement content criteria to discriminate between honest and deceptive statements.

Comparing the Cognitive Interview to Reality Interview

The CI and the RI are two interviews that are formulated to have both the structure and the content necessary for DRE. The two-alternative, forced-choice questions of the RI are included to facilitate the detection of deception. The first block of these forced-choice questions begins after the participant has completed the mental reinstatement of context mnemonic. This placement is crucial. The mental reinstatement of context mnemonic helps inoculate the participant's memory against contamination (Memon, Meissner, et al., 2010; Memon, Zaragoza, et al., 2010), and the order of the RI is designed to take advantage of this protective effect (Colwell et al., 2002, 2008). Forced-choice questions should *not* be used prior to the elicitation of two free narratives: the first from a general, open-ended free recall and the second from the mental reinstatement of context mnemonic. They should require the respondent to think deeply about the event (e.g., visuospatial questions are best), and they should be about factors that the respondent is not likely to have practiced as part of his or her lie script. Inferences (e.g., Was the gun closer to the door or to the window? Did anyone intend to harm anyone else?) require more cognitive effort than simple recall (Colwell et al., 2002), thereby maximizing differences between honest and deceptive respondents.

A major challenge with forced-choice questions is to avoid leading the respondent. There are two general strategies to do this. In those cases where a significant amount of information is not available at the time of the interview (which is likely the case in most preliminary investigative interviews), questions should require very general inferences. Examples of these are, "Was there a crime committed," or, "Did anyone speak with an accent." When information is available regarding the target event prior to the interview, the forced-choice questions can be global inferences, or they can be carefully constructed so that one of the choices is absolutely correct.

The basic task of certain types of deception is to inhibit memory for the original event while providing information from a lie script in a manner that avoids contradictions and appears confident. The forced-choice inferences interfere with this inhibition of the original memory in two ways: (1) they provide information from the target event as one of the response choices whenever possible and (2) they force respondents at least to think outside their script and, at best, to think back to the target event. The first is akin to a Stroop Task, where the automatic tendency to process information from the target event will compete with the effortful attempt to suppress that information. The second is simply another form of an unanticipated question.

There will be times when the respondent is deceptive but has no memory for the target event. In these cases, forced-choice questions increase the cognitive demand placed upon respondents because they must choose carefully while attempting to determine what the interviewer does and does not know about the event. In instances in which a significant amount of information about the target event is known, the forced-choice questions can provide an additional cue to credibility, in a manner akin to symptom validity testing. Simply put, people who are being deceptive often perform at or below chance, or at least significantly worse than what should be expected, indicating that they are deliberately missing questions to manipulate the interviewer (e.g., Colwell & Colwell, 2011; Colwell & Sjerven, 2005; Hiscock & Hiscock, 1989; Rogers & Bender, 2003). Recent research also indicates that forced-choice questions can be used to screen a large number of witnesses to focus on those who either are very cooperative or are working hard to hide information (Gavigan et al., 2012).

The authors have compared the RI to the CI in two studies using male and female inmates who witnessed a staged theft. All participants witnessed the theft. Those in the honest group were asked to describe what they had seen and cooperate in the investigation of the thief. Those in the deceptive group were instructed to answer questions in such a way that investigators would not be able to convict the real thief. In the first study, the dependent measures were TTR, response length, and coherence. Results indicated a ceiling effect, with both interviews performing in the mid-90% range in accurately classifying statements as honest or deceptive (93% for RI, and 94% for the CI; Colwell et al., 2002).

In the second study, the open-ended narratives elicited by free recall and each of the mnemonics were assessed, and the dependent measures were the amount, type, and location of details (Hiscock-Anisman et al., 2012). The actual answers to the forced-choice questions were not considered in this study. Therefore, raters coded what appeared to be identical interview formats (note: the forced-choice questions were omitted from the transcripts). The RI led to significant improvement over the CI in predictive accuracy (90% vs. 71%). This means that 90% of RI statements were accurately classified as honest or deceptive, while only 71% of the CI statements were accurately classified as honest or deceptive. The amount of information provided at free recall was the same for both interviews, which was expected. However, during the mnemonic phase of the interview, honest respondents in the RI provided more detail than did honest respondents in the CI. Also, deceptive respondents in the RI provided less detail than did deceptive respondents in the CI. This study demonstrated that RI is better able to generate DRE. The forced-choice questions made deception more difficult and obvious while providing yet another memory cue for honest respondents. The differences between the CI and RI were primarily in the form of the amount of words and details added during the mnemonic section of the interviews. There was not a corresponding difference in how carefully phrased statements became during the mnemonic section as measured by the TTR. This, along with a ceiling effect, appears to be why there was no difference in predictive accuracy of the CI vs. the RI in the original Colwell et al. (2002) study.

Assessment Criteria Indicative of Deception: Combining Differential Recall Enhancement with Content Analysis

The Assessment Criteria Indicative of Deception (ACID; Colwell et al., 2008) system integrates interviewing for DRE with dependent measures that highlight vividness and spontaneity for honest respondents, and highlight careful phrasing and control of information for deceptive respondents (Colwell et al., 2007, 2012). Optimally, the ACID approach uses an RI to elicit the statement; a CI, structured as above, can be used, but this has been shown to be less effective (Hiscock-Anisman et al., 2012). The dependent measures for the ACID system are response length,

TTR, amount of details, coherence,[4] and whether the respondent admitted that he/she could possibly be mistaken. Response length, TTR, and the number of details are tallied for free recall, and then separately for the mnemonics phase of the interview. Response length is simply the total number of words provided in the statement. TTR is scored by computer software, first for the free recall phase and then averaged across responses to the mnemonics phase. Finally, details are tallied as the number of specific descriptors used in the statement. In order for a detail to be counted in the mnemonics phase, it must be unique—that is, it must not have been provided during the free recall phase. Only new details are counted.

As seen in Table 11.5, this system has been used successfully with university students, male and female prison inmates, children, people speaking English and Arabic, and US military personnel who experienced severe anxiety and distress as part of their training. ACID has been used to study the statements of victims, witnesses, and perpetrators. Finally, ACID can also be applied to written transcripts of interviews, instant messenger interactions over the Internet, and audio statements assessed in real time.

Perhaps the best example of the utility of ACID was a study examining statements provided by college students regarding the theft of an exam key (Colwell et al., 2008). University students were required to enter what they believed to be a professor's office and steal or replace what they thought was an exam key. Students were told that the professor who used the office did not know of the study and, if they were caught, the professor would be angry. It was also stated that the police would be called, and the student would be arrested, and would have to wait until either the Department Chair or the Principal Investigator could come and explain things for them (note: this was a deception, but students reported that they believed this part of the experiment during debriefing). After completing the illicit act, participants were assigned to either report honestly (i.e., answer completely and help the investigator) or deceptively (i.e., answer so that they are not found guilty of anything). Participants were also offered $100 for the "two most convincing" statements. The students had approximately one week to practice their statements prior to returning for their interview. The interview followed the RI format provided in Table 11.3. The only answer from the forced-choice questions that was analyzed was whether the participants admitted that they could have been mistaken. The other dependent measures were the number of details provided during free recall (i.e., external-free recall, contextual-free recall, and internal-free recall), the number of new details added during the mnemonics (i.e., external-mnemonics, contextual-mnemonics, and internal-mnemonics), and the total number of words provided during the mnemonic section of the interview. On the basis of these eight variables, 86.8% of statements were accurately classified as honest or deceptive (78.9% of honest and 94.7% of deceptive statements were accurately classified). Honest statements were longer and more detailed during the mnemonics, and more likely to

---

[4] The authors suggest using an expanded version of coherence with children. For children, whether they disclose sensitive information should be scored as a "yes or no." In addition, the number of serious contradictions should be counted.

Table 11.5 Studies using all or part of the ACID system

Citation	Statement type	How decisions were made	Accuracy of decisions
Colwell et al. (2002)	Inmate transcribed statements, staged theft w/ live actors Interviewed with CI and RI	TTR, response length verbal hedges, coherence Discriminant function analysis	91.9%
Colwell et al. (2007), Experiment 1	Student hand-written statements, videotaped theft, videotaped interviewer Interviewed with CI	Amount and distribution of details Discriminant function analysis	81.0%
Colwell et al. (2007), Experiment 2	Inmate transcribed statements, staged theft w/ live actors Interviewed with RI	Amount and distribution of details Discriminant function analysis	95.0%
Colwell et al. (2008)	Student transcribed statements, theft from professor's office Interviewed with RI	Amount and distribution of details, admitting mistakes Discriminant function analysis	86.8%
Colwell et al. (2009)	Transcripts from students and inmates from previous studies	Student rater judgments Pre-ACID training Post-ACID training	57.0% 77.0%
Suckle-Nelson et al. (2010)	Inmate transcribed statements, staged theft w/ live actors Interviewed with RI	TTR, response length, amount and distribution of details Males Females Discriminant function analysis	88.3% 89.8%
Morgan, Hazelett, Colwell (2011)	Military personnel statements in high-stress advanced training Interviewed with CI	TTR, response length, amount and distribution of details Discriminant function analysis	82.0%

(continued)

Table 11.5 (continued)

Citation	Statement type	How decisions were made	Accuracy of decisions
Ansarra et al. (2011)	Student statements re: theft from classroom Combined sample, CI and RI	Amount and distribution of details Discriminant function analysis	80.0%

Montalvo et al. (in press)	Written or audio statements from previous research	Student rater judgments after 3-h ACID training
		  Untrained audio
		  Untrained written
		  Trained audio
		  Trained written
			51.0%
			55.0%
			71.0%
			71.0%

Hiscock-Anisman, Colwell et al. (2012)	Written or audio statements from previous research	Police officer rater judgments after 8-h ACID training
		  Untrained
		  Trained
			56.0%
			90.0%

Colwell, Hiscock-Anisman et al. (2011)	Arabic-speaking community residents who stole from hotel room Interviewed with CI	TTR, response length, amount and distribution of details Discriminant function analysis	83.3%

Colwell, Colwell et al. (2011)	Written transcripts from previous studies	Forensic professional rater judgments after 3-h ACID training
		  Pre-training
		  Post-training
			58.2%
			70.0%

Williams et al. (2012)	Children's honest or deceptive statement re: scavenger hunt Interviewed with RI	Amount and distribution of details, number and location of contradictions / sensitive disclosures, admitting mistakes Discriminant function analysis	87.0%

Hiscock-Anisman, Morrissey et al. (2012)	Inmate-transcribed statements, staged theft w/ live actors	Response length, amount and distribution of details
		  RI
		  CI
		Discriminant function analysis
			90.0%
			71.0%

Note: In all of the above-mentioned training studies, participants were trained to locate and track differences between honest and deceptive statements previously obtained. This was a demonstration of how people can be trained to perform credibility assessment and detecting deception within the ACID framework. Learning to interview, which is the most important part of ACID, requires a 2–4-day training session.

contain an admission of a potential mistake, compared to deceptive statements. Consistent with DRE, the most powerful predictors were obtained during the mnemonic segment of the interview. This study demonstrated the utility of ACID with a student sample engaged in what was believed to be an illicit act. Deceivers were able to either omit certain information or to otherwise modify an existing memory during the investigative interview. This is arguably the most common type of deception that is encountered in real investigations and has, therefore, been the most common type of situation studied in ACID research (Colwell et al., 2002, 2008; Colwell, Hiscock-Anisman, et al., 2006; Suckle-Nelson et al., 2010). It is, after all, considerably simpler to tell a partial truth than it is to wholly fabricate.

Another important scenario facing investigators is a deceptive respondent who is wholly or largely fabricating; that is, describing an event they have not actually witnessed or performed. In one such study, US military personnel were asked to either respond honestly or deceptively about undergoing torture and interrogation as part of their training (Morgan, Hazlett, & Colwell, 2011). Honest respondents had undergone torture and interrogation as part of their training, whereas deceptive respondents were military personnel who were qualified for this same training, but who had not been through the process. Rather, deceptive respondents were provided with a description taken from the Internet that had been posted by someone who went through the training, and were asked to respond as if they had been through the same. In this study, a CI was used to elicit statements, which were analyzed on the basis of the TTRs, response length, and the amount of detail at free recall and the amount of new detail added during the mnemonics. This allowed for an 82% rate of accurately classifying statements as honest or deceptive. Honest statements had lower TTRs, longer responses, and more detail. Again, the largest effects were seen during the mnemonic section of the interview.

Moderators of Assessment Criteria Indicative of Deception

Gender

The highest predictive accuracies in ACID research to date have occurred when the sample is either all male or all female (or split by gender) and when statistical software makes the predictions using a discriminant function analysis. These differences due to gender were verified in a recent study by Suckle-Nelson et al. (2010). This study demonstrated that women who responded honestly were able to provide more information than were men who responded honestly. Also, women who responded deceptively were more aware of the need to keep their statement short and careful than were men who responded deceptively. Importantly, men who responded honestly were more likely to provide an incoherent story than were women who responded deceptively. Research has shown that women in the US tend to have improved attention, memory, interpersonal, and verbal ability compared to men (Crawford, 1995). Those differences are likely the partial cause of these observations.

Language

Initial research using ACID has shown that the technique demonstrates significant success with English speakers. All and parts of the system have also been used to discriminate honest from deceptive statements from Arabic speakers. In these studies, a sample of Arabic speakers was questioned through an interpreter, and the interpreter's English translation of the Arabic speaker's responses was coded (Colwell, Hiscock-Anisman, Hazlett, & Morgan, 2011). As seen in Table 11.5, ACID was able to discriminate honest from deceptive responding at an 83.3% level of accuracy. It is important to note that this study employed a CI rather than an RI because the CI is more user-friendly. Further research should employ the RI to generate a more accurate estimate of the ability of ACID through an interpreter.

The authors attempted to use ACID with Chinese speakers, using pictograms rather than verbal statements to score the dependent variables. This study was promising in that the strategies of impression management described by Chinese respondents did not differ in many ways from the strategies of impression management listed in Table 11.2 (Hsieh et al., 2012). However, the stimulus chosen for the event was faulty, and the use of pictograms may have also been inappropriate. The stimulus for this research was faulty because Chinese and US students were each asked to either respond honestly about a time someone with authority mistreated them, or to lie and make a false-allegation that someone with authority had mistreated them. All the US students in the honest group had experiences where a professor, teacher, parent, or coach had mistreated them, and they were willing to disclose. Similarly, the US students did not have any difficulties making false allegations. However, the authors learned from communication with the Chinese scholars that Chinese people are generally taught that any incident where it appears an authority figure is mistreating someone represents a misperception, and a chance for personal growth on behalf of the person who thought he or she was mistreated. In this study, the authors asked the participants to respond honestly about a situation that, in their culture, does not exist. Additionally, ACID variables were created to be scored on written words. However, because the strategies of impression management and deception that were described by the Chinese participants were the same as those described by the US participants, it is likely that ACID will work with the Chinese statements. Future research should give careful attention to the event chosen (e.g., one that does not violate cultural assumptions of the participants) and also score the ACID content criteria using audio rather than written statements.

It is important to note that ACID, or part of ACID, has been used in the assessment of people whose first language was Spanish but who were speaking English (Colwell et al., 2002, 2007; Suckle-Nelson et al., 2010), that is, because these samples were drawn from Texas prisons and approximately 10% of participants spoke Spanish before learning to speak English (Colwell, 1997). Yet, there was no difference in the ability to detect deception in any of these studies as a function of ethnicity. Also, ACID research has included English speakers from across the US, Canada, and Scotland, Arabic speakers from Morocco, and Chinese speakers from

China. The technique worked well with all of these samples except for the flawed Chinese study. Even in that study, the strategies described by participants regarding their attempts at impression management and deception were essentially the same as the strategies described by a matched sample of US college students. This convergence of verbal behavior and strategies of deception indicates that ACID may be assessing basic aspects of interpersonal deception regarding an event. After all, DRE is based upon memory and cognition, and these should be common regardless of ethnicity or culture. It may be possible to synthesize a uniform theory of interpersonal deception using these and related findings.

Training and Modality

Perhaps the most impressive aspect of ACID research is the recent findings related to training and application. These include the following: (1) ACID can be trained to a significant degree with a half-day workshop (e.g., participants are able to improve from chance to the 70% range), (2) ACID can be applied to real-time audio recordings rather than just written transcripts and (3) a one-day training workshop is sufficient to improve police officers' ability to detect deception from either transcribed or audio statements from chance levels to almost 90% success (Hiscock-Anisman et al., 2012). To date, almost all statement analysis systems have required many days of training and have been done using verbatim transcripts. These are tedious and make application difficult, at best. However, a series of studies has shown that ACID can be easily trained, with no difference in the ability of those trained to detect deception by reading or by listening to statements. This ability ranges from the mid-70% range following a half-day training to 90% following a full-day training (Colwell & Colwell, 2011; Hiscock-Anisman et al., 2012; Montalvo et al., in press). In fact, ACID can even be applied to the statements obtained via instant messenger in computer-mediated interactions (Werdin et al., 2012).

All of these training studies have one very important feature – the statements provided for making judgments of honest vs. deceptive all come from unique events. The participants (e.g., college students, forensic professionals, police officers) were each presented with a number of honest or deceptive statements. Each statement was the only one given about a particular event. This means that each participant would have two statements from witnesses regarding thefts, two statements from suspects regarding what they did during the time of two different alleged thefts, and two statements from respondents who allege that they were mistreated by their boss or professor. Each statement had to be judged on its own merit as there was no other evidence regarding the event described in each. Importantly, participants were not able to compare the descriptions provided on one statement with the description of the same event provided on another. The findings from training studies have indicated that a full day is better than a half day (Colwell et al., 2009, 2012; Hiscock-Anisman et al., 2012) and that decisions can be made just as well from audio or written statements (Kradas et al., 2012; Montalvo et al., in press).

Applications, Future Research, and Limitations

One area of emerging interest is computer-mediated communication (see Hancock & Woodworth, present volume). This area has been of interest to the authors since the beginning of their research. Colwell's (1997) research, for example, used software to score TTR and response length. This led to a natural grouping among the ACID dependent measures – TTR and response length are scored by computer (and admitting potential mistakes could easily be scored by computer), whereas the amount of detail presented at free recall and the amount of new detail presented during the mnemonics is scored by trained raters. There is a natural tendency in automated applications to emphasize TTR and response length, and there is a natural tendency in interpersonal interactions to just use the amount and type of details. Future research should be done to compare the validity of each of these simplified approaches. There is some reason to believe that the two may work as well as one another (Morgan et al., 2011), although some loss is likely in predictive accuracy from using less content criteria (Suckle-Nelson et al., 2010). This loss of accuracy may be outweighed by the ability to listen to a real-time audio of an interview and make a decision regarding honesty vs. deception in the 88–90% range (Hiscock-Anisman et al., 2012).

One of the most challenging areas for investigative interviewing and statement analysis is communication via instant messenger. This challenge also allows for potential insight into the component processes of interpersonal deception. ACID has been based upon the findings that deceptive respondents work harder than honest respondents due to the need to (1) track information and avoid releasing sensitive details or making contradictions and (2) appear calm and confident in the interpersonal setting. Instant messenger interactions provide the chance to review and edit prior to sending, and allow for one to see the history of the interaction. Similarly, there is no face-to-face interaction, so there is less behavior to control (see Hancock & Woodworth, present volume). Werdin et al. (2012) studied instant messenger interactions obtained from men or women who were trying either to tell the truth about their gender or lie about their gender. Honest respondents described the last time they did something with their same-sex best friend, while deceptive respondents were required to fabricate an interaction as if they were the other gender and were spending time with their best friend of that same gender. These participants went through the standard ACID technique. It was possible to accurately classify 30 of 37 statements as honest or deceptive. Importantly, honest statements were longer and more detailed at free recall, but they were not significantly longer or more detailed during the mnemonics. The differences were all in the expected direction, but they were not significant. Nevertheless, these findings could give some insight into the process of deception. The authors are currently trying to replicate this study, and are also studying what will happen if mirrors and cameras are placed in front of the respondents. If the expected differences return as a result of re-introducing the video information, it will underscore the amount of effort expended by deceivers in trying to appear calm and confident. Similarly, another variation will be investigated where respondents are unable to see their response history and so will have to track information with no additional cues. This manipulation will provide insight into the amount of effort expended in working memory during deception.

The principle of DRE, in general, and the ACID system, in particular, can apply to any situation where an honest respondent should have formed an episodic memory. This means that it can be applied to eliciting and assessing information about what happened during a certain period of time. An example of an area that could see future applications is the assessment of Post Traumatic Stress Disorder (e.g., regarding allegations of abuse). In contrast, this approach will not work when questioning people about their attitudes. It is also not likely to work when questioning about future plans (unless you can have a person describe what he or she has done to prepare for his or her future behavior). Similarly, these techniques are not likely to assist in detecting deception about what a person may be hiding in his or her clothing. Finally, this approach is not likely to work when the respondent actually believes what he or she is saying. The latter is an interesting empirical issue, and future researchers would do well to consider whether this type of assessment ceases to assist in detecting deception when the deceiver comes to believe his or her deception is true. Related to this, DRE and ACID are not likely to work when people are mistaken. This system is not designed to detect memory errors, only deliberate deception.

The most important area to study at this point is real-world application. There have been a number of lab-based studies, but no, "real world," evidence to date. This type of research is expensive and difficult because it requires cooperation with an investigative agency. Moreover, it requires that investigators are willing to seriously apply these techniques in their own work, rather than the techniques they have used for the entirety of their career. Professionals in law enforcement and forensics have been trained in ACID. The response has been positive. However, there is still no available data regarding systematic application by professional investigators.

Summary and Conclusions

There has been a large body of research over the past two decades dealing with the importance of proper interviewing in order to obtain information and detect deception. This has led to a focus on those techniques that help honest respondents remember and provide information, while hindering attempts at deception. This interaction effect between question type and honesty of responding is DRE. Many researchers are working on variations of this, including those studying cognitive load, strategic or tactical interviewing, and ACID. ACID is a systematic approach to interviewing and assessment with content criteria derived from CBCA, RM, and research into interpersonal deception and impression management. ACID derives statements using either the CI or the RI, with the RI being preferred when detecting deception is the primary goal of the interview. ACID has been studied in numerous settings, and it can be trained to students and professionals alike. It has been used with English interpretations of Arabic statements. Also, English speakers from the US, Canada, and Europe, as well as Chinese speakers from China and Arabic speakers from Morocco all approach the process of interpersonal deception in the same way. Therefore, it appears that DRE and ACID are getting at basic aspects of human interactions that apply across cultures. This technique is most capable when dealing with face-to-face interviews and statements involving episodic memory. Other types of deceptions are outside the ability of this technique. Some areas of future research are computer-mediated communication and PTSD. This line of research has potential to inform actual investigative interviews, as well as provide insight into the process of interpersonal deception.

Acknowledgement The authors thank Lori Colwell, Ph.D., for her comments on previous versions of this chapter.

References

Akehurst, L., Koehnken, G., & Hofer, E. (1995). Content credibility of accounts derived from live and video presentations. *Legal and Criminological Psychology, 6*, 65–83.

Ansarra, R., Colwell, K., Hiscock-Anisman, C., Hines, A., Fleck, R., Kondor, S., & Cole, L. (2011). Augmenting ACID with affective details to assess credibility. *European Journal of Psychology Applied to the Legal Context, 3*(2), 1–10.

Blandon-Gitlin, I., Pezdek, K., Lindsay, S., & Hagen, L. (2009). Criteria-based content analysis of true and suggested accounts of events. *Applied Cognitive Psychology, 23*(7), 901–917.

Blandon-Gitlin, I., Pezdek, K., Rogers, M., & Brodie, L. (2005). Detecting deception in children: An experimental study of the effect of event familiarity on CBCA ratings. *Law and Human Behavior, 29*(2), 187–197.

Boychuk, T. D. (1991). *Criteria-based content analysis of children's statements about sexual abuse: A field-based validation study*. Unpublished doctoral dissertation. Arizona State University: Tempe, Arizona.

Buckley, J. P. (2006). The Reid Technique of interviewing and interrogation. In T. Williamson (Ed.), *Investigative interviewing: Rights, research, regulation* (pp. 190–206). Devon, UK: Willan Publishing.

Colwell, K. (1997). *Interviewing techniques and the psycholinguistic assessment of statement credibility*. Unpublished master's thesis. Sam Houston State University: Huntsville, Texas.

Colwell, L. H., & Colwell, K. (2011). Assessing feigned cognitive impairment in defendants hospitalized for competency restoration: Further validation of the TOMI. *Journal of Forensic Psychology Practice, 11*, 293–310.

Colwell, L. H., Colwell, K., Hiscock-Anisman, C., Hartwig, M., Cole, L., Werdin, K., & Youschak, K. (2012). Teaching professionals to detect deception: The efficacy of a brief training workshop. *Journal of Forensic Psychology Practice, 12*, 68–80.

Colwell, K., Hiscock, C. K., & Memon, A. (2002). Interviewing techniques and the assessment of statement credibility. *Applied Cognitive Psychology, 16*, 287–300.

Colwell, K., Hiscock-Anisman, C. K., Corbett, L., Bonilla, Y., Memon, A., & Hauselt, W. J. (2011). Change in suspect's memory as a result of deception. *American Journal of Forensic Psychology, 29*(4), 1–9.

Colwell, K., Hiscock-Anisman, C.K, Hazlett, G., & Morgan, C.A. (2011). *Credibility assessment of suspects speaking Arabic through English interpreters*. Paper presented at the Annual Conference of the American Psychology and Law Society, Miami, Florida.

Colwell, K., Hiscock-Anisman, C., Memon, A., Colwell, L. H., Taylor, L., & Woods, D. (2009). Training in Assessment Criteria Indicative of Deception (ACID) to improve credibility assessment. *Journal of Forensic Psychology Practice, 9*, 199–207.

Colwell, K., Hiscock-Anisman, C., Memon, A., Rachel, A., & Colwell, L. (2007). Vividness and spontaneity of statement detail characteristics as predictors of witness credibility. *American Journal of Forensic Psychology, 25*, 5–30.

Colwell, K., Hiscock-Anisman, C. K., Memon, A., Taylor, L., & Prewett, J. (2008). Assessment Criteria Indicative of Deception (ACID): An integrated system of investigative interviewing and detecting deception. *Journal of Investigative Psychology and Offender Profiling, 4*, 167–180.

Colwell, K., Hiscock-Anisman, C., Memon, A., Woods, D., & Michlik, P. (2006). Strategies of impression management among deceivers and truth-tellers: How liars attempt to convince. *American Journal of Forensic Psychology, 24*(2), 31–38.

Colwell, L. H., Miller, H. A., Miller, R. S., & Lyons, P. M. (2006). US police officers' knowledge regarding behaviours indicative of deception: Implications for eradicating erroneous beliefs through training. *Psychology, Crime, & Law, 12*(5), 489–503.

Colwell, K., & Sjerven, E. R. (2005). The 'Coin-in-Hand' strategy for forensic assessment of malingering. *American Journal of Forensic Psychology, 23*, 83–89.

Crawford, M. (1995). *Talking difference: On gender and language*. Thousand Oaks, CA: Sage Publications, Inc.

Dando, C. J., & Bull, R. (2011). Maximising opportunities to detect verbal deception: Training police to interview tactically. *Journal of Investigative Psychology and Offender Profiling, 8*(2), 189–202.

Esplin, P.W., Boychuk, T.D., & Raskin, D.C. (1988). *A field validity study of criteria-based content analysis of children's statements in sexual abuse cases*. Paper presented at the NATO Advanced Study Institute on Credibility Assessment, Maratea, Italy.

Fisher, R., Geiselman, E., & Amador, M. (1989). Field test of the cognitive interview: Enhancing the recollection of the actual victims and witnesses of crime. *Journal of Applied Psychology, 74*(5), 722–727.

Gavigan, B.J., Fede, J., Richards, E., Hiscock-Anisman, C.K., Pankratz, L., & Colwell, K. (2012). *A forced-choice test to detect witness deception*. Poster presented at the Annual Conference of the American Psychology and Law Society, San Juan, Puerto Rico.

Hartwig, M., & Bond, C. F. (2011). Why do lie-catchers fail? A lens model meta-analysis of human lie judgments. *Psychological Bulletin, 137*(4), 643–659.

Hartwig, M., & Doering, N. (2009). *Strategies of the deception game: A social cognitive theory of the psychology of innocence and guilt*. Paper presented at the annual conference of the American Psychology-Law Society, San Antonio, Texas.

Hartwig, M., Granhag, P., Strömwall, L. A., & Kronkvist, O. (2006). Strategic use of evidence during police interviews: When training to detect deception works. *Law and Human Behavior, 30*(5), 603–619.

Hernández-Fernaud, E., & Alonso-Quecuty, M. (1997). The cognitive interview and lie detection: A new magnifying glass for Sherlock Holmes? *Applied Cognitive Psychology, 11*(1), 55–68.

Hines, A., Colwell, K., Hiscock-Anisman, C., Garrett, E., Ansarra, R., & Montalvo, L. (2010). Impression management strategies of deceivers and honest reporters in an investigative interview. *European Journal of Psychology Applied to the Legal Context, 2*(1), 73–90.

Hiscock, M., & Hiscock, C. K. (1989). Refining the forced-choice method for the detection of malingering. *Journal of Clinical and Experimental Neuropsychology, 11*(6), 967–974.

Hiscock-Anisman, C. K., Colwell, K., Danna, M., Rodriguez, N., Sorcinelli, A., & French, M. N. (2012). *Using ACID to help police detect deception*. Poster presented at the Annual Conference of the American Psychology and Law Society, San Juan, Puerto Rico.

Hiscock-Anisman, C.K., Morrissey, D., Willet, S., Evans, M., Belarde, D., & Colwell, K. (2012). *Comparing the Reality Interview and the Cognitive Interview: Two-alternative, forced-choice questions and differential recall enhancement*. Manuscript in preparation.

Hofer, E., Akehurst, L., & Metzger, G. (1996). *Reality monitoring: A chance for further development of CBCA*? Paper presented at the annual meeting of the European Association of Psychology and Law, Sienna, Italy.

Hsieh, C., Hiscock-Anisman, C.K., Colwell, K., Florence, S., Sorcinelli, A. & French, M.N. (2012). *Strategies of impression management and deception among Chinese and English speakers*. Paper presented at the Annual Conference of the American Psychology and Law Society. San Juan, Puerto Rico.

Inbau, F. E., Reid, J. E., Buckley, J. P., & Jayne, B. C. (2004). *Criminal interrogations and confessions* (4th ed.). Sudbury, MA: Jones & Bartlett Publishers, Inc.

Johnson, M. K., & Raye, C. L. (1981). Reality monitoring. *Psychological Review, 88*, 67–85.

Karim, A., Schneider, M., Lotze, M., Veit, R., Sauseng, P., Braun, C., & Birbaumer, N. (2010). The truth about lying: Inhibition of the anterior prefrontal cortex improves deceptive behavior. *Cerebral Cortex, 20*(1), 205–213.

Koehnken, G., Schimossek, E., Aschermann, E., & Hofer, E. (1995). The cognitive interview and the assessment of the credibility of adults' statements. *Journal of Applied Psychology, 80*(6), 671–684.

Kradas, M., Henry, C., Williams, S., Talwar, V., Marsland, K.W., & Colwell, K. (2012). *Reliability and validity of Assessment Criteria Indicative of Deception (ACID) with audio and written statements*. Manuscript in preparation.

Lamb, M. E., Sternberg, K. J., Esplin, P. W., & Hershkowitz, I. (1997). Criteria-based content analysis: A field validation study. *Child Abuse & Neglect, 21*, 255–264.

Landry, K., & Brigham, J. C. (1992). The effect of training in criteria-based content analysis on the ability to detect deception in adults. *Law and Human Behavior, 16*, 663–675.

Loftus, E. F., & Palmer, J. C. (1974). Reconstruction of automobile destruction: An example of the interaction between language and memory. *Journal of Verbal Learning and Verbal Behavior, 13*(5), 585–589.

Masip, J., Sporer, S. L., Garrido, E., & Herrero, C. (2005). The detection of deception with the reality monitoring approach: A review of the empirical evidence. *Psychology, Crime, & Law, 11*(1), 99–122.

Melton, G. B., Petrila, J., Poythress, N. G., & Slobin, C. (2007). *Psychological evaluations for the courts: A handbook for mental health professionals and lawyers* (3rd ed.). New York, NY: The Guilford Press.

Memon, A., Fraser, J., Colwell, K., Odino, G., & Mastroberadino, S. (2009). Distinguishing truthful from invented accounts using Reality Monitoring criteria. *Legal and Criminological Psychology, 15*(2), 177–194.

Memon, A., Meissner, C. A., & Fraser, J. (2010). The Cognitive Interview: A meta-analytic review and study space analysis of the past 25 years. *Psychology, Public Policy, & Law, 16*(4), 340–372.

Memon, A., Omerod, T.C., & Dando, C.J. (2012). *Truth or lies: Reality monitoring and deception detection*. Manuscript under review.

Memon, A., Zaragoza, M., Clifford, B. R., & Kidd, L. (2010). Inoculation or antidote? The effects of cognitive interview timing on false memory for forcibly fabricated events. *Law and Human Behavior, 34*(2), 105–117.

Montalvo, L., Hallinan, C., Hiscock-Anisman, C.K., Morrissey, D., Bonilla, Y., Colwell, K., & Kradas, M. (in press). Using ACID to improve credibility assessments with written and audio statements. *American Journal of Forensic Psychology*.

Morgan, C. A., Hazlett, G., & Colwell, K. (2011). Efficacy of forensic statement analysis in distinguishing truthful from deceptive eyewitness accounts of highly stressful events. *Forensic Sciences, 56*(5), 1227–1234.

Porter, S., & Yuille, J. C. (1995). Credibility assessment of criminal suspects through statement analysis. *Psychology, Crime, & Law, 1*(4), 319–331.

Porter, S., & Yuille, J. C. (1996). The language of deceit: An investigation of the verbal clues to deception in the interrogation context. *Law and Human Behavior, 20*(4), 443–458.

Rogers, R., & Bender, S. D. (2003). Evaluation of malingering and deception. In A. M. Goldstein (Ed.), *Handbook of psychology: Forensic psychology* (Vol. 11, pp. 109–129). Hoboken, NJ: John Wiley and Sons, Inc.

Ruby, C. L., & Brigham, J. C. (1998). Can criteria-based content analysis distinguish between true and false statements of African American speakers? *Law and Human Behavior, 22*, 369–388.

Scheck, B., Neufeld, P., & Dwyer, J. (2001). *Actual innocence: When justice goes wrong and how to make it right.* New York, NY: Signet.

Steller, M., Wellershaus, P., & Wolf, T. (1988). *Empirical validation of criteria-based content analysis.* Paper presented at the NATO Advanced Study Institute on Credibility Assessment, Maratea, Italy.

Suckle-Nelson, J. A., Colwell, K., Hiscock-Anisman, C., Florence, S., Youschak, K. E., & Duarte, A. (2010). Assessment Criteria Indicative of Deception (ACID): Replication and gender differences. *Open Criminology, 3*, 23–30.

Undeutsch, U. (1954). *Die Entwicklung der gerichtspsychologischen Gutachtertätigkeit.* Oxford, England: Hogrefe, Verlag Fuer Psychologie.

Vallano, J. P., & Compo, N. S. (2011). A comfortable witness is a good witness: Rapport building and susceptibility to misinformation in an investigative mock-crime interview. *Applied Cognitive Psychology, 25*(6), 960–970.

Verkampt, F., & Ginet, M. (2010). Variations of the cognitive interview: Which one is the most effective in enhancing children's testimonies? *Applied Cognitive Psychology, 24*, 1279–1296.

Vrij, A. (2005). Criteria-based content analysis: A qualitative review of the first 37 studies. *Psychology, Public Policy, & Law, 11*(1), 3–41.

Vrij, A., Akehurst, L., Soukara, S., & Bull, R. (2002). Will the truth come out? The effect of deception, age, status, coaching, and social skills on CBCA scores. *Law and Human Behavior, 26*(3), 261–283.

Vrij, A., Edward, K., Roberts, K. P., & Bull, R. (2000). Detecting deceit via analysis of verbal and nonverbal behavior. *Journal of Nonverbal Behavior, 24*, 239–263.

Vrij, A., Fisher, R., Mann, S., & Leal, S. (2006). Detecting deception by manipulating cognitive load. *Trends in Cognitive Sciences, 10*(4), 141–142.

Vrij, A., Leal, S., Granhag, P., Mann, S., Fisher, R.P., Hillman, J., & Sperry, K. (2009). Outsmarting the liars: The benefit of asking unanticipated questions. *Law and Human Behavior, 33*(2), 159–166.

Werdin, K., Colwell, K., Hiscock-Anisman, C.K., Hartwig, M., Bessenoff, G., & Fede, J. (2012). *ACID and computer-mediated deception: The use of Assessment Criteria Indicative of Deception to assess credibility via instant messaging.* Manuscript under review.

Williams, S.M., Talwar, V., Rodriguez, N., Fede, J., Colwell, K., & Hiscock-Anisman, C.K. (2012). *The mistakes of child lie tellers: Using the assessment criteria indicative of deception (ACID) system with children.* Poster presented at the Annual Conference of the American Psychology and Law Society, San Juan, Puerto Rico.

Winkel, F. W., & Vrij, A. (1995). Verklaringen van kinderen in interviews: Een experimenteel onderzoek naar de diagnostische waarde van Criteria Based Content Analysis. *Tijdschrift voor Ontwikkelingspsychologie, 22*, 61–74.

Yuille, J. C., Hunter, R., Joffe, R., & Zaparniuk, J. (1993). Interviewing children in sexual abuse cases. In G. S. Goodman & B. L. Bottoms (Eds.), *Child victims, child witnesses: Understanding and improving testimony* (pp. 95–115). New York, NY: Guilford Press.

Zaparniuk, J., Yuille, J., & Taylor, S. (1995). Assessing the credibility of true and false statements. *International Journal of Law and Psychiatry, 18*(3), 343–352.

Chapter 12
The ABC's of CBCA: Verbal Credibility Assessment in Practice

Dorothee Griesel, Marguerite Ternes, Domenica Schraml, Barry S. Cooper, and John C. Yuille

Introduction

Statement validity analysis (SVA) was developed during the 1960s and 1970s in the context of evaluating child witness statements of sexual abuse (e.g., Undeutsch, 1967, 1989). Criteria-Based Content Analysis (CBCA) is one component of SVA used to distinguish between event-based and intentionally fabricated statements of child and adult witnesses concerning sexual interactions and other topics (Vrij, 2005). It has become a widely accepted method of credibility assessment in many European courts (see Köhnken, 2004). The last author of the present chapter (JY) was instrumental in bringing this procedure to North America in the late 1980s (e.g., Yuille, 1988) and research conducted by him and other coauthors (DG, MT, BC) is presented in this chapter. Two of the authors (DG, DS) serve as expert

---

D. Griesel(✉) • D. Schraml
Gesellschaft für Wissenschaftliche Gerichts- und Rechtspsychologie—Aussagepsychologie,
GWG, Rablstraße 45, 81669 Munich, Germany
e-mail: griesel@gwg.info

M. Ternes
Department of Psychology, University of British Columbia, Vancouver, BC, Canada

B.S. Cooper
The Forensic Alliance, Vancouver, BC, Canada

University of British Columbia-Okanagan, Kelowna, BC, Canada

University of British Columbia, Vancouver, BC, Canada

Simon Fraser University, Burnaby, BC, Canada

Forensic Psychiatric Hospital, Port Coquitlam, BC, Canada

J.C. Yuille
The Forensic Alliance, Salt Spring Island, BC, Canada

University of British Columbia, Vancouver, BC, Canada

witnesses who provide testimony on statement credibility in German courts. This chapter, thus, offers insights from both researchers' and practitioners' points of view, as well as from European and North-American perspectives. It offers a discussion of common misunderstandings of CBCA as well as case examples to demonstrate individual CBCA criteria definitions and rating heuristics.

The first part of the chapter provides a review of the research that has been conducted on CBCA during the past 20 years. As a comprehensive review of the respective studies was provided by Vrij (2005), and to avoid redundancy, the present summary is focused on a number of theoretical misconceptions about CBCA, which have direct implications for practice. The second part of the chapter provides case examples for CBCA criteria to address some of these misconceptions and to illustrate how the method can be applied meaningfully in the context of a hypothesis-testing approach. This amalgamation of criteria definitions and rating heuristics is meant to be helpful to practitioners who wish to familiarize themselves with SVA. It is also meant to inform researchers in terms of how to design research that resembles a comprehensive, forensic assessment context.

Insights, Limitations, and Misconceptions in CBCA Research

Many studies indicate that CBCA can differentiate truthful and deceptive statements better than chance. That is, CBCA criteria suggestive of credibility are more likely to be found in verbal accounts known to be true than in verbal accounts known to be fabricated. This has been found to be true both for children's (e.g., Akehurst, Bull, Vrij, & Koehnken, 2004; Akehurst, Manton, & Quandte, 2011; Esplin, Houed, & Raskin, 1988; Granhag, Strömwall, & Landström, 2006; Kim, Choi, & Shin, 2011; Roma, San Martini, Sabatello, Tatarelli, & Ferracuti, 2011; Steller & Köhnken, 1989; Strömwall, Bengtsson, Leander, & Granhag, 2004; Yuille, 1988; for review, see Vrij, 2005) and for adults' statements (e.g., Blandón-Gitlin, Pezdek, Lindsay, & Hagen, 2009; Schelleman-Offermans & Merckelbach, 2010; Ternes, 2009; Vrij & Mann, 2006; Vrij, Mann, Kristen, & Fisher, 2007; for review, see Vrij, 2005), with accuracy ratings ranging from 55 to 90% for trained CBCA coders. A few studies have also examined verbal clues to deception in offenders (Colwell, Hiscock, & Memon, 2002; Cooper, Ternes, Griesel, Viljoen, & Yuille, 2007; Lee, Klaver, & Hart, 2008; Ternes, 2009; Ternes, Cooper, & Yuille, 2010; Willén & Strömwall, 2011) and (mock) suspects of crime (Gödert, Gamer, Rill, & Vossel, 2005; Porter & Yuille, 1996). Few criteria seemed to work in a suspect/offender context; however, conclusive evidence is difficult to obtain for methodological reasons (e.g., ceiling effect; Ternes, 2009) and motivational issues (e.g., an accused suspect who has the right to remain silent may not provide a statement at all).

Throughout all of the aforementioned research, a number of limitations and issues have been highlighted about CBCA (also see Colwell, Hiscock-Anisman, & Fede, present volume). These are outlined and addressed in the following paragraphs and suggestions for practitioners are offered.

The Quality of the CBCA Judgment Depends on the Quality of the Interview

A number of idiosyncrasies across studies have limited the ability to generalize the research findings. For example, some CBCA studies have used primarily open-ended questions, some have used primarily closed questions, some have had participants write out their statements, rather than participating in an interview, and some have enforced length or time limits on the participants' statements (e.g., Buck, Warren, Betman, & Brigham, 2002; Köhnken, Schimossek, Aschermann, & Höfer, 1995; Lee et al., 2008; Steller & Wellershaus, 1996; Vrij et al., 2007). As a proper interview, with mainly open-ended, nonleading questions, is a component of SVA, this should be standard across studies. Research has shown that the type of question asked affects CBCA judgements: responses to open-ended questions tend to contain a greater number of CBCA criteria (Hershkowitz, Lamb, Sternberg, & Esplin, 1997). Moreover, Vrij et al. (2007) found that using accusatory interviews, which consisted of suggestive accusations and statements, did not result in verbal cues to credibility and these interviews were not effective at eliciting the verbal clues to credibility necessary for CBCA to effectively discriminate between true and fabricated narratives.

Some CBCA Studies Are of Limited Ecological Validity

Two common research paradigms have been applied to research the validity of CBCA in distinguishing truthful and fabricated accounts: laboratory and field research (Horowitz et al., 1997, 1998; Ruby & Brigham, 1998). In both field and laboratory studies, CBCA-trained judges review accounts of events that have been determined to be true or false, and assess whether each of the CBCA criteria are present in each account. In most laboratory studies, the participants are asked to describe what they witnessed immediately following a staged event, a film, or a slide show. However, when CBCA is applied in the legal context, it is generally applied to a statement about a crime by a victim, perpetrator, or bystander. Attempts have been made to approximate experimental parameters to possible forensic contexts. For instance, some research has had participants provide statements about events that they considered negative, emotional, and characterized by a lack of control, to simulate important characteristics of sexual abuse (e.g., Landry & Brigham, 1992; Ruby & Brigham, 1998; Santtila, Roppola, Runtti, & Niemi, 2000), and some laboratory research has used a mock crime situation so that participants believed they were witness to an actual crime (e.g., Gödert et al., 2005; Porter & Yuille, 1996), increasing the ability of these research study results to generalize to the legal context. However, most CBCA laboratory research has examined statements about relatively benign events, such as descriptions of videotaped events or nonthreatening interactive events (e.g., Akehurst et al., 2004; Vrij, Edward, Roberts, & Bull,

2000a; Vrij, Kneller, & Mann, 2000b; Zaparniuk, Yuille, & Taylor, 1995). The activities described in some laboratory studies were short and involved only minimal interaction (e.g., Blandón-Gitlin et al., 2009).

In contrast, in most field studies, real-life witnesses report crimes, often after a considerable delay. These procedural disparities mean that different storage and retrieval processes are likely to have taken place for accounts elicited in the laboratory and the field (see Hervé, Cooper, & Yuille, present volume). Whereas some of the laboratory research investigating CBCA is simply not applicable to situations in the criminal justice system where CBCA is likely to be applied, the experimental paradigm is useful to explore selected variables and conditions in isolation, which might then inspire more comprehensive research.

Risk of a Truth Bias and How it Can be Reduced

Most studies have revealed a truth bias. That is, the procedure usually produces more false positive (i.e., the statement is "credible") than false negative (i.e., the statement is "not credible") errors (e.g., Landry & Brigham, 1992). Contrary to other approaches to evaluating truthfulness, CBCA is focused on clues to credibility rather than deception. Although it can differentiate between event-based and fabricated statements, this differentiation only works one-way. That is, CBCA can lead an evaluator to assume that an account could not have been produced unless the person had experienced the event reported in the account. A common misconception is that the absence of CBCA criteria in a statement is indicative of deception (e.g., "The CBCA system is designed to identify reports of nonexperienced events by the absence of memory indices"; Hershkowitz, 2001, p. 1407). However, if the statement does not contain enough CBCA criteria, this is not proof of a lie. Other explanations have to be considered. For example, the person may not have wanted to provide a rich account (note: in forensic situations, this might happen if the witness wants to protect the accused). In order to avoid a truth bias, it is crucial that CBCA is used in the context of SVA. The central issue is if the quality of the account could have been produced by the person without having experienced the event in question. Thus, the person's intellectual and verbal abilities as well as his/her knowledge in the area the questionable account is concerned with set the threshold for the decision whether potential CBCA criteria are powerful enough to prove that he/she could not have invented the account.

This demonstrates the importance of a hypothesis-driven approach: CBCA can only be applied in a meaningful way if ideas have been developed as to how the statement could have originated, assuming that it is a lie. Following the principle of falsifiability (Popper, 1959), the lie hypothesis could only be rejected if sufficient data (i.e., CBCA criteria) exist to suggest the opposite (i.e., a genuine experience underlying the statement). Often, research studies—particularly laboratory research—lack the contextual information necessary for such decisions. This might be a reason for the truth bias found in the literature.

Related to the above, research suggests that combining various channels (e.g., verbal clues to credibility and nonverbal clues to deception) improves the level of accuracy in distinguishing truth from lies (e.g., O'Sullivan, present volume; ten Brinke & Porter, present volume; Vrij, Akehurst, Soukara, & Bull, 2004a; Vrij, Edward et al., 2000a), which supports the idea that CBCA used in isolation should not be the sole determinant of credibility.

Can Event-Based and Erroneously False Statements be Differentiated?

It has been noted that CBCA does not have the potential to distinguish erroneously false statements from truthful accounts (Vrij, 2005). Indeed, Undeutsch's hypothesis that event-based accounts and lies differ for motivational and cognitive reasons does not apply to erroneously false statements (e.g., generated via suggestive processes). Thus, CBCA is only applicable to differentiate between a lie and a truthful account. Someone who reports a subjectively true story that is objectively/historically false will not attempt to conceal a "lie" (i.e., not be deceptive). Therefore, the motivational CBCA criteria will not apply in this context. The question is whether the person would cognitively be able to produce a statement that resembles an event-based memory in terms of other CBCA criteria.

The aforementioned issue has not been well researched. In fact, such undertakings are difficult because false memories and their recovery have to be induced (see Volbert, 2004). Here, laboratory studies are valuable. For instance, Blandón-Gitlin et al. (2009) found that accounts of true events received significantly higher total CBCA scores than suggested events (i.e., false memories) or fabricated events (i.e., lies). In contrast, Erdmann, Volbert, and Böhm (2004) demonstrated that accounts of pseudo-memories can be as rich as event-based statements and are, thus, difficult to differentiate by means of CBCA. To date, there is insufficient empirical evidence to show that accounts of pseudo-memories can be reliably differentiated from accounts of true events. Thus, CBCA remains a means by which only the hypothesis of a conscious lie can be falsified (Volbert, 2008). Based on a growing body of research on suggestive processes, other criteria and test strategies have been introduced to differentiate between false (erroneous) and reliably event-based memories (see Volbert, 2004).

Certain Circumstances Demand Caution

CBCA judgments have generally been found to be affected by age, verbal ability, social skills, and fantasy-proneness, irrespective of the truthfulness of the statements (Buck et al., 2002; Pezdek et al., 2004; Roma et al., 2011; Santtila et al.,

2000; Schelleman-Offermans, & Merckelbach, 2010; Vrij, Akehurst, Soukara, & Bull, 2002, 2004b; Vrij et al., 2004a). CBCA judgments have also been found to be affected by coaching. Vrij, Kneller, et al. (2000, 2002) have investigated the impact of teaching participants some CBCA criteria prior to being interviewed and showed that the narratives of participants who had been coached on how to make their account appear credible contained more CBCA criteria than the narratives of participants who had not received such coaching.

Other issues are relevant as well. Pezdek et al. (2004) found that CBCA scores were related to a child's familiarity with the event in question. Specifically, children who had been asked to recall a traumatic medical procedure they had experienced multiple times included a greater number of CBCA criteria in their accounts than children who had been asked to recall a traumatic medical procedure they had experienced only once. However, Strömwall et al. (2004) did not find that event familiarity affected children's CBCA scores for accounts about health examinations.

The above research suggests that, for credibility assessors, it is crucial to examine factors outside of CBCA in order to set an adequate threshold for the decision whether or not the CBCA criteria found in a particular account can be considered clues to a real experience underlying the statement. For young children, this threshold will be lower than that for older children and adults. Irrespective of the age of the witness, it is also crucial to assess for his/her familiarity with the area the statement is concerned with (e.g., for sexual abuse: knowledge about sexual practices and body functions). The question is whether the witness could have transferred his/her theoretical knowledge (or experiences from other events) onto his/her statement concerning the event in question. Finally, one should try to find out from a witness about his/her knowledge of the method (CBCA) itself. In some cases of high familiarity or a great likelihood of coaching, CBCA may not be applicable.

CBCA Is a Qualitative Method

Our examination of the research on CBCA has revealed limitations in some study designs that may suggest a lack of understanding of the theoretical underpinnings and proper applications of CBCA. The decision whether an account is credible ought to be based on a qualitative judgment rather than a summation of criterion scores. Vrij et al. (2007) maintain that they tend to use total CBCA scores in research because "total CBCA scores are typically used in real-life cases" (p. 505). If this is the case, then expert assessors have not been applying CBCA the way it was meant to be applied (e.g., Steller, 1989). Indeed, CBCA is not a standardized test with set norms suggesting certain interpretations. There are no commonly agreed-upon "decision rules" to determine whether a statement is credible (e.g., Tye, Amato, Honts, Devitt, & Peters, 1999). CBCA is a complex qualitative procedure, arguably akin to the structured clinical judgment approach used in the risk for recidivism area (Cooper, Griesel, & Yuille, 2007). A composite or total score would be hard to interpret, as certain criteria should be given more weight than others. For example, *Logical structure* and an *Appropriate amount of detail* are, according to some practitioners, mandatory for credible accounts, whereas *Unusual details* or *Unexpected complications* are optional (Steller & Köhnken, 1989). A similar problem emerges if one attempted to establish a required minimum total score for credible statements. As mentioned above, in cases involving children, even a very low CBCA total score could be meaningful depending on the child's age and knowledge in the area. Thus, CBCA should be viewed as a semi-standardized, qualitative approach, rather than a quantitative approach.

How much Training Is Necessary?

Research has shown that training matters. Although some practitioners suggest that several days of intense training are necessary to become a reliable CBCA coder (e.g., Köhnken, 2004; Yuille, 1988), even short training sessions have been shown to improve raters' accuracy, defined as the ability to differentiate true statements from false statements (e.g., Landry & Brigham, 1992; Steller, 1989). In the authors' opinion, proper identification of potential CBCA criteria in a statement can be reached with relatively little training. However, extensive training and practical experience is necessary to decide whether the criterion "counts" under the given circumstances (i.e., whether it provides a clue to a genuine experience underlying the statement). Since no standard procedure exists to assess a person's cognitive and verbal abilities (i.e., as they apply to CBCA), a certain degree of psychological experience is required to reach an adequate judgment. Relevant information can be derived from the person's biography, his/her style of speech, a behavioral analysis, and sometimes psychometric test results (Steller, 2008). Also, the other components of SVA such as a properly conducted interview (e.g., Fisher & Schreiber, 2007) or the assessment of possible suggestive influences in the statement's genesis require considerable training and practical experience.

Which CBCA Criteria Are most Informative?

Schwind (2007) conducted a field study to analyze the internal consistency of CBCA to examine to which degree the criteria measure the same construct. Schwind also examined the individual criteria's selective power in order to determine which represents the construct best. A total of 138 written credibility assessments on statements from child and adult witnesses who claimed to have experienced various forms of sexual abuse and sexual violence (i.e., 91% of all cases), physical violence, blackmail, or insult were analyzed. The assessments had been prepared by expert witnesses contracted by the prosecution and by various criminal courts.

All assessments were based on SVA, as required by the German Supreme Court's ruling (Supreme Court [BGH], 1999), which has set a number of minimum standards for credibility assessments. For all 138 assessments and all CBCA criteria, an internal consistency (i.e., Cronbach's α) of .85 was obtained (note: 19 CBCA criteria were used; Steller & Köhnken, 1989). Thus, this research suggests CBCA captures one underlying construct. The removal of the motivational CBCA criteria from this analysis led to a decrease of Cronbach's α compared to the analysis that included all 19 criteria. In line with the context in which SVA was developed, the criteria showed highest reliability for child witnesses and for statements of sexual abuse, when the age of the witness and the type of alleged offence was controlled in the analyses.

Concerning the individual criteria's selective power, item-total correlations were calculated. *Logical structure, Quantity of detail, Contextual embedding, Description of interactions, Reproduction of conversation, Accounts of subjective mental states,* and *Attribution of perpetrator's mental state* revealed item-total correlations above 0.5 in all witness groups. This research suggests that these criteria best represent the underlying construct (i.e., event-base of the account). Indeed, they played the most important role in the experts' decisions regarding statement credibility. Whereas *Unstructured production, Reporting of unexpected complications during the incident, Unusual details, Self-depreciation,* and *Pardoning the perpetrator* showed a medium selective power (i.e., r's between 0.5 and 0.3), the item-total correlations of the criteria *Related external associations, Raising doubts about one's own testimony, Admitting lack of memory, Superfluous details,* and *Spontaneous corrections* were all below 0.3. Thus, these latter criteria were less representative of the underlying construct (i.e., an event-base of the account) and were also less useful in determining whether a genuine experience was underlying the statement.

To summarize, CBCA cannot be applied meaningfully unless it is used in the context of SVA. This includes a hypothesis-driven approach, a suitable interview to elicit the statement in question, and the assessment of contextual information such as the person's intellectual (particularly verbal) abilities, his/her social (particularly deceptive) skills, his/her familiarity with the type of experience in question, and possible coaching influences. The idea of the statement being representative of a cognitive performance is central in this evaluation. After CBCA criteria are identified in a given statement, the assessor considers all available contextual information and decides if the person could and would have fabricated his/her statement. CBCA is not suitable to test hypotheses related to suggestive processes that might have led to the statement in question. It only serves to test the lie hypothesis. According to falsifiability theory, CBCA/SVA cannot confirm the lie hypothesis. However, the idea that deception underlies the account can be rejected if the assessor concludes that the person, with his/her given abilities and background knowledge, could not have provided the statement unless he/she had experienced it. Thus, SVA is not a standardized, quantitative test but a complex, qualitative method that requires considerable psychological knowledge and training.

Practical Considerations in Rating the CBCA Criteria

Following is a demonstration of individual CBCA criterion scoring based on approximately 180 SVA assessments conducted by the first or third author (DG, DS) of real child and adult court witnesses' statements as well as statements obtained in the context of two large field investigations on adult sex trade workers' (Griesel & Yuille, 2012; $N=119$) and adult male incarcerated offenders' reports of violence (Cooper, 2005; Cooper & Yuille, 2007; Ternes, 2009; $N=150$; see Yuille, present volume). No ground truth was known for the reported events, save for the study with male offenders (e.g., official file information was examined—i.e., the criminal profile reports). Only the commonly known 19 CBCA criteria are discussed (e.g., Vrij, 2005) even though other criteria have been suggested (e.g., by the last author, JY) and discussed in the literature (e.g., Arntzen, 2007; for review see Greuel et al., 1998).

The purpose of this section of the chapter is not a comprehensive evaluation of each case presented but merely a discussion of considerations that influenced the ratings of individual criteria in the context of the case/research. Brief definitions of each CBCA criterion are provided below; more detailed descriptions are provided elsewhere (e.g., Köhnken, 2004; Steller & Köhnken, 1989; Vrij, 2005). Whenever possible, hypotheses were developed (e.g., based on forensic file information) to explain the genesis of the statement, assuming that it was a lie (see falsifiability theory above). Each case presentation begins with a brief description of the specific episode that was the subject of a respective statement. For confidentiality purposes and reading ease, all identifying information has been changed. All statements presented here were elicited by means of adequate interviewing (e.g., via the Step-Wise Interview Guidelines; Yuille, Cooper, & Hervé, in press; Yuille, Marxsen, & Cooper, 1999; or the Cognitive Interview; Fisher & Geiselman, 1992). The fact that, for some criteria, several examples are provided, whereas a few criteria are not illustrated by any case material, might reflect the frequency with which the pertinent criteria occur. It should be noted that some of the statements contain rather graphic and sometimes gruesome details. This cannot be avoided in a forensic context.

Criterion 1: Logical Structure/Coherence

The criterion of *Logical structure/coherence* requires that an account contains no contradictions and follows the laws of nature. It is a basic requirement for any account. *Case example*: A 21-year-old male Caucasian incarcerated offender, Mr. Smith, participated in Cooper's (2005) and Ternes' (2009) field investigation of violent offenders' memories for violence (see also Cooper & Yuille, 2007). His index offence was aggravated assault and he had been incarcerated for 2 years up to the point of his research interview. Via the Step-Wise Interview (Yuille et al., 1999; in press), he was asked to talk about a violent act that he did not remember well (i.e., a "poor" memory). He indicated he did have such a memory, and the respective event reportedly happened 3.5 years before his research interview. He described how he damaged his friend's apartment in an LSD-induced rage. He claimed that he was drinking with a couple of friends when they "slipped a couple of hits of acid" in his drink. He did not have a recollection of his violent actions—he only remembered hearing his friends suggesting that he sleep it off. *Hypotheses*: Due to the research context, no complete SVA assessment was conducted. Due to insufficient context information, no hypothesis testing was possible. Nevertheless, CBCA was applied and is presented here to illustrate an individual criterion. The following includes excerpts from his statement:

> He stated that when he woke up: "I walked down the stairs, looked around the entire apartment, the fridge, the fridge was picked up and thrown across the room. Um the walls were, the wall was smashed through, uh the stove was, every, the entire apartment was just completely destroyed." A few lines later, in the same narrative, the participant continued, "I was, apparently, I was picking up couches, like I just threw the stove across the room it just … I don't remember." As the interviewer went through the event with the participant, following the initial free narrative, she asked for more information about what he saw when he woke up. At this point, he stated that one of his friends was "sittin' there with an apron on, cooking something at the stove." Only a few lines later, as he continued to describe the damage to the apartment, the participant stated that "the stove was pushed across the hallway … the stove was pulled out from the kitchen and there was rips in the carpet cause I guess I shoved it across the carpet, right, and the stove thing ripped some of the carpet and I shoved it all the way down the linoleum hallway and slammed into the door, so it was blocking the door."

Discussion: The above statement does not fulfill the requirement of *Logical structure/coherence*, since Mr. Smith described that he saw the stove being damaged and ripped out; yet, he mentioned his friend cooking on the very same stove a while after. These two pieces of information are contradictory. Such violations of the coherency criterion are very rare because liars usually are careful that their stories make sense. *Logical structure/coherence* is easy to rate and is necessary for the statement to fulfill the basic requirements for a judgment as "credible" (see Schwind, 2007). It is rated at the overall level of the statement. In this particular case, the account might have been insufficiently coherent because, for the purposes of research, Mr. Smith was asked to recall a poor memory. Thus, making sense was likely not a priority to him in this context.

Criterion 2: Unstructured Production/Spontaneity

The criterion of *Unstructured production/spontaneity* can only be applied to longer statements and refers to an unorganized and disconnected way of telling the account during the free narrative stage of the interview. *Case example*: A 17-year-old-girl, Ivy, was referred for an SVA of her report of sexual abuse by her uncle. She claimed about 15 individual episodes of abuse (e.g., uncle kneading her breasts, sticking his finger into her vagina, having Ivy watch him masturbate, having Ivy masturbate his penis). Some of these situations had happened repeatedly, she said. Supposedly, the abuse had started 3 years previous to her assessment, when she moved in with her aunt and uncle. According to file information, Ivy spontaneously informed her mother's friend of her abuse. When her mother heard about this, she told Ivy to "stop lying." A few months later, Ivy told a teacher about the abuse. The school informed the authorities and Ivy was placed in foster care about 1 year prior to the assessment. According to file information, Ivy's intellectual development was comparable to an 8–10-year-old child. The accused uncle reported that he had cuddled with Ivy and "sexually educated" her but denied any intentional sexual interactions. He reported to have watched pornographic movies on occasion, while masturbating. He said Ivy might have seen him do this. Ivy was interviewed by the police, and—6 months later—by one of the authors for SVA. *Hypotheses*: The hypothesis of a partial invention or an aggravated depiction of sexual interactions was the primary hypothesis underlying the analyses. Due to the possibility that she might have seen pornographic movies, another hypothesis concerned the possibility that she transferred her (sexual) knowledge from these perceptions to her statement concerning the uncle. Hence, the analysis was particularly focused on those parts of her statement that could prove an involvement of her uncle. The alternative (truth) hypothesis was that Ivy's account was based in the experience of sexually abusive interactions with her uncle; as claimed by Ivy. The following is a description of Ivy's statement:

> Ivy provided her statement in a highly disorganized fashion that did not follow a chronological order. For instance, certain details were merely mentioned at different points throughout her report but she did not provide a cohesive account of any of the alleged abusive actions. Each time, Ivy's story came out in an unorganized way, yet the details ended up fitting together and making sense (see *Logical structure/coherence*). When two interviews were compared to each other, a high degree of consistency became apparent. For example, in her police interview, she merely stated that the accused had denied her pocket money until she would masturbate him. Then, in the assessment interview, she provided a detailed account of masturbating her uncle's penis in the bathroom and spontaneously brought up the detail of her pocket money again. According to Ivy, her uncle had said that she had to do him this favor in order to receive her money and he gave her instructions on how to touch his penis. At a different point in time in the SVA interview, she explained that her uncle once kept her pocket money because she did not agree to have her picture taken by him. She had already mentioned the uncle's attempt to take her picture in her police interview; however, the detail was only later connected to the issue of her pocket money. Bit by bit, the story of her sexual abuse came together coherently. Single details (e.g., concerning contextual details) began to fit into the overall report.

Discussion: Considering the long duration of Ivy's alleged abuse (i.e., 2 years), her low intellectual abilities, the length of her account (e.g., many individual situations), and the consistency of her claims over time, it had to be assumed that the *Unstructured production/spontaneity* of her statement was only possible based on genuine experiencing. It is unlikely that Ivy could have invented such a complex story and told it in such a disorganized fashion, yet kept all the details consistent.

Criterion 3: Appropriate Quantity of Detail

No case is presented here. In a way, *Appropriate quantity of detail* is straightforward to rate; that is, sufficient details have to be provided for the listener to understand the account. The presence of this criterion, together with *Logical structure/coherence*, is a minimum requirement that every statement has to fulfill to be judged as credible (Greuel et al., 1998). However, the decision whether the amount of details (e.g., who, where, when, what, how) is appropriate is more complex: it depends on factors that research has found to influence the quality of witness statements (e.g., age, verbal skills, coaching, event familiarity). Furthermore, the time passed since the event in question, the number of previous retellings, and the subjective meaning attached to it need to be taken into account as well (see Hervé et al., present volume). Events of impact are thought to be remembered more easily and in more detail than benign events (see Yuille & Daylen, 1998) and the decision about what is deemed an *Appropriate quantity of detail* should be made in comparison to the interviewee's baseline verbal abilities. The rating of this criterion requires considerable knowledge of psychological processes and contextual case facts.

Criterion 4: Contextual Embedding

The criterion of *Contextual embedding* requires that the statement includes references to the situational circumstances of the person at the time of the alleged event (e.g., time, place). *First case example*: Ivy's case (see above) is used to illustrate this criterion. As part of her statement, she reported the following:

> She had developed an abscess on her buttocks during a church camp. Ivy reported the following (translated from German): "We rode our bikes there and had to sit on big rocks or on a pile of wood. When we came back home on Friday, something hurt on my behind. It became bigger and bigger." At a later time during her free narrative, she reported: "He had a substitute key to our apartment and came to smear my abscess with cream. This was after the surgery." Later she added: "And he would always touch my breasts. And I had had surgery on my abscess that needed to be smeared. Mom had said he (my uncle) was supposed to do it. And then he massaged my abscess and then he went further and then he turned me over and touched me from the front. And then I told him that I didn't like this. And he would keep sticking his finger into my vagina ... And I told him I didn't like that so he stopped and went to wash his hands. I put my clothes back on and he helped me with it."

Discussion: The above passage describes a script memory (i.e., a general description of what happened in repeated similar episodes; see Hervé et al., present volume; Paz-Alonso, Ogle, & Goodman, present volume; Yarbrough, Hervé, & Harms, present volume). It illustrates the criterion of *Contextual embedding* (e.g., the church camp, during which the abscess was developed, followed by surgery and the need to cream the scar near her genital area). Importantly, the sexual touching is related to Ivy's living context and biography. Such links represent a high cognitive performance and are difficult to invent. Therefore, they provide a clue that Ivy actually experienced the alleged abuse. The reader might notice that the above passage also contains examples of other criteria (e.g., *Unstructured production/spontaneity; Details characteristic of a particular act;* see below). Double scoring is possible in CBCA (Steller, 1989), which provides further evidence that it is not a quantitative scale.

12 The ABC's of CBCA 305

Second case example: Another case vignette is described to juxtapose the first case. It demonstrates that merely naming contextual details does not necessarily add to the credibility of a statement. This case concerns a 28-year-old woman, Ms. Dayton, who was referred for SVA (note: she had 9 years of formal education). She had accused her long-term ex-boyfriend, whom she had two children with, to have sexually assaulted her many times towards the end of their relationship. *Background and hypotheses*: After several attempts to separate from her (now ex-) boyfriend, Ms. Dayton had an affair with his brother-in-law. At the time of the assessment, she expected a child from the latter. After a fight between the two men, she was interviewed as a witness by the police. During the police interview, she accused her ex-boyfriend of sexually assaulting her. Thus, one hypothesis was that she had told a partial lie concerning the unwanted, violent nature of the described sexual interactions. This became the central focus of the analysis. Her motivation could have been to protect and support the father of her unborn child. The alternative hypothesis was that the account was founded in the experience of sexual violence by her ex-boyfriend. The following is a (translated) excerpt from her statement that describes the first alleged sexual assault:

> "It was September ... the situation was the same as usual, always back and forth. On that day, I didn't want to sleep at home (note: her own apartment) because the day had been so stressful with him (note: her ex-boyfriend). I would always lie down with my daughter in her bed (note: she had earlier described the lower half of a bunk bed) when he would become too pushy. That evening, I did it the same but he didn't like that again. He was real mad and kept saying, 'lie down with me, not the child' ... And I was so tired that day. I started sleeping at some point. Then I woke up ... All of a sudden, the girl was gone from the bed and he was lying next to me. He started again with his touching. I said 'let it be, go out of the bed, let me alone.' But he did not care and went on to touch me between my legs. I told him to leave the bed already ... and he was real mad. 'You can't tell me to leave, this is my place as much as it is yours', he said. And he continued to touch me all over. He tore down my pants and I turned around for him to let go of me. I tucked my covers in but he pulled them away and inserted it from behind. And I tried to push him off ... his face scratched. He had lots of scratches on his face. He kept turning me and, at some point, I was so mad that I pushed him hard ... he was then interrupted." In a later interview, Ms. Dayton denied to have pushed him.

Discussion: Of course, criteria that are missing from an account can never serve to prove a lie. That said, the above excerpt demonstrates that much contextual information was provided (e.g., in the formerly common apartment; in the children's room; in the girl's part of the bunk bed; after children were asleep), yet none of these contextual details tie in with the alleged core interactions (i.e., a sexual assault). Since it had to be assumed that Ms. Dayton had experienced sexual interactions with her ex-boyfriend (i.e., event familiarity), the focus of SVA was not to prove that sexual contact had happened. Instead, the question was if the sexual contact was violent. From the statement, this did not become clear. Although Ms. Dayton provided a lengthy and detailed statement, it remained unclear how the alleged sexual assault ensued (e.g., how positions in the tight space of a bunk bed were assumed; how he forced her into sexual interactions; how the situation ended).

Criterion 5: Descriptions of Interactions

According to Schwind (2007), *Descriptions of interactions* is another powerful criterion in CBCA assessments. The criterion requires a description of mutually connected actions and reactions (Greuel et al., 1998). Two cases are presented: one fulfills the criterion; the other does not. *First case example*: A 45-year-old woman, Mrs. Wilhelm, was referred for an SVA assessment. She claimed that her second husband had physically abused her on several occasions. *Background information*: Mrs. Wilhelm completed 9 years of schooling and, later, vocational training as a baker. After giving birth to two boys in her first marriage, she was married a second time (i.e., to the accused). Mrs. Wilhelm reported that her husband was an abusive alcoholic but had often promised to stop consuming alcohol and to stop assaulting her. She said her sons showed great affection towards him. Therefore, according to Mrs. Wilhelm, for a long time, she did not report the alleged abuse to the authorities. After many years, she separated from her husband during a stay at a psychiatric clinic when she first talked about the abuse. *Hypotheses*: The file did not reveal any information that suggested that Mrs. Wilhelm might have been subject to any suggestive processes in the course of her stay in the psychiatric clinic; the hypothesis of an intentional lie was tested. The alternative hypothesis was that her statement was based on a true experience. A summary of one alleged episode of abuse is as follows:

> Mrs. Wilhelm described that her husband once came home drunk. Supposedly, this had happened when they still lived with her parents-in-law. She stated he woke her up and brought her into a small room that served as a living room. He accused her of cheating on him but Mrs. Wilhelm reported that she told him, this was not true. Her husband then pulled some of her hair out, grabbed her neck, and choked her while pushing her against a window. Mrs. Wilhelm indicated her husband threatened to kill her by throwing her out of the window. She then scratched his arm to stop him. She stated that, by caressing his arm, she was able to calm him down enough for him to stop. Pretending that she had to use the bathroom, she then left the room and called the police from downstairs. The next day, she cut her hair to prevent him from pulling it again.

Discussion: The above demonstrates a *Description of an interaction*. A chain of actions and reactions is described, rather than a simple list of actions committed by the supposed perpetrator. Mrs. Wilhelm described an action by her husband (i.e., pulling her hair; pushing her against the window) then her own reaction (i.e., scratching, then caressing his arm) and then her husband's reaction to that (i.e., he stopped choking). This report of such intertwined actions and reactions would take a considerable effort to invent. Also, mentioning that she cut her hair provides evidence for *Contextual embedding* (see criterion 4). Considering Mrs. Wilhelm's rather average intellectual and verbal abilities, it seemed likely that this part of her statement was event-based.

Second case example: A 36-year-old, incarcerated man, Mr. Taylor, participated in the study of offenders' memories for violence introduced above (Cooper, 2005; Ternes, 2009). At the time of his research interview, he had been incarcerated for 18 years for second degree murder. He was Aboriginal and reported to have 17 years of education. He was asked to describe an act of instrumental (i.e., planned) violence he had committed (see Cooper & Yuille, 2007). Mr. Taylor reported that, 20 years previous to the research interview, he was working with some people who had "problems" with a "rat" (i.e., someone who had betrayed them). Supposedly, he was paid 150,000 dollars to deliver a "noticeable, very violent" message to this person. In the research interview, he indicated that he kidnapped the man, brought him to a warehouse, and tortured him in order to find out how much information he had divulged. He stated, he kidnapped him in front of his wife by putting a gun to the back of his head; he then "threw" him into a van. Mr. Taylor indicated that, at the warehouse, he sliced two fingers off the man, who then told him the information he was seeking. The rest of the torture was reportedly "for show." He said, he cut off all the victim's fingers and toes and that, when the victim passed out, he cut off his eyelids so that he would not further lose consciousness. Mr. Taylor continued by stating that he proceeded to skin his victim by using a hot knife so that he would not bleed to death. He noted, the man died of a "Colombian necktie," explaining that such is when the tongue is pulled out through a slit made in the throat. *Hypotheses*: No complete SVA was conducted; hence no hypothesis testing was possible (e.g., due to the research context, no information was collected about this offender's experiences and interests such as hunting and his knowledge of other offenders' crimes; thus little was known about his event familiarity). The following verbatim passage from his statement serves to illustrate the criterion of *Description of interactions* in isolation:

> I didn't start cutting off the fingers right away. I used nut crackers on his nails, um, on his knuckles first. To start gauging how much information that he had given. And uh, by the time I had broken all his knuckles, I was satisfied that he wasn't lying anymore. I called and let the appropriate people know what he had given up and hadn't given up and then I went back to work on him. I kept asking him the same questions over and over and over. What did you say, who did you say it to. Who is the name of the undercover guy that is working and all that stuff. Then, I started cutting fingers off ... every time I cut it, a digit off or something, I put the pruning shears back into the fire. I made like a barbecue so it would cauterize it as it was cutting so he wouldn't bleed to death. One after another ... after I was done with the finger and the toes, that's when I stopped for a little while. I went and had something to eat. Came back, it was just after eight in the evening when I started to peel his skin off. And that took pretty much the rest of the night into the next day. He kept passing out. And I had to stop every once in a while to let the knife get hot again.

Discussion: The above is a poor example of a *Description of an interaction*. Good examples would follow a pattern of intertwined actions and reactions (A-B-A), where an action of one person is described, followed by a reaction of another person, followed by a reaction of the first person again (see Mrs. Wilhelm's statement above). Mr. Taylor's statement, however, follows the pattern A-A-A ("I used nut crackers," "I had broken all his knuckles," "I called," "I kept asking," "I started cutting off fingers," etc.). Despite the lengthy, detailed, and charged presentation of the statement, Mr. Taylor did not describe any concrete reaction of the supposed victim, except that the man stopped lying and kept passing out. However, these are not descriptions at a behavioral level (e.g., a description of what the supposed victim said was the truth; a description of how the offender noticed that his victim had passed out). Subsequent to his interview, it was found out that this research participant had a long history of deceptive statements.

Criterion 6: Reproduction of Conversation

The criterion *Reproduction of conversation* is a particular kind of a *Description of an interaction*. It is fulfilled if a complex sequence of conversation is reported, e.g., if the person describes a chain of connected, intertwined questions and answers (Greuel et al., 1998). *Case example*: Ivy's case (see above) is used again to illustrate this criterion. At one point in her statement, the following was indicated:

> "He used to have pictures on his computer. Once he called me and showed me some of them." Later, Ivy said, "once in a while, he sat upstairs and would play around with his computer. And my aunt doesn't know he has these sex photos on there to look at." She was later asked to expand on these previous remarks. Ivy reported: "Once he said that supposedly he cannot delete these pictures." Assessor: "And how did this topic come up?" Ivy: "Because I went upstairs and wanted to go into my room and I told him ... I saw him sitting at his computer. So I went there. Up to that point, he was looking at some sort of music but when I came, he said, 'I have to show you something.' And then he clicked and showed me these pictures and said, 'You can't tell anyone about this!' I asked him, 'Then why don't you delete these pictures?' and he said, 'I can't do that'... because my aunt didn't know about them." Assessor: "Do you remember what you saw in these pictures?" Ivy: "Two women or one woman and a man, I don't know, I didn't look at it closely because I was about to go, I wasn't interested in the picture."

Discussion: Ivy's example indicates a *Reproduction of a conversation*. It contains specific contents and it is clear from Ivy's report who said what. Considering her low intellectual abilities, and in the context of the overall assessment, this episode was counted as a clue to a genuine experience.

Criterion 7: Unexpected Complications During the Incident

The criterion *Unexpected complications during the incident* is met if unsuccessful, incomplete, or interrupted actions are described (Greuel et al., 1998). *First case example*: Mrs. Wilhelm's case (see above) is used again to illustrate this criterion. At one point in time in her interview, she reported the following episode:

> Shortly after her wedding, she and her husband went to a carnival party at a pub. She said her husband got drunk, and that he later saw her chatting with some elderly men. He came up to her, pulled her out of the pub and pushed her into the mud on the ground in front of the pub. Mrs. Wilhelm further reported that her husband also fell into the dirt because she clung on to him.

Discussion: The part of Mrs. Wilhelm's statement that describes her husband falling down with her illustrates an account of an *Unexpected complication*. Mrs. Wilhelm's reported clinging ties in with her husband's questionable abuse (i.e., pushing). The detail would not have been necessary if Mrs. Wilhelm had invented her husband's pushing. Therefore, from a motivational point of view, this detail would not have been an "obvious" one to include in a fabricated statement; hence it would be difficult to invent. In the context of the overall assessment, this detail was rated as a clue to a genuine experience.

Second case example: This case concerns another participant from the above described field study (Cooper, 2005; Ternes, 2009), Mr. Lee. At the time of his research interview, he was a 30-year-old offender incarcerated for living off the avails of prostitution. His research interview occurred in his third year of incarceration for this offence. He reported to have 11 years of education. He was asked to describe an act of reactive violence. Mr. Lee indicated that he had engaged in such an act about 7 years previous to the interview, around the time when he had started "selling a bit of crack." He described a fight in a "crack house" that involved several men, noting the house had hardwood floors. Reportedly, he was under the influence of marijuana at the time. *Hypotheses*: No hypothesis testing was possible due to the lack of sufficient background information in the research context. CBCA was applied to illustrate individual criteria in isolation. The following includes a verbatim excerpt from Mr. Lee's research interview:

> Mr. Lee reported that, in the course of the fight, he had been shot in the hand. He described grappling with one of the men and stated, in his own words that, at one point in time, "I'm bleeding pretty good out of my hand, so it's getting pretty slippery on this floor, so we ended up uh, wrestling. He grabs me, I slip on the blood, I fall." He described that he fell down the stairs and the other man "pretty much" used him "as a sled."

Discussion: The slipping is an example of an *Unexpected complication*, which ties in with the earlier shooting of Mr. Lee's hand. Such a chain of actions is generally not easy to fabricate. A complete SVA assessment would require an analysis of Mr. Lee's verbal and cognitive abilities as well as his knowledge and experience with fights and shootings in order to judge whether he could have invented this statement. Note: the information that this event reportedly happened when he first started selling crack provides evidence of *Contextual embedding* (see above).

Criterion 8: Unusual Details

The criterion *Unusual details* is defined by the rarity of the details provided; however, they are not unrealistic details (Greuel et al., 1998). *Case example*: Griesel (2008; Griesel & Yuille, 2012) conducted a field study in which sex trade workers were asked to talk about sexually violent events they had experienced. One participant, a 29-year-old female, Ms. Parker, entered the sex trade when she was 12 years old and quit prostituting herself at the age of 17. She reported to have 9 years of formal education and to have experienced several types of childhood abuse (including sexual abuse). Although she had a history of drug abuse, she was clean and sober at the time of her research interview. When she was asked to recall a sexual assault she remembered well via the Step-Wise Interview (Yuille et al., 1999), she reported an event that occurred when she was 14 years old (note: she denied being under the influence of any drugs at the time). She reported that a friend of her pimp took her to a hotel room and anally sexually assaulted her. *Hypotheses*: Due to the research context and lack of sufficient background information, no concrete hypotheses could be tested. CBCA was applied only to discuss the rating of individual criteria. Following is a verbatim excerpt from the research interview with Ms. Parker:

> I go about, you know, what I would normally do in any situation. So, got undressed and was there and, and uh, but he wasn't into normal things, and um. He uh, he pinned me down onto the bed, and um. Took uh, took out a bottle of roll-on deodorant. And proceeded to cover my entire body, including my face, my eyes, in my ears, um. Like literally cover my entire body with this roll-on deodorant … it's kind of got this dry, um, sticky, unclean feeling to it, um. And I, he was hu-, this guy was huge and I couldn't get up … he has me pinned down onto the bed, he's got me covered in this crap that … and I mean my whole body. There wasn't a single part of my body that, that was … that didn't have this stuff on it, and the smell of it, um, I mean it was incredibly sick, sweet, it was a really sweet smelling deodorant, like I don't, you know, they all have different scents and this one was just overly potently fruity kinda sweet smelling and, and it was so sticky and then he started to roll over me. Like to rub it off my onto him, and um, which was really hurting me especially in the abdomen area cause he was really, really big and he just kept rolling back and forth over me … and then he um, and I, I mean my face was in the bed so I couldn't, um, see what was going on. And um, I had never had anal sex before this point and he um, decided that was where he was going. But before that, he took the little roller thing off and literally poured the rest of this bottle, of deodorant, like the liquid deodorant, all over my ass and, in it and um, and then (smacks hands together) you know, proceeded to do, to put himself in, in my ass which I'd never had that before. Was the most, one of the most painful experiences of my life … the deodorant actually made it less lubricated because it was sticky and tacky and, and so every time he went in and out it was, it was like, I felt like my skin was ripping. And I was bleeding.

Discussion: The details about the deodorant being poured all over Ms. Parker's body illustrate an unusual use of deodorant. It is a great example of an *Unusual detail*. If the statement was invented, such information would be difficult to fabricate, unless Mr. Parker had had similar experiences elsewhere (event familiarity). The deodorant detail is highly informative because it is tied to the account of the alleged anal sexual assault. Interestingly, the cited passage also involves an account of Ms. Parker's *Subjective mental state* (see below; the deodorant's scent; being hurt from the man rolling onto her; being hurt from anal intercourse) as well as information about the *Contextual embedding* (see above; e.g., hotel room; first anal intercourse). Again, double coding is possible in CBCA since it is a qualitative procedure. In this case, Ms. Parker provided an example of a detailed and rich statement, with remarkable hints to a genuine experience.

Criterion 9: Superfluous/Peripheral Details

The criterion of *Superfluous/peripheral details* is met if many details are provided in a statement that are irrelevant for understanding the event in question (see Greuel et al., 1998). *Case example*: A 20-year-old woman, Ms. Heuser, was referred for an SVA assessment. She claimed that the former boyfriend of her mother had sexually abused her from the ages of 12–18. The man and her mother had separated but remained friends soon after the abuse had reportedly started. Ms. Heuser claimed that, over the course of the years, her and her abuser had provided oral sex to each other, and had had sexual intercourse with each other in various ways. Ms. Heuser reported that, throughout the time of the alleged abuse, she had been in several short relationships with peers. When she was 18 years old, she reported her mother's ex-partner to the police. Ms. Heuser reported a total of 20 different, individual episodes of sexual abuse (e.g., the first instance of oral sex; the first instance of vaginal intercourse). *Hypotheses*: There were several hypotheses tested in the SVA assessment: One of them was that Ms. Heuser could have made up the entire story. Another was that she could have falsely transferred her sexual knowledge from other relationships onto her statement concerning the accused. As the accusation in this case was not about adult sexual assault, but child sexual abuse, the crucial question was whether Ms. Heuser had experienced any sexual interactions with her mother's ex-partner as a child. The alternative hypothesis was that she provided a true statement based in a real experience. Two (translated) excerpts from her lengthy overall statement are as follows:

> When Ms. Heuser described how the accused gave her oral sex for the first time, she mentioned: "... soon after the first time (reference to the pervious incident), I remember we were sitting on my mother's bed ... not where the head goes but on the side ... It was dark, and in the hallway a lamp was shining, the lighting was kind of dim."
> Ms. Heuser also described a series of incidents when the accused had sexual intercourse with her in the back of a vehicle while they were in a car wash. Ms. Heuser said: "He used to have tissues in the car to wipe himself off. He used to jump out of the car and would clean all windows with some sort of windshield wiper because little drops of water would be on them. I still remember that, while he did this, I would get dressed again slowly and watch him manually clean his car."

Discussion: The aforementioned details (e.g., the lamp; wiping the windshield) were spontaneously mentioned by Ms. Heuser. They can be considered *Peripheral details* because they are not central to any of the reported abusive actions (e.g., oral sex, vaginal intercourse in the car wash). Yet, they are described in conjunction with sexual interactions and, in combination with all the other CBCA criteria that were present in her statement (not discussed here), add to the sense that Ms. Heuser's statement was based on actual experiencing. The peripheral details also tie in with the *Contextual embedding* (see above) of each event, which is important in differentiating Ms. Heusers' statement of abuse with the accused from sexual experiences with her boyfriends. That is, they hint at the fact that the accused might have been involved in the reported incidents.

Criterion 10: Accurately Reported Details Misunderstood

The criterion *Accurately reported detail misunderstood* is rated if a phenomenon is described but its meaning is not understood or is incorrectly interpreted. If this criterion is present, it usually only happens in children's statements (see Colwell et al., present volume). *Case example*: Florian, an 8-year-old boy, was referred for an SVA assessment, and consequently provided a statement alleging he was abused by his adult brother. The alleged abuse became known after Florian tried to engage another boy at a birthday party into sexual play. In this context, he told the other boy that his brother had stuck his "wiener" into his (Florian's) "bum." When the other boy told his parents about this conversation, Florian was asked further questions by his friend's parents and his own foster parents about the alleged experiences with his brother. Eventually, the local child welfare office reported the abuse to the police, and Florian was formally interviewed. He reported several acts of oral and anal intercourse. Florian indicated that his brother had also watched pornographic movies with him, which contained depictions of oral and anal intercourse between a man and a woman. *Hypotheses*: Considering the context in which the statement first originated, it had to be considered that Florian lied intentionally in order to justify his sexual play with a friend at the party. Also, it had to be tested if Florian could have transferred the knowledge he acquired from watching the aforementioned pornographic movies onto the contents of his statement concerning sexual interactions with his older brother (i.e., a partial lie—viewing pornography being true). The alternative hypothesis was his entire account was true (i.e., being shown pornographic movies by his brother; engaging in sexual interactions with him). The following is an excerpt from his statement:

> Florian reported one situation that had supposedly taken place in a hut with a ladder and a slide on a playground. There, he and his brother sat next to each other and the accused opened Florian's pants, took his penis out and sucked on it. Florian described that his pants had been pulled down to his knees. Florian explained that his penis had become "big" at that time. After that, his brother reportedly did "the same" on himself. When asked, Florian reported that, while he was getting dressed again, his brother had opened his own pants and taken out his "wiener." Florian proceeded to demonstrate a masturbatory gesture. The assessor asked: "How long did he do this? Did something else happen?" Florian: "Something white came out." Assessor: "Where and when did that come out?" Florian: "What?" Assessor: "Where and when did it come out?" Florian: "I don't know." Assessor: "Where did it come from?" Florian: "From his wiener." Assessor: "And what happened next?" Florian: "It was flowing out." Assessor: "Where?" Florian: "Into his pants." Assessor: "Did your brother take off his pants entirely?" Florian: "They were like mine before." Assessor: "You mean they were down to his knees?" Florian: "Yes." Assessor: "And his underwear?" Florian nodded his head. Assessor: "Have you ever seen something white coming out?" Florian: "No." Assessor: "What did that white stuff look like? Can you describe that a little more?" Florian: "It was all white and was something like … like cream. Like a … What's that called? Like cream so that your skin doesn't dry out … bodymilk … or whatever that's called."

Discussion: Florian's description of "bodymilk" that supposedly came out of the accused's penis represents an *Accurately reported detail misunderstood*. When asked, Florian denied that the pornographic movies he had watched contained anything similar. Assuming this background information was true, it could be assumed that he did not have any alternative sources of knowledge to construct the above described part of his statement. This criterion is powerful because it cannot be assumed that the boy could have entirely invented such a phenomenological accurate description of male masturbation. Although he had knowledge of pornographic material, it was not viewed as likely that he transferred the "bodymilk" detail because he denied that he had ever seen anything like that before (assuming this denial was true). This demonstrates how careful the circumstances of a witness have to be assessed before a judgment can be made as to whether a criterion represents a clue to a genuine experience.

Criterion 11: Related External Associations

The occurrence of this criterion is extremely rare in our experience. According to Arntzen (2007), it is fulfilled if a witness talks about a conversation with the person he/she was supposedly involved with that refers to a different yet similar experience. The report of related actions has to resemble the core of the event in question; however, these interactions would have been experienced at another time. For instance, in case of an incestuous relationship between a father and a daughter, she might report a conversation with him that concerned a sexual experience with her boyfriend (e.g., reference to a specific sexual act; reference to the boyfriend's body shape). The interlacing of the reported act in question with the reported conversation is key to this criterion. It is particularly useful to test the hypothesis of knowledge from other experiences being transferred onto the person accused in the present statement (Greuel et al., 1998).

This criterion did not come up in any of the case and research material reviewed in preparation for this chapter. According to Schwind (2007), this criterion was rarely encountered by other credibility assessors as well; therefore, it did not have good selective power.

Criterion 12: Accounts of Subjective Mental State

The criterion *Account of a subjective mental state* is satisfied if emotional or bodily reactions or cognitive reflections are reported related to the event in question (Greuel et al., 1998). *Case example*: Mrs. Wilhelm's case is used again to illustrate this CBCA criterion. The relevant part of the summary of her report is as follows:

> Mrs. Wilhelm reported that, soon after her wedding, she had tossed her wedding ring into a corner of their apartment. She indicated she was furious after her husband had beaten and pushed her into the mud in front of a pub after the aforementioned (see above) carnival party where he was intoxicated. She said that she later searched for the ring to no avail.

Discussion: The report of Mrs. Wilhelm's rage is an example of an *Account of a subjective mental state*. It is presented in the form of a behavioral act (i.e., tossing a ring), which was supposedly provoked by her husband's abusive behavior (i.e., pushing her in the dirt). As such, this detail is not a mere statement of Mrs. Wilhelm's mental state (e.g., "I was mad") but is tied in with the core of her story (i.e., the questionable abuse). Interestingly, the detail of tossing the ring is also connected with the overall story of her marriage (i.e., she subsequently searched for the ring). Hence, this example also serves as an illustration of *Contextual embedding* (see above).

Criterion 13: Attribution of Perpetrator's Mental State

The criterion of *Attributions of perpetrator's mental state* is met if the witness reports emotional reactions of the accused, e.g., by reporting physical or physiological processes. In the case of an offender's statement, the criterion could be met if the statement provider provides an attribution of another person's mental state. *First case example*: Mrs. Wilhelm's case is used again to illustrate the rating of this criterion. The relevant summary of her account is as follows:

> Mrs. Wilhelm reported that her husband once returned home intoxicated at night and assaulted her on her nose. She indicated that, shortly before this event, she had had surgery on her nose. She recalled that the assault hurt so badly that, for the first time, she actually cried for help and defended herself by striking back at her husband's chin. She reported that he seemed amused by such and commented that she "strikes like a smith [strong and powerful]."

Discussion: Among other criteria (e.g., the *Description of an interaction*; see above), this section fulfills the criterion of an *Attribution of the perpetrator's mental state* (i.e., her husband's change from aggression to amusement). His state was not merely claimed (e.g., "he was aggressive," "he had fun"), which would have been easier to invent, but was derived from Mrs. Wilhelm's description of interwoven actions and reactions. Again, this detail ties in with the core of her statement (i.e., abusive behaviors by her husband) and can therefore be considered a clue to credibility.

Second case example: A second case is presented as a less pronounced example of this criterion. The aforementioned 36-year-old Mr. Taylor from Cooper's (2005) and Ternes' (2009) field study on violent offenders' crimes also reported an incident of reactive violence—stabbing another inmate in prison. *Hypotheses*: Due to the research context, no SVA assessment was conducted; hence no hypothesis testing was possible. CBCA criteria were coded in isolation. The following is an excerpt from Mr. Taylor's statement:

> I remember looking along the dining hall, seeing all the amazed looks on people's faces. I guess they figured I was just some kind of punk white boy in there, not standing up for himself.

Discussion: The mentioning of "amazed looks" concerns the report of the inner reactions of other inmates who witnessed the reported stabbing, hence it could be considered an *Attribution of another persons' mental state*. Technically, the cited statement fulfills this criterion. However, the other persons' amazement is merely named but not explained on a descriptive level (e.g., a description of faces with their mouths wide open). Also, in his statement, the offender formulates a guess about other people's thoughts. This part cannot be counted as a clue to the statement's credibility because the offender draws the information from his thoughts, not his memory (i.e., "I guess"). The possibility that he constructed and added this detail retrospectively has to be considered. Possibly, it mirrors the way he wished to be seen by others (not as "some kind of punk white boy"; i.e., a motivational factor). This illustrates how each criterion has to be discussed and evaluated in context, the question being if this person could have cognitively invented the detail. The conclusion offered in this case does not imply that the stabbing did not happen the way the offender described it; it only means this criterion, on its own, is not suitable to prove the statement's credibility.

Criterion 14: Spontaneous Correction

The criterion *Spontaneous correction* is satisfied if the statement provider spontaneously corrects his/her statement, thereby showing a critical perspective on his own (supposed) memory. *Case example*: Mr. Lee from the field study on violent offenders' memories (Cooper, 2005; Ternes, 2009) reported being shot in the hand during an act of reactive violence (see above). *Hypotheses*: CBCA criteria were coded without a formal SVA assessment; hence, no hypotheses were tested. The following is an excerpt from Mr. Lee's statement in the form of an introduction to his act of violence:

> It was rush hour on Friday, and uh, we went into this house to get some pot and, like we walked in, first, you know the memory's a little bit shagged. I need to go back a second. First we didn't go there directly to buy, to buy pot. We got a call on the cell phone saying ... our buddy ... He was screaming in pain and there was some noise and some, some, something was going on up there, so he called us, so that's why we went directly down there, but we didn't get pot anyway.

Discussion: The above excerpt from Mr. Lee's statement includes a *Spontaneous correction* (i.e., about going to a house to purchase marijuana). Whether or not it can be considered as fulfilling a CBCA criterion has to be carefully evaluated. On the one hand, a liar would not be expected to include "a mistake" in his/her statement and correct him/herself (note: if an interviewer challenges him/her on a contraction and then the story changes, this is merely a correction, not a spontaneous correction). Evidence towards this criterion counts only if the correction is spontaneous and improves the statement (e.g., adds more precision to an action that was already mentioned). On the other hand, a correction might simply be an effort to resolve a contradiction in the statement, which could happen, for example, if the person did not carefully prepare the lie. This could match Lee et al.'s (2008) observation that *Spontaneous corrections* were more often present in false than in truthful narratives. Therefore, it is important that the correction occurs spontaneously, as in the above cited case, not when the person is prompted to explain seemingly contradictory parts of the statement. Nevertheless, this criterion is difficult to rate without the context of other potential CBCA criteria.

Criterion 15: Admitting Lack of Memory

The literature from the 1980s suggests that *Admitting lack of memory* could be a hint towards an event-based account (e.g., Steller & Köhnken, 1989). *Case example*: A 36-year-old Aboriginal offender, Mr. Morris, with 12 years of education, participated in the aforementioned field study of memory for violent crimes (Cooper, 2005; Ternes, 2009). In the research interview, he reported an instrumentally violent crime he had committed when he was 18 years old. He reported to have been under the influence of marijuana at the time. He explained that he was paid by a pizza service to hurt the owner of another, competing pizza service. Supposedly, this was his first such "contract." He described that, together with an accomplice, he beat a man and the man's son with a club after they had pulled up in their pizza delivery vehicle. Mr. Morris indicated that, before the "hit," he and his accomplice had collected money from a female acquaintance who was working as a prostitute for his accomplice. *Hypotheses*: As with the other study participants, no formal SVA assessment was performed, and no specific hypotheses were tested as to how this account could have originated. The following includes an excerpt from Mr. Morris' research transcript:

> When asked by the interviewer what his female acquaintance was wearing that day, Mr. Morris admitted that he did not remember: "No, I, I, didn't even really look over at her much that day, because I was just pretty much just listening. I remember hearing a few things, but I was really looking out the window. Like I remember looking out the window a lot that day. I was just off in my own world." Earlier in his statement, he had stated: "Umm, I remember sitting and rolling my joints up and I remember thinking how good this is going to be for my career and all that, I am going to be a hit man now. I remember going through those thoughts, and I was pretty much going through those thoughts all day."

Discussion: The aforementioned research participant *Admitted lack of memory* for his female acquaintance's clothing. Motivationally speaking, admitting lack of memory is not expected from someone who tells a lie because it is assumed that liars are motivated to provide a complete account and to answer all questions asked of them. Note that Schwind's research (2007) demonstrated that not many experts use this criterion in actual SVA assessments. Our experience suggests that the criterion occurs both in statements that are deemed credible and not-credible. Evidence towards this criterion should be applied in combination with other criteria (e.g., *Appropriate amount of detail*, *Coherence*) because the central (i.e., questionable) part of a statement should be comprehensible (see also Greuel et al., 1998).

Criterion 16: Raising Doubts About One's Own Testimony

The criterion is fulfilled if the person mentions objections to his/her own account. This criterion has not been encountered by the authors in their research material or case work evaluated for this chapter. It was shown to be rare in other experts' SVA assessments, too, and it correlated only marginally with statement credibility in Schwind's (2007) study of internal consistency.

Criterion 17: Self-deprecation

The criterion *Self-deprecation* is met if the person portrays him/herself or his/her actions in an unfavorable fashion, e.g., by reporting own mistakes or taking part in an abusive action (Greuel et al., 1998). *Case example*: An 11-year-old boy, Lovis, was referred for an SVA assessment based on his report of being sexually abused by an elderly man who was the uncle of his mother's boyfriend. The alleged abuse was detected after Lovis' mother observed the accused kiss Lovis on his mouth one morning. When Lovis was asked if the accused had "touched" him, Lovis responded in the affirmative. In subsequent interviews by a social worker and the police, Lovis disclosed further details. *Hypotheses*: One hypothesis in this case concerned the possibility of a coached statement (e.g., applying sexual knowledge gained from informal questioning and formal interviews to the statement). Thus, it had to be tested if Lovis was able to provide autonomous supplements to the information that had been communicated to him during previous interviews (as documented in the file). The following includes two translated excerpts from Lovis' interview:

> Lovis reported that the accused visited his family several times during a period of time that started about 1 year prior the disclosure of the alleged abuse. Each time, the accused slept in Lovis' room on an extra mattress. Lovis reported that they used to kiss each other "good night" and "good morning." He reported that on one particular morning: "I waited until he was awake and then he said, 'why haven't you come down here?' So I went down there and we cuddled a little bit. And then it started that he teased me ... not that he touched me down there ... And then I started to pull his pants down. Yah. And then it all developed. He never hurt me or asked something of me. In the beginning, he used to rub me and my penis became hard. He moved my foreskin back and forth quickly, again and again."
>
> Lovis also reported that he had become curious and wanted to insert his penis into the accused's rectum: "Yah, then ... I had a hard-on, I believe. And then I ... he was lying on his tummy ... I lay onto him, with my tummy against his back, and tried to stick my penis in his hole. I don't know any more if it worked or if it didn't work" Assessor: "Why don't you know this?" Lovis: "I don't know, I forgot ..." Assessor: "Can you tell me how you tried to stick it in there?" Lovis: "I spread his bum cheeks a little bit apart so that I could see the hole, and then I tried to get in with my penis but it didn't work." When asked, Lovis denied that the accused had ever tried to do the same with him.

Discussion: The above is particularly valuable because Lovis reported that he initiated sexual acts with the accused. Thus, it counts as evidence of *Self-deprecation*. According to file information, the possibility that Lovis initiated sexual contact had never been suggested to him in any interview. From a motivational point of view, the evidence towards self-deprecation would not be expected from a child who attempted to wrongfully accuse a person of sexually abusing him.

Criterion 18: Pardoning the Perpetrator

The criterion *Pardoning the perpetrator* is met if a witness exonerates the accused perpetrator or refrains from incriminating him/her further (Greuel et al., 1998). *Case example*: Ivy's case is used again to illustrate this criterion. The following includes *excerpts* from Ivy's statement:

> Above it was described how Ivy's uncle would smear cream on an abscess near her genital area. In this context, Ivy said: "And I told him I didn't like that so he stopped and went to wash his hands."

> Another time during her interview, Ivy said that the accused had announced that he wanted to take pictures of her breasts and her vagina. Reportedly, Ivy said she did not want this to happen. She noted that he refrained from getting the camera.

Discussion: The fact that Ivy refrained from further incriminating her uncle (i.e., he stopped an abusive act; he did not use violence; he refrained from planned pornographic production) fulfills the criterion of *Pardoning the perpetrator*. From a motivational point of view, this is unexpected from a witness who means to portray the perpetrator and his abuse as maximally drastic.

Criterion 19: Details Characteristic of a Particular Act

This criterion is met if the witness reports several details throughout his/her statement that cannot be expected from him/her based on common knowledge, yet the details correspond with known offender patterns (e.g., the grooming behavior of a seductive pedophile). *First case example*: Ivy's case is used again to illustrate this criterion. The below includes part of the SVA assessor's formulation:

> When Ivy's statements of individual episodes of her alleged abuse by her uncle were organized into chronological order, it became apparent that the abuse had started with the touching of her breast and progressed to more serious forms of abuse (e.g., having Ivy touch his genitals; inserting fingers into her vagina) which were slowly and progressively introduced as part of normal bodily care actions.

Discussion: Based on the background information provided from Ivy (e.g., her general knowledge about child sexual abuse), the increasing severity of the sexual interactions she reported with her uncle cannot be considered part of her general knowledge base. The aforementioned development is typical of incestuous relationships, where there is a gradual increase in the severity of the abuse (e.g., Arntzen, 2007; Leclerc, Proulx, & Beauregard, 2009). Hence, it is evidence towards *Details characteristic of a particular act*. Her description of an episode where her uncle used the pretext of body care (i.e., applying cream to an abscess on her buttock) to insert a finger into her vagina also demonstrates a *Detail characteristic of an act* of progressively severed sexual abuse. Indeed, it is not uncommon for perpetrators to introduce sexual activity in the context of normal activities (e.g., Berliner & Conte, 1990). It is unlikely that Ivy could have invented the gradual progression of her abuse and the context of bodily care in one of the specific abuse situations based on her general sexual knowledge.

Second case example: Lovis' case is also used again to illustrate this criterion (see above). Below is a summary of part of his statement to the credibility assessor:

> Lovis and his uncle had started out by kissing each other "good night." Lovis reported that they then pulled each other's pants down and touched each other's penises "for fun." He reported taking the initiative in an attempt to penetrate his uncle anally (see above). In addition, he stated that, on other occasions, his uncle had sucked his (Lovis') penis. Lovis denied that his uncle had ever asked him to perform such an act on him. Lovis said he had always liked the uncle, who gave him presents, bought him exactly the toys he had wanted,

let him play with the computer and would never become mad at him for mistakes he made. He said that he never knew that the behaviors he and the uncle had engaged in were considered abusive.

Discussion: The description of gradually more intense and intimate touching coupled with evidence of grooming behavior (e.g., presents) fulfills the criterion of *Details characteristic of a particular act*. The same is true for the reported reciprocity of sexual touching. Considering Lovis' background experience (i.e., no other sexual abuse), it seemed unlikely that he could have invented these aspects of his statement. Such specific details are known to those working in this area but usually not a child witness. Hence, together with some of the other CBCA criteria found in his account (not all discussed here), they provide a strong clue to a genuine experience underlying the statement.

Conclusion

The partial intent of this chapter was to demonstrate some of the logic behind CBCA and to dispel some misconceptions about its use in research and practice. The other focus was to explain the reasoning behind the ratings of individual CBCA criteria via cases from research and clinical practice. Clearly, a multiple hypothesis-driven approach is necessary for SVA assessments, which includes CBCA. Some of the factors that have been discussed in the literature (e.g., age, event familiarity, coaching affecting CBCA ratings) do not necessarily limit the applicability of SVA, if proper hypotheses are formed and evidence is gathered to take these challenges into account (e.g., possibility of knowledge transfer; evaluation of cognitive and verbal abilities necessary to invent the statement; possibility of a partial lie). Although some CBCA criteria can be more powerful than others, a meaningful pattern of several criteria is usually necessary to judge an account as credible. Such decisions are qualitative (e.g., no "scores," no standardized minimum amount of criteria), and the frame of reference is always within the individual—a comparison of the person's statement with other individuals' CBCA performance is not useful.

Behavioral channels other than verbal content have been discussed as clues to deception in the literature (e.g., Ekman, 2009; ten Brinke & Porter, present volume). These could be used by an SVA assessor to obtain and assess more precise and complete information during the interview, which would form the basis for an SVA evaluation (e.g., together with file information, etc.). For instance, an observation of a micro-expression, or a change in verbal style or body language might provide important clues related to a critical passage of a statement (Cooper, Hervé, & Yuille, 2009).

The above notwithstanding, SVA is not a tool to identify deception. As explained above, there are only two possible outcomes of SVA: credible or not credible. The former implies that no theory other than an actual experience explains the origin and the high quality of the statement. The latter suggests that several origins of the statement are possible (e.g., an intentional lie; the witness' lack of motivation to provide more details and/or details of a higher quality). Therefore, the absence of CBCA criteria does not mean anything other than the statement was not suitable to provide evidence of credibility. It is not the job of an SVA assessor to prove a lie.

At the beginning of the chapter, a relatively new area of research—verbal credibility assessments on offender statements—was introduced. Some of our case examples were derived from a large field study on violent offender's narratives of violence. It is hoped that some of the reasoning in the above case presentations will inspire future research and practice in the area of verbal credibility assessment with offenders and other relatively neglected populations.

References

Akehurst, L., Bull, R., Vrij, A., & Koehnken, G. (2004). The effects of training professional groups and lay persons to use Criteria-Based Content Analysis to detect deception. *Applied Cognitive Psychology, 18*, 877–891.

Akehurst, L., Manton, S., & Quandte, S. (2011). Careful calculation or a leap of faith? A field study of the translation of CBCA ratings to final credibility judgements. *Applied Cognitive Psychology, 25*, 236–243.

Arntzen, F. (2007). *Psychologie der Zeugenaussage: System der Glaubhaftigkeitsmerkmale.* München: C.H. Beck.

Berliner, L., & Conte, J. R. (1990). The process of victimization: The victims' perspective. *Child Abuse & Neglect, 14*(1), 29–40.

Blandón-Gitlin, I., Pezdek, K., Lindsay, D. S., & Hagen, L. (2009). Criteria-based Content Analysis of true and suggested accounts of events. *Applied Cognitive Psychology, 23*, 901–917.

Buck, J. A., Warren, A. R., Betman, S. I., & Brigham, J. C. (2002). Age differences in Criteria-Based Content Analysis scores in typical child sexual abuse interviews. *Applied Developmental Psychology, 23*, 267–283.

Bundesgerichtshof (BGH [German Supreme Court]; 1999). *Grundsatzurteil zu den Mindeststandards aussagepsychologischer Begutachtungen,* 30.07.1999, 1 StR 618/98—LG Ansbach.

Colwell, K., Hiscock, C. K., & Memon, A. (2002). Interviewing techniques and the assessment of statement credibility. *Applied Cognitive Psychology, 16*, 287–300.

Cooper, B.S. (2005). *Memory for mayhem.* Unpublished doctoral dissertation. University of British Columbia, Vancouver, BC.

Cooper, B. S., Griesel, D., & Yuille, J. C. (2007). Clinical-forensic risk assessment: The past and current state of affairs. *Journal of Forensic Psychology Practice, 7*(4), 1–63.

Cooper, B. S., Hervé, H. F., & Yuille, J. C. (2009). Evaluating truthfulness: Detecting truths and lies in forensic contexts. In R. Bull, T. Valentine, & T. Williamson (Eds.), *Handbook of the psychology of investigative interviewing* (pp. 301–328). Chichester: Wiley-Blackwell.

Cooper, B.S., Ternes, M., Griesel, D., Viljoen, S., & Yuille, J.C. (2007). *An examination of the credibility of Canadian offenders' accounts of instrumental and reactive homicides.* Invited paper presented at the 30th International Congress on Law and Mental Health, Padua, Italy.

Cooper, B. S., & Yuille, J. C. (2007). An investigation of violent offenders' memories for instrumental and reactive violence. In S. A. Christianson (Ed.), *Offenders' memories for violent crimes* (pp. 75–98). Chichester: Wiley.

Ekman, P. (2009). *Telling lies: Clues to deceit in the marketplace, politics, and marriage.* New York: Norton.

Erdmann, K., Volbert, R., & Böhm, C. (2004). Children report suggested events even when interviewed in a non-suggestive manner: What are its implications for credibility assessment? *Applied Cognitive Psychology, 18*(5), 589–611.

Esplin, P. W., Houed, T., & Raskin, D. C. (1988). *Application of statement validity assessment.* Maratea: Paper presented at NATO Advanced Study Institute on Credibility Assessment.

Fisher, R. P., & Geiselman, R. E. (1992). *Memory-enhancing techniques for investigative interviewing: The cognitive interview*. Springfield, IL: Charles C. Thomas.
Fisher, R. P., & Schreiber, N. (2007). Interview protocols for improving eyewitness memory. In M. P. Toglia, J. D. Read, D. F. Ross, & R. C. L. Lindsay (Eds.), *The handbook of eyewitness psychology* (Vol. 1, pp. 53–80). Mahwah, NJ: Lawrence Erlbaum.
Gödert, H. W., Gamer, M., Rill, H.-G., & Vossel, G. (2005). Statement validity assessment: Interrater reliability of Criteria-Based Content Analysis in the mock-crime paradigm. *Legal and Criminological Psychology, 10,* 225–245.
Granhag, P. A., Strömwall, L. A., & Landström, S. (2006). Children recalling an event repeatedly: Effects on RM and CBCA scores. *Legal and Criminological Psychology, 11,* 81–98.
Greuel, L., Offe, S., Fabian, A., Wetzels, P., Fabian, T., Offe, H., & Stadler, M. (1998). *Glaubhaftigkeit der Zeugenaussage. Theorie und Praxis der forensisch-psychologischen Begutachtung*. Weinheim: PVU.
Griesel, D. (2008). *An investigation of trauma and its cognitive and emotional consequences in prostituted victims of sexual crimes*. Vancouver: Unpublished doctoral dissertation. University of British Columbia.
Griesel, D., & Yuille, J. C. (2012). Sex trade workers' narratives of sexual violence: A field investigation. *Memory*. doi:10.1080/09658211.2012.654797.
Hershkowitz, I. (2001). A case study of child sexual false allegation. *Child Abuse & Neglect, 25,* 1397–1411.
Hershkowitz, I., Lamb, M. E., Sternberg, K. J., & Esplin, P. W. (1997). Relationships among interviewer utterance type, CBCA scores and the richness of children's responses. *Legal and Criminological Psychology, 2,* 169–176.
Horowitz, S. W., Lamb, M. E., Esplin, P. W., Boychuk, T. D., Krispin, O., & Reiter-Lavery, L. (1997). Reliability of Criteria-Based Content Analysis of child witness statements. *Legal and Criminological Psychology, 2,* 11–21.
Kim, T. K., Choi, S., & Shin, Y. J. (2011). Social factors influencing competency of children's statements on sexual trauma. *Child Abuse & Neglect, 35,* 173–179.
Köhnken, G. (2004). Statement validity analysis and the 'detection of the truth'. In P. A. Granhag & L. Strömwall (Eds.), *The detection of deception in forensic contexts* (pp. 41–63). New York, NY: Cambridge University Press.
Köhnken, G., Schimossek, E., Aschermann, E., & Höfer, E. (1995). The cognitive interview and the assessment of the credibility of adults' statements. *Journal of Applied Psychology, 80,* 671–684.
Landry, K. L., & Brigham, J. C. (1992). The effect of training in Criteria-Based Content Analysis on the ability to detect deception in adults. *Law and Human Behavior, 16,* 663–676.
Leclerc, B., Proulx, J., & Beauregard, E. (2009). Examining the modus operandi of sexual offenders against children and its practical implications. *Aggression and Violent Behavior, 14*(1), 5–12.
Lee, Z., Klaver, J. R., & Hart, S. D. (2008). Psychopathy and verbal indicators of deception in offenders. *Psychology, Crime, & Law, 14,* 73–84.
Pezdek, K., Morrow, A., Blandon-Gitlan, I., Goodman, G. S., Quas, J., Saywitz, K. J., Bidrose, S., Pipe, M.-E., Rogers, M., & Brodie, L. (2004). Detecting deception in children: Event familiarity affects Criterion-Based Content Analysis ratings. *Journal of Applied Psychology, 1,* 119–126.
Popper, C. R. (1959). *The logic of scientific discovery*. New York: Basic Books.
Porter, S., & Yuille, J. C. (1996). The language of deceit: An investigation of the verbal clues to deception in the interrogation context. *Law and Human Behavior, 30,* 443–458.
Roma, P., San Martini, P., Sabatello, U., Tatarelli, R., & Ferracuti, S. (2011). Validity of Criteria-Based Content Analysis (CBCA) at trial in free-narrative interviews. *Child Abuse & Neglect, 35,* 613–620.
Ruby, C. L., & Brigham, J. C. (1998). Can Criteria-Based Content Analysis distinguish between true and false statements of African-American speakers? *Law and Human Behavior, 22,* 369–388.
Santtila, P., Roppola, H., Runtti, M., & Niemi, P. (2000). Assessment of child witness statements using Criteria-Based Content Analysis (CBCA): The effects of age, verbal ability, and interviewer's emotional style. *Psychology, Crime, & Law, 3,* 159–179.

Schelleman-Offermans, K., & Merckelbach, H. (2010). Fantasy proneness as a confounder of verbal lie detection tools. *Journal of Investigative Psychology and Offender Profiling, 7*, 247–260.

Schwind, D. (2007). *Glaubhaftigkeit von zeugen vor gericht. Trennschärfe der realkennzeichen anhand von aussagepsychologischen gutachten*. Saarbrücken: VDM.

Steller, M. (1989). Recent developments in statement analysis. In J. C. Yuille (Ed.), *Credibility assessment* (pp. 135–149). Dordrecht: Kluwer Academic.

Steller, M. (2008). Glaubhaftigkeitsbegutachtung. In R. Volbert & M. Steller (Eds.), *Handbuch der Rechtspsychologie* (pp. 300–310). Göttingen: Hogrefe.

Steller, M., & Köhnken, G. (1989). Criteria-based statement analysis. In D. C. Raskin (Ed.), *Psychological methods in criminal investigation and evidence* (pp. 217–245). New York, NY: Springer.

Steller, M., & Wellershaus, P. (1996). Information enhancement and credibility assessment of child statements: The impact of the cognitive interview technique on Criteria-Based Content Analysis. In G. Davies, S. Lloyd-Bostock, M. McMurran, & C. Wilson (Eds.), *Psychology, law, and criminal justice: International developments in research and practice* (pp. 118–126). New York, NY: de Gruyter.

Strömwall, L. A., Bengtsson, L., Leander, L., & Granhag, P. A. (2004). Assessing children's statements: The impact of a repeated experience on CBCA and RM ratings. *Applied Cognitive Psychology, 18*, 653–668.

Ternes, M. (2009). *Verbal credibility assessment of incarcerated violent offenders' memory reports*. Vancouver: Unpublished doctorial dissertation. University of British Columbia.

Ternes, M., Cooper, B.S., & Yuille, J.C. (2010). *Psychopathy and verbal credibility assessment in male violent offenders*. Paper presented at the American Psychology and Law Society's conference, Vancouver, BC.

Tye, M. C., Amato, S. L., Honts, C. R., Devitt, M. K., & Peters, D. (1999). The willingness of children to lie and the assessment of credibility in an ecologically relevant laboratory setting. *Applied Developmental Science, 3*, 92–110.

Undeutsch, U. (1967). Beurteilung der Glaubhaftigkeit von Aussagen. In U. Undeutsch (Ed.), *Handbuch der Psychologie, Forensische Psychologie* (Vol. 11, pp. 26–181). Göttingen: Hogrefe.

Undeutsch, U. (1989). The development of statement reality analysis. In J. C. Yuille (Ed.), *Credibility assessment* (pp. 101–120). Dordrecht: Kluwer Academic.

Volbert, R. (2004). *Beurteilung von aussagen über traumata: Erinnerungen und ihre psychologische Bewertung*. Bern: Hogrefe.

Volbert, R. (2008). Glaubhaftigkeitsbeurteilung—mehr als merkmalsorientierte Inhaltsanalyse. *Forens Psychiatr Psychol Kriminol, 2*, 12–19.

Vrij, A. (2005). Criteria-based content analysis: A qualitative review of the first 37 studies. *Psychology, Public Policy, and Law, 11*(1), 3–41.

Vrij, A., Akehurst, L., Soukara, S., & Bull, R. (2002). Will the truth come out? The effect of deception, age, status, coaching, and social skills on CBCA scores. *Law and Human Behavior, 26*, 261–283.

Vrij, A., Akehurst, L., Soukara, S., & Bull, R. (2004a). Detecting deceit via analyses of verbal and nonverbal behavior in children and adults. *Human Communication Research, 30*, 8–41.

Vrij, A., Akehurst, L., Soukara, S., & Bull, R. (2004b). Let me inform you how to tell a convincing story: CBCA and reality monitoring scores as a function of age, coaching, and deception. *Canadian Journal of Behavioural Science, 36*, 113–126.

Vrij, A., Edward, K., Roberts, K. P., & Bull, R. (2000). Detecting deceit via analysis of verbal and nonverbal behavior. *Journal of Nonverbal Behavior, 24*, 239–263.

Vrij, A., Kneller, W., & Mann, S. (2000). The effect of informing liars about Criteria-Based Content Analysis on their ability to deceive CBCA raters. *Legal and Criminological Psychology, 5*, 57–70.

Vrij, A., & Mann, S. (2006). Criteria-Based Content Analysis: An empirical test of its underlying processes. *Psychology, Crime, & Law, 12*, 337–349.

Vrij, A., Mann, S., Kristen, R. P., & Fisher, R. P. (2007). Cues to deception and ability to detect lies as a function of police interview styles. *Law and Human Behavior, 31*, 499–518.

Willén, R. M., & Strömwall, L. A. (2011). Offenders' uncoerced false confessions: A new application of statement analysis? *Legal and Criminological Psychology*. doi:10.1111/j.2044-8333.2011.02018.x.

Yuille, J. C. (1988). The systematic assessment of children's testimony. *Canadian Psychology, 29*, 247–262.

Yuille, J.C., Cooper, B.S., & Hervé, H.F. (in press). The step-wise guidelines for child interviews: The new generation. In: M. Casonato, Pfafflin (Eds.), *Handbook of pedosexuality and forensic science*.

Yuille, J. C., & Daylen, J. (1998). The impact of traumatic events on eyewitness memory. In C. P. Thompson, D. J. Herrmann, J. D. Read, D. Bruce, D. G. Payne, & M. P. Togila (Eds.), *Eyewitness memory: Theoretical and applied perspectives* (pp. 155–178). Mahwah, NJ: Lawrence Erlbaum.

Yuille, J. C., Marxsen, D., & Cooper, B. S. (1999). Training investigative interviewers: Adherence to the spirit, as well as the letter. *International Journal of Law and Psychiatry, 22*(3–4), 323–336.

Zaparniuk, J., Yuille, J. C., & Taylor, S. (1995). Assessing the credibility of true and false statements. *International Journal of Law and Psychiatry, 18*, 343–352.

Chapter 13
An "Eye" for an "I": The Challenges and Opportunities for Spotting Credibility in a Digital World

Jeff Hancock and Michael Woodworth

Rarely a day goes by without a new scandal that involves some kind of deception or fraud that has been perpetrated with the assistance of the Internet. Commonly, these deceptions involve people lying about who they are. These kinds of identity fraud stories are particularly compelling given the apparent ease with which individuals can craft a false identity or make false statements when they are hidden behind a computer screen. While lies about some aspect of one's identity or life are generally innocuous, this type of deception can also have disastrous consequences. The recent case of William Melchert-Dinkel illustrates this point. Melchert-Dinkel used a number of aliases, including posing as a suicidal female nurse named "li Dao" who actively encouraged individuals on the Internet to end their own lives. In a landmark decision, Judge Neuville referred to his actions as "lethal advocacy" and found that Melchert-Dinkel was guilty of aiding suicide in connection with the deaths of a Canadian female university student and an adult man in the UK.

Given that online environments consist of primarily text and, in some cases, photos, conventional wisdom considering credibility in the digital world dictates that it is easier to lie about who you are or what you are doing in comparison to face-to-face communication (see Colwell, Hiscock-Anisman, & Fede, present volume). Indeed, almost everyone has beliefs about how technology affects deception and deception detection. However, many of these beliefs are unwarranted and often the product of powerful psychological biases. But with billions of messages exchanged daily on the Internet regarding business, politics, national security, and interpersonal relationships, these misconceptions and errors can be deeply consequential.

We begin this chapter by examining some of the errors people make in judging deception and credibility online, including beliefs about how often people lie in

---

J. Hancock (✉)
Cornell University, New York, USA
e-mail: ith34@cornell.edu

M. Woodworth
University of British Columbia – Okanagan,
Vancouver, Canada

digital contexts and the relative difficulty of detecting these deceptions. We then describe a number of studies we have conducted that empirically investigate people's ability to detect deception in text-based online communication, such as email, text messaging, online chat or status updates on Facebook, and what psychological factors appear to play a role. Given that the online world is rife with text, we describe a series of studies we have conducted looking at how the language of online messages can be mined to discover differences between truthful and deceptive messages. We also examine a similar but new line of work that examines how personality traits, such as psychopathy, can be potentially detected from language, and how this might play a role in how to judge credibility in online environments.

Finally, we end the chapter with a novel approach to credibility in digital contexts. The central idea revolves around the challenge of detecting deception after the fact. Given this difficulty, our approach suggests that structuring honesty may be a more fruitful approach for credibility online. In particular, we suggest using subtle primes and psychological constraints to reduce the likelihood that an individual will lie in a particular context. This approach aims to reduce the chance that deception will occur, rather than trying to detect it post conversation. We sketch out our initial thinking in this area and follow up with some promising new results.

Beliefs about Digital Deception

Most people believe that the Internet is awash with deception (Keyes, 2004), a belief that is supported by frequent media reports of people caught in a lie facilitated by some online technology. An apt observation is that, "on the Internet, no one knows you're a dog" (see Walther, 1996, p. 22). The idea that technology affords more deception than face-to-face interactions is not new to the Internet. Every time new technologies are developed that allow people to communicate at a distance, from the telephone and telegraph to the invention of the alphabet, the public has registered concerns about increases in lying (see Hancock, 2007). These beliefs about deception, however, run contrary to several studies that have examined how often people lie to each other online versus face to face or on the phone. In one series of diary studies that we conducted, participants reported lying least often in email (Hancock, 2004). In fact, in most studies, including DePaulo et al.'s (1996) seminal diary study on deception, the telephone is the medium of choice, with rates of lying in telephone conversations higher than typical Internet-based technology (see Hancock & Gonzales, in press).

The aforementioned results are inconsistent with the conventional wisdom that, when there are fewer cues, people should lie more often. We call this the *cue-availability heuristic* (Toma & Hancock, 2012) in which people assume that when there are fewer cues available in a communication medium, lies are more likely since fewer cues lower the chances of getting caught. According to this logic, people should lie more in text-based communication than in media that have more vocal or physical cues, such as the telephone or face-to-face. Why is it that people believe this to be the case when it comes to new technologies?

The most likely answer to this question relates to the recency of digital communication. Humans evolved communicating with one another when all members of the communication were physically present. This evolutionary trait has been in effect since humans began using speech, at least making it approximately 6–1,00,000 years old. Given this timescale, the ability to communicate at a distance is extremely new, with the invention of the alphabet around 3,000 years ago, and the use of email and text messaging only about 20 years old. Our systems, therefore, are potentially biased to be less trusting when not physically interacting with one another. Some of our own research described below calls into question how suspicious individuals are in online environments. This suggests that it may, in fact, be that individuals are still not comfortable deceiving in this relatively new communication medium—at least not at the rate that many people believe deception occurs online.

To examine the cue availability heuristic and its role in beliefs about deception and technology, we conducted a study that drew upon two well-established biases, one from psychology and one from communication studies. The first is the *double-standard effect*, in which individuals tend to believe that other people use deception more than they do themselves (Gordon & Miller, 2000). This perspective difference is due to biases in the way people perceive lies told by the self versus others, with lies told by the self perceived as more justified than those told by others. Saxe (1991) has also argued that this kind of self–other asymmetry in people's beliefs about deception is critical to advancing our understanding of beliefs about deception, whether it be of the digital variety or not. The second bias is the *third person effect* (see Davison, 1983), which suggests that people do not like to perceive themselves as vulnerable to media effects because such an admission violates their sense of the self as in control of decisions and behaviors. For example, people tend to believe that advertising has a persuasive impact on others, but not on them. This effect has been demonstrated for many media dynamics (Perloff, 2002).

The question, then, is whether the combination of the third person effect and the double standard effect can explain people's beliefs about deception in digital contexts. We (Toma, Jiang, & Hancock, under review) recently examined this question by asking participants in a national survey first about their beliefs about how often *other* people lie face to face, on the telephone, in email and text messaging (1 = not at all, 7 = all the time). We then asked them about their *own* lying behavior across these media. Finally, we asked them for their rationale, and whether cues were important and whether certain reasons, such as self-protection, played a role in their thinking.

The results revealed the double standard of deception—overall, people thought that others lied more than they did. But, the self-other difference was significantly larger when participants judged deception in email and text messaging, revealing a third person effect. That is, the double standard of deception is intensified for online media, with our participants believing that other people lie much more than they do in email and text messaging. When we asked them why they lie versus why others lie, the cue availability heuristic was apparent. People argued that other people use digital media to lie because there are no nonverbal cues to be detected and, therefore, they are less likely to be discovered than they are in face-to-face interactions. In contrast, participants argued that their own lying behavior was not driven by cues but by justifiable reasons, such as protecting one's privacy. Thus, consistent with the third person effect, participants felt that others would be more affected by online media. Other people, relative to the self, were expected to engage in more deceptive behavior online, and for less noble reasons.

The aforementioned study makes clear that some people's beliefs about deception and credibility in online media are subject to important psychological biases, such as the self-other asymmetry that drives the double standard effect, and the media-based third person effect. Given these biases, it is important to look at how these kinds of biased beliefs may play a role in detecting deception in online contexts.

Detecting Deception Online

Considering the biases outlined above, are individuals *actually* more suspicious when interacting within computer-mediated contexts? They certainly appear to believe that, contrary to their own relatively low level of deception, others are engaging in a higher level of deception within online contexts. For example, Caspi and Gorsky (2006) found that 79% of participants believe that deception is widespread online while only 19% reported engaging in online deception themselves. In face-to-face situations, humans tend to err on the side of assuming that their conversational partner is telling the truth, and this truth bias appears to be difficult to extinguish (e.g., Vrij, 2008). It is believed that one of the numerous factors that may account for this truth bias is that many individuals erroneously believe that, if they can see a person, they will be able to detect deception (e.g., "I could tell by looking into their eyes"; Hancock, Woodworth, & Goorha, 2010; ten Brinke & Porter, present volume). Unfortunately, in many cases, individuals are not particularly good at detecting deceit, potentially inflating their confidence that others are being truthful (e.g., Porter, Woodworth, & Birt, 2000).

Woodworth, Hancock, Agar, Cormier, and Carpenter, (2010) examined the role of suspicion specifically in synchronous computer-mediated communications. One hundred and two undergraduate student dyads were asked to discuss four topics meant to approximate what they would typically discuss online (e.g., relationship issues and status and identity issues). One participant, the sender, was deceptive during two topics and truthful during the other two. Suspicion was also manipulated across three conditions ranging from low to high suspicion (e.g., "there is a strong likelihood that your communication partner is lying to you"). Deception detection accuracy was operationalized as the absolute difference between the sender's rating of their truthfulness (on a scale from 0, completely untruthful, to 10, completely truthful) and the receiver's rating of the sender's truthfulness (on the same scale). Surprisingly, level of suspicion did not significantly impact deception detection accuracy with all three levels of the suspicion manipulation achieving between 55 and 59% accuracy rates. Even when participants were led to be highly suspicious of their interaction partner, this did not positively impact their ability to detect deceit. Interestingly, the sample was comprised of psychology students who will typically have more education and are likely to be more computer savvy than the general population. Independent of the suspicion manipulation, they should have presumably been more suspicious compared to individuals in the community.

One explanation parsimonious with face-to-face theory is that, regardless of the communication medium, it is far too stressful and incongruent with our instinct to always have to be guarded or wary of being deceived. It may be that this truth bias is ingrained at a level that has not trumped our common-sense knowledge of computer-mediated concerns (e.g., lack of nonverbal cues, or the fact that, in this particular experiment, individuals were interacting with anonymous strangers). Participants were far more likely to judge that the sender was truthful on all four of the topics (i.e., 61% of receivers) than deceptive on all four topics (i.e., only 1%). This demonstrated that lack of suspicion is concerning considering that, for an increasing number of individuals, computer-mediated communication is their primary means of social communication (e.g., Hancock, 2007). So, while individuals report generally believing that others are being deceptive more than themselves in online situations, they intriguingly appear to let their guard down during their own individual online interactions and defer to the truth bias, perhaps particularly in situations where they are familiar with the person they are interacting with and have built up some trust.

Unfortunately, because there is still an overall lack of comparison for how to accurately judge the veracity of information in online contexts, the default for being more sensitive for distressing information may be to assume that an individual is being deceptive about this "high stake" or serious information. The recent case of Cameron Moffat and Kruse Wellwood, who murdered 16 year-old Kimberly Proctor, is a perfect example of individuals being unable to correctly determine the honesty of the sender in an online context. Moffat admitted that, in the days leading up to the murder, he discussed different potential techniques for committing murder with "over a dozen people" in various online forums. One can only assume that, if he had similar conversations with these individuals in face-to-face contexts, somebody would have notified a parent or the authorities. However, their default assumption was likely that he was joking about such heinous information and would never have been honestly reporting intent to commit murder. Adding to the confusion, some of these conversations about the "real world" occurred within the online discussion group for the online fantasy game "World of Warcraft." Sadly, if the police had been notified about some of these online interactions, this tragedy could have potentially been avoided. In addition to this surprising general lack of suspiciousness (and lack of clarity around the norms of what is honest intent within online contexts), there are a number of other issues that potentially compound the difficulty of detecting deceit in online contexts. A strong motivation to lie, such as in a high-stakes situation (e.g., punishment if caught), has always been considered one of the few variables that consistently serve to impede deceptive individuals (e.g., Depaulo, Kirkendol, Tang, & O'Brien, 1988). It is thought that the cognitive effort necessary to construct a lie when the individual is highly motivated may provide additional effective cues (considered to be largely nonverbal) for a receiver trying to ascertain the truth (see O'Sullivan, present volume). This has commonly been referred to as the *motivational impairment effect*. While the double standard effect discussed above suggests that individuals often feel they have genuine and pure motivations to lie in an online environment, individuals are often highly motivated to tell a variety of harmful and nefarious lies as well.

Hancock et al. (2010) conducted the first empirical study to examine if the aforementioned well-documented impairment effect would translate to the computer-mediated context where dyads were asked to communicate with each other in instant messenger. Motivation was manipulated so that individuals in the "high" motivation category were informed that deception was a "very important skill" and that being able to successfully deceive was indicative of future successes in both employment and social contexts. The results indicated that, contrary to decades of face-to-face research, "high motivation" participants were the most successful at deceiving their partners, with increased motivation enhancing their success at deceiving. It would appear that a combination of the features available in the computer-mediated context is responsible for this novel finding. The exclusive availability of verbal cues (and lack of availability of nonverbal cues), combined with aspects of online interactions such as the opportunity to edit and plan out messages, may facilitate liars who are motivated enough to take advantage of these features. For example, any "late" or prolonged response latency in a face-to-face context has repeatedly been shown to be a perceived indicator of deception, potentially due to the extra time that is perceived that to be needed to craft a successful lie (e.g., Boltz, Dyer, & Miller, 2010), while in online communication, latencies of varying degrees are quite normal and expected. One has to wonder if the results would have been even stronger if the researchers had been able to manipulate motivation in a manner that more adequately approximated real-life situations. Presumably, many of the kinds of high-stakes lies that are told in online environments by sexual predators and other deceptive criminals would invoke a level of motivation that is difficult to create within an experimental paradigm.

Computer-mediated communication has become increasingly prevalent and, for many, is fast becoming the primary means of communication in some aspects of their life (Hancock, 2007). However, this type of communication is faced with a unique set of challenges for detecting deception, which include a general lack of suspiciousness and a set of features that benefit the goals of the highly motivated deceiver. Sadly, on the day she was murdered, Kimberly Proctor was lured and manipulated to meet up with Moffat and Wellwood by a number of text messages and no face-to-face communication. Fortunately, a number of studies outlined below suggest that, if the receiver is on the lookout for specific types of cues within the language of his or her communication partner, it may increase his or her confidence in the veracity of the information.

Linguistic Assessments of Deception Online

As outlined above, the digital world of communication is composed almost entirely of text. Almost all messages exchanged online involve a verbal message. Given the longstanding emphasis on nonverbal cues to assess deception, the textual nature of the digital world seems to pose a challenge. Where there are challenges, however, there are also opportunities. In fact, one of the transformative aspects of digital communication for deception is that, unlike speech, everything that is communicated online leaves a digital trace. Even when speech is recorded, it still must be transcribed. Online, everything is already typed, producing a massive amount of text that can be analyzed.

Importantly, research on face-to-face deception has revealed important linguistic differences between deceptive and nondeceptive individuals. For example, Arciuli, Mallard, and Villar, (2010) found that individuals who were lying were significantly less likely to interject their speech with instances of "um" than truthful participants. The authors speculated that this type of speech utterance was associated with more natural and effortless speech, which would be difficult for many liars due to the cognitive stress of the lie. Interestingly, this potential linguistic clue to deception has also previously been found to increase during lying, presumably as an indicator of the increased cognitive demands of telling a lie (e.g., Vrij, Edward, Roberts, & Bull, 2000). The differences between face-to-face communication and computer-mediated communication (i.e., the parameters and affordances offered discreetly by each) offer an interesting opportunity to enhance our understanding of one by studying the other. For example, perhaps the nonverbal cues found in deceitful face-to-face communicators (e.g., Vrij, 2008) translate into textual evidence online. Further research on the topic would be welcomed as a way to better understand the similarities and differences between on and offline communication.

A substantial amount of recent work has also begun to examine the linguistic nature of deception in online contexts. This research has been driven by important advances in natural language processing, or the ability for computers to parse language, which is a potential boon to deception researchers. Researchers can now use computer programs to efficiently parse and count patterns in verbal messages, an approach that coincides with recent calls for researchers to focus more on verbal aspects of deception (Vrij, 2008). For example, a recent study by Duran, Hall, McCarthy, and McNamara, (2010) found that deceptive individuals were more likely to include redundancies, or the repetition of key information.

Consider one model that uses a very simple word-counting computerized approach to deception and language, the empirically derived Newman–Pennebaker (NP) model of deception. This model predicts several language features associated with deception, including fewer first person singular terms, fewer instances of exclusive conjunctions (e.g., words such as except, but, without) and more negative emotion terms (Newman, Pennebaker, Berry, & Richards, 2003). While this model was derived from controlled laboratory studies, this linguistic pattern has also been observed in deception by prison inmates (Bond & Lee, 2005) and, most recently, in courtroom testimonies of 46 defendants who were either found guilty of a crime and of perjury versus a group of defendants found guilty but who were later exonerated (e.g., in most cases by DNA evidence; Pennebaker, 2011). In this latter study, the strongest effects were from the use of first person singular pronouns. The more defendants used first person singular pronouns, the more likely they were to be innocent. This pattern suggests that use of first person singular reflects ownership of a person's story. Use of exclusive words indicate that people are making a distinction between what they did do and what they did not do—essentially a marker of cognitive complexity.

We have also found similar patterns within laboratory studies (Hancock, Curry, Goorha, & Woodworth, 2008) and in political speech (Markowitz, Hancock, & Bazarova, 2011), and we have begun looking at how a variety of language processes, including negations, obligatory evidentiality, affect terms, coherence, and linguistic style matching markers can signal honesty/deception in text-based communication (see Hancock, 2004, 2007; Hancock and Gonzales, in press). In one project that shows how digital data can transform the analysis of deception beyond the Internet, we (Liu, Hancock, Zhang, Xu, Markowitz, & Bazarova, 2012; Markowitz et al., 2011) compared a corpus available on the Internet of false and non-false statements produced by officials in the Bush administration in the run up to the Iraq war. The false statements were identified by the non-partisan Center for Public Integrity, who used the 911 Commission conclusions that Iraq did not have weapons of mass destruction (WMD) or direct links to Al Qaeda at the time of the war, to identify a total of 535 false statements.

We applied the NP model of deception to the false and non-false statements collected by the Center for Public Integrity. Consistent with the model's predictions, false statements about WMD and links to Al Qaeda contained substantially and statistically significant reduced rates of first person singular ("I") and exclusive terms ("except," "but") but contained more negative emotion terms and action verbs. Using this extremely simple model, we were able to classify approximately 76% of the statements correctly as either false or not false, suggesting that the language of the statements can predict whether or not the statement would turn out to be true of false. We have now begun examining other instances in which Western (i.e., English speaking) leaders made false claims and/or deployed misinformation (e.g., Churchill's deceptions during WWII).

It is tempting to begin to think of a set of consistently accurate verbal cues that predict deception, no matter what the context. For example, the decrease of first person singular across a wide range of studies suggests that it might be a reliable cue in verbal deception detection. While we believe that it is important to look at theoretically important cues regardless of the context, our research across a number of different studies has lead us to conclude that verbal cues are likely to be much more sensitive to contextual factors (such as the type of conversation, what the lie was about, whether the deception could be verified or is simply a person's opinion) than current assumptions around nonverbal behavior (see Ekman, 2001). We argue here that researchers should tailor their predictions for verbal cues to deception to the specific context, although we are still working to determine which key factors must be considered.

Consider, for example, three cues and how they operate across three very different studies. The cues are derived from the NP model (Newman et al., 2003): first person singular, which is expected to decrease during deception due to psychological distancing; conjunctives, which are also expected to decrease as deceptive language is often less complex than truthful; and more negative emotion terms, which should "leak" out given increases in anxiety around lying.

We have run three radically different studies to examine the aforementioned issues. The first was an experiment in which students chatted with each other over instant messaging about four topics, two truthfully and two deceptively (Hancock et al., 2008). In the second study, we looked at deceptive and truthful online dating profiles (Toma & Hancock, 2012). In this study, we examined how the free form text from the "about me" section changed with lies about the dater's height, weight, and age. In the third study, we compared honest and deceptive hotel reviews (Ott, Choi, Cardie, & Hancock, 2011). Here, we asked one group of participants to write a five star review of a specific hotel as if they had actually stayed there and compared that to actual reviews of that hotel that presumably were honest.

What we found was that first person singular decreased, as predicted by the NP model, for both the chat and dating profiles deceptions, but actually increased for the deceptive hotel reviews. For conjunctions, we found that they decreased as expected for both the chats and the hotel reviews, but did not differ across deceptive and truthful dating profiles. Lastly, we found that negative emotion terms actually increased for both hotel and online dating deceptions but did not differ for the chats.

As we can see, the cues frequently differed across honest and deceptive accounts, but the differences may be systematic rather than random across the contexts. For instance, first person singular decreases when people may feel guilty about their deception, which might be the case in the deceptive chats and dating profiles where our participants were lying about aspects important to the self, such as important beliefs and identity. In contrast, in the hotel reviews, the whole point of the lie was to convince readers that they were actually there; thus, the liars over-emphasized first person singular. Conjunctives appear to be sensitive to how cognitively demanding the deception is. This is likely the case for the hotel reviews, which would require recreating a scene and an experience and, for the chats, which would require lies in real-time. In contrast, when creating an online dating profile and lying about aspects of the self, in which one has the time to construct and edit the well-known topic of the self, the cognitive demand should be moderated. Lastly, negative emotion terms appear to be sensitive not only to "leaked" emotion, but also to be a strategically deployed cue. Negative emotion terms were reduced in the two contexts in which the lies involved "selling" something (over and above the deceit in and of itself) – either how attractive the dater was or in how wonderful a hotel is. While it is impossible to know if these post hoc speculations can explain the pattern of results across these three different studies, we argue in this chapter that it is critical to consider how psychological dynamics and objectives differ across deceptions.

Taken together, we believe that the ability to analyze texts from a variety of domains points to a context-dependent approach to deception online. Deception researchers should consider the context when developing predictions about verbal cues, rather than trying to identify universal cues of deception that should apply to every context (see O'Sullivan, present volume). Why, for example, would we expect deceptions in an insurance fraud to be the same as deceptions about hotel reviews or about rationales for taking a country to war? In the digital world and with new tools for parsing language, we should instead consider the specific circumstances and intent when constructing theoretically derived verbal predictions.

The Potential Role of Personality for Online Deception and Manipulation

When considering other context-driven variables that may impact credibility in online environments, the personality of both the deceiver and the individual being deceived are also important to keep in mind. An individual's language is arguably one of the best ways to glean important insights into his or her thoughts and beliefs. An increasing number of research projects have utilized automatic linguistic analysis programs to examine the language of other types of clinical populations and found that they can successfully differentiate between a variety of individual factors (e.g., Tausczik & Pennebaker, 2010). Previous research suggests that language may reveal important insights into both the personality and psychological make-up of an individual. Oberlander and Gill (2006) conducted an automated analysis of the email communication of a group of students and found a number of consistent linguistic style patterns based on the personality of the participant. For instance, a higher level of extraversion was associated with a preference for adjectives, whereas lower levels of neuroticism were linked to a preference for adverbs (see also Pennebaker, Mehl, & Niederhoffer, 2003).

Until recently, no automated language analysis programs had been employed to analyze the speech production of criminals and, more specifically, of psychopathic offenders. Previous studies that employed human coders have suggested particular language characteristics of psychopathic offenders. For example, Porter and Woodworth (2007) found that individuals scoring higher on psychopathy were more likely to exaggerate the reactivity of the homicide they committed and to omit some core detail of the incident than those scoring low on psychopathy. However, using automated language programs is arguably preferable in some cases, considering that many of the aspects of language measured with these programs are not consciously controllable by the speaker or measurable by human coders. Further, they are arguably more efficient than human coders both in terms of consistency and speed by which large amounts of text can be analyzed. Psychopaths are known to be particularly skilled at manipulating, deceiving, and controlling their self-presentation, making an automated enquiry into their language production another way to potentially obtain important insights into their behavior. Further, if they are demonstrating particular types of language patterns, it might be possible to more readily detect them in online environments where the vast majority of information will be text based.

Hancock, Woodworth, and Porter, (2011) used text analysis tools to examine the crime narratives of 14 psychopathic and 38 non-psychopathic homicide offenders. Psychopaths showed reliable differences relative to their nonpsychopathic counterparts such as focusing more on material needs during their narratives (e.g., food, drink, money) and making fewer references to social needs (e.g., family, religion/ spirituality). Psychopaths also used more past tense and less present tense verbs in their narratives, suggesting a greater psychological and emotional detachment from the incident. Consistent with the above, their language was less emotionally intense and pleasant.

The above study was one of the first to suggest that language may be used as a red flag by certain types of aversive personalities; in this case, the psychopathic personality, who is known to have a penchant for manipulation lying, and an ability to sense weaknesses (such as fear) in other individuals (e.g., Woodworth & Waschbusch, 2008). Interestingly, Wheeler, Book, and Costello, (2009) found that individuals who possess a high number of psychopathic traits were also better able to discern more vulnerable individuals from less vulnerable individuals, based on gait and other nonverbal cues. Further, individuals with a particularly concerning combination of personality characteristics known as the Dark Triad (Paulhus & Williams, 2002) which is a combination of subclinical psychopathy, narcissism, and Machiavellianism engage in the manipulation of others and the use of exploitation (Jonason, Li, & Teicher, 2010). Black, Woodworth, and Porter, (in preparation) are conducting one of the first research projects that explores whether Dark Triad individuals also will have an enhanced ability to detect vulnerability in individuals, as well as the verbal and nonverbal cues that they use to detect vulnerability. Once researchers possess a deeper understanding of the cues that Dark Triad individuals use to detect vulnerability in face-to-face interactions, this knowledge will lead to an investigation to determine whether exploitative and deceptive individuals are able to detect vulnerability in an online setting without the presence of any traditional nonverbal cues.

These types of studies lead to the troubling question of whether certain personalities or individuals are actually more prone to being preyed upon or deceived in online environments. For example, face-to-face research has demonstrated that some individuals are more vulnerable to being taken advantage of than others due to their own personality traits, such as low self-esteem and low assertiveness (e.g., Egan & Perry, 1998). Whether or not similar results would be obtained in an online environment remains to be seen. However, it is important for individuals interacting within computer-mediated domains to both create an environment and present in a manner where they can be most confident of the veracity of the sender of information.

Structuring Honesty—Promoting Truth Versus Detecting Deception

As has been made clear by numerous meta-analyses (e.g., Bond & DePaulo, 2006), deception detection is difficult for humans, who often perform effectively at chance in laboratory settings. Although much of the literature has focused on assessing credibility or detecting deception, another approach that might be useful is reducing the likelihood that an individual will *produce* a lie when given the opportunity. Given that deception detection is difficult, researchers should focus on reducing the chance of a lie before it occurs.

How might the aforementioned be accomplished? One approach is to prime honest behavior. Evidence from evolutionary psychology suggests that pro- and antisocial behaviors can be manipulated using subtle primes. For example, in one study, researchers alternated a photo placed on a cup used to collect donations for the use of cream for coffees (Bateson, Nettle, & Roberts, 2006). One week, the photo had a pair of human eyes; the next, the photo was of flowers. At the end 10 weeks, the eye photo cup had collected significantly more than the flower cup. In another study, Haley and Fessler (2005) found that simple cartoons of eyes could prime a sense of surveillance and enhance cooperation in a dictator game. In particular, when players had two black dots over one dot on their computer screen, which represents two eyes and a nose, they gave more money to their partner in a money-splitting game than when there was one dot over two dots. In conversations, social psychologists have been able to prime more polite and more rude behavior by manipulating the kinds of words used in a conversation (Chartrand & Bargh, 1999).

These studies, while not focusing on deception per se, but the larger category of dishonest behaviors, suggest that individuals might be primed to be more honest in a certain situation where honesty is particularly important, such as in a witness report or a resume. Thus, we argue that the digital environment could be modified to prime more honest behavior. Imagine a witness report for an insurance claim that is filled out online. On the form could be placed the two dots above one dot configuration, perhaps as a logo, which has been shown to prime more pro-social behavior. Could it also prime the witness to be more honest in completing their report? If this was the case, the applications seem endless given the wide range of human activities now conducted online.

A second approach to enhancing honesty and credibility online would be to attempt to constrain people's ability to lie. One important lack of constraint in some digital contexts is that people can behave anonymously, such as in Internet chat rooms. But, in many other digital domains, there are connections between the person's virtual behavior or identity and their real-world identity—these connections are called *warrants* (Walther & Parks, 2002). Facebook, for example, made it clear to users from the beginning that their profiles should be for real individuals, and they initially implemented this policy by requiring an email from a university domain (e.g., @harvard.edu). Because Facebook profiles are tightly connected to their real-world identities, they should be credible and accurate. Recent research suggests this is the case. Back et al. (2010) found that individuals can accurately assess other individuals' personality traits using only Facebook information about that individual. Other work has found that the more warranted an identity is in an online space (e.g., photo, real name, presence of real-world friends), such as email or social networking sites, the more honest that person reported being in that space (Warkentin, Woodworth, Hancock, & Cormier, 2010).

Taken together, these studies suggest that the communication environment online can be manipulated to increase the degree to which people produce credible, honest behavior online. First, primes can plausibly be inserted into an environment that should lead to more honest behavior. Second, warrants that connect an individual to their real-world identity should lead to more honest behaviors and credible communication than unwarranted situations. However, certain personality types, such as those scoring high on psychopathy (or on the dark triad), will likely be much more resistant to conventional means that may attempt to appeal to their conscience or empathy as a human being.

Conclusion

In summary, a review of deception in computer-mediated communication reveals that there are important implications across a variety of online communication settings. Many individuals are now conducting a substantial amount of their social interactions online, and often appear to be willing to divulge an inordinate amount of personal information. This is particularly true for teenagers, and even children who are still in the 10–12-year-old age range (e.g., Lenhart, Purcell, Smith, & Zickuhr, 2010). Business interactions and networks have also become increasingly geared toward online communication (e.g., Logsdon & Patterson, 2009). Identifying deception still poses unique challenges in online environments. For example, there is a lack of social norms available for what even constitutes deception. The recent divorce proceedings of Amy Pollard and her spouse David help to illustrate just how difficult this task may be. Pollard accused her spouse of engaging in what she believed was serious deceptive behavior online. She caught her husband engaging in online sexual activity between his avatar and another participant's female avatar (i.e., a virtual call girl), and believed this to be tantamount to cheating. Based on the fact that her spouse had engaged in digital adultery, she filed for divorce citing "unreasonable behavior."

Everyone will have a different opinion regarding both the seriousness of this behavior as well as whether this would constitute deceptive behavior truly indicative of infidelity. Interestingly, although it is clear that Pollard felt she had been deceived, in this case, what is unclear is the type (or nature) of deception that her (ex) husband had actually engaged in. Understanding the veracity (or seriousness) of the information provided in computer-mediated contexts was also a frustrating challenge in the Kimberly Proctor murder case outlined above. Further, it appears that the truth bias that is so evident in face-to-face environments is also present in online environments, despite individuals' expectations that others will lie more often (and for less selfless reasons) than themselves. Further complicating the matter, highly motivated individuals, who have unparalleled access to potential victim pools in online environments, appear to benefit from features inherent in online communication, as well as the lack of traditional nonverbal cues.

Despite these troublesome aspects of online communication, the increasing prevalence of computer-mediated communication also affords many chances for us to improve our understanding of both deception as well as social interaction. Research conducted in online contexts discussed in this chapter has demonstrated that the type of language deceptive individuals will produce will vary across both context as well as the motivations of the deceiver. Further, it would appear that certain personality types, such as psychopaths, engage in specific patterns of language use that may facilitate their detection both in online and face-to-face environments. Research is also beginning to suggest particularly effective parameters that could be employed to facilitate honest communication online. These include creating an environment that requires individuals interacting online to provide a variety of warrants to decrease their feelings of anonymity. Priming individuals in computer-mediated communication with social cues that in face-to-face contexts have been effective in instilling increased responsibility (e.g., including a simple image of being watched) may also be effective for reducing the amount of deceptive behavior online. While deception may currently be posing unique challenges for online communication, this environment also arguably provides us with distinct opportunities to improve our ability to understand both the mechanics of deception as well as parameters aimed at increasing our success at accurately gauging deceit.

References

Arciuli, J., Mallard, D., & Villar, G. (2010). "Um, I can tell you're lying": Linguistic markers of deception versus truth telling in speech. *Applied Psycholinguistics, 31*, 397–411.
Back, M. D., Stopfer, J. M., Vazire, S., Gaddis, S., Schmukle, S. C., Egloff, B., & Gosling, S.D. (2010). Facebook profiles reflect actual personality, not self-idealization. *Psychological Science, 21*, 372–374.
Bateson, M., Nettle, D., & Roberts, G. (2006). Cues of being watched enhance cooperation in a real-world setting. *Biology Letters, 2*, 412–414.
Black, P. J., Woodworth, M., & Porter, S. (in preparation). The influence of the dark triad on the ability to detect vulnerability in others.
Boltz, M. G., Dyer, R. L., & Miller, A. R. (2010). Are you lying to me? Temporal cues for deception. *Journal of Language and Social Psychology, 29*, 458–466.
Bond, C. F., & DePaulo, B. M. (2006). Accuracy of deception judgments. *Personality and Social Psychology Review, 10*, 214–234.
Bond, G. D., & Lee, A. Y. (2005). Language of lies in prison: Linguistic classification of prisoners' truthful and deceptive natural language. *Applied Cognitive Psychology, 19*, 313–329.
Caspi, A., & Gorsky, P. (2006). Online deception: Prevalence, motivation, and emotion. *Cyberpsychology & Behavior, 9*, 54–59.
Chartrand, T. L., & Bargh, J. A. (1999). The chamelion effect: The perception–behavior link social interaction. *Journal of Personality and Social Psychology, 76*, 893–910.
Davison, W. P. (1983). The third-person effect in communication. *Public Opinion Quarterly, 47*, 1–15.
DePaulo, B. M., Kirkendol, S. E., Kashy, D. A., Wyer, M. M., & Epstein, J. A. (1996). Lying in everyday life. *Journal of Personality and Social Psychology, 70*, 979–995.
DePaulo, B. M., Kirkendol, S. E., Tang, J., & O'Brien, T. P. (1988). The motivational impairment effect in the communication of deception: Replication and extension. *Journal of Nonverbal Behavior, 12*, 177–202.
Duran, N. D., Hall, C., McCarthy, P. M., & McNamara, D. S. (2010). The linguistic correlates of conversational deception: Comparing natural language processing technologies. *Applied PsychoLinguistics, 31*, 439–462.
Egan, S. K., & Perry, D. G. (1998). Does low self-regard invite victimization? *Developmental Psychology, 34*, 299–309.

Ekman, P. (2001). *Telling lies: Clues to deceit in the marketplace, politics, and marriage*. New York, NY: Norton & Company, Inc.

Gordon, A. K., & Miller, A. G. (2000). Perspective differences in the construal of lies: Is deception in the eye of the beholder? *Personality and Social Psychology Bulletin, 26*, 46–55.

Haley, K. J., & Fessler, D. M. T. (2005). Nobody's watching? Subtle cues affect generosity in an anonymous economic game. *Evolution and Human Behavior, 26*, 245–256.

Hancock, J. T. (2004). Verbal irony use in computer-mediated and face-to-face conversations. *Journal of Language and Social Psychology, 23*, 447–463.

Hancock, J. T. (2007). Digital deception: When, where and how people lie online. In K. McKenna, T. Postmes, U. Reips, & A. N. Joinson (Eds.), *Oxford handbook of internet psychology* (pp. 287–301). Oxford: Oxford University Press.

Hancock, J. T., Curry, L., Goorha, S., & Woodworth, M. T. (2008). On lying and being lied to: A linguistic analysis of deception. *Discourse Processes, 45*, 1–23.

Hancock, J.T. & Gonzales, A. (in press) To lie or not to lie online: The pragmatics of deception in computer-mediated communication. In S. Herring, D. Stein, & T. Virtanen (Eds.) *Handbook of pragmatics of computer-mediated communication*. Berlin, Germany: Mouton de Gruyter.

Hancock, J. T., Woodworth, M. T., & Goorha, S. (2010). See no evil: The effect of communication medium and motivation on deception detection. *Group Decision and Negotiation, 19*, 327–343.

Hancock, J. T., Woodworth, M., & Porter, S. (2011). Hungry like the wolf: A word pattern analysis of the language of psychopaths. *Legal and Criminological Psychology*. doi:10.1111/j.2044-8333.2011.02025.x.

Jonason, P. K., Li, N. P., & Teicher, E. A. (2010). Who is James Bond? The dark triad as an agentic social style. *Individual Differences Research, 8*, 111–120.

Keyes, R. (2004). *The post-truth era: Dishonesty and deception in contemporary life*. New York, NY: St. Martin's Press.

Lenhart, A., Purcell, K., Smith, A., & Zickuhr, K. (2010). Social media & mobile internet use among teens and young adults. In *Pew Internet & American Life Project*. Retrieved from http://www.pewinternet.org/Reports/2010/Social-Media-and-Young-Adult.

Liu, X., Hancock, J. T., Zhang, G., Xu, R., Markowitz, D., & Bazarova, N. (2012). *Exploring linguistic features for deception detection in unstructured text*. Presentation at the Proceedings of the International Conference on System Sciences, Hawaii, USA

Logsdon, J. N., & Patterson, K. D. W. (2009). Deception in business networks: Is it easier to lie online? *Journal of Business Ethics, 90*, 537–549.

Markowitz, D., Hancock, J. T., & Bazarova, N. (2011). *The language of presidential lies: How words can reflect lies about war, personal scandal and state secrets*. Presentation at the 97th Annual Meeting of the National Communication Association, New Orleans, LA.

Newman, M. L., Pennebaker, J. W., Berry, D. S., & Richards, J. M. (2003). Lying words: Predicting deception from linguistic styles. *Personality and Social Psychology Bulletin, 29*, 665–675.

Oberlander, J., & Gill, A. J. (2006). Language with character: A stratified corpus comparison of individual differences in e-mail communication. *Discourse Process, 42*, 239–270.

Ott, M., Cardie, C., Choi, Y., & Hancock, J.T. (2011). Finding deceptive opinion spam by any stretch of the imagination. *Proceedings of the 49th Annual Meeting of the Association for Computational Linguistics (ACL 2011)*, 309–319.

Paulhus, D. L., & Williams, K. M. (2002). The dark triad of personality: Narcissism, machiavellianism, and psychopathy. *Journal of Research in Personality, 36*, 556–563.

Pennebaker, J. W. (2011). *The secret life of pronouns*. New York, NY: Bloomsbury Press.

Pennebaker, J. W., Mehl, M. R., & Niederhoffer, K. G. (2003). Psychological aspects of natural language use: Our words, our selves. *Annual Review of Psychology, 54*, 547–577.

Perloff, R. (2002). The third person effect. In J. Bryant & D. Zillmann (Eds.), *Media effects: Advances in theory and research* (pp. 489–505). Mahwah, NJ: Lawrence Erlbaum Associates, Inc.

Porter, S., & Woodworth, M. (2007). "I'm sorry I did it ... but he started it": A comparison of the official and self-reported homicide descriptions of psychopaths and non-psychopaths. *Law and Human Behavior, 31*, 91–107.

Porter, S., Woodworth, M., & Birt, A. R. (2000). Truth, lies, and videotape: An investigation of the ability of federal parole officers to detect deception. *Law and Human Behavior, 24*, 643–658.

Saxe, L. (1991). Lying: Thoughts of an applied social psychologist. *American Psychologist, 46*, 409–415.

Tausczik, Y., & Pennebaker, J. W. (2010). The psychological meaning of words: LIWC and computerized text analysis methods. *Journal of Language and Social Psychology, 29*, 24–54.

Toma, C., & Hancock, J. T. (2012). What lies beneath: The linguistic traces of deception in online dating profiles. *Journal of Communication, 62*, 78–97.

Toma, C., Jiang, C., & Hancock, J. T. (under review). The deception-media double standard: Self-other asymmetry in beliefs about deception across media. *Cyberpsychology, Behavior and Social Networking*.

Vrij, A. (2008). *Detecting lies and deceit: Pitfalls and opportunities*. West Sussex, England: Wiley.

Vrij, A., Edward, K., Roberts, K. P., & Bull, R. (2000). Detecting deceit via analysis of verbal and nonverbal behavior. *Journal of Nonverbal Behavior, 24*, 239–263.

Walther, J. B. (1996). Computer-mediated communication: Impersonal, interpersonal, and hyperpersonal interaction. *Communication Research, 23*, 3–43.

Walther, J. B., & Parks, M. R. (2002). Cues filtered out, cues filtered in: Computer-mediated communication and relationships. In M. L. Knapp & J. A. Daly (Eds.), *Handbook of interpersonal communication* (3rd ed., pp. 529–563). Thousand Oaks, CA: Sage.

Warkentin, D., Woodworth, M., Hancock, J.T., & Cormier, N. (2010). Warrants and deception in computer mediated communication. *Proceedings of the ACM Conference on Computer-Supported Cooperative Work (CSCW2012)*, 9-12.

Wheeler, S., Book, A., & Costello, K. (2009). Psychopathic traits and perceptions of victim vulnerability. *Criminal Justice and Behavior, 36*, 635–648.

Woodworth, M., Hancock, J., Agar, A., Cormier, N., & Carpenter, T. (2010). *Suspicion in synchronous computer-mediated communication: Preliminary results*. Presentation at the Proceedings of the International Conference on System Science, Hawaii, USA.

Woodworth, M., & Waschbusch, D. (2008). Emotional processing in children with conduct problems and callous/unemotional traits. *Child: Care, Health and Development, 34*, 234–244.

Index

A
Absent-mindedness, 66, 67, 149
Abuse disclosure. *See* Disclosure, of abuse
Academic psychology, 5
ACID. *See* Assessment criteria indicative of deception (ACID)
Active forgetting, 103, 104
Adjusted Rand Index, 203
Alexandria case, in Sweden, 154
Amnesia, 103, 104
Andrew, Hurricane, 160
ANS. *See* Autonomic nervous system (ANS)
Arousal sensitivity, 102, 110–121, 123, 124, 126–131, 133
Assessment criteria indicative of deception (ACID), 260, 287–289. *See also* Deception
Attitudes, 34, 39, 47, 91, 288
Audit Commission, 44
Autobiographical memory, 192, 194. *See also* Narrative memory
Autonomic nervous system (ANS), 102, 112, 116, 117, 120–123, 125, 128–132

B
BAI. *See* Behavioural Analysis Interview (BAI)
Behaviorism, 5, 7
Behavioural Analysis Interview (BAI), 42
Behavioural memory, 149
Beliefs, 3–5, 9, 12, 16, 34, 35, 38, 39, 46–51, 60, 61, 63, 69, 74, 76–78, 82, 89, 173–187, 191, 225, 230, 233, 234, 240, 247–254, 325–328, 333, 334
Benefit claim 39
Benefit Fraud Inspectorate (BFI), 44, 45
Benefit fraud investigation. *See also* Benefit fraud suspects
Benefit fraud investigators, 35
Benefit fraud suspects, 33
BFI. *See* Benefit Fraud Inspectorate (BFI)
Bias
deception, 223
interviewer, 76
memory, 69
truth, 244
Biological variables, of eyewitness memory
perpetuating factors, 124–125
precipitating factors, 119–121
predisposing factors, 110–117
Biopsychosocial model, of eyewitness memory, 99
memory patterns, 109–110
Bivalent logic, 22
Blum, Bennett, 62
"Boy-who-cried-wolf" effect, 245
British Common Law, 261

C
Camp Erika (prisoners), 195
Canadian Dangerous Offender, 232
CBCA. *See* Criteria-Based Content Analysis (CBCA)
Chamberlain, 74
Childhood abuse 195
Children's memory. *See also* Child sexual abuse (CSA)
Child sexual abuse (CSA), 143
CI. *See* Cognitive Interview (CI)
Civil standard of proof, 24, 26
Close-ended question, 86

Clues
    to deception, 247–254
CM. *See* Created memory (CM)
Coaching, 298, 300
Coercive tactics, 90–91
Cognitive-interpretative system, 102
Cognitive Interview (CI), 68, 80, 105, 260, 272, 273, 275–277, 279, 284, 285, 288, 301
Cognitive load hypothesis, 260
Cognitive/memory processes, 66–69
Coherence, 261–263, 301–304
Common law jurisdictions, 191–192
Common law trials, 19–29
Communication channels, 240, 244, 249
Complex event, 178
Compound questions, 87
Computer-mediated communication, 287, 289, 328–330, 337, 338
Content analysis 279–284
Contradictory statements, 177, 178
Cory (Justice), 225
Court, 6, 12, 21, 22, 38, 43, 51, 71, 78, 90, 106, 134, 148, 156, 187, 192, 211, 224, 229, 233, 234, 261, 293, 294, 299–301
Created memory (CM), 103, 109
Credibility assessment, 19–29, 221, 222, 224, 225, 231–234, 259–261, 293, 299, 300. *See also* Verbal credibility assessment
    CBCA, 261–263
    reality monitoring, 263–265
Crime 100–101
Criminal justice system, 38
Criminal offence, 191
Criminal sentencing, 28
Criminal standard of proof, 25
Criteria-based content analysis (CBCA), 70, 156, 157, 240, 270, 288
    Undeutsch hypothesis, 261
    verbal credibility assessment, 293
        accounts of subjective mental state, 313
        accurately reported details misunderstood, 311–313
        appropriate quantity of detail, 302–304
        attribution of perpetrator's mental state, 314–315
        contextual embedding, 304–305
        descriptions of interactions, 306–308
        details characteristic of particular act, 318–319
        logical structure/coherence, 301–302
        pardoning the perpetrator, 317–318
        raising doubts about one's own testimony, 316
        related external associations, 313
        reproduction of conversation, 308
        self-deprecation, 316–317
        spontaneous correction, 315
        superfluous/peripheral details, 310–311
        unexpected complications during the incident, 308–309
        unstructured production/spontaneity, 302–303
        unusual details, 309–310
"Crocodile tears," 231
CSA. *See* Child sexual abuse (CSA)
Cue-availability heuristics, 326–327
Cues, to deception, 225–228

D
Dangerous Decisions Theory (DDT), 228–233
Dark triad, 335, 337
DDT. *See* Dangerous Decisions Theory (DDT)
Dean, John, 195
Deceit. *See* Deception
Deception, 213.
    ACID, 279–284
    detection, clues to, 247–254
    digital, 326, 328
    moderators, 284–286
Demeanor evidence, 19–21, 23, 29
Department for Work and Pensions (DWP), 33, 43–45
Differential recall enhancement (DRE), 259, 276–277
Digital world 325
    digital deception, 326–328
Disclosure, of abuse, 148–155, 162, 164
Dissociative amnesia, 103, 104
Dissociative memory (DM), 103, 107
    external focus, 108
    internal focus, 108–109
Distinctive events, 162
Distractions, in interview. *See* Observation and listening
DM. *See* Dissociative memory (DM)
DRE. *See* Differential recall enhancement (DRE)
DWP. *See* Department for Work and Pensions (DWP)

E
Ecological validity, 106, 242, 295–296
Email, deception in, 326, 327
Emotion
    facial expressions, 227, 244

multidimensional nature, 101–102
Emotional lie, 71
Emotional memory, 159
Episodic memory. *See* Narrative memory
Erroneously false statements, 297
European courts, 293
Event-based statements, 297
Event familiarity, 263, 298, 300, 304, 305, 307, 310, 319
Evidence scholarship, 22–23
Experimental methodology, 4
Experimental psychology, 4–6
Experimental research, 158, 163, 164, 174, 254
Experimental witnesses, 176
The Expert Belief Group, 247
Expert lie detectors, 239
    language, contribution of, 240
        deception, clues to, 247–254
        deceptive judgment, 244–246
        idiographic analysis, 254
        modality dissection, 243–244
        think aloud protocol, 249
        truth wizards, 244, 249, 250
        verbal and nonverbal behaviors, 241–243
        verbal content analysis, 240–241
External focus, of dissociative memory, 108
Eyewitness
    consistency, 174
    hypersensitive/hyposensitive, 111–133
    identification, 11–12
    metacognition, 180
    and personality, 117
    research, 7–8
    sensitivity to arousal, 102
    testimony, 178
Eyewitness memory, 3, 4, 8, 13
    biopsychosocial model (*see* Biopsychosocial model, of eyewitness memory)
    field research, 5–6
    hypersensitive/hyposensitive, 111–133
    patterns, 102
        active forgetting, 104
        created memory, 109
        dissociative amnesia, 104
        dissociative memory, 107–109
        normal forgetting, 103–104
        red out, 105–106
        remarkable memory, 106–107
        script memory, 107
        SDM, 105
    perpetuating factors, 124
        biological variables, 124–125
        psychological variables, 125–126
        social variables, 126–127
    and personality, 117
    precipitating factors, 119
        biological variables, 119–121
        psychological variables, 121–123
        social variables, 123–124
    predictions, 127–133
    predisposing factors, 110
        biological variables, 110–117
        psychological variables, 117–118
        social variables, 118–119

F
Face-to-face interactions, 326
Face-to-face theory, 329
Facial expression, 227, 233, 241, 243, 244, 247, 250
Factual lie, 71
False memory, 109, 133
False reports, of CSA, 156–158
Familiarity. *See* Event familiarity
Field research, 3, 9, 11–15, 123, 133, 134, 143, 144, 158–165, 221–234, 295
Field study, 12, 15, 48, 106, 227, 299, 309, 314–316, 320
Flashbulb memory, 159
Folk Psychology, 4
Forensic memory research, challenge for. *See* Methodolotry
Forensic psychology
    error, consequences for, 8
Free Recall, 276
The Free Response to Item Group, 247, 248
Fuzzy logic, 19–29

G
Geiselman effect, 275
Gender, and ACID, 284
The General Belief Group, 247
German courts, 294, 299
Gupta, Madan, 22

H
Historical approach, to benefit fraud investigation, 36–40
Hitler, 74
Honesty determination, 224
Hypersensitive/hyposensitive eyewitness memory, 111–133
Hypothesis-testing approach, 294, 302, 307, 309, 314

I

Identification, of witnesses. *See*
    Eyewitness:identification
Idiosyncrasy error, 75
Illusory memory, 109
Impairment effect. *See* Motivational
    impairment effect
Impression management
  objective clues
    appearing calm and cooperative,
      269–271
    lie script, 268–269
  subjective clues, 265–267
Improper phrasing, of questions, 86–88
Inconsistency, 173
  beliefs about, 181–182
  consistency and deception, scientific
    evidence, 182
  differential preparation, 184–185
  retrieval strategies, 185–186
  and deception, 181
  framework, 178
    analysis by components, 180–181
    mental representation, 179
    metacognition, 180
    retrieval processes, 179–180
  in legal framework, 174–175
  and memory inaccuracy, 174–175
  practical implications, 187
  scientific research on, 175
    experimental testing, 176
    inaccuracy of inconsistent statements,
      177
    inconsistent *vs.* consistent witnesses,
      177–178
Inconsistent reports, 192–194, 210
Inconsistent statements, inaccuracy of, 177
Inconsistent *vs.* consistent witnesses, 177–178
Inferential Interview. *See* Reality interview (RI)
Intent lie, 71
Internal focus, of dissociative memory, 108–109
Internet, 325
  digital deception, beliefs about, 326–328
  promoting truth *vs.* deception detection,
    335–337
  online deception
    detection, 328–330
    linguistic assessments, 330–334
    personality for, 334–335
Interpersonal dynamics and recall
    enhancement, 274
Interruption, during interview, 88–90
Interview(s). *See also* Interviewing
  cognitive (*see* Cognitive interview)
  goal, 59
  improper phrasing, of questions, 86–88
  interruption during, 88–90
  interviewee, knowledge about (*see*
    Interviewee)
  observation and listening, 84–86
  planning, 79–83
  preparation, 184–185
  questions, 176, 179–181, 183–186
  reality (*see* Reality interview)
  repeated, 191
    about repeated autobiographical events,
      195–198
    case study, 198–208
    crime victims' recollections, 208
    laboratory work, 209
    limitations, 210–211
    recency and primacy effect, 209
    report consistency and perceived
      credibility, 192–194, 210
    trauma, 196
  step-wise (*see* Step-wise interview)
Interviewee
  background determination, 82–83
  gathering knowledge, 80–81
  mental health issues, review of, 82
  personality style, 81–82
  physical state, 82
Interviewer
  bias, 76
  misleading
    concealment, 71
    falsification, 71
  wrong assumptions made by, 78–79
Interviewing. *See also* Interview(s)
  importance, 59–60
  investigative (*see* Investigative
    interviewing)
  sins of
    coercive tactics, 90–91
    corroborating information, failure of, 91
    idiosyncrasy error, 75
    improper phrasing of questions, 86–88
    improper planning, 79–83
    lack of observation and listening, 84–86
    lack of rapport, 83–84
    lying and truth telling, 70–74
    memory, misunderstanding, 62–70
    "me" theory, of personality, 60–62
    multiple explanations, 78–79
    Othello error, 74–75
    Pinocchio error, 74
    poorly timed question, 88–90
    self-awareness, absence of, 76–78

Interview quality, and CBCA judgment quality, 295
Investigative interviewing, 271–273
  of benefit fraud suspects, 33
  and credibility assessment, 269
  errors made in, 59
    coercive tactics, 90–91
    corroborating information, failure of, 91
    idiosyncrasy error, 75
    improper phrasing of questions, 86–88
    improper planning, 79–83
    lack of observation and listening, 84–86
    lack of rapport, 83–84
    lying and truth telling, 70–74
    memory, misunderstanding, 62–70
    "me" theory, of personality, 60–62
    multiple explanations, 78–79
    Othello error, 74–75
    Pinocchio error, 74
    poorly timed question, 88–90
    self-awareness, absence of, 76–78
  goals, 271

J
James, William, 6
Judges, 19–23, 27
Judges' Rules, 36
Judgment, 25, 77, 78, 91, 182, 206, 207, 210, 211, 223, 228–233, 240, 243–247, 262, 286, 295, 297–299, 302, 313

L
Laboratory research, 3–5, 12, 13, 15, 71, 122, 127, 155, 158, 159, 254, 295, 296
Laboratory study, 6–8, 10, 12–14, 123, 143, 158, 165, 176, 182, 183, 193, 295–297, 331, 332
Lambert, Wallace, 7
Language
  and ACID, 285–286
  and lie detection
    deception, clues to, 247–254
    deceptive judgment, 244–246
    idiographic analysis, 254
    modality dissection, 243–244
    and speech, 240
    think aloud protocol, 249
    truth wizards, 244, 249, 250
    verbal and nonverbal behaviors, 241–243
    verbal content analysis, 240–241
LAs. See Local authorities (LAs)

Latent Semantic Analysis, 240
Law enforcement, 14, 34, 59–62, 91, 92, 99, 115, 133, 182, 251, 270, 288
Leakage, and lying, 73
Lehmann, Alfred, 7
Liars
  differential preparation, 184–185
  rehearsal, 184
  retrieval strategies, 185–186
  vs. truth-tellers, 183
Lie
  emotional, 71
  factual, 71
  intent, 71
  leakage, 73
  opinion, 71
  script, 268–269
  and truth telling, 70–74
Lie detection, and language
  deception, clues to, 247–254
  deceptive judgment, 244–246
  idiographic analysis, 254
  modality dissection, 243–244
  and speech, 240
  think aloud protocol, 249
  truth wizards, 244, 249, 250
  verbal and nonverbal behaviors, 241–243
  verbal content analysis, 240–241
Linguistic assessments, of online deception, 330–334
Local authorities (LAs), 33, 34, 38, 43–45
Logical Positivism, 5
Logical structure. See Coherence
Long-term autobiographical memory, 192, 200
Long-term memory (LTM), 128–130, 192
Lundholm, Helge, 7
Lying. See Lie

M
McCurdy, Harold, 7
Memory. See also Memory variability in eyewitnesses
  absent-mindedness, 66, 67, 149
  accuracy, 151, 174
  and age, 161–162
  behavioural, 149
  bias, 69
  blocking, 67–68
  consistency (see Memory consistency)
  created, 109
  and credibility assessment
    CBCA, 261–263
    reality monitoring, 263–265

Memory (*cont.*)
  dissociative, 107
    external focus, 108
    internal focus, 108–109
  emotional, 159
  false, 109, 133
  flashbulb, 159
  illusory, 109
  inaccuracy and inconsistency, 174–175
  lack of understanding, 62–70
  main properties/characteristics, 62–63
  misattribution, 68
  narrative, 64, 99
  for past events, 69
  patterns, 109–110
  persistence, 69
  procedural, 64
  processes, 66–69
  prospective, 64
  reconstruction, 66, 69, 103
  remarkable, 106–107
  report, 144, 149, 158, 160, 164
  retrieval processes, 179–180, 185–186
  script, 64, 107
  semantic, 64
  for significant event, 66
  state-dependent, 105
  suggestibility, 68–69
  transience, 67
  trauma on, 158
  of traumatic events, 149
  verbal, 149
Memory consistency. *See also* Report consistency
  and deception
    scientific evidence, 182
    scientific evidence: differential preparation, 184–185
    scientific evidence: retrieval strategies, 185–186
Memory patterns, 69, 102
  active forgetting, 104
  created memory, 109
  dissociative amnesia, 104
  dissociative memory, 107–109
  normal forgetting, 103–104
  red out, 105–106
  remarkable memory, 106–107
  script memory, 107
  state dependent memory, 105
Memory variability in eyewitnesses. *See also* Memory
  biopsychosocial perspectives on crime, nature of, 100–101

  emotion, multidimensional nature of, 101–102
  implications, 133–134
  memory patterns, 109–110
  perspectives, 110–127
  predictions, 127–133
  reconstructive and variable nature, 102–109
Mental representation, of inconsistency, 179
Metacognition, of eyewitnesses, 180
"Me" theory, of personality, 60–62
Methodolotry, 3
  actual crimes and witnesses, 13
  brief history, 4–7
  contemporary eyewitness research, 8–9
  cure for, 15–16
  eyewitness
    identification, 11–12
    research, 7–8
  psychology, broader impact on, 15
  reasons for, 13–15
  stress, effect of, 9–10
  weapon focus effect, 11
Misattribution memory, 68
Mnemonics and recall enhancement, 275–276
Modality
  and ACID, 286
  expert lie detectors, dissection by, 243–244
Moderators, of ACID
  gender, 284
  language, 285–286
  training and modality, 286
Moffat, Cameron, 329
Motivational impairment effect, 36, 231, 329
Mullins-Johnson, William, 232
Multidimensional nature, of emotion, 101–102
Multiple choice question, 87
Munsterberg, Hugo, 6

N
Narrative memory, 64, 99
  vs. script memory, 65
Neurocognitive functioning, 116
Newman–Pennebaker (NP) model of deception, 331, 332
Nonexperimental approach, 4
Non-leading questions, 88
Nonverbal and verbal behaviors, behavioral measurement of, 241–243
Nonverbal cues, to deception, 42, 222, 248, 249, 327, 329–331, 335, 337
Normal forgetting, 103–104

O

Objective clues
  appearing calm and cooperative, 269–271
  lie script, 268–269
Observation and listening, 84–86
Offender memory, 14, 100, 301, 306, 315
O'Halloran (Chief Justice), 20
Online deception
  chat, 326, 333
  detection, 328–330
  linguistic assessments, 330–334
  media, 327–328
  personality for, 334–335
On the witness stand, 6
Open-ended question, 86, 87
Opinion lie, 71, 253
Othello error, 74–75

P

PACE, 36–40, 51
Paivio, Allan, 7
PEACE model, 40–51
Perceived credibility, and consistent report, 192–194
Perceptions of credibility, 192, 206, 210, 212
Perpetuating factors, of eyewitness memory, 124
  biological variables, 124–125
  psychological variables, 125–126
  social variables, 126–127
Persistent memory, 69
Personality
  and eyewitness, 117
  "me" theory, 60–62
  for online deception, 334–335
Personal Remembered Lie Group, 247, 249
Pinocchio error, 74
Planning, an interview, 79–83
Police, deception detection by, 222–224
Police and Criminal Evidence Act, 36
Police officers interview training, 40–42
Policy, 12, 19, 44, 336
Positivism, 4
Post-traumatic stress disorder (PTSD), 101, 118–119, 126, 130, 133, 289
POW. *See* Prisoner of war (POW) training
Precipitating factors, of eyewitness memory, 119
  biological variables, 119–121
  psychological variables, 121–123
  social variables, 123–124
Predisposing factors, of eyewitness memory, 110
  biological variables, 110–117
  psychological variables, 117–118
  social variables, 118–119
Pre-interview rehearsal, 184
Primacy and recency effect, 209
Prisoner of war (POW) training, 10
Procedural memory, 64
Proctor, Kimberly, 329
Progressive Movement, 5
Prosecution, 22, 28, 35, 37–40, 43, 44, 191, 223, 232, 299
Prospective memory, 64
Provincial Appellate Courts, 21, 22
Pseudo-memory, 297
Psychological variables, of eyewitness memory
  perpetuating factors, 125–126
  precipitating factors, 121–123
  predisposing factors, 117–118
Psychopathy, 326, 334, 335, 337
PTSD. *See* Post-traumatic stress disorder (PTSD)

Q

Questions
  close-ended, 86
  compound, 87
  improper phrasing, 86–88
  improper timing, 88–90
  interruption, 88–90
  multiple choice, 87
  non-leading, 88
  open-ended, 86
  timing, 88–90

R

Rapport, 83–84
RCCP. *See* Royal Commission on Criminal Procedure (RCCP)
Reality interview (RI), 260, 272, 273, 276, 280, 285, 288
Reality monitoring (RM), 240, 263–265, 288
Real-life events, 9
Reasonable doubt standard, 24
Recall enhancement. *See* Differential recall enhancement (DRE)
Recency and primacy effect, 209
Red out, 103, 105–106
Reid model/technique, 41–42
Relative plausibility theory of evidence, 23
Remarkable memory (RM), 103, 106–107
Reminiscence effect, 193–194

Repeated interviews. *See* Interview(s)
Report
    false report, 144, 156–158, 164, 165
Report consistency
    across robberies, 204
    and perceived credibility, 192–194
Reproductive recall, 179
RI. *See* Reality interview (RI)
RM. *See* Reality monitoring (RM); Remarkable memory (RM)

S

Scientific case study, of CSA, 148–155
    false reports, 156–157
    limitations, 157–159
    main characteristics, 145–147
Scientific case study paradigm, 144
Scientific research, on inconsistency, 175
    experimental testing, 176
    inconsistent statements, inaccuracy of, 177
    inconsistent *vs.* consistent witnesses, 177–178
Script memory (SM), 64, 103, 107
SDM. *See* State-dependent memory (SDM)
Self-awareness, absence of, 76–78
Semantic memory, 64
Sentencing, 27
Sexual abuse. *See* Child sexual abuse (CSA)
Short-term memory (STM), 128–130
SI. *See* Step-wise interview (SI)
Sins of interviewing. *See* Investigative interviewing:errors made in
"Skills erosion," 50
SM. *See* Script memory (SM)
Social psychology, 15
Social security benefit fraud, 33, 34, 37
Social security prosecutions (UK), 37
Social variables, of eyewitness memory
    perpetuating factors, 126–127
    precipitating factors, 123–124
    predisposing factors, 118–119
Sophonow, Thomas, 225, 234
Southin (Justice), 192
Standard of proof, 24–26
    criminal, 24, 25
    civil, 24, 26
State-dependent memory (SDM), 103, 105
Statement analysis, 259–261, 286, 287
Statement validity analysis (SVA), 293–296, 299–303, 305–307, 309–311, 314–320
Statutes of Limitations, 191

Step-wise interview (SI), 48, 105, 144, 199, 260, 272, 301, 309
Stimulus event, 100–101
STM. *See* Short-term memory (STM)
Stoppel, Barbara, 225
Stress, 9–10, 101, 106, 107, 118, 120, 122, 123, 134
Stroop Task, 278
Subjective clues, 265–267
Suggestion, 59–92, 103, 109, 227, 229, 294
Suggestive processes, 297, 300, 306
Suggestibility memory, 68–69
Superficial encoding, 268
Suspect, 33–54, 71, 72, 76–79, 83–85, 89, 173, 181, 182, 186, 187, 223, 226, 228, 230, 241, 242, 269, 286, 294
SVA. *See* Statement validity analysis (SVA)

T

Traditional logic *vs.* fuzzy logic, 22
Training, 286
Transience, 67
Trauma, 101, 105–107, 110, 118, 119, 122, 126, 130, 132, 196
Technology, and deception, 325–327
Testimonial inconsistency. *See* Inconsistency
Text-based online communication, and deception, 326
Text messaging, deception in, 326, 327
Think aloud protocol, 249
Third person effect, 327–328
Timing, of questions, 88–90
Titchener, 4–5
Truscott, Steven, 231
Trustworthiness, intuitive judgments of, 229
Truth
    bias, 244, 296–297
    and deception, 233–234
    and opinion, 245, 248, 250–252
    telling, 70–74
    wizards, 244, 249, 250
Truth-tellers
    differential preparation, 184–185
    vs. liars, 183
    retrieval strategies, 185–186
The Truth Wizard Project, 250, 253
Type-token ratio (TTR), 270, 279, 280, 287

U

UK, benefit fraud. *See* Benefit fraud suspects
Undeutsch hypothesis, 70, 241, 261
Units of information, 200

V

Validity, ecological. *See* Ecological validity
VCUG. *See* Voiding Cystourethrogram Fluoroscopy (VCUG)
Verbal and nonverbal behaviors, behavioral measurement of, 241–243
Verbal channel, 246
Verbal content analysis, 240–241
Verbal credibility assessment, 293
    accounts of subjective mental state, 313
    accurately reported details misunderstood, 311–313
    appropriate quantity of detail, 302–304
    attribution of perpetrator's mental state, 314–315
    circumstances demanding caution, 297–298
    contextual embedding, 304–305
    descriptions of interactions, 306–308
    details characteristic of particular act, 318–319
    event-based statements *vs.* erroneously false statements, 297
    informative CBCA, 299–300
    interview quality and judgment quality, 295
    lack of memory, 315–316
    logical structure/coherence, 301–302
    misconceptions, 294
    pardoning the perpetrator, 317–318
    qualitative method, 298–299
    raising doubts about one's own testimony, 316
    related external associations, 313
    reproduction of conversation, 308
    self-deprecation, 316–317
    spontaneous correction, 315
    superfluous/peripheral details, 310–311
    training, 299
    truth bias, 296–297
    unexpected complications during the incident, 308–309
    unstructured production/spontaneity, 302–303
    unusual details, 309–310
Verbal cues, 222, 248, 249, 295, 330, 332, 333
Verbal memory, 149
Victim, witness, 59, 62
Videotaped deception scenario, 248
Violent crime, 6, 9, 62, 100, 104, 106, 316
Vocal quality, 242, 246
Voiding Cystourethrogram Fluoroscopy (VCUG), 161

W

Warrants, 336–338
Wartime stressors, reports of, 195
Watson, John B., 5
Weapon focus effect, 11
Wellwood, Kruse, 329
Wigmore, John, 6, 9
Witnesses. *See also* Eyewitness
    contradictory statements, 177
    credibility assessment, 19–29
    demeanor, 20
    experimental, 176
    inconsistent *vs.* consistent, 177–178
    law trials (*see* Common law trials)
    metacognition, 180
"World of Warcraft," 329
Wrong phrasing, of questions, 86–88
Wundt, Wilhelm, 4, 7
Wundtian psychology, 5

Y

Yuille, John, 7

Z

Zadeh, Lotfi, 22